ADVISORY BOARD

THE WESLEYAN EDITION OF THE
WORKS OF HENRY FIELDING

———

AN ENQUIRY INTO THE CAUSES
OF THE LATE INCREASE OF ROBBERS
AND RELATED WRITINGS

HENRY FIELDING

An Enquiry into the Causes
of the
Late Increase of Robbers
and Related Writings

EDITED BY
MALVIN R. ZIRKER

WESLEYAN UNIVERSITY PRESS
MIDDLETOWN, CONNECTICUT

Published in the United States by
Wesleyan University Press.

Published simultaneously in Great Britain by
Oxford University Press
Copyright © 1988 by Oxford University Press

Library of Congress Cataloging-in-Publication Data
Fielding, Henry, 1707–1754.
An enquiry into the causes of the late increase
of robbers, and related writings.
Includes index.
1. Robbery—Great Britain. 2. Poor—Great Britain.
3. Brigands and robbers—Great Britain. I. Zirker,
Malvin R.   II. Title.
HV6665.G7G63   1988   364.1'522'0942   87–21024
ISBN 0–8195–5166–X

All inquiries and permissions requests should be
addressed to the Publisher, Wesleyan University Press,
110 Mt. Vernon Street, Middletown, Connecticut 06457.

Distributed by Harper & Row Publishers,
Keystone Industrial Park, Scranton, Pennsylvania 18512.

First American Edition

TO JOAN

PREFACE

THE purpose of the Wesleyan edition is to provide a critical unmodernized text of Fielding's works. Its principles are set forth in the Textual Introduction following the General Introduction, and the details of bibliographical description, along with a record of textual changes made, may be found in the textual appendixes. In the Introduction, the discussion of *A Proposal for Making an Effectual Provision for the Poor* immediately follows that of *An Enquiry Into the . . . late Increase of Robbers* because these two pamphlets are in many ways complementary. Fielding's texts, however, are printed in this volume in the order of their publication.

The Wesleyan edition does not attempt 'readings' of Fielding's works or, more pertinent in the case of the six pamphlets printed in this volume, evaluations of his social and political attitudes. The primary intention of the Introduction and the annotations is to clarify the texts and to supply the reader with the historical information necessary for an understanding of pamphlets topical in origin and concerned with issues largely forgotten. What is known about the circumstances of composition and publication, and our knowledge is relatively meager, also forms a part of the editor's responsibilities.

Aside from their chronological proximity (they span the period 1749–53), two points of connection unite these six works. Each is a product of Fielding's activity as justice of the peace for Westminster and Middlesex and each, with the exception of *A True State of the Case of Elizabeth Canning*, focuses on social and legal problems relating to the poor or the 'lower orders of Mankind'. These two points are themselves connected. Then, as now, a magistrate's court or police court had largely to do with the misdemeanours or crimes of lower-class offenders. Thus the question of class attitudes in these pamphlets poses a special problem for editorial objectivity. While the particular issues Fielding addresses may be fixed in the past, attitudes about class and notions about the poor are perennially divisive topics, and Fielding's conservative social views invite and have elicited reproachful commentary. A reader unfamiliar with the writings in this volume may well share the shock I experienced when I first read *An Enquiry into the Causes of the late Increase of Robbers*, and may wish, as I did, to uncover an underlying irony which would harmonize its statement with the apparently more generous values of *Tom Jones*. But no such irony exists.

We must accept, if regretfully, Fielding's failure to escape the assumptions and attitudes of his time and class. The intention of my commentary has been to illuminate the historical context which renders his views comprehen-

sible and even predictable. Fielding was not a 'reformer who set himself
squarely against the point of view and corrupt tendencies of his time',[1] but, at
least as a justice of the peace, was very much a man of his age who, with
obligations to his office and to the men in power who utilized that office,
attempted solutions to social questions still unresolved.

The citations in this volume to statutes and legal books require some
comment. There are two methods of quoting an act: 1) by its short title, if
any, e.g. The Vagrancy Act of 1744; 2) by reference to the regnal year in
which the act passed, e.g. 17 Geo. II, c. 5. 'Reference is also made to any
particular section of the act by its number. Local acts are referred to by small
Roman numerals, e.g., 62 & 63 Vict. c. xi; private acts by italicized numerals,
e.g., 62 & 63 Vict. c. *10*.'[2] Thus 17 Geo. II, c. 5 means the Fifth Chapter
(act) passed in the session of Parliament held in the seventeenth year of
George II's reign. In checking Fielding's citations to statutes or in quoting
from statutes I have used *Pickering's Statutes at Large* (1762). Some minor
inconsistencies of this edition of the statutes (inconsistencies characteristic
of Fielding's own practice) have been retained. Thus the name of the
monarch is sometimes latinized, e.g. 'Car. II.', and sometimes not, e.g. 'Will.
III.'. Where Fielding's citation of a statute is clear, no confirming comment
has been added. Occasionally additional information to Fielding's footnote
citations has been placed in brackets immediately following his text.
Whenever possible I have used the same editions of law reports and books of
legal authority as Fielding cites or as were in his library. The reader
interested in looking at these texts will not find my use of old editions an
impediment, for nearly all modern reprints indicate the pagination or
foliation of the original editions. The law reports Fielding cites have been
reprinted in *English Reports*.[3]

This edition was undertaken in a state of dark ignorance about
eighteenth-century English law, an ignorance that many years of inefficient
buffeting of unfamiliar books gradually lessened but never entirely removed.
I am grateful to Hendrik Hartog, Morris Arnold, and Barbara Singer who
helped unravel some of these mysteries of legal citations and directed me to
those dark corners of law libraries to which '3 *Keb.*', '*H.P.C.*', and 'I *Vent.*'
had repaired. I am especially grateful to John H. Langbein of the University
of Chicago Law School who read my manuscript and allowed me to read
drafts of several of his articles, now published.

I also owe thanks to the staffs of a number of libraries, and it is a pleasure
to acknowledge here the courtesies I received at the Lilly, Newberry, and

---

[1] Frederic T. Blanchard, *Fielding the Novelist: A Study in Historical Criticism* (New Haven, Conn.,
1926), p. 576.
[2] Percy H. Winfield, *The Chief Sources of English Legal History* (Cambridge, Mass., 1925), pp. 76–7.
[3] Ed. Max A. Robertson *et al.* (London, 1857).

Huntington Libraries; the William Andrews Clark Memorial Library, the Library of Congress, the Law Library of Indiana University, and the Cook County Law Library (Chicago); and abroad, the British Library, the Bodelian Library, Cambridge University Library, the London Library, the Guildhall Library, the Institute of Advanced Legal Studies (London), and the Public Record Office. William Cagle, Lilly Librarian, gave generously of his time and expertise, and Anthony Shipps, of Indiana University Library, saved me many hours of labor with his extraordinary skills of librarianship. I also wish to thank Aubrey Diller, James Halporn, Timothy Long, and Sarah Strickland.

Ralph Wilson Rader and Ian Watt read portions of the manuscript and have, over the years, provided friendly counsel. Martin C. Battestin and Hugh Amory, who kindly read the manuscript, shared their knowledge of Fielding liberally and made many helpful suggestions. Fredson Bowers's guidance on bibliographical matters has been invaluable. For his solution to the puzzling printing history of *Bosavern Penlez* I am particularly thankful. William B. Coley, the general editor of the Wesleyan edition, has provided abundant patience and encouragement. I have profited greatly from his exacting and acute criticism.

My daughters, Elizabeth and Christina, have accorded my labors a respect and trust one would not care to justify. This work is dedicated to Joan McTigue Zirker.

M. Z.

Bloomington, 1983

CONTENTS

ILLUSTRATIONS

Title-page facsimiles in the text are from copies in the Lilly Library, Indiana University, except for the facsimile for the second edition title-page of *Elizabeth Canning*, which is reproduced with the kind permission of the Newberry Library, Chicago.

ABBREVIATIONS

Amelia	Henry Fielding. *Amelia*, ed. W. H. Henley. London, 1903.
Baker	*A Catalogue of the Entire and Valuable Library of the Late Henry Fielding, Esq; . . . sold by Auction by Samuel Baker.* [London, 1755].
BL	British Library.
Blackstone, *Comm.*	Sir William Blackstone. *Commentaries on the Laws of England; in Four Books* (London, 1765–9), ed. Thomas M. Cooley. Chicago, 1872.
Bosavern Penlez	Henry Fielding. *A True State of the Case of Bosavern Penlez.* London, 1749.
Bracton	Henry of Bratton. *De Legibus et consuetudinibus Angliae*, ed. George E. Woodbine. 2 vols., Cambridge, Mass., 1968–.
CGJ	Henry Fielding. *The Covent-Garden Journal*, ed. Gerard Edward Jensen. 2 vols., New Haven, Conn., 1915.
Charge	Henry Fielding. *A Charge Delivered to the Grand Jury . . . for the City and Liberty of Westminster.* London, 1749.
Coke, *Inst.*	Sir Edward Coke. *The Institutes of the Laws of England.* Four Parts. London, 1628–44.
Cross	Wilbur L. Cross. *The History of Henry Fielding.* 3 vols., New Haven, Conn., 1918.
DNB	*Dictionary of National Biography.*
Dudden	F. Homes Dudden. *Henry Fielding, his Life, Works, and Times.* 2 vols., Oxford, 1952.
ECS	*Eighteenth-Century Studies.*
ELH	*English Literary History.*
Elizabeth Canning	Henry Fielding. *A Clear State of the Case of Elizabeth Canning.* London, 1753.
Enquiry	Henry Fielding. *An Enquiry Into the Causes of the late Increase of Robbers, &c. with some Proposals for Remedying this Growing Evil.* London, 1751.
Examples of Providence	Henry Fielding. *Examples of the Interposition of Providence in the Detection and Punishment of Murder.* London, 1752.
GM	*The Gentleman's Magazine.* London, 1731–1914.
Godden	G. M. Godden. *Henry Fielding, A Memoir.* London, 1910.
Hale	Sir Matthew Hale. *Historia Placitorum Coronae*, ed. Sollom Emlyn. 2 vols., London, 1736.
Hawkins	William Hawkins. *A Treatise of the Pleas of the Crown.* 2nd edition. 2 vols., London, 1724, 1726.
Henley	*The Complete Works of Henry Fielding, Esq. With an Essay on the Life, Genius and Achievement of the Author, by William Ernest Henley, LL.D.* 16 vols., London, 1903.

Holdsworth	Sir William Holdsworth. *A History of English Criminal Law.* 16 vols., London, 1922–66.
JHC	*Journals of the House of Commons.*
JJ	Henry Fielding. *The Jacobite's Journal and Relating Writings,* ed. W. B. Coley. Oxford and Middletown, Conn., 1975.
Jonathan Wild	Henry Fielding. *Jonathan Wild,* ed. W. E. Henley. London, 1903.
Jones	B. Maelor Jones. *Henry Fielding, Novelist and Magistrate.* London, 1933.
Joseph Andrews	Henry Fielding. *Joseph Andrews,* ed. Martin C. Battestin. Oxford and Middletown, Conn., 1967.
Loeb	The Loeb Classical Library.
Miscellanies (1743)	*Miscellanies, by Henry Fielding Esq; Volume One,* ed. Henry Knight Miller. Oxford and Middletown, Conn., 1972.
MP	*Modern Philology.*
N&Q	*Notes and Queries.*
OED	*Oxford English Dictionary.*
PMLA	*Publications of the Modern Language Association.*
PQ	*Philological Quarterly.*
Proposal	*A Proposal for making an Effectual Provision for the Poor, for Amending their Morals, and for Rendering them Useful Members of Society.*
Radzinowicz	Leon Radzinowicz. *A History of English Criminal Law and its Administration from 1750.* 4 vols., London, 1948–68.
Rapin	M. Rapin de Thoyras. *The History of England,* trans. Nicholas Tindal. 4th edition. 21 vols., London, 1757.
RES	*Review of English Studies.*
Sedgwick	Romney Sedgwick. *The History of Parliament: The House of Commons, 1715–1754.* 2 vols., New York, 1970.
Select Trials	*Select Trials . . . at the Sessions-House in the Old-Bailey.* 4 vols., London, 1764.
State Trials	T. B. Howell. *Complete Collection of State Trials and Proceedings for High Treason and Other Crimes and Misdemeanors from the Earliest Period.* 33 vols., London, 1809–26.
Statutes at Large	*The Statutes at Large, from Magna Charta to . . . 1761,* ed. Danby Pickering. Cambridge, 1762.
Tom Jones	Henry Fielding. *Tom Jones,* ed. Martin C. Battestin. 2 vols., Oxford and Middletown, Conn., 1974.
TP	Henry Fielding. *The True Patriot,* ed. Miriam Austin Locke. University of Alabama, 1964.
Voyage to Lisbon	Henry Fielding. *The Journal of a Voyage to Lisbon,* ed. Harold E. Pagliaro. New York, 1963.
Zirker, *Social Pamphlets*	Malvin R. Zirker, Jr. *Fielding's Social Pamphlets.* Berkeley and Los Angeles, 1966.

GENERAL INTRODUCTION

I. BIOGRAPHICAL CONTEXT

THE winter of 1748–9 marked both the publication of *Tom Jones* and the active commencement of Fielding's tenure as magistrate for the city and liberty of Westminster and county of Middlesex. Hence it was on the one hand the triumphant culmination of 'some Thousands of Hours' of labor,[1] and on the other the beginning of a brief (some four and a half years), intense, and in many ways impressive career as a magistrate. Fielding's magistracy affected his writings profoundly. In fact, with the exception of the revised version of *The Author's Farce* (1750) and *Jonathan Wild* (1754), everything he published after *Tom Jones*, including the *Covent-Garden Journal, Amelia*, and *The Journal of a Voyage to Lisbon*, as well as the pamphlets printed in this volume, shows the impress of his Bow-Street experience.

The appointment was probably not so much a reward for his literary genius as it was the modest and perhaps disappointing recompense for years of faithful and obliging journalism in the service, if not the commission, of the Pelham Administration.[2] In 1754, in desperate ill health and looking back on his career as a magistrate, Fielding wrote bitterly of the modest rewards he had enjoyed as 'principal justice of peace in Westminster'.[3] In 1749, however, despite the low reputation of the office, he must have viewed his prospects more optimistically. The magistracy offered some security from the uncertainties of pamphleteering and journalism (the last issue of the *Jacobite's Journal* had appeared, appropriately, on Guy Fawkes Day, 5 November 1748), and it must surely have seemed a more promising sinecure than that of 'High Steward to the Warden of the New Forest', which post it is probable that the Duke of Bedford had granted him early in 1748.[4]

---

[1] *Tom Jones*, XI. ii. 571. On the composition of *Tom Jones*, which was undertaken perhaps as early as the spring of 1745, see the General Introduction to *Tom Jones*, pp. xxxv–xlii.

[2] In 1745 Fielding published three pamphlets warning of the consequences of a successful Jacobite invasion: *A Serious Address to the People of Great Britain, The History of the Present Rebellion*, and *A Dialogue between the Devil, the Pope, and the Pretender*. The *True Patriot* began its run on 5 Nov. of the same year (the last issue appeared 17 June 1746). Two political pamphlets of 1747, *A Dialogue between A Gentleman from London . . .*‌ *and an Honest Alderman of the Country Party* and *A Proper Answer to A Late Scurrilous Libel . . .* , are printed in *JJ*. The *Jacobite's Journal* ran from 5 Dec. 1747 to 5 Nov. 1748.

[3] *Voyage to Lisbon*, pp. 34–5 and n. Fielding says that because he administered his post honestly he had reduced 'an income of 500£ a year of the dirtiest money upon the earth, to little more than 300£; a considerable proportion of which remained with my clerk.' The commentary surrounding this passage makes his disillusion with his office clear and underscores the failure of his 'great Patron', here probably the Duke of Newcastle, to support its operation decently.

[4] The evidence for this appointment is presented in M. C. with R. R. Battestin, 'Fielding, Bedford, and the Westminster Election of 1749', *ECS* 11 (1977–8), 146.

Moreover, Fielding had increasing family obligations. His marriage to his first wife's maid, Mary Daniel, had taken place 27 November 1747, and a son, William, had been born 25 February 1748. A daughter, Mary Amelia, was baptized 6 January 1749. To a man once again embarking on family life, his appointment to an office with at least the reputation of being lucrative offered some apparent stability as well as a fresh opportunity to pursue his legal career.

The major documents testifying to Fielding's allegiance to the Pelham Administration during the period 1745 to 1748 are the *True Patriot* and the *Jacobite's Journal*. It has never been demonstrated, though it has often been suspected, that either of these newspapers was undertaken directly at the request of Fielding's political friends or patrons.[5] The same uncertainty as to the precise impulse behind Fielding's good offices as government magistrate hovers over most of the works in this volume. With the exception of *A True State of the Case of Elizabeth Canning*, which arose from circumstances totally unpredictable and essentially unpolitical, all of these pamphlets serve the interests of the Pelham Administration and, taken as a whole, clearly reflect Fielding's eager readiness to praise English government under George II and his willingness to court the favor of such powerful men as Lord Chancellor Hardwicke, Henry Pelham, and the Duke of Bedford. Even *Examples of the Interposition of Providence in the Detection and Punishment of Murder*, despite its pieties, may be seen as an attempt welcome to the government to coerce the good behavior of the lower classes. That any of these pamphlets was written either at the invitation or the command of such figures of power, or shows Fielding to be writing from within the circle of those privy to government policy cannot, however, be shown. Rather, the evidence presented in the following pages indicates that Fielding simply seized those opportunities appropriate to his office to further government interests or, as with *An Enquiry Into the Causes of the late Increase of Robbers* (1751) and *A Proposal for Making an Effectual Provision for the Poor* (1753), offered his own elaborate solutions to problems Parliament currently was debating. Undoubtedly he hoped that these demonstrations of his loyalty and displays of his skills would win further favor, but though he wrote essentially as a political appointee whose voice could not be entirely his own, one never senses in these writings that Fielding speaks against his conscience.

The vexed and confusing questions surrounding his successive appointments to the Middlesex and Westminster commissions of the peace seem now to have been satisfactorily answered. The documents pertaining to his commissions, some of which G. M. Godden apparently found but failed to document in her valuable, pioneering study of Fielding,[6] have for the most

---

[5] See *JJ* pp. lv–lvi; and *TP* p. 5.
[6] Godden, pp. 173 and 195 ff.

part been located and described in two important articles, one by William B. Coley and the other by Martin with Ruthe Battestin.[7] The process of qualification for the Middlesex commission was initiated as early as June of 1747 but was not perfected until the spring of 1749. Though Fielding had begun to sit as justice of the peace for the city and liberty of Westminster by 2 November 1748,[8] he could not sit for Middlesex until he had satisfied the requirement that he hold property valued at £100 per annum. His request to the Duke of Bedford for the lease of houses valued at this amount is well known;[9] now it is certain that Bedford complied with his request.[1]

The low reputation of these commissions, which Fielding was obliged to seek eagerly and for which, at least in the matter of the property qualification, he was to render abject thanks to the Duke of Bedford,[2] has never been in doubt. Probably the most often quoted anecdote concerning Fielding and the office of 'trading justice'[3] is that found in a note to Paul Whitehead's 'An Epistle to Doctor Thompson' [1751]: 'It is reported, that during the time Mr. Addison was Secretary of State, when his old Friend and Ally, Ambrose Phillips, applied to him for some preferment, the Great Man, very coolly answered, that "He thought he had already provided for him, by making him Justice for Westminster." To which the Bard, with some indignation, replied, "Though Poetry was a trade he *could not* thrive by, yet he scorned to owe his subsistence to another, which he *ought not* to live by."—However Great Men, in our days, may practice the Secretary's *prudence*, certain it is, the Person here pointed at [Fielding] was very far from making a precedent of his Brother Poet's *principles*.'[4] There is abundant evidence in the literature of the period (not least in Fielding's own portraits

[7] W. B. Coley, 'Fielding's Two Appointments to the Magistracy', *MP* 63 (1965–6), 144–9; M. C. with R. R. Battestin, 'Fielding, Bedford, and the Westminster Election', pp. 143–85.

[8] Archibald Bolling Shepperson first demonstrated that Fielding was hearing cases at this early date ('Additions and Corrections to Facts about Fielding', *MP* 51 [1954], 217–20.

[9] First printed in Godden, pp. 196–7. Sidney and Beatrice Webb state that this modest property qualification was often and easily avoided (*The Parish and the County* [London, 1906], p. 324).

[1] Fielding's letters of thanks to Bedford and his principal agent, Robert Butcher, are printed for the first time in the article cited above by M. C. with R. R. Battestin: items 8 and 9 of the appendix.

[2] Fielding closes his letter to Bedford 'with unspeakable Gratitude and Devotion'; in that to Butcher he regrets that he is 'not yet able to throw myself at [Bedford's] Feet'.

[3] The term refers to those justices, notoriously common in the London metropolitan area, who supposedly made a trade of their office by seeking out 'business' for the sake of the generally modest fee involved. See S. and B. Webb, *The Parish and the County*, pp. 321 ff.

[4] *The Poems and Miscellaneous Compositions of Paul Whitehead*, ed. Captain Edward Thompson (London, 1777), p. 114 n. The apologist for Con Phillips (who may have been Whitehead) also ridiculed Fielding as trading justice:

At present, we shall leave him in the vain Possession of his mercenary Tribunal; issuing forth *Twelve-penny Citations* to his *legal Warehouse*, and earning a scandalous Subsistance by the Sale of that Justice, which, to be rendered *respectable*, ought to be *less venal* and *less exercised*.

But when the Dispensation of Justice is made a *Trade*, no Wonder the *Rod* of Authority should become a *Scorpion* in the Hands of those, whose Backs would much better justify the Application of it (*An Apology for the Conduct of Mrs. Teresia Constantia Phillips* [London, 1748–9], iii. 321).

of trading justices in *The Coffee-House Politican* and *Amelia*) of the widespread opprobrium of the office.[5] Early in the century (1716) Thomas Baston attacked 'trading justices', observing, ''Tis a common proverb amongst Us, As Corrupt as a Middlesex Justice: And indeed they are corrupt enough.'[6] Towards its close (1780) Burke remarked that 'The Justices of Middlesex were generally the scum of the earth—carpenters, brickmakers, and shoemakers; some of whom were notoriously men of such infamous characters that they were unworthy of any employ whatever, and others so ignorant that they could scarcely write their own names.'[7] Fielding's most famous predecessor, Sir Thomas De Veil, who also seems to have acted as the principal magistrate for Middlesex and Westminster,[8] was not trained to the law but acquired a knowledge of his office on his own. His memoirist observes that De Veil's fellow justices are 'a sort of people that have never stood in a very fair light, either with their superiors or inferiors: by the former they are generally considered as low, needy, and mercenary tools, who subsist on their commissions, and may be put upon any thing by such as have either power or interest sufficient to affect them. On the other hand, they are hated and dreaded by the common people, who fancy they have far greater powers than they really have.'[9] De Veil himself stressed the corruptions surrounding his office and the dangers inherent in the fee system which provided the only official remuneration for justices of the peace.[1]

That the appointment to this office proved to be the culmination of Fielding's legal career surely is a mournful fact in the biography of a man abundantly possessed of merit and talent. It was so considered by some of his contemporaries. Lady Mary Wortley Montagu commented that 'the highest

---

[5] It is not clear to what extent this low reputation is owing to class bias. Traditionally the justice of the peace was drawn from the gentry and was a man of substance who expected no gain from his office. When this essentially rural tradition was translated to the city where gentlemen willing to undertake a heavy case load of urban crime were rare, the justice of the peace was likely to be a man who accepted the office for profit and whose social standing invited the sneers of such as Burke (quoted below). The actual extent of the venality of London trading justices is unknown. They could scarcely have been more ignorant of the law than Fielding's Squire Western.

[6] *Thoughts on Trade and a Publick Spirit* (London, 1716), p. 127.

[7] *Parliamentary History*, 8 May 1780, xxi. 592; cit. by S. and B. Webb, *The Parish and the County*, p. 325.

[8] The writer of *Memoirs of the Life and Times of Sir Thomas Deveil* (London, 1748) attempts a history of this unofficial office (pp. 22 ff.). The Webbs state that at least in the 18th century 'there existed what was called "the Court Justice"—one of the Justices of the Peace for the Metropolitan area, to whom the Government gave instructions, and on whom it relied for prompt and obedient action in any emergency' (ibid., p. 337).

[9] *Memoirs*, p. 18.

[1] In *Observations on the Practice of a Justice of the Peace: Intended for such Gentlemen as Design to Act for Middlelex* [sic] *or Westminster* (London, 1747). De Veil enjoyed numerous government rewards, financial and titular, for his services (see *Memoir*, p. 67; S. and B. Webb, *The Parish and the County*, pp. 339 ff.), including 'a lucrative employment in the *Customs*.' One remembers that Fielding asked unsuccessfully for 'the Place of Solicitor to the Excise' (Cross, ii. 242).

of his preferment [was] raking in the lowest sinks of vice and misery' and thought it 'a nobler and less nauseous employment to be one of the staff officers that conduct nocturnal weddings'.[2] Later, Sir John Hawkins ungenerously and inaccurately remarked that '[Fielding] was, in his early life, a writer of comedies and farces, very few of which are now remembered; after that, a practising barrister with scarce any business; then an anti-ministerial writer, and quickly after, a creature of the duke of Newcastle, who gave him a nominal qualification of 100£ a year, and set him up as a trading-justice, in which disreputable station he died.'[3] Curiously, Hawkins himself was in the commission of the peace for Middlesex, perhaps recommended to Newcastle for that post by Paul Whitehead.[4]

Fielding had begun his pursuit of a legal career with high ambitions. Cross states that after the publication of the *Miscellanies* in 1743, Fielding for several years devoted himself wholly to the law and 'was making extraordinary efforts to succeed'.[5] He is probably correct in asserting that 'Fielding . . . once had the ambition to end his career on the King's Bench like his kinsmen among the Goulds'.[6] Perhaps Fielding's initial hope for advancement lay in the mysterious work on criminal law which was announced for publication early in 1745 ('TWO VOLUMES *in Folio*' entitled 'An Institute of the Pleas of the Crown') but which never appeared and about which little is known.[7] In any case, the kind wishes of that rare figure—an anonymous writer sympathetic to Fielding—were not to be realized:

> Accept the hearty Wish, nor take it ill,
> Plainess is Elegance with pure Good Will.
> O! may the plural Fee so fertile rise,
> *Briareus'* Hands to take shall scarce suffice:
> May the vast Toil be paid with vast Rewards;
> May Furry Honours crown the Muse-lost Bard:
> May to the *Orator* the *Member* follow,
> And yield at last a *Talbot* from *Apollo*.[8]

What is remarkable, of course, is what Fielding made of his meager opportunities. As Martin Battestin says, Fielding 'did much to reform a corrupt and despised office, restoring it from the abuses of venal and

---

[2] *Letters of Lady Mary Wortley Montagu*, ed. W. Moy Thomas (London [1861]), ii. 282–3.

[3] *The Works of Samuel Johnson* (London, 1787), i. 214.

[4] Bertram H. Davis, *A Proof of Eminence: the Life of Sir John Hawkins* (Bloomington, In., 1973) p. 176.

[5] Cross, ii. 1–2.   [6] Ibid., p. 96.

[7] See W. B. Coley, 'Henry Fielding's "Lost" Law Book', *MLN* 76 (1961) 408–13; and Hugh Amory, 'A Preliminary Census of Henry Fielding's Legal Manuscripts', *PBSA* 62 (1968), 587–601.

[8] *The Young Senator. A Satyre. With an Epistle to Mr. 'Fielding', on his Studying the Law* (London, 1738), p. 18.

incompetent petty tyrants . . . to its proper function as an instrument for administering justice and preserving the social order'.[9] His initiatives in establishing a stable body of thief-takers and creating a central police court have won him a secure position as one of the founders of the British police system.[1] The best evidence, however, of his ability to bring some measure of dignity and high seriousness to those dreary scenes and activities spreading from Bow Street and Westminster to the outreaches of Middlesex lies in the pamphlets collected in the present volume. Though they are all, in one way or another, occasional pieces prompted either by the immediate pressure of events or directed to issues current and topical, taken together they represent an energetic, sincere, and informed response to the obligations and opportunities of his office. They show Fielding to be an accomplished jurist who, within the limitations of a conservative and traditional world-view, sought, in a broad sense, to see justice done. One must not minimize the limitations imposed by Fielding's conservative social outlook.[2] One looks in vain in these pamphlets for any sign of dissatisfaction with the traditional structures of society. What one finds is acceptance of fixed social roles, of class privilege and class disequalities, and approval of an antiquated and often brutal criminal code, a code which Fielding, unlike many of his contemporaries, wished to apply rigorously. But even in the *Proposal*, surely the grimmest of these pamphlets, where Fielding advocates an enormous workhouse to set the poor at work, one finds at least fleeting expression of sympathy for the misery and suffering of the poor:

if we were to make a Progress through the Outskirts of this Town, and look into the Habitations of the Poor, we should there behold such Pictures of human Misery as must move the Compassion of every Heart that deserves the Name of Human. What indeed must be his Composition who could see whole Families in Want of every Necessary of Life, oppressed with Hunger, Cold, Nakedness, and Filth, and with Diseases, the certain Consequence of all these; what, I say, must be his Composition, who could look into such a Scene as this, and be affected only in his Nostrils?[3]

At mid-century, desperate though the conditions of the poor in London were, compassionate and knowledgeable observations such as these, especially in writings directly about the poor, are sadly rare.

---

[9] 'Fielding, Bedford, and the Westminster Election', p. 149.
[1] Fielding's pre-trial initiatives as court justice of the peace are conveniently summarized in John H. Langbein's important article, 'Shaping the Eighteenth-Century Criminal Trial: A View from the Ryder Sources', *The University of Chicago Law Review*, 50 (1983), 60–7.
[2] For discussion of Fielding's conservatism, see Zirker, *Social Pamphlets, passim*.
[3] Below, p. 230.

2. A CHARGE . . . TO THE GRAND JURY

Fielding was elected Chairman of the Westminster quarter sessions in May 1749,[1] and apparently continued to enjoy that honor until his declining health ended his attendance at quarter sessions.[2] It is important to be clear about the jurisdiction of the Westminster quarter sessions, which were held four times a year out of term in Westminster. As Fielding indicates (*Charge*, p. 12) and as the range of offences he touches upon in the *Charge* implies, the Westminster quarter sessions centered on the hearing of misdemeanor cases, cases involving 'public nuisances', and were not addressed to 'crimes of the deeper dye'. Such crimes would be preferred either to Middlesex general sessions, held six times a year at Hicks's Hall, St John Street, Clerkenwell, and twice a year (April and October sessions) at Westminster Hall; or, if within the jurisdiction of the city of London, at the Old Bailey Sessions House adjoining Newgate Prison. Elizabeth Canning was indicted for perjury at Hicks's Hall, where too a grand jury found the bill of indictment against Heartfree.[3]

Since in some unofficial capacity Fielding seems to have been considered, and considered himself, 'principal magistrate' for the metropolis of London, and since he was in fact listed in His Majesty's commission for the county of Middlesex as well as for the city and liberty of Westminster, these wider authorities have misleadingly been attached to his charge to the Westminster grand jury. This misconception has been furthered by the tradition that Fielding was chairman of the Middlesex sessions, a notion first started by an announcement in the *General Advertiser*, 17 May 1749, erroneously stating that 'Counsellor Fielding' was chosen 'Chairman of the Sessions at Hicks Hall for the County of Middlesex',[4] and still repeated in a 1979 biography of Fielding.[5] In fact with respect to the legal machinery at work in London and the county of Middlesex, the authority of the Westminster quarter sessions was relatively modest, and it was misleading for Cross to describe Fielding's *Charge* as a 'manifesto' addressed to the citizens of Middlesex (ii. 230).

---

[1] Godden has noted the following entry in the *Sessions Book* of Westminster, 1749: 'May. 1749, Mr.Fielding elected chairman of this present Session, and to continue until the 2nd day of the next' (p. 204 n.).

[2] Godden states that on 12 Jan. 1750 'Fielding was again elected as chairman "for the two next Quarter Sessions"; which election was repeated, "for the two next Sessions," in July' (ibid., p. 220). According to Anthony Babington, there is reason to believe that Fielding 'stayed on as Chairman throughout the whole of the time he was an active member of the Westminster Commission' (*A House in Bow Street: Crime and the Magistracy, London 1740–1881* [London, 1969], p. 77). Standing chairmanships were customary (S. and B. Webb, *The Parish and the County*, [London, 1906], p. 435).

[3] *Jonathan Wild*, IV. i, 146.

[4] Godden, p. 204. See also Mary Margaret Stewart, 'Notes on Henry Fielding as Magistrate', *N & Q* 214 (1969), 348–50; and 'A Correction and Further Note Concerning Henry Fielding as Magistrate', *N & Q* 218 (1973), 13–15.

[5] Pat Rogers, *Henry Fielding, a Biography* (New York, 1979), p. 179.

If the authority addressed by Fielding's *Charge* was limited, one imagines that the occasion none the less possessed considerable grandeur. The list of justices of the peace in the Westminster Commission who formed the bench for the quarter sessions indicates a distinguished audience. The Right Honourable George Lord Carpenter was probably the son of the George Carpenter who had sat for Westminster in the House of Commons (1722–7) and who had been raised to the peerage in 1719.[6] Sir John Crosse came of a substantial Westminster family (originally brewers) and was to sit for Westminster (1754–61). Among the more professional magistrates one notes the name of Thomas Lediard, a particularly active magistrate who, like Fielding, used the front of his house in New Palace Yard as a courtroom.[7] It was to Lediard that Virtue Hall was to recant her confession in the Elizabeth Canning case.

If one accepts the arguments of Douglas Hay in 'Property, Authority, and the Criminal Law',[8] one could see Fielding's delivery of his *Charge* as dramaturgical enactment, as performance in that licensed theater of the ruling class. The association of stage and court is at least as old as the *Eumenides*, but Hay's perspective is markedly more political than religious. He sees the criminal law as an 'ideological system', as a 'specific set of ideas designed to vindicate or disguise class interest' (p. 26 and n.), and from this perspective comments on the 'majesty' of the courtroom scene: 'In the court room the judges' every action was governed by the importance of spectacle. Blackstone asserted that "the novelty and very parade of . . . [their] appearance have no small influence upon the multitude": scarlet robes lined with ermine and full-bottomed wigs in the seventeenth-century style, which evoked scorn from Hogarth but awe from ordinary men.'[9] Hay's definition of ideology is probably more appropriate to his own perspective than to eighteenth-century law, but his observations about legal spectacle are pertinent to the traditional public performance that Fielding's *Charge* represents.

The presiding justice's charge to the grand jury was one of the signal public events in the legal process of assizes and quarter sessions. The ceremonies attached to assizes were generally grander, for they involved the semi-annual visitation of the king's justices to the counties, an event that the principal gentlemen of the county inevitably attended either as members of

---

[6] Carpenter was a friend of the Hon. Alexander Murray and Sir George Vandeput, central figures in the Westminster election of 1749 (see below, pp. xlv ff.).

[7] Hugh Phillips, *Mid-Georgian London* (London, 1964), p. 19 and p. 152. Lediard had succeeded Fielding as Chairman of the Westminster Sessions by July 1753; his *Charge . . . to the Grand Jury . . . for Westminster* directed against Bolingbroke's *Works* (1752) was published in 1754.

[8] In *Albion's Fatal Tree: Crime and Society in Eighteenth-Century England* (New York, 1975), pp. 17 ff.

[9] Ibid., p. 27. Hay's argument that the 'manipulation of the law by the wealthy and powerful' amounts to a 'ruling-class conspiracy', is refuted by John H. Langbein in 'Albion's Fatal Flaws', *Past and Present*, 98 (1983), 96–120.

the bench or of the grand jury or as participants in the social affairs surrounding the arrival of His Majesty's justice. There were no assizes for London or Middlesex, the king's courts being ready at hand in Westminster Hall, but quarter sessions in Westminster and in London and general sessions for Middlesex provided frequent occasion for judicial pronouncement and ceremony.

The charge to the grand jury followed the swearing of the grand jurors and preceded the calling of prosecutors and witnesses. As Fielding points out, the grand jury was not only to determine whether indictments brought before it were to be found 'true bills' or not, it was also empowered to 'present' offences to the petit jurors on its own initiative. Consequently, as E. G. Dowdell notes, the charge was of great importance and 'the Chairman had great influence on the character of the presentments initiated by the Grand Jury and, one suspects, not a little affected their willingness to find bills at the instance of others'.[1] Relatively few of the many thousands of charges delivered to grand juries in the eighteenth century have survived (the Webbs cite only ten charges published in the eighteenth century before Fielding's),[2] but we may safely assume that, when not totally perfunctory,[3] the chairman's charge focused on those social disorders he considered particularly in need of redress.

Fielding must have prepared his maiden charge with an especially sharp sense of the moment not only as an occasion fraught with legal tradition but also as one full of significance for his personal fortunes. Whatever satisfaction he derived in imagination from being read 'with Honour, by those who never knew nor saw me, and whom I shall neither know nor see', or in fact from that 'much plumper Dame, whom no airy Forms nor Phantoms of Imagination cloathe' (*Tom Jones*, XIII. i, 683–4), the immediate benefits of *Tom Jones* were now in the past. For his present occasions it must have seemed that his fortunes lay, once more, with the law, heretofore an indifferent mistress.

Certainly, and I shall say more of this in a moment, he intended to display a distinguished expertise in his profession. But he must have been aware also of the ironies and incongruities potential in his situation, at least as they would be perceived and publicized by his large circle of enemies and detractors. To speak in formal garb and measured periods of the disorders fostered by too frequent public amusements and by unlicensed theaters or of the scandalous and mischievous nature of the public press, was to invite

[1] *A Hundred Years of Quarter Sessions* (Cambridge, 1932), p. 2.

[2] S. and B. Webb, *The Parish and the County*, p. 448. A good number more are listed in the recent *A Bibliography of Eighteenth Century Legal Literature* by J. N. Adams and G. Averley (Newcastle Upon Tyne, 1982), pp. 403–5. But this bibliography records only fifteen charges, including Fielding's, addressed to London grand juries in the first half of the 18th century.

[3] As they must often have been when chairmen served many years consecutively.

rebuke.[4] Cibber's memorable if not wholly accurate comment on Fielding's responsibility for the Licensing Act of 1737 ('this Drawcansir in wit . . . to make his poetical fame immortal, like another Erostratus, set fire to his stage by writing up to an Act of Parliament to demolish it'[5]), is one memento of Fielding's injudicial past. As both dramatist and journalist, he had contributed vigorously to the violent world of eighteenth-century politics and had lashed the guilty by name.

Less than eight months intervene between Fielding's *Charge* and the last number of the *Jacobite's Journal* (Fielding in fact had begun his magisterial duties three days before the last issue of that newspaper[6]), and Fielding's ironic creation of John Trottplaid stood in stark enough contrast to His Majesty's justice. Fielding always assumed the literary and moral superiority of his journalism over 'the low, quibbling, unintelligible Articles of a *London Evening Post*; or the more than Cimmerian-Darkness of the Bellman of *Westminster*, or of the Argus, with all his Eyes out, of *Old England*',[7] and the assumption in the *Charge* of the social meanness of scribblers for the public press was gallingly familiar: 'to the Shame of the Age be it spoken, there are Men who make a Livelihood of Scandal. Most of these are Persons of the lowest Rank and Education, Men who lazily declining the Labour to which they were born and bred, save the Sweat of their Brows at the Expence of their Consciences; and in order to get a little better Livelihood, are content to get it, perhaps, in a less painful, but in a baser Way than the meanest Mechanic' (p. 29).

In the *Jacobite's Journal* Fielding's indulgence in the give and take of personal insult publicly displayed is nowhere more sharply represented than in his attack on the mimic and comedian Samuel Foote, an attack pertinent here because it is clearly Foote whom Fielding has in mind in the *Charge* when he rebukes that furious 'appetite for Pleasure' that leaves the public 'not content with three Theatres, they must have a fourth; where the Exhibitions are not only contrary to Law, but contrary to Good-Manners, and where the Stage is reduced back again to that Degree of Licentiousness

---

[4] Such as that delivered in *An Apology for the Conduct of Mrs. Teresia Constantia Phillips* (1748–9):

But, gentle Readers, must it not be pleasant enough to hear this *Mite of Magistracy* haranguing his gaping Brethren upon the *Licentiousness of the Press*, which he himself had so many Years polluted; and thundering out his *harmless Vengeance*, against the honest Exercise of that *Liberty*, which he had so shamefully *abused*? . . .

No sooner had this *new Convert to the Gospel and the Ministry*, by a most flagrant Prostitution of his Tongue and Pen, wriggled himself into a *little dirty Authority*; but he at once commences Zealot in the Work of Reformation (iii. 318–19).

[5] *An Apology for the Life of Mr. Colley Cibber*, ed. Robert W. Lowe (London, 1888), i. 349.

[6] Archibald Bolling Shepperson has shown that Fielding was active as a Westminster magistrate by 2 Nov. 1748 ('Additions and Corrections to Facts about Fielding', *MP* 51 [1954], 217). The last issue of the *Jacobite's Journal* appeared 5 Nov. 1748.

[7] *JJ* no. 1 (5 Dec. 1747), pp. 96–7.

which was too enormous for the corrupt state of *Athens* to tolerate.'[8]

The story of Fielding's quarrel with Foote has been told by scholars sympathetic both to Fielding and to Foote.[9] Fielding, who appears to have been the aggressor, had attacked Foote in the *Jacobite's Journal* as a bad actor ('fit only . . . to give Tea') and a libeller.[1] But it was at his puppet theater in Panton Street[2] that Fielding most actively pursued the attack. His advertisement in the *General Advertiser* for 14 April 1748 announced that 'Mimicking' (i.e., Foote) would be among the 'Comical Humours of the Town' satirized in the performance of 18 April—the same day Foote was to initiate his *Auction of Pictures* wherein one of the portraits 'sold' was of Fielding. By April 30, Fielding's anger required more durable expression, and he hailed Foote before his 'Court of Criticism' in the *Jacobite's Journal*, found him guilty of indecent personal abuse, and passed sentence: 'I . . . proceed . . . to pronounce the Judgment of the Court; which is, that you *Samuel Fut* be p–ssed upon, with Scorn and Contempt, as a low Buffoon; and I do, with the utmost Scorn and Contempt, p–ss upon you accordingly.

'The Prisoner was then removed from the Bar, mimicking and pulling a Chew of Tobacco from his Mouth, while the P–ss ran plentifully down his Face.'[3]

However one judges Fielding here, the incident certainly dramatizes the potential embarrassment he faced as spokesman for the legal establishment, especially as a censor of disruptive public amusements and indecorous journalism. He ran his puppet theater, in fact, by the same subterfuge used by Foote, offering the performance gratis and charging only for 'the very best of / TEA, COFFEE, CHOCOLATE, and JELLIES'.[4] Battestin adduces abundant evidence that contemporaries, especially in the pages of *Old England*, found a rich vein of ridicule in the incongruities between Fielding as puppet-master and Fielding as justice of the peace even before his election as chairman of the Westminster quarter sessions. As we shall see, the political quarrels surrounding the *Case of Bosavern Penlez* intensified such attacks on Fielding.

One other incident lies behind Fielding's censure of the unlicensed performances at the Haymarket, where Foote's activities both as mimic and comedian continued until just four weeks before Fielding's delivery of the

---

[8] *Charge*, below, p. 24. Because of his personal satires, Foote had acquired the nickname of 'the English Aristophanes'.

[9] See Martin C. Battestin, 'Fielding and "Master Punch" in Panton Street', *PQ* 45 (1968), 191–208; and Simon Trefman, *Sam. Foote, Comedian, 1720–1777* (New York, 1971), pp. 15–40.

[1] *JJ* no. 10 (6 Feb. 1748), p. 153; and no. 22 (30 Apr. 1748), pp. 264–5.

[2] See Martin Battestin's article cited above for Fielding's management of this puppet theater.

[3] *JJ* no. 22, p. 266. Fielding was fond of chewing tobacco.

[4] In *JJ* no. 22 (p. 264), Fielding complained against this transparent device to evade the restrictions of the Licensing Act of 1737.

Charge to the Jury and which now included attacks on Fielding's friends Garrick and Woodward. The famous Bottle-Conjuror's hoax, which resulted in a riot causing, in the estimate of the owner of the theater, John Potter, £4,000 in damages, took place on 16 January 1749. Just such an event was what Fielding as magistrate was concerned to decry when he called the attention of the grand jurors to 'This Fury after licentious and luxurious Pleasures'. In this instance, however, it is at least amusing to note that the Duke of Richmond, whom Fielding praises and whose intense pursuit of Sussex smugglers brought him knowledge useful to Fielding in tracking down gangs of London criminals,[5] may in part have been responsible for this riot, which incidentally deprived Foote of his theater for some time. At least such is the implication of an account appearing in *Town and Country Magazine* (September 1772, p. 457):

This was a scheme planned by the late Duke of Montague, in company with the Duke of Richmond, and some other noblemen of distinguished taste and humour; who conversing upon the credulity of the English nation, the first of these noblemen offered a wager of 100 guineas that if an advertisement was publish'd setting forth that on such a day a man would get into a bottle, the inhabitants of this metropolis would flock to pay for being spectators of an impossibility. The event confirmed his Grace's opinion, and of course won him the bet; but it was fatal to the proprietors of the House in the Haymarket, who sustained considerable loss from the resentment of the audience at being imposed upon, as no such exhibition was attempted.[6]

In his *Charge* Fielding betrays no consciousness of past or impending animadversions on his position as magistrate or as chairman of the grand jury. His *Charge* is a masterly and assured model of its kind, confident and dignified in tone, precise in application, rich in legal allusion, and thoroughly at ease with the perspective of judicial tradition. Its measure may best be taken by comparing it to the other extant examples of its kind, few though they are. Model charges may be found in handbooks and treatises concerned with the office of justice of the peace—Fielding mentions (*Charge*, p. 16) the one in Lambarde's *Eirenarcha*—but such examples tended to be inclusive lists of indictable offenses within the grand jury's jurisdiction, offering the king's plenty in inchoate form. Five charges by Sir John Gonson, delivered in 1728–9; three by Whitlocke Bulstrode, in 1718 and 1722; and one each by Sir Daniel Dolins (1725), William Cowper (1719), and William Hay (1733) better illuminate the distinction of Fielding's *Charge*.[7]

---

[5] See *Enquiry*, below, p. 126 and n. 6.

[6] Cited by George Winchester Stone, Jr., *The London Stage, 1747–1776: A Critical Introduction* (Carbondale, 1968), p. cxcviii.

[7] See *Sir John Gonson's Five Charges to Several Grand Juries*, 3rd edn. (London, 1730); and *The Charge of Sir Daniel Dolins, Kt* (London, 1725). The three *Charges* of Whitlocke Bulstrode and that of William Cowper are bound together, BL 883. e. 17. William Hay's *Charge* is reprinted in *Works* (London, 1794), i. 303–16 (for Hay, see *Proposal*, below, p. lxxv and n. 6). Nearly all of these charges

Most of these charges employ the same division Fielding found useful and distinguish offences against God, king, and fellow subject. They are likely to begin with praise of the jury system and of English justice and to include praise of the House of Hanover. Offenses such as Fielding mentions are customarily cited—blasphemy, misprisions, 'Riots, Routs, and unlawful Assemblies', gambling, bawdy-houses, libels—as are some that, surprisingly, Fielding ignores, such as the evils of gin-drinking and drunkenness. Some of the charges are strongly topical. Gonson's fifth *Charge*, for instance, is largely directed at *Mists'* libellous twenty-fourth number (August, 1728); Bulstrode's second *Charge* focuses on deistical and atheistical writers such as Toland.

There are relatively few legal or historical references in these charges. Only Gonson demonstrates anything like Fielding's range of learning. His first *Charge*, for instance, begins with a Hobbesian account of the origins of society, and observes that 'it is one of the most valuable Parts of our Constitution, that no Man can be convicted, or attainted of any Crime, before two Juries pass upon him, of at least Twenty four Persons' (p. 15), and he cites the passage in Fortescue's *De Laudibus* that Fielding cites for the origin of the jury system. His fourth *Charge* includes references to Horne's *Mirror of Justice*, Coke, Bracton, Britton, Nathaniel Bacon, Petyt, and Machiavelli's *Discourse*, all writers whom Fielding cites either in the *Charge* or the *Enquiry*. But there is nothing in any of these charges comparable to Fielding's easy allusions to historians like Daniel, Echard, Rapin, and Spelman; his learned citation of law reporters like Keble, Croke, Anderson, and Kelying; or his familiarity with legal 'books of authority' like Bracton's *De Legibus et consuetudinibus Angliae*, Coke's *Institutes*, the Year Books, and the *Custumier de Normandy*. Unique too is his willingness to debate with Coke a learned topic such as the origin and antiquity of the Court of Star Chamber, or his ability to grace his observations with classical allusions.

It is Fielding's display of erudition which most clearly distinguishes his *Charge* from others of its kind, for in an occasional and formulaic address any attempt at an original disquisition on the law would have been inappropriate. Earlier, in *Joseph Andrews*, he had commented ironically on the absence of any instruction from the bench at quarter sessions. To the observation that 'it is usual for the young Gentlemen of the Bar to repair to these Sessions, not so much for the sake of Profit, as to shew their Parts and learn the Law of the Justices of Peace: for which purpose one of the wisest and gravest of all the Justices is appointed Speaker or Chairman, as they modestly call it, and he reads them a Lecture, and instructs them in the true Knowledge of the

include the formulaic compliment that it was '. . . *a very Learned and Useful Charge, and highly tending to the Service of His Majesty and His Government*' and record that it is printed at the desire of the justices of the peace and the grand jurors.

Law', Parson Adams, with his childlike clarity of observation, gently enters a demurrer: ' "You are here guilty of a little Mistake . . . which if you please I will correct; I have attended at one of these Quarter Sessions, where I observed the Counsel taught the Justices, instead of learning any thing of them" ' (II. iv. 107). In *Amelia*, Justice Thrasher's profound ignorance of the law was to prompt the more bitterly ironic comment that 'I own, I have been sometimes inclined to think that the office of a justice of peace requires some knowledge of the law'. The narrator goes on to observe that 'the statutes which relate to this office . . . [make] themselves at least two large volumes in folio; and that part of his jurisdiction which is founded on the common law [is] dispersed in above a hundred volumes' (I. ii. 17). These hundred legal volumes and more were in Fielding's library, and the *Charge to the Grand Jury*, as well as the other writings in this volume, leave no doubt that Fielding had assimilated them. The *Charge* is both a public display of his credentials and an anticipatory response, inevitably unheeded, to those who would ridicule his sober posture at the bench.

Only a legal historian can speak with authority on the extent of Fielding's expertise in the law (none such, 'war and wys', who have written about Fielding have questioned it). My impression is that he was not merely competent but learned in his profession and possessed an easy and confident command of the legal literature of his day and an assured comprehension of the legal principles and processes with which he dealt. Murphy tells us that Fielding's 'application, while he was a student in the Temple, was remarkably intense',[8] and he has also recorded that 'Mr. Fielding is allowed to have acquired a respectable share of jurisprudence, and, in some particular branches, he is said to have arisen to a great degree of eminence; more especially in crown-law, as may be judged from his leaving two volumes in folio upon that subject. This work still remains unpublished in the hands of his brother, Sir John Fielding; and by him I am informed, that it is deemed perfect in some parts'.[9] We can accept these statements about Fielding's qualifications without question.

It is also my impression, however, that Fielding's legal allusions fall within a range customary and conventional to his subject matter. Sir William Holdsworth has remarked that 'the two great sources of our English law are the statute book and the law made by the lawyers to be found in reports of decided cases, in the plea rolls, and in books of authority'.[1] Fielding of course owned the *Statutes at Large* (the first item in the list of books selected for special attention at the head of Baker's sale *Catalogue of . . . Books of Henry*

---

[8] Arthur Murphy, 'An Essay on the Life and Genius of Henry Fielding, Esq.,' In *The Works of Henry Fielding, Esq.* (London, 1762), i. 28.

[9] Ibid., p. 29.

[1] *Sources and Literature of English Law* (Oxford, 1925), p. 4.

Fielding[2] is 'Statutes at large down to the 26th Year of the Reign of the present King, 34 vol.'), and he cites them nearly always with scrupulous accuracy. He owned many of the privately compiled reports of cases published in the sixteenth, seventeenth, and eighteenth centuries which were ascribed, not always accurately, to distinguished judges (the second item in the list just mentioned is 'Almost all the Reports in Law'); and he owned, and used, the Year Books, roughly the medieval equivalent of the modern law report. He also owned most of the standard 'books of authority' of his day, books clearly established in received opinion as central to the study and application of the law.

My hope is that the annotations to the *Grand Jury* sufficiently identify and place in context most of these books of authority. The point to be made here is that none of the authorities that Fielding cites is unusual or unexpected, especially when his context is criminal law. The section in Bracton's *De Legibus et consuetudinibus Angliae* on crown law (*De Corona*) was, and still is, recognized as the most important early treatise on that subject. Britton and Fleta had long been identified as important supplementary texts.[3] The Year Books, despite being printed in law-French, a dialect Blackstone calls 'barbarous', and which, he continues, 'joined to the additional terrors of a Gothic black letter, has occasioned many a student to throw away his Plowden and Littelton, without venturing to attack a page of them',[4] continued to be cited with regularity in the eighteenth century (and they are still cited today).

Fielding's most important authorities are Coke, Sir Matthew Hale, and William Hawkins.[5] Coke, of course, was everybody's authority. He was the first legal writer since Bracton to attempt a complete exposition of English law. Fielding had remarked in *Tom Jones* (III. iii, 126) that Coke's *Commentary on Littelton* was 'of equal Authority with the Text', and he makes

---

[2] For his auction of Fielding's library, held 10–13 Feb. 1755, Samuel Baker published *A Catalogue of the Entire and Valuable Library of Books of the Late Henry Fielding, Esq.* (BL S–C Sotheby. 2. [3]). It is reprinted, with commentary, by Hugh Amory in *Sale Catalogues of Libraries of Eminent Persons* (London, 1973), vii. 123–58; and by Ethel Margaret Thornbury in *Henry Fielding's Theory of the Comic Prose Epic*, University of Wisconsin Studies in Language and Literature, 30 (Madison, 1931), pp. 168–89.

[3] In the 'Proeme' to the *Second Part of the Institutes* (completed by 1628; published 1641), Coke had written, 'We in this second Part of the *Institutes*, treating of the ancient and other Statutes have been inforced almost of necessity to cite our ancient Authors, *Bracton, Britton*, the *Mirror, Fleta*, and many Records, never before published in print, to the end the prudent Reader may discerne what the Common Law was before the making of every of those Statutes, which we handle in this Work, and thereby know whether the Statute be introductory of a new Law, or declaratory of the old, which will conduce much to the true understanding of the Text its selfe.'

[4] *Comm.* iii. 318.

[5] 'Five stars of the first magnitude have shone in the firmament of legal literature—Glanvill, Bracton, Littleton, Coke, and Blackstone. Others nearly as bright as they, are the writers of Fitzherbert's *Natura Brevium*, Hale's History of the *Pleas of the Crown*, and Hawkins's *Pleas of the Crown* . . .' (Percy H. Winfield, *The Chief Sources of English Legal History* [Cambridge, Mass. 1925], p. 254). For Hawkins see *Charge*, below, p. 4 n. 2.

substantial use of the second, third, and fourth *Institutes* (which treat, respectively, early statutes, criminal law, and the jurisdiction of the courts) and Coke's *Reports* as well as the more famous *Commentary* (from which Fielding draws information on Anglo-Saxon England). Hale's *Historia Placitorum Coronae* was left unfinished at his death in 1676. None the less, in 1680 the House of Commons ordered it to be printed (though it was not to be published until 1736). It was the first attempt at a history of criminal law, and 'Ever since its first publication it has been regarded as a book of highest authority'.[6] All commentators agree that Hale, who rose to be chief justice of the King's Bench and who was learned in science, mathematics, and theology, was a legal historian of the highest distinction. David C. Douglas writes that 'When [Hale] addressed himself to write the History of the Common Law he wrote as a practical lawyer speaking with the authority of a fine scholar noted for his impartiality'.[7] Holdsworth states flatly that 'Hale was the greatest common lawyer since Coke'.[8] Hale's text, like Coke's (and unlike Hawkins's, which attempts a schematic outline of criminal law), offers commentary and opinion generously. Fielding's firm command of Coke, Hale, and Hawkins reflects his mastery of his subject and his professional awareness of where the law was to be found.

Lawyers, as we know, are as fond of precedents and authorities as editors are of footnotes. 'To say truth, although it is not necessary for counsel to know what the history of a point is, but to know how it now stands resolved, yet it is a wonderful accomplishment, and without it a lawyer can not be accounted learned in the law.'[9] Fielding seems unusually eager to be accounted learned in the law, a point 'Aretine' in *Old England* made with customary brutality. Aretine dreams of an apparition with 'the Gesture, and Manner peculiar to the Master of a Puppet-Shew' who declares 'he was come to tell them of Laws, whereof some of them had not been heard of for a thousand, and others for 300, Years before'. The apparition, who is armed with '*Golden* Preparations, or rather the *Remains of Gould*' and who speaks of 'Spellman, Bracton, Fortescue and Lambard', disappears when the dreamer is awakened by 'a noisy Cry in the Street of, *Justice Foundling's Charge!—a whole Shilling Book for so small a Price as One Ha'penny:*—a Grub Edition, I suppose'.[1] The charge of pedantry is perhaps not without point. One can

---

[6] Holdsworth, *Sources*, p. 153.

[7] *English Scholars, 1660–1730*, 2nd rev. edn. (London, 1951), p. 121.

[8] *Some Makers of English Law* (first published 1938; Cambridge, 1966), p. 144. On the influence of Hale's *A Discourse Touching provision for the Poor* on Fielding's *Enquiry* and *Proposal*, see below, pp. lxxix and 101

[9] Roger North, *A Discourse on the Study of the Laws*, as quoted by Sir William Holdsworth, *The Historians of Anglo-American Law* (Hamden, Conn., 1966 [first pub. 1928]), p. 27.

[1] *Old England*, 5 Aug. 1749. '*Golden* Preparations' and 'the *Remains of Gould*' allude to Fielding's supposed possession of the legal manuscripts of his maternal grandfather, Sir Henry Gould (see below, p. xlix, n. 3).

only observe that the learned context which Fielding provides here for his remarks to the grand jurors of Westminster is characteristic of all the pamphlets in this volume. Inevitably, even in *Examples of the Interposition of Providence in the Detection and Punishment of Murder*, contemporary and practical issues are seen in the light of a complex historical, legal, social, or religious tradition. In this regard, however, only the *Enquiry* is quite as ambitious as *A Charge delivered to the Grand Jury*.

The *Charge* was published 21 July 1749.[2] A modest printing of 750 copies is recorded in Strahan's ledger for that month.[3] On the day of its publication, Fielding sent a copy of the *Charge* and his 'Draught of a Bill for the better preventing Street Robberies' (see below, p. lvii–lviii) to Hardwicke. In an accompanying letter, Fielding politely remarks that he is 'but too sensible how unworthy [the *Charge*] is of your Notice'.[4] Nevertheless, in sending a copy to the Lord Chancellor, to whom appropriately he was to dedicate the *Enquiry*, Fielding was asserting his consciousness of his achievement and hinting, one imagines, that his capacities merited larger responsibilities.[5]

3. BOSAVERN PENLEZ

After his delivery of the *Charge to the Grand Jury* on Thursday, 29 June 1749, Fielding left London presumably for a weekend of rest and celebration of the success of his address. During the course of his *Charge* he had recommended that the grand jurors present to the court any information they might have about bawdy-houses, the cause of 'many Mischiefs' and which tended 'directly to the Overthrow of Men's Bodies, to the wasting of their Livelihoods, and to the indangering of their Souls' (p. 23). Moreover, Fielding argued, brothels had 'become in a Manner the Seminaries of

---

[2] Both the *London Evening-Post* and the *Whitehall Evening-Post* for July 18–20 advertise the publication of the *Charge* 'tomorrow'; the *General Advertiser* for Friday, 21 July, and the *London Evening-Post* for 20–2 July, carry the 'This day is published' announcement. The *Monthly Review* for July 1749 (i. 239–40) compliments 'This ingenious author and worthy magistrate' who 'has, in this little piece, with that judgment, knowledge of the world, and of our excellent laws (which the publick, indeed, could not but expect from him) pointed out the reigning vices and corruptions of the times, the legal and proper methods of curbing and punishing them, and the great necessity of all magistrates . . . vigorously exerting themselves in the duties of their respective offices' (as quoted by Cross, ii. 231).

[3] BL Add. MSS 48800, fo. 71: 'Fielding's Charge to the Grand Jury 4 1/2 Sheets No. 750 @ 16p— 3:12:–
Extraordinary Corrections in D°— –:7:6.'
There was no second edition, and though fewer copies of the *Charge* were printed than of any other pamphlet in this volume, Millar was still advertising its sale in 1753 (in the list of books by Fielding printed at the end of the *Proposal*). A Dublin edition was published by Faulkner in 1749 which corrects some minor typographical errors but appears to have no textual authority.

[4] BL Add. MSS 35590, fo. 334 (as quoted by Cross, ii. 244).

[5] Arthur Murphy printed the *Charge* in his 1762 edition of Fielding's *Works*, though the decision to include it may have come late in the planning of the editions. See Hugh Amory's recent account of the planning and printing of the Murphy edition, 'Andrew Millar and the First Recension of Fielding's *Works* (1762)', *Trans. Cambridge Bibliographical Society*, 8 (1981), 65–6.

Education of those youth' who, 'however vitiated and enervated their Minds and Bodies may be with Vices and Diseases', were 'born to be the Governors of our Posterity' (p. 23). A little more than forty-eight hours after Fielding had instructed the grand jurors, three sailors belonging to a man-of-war, the *Grafton*, were robbed of '30 guineas, 4 moidores, a bank note of £20, two watches, etc.',[1] at a brothel near St Mary's-le-Strand owned by a man named Owen. When they protested, they were beaten away from the house by 'bullies'. The angry sailors returned that night with 'great numbers of armed sailors who, entirely demolished the goods, cut the feather-beds to pieces, strew'd the feathers into the street, tore the wearing apparel, and turn'd the women naked into the street; then broke all the windows, and considerably damaged an adjacent house'.[2]

Thus began three days of rioting along the Strand which, considering the ordinariness of the occasion and the low degree of the rioters and the objects of their wrath, were to have extraordinary repercussions. Before the ghost of Bosavern Penlez was finally laid, Fielding the magistrate was to appear before the public more notoriously than in any instance save the even more embarrassing case of Elizabeth Canning. And the Pelham Administration, for which Fielding acted as spokesman, was nearly to lose the election of its candidate for the important and prestigious Westminster seat at stake in the by-election of 1749. The connection between the riots on the Strand, Fielding's *A True State of the Case of Bosavern Penlez*, and the Westminster election of 1749 has been clearly made only in the past decade.[3] Before I review our knowledge of this relationship, however, it will be useful to set forth the sequence of events in the rioting itself for which the best evidence, because of the sworn depositions he prints, is Fielding's own account, supplemented by the information contained in the anonymous *The Case of the Unfortunate Bosavern Penlez*. This latter pamphlet, which was published eleven days before Fielding's *Bosavern Penlez* but which seems partly informed as to what Fielding was to say, provides a very different perspective on the events of 1–3 July 1749.

When the angry sailors from the *Grafton* began their assault on Owen's house the evening of Saturday, 1 July, at first only two beadles opposed them. Recognizing their helplessness, the beadles summoned constables. They too were unable to stop the rioters, who demolished the house and fired its contents. One of the constables, John Carter, called fire-fighters to control the fire, and he was also able to convince General Campbell to come

---

[1] *GM*, 'Historical Chronicle' for July, 1749.   [2] Ibid.

[3] See Nicholas Rogers, 'Aristocratic Clientage, Trade and Independency: Popular Politics in Pre-Radical Westminster', *Past and Present*, 61 (1973), 70–106; Peter Linebaugh, 'The Tyburn Riot Against the Surgeons', *Albion's Fatal Tree: Crime and Society in Eighteenth-Century England* (New York, 1975), pp. 65–117; and M. C. with R. R. Battestin, 'Fielding, Bedford, and the Westminster Election of 1749', *ECS* 11 (1977–8), 143–85.

with a detachment of soldiers from nearby Somerset House. The rioters fled. Four arrests were made, but these prisoners were later rescued by their companions. The mob reassembled before another bawdy-house close by kept by a man named Stanhope,[4] but this time the soldiers, reinforced with a detachment of forty soldiers from the Tilt Yard in Whitehall, prevented the destruction of the house.

The next morning Stanhope, expecting more trouble that evening, came to Saunders Welch,[5] who rather unhelpfully told him to apply to a magistrate. Stanhope's fears were confirmed that night when the sailors returned and sacked his house. The constable, Carter, urged by respectable neighbors of Stanhope, went to the Tilt Yard for soldiers. He was refused assistance without a magistrate's authority and before he obtained that authority Saunders Welch appeared with a troop of soldiers. Returning along the Strand from the City, Welch had met Peter Wood, proprietor of a reputed bawdy-house, the Star, who had told him that Stanhope's house was burned and that his was next. Welch with difficulty had been successful in obtaining troops and as they neared the scene of rioting at 1 a.m. he had the soldiers beat their drums. This timely alarm obliged the rioters to flee Wood's house before they could fire its contents, which they had thrown into the street. Benjamin Lander, who proved to be merely a curiosity seeker, was the only one arrested in the house. Several others accused by Peter Wood of having been in the house were also arrested and sent to the New Prison, Clerkenwell. Welch stayed until 3 a.m. to prevent further attacks.

Just about the time Welch had arrived at the Star, a watchman was alerted that there was a man with stolen goods in Bell Yard, a few streets east of Wood's house. On the approach of the watchman, the suspect fled, but he was pursued and captured by a second watchman and taken to a watchhouse. When he was unable to account for the goods in his possession ('ten lac'd Caps, four lac'd Handkerchiefs, three Pair of lac'd Ruffles, two lac'd Clouts, five plain Handkerchiefs, five plain aprons, and one lac'd Apron'), he was sent to New Prison. This was at about 2 a.m. on Monday. The prisoner was Bosavern Penlez, a peruke-maker, son of an Exeter clergyman, who lived in the neighborhood.

Fielding was back in Bow Street by noon on Monday where Saunders Welch brought him up to date about the events of the past weekend. Fielding sent for the prisoners, Bosavern Penlez now among them, and after he had heard the evidence, including testimony from Peter Wood and his wife and servant, he committed them (variously reported as seven or nine offenders) to Newgate. The transportation of the prisoners to Newgate was accomplished only with difficulty, for sailors and other rioters had converged on Bow

[4] See *Bosavern Penlez*, p. 49 and n. 9.
[5] For Welch see *Bosavern Penlez*, p. 50 and n. 2.

1. The Tars' Triumph, showing the destruction of the Star Tavern

2. The Sailors Revenge or the Strand in an Uproar

Street threatening a rescue, and they paid little attention to Fielding's exhortation that they return to their homes, or to Welch, who went among them advising them to disperse. On information that more rioting was intended that evening, Fielding and Welch stayed up on Monday night with a guard of some forty soldiers. The next day, 3 July, Fielding sent Welch to the secretary of war for more troops and wrote to the Duke of Bedford implying that a large detachment of soldiers was probably needed that evening (see *Bosavern Penlez*, below, p. 52–3, n. 4). The main rioting, however, was at an end.

It is clear from this account of events that Fielding, Welch, the various parish officers involved, and the military officers, who released troops without proper civil authority, took the disorders of 1–3 July very seriously. The uncertainty of the mob's disposition, the very real danger from the fires in close and crowded streets, and the presence of many substantial and respectable shops and businesses in the immediate neighborhood of the disorders surely warranted this concern. By the time of the trial of Penlez, Wilson, and Lander, however (and even more strenuously as the execution date of Penlez and Wilson approached), public opinion, at least that part of it that may still be heard, had turned against the civil authorities. Before describing the public outcry in October and November and attempting some account of its origins, I will pursue the chronology of events following the three days of rioting in July.

The grand jury at Hicks's Hall found an indictment on 7 July 1749 against Penlez, Wilson, Lander, and a fourth accused (who was to die in prison before the trial). The jury refused to indict two others.[6] The trial itself was deferred to the September sessions at the Old Bailey, until which time Wilson, who was sick, was released on bail at the intercession of a 'noble Person'. Fielding's *Charge to the Grand Jury* was published *c.*20 July.

The first instance I have noted of public reproof of the government's handling of the Strand riots and Fielding's role therein appeared, predictably, in the pages of *Old England*. Its attack was almost certainly personally motivated, for the first report of the riot to appear in its pages (8 July) consists of no more than a perfunctory account of the rioting lifted from other newspapers, and praises London magistrates generally. There is no mention of Fielding. By the following week, however, Argus Centoculi, '*Inspector-General* of Great-Britain', had learned that Fielding was the principal magistrate involved, and the nature of the commentary changes radically. The leader of 15 July is devoted entirely to the Strand riots. It begins with an encomium to British sailors and sternly rebukes politicians who accept court appointments (an association that anticipates the political

---

[6] Linebaugh, 'The Tyburn Riot Against the Surgeons', p. 93.

rhetoric that was to figure in the Westminster election discussed below). Argus Centoculi goes on to claim that the 'honest tars', though not blameless, acted understandably in their attacks on bawdy-houses considering the varied temptations that the vast number of these houses afforded. In fact, he suggests, since they are both numerous and inevitable, the wisest policy might be to license them, a proposal only someone like Fielding, a corrupt protector of bawdy-houses, would protest. The last paragraph of this essay makes its charge clearly enough, reminding the reader as well of the incongruities attached to Fielding's magistracy:

The late *worshipful Puppet-Shew* Writer may, in his present State of Transformation, imbitter his rueful Aspect at a Proposal to incorporate the incorrigible Spinsters of his Neighborhood into a legal Body, which may abridge the Perquisites of the good *old Shop*, and lessen the *Trade thereof*. To him I answer, that the scandalous Connivance at, if not the Protection of, Brothel Houses, has been but too long the prevailing Practice among a certain *worshipful Order* of Men, *for divers valuable Considerations thereunto moving*. Whether he knows this by *Experience*, and if from a Customer he is become a Patron, is submitted to himself.

The malice of this attack (continued the following week but directed against Fielding's *Charge to the Jury*) was followed by more sober signs of public dissatisfaction only after another month had passed, and this interval of silence supports the view that the sympathy for sailors in *Old England* was no more than a brush to tar Fielding with. Bosavern Penlez had not been mentioned.

The jury that convicted Penlez and Wilson and acquitted Lander on 6 September 1749 was another matter. It was dissatisfied with its verdict, a verdict based largely on the testimony of Peter Wood and his wife. Wood had had several informations preferred against him for keeping a disorderly house and he was in such ill repute that he was obliged to enter his house in the rates under a servant's name. He was to suffer future prosecutions for keeping a disorderly house.[7] At the trial one witness had asserted that he 'would not hang a dog or a cat' on the evidence of Wood and his wife.[8] Moreover, that they had sworn, apparently incorrectly, that Lander had taken part in the destruction of their property and had knocked Mrs Wood down, strongly impugned their testimony against Penlez and Wilson as well. Was not Wood, after all, 'ready to run at every one, like a mad Dog, . . . indifferent who it was he hang'd by his Oath? since whoever he hang'd, if he was but an honest Man, stood in the Light of an enemy to him.'[9]

[7] Hugh Phillips, *Mid-Georgian London* (London, 1964), p. 183.

[8] *The Proceedings on the King's Commission of the Peace . . . for the City of London*, September sessions, 1749, p. 134. This publication is more often referred to as *Old Bailey Sessions Papers* (see *Elizabeth Canning*, below, p. 307, n. 9).

[9] *The Case of the Unfortunate Penlez* (London, 1749), p. 30. Hereafter cited as the *Unfortunate Penlez*.

Still, without evidence to contradict Wood's sworn testimony, the jury had felt itself obliged to convict Penlez and Wilson, but it had recommended mercy, which meant in effect that it asked the trial judge (Chief Justice John Willes) to pass that recommendation on to the secretary of state who in turn would request His Majesty's pardon. Probably the jurymen thought a pardon would be granted. When it appeared later that none was forthcoming and the rumor circulated that Penlez had also been indicted for theft, 'they had the Goodness to form and forward a Representation, tending to invalidate any ill Effect from this Charge of Theft, . . . since nothing of it appeared to them at the Trial'.[1]

Thus the circumstances of Penlez's and Wilson's conviction would not have seemed convincing, especially to anyone inclined to view the destruction of a bawdy-house as a public-spirited act wherein 'the Mob proceeded in their summary Way, to do the Work of a Number of fruitless Presentments'.[2]

On 28 September the parishioners of St Clement Danes (St Clement was the patron saint of sailors) expressed their disapproval of Penlez's conviction by voting in a vestry meeting to ask for the attorney general's opinion 'in order totally to suppress the Notorious Bawdy-Houses between the Church-Yard and Temple-Bar' (*London Evening-Post*, 5–7 October). The next day three hundred 'principal inhabitants' of the parish of St Clement Danes (over eight hundred according to the writer of the *Unfortunate Penlez*) petitioned the Duke of Newcastle, acknowledging that Wilson and Penlez had broken the law but pleading their youth, their good character, and the absence of criminal design, and pointing to the subordinate role they had played in the rioting. Newcastle reportedly passed this petition on to the King (it is printed in *The General Advertiser*, 11 October 1749; and *The Whitehall Evening-Post*, 7–10 October 1749). A flurry of further petitions followed, one from a 'worthy and honourable Gentleman' to the Privy Council (*The Whitehall Evening-Post*, 12–14 October); another from a 'worthy Society of Gentlemen of Distinction', presented first to 'the highest Dignity in the Law' and later to 'some other noble Personages' (ibid, 14–17 October); and a third from 'several Gentlemen of great Repute' to His Majesty at Kensington (*London Evening-Post*, 12–14 October).

Surprisingly the government held firm against Penlez.[3] Wilson was reprieved the night of 17 October (he was pardoned 27 October 1749). But on 18 October Bosavern Penlez rode in one of the six carts proceeding to

---

[1] The *Unfortunate Penlez*, p. 28.   [2] Ibid., p. 24.

[3] Just barely, if the following anecdote is to be believed: 'It is said that the king was disposed to have pardoned them both; but that Lord Chief Justice Willes, before whom they were tried, declared in council that no regard would be paid to the laws except one of them was made an example of. Our account informs us that the king was still inclined to pardon them both, and that the Chief Justice was three times sent for and consulted on this occasion; but that he still persisted in his former opinion' (*The Newgate Calendar*, ed. Andrew Knapp and William Baldwin [London, 1824], ii. 61).

Tyburn where he was hanged with fourteen others (all sailors except one woman, who was the wife of a seaman).[4] The threat of a rescue was considerable. Large numbers of armed sailors had gathered at Tyburn and the crowds in the streets along the way from Newgate to the gallows were unusually large. Theodore Janssen, Sheriff of London (he became Lord Mayor in 1754) led the accompanying guard. Saunders Welch and his constables were among his retinue. Perhaps because he refused the proffered aid of a military guard and relied instead on an unusually large number of under-officers and constables, Janssen maintained order, though not without difficulty. According to one account, Janssen 'spoke to the mob, told them, that when the law was performed, they should have what bodies they required; and partly by fair means, and partly by threatening to read the proclamation against riots, prevented any violence, saw the execution done with as little disorder as possible, . . . and . . . had the pleasure of seeing this tumultuous assemble disperse without any of the usual ill consequences of frays and fighting'.[5] Late in October, a 'Monumental Inscription intended for PEN LEZ', sharply critical of the government, summarized his 'case':

To the Memory of the unfortunate
BOSAVERN PEN LEZ,
Who finished a Life, generally well reported of,
By a violent and ignominious Death.
He was the Son of a Clergyman,
To whom he was indebted for an Education, which he so wisely improv'd
As to merit the Love and Esteem of all that knew him.
But actuated by Principles, in themselves truly laudable
(When rightly directed, and properly restrain'd)
He was hurried by a Zeal for his countrymen,
And an honest Detestation of Public Stews
(The most certain Bane of Youth, and the Disgrace of Government)
To engage in an Undertaking, which the most Partial cannot defend,
And yet the least Candid must excuse.
For thus indeliberately mixing with Rioters, whom he accidentally met with,
He was condemn'd to die:
And of 400 Persons concerned in the same Attempt, he only suffer'd,
Tho' neither Principal, nor Contriver.

How well he deserved Life, appears
From his generous Contempt of it, in forbidding a Rescue of himself;
And what Returns he would have made to Royal Clemency,
Had it been extended to him, may fairly be presumed
From his noble Endeavours to prevent the least Affront to that Power,
Which, tho' greatly importun'd, refused to save him.

[4] Linebaugh, 'The Tyburn Riot Against the Surgeons', p. 98.
[5] *The Right Method of Maintaining Security in Person and Property* (London, 1751), pp. 54–5.

> What was denied to his Person, was paid to his Ashes,
> By the Inhabitants of St. Clements Danes,
> Who order'd him to be interr'd among their Brethren,
> Defray'd the Charges of his Funeral,
> And thought no Mark of Pity or Respect too much
> For this Unhappy Youth,
> Whose Death was occasioned by no other Fault
> But a too warm Indignation for their Sufferings.
>
> By his sad Example, Reader be admonish'd
> Of the many ill Consequences that attend an intemperate Zeal.
> Learn hence to respect the Laws—even the most oppressive;
> And think thyself happy under that Government
> 'That doth *truly* and *indifferently* administer Justice,
> 'To the Punishment of Wickedness and Vice,
> 'And to the Maintenance of God's True Religion and Virtue.'[6]

This inscription, which defiantly and publicly asserts Bosavern Penlez's essential innocence, doubtless reflected common opinion. Its rebuke of public stews, 'the Disgrace of Government', its ironic admonition to the reader to respect the laws, 'even the most repressive', and the more bitter indirection of its celebration of a government 'That doth *truly* and *indifferently* administer Justice', indicate how deeply anger and disaffection ran against 'that Power, / Which, tho' greatly importun'd, refused to save him'. The sentimental view of Penlez as a young man of good background and character hurried on by a patriotic zeal for the seamen's cause and a natural antipathy to whorehouses, especially those insulting the parishioners of St Clement Danes (his 'Death was occasioned by no other Fault / But a too warm Indignation for their Sufferings) both reminds us of that familiar truth about lapidary inscriptions and shows how much the time wanted a hero.

The opening lines of the inscription perhaps suggested a title to the author[7] of *The Case of the Unfortunate Bosavern Penlez* (announced as 'to be published' 1 November 1749; published 7 November). This pamphlet certainly contains many of the attitudes expressed in the inscription, and it is easily the fullest and best informed pro-Penlez document we have. It was perceived as a statement of 'the case' competing with Fielding's (advertisements for the two pamphlets soon regularly ran together, the anonymous author distinguished by the phrase 'By a Gentleman not Concerned'), but one can scarcely call it, as Linebaugh does, 'an attack on the frankly polemical and self-interested account of Henry Fielding',[8] if for no other

---

[6] *GM*, Oct. 1749, p. 465.
[7] Perhaps John Cleland. Roger Lonsdale makes this attribution in 'New Attributions to John Cleland', *RES*, NS 30 (1979), 270–5.
[8] 'The Tyburn Riot Against the Surgeons', p. 90.

reason than that it was published before Fielding's. It does allude to details that appear to bespeak some knowledge of what Fielding was to say. The pamphleteer is aware, for instance, of the 'Circumstance of this miserable Bundle [Penlez's booty], which it seems was started but a day or two before the Execution' (p. 26). His comment that it was '*the great Means of preventing Mercy from being extended to this unhappy young Man*' (ibid.) could be taken as an aspersion on Fielding's acknowledged intervention. One could as easily, however, make a case for Fielding's pamphlet being a response to the *Unfortunate Penlez*. It is more likely that neither writer had seen the work of the other and that those points of connection between the two pamphlets reveal the inevitably contrasting views of polemicists on opposite sides of a question.

It is in fact the consistently divergent attitude of the *Unfortunate Penlez*, rather than any question of influence one way or another, that illuminates Fielding's pamphlet, for it effectively characterizes those attitudes that Fielding was concerned to oppose or change. The pamphlet begins with an extended description of the operation of bawdy-houses which is sympathetic to the 'fallen Angels' in the clutches of those 'obscene Foxes', the bawdy-house keepers. Once the villainy of the keepers is established, the writer describes the rioting on the Strand. He is tolerant throughout of the 'honest tars'—'true brave fellows', 'jovial sailors', 'a Parcel of Brave unthinking Fellows'—who 'in the Heat of young Blood, as a pleasant Frolick,' undertook to revenge 'the Cause of their injur'd Brother'. He emphasizes the good behavior of the crowd, the orderliness of their procedure ('notwithstanding the Crowd gather'd together on this Occasion, a Child of five Years old might have crossed the Street in the thickest of them, without the least Danger'), their scrupulous choice of houses to attack, and the general approval respectable onlookers accorded to their activities. He asserts that on the first night of rioting the soldiers appeared to look on with approval and were 'a little cast down and abash'd at the Nature of the Service they were order'd upon'. 'They loiter'd about, rang'd themselves on both Sides the Street, or stood very compos'd round the Remains of the Bonfire, as if that had been what they were sent to Guard, and not the Bawdy-Houses' (p. 20). The second night they carefully beat their drums (cf. Welch's account here) to warn the sailors of their coming. No goods were 'embezzled or diverted' from the bonfires 'except an old Gown or Petticoat, thrown at a Hackney Coachman's Head, as a Reward for a dutiful Huzza as he drove by' (p. 22).

The pamphleteer bitterly attacks Wood's character and impugns his testimony at the trial. He represents Penlez, whose character is excellent ('supported by a Cloud of Attestations'), and whose only crime was to become 'flustered with Liquor' and hence unable to account for his actions or the 'miserable Bundle', as an innocent victim of the confused scene. Penlez, he asserts, was 'drawn in quite unpremeditately [*sic*] to join in this fatal Frolick'. The writer points to the widespread sympathy for Penlez and the frantic attempts to win him a pardon, and generally condemns the injustice of the government's action as an outrage to an Englishman's notion of liberty and his sense of fair play. Penlez's dignified behavior at his execution and the respectful response of the crowd to Janssen's orchestration of the execution only confirm for the pamphleteer the peruke-maker's modest innocence and the 'old British Spirit' of his peers.

'Riot' in fact is a misnomer for the 'excesses' in the Strand and if one wishes to look for a 'Riot in Form, with Circumstances that cry'd yet louder for the Cognizance of the Law' one has to seek no farther than the previous January when 'Gentlemen' tore up the theatre in the Haymarket (see above, p. xxviii), a connection that naturally leads to the observation that 'nothing begets a greater Contempt or Irreverence to the Laws, than the partial Administration of them; and above all, when the Partiality is seen, to run with too staring a Bias in Favour of the Rich, in Contra-distinction to the Poor' (p. 42).

Though it is perhaps not always syntactically sound, and though it lacks Fielding's power of generalization, *The Case of the Unfortunate Bosavern Penlez* is a creditable performance. It contains what appear to be first-hand details and makes a cogent and suasive case for precisely that point of view which Fielding wished to oppose. Directly or indirectly, Fielding's argument answers most of the assertions in the pamphlet, placing the imperative of the law and the sobrieties of property and order against the vaguely republican sympathies of the pamphleteer. Fielding does not mention Wood's testimony, for obvious reasons. Instead he presents evidence to prove that Penlez was a thief. The anonymous pamphleteer discounts the bundle and appears ignorant of the depositions of the arresting officers which Fielding prints. Despite Fielding's firm, clear, and accurate argument in *A True State of the Case of Bosavern Penlez*, however, he does not satisfactorily explain the unpopular decision to hang Penlez. The author of the *Unfortunate Penlez* wonders why a pardon which would have been so popularly received was withheld and can only conclude 'Some deep abstruse Reason of State . . . prevailed over an Occasion of gratifying large Bodies of Men, and indeed, the whole Town in general' (p. 47).[9] His puzzlement is only fully shared

---

[9] That this writer goes out of his way to defend the Duke of Bedford against the charge that he had been 'disserviceable' to Penlez and Wilson, indicates that the *Unfortunate Penlez* was not written simply in opposition to Bedford and Trentham: 'And here it is but common Justice to mention an infamous Suggestion, in order to explode it, of a great Person, of whom a Number of Tenures, of the Nature of those aimed at in the last Riot, are supposed to be held, from having been disserviceable to the condemn'd Parties: This was so far from the Truth, that, by the justest Account, no Life would have been taken away on this Occasion, had his Opinion prevail'd: So that this malicious scandalous Rumour

when one considers the execution in the context of the Westminster election which followed a month after Penlez's death.

In the general election of 1747 Granville Leveson-Gower, Lord Trentham (1721–1803), was one of the successful court candidates for the two Westminster seats in the House of Commons. Some time during the summer of 1749 (*Old England* heard rumour of his appointment as early as 5 August) he was appointed a Lord of the Admiralty, which meant that under the Regency Act of 1706 he had to present himself for re-election to allow his constituents to approve the fact that their representative was now the king's servant. His original election had been sharply contested (though Trentham won by a wide margin, his brother-in-law, the Duke of Bedford, had contributed to a tavern bill of £4,400, and Fielding had written his *Dialogue Between a Gentleman from London . . . and an Honest Alderman of the Country Party* at least partly in his support.[1] The 1741 Westminster election had also been a bitter contest and consequently the Administration had had ample warning that the third election in the decade was likely to be troublesome. Such certainly proved to be the case. Nicholas Rogers characterizes it as 'one of the most violent and vituperative struggles of the half-century'.[2]

Two issues dogged Trentham's campaign. One was the charge that he patronized a troupe of French players who were appearing at the Haymarket and had defended them with his sword when 'anti-Gallicans' interrupted their performance on 14 November 1749. The intention was to brand him as a Francophile aristocrat insensitive to English values. The second was the accusation that he and the court party he represented were responsible for the execution of Bosavern Penlez. Summing up the election campaign, the *Gentleman's Magazine* remarked (19 [November 1749], 522), 'The execution of *Penlez* was . . . made a handle of clamour against Lord *T———m*, as if he had refused to sign or present a petition in his behalf; but all this groundless discontent had been prevented, if the judge at the *Old Baily* had permitted a trial of him on the indictment for felony, on which he was arraign'd, as the fullest evidence of that fact would have then appear'd in the sessions book; and, perhaps, have prevented a petition in his favour, or have satisfy'd the

could only arise, or be receiv'd, by those who impute to others the Meanness of their own Hearts' (p. 51).

[1] See *JJ* pp. xxxiii–xxxv.
[2] 'Aristocratic Clientage', p. 77. Trentham was financed by his father, Lord Gower, and by the Duke of Bedford. Sedgwick (i. 287) states that George II, 'actuated less by regard for Bedford and Gower than by indignation at being flouted in his own parish', insisted that the government also support Trentham's campaign. Lord Gower had deserted to the Broad-Bottom Administration in 1744 and his family was obnoxious to the Tories, which in part accounts for the spirited opposition which developed. Sir John Perceval, Earl of Egmont, leader of the opposition for the Prince of Wales, backed Sir George Vandeput. Both Lord Gower and Vandeput had subscribed to Fielding's *Miscellanies*.

petitioners, and justify'd rejecting it.' In the case of Penlez, the intention of the opposition, apparently run by a group which called itself the Independent Electors of Westminster,[3] was to taint Trentham with the oppressions of an administration indifferent to the liberties of a free people, an administration which did not scruple to employ a repressive act like the Riot Act and which callously ignored the appeals of its citizenry to spare an innocent victim.

Both issues figure repeatedly in the press and in the letters, squibs, and broadsides that circulated abundantly during the campaign,[4] and they often appeared in conjunction with one another. For instance, Peter Wood, 'distinguished for Service and Pleasure [to] the public in General', purportedly announced his candidacy: 'Mr. Wood desires the Worthy Electors to excuse his not making his Personal Application, *a late Affair hindering him from it*; but hopes they will take notice, That he was no Way concern'd in the Vindication of the FRENCH STROLLERS'.[5] In the guise of a Francophile aristocrat, scornful of cits and tradesmen, a mock Trentham supporter argues that should Trentham lose, 'our Candidate may petition; and it is not the first Time our Court Friends have voted *Seven* a greater number than *Seventy*.—If they should be a little squeamish . . . we can raise a Riot *quand il nous plaira*, and that of Course will make a void Election, besides the Pleasure of *Penlezing* some of our Adversaries'.[6]

Trentham issued a signed statement from 'Grosvenor-Street, Nov. 23, 1749' denying that he was 'active in the Disturbance at the *French* Playhouse'. A close parody, issuing from 'Temple-Bar, Nov. 24, 1749' signed 'P——r W—D' shortly followed. It reads in part, 'I do declare, *Upon my Honour*, that I neither on the Bench nor in the Gallery, nor uttered my Evidence, or made use of any Perjury to condemn or hang any of the Prisoners'.[7] An 'honest Elector of Westminster' contributed an epitaph on 'the unfortunate Bosavern Penlez' ('Unfortunate Fellow he died, / Lamented by all that is good; / No Female in *London* but cried, / Excepting the Daughters of *Wood* ');[8] and the shade of Bosavern Penlez, writing from 'St. Clement's Church-Yard', contributed an acrostic on Trentham:

---

[3] The Administration emphasized the supposed Jacobite sympathies of this group (see *JJ* pp. xxix–xxx) and tried to brand all of Vandeput's supporters as Jacobites. According to Rogers, this anti-ministerial society 'functioned most successfully once the agitation was under way. It was principally an organ of redress, waiting upon event, capitalizing upon electoral irregularities' (Rogers, 'Aristocratic Clientage', p. 96). Rogers stresses the real independency of the opposition to Trentham.

[4] They are preserved in three collections: *T——t—m and V—d——t. A Collection of the Advertisements and Hand-Bills . . . Published on both Sides during the Election for . . . Westminster* (London, n.d.); *A True and Impartial Collection of Pieces in Prose and Verse . . . Westminster Election* (London, 1749); and *A Genuine and Authentic Account of the . . . Election for . . . Westminster* (London, n.d.). See also *A Dialogue between Two Free Electors, Dick and Tim on a certain Day of the Poll for L—d T——th—m and Sir G——e V–D–P–T* (London, 1749); and *The First Chapter of Tear'em the Son of Gore'am, in the Apocripha* (2nd edn., London, 1750).

[5] *T——t—m and V—d——t*, p. 5. [6] *A True and Impartial Collection*, p. 21.
[7] *A Genuine and Authentic Account*, p. 17. [8] Ibid., p. 52.

T ruant to thy promis'd Trust;
R ebel daring where thou durst;
E ager to promote French Strollers,
N one but Poltroons are thy Pollers:
T ribes of Nose-led Clerks, and Placemen,
H ackney Voters (Bribes disgrace Men)
A ll forswear thro thick and thin,
M eanness theirs, but thine the Sin.

Signing himself 'Yours in the Spirit', Penlez assured his readers that they 'may take the Ghost's Word for a Thousand Pounds'.[9]

The editor of one collection of election material describes a number of 'Figures' exhibited during the election, including 'A Person carried about in a Coffin dress'd in a Shroud, attended by a Number of Lights, &c. designed to represent *Penlez* who was Executed for the Riot at the Bawdy-house in the Strand; who frequently sat up and harangued the Populace for his unhappy Fate, &c.'[1] Rogers cites an observer's response to this tableau: 'Penley's [*sic*] Ghost . . . (wch they have carried about in Triumph & surely a high insult on Governmt) has raised more People to vote for St. Clems. than there are Houses in the Parish.'[2]

During the course of the election there had been bitter charges of physical intimidation (especially by Bedford's 'bruisers'), financial intimidation (again especially by Bedford as landlord), and illegal voting. It was in reference to the latter charge that a letter from Newgate, signed by Jemmy Twitcher, Robin of Bagshot, and Mat of the Mint, among others, reminded the agents of a '*noble Candidate*' that they had not polled once and offered his Lordship their votes 'upon *very easy terms*', assuring him 'UPON OUR HONOUR' (Trentham had sworn 'upon his Honour' in his announcement concerning the French players) 'we were no way concerned with the late Mr. Penlez in the Demolition of the Bawdy-houses'. A postcript to this letter alludes to the very active role Fielding played as magistrate during the polling, particularly his release of one accused of being the leader of Bedford's 'bruisers'.[3]

So closely associated were the issues of the French players and Bosavern Penlez's execution that Fielding himself, if we accept Martin Battestin's attribution to Fielding of an electioneering broadsheet entitled the *Covent-Garden Journal* (5 December 1749),[4] attempted to laugh away this

---

[9] Ibid., p. 38. [1] *T—t—m and V—d—t*, p. 42.

[2] 'Aristocratic Clientage', p. 100.

[3] *A Genuine and Authentic Account*, p. 53. Martin Battestin provides a full account of Fielding's activities during the polling ('Fielding, Bedford, and the Westminster Election', pp. 154 ff.), and concludes that 'There is no proof that Fielding conducted himself improperly on the bench' (p. 157). Fielding cast his vote for Trentham.

[4] 'Fielding, Bedford, and the Westminster Election', pp. 166 ff.

conjunction of embarrassments. The writer of the '*Introductory Essay*' of this
paper begins with the ironic assertion that there can be no liberty that 'can be
controul'd by Power' and to demonstrate the government's suppression of
English liberties adduces the evidence of the recent turmoil: 'Is there any
Man so corrupt, so bribed, so great a Friend, Patron, Protector and
Champion of *French* Strollers as not to own that the Case of *Bosavern Penlez*
was a Denial of all that I have here asserted. To take away the life of a Man
merely because he was an Enemy to Houses of evil and bad Fame, is a Thing
unknown in any Country where *French* Strollers have not been encouraged.'
He follows this extravagantly illogical demonstration with an equally absurd
rhetorical question intended to confound the opposition propaganda and to
remind the reader of the real reasons for Penlez's execution: 'Perhaps it will
be said that he was not only a rioter, but a Thief; to which I answer, what are
the *French* Strollers?' Writing some years later, Horace Walpole summarized
the election campaign against Trentham (he reduces it to Jacobite
resentment against Lord Gower, Trentham's father, for deserting to the
court party), and he too remembered the dominance of the same issues: '[the
Jacobites] had fomented a strong spirit against Lord Trentham, on his
declining to present a petition to the King in favour of a young fellow hanged
for a riot; and on his countenancing a troop of French players in the little
theatre in the Haymarket'.[5]

After two weeks of voting, the polls closed on 8 December 1749, and
Trentham was declared the winner (4,811 votes to 4,654). A scrutiny was
called for, the results of which, announced in May 1750, confirmed
Trentham's victory (this time by 4,103 votes to 3,933), but the scrutiny in
turn occasioned further angry repercussions which did not subside until
1751.[6] The election cost Bedford nearly £4900 in tavern bills alone,[7] and
according to one observer, permanently changed Westminster voting
patterns:

I think in all future Elections the power of the Court is weakened & the lower Class
of voters will determine Victory which ever side they take—my reason is, that you
have now opened a door to about 1500 of a lower class of the People than ever Voted
before, & who will be influenced from popular Cryes or Caprice or Money. for when
we see what a *French Play* and *Penley's Ghost* has done at this Juncture, can any
Juncture be without Scarcrows of such base materials . . . in short whoever has the

---

[5] *Memoirs of the Reign of King George the Second*, ed. Lord Holland, 2nd edn., revised (London,
1847), i. 13–14.
[6] Sedgwick (i. 287) briefly summarizes this later history of the election, as do Rogers and Battestin
in the articles cited (see p. xxxiv n. 3 above).
[7] 'The Duke of Bedford paid the election, which he owns to have cost £7,000, and Lord Gower
pays the scrutiny, which will be at least as much' (Walpole to Mann, 31 Jan. 1750, cit. Sedgwick, i.
287).

leading of these New Established voters in St. Johns and St. Margarets [court parishes] will in future Elections turn the Scale which way they will.[8]

In St Clement Danes (including St Mary-le-Strand) and St Martin's, the parishes least subject to court influence and both directly affected by the Strand riots, the vote had been overwhelmingly for Vandeput (686 to 198; 1,267 to 694, respectively).

The decision to execute Penlez, then, proved an impolitic one. Even though his death preceded the official announcement of Trentham's appointment to the Admiralty by three weeks, it was known well before then that Trentham would have to stand for re-election for a seat central to national politics. 'Westminster elections were the cockpits of party strife during the Augustan era', according to Nicholas Rogers,[9] and the Administration must have anticipated that the unpopularity of Penlez's execution would take political shape in the coming months. The government, of course, may simply have miscalculated the extent of the opposition it was to face. Its nervousness over the large numbers of disbanded soldiers and sailors after the Treaty of Aix-la-Chapelle[1] also doubtless affected its decision to remain firm against appeals for mercy to a rioter. A drunken peruke-maker perhaps seemed a safer sacrifice to the principle of exemplary punishment than one of the sailors, who were spared but none the less warned.

The precise nature of Fielding's attitude toward and the extent of his involvement in the decision to execute Penlez also remains unclear. Certainly he exposed himself to renewed attacks in the pages of *Old England*. Its leader for 25 November 1749, for instance, is largely an attack on Fielding and his pamphlet on Penlez, accusing him of pursuing Penlez beyond the grave and suggesting that his financial alliance with bawdy-houses explained his refusal to support a pardon.[2] It ridicules the inappropriateness of a magistrate/playwright/puppet-master invoking such a dangerous law as the Riot Act (even if he owns Judge Gould's law notes[3]), and concludes sneeringly that Penlez 'was not so mean neither; for it appears

---

[8] Cit. Rogers, 'Aristocratic Clientage', p. 102.   [9] Ibid., p. 73.

[1] 'The approach of peace, amidst all the joy which it naturally produces, has raised not only compassion, but terror in many private Gentlemen, and no less, I suppose, to those in public stations, who consider well the consequences of discharging so many men from their occupations in the army, the fleet, and the yards for building and repairing the navy. As one half of these poor men will not be able to get employment, there is great, and just apprehension, that necessity will compel them to seize by violence, what they can see no method to obtain by honest labour' (*GM* 18 [1748], 293).

[2] Sir John Fielding too was frequently accused of protecting bawdy-houses, and was forced to explain the difficulties involved in prosecuting them (R. Leslie-Melville, *The Life and Work of Sir John Fielding* [London, 1934], pp. 91 ff.).

[3] Alluding to Fielding's maternal grandfather, Sir Henry Gould, Judge of the Queen's Bench, whose legal manuscripts Fielding may have inherited.

he was the son of a clergyman, which must be allowed to be at least equal with that of a Soldier'. These attacks continued in the leaders of 9 and 16 December.

Because of its self-serving impulse, recent commentators have found Fielding's *Bosavern Penlez* unconvincing as a description of the rioting itself. Linebaugh's characterization of it as 'frankly polemical and self-interested' has already been quoted. He accepts the view of the rioting presented in the *Unfortunate Penlez* and suggests that Fielding's account is merely a rationalization trumped up for use in the Westminster election. Janssen's success in carrying out the execution without military aid demonstates, he argues, that troops were not needed to suppress the riots. The execution, in fact, was necessary only in order to prove that the rioting had indeed been serious.[4] On Fielding's remark that 'The Cry against Bawdy-Houses might have been easily converted into an Out-cry of a very different Nature, and Goldsmiths might have been considered to be as great a Nuisance to the Public as Whores', Nicholas Rogers comments, 'this was a trumped-up case if ever there was one, and it was never substantiated. The public were not prepared to regard the demolition of brothels as an assault upon property in general'.[5]

Aside from specious postulation of alternative methods to control the rioting, there is little reason to question the sincerity or essential accuracy of Fielding's account of events. His view, inevitably and properly an official one, comprehends one valid response to the pressure of an event that not even hindsight can perceive with perfect clarity. Obviously the reports given him by the parish officers and by Welch convinced him on the Monday of his return to Bow Street that the riots had been dangerous. The mob outside his courtroom confirmed their accounts. If Janssen was able to control his mob by the force of his authority (and a larger than usual party of constables), one can only observe that Fielding, speaking from the window of his office, was unable to make a similar impression. No one else in a position of authority, except for Welch, tried. It is hard to imagine being present on the Strand during those nights without feeling fear.

Penlez remains a pathetic object, truly the 'unfortunate Penlez'. He seems ridiculously small fry to fall in the maw of the law, a puny object to expose to the rigors of the Riot Act with its strictures against rebellion and insurrection. That he was guilty of stealing the 'miserable bundle' of linen seems clear enough, but it is not at all clear that a jury would ever have convicted him of a capital offence for his theft. Eighteenth-century juries commonly spared a thief's life either by finding him guilty but of a lesser offence, one that did not carry the death penalty, or by undervaluing the

[4] Linebaugh, 'Tyburn Riots', p. 98.
[5] 'Aristocratic Clientage', p. 100.

goods he had stolen (theft from a dwelling house of goods valued under 40*s.* was not capital).[6] Such 'pious perjury', as Blackstone called it, was especially common when the culprit was a first offender of good reputation. Fielding, however, considered Penlez a thief, and one imagines that it is this fact, exactly as he states, which convinced Fielding that Penlez did not deserve mercy. All of the evidence of the works printed in this volume indicates that Fielding largely accepted the harsh criminal code of his day. Indeed, unlike Blackstone, who saw its uneven enforcement as a generous moderation of its severity, Fielding consistently argued for its uniform and rigorous application. He need not have strained his conscience to argue for Penlez's execution and there is no reason to think that his argument in *Bosavern Penlez* is merely a ministerial one. These observations are not inconsistent with the view that Fielding wrote *Bosavern Penlez* as much to support the Pelham Administration as to explain his own role in the affair. More particularly, his pamphlet served the cause of the Duke of Bedford's candidate, Trentham, a cause to which he later contributed a number of other helps.

Bosavern Penlez was not published until 18 November,[7] a month after Penlez's execution and just four days before the polling began for the Westminster election. Strahan's ledger, however, indicates that it was printed in September: 'Sep.ʳ [1749] Fielding's Account of Penlez 3 1/2 Sheets No. 1000 @ 18ˢ p Sheet—3:3' (BL Add. MSS 48800, fo. 71). The especial political timeliness of the publication date of Fielding's pamphlet in combination with an implied date of composition in September is puzzling. Martin Battestin, conscious of the entry in Strahan's ledger indicating that *Bosavern Penlez* was printed in September, suggests that 'there is reason to believe that, anticipating how awkward this issue would be for Bedford's party in the election, he deliberately withheld publication of the pamphlet for some months, timing its release to coincide with the announcement of Trentham's candidacy and the start of the polling'.[8] But it is not really possible to read *Bosavern Penlez* as a work written in its entirety much before mid-October. In his pamphlet, Fielding knows that Penlez was executed (18 October), and that Wilson was reprieved (17 October), and seems fully aware of the clamor raised over these events during the first two weeks in October. Only the long middle section of the pamphlet, which describes the Riot Act and its history, presents the depositions of Welch and the parish officers, and reflects on the riot (pp. 35–56) could conceivably have been written in September. Thus if one were to accept Strahan's entry, one would

[6] Fielding complains in the *Enquiry* (p. 128) of such evasions of the law.

[7] The *General Advertiser* for Tuesday 14 Nov. carries an 'in a few days will be published' notice for *Bosavern Penlez*; on 17 Nov. it announces publication for 'tomorrow'; and on Saturday, 18 Nov. the 'This day at Noon will be published' notice appears. The *London Evening-Post* and the *Whitehall Evening-Post* also announce publication of *Bosavern Penlez* for 18 Nov.

[8] 'Fielding, Bedford, and the Westminster Election', p. 165.

be obliged to posit that Strahan set Fielding's MS in type in September and kept it standing for nearly two months until Fielding revised the opening and conclusion of his pamphlet in standing type. Far more likely is Professor Bowers's suggestion that the listing of *Bosavern Penlez* for September is simply an error arising from Strahan's failure to enter 'October' in the margin of his ledger (for Bowers's argument see the Textual Introduction, below, pp. cxvii–cxviii). This suggestion, which implies composition and printing in October, is in accord with the bibliographical facts, makes full sense of the pamphlet actually printed, and confirms the political pertinence of its composition.

A second entry in Strahan's ledger records 'Nov.^{r} [1749] Fielding's Account of Penlez. 2^d Edit. No. 1000, deducting for 3 1/3 Sheet Stand.^{g}— 2:11:'. This second edition, not so identified on the title-page (and hence not previously identified) may be distinguished from the first by its variant press figures and the variant use of round and square brackets surrounding page numbers. Much of it was printed from standing type, only pages 1–8 (sheet B), 13 (C3), 15 (C4), 16 (C˅), 26 (E1˅), and 31 (E4) being reset. This second edition, which was not revised by Fielding, was announced for publication by the *General Advertiser* on 16 December 1749, and again on 18 December. Though the polls were by then closed and the election officially over, Penlez's execution was still a political issue, as is indicated by the nearly simultaneous publication of the second edition of the *Unfortunate Penlez* (see the *London Evening-Post* for 19–21 December).

4. THE ENQUIRY.

After the publication of *A True State of the Case of Bosavern Penlez* in November 1749, over a year passed before Fielding's *An Enquiry into the Causes of the late Increase of Robbers* appeared in print (January 1751). This considerable period of silence (perhaps briefly broken by some fugitive campaign literature for the Westminster election late in 1749[1]) is remarkable in a remarkably active writing career but may reasonably be accounted for. At least by December of 1749 Fielding was planning his next novel, *Amelia*, or had actually begun its composition. Such is the implication of a letter from Richardson to Lady Bradshaigh written late in November or early in December of 1749, in which Richardson distinguishes himself from 'fashionable' and prolific writers like Fielding ('So long as the world will receive Mr. Fielding will write') and notes that 'some of his [Fielding's] next scenes [will] be laid' in Newgate.[2] This information, which Richardson could

---

[1] On Fielding's campaign pieces, see M. C. with R. R. Battestin, 'Fielding, and Bedford, and the Westminster Election', *ECS* 11 (1977–8), 161 ff.

[2] *Selected Letters of Samuel Richardson*, ed. John Carroll, (Oxford, 1964), pp. 133–4.

have got from the Collier sisters,[3] Sarah Fielding, or, as Richardson's biographers suggest, from 'Bookselling friends',[4] pushes the composition of *Amelia* considerably forward from the date traditionally assigned[5] and obviously helps account for Fielding's silence. Also, a series of mainly distressing domestic events in 1749–50 must have occupied his attention. His second child with Mary Daniel, Mary Amelia (named for Fielding's wife and the novel now underway?), was buried on 17 December 1749. Another daughter, Sophia, was born 21 January 1750. Three of Fielding's sisters, Catherine, Ursula, and Beatrice, died between July 1750 and February 1751. Fielding himself had been seriously ill in December of 1749.[6] These events and his work on *Amelia*, in combination with the composition of the *Enquiry* and his very active commitment to his magistracy, comprise a sufficiently crowded calendar for 1750.

The *Enquiry* may be seen as the major result of Fielding's activities as magistrate and as innovating creator of that police force which historians have come to see as the progenitor of Scotland Yard. The *Enquiry* is easily the most distinguished and ambitious of Fielding's social pamphlets (only the *Charge* betrays·similar longings for immortality but its scope is much slighter), and it reflects, within the limits of its context, Fielding's impressive learning, his considerable but necessarily imperfect grasp of the implications of the social and cultural changes he perceived to be taking place, and his first-hand experience of the crime and poverty pervading the 'lower ranks' of the London world and continually impinging on the lives of the respectable and genteel.

We know that from Fielding's first institution as justice of the peace a steady concourse of petty and pathetic offenders appeared before him for the dispensing of justice.[7] Archibald Shepperson records that between November 1748 and January 1749, the very beginning of his tenure in office, Fielding committed sixty-four persons to the Gatehouse Prison in Westminster.[8] Most of these committals were for what one would consider minor offences, though they might in fact have cost the perpetrator his life. Early in January 1751, the month the *Enquiry* was published, a string of characteristic cases was reported in the *General Advertiser*:

---

[3] Jane and Margaret Collier were friends of Fielding and his sisters and of Richardson. T. C. Duncan Eaves and Ben D. Kimpel note that 'by 1750 one of the Misses Collier was staying with Richardson as part of his family' (*Samuel Richardson, a Biography* [Oxford, 1971], p. 203).

[4] Ibid., p. 299.

[5] Both Cross (ii. 311) and Dudden (ii. 798) suggest Fielding began *Amelia* after he had completed the *Enquiry*.

[6] Dudden, ii. 756.

[7] Some account of characteristic cases which came before Fielding may be found in Cross (ii. 223–5); Dudden (ii. 733–4); and in the article by Archibald Shepperson cited in the following note.

[8] 'Additions and Corrections to Facts about Fielding', *MP* 51 (1954).

January 2   On Monday last a Fellow, dress'd like a Farmer, with Boots and Whip, &c. was detected in Holborn picking a Gentleman's Pocket, who immediately seized him and being carried before Mr. Justice Fielding, he was committed to Newgate, and the Gentleman bound over to prosecute.

January 4   [Yesterday] was committed to Tothill-fields Bridewell, by Justice Fielding, one Ann Nicholls, for stealing a Silk Gown, a Pair of Silver Buckles, and other things.

January 8   Yesterday one Wilson was committed to the Gatehouse by Justice Fielding, for stealing several Pewter Pots, the Property of Mr. Franklin in Earl-street near the Seven Dials.

January 10   Yesterday two Soldiers were committed to Clerkenwell Bridewell, by Justice Fielding for beating in a violent manner a Watchman on his Duty, who detected them as they were attempting to break in the Angel-Inn near St. Giles's Church.

January 12   When James Farrow was under examination at Justice Fielding's on Thursday last, on Suspicion of having broke open a Chamber in the house of Mrs. Collingwood, and stolen goods . . . a Maid Servant of the Justice declared that she saw the Prisoner . . . throw something over the Wall into the next Yard, which being immediately fetched, a remarkable Silver Groat was found [which Mrs. Collingwood identified].

One imagines that such was the daily fare, but Bow Street knew the '*Calibash* and *Calipee*' of crime as well and could 'hash and ragoo' it with annals fit, if not for commemoration in half-acre tombs, then for celebration in Newgate Calendars. The cases of Bosavern Penlez and Elizabeth Canning are the most notable instances in Fielding's career of distinguished criminal fare, but there are hints of other events that indicate his involvement in controlling what may fairly be called organized crime and which must have shaped the ideas and attitudes of the *Enquiry* and, not incidentally, have consumed much of his energies in 1750.

One may mention first, if only for the evidence it provides that Fielding was a magistrate on whom the powerful relied, a case obscurely alluded to in a letter from Fielding discovered by G. M. Godden and first published in 1910. The letter (dated 25 November 1750) is addressed to Hutton Perkins in Lincolns Inn Square, who was secretary to the Lord Chancellor, and reads as follows: 'I have made full enquiry after the three Persons and have a perfect account of them all. Their characters are such that perhaps three more likely Men could not be found in the Kingdom for the Hellish Purpose mentioned in the Letter. As the Particulars are many and the Affair of such Importance I beg to see you punctually at six this evening when I will be alone to receive you . . .'[9] A day or two earlier, Hardwicke had received a

---

[9] *Henry Fielding, a Memoir*, p. 222.

letter from an anonymous and semi-literate informer which clarifies Fielding's report to Perkins. Apparently Hardwicke was held responsible by three keepers of disreputable houses (located near the scene of the Penlez riots) for the destruction of their gaming tables, and they plotted his death. The informer warns Hardwicke of his danger and says that 'Was enquiry to be made after the caricters of these three persons, it will appear that they are wicked and desperate men of very bad caricters'.[1] Clearly Hardwicke had alerted Fielding, who quickly responded with alarming confirmation of the informer's account. Nothing more is known of the incident.[2]

We may be somewhat more precise about a reference in the *Enquiry* itself to organized gangs of criminals in London early in 1750. On p. 126 below, Fielding remarks on the organized dealings in stolen goods that take place in London and feed the criminal life of the city: 'Among the *Jews* who live in a certain Place in the City, there have been, and perhaps still are, some notable Dealers this Way, who in an almost public Manner have carried on a Trade for many Years with *Rotterdam*, where they have their Warehouses and Factors, and whither they export their Goods with prodigious Profit, and as prodigious Impunity. And all this appeared very plainly last Winter in the Examination of one *Cadosa* a *Jew*, in the Presence of the late excellent Duke of Richmond, and many other Noblemen and Magistrates.' The *Whitehall Evening-Post* for 3–6 February reported 'We hear that near forty Highway-men, Street-Robbers, &c. have been committed within a Week past to several Prisons by Justice Fielding'. About a fortnight later the same paper reported 'Tuesday [20 Feb.] a great Number of Felons were re-examined before Justice Fielding in Bow-Street', some of whom were sent to Clerkenwell, others to Newgate, and among the latter was 'Samuel Cadoza, for receiving stolen Goods'. The *General Advertiser* for 21 Feb. carried a similar announcement naming 'Sam. Cadoza, a Jew.' The *Penny London Post* for 21–3 February had the same story and added 'There are more Street Robbers and notorious and dangerous Villains to be try'd this Sessions than were in the December Sessions 1745, when the Black Boy Alley Gang were try'd'.[3] Thus we have a picture of Fielding 'breaking' a group of criminals

---

[1] The anonymous letter is printed in Philip C. Yorke, *The Life and Correspondence of Philip Yorke, Earl of Hardwicke* (Cambridge, 1913), ii. 108–10.

[2] It may account, however, for Fielding's use of large numbers of troops in a raid on a gambling house in the Strand three months later (1 Feb. 1751), an event widely reported in the newspapers. Fielding first sent 40 soldiers to close the house, but 80 were finally required. They entered with bayonets fixed, destroyed three gaming tables, valued at £60 each, and made 45 arrests. Fielding committed 39 prisoners to the gatehouse.

[3] This notice identifies a principal evidence against these 'villains' as 'one Lewis'. This was Thomas Lewis, whose case as reported in *Select Trials* (ii. 1 ff.) elaborates Fielding's involvement with this gang of thieves. Immediately on his release after his testimony against his companions in February, Lewis and four other men engaged in a series of robberies, including among their victims Lord Hervey, the Countess of Albemarle, and the Dean of Peterborough. William Pentlow, one of Fielding's constables, assisted in their arrest and identified them at their trial. When they impugned

who had enjoyed a common factor and whose takings had flowed easily to a foreign market. The presence of the Duke of Richmond, whose formidable pursuit of smugglers in his home county of Sussex had attracted much attention and won him praise as a public benefactor,[4] suggests the possibility of a still larger dimension to Fielding's police work in this case, for we know that Fielding had complied with Richmond's request in the spring of 1749 to examine some of the Sussex smugglers.[5] The presence of 'other Noblemen and Magistrates' reminds us, incidentally, of the very public nature of the office at Bow Street (an office literally crowded with genteel spectators for his examinations of Elizabeth Canning), and Walpole's anecdote about his friends interrupting Fielding at supper with a criminal complaint shows that Fielding's time was scarcely his own.[6]

Several months after the Cadoza Case, Fielding was again involved in a large-scale assault on criminal gangs, as the 'Historical Chronicle' for August in the *Gentleman's Magazine* informs us: 'So many highway-men and street-robbers are in custody on the impeachment of their accomplices, that the little prisons are quite full.' This notice concludes with the advice that these rogues may be seen on their examinations 'at justice Fielding's'. We can infer that Fielding speaks from the common experience of Londoners when he remarks near the beginning of the *Enquiry* that 'The great Increase of Robberies within these few Years, is an Evil which to me appears to deserve some attention' and goes on to assert that 'the Streets of this Town, and the Roads leading to it, will shortly be impassable without the utmost Hazard; nor are we threatned with seeing less dangerous Gangs of Rogues among us, than those which the Italians call the Banditi.'[7] The desperation

his integrity, Fielding testified to his character, declaring 'he sincerely believed there was not an honester, or braver man than he, in the King's Dominions'. Fielding's affidavit in the Public Record Office (Treasury Board Papers (TI) 342. f. 27) attests that Pentlow arrested Thomas Lewis who 'discovered' the 'great Gang of street Robbers last winter'. It is dated 3 May 1750.

[4] For a detailed account of the Duke of Richmond's campaign against smugglers, see Cal Winslow, 'Sussex Smugglers', in *Albion's Fatal Tree* (New York, 1975), pp. 119–66. Richmond's activities began in the autumn of 1748 and continued until his death in August 1750. He received support from Pelham, Newcastle, and Hardwicke; his agents were active in London and Holland. Isaac Maddox, Bishop of Worcester (see *Examples of Providence*, below, pp. lxi and 177), eulogized Richmond: 'The Bravery, Benevolence, and Love to his Country, which always adorned his Mind, excited this noble Person, totally regardless of the Danger or Fatigue, to bring to public Justice some of the most enormous Offenders in the Smuggling Way' (*The Expediency of Preventative Wisdom*, 3rd edn. [London, 1751], pp. xx–xxi). For Fielding's earlier relationship with Richmond, see *Enquiry*, below, p. 126 and n. 6.

[5] Mary Margaret Stewart prints Fielding's letter, dated 'Bow Street Ap.¹ 8 1749', revealing his service to Richmond and discusses their relationship ('Henry Fielding's Letter to the Duke of Richmond', *PQ* 50 [1971], 135–40).

[6] The Walpole anecdote is in *Letters of Horace Walpole*, ed. Toynbee, ii. 383–4. An engraving of 1779 (reproduced as the frontispiece to R. Leslie-Melville's *The Life and Work of Sir John Fielding* [London, 1934]) shows John Fielding's Bow-Street courtroom filled with onlooking ladies and gentlemen.

[7] Below, p. 75. Dudden (ii. 759–60) usefully reviews this outbreak of violence.

of the government before such increasingly outrageous depredations is reflected in its proclamation, noted in the *Gentleman's Magazine* for December 1750, of a £100 reward for the capture of offenders between 20 September 1750 and 20 December 1751. Earlier in 1750 a royal proclamation printed in the *London Gazette* (27–30 January) had offered £100 for the capture of 'Thomas Jones, otherwise Harper' who had been rescued from prison by more than twenty armed men.[8] This proclamation took notice of the 'frequent Murders, Robberies, and other Outrages'.

Fielding was necessarily immediately involved in the response to these public disorders, and, moreover, he strongly objected to rewards under proclamation, which he saw as expensive, ineffectual, and susceptible of the worst abuse.[9] His distrust of these awards perhaps arose from an early encounter with the notorious thief-taker, Stephen McDaniel, who was to prove such an embarrassment to John Fielding in 1754.[1] In his *A Plan for Preventing Robberies within Twenty Miles of London*, John Fielding recalls his brother's meeting with McDaniel, which must have taken place before 8 August 1750, the date of Richmond's death:

I remember . . . McDaniel came some years ago wounded to my brother, and swore he had been robbed and shot at by two persons whom he produced; and though he swore positively to them and the fact, yet that magistrate conceived so ill an opinion of the prosecutor in the course of his examination, that the prisoners, though charged with a capital offence, were both admitted to bail, to the great satisfaction of his grace, the late Duke of Richmond, and several gentlemen then present, and were afterwards acquitted at the Old Bailey.[2]

The pressing concerns of office, then, must have fully occupied Fielding's time and attention in 1750 and earlier. His first attempt that we know of to effect some kind of official response to these disorders was in a 'Draught of a Bill for the better preventing street Robberies' which he sent in a letter to

[8] The account in *Select Trials* (ii. 94 ff.) of Quin, Dowdell, and Talbot 'for the Highway' in May 1751 indicates that these three men, with others, had been extremely active in 1750 and earlier. They had taken part in the rescue of Jones and clearly were part of a substantial gang.

[9] In the *Voyage to Lisbon*, Fielding claimed credit for preventing the government from reviving the practice of rewards under proclamation and stated that such rewards cost the government 'several thousand pounds within a single year'. 'All such proclamations', he went on to observe, 'instead of curing the evil, had actually encreased it; had multiplied the number of robberies; had propagaged the worst and wickedest of perjuries; had laid snares for youth and ignorance; which, by the temptation of these rewards, had been sometimes drawn into guilt; and sometimes, which cannot be thought on without the highest horror, had destroyed them without it' (p. 36).

[1] For McDaniel, see Leslie-Melville, *Sir John Fielding*, pp. 63 ff.; Radzinowicz, ii. 326 ff.; and *State Trials*, xix. 746–814. McDaniel had been a thief-taker perhaps as early as 1740. In 1754 it was revealed that he and others had persuaded two young men to commit a robbery in order to 'capture' them for the sake of the reward. Since the victim of the robbery was a member of McDaniel's gang, it was unclear if any robbery could be said to have taken place, and McDaniel was acquitted. Several further trials took place. Clearly neither Henry nor John Fielding wanted any part of such a thief-taker.

[2] (London, 1755), p. 5.

Hardwicke 21 July 1749 along with a copy of his *Charge to the Grand Jury*.[3] Unfortunately we do not know the contents of this draft, but the inference of Hugh Amory[4] that it contained essentially the same plan that Fielding presented to the Duke of Newcastle in 1753 is certainly reasonable.[5] One of the essential points of Fielding's plan was the retention of trustworthy and experienced constables, professional thief-takers in the government's employ, who could be sharply distinguished from the likes of McDaniel. A passage in John Fielding's *Plan for Preventing Robberies* both confirms Henry's deep involvement in controlling crime in 1749–50 and suggests his early pursuit of a professional police force:

The winter after the late Henry Fielding Esq; came to Bow-Street, the town was infested by a daring gang of robbers, who attacked several persons of fashion, and gave a general alarm through the City and the Liberty of Westminster; and as that magistrate then enjoyed a good share of health, he spirited up the civil power, and sent several bodies of constables with the advantage of having Mr. Welch at their head, into different parts of the town, by whose bravery and activity those disturbers of the peace were quickly apprehended and brought to justice: and though, the year after, most of these constables were out of office, yet some of them, being actuated by a truly public spirit against thieves, and being encouraged by the said magistrate, continued their diligence, and were always ready, on being summoned, to go in pursuit of villains.[6]

John Fielding goes on to observe that gradually more constables and 'other persons' were persuaded to 'serve the public in the same way', and he emphasizes the point that such men were all reputable householders.

Whatever the content of Fielding's 'Draught', the *Enquiry* represents his public contribution to the immediate social problems that had engaged him and had aroused both the public and the government. The scope of its allusions, the fullness of its coverage, and the elaborateness of its documentation, were other evidence wanting, confirm the ambitious and considered nature of this pamphlet. We know, however, that its composition was under way at least by 9 October 1750 when the following notice appeared in the *General Advertiser*: 'We hear that an eminent magistrate is now employed in preparing a pamphlet for the press in which the several causes that have conspired to render robberies so frequent of late will be laid open; the defects of our laws enquired into, and methods proposed which may discourage and in a great measure prevent this growing evil for the

---

[3] Godden, *Fielding*, pp. 209–10. See above, p. xxxiii.

[4] 'Henry Fielding and the Criminal Legislation of 1751–2', *PQ* 50 (1971), 189–90.

[5] For Fielding's Plan, see *Voyage to Lisbon*, pp. 32 ff.; John Fielding's *Plan for Preventing Robberies* and *An Account of the Origin and Effects of a Police Set on Foot by . . . the Duke of Newcastle in the Year 1753, upon a Plan . . . by the late Henry Fielding* (London, 1758); and Leslie-Melville, *Sir John Fielding*, pp. 47 ff.

[6] pp. 1–2.

future'.[7] This notice, which accurately reflects the distinction on the title-page of the *Enquiry* between causes and remedies, suggests that already by this date Fielding's strategies were formulated. A little more than three months later, on 19 January 1751, the *Enquiry* was published.[8] Two days later in his address opening Parliament, the king exhorted his audience 'to make the best use of the present State of Tranquillity, for improving the Trade and Commerce of my Kingdoms; for enforcing the Execution of the Laws; and for suppressing those Outrages and Violences, which are inconsistent with all good Order and Government; and endanger the Lives and Properties of my Subjects'.[9] Shortly afterwards, on 1 February, a Committee was appointed 'to revise and consider the Laws in being, which relate to Felonies, and other Offences against the Peace; and to report their Opinion thereupon, from time to time, to the House, as to the Defects, the Repeal, or Amendment, of the said Laws'.[1] Fielding's *Enquiry* had appeared at an opportune time.[2]

For over two years Fielding had observed the spectrum of criminal life and had taken note of the varieties of poverty and human desperation and misery. He was intimate with the ploys of habitual criminals (my impression is that 'professional' grants too much expertise to this eighteenth-century context) and alert to the inadequacies and misdirections of the traditional legal machinery that was to control them. Much more than practical expertise, however, went into the writing of the *Enquiry*. To it Fielding also brought the sophistication of a man of letters, the knowledge of a historian, and the perspective of an accomplished student of English law and legal precedents. This pamphlet, far more than any other in this volume, reflects Fielding's mature view of his society and his cultural milieu and at the same time effectively expresses a mid-century view of poverty and crime that captures many of the common opinions of his day.

I have argued previously that the *Enquiry* (and the *Proposal*) is a document which, both in its general attitudes to crime and poverty and in the specific 'remedies' it advances for the relief of these evils, should be regarded as a distinguished but essentially conventional expression of widely shared

---

[7] Cit. Cross, ii. 255.   [8] See below, p. lxxi and n. 5.

[9] *JHC* xxvi. 3.

[1] *JHC* xxvi. 27. For this important Committee of 1751, see Radzinowicz, i. 399 ff.

[2] The coincidence of Fielding's pamphlet with the king's remarks and the formation of this select committee has led to considerable speculation about the possibility of Fielding's influence on the committee and the legislation which stemmed from its recommendations. I argued my skepticism concerning Fielding as 'man behind the scenes' in *Social Pamphlets* (pp. 32–42). Later Hugh Amory analyzed this committee's activities and reached similar conclusions (see p. lviii n. 4, above). I think this skepticism is in the main correct, especially with regard to the Acts in question. It should be noted, however, that while the initial nine Resolutions of this committee, reported on 1 Apr. 1751, bear little resemblance to Fielding's *Enquiry*, eight of the sixteen further Resolutions reported on 23 Apr. are generally similar to points Fielding made in the *Enquiry* (*JHC* xxvi. 159–60 and 190). Perhaps the *Enquiry* enlarged the number of causes of crime that the Committee was willing to consider.

opinion.³ Before considering from a different perspective some of the legal and historical dimensions of Fielding's argument, however, some review of these earlier findings may be useful.

Though Fielding's title suggests that his subject is crime, the *Enquiry* is equally an essay on the state of the poor, for Fielding, like many of his contemporaries, clearly perceived the interconnection between the two. It is one of many such pamphlets, which were particularly common in the 1750s. In one of the appendices to F. M. Eden's *The State of the Poor* (London, 1797) pamphlets on the poor are catalogued chronologically. For the decade of the thirties Eden has only two entries; for the forties, only three. He lists eighteen different pamphlets which appeared between 1750 and 1760, some of which underwent second printings. Eden missed a good number of pamphlets but his chronological proportions are roughly accurate. His tabulation does not take into account the many legal and economic documents that also consider the poor and crime.⁴ Fielding knew this pamphlet literature. His remark in the *Proposal* that to the study of the laws relating to the poor and to his experience in applying them he has 'likewise added a careful Perusal of every thing which I could find that hath been written on this Subject, from the Original Institution in the 43rd of *Elizabeth* to this Day' applies equally to the *Enquiry*.

There is little in fact in the *Enquiry* that does not find its parallel or analogue in this pamphlet literature. Even Fielding's language often betrays a conditioned rather than original response to his subject. For instance his recurrent epithets for the poor—the 'Commonalty', 'People of the lower Sort', the 'inferior part of Mankind', the 'thoughtless and tasteless rabble', 'the very Dregs of the People'—are a conventional part of this literature, as are many other rhetorical 'turns' in his pamphlet. 'Too frequent Diversions', gin-drinking, and gambling, Fielding's three categories of 'Voluptuousness' among the poor, which he offers as the basic incitements to that luxury which lies at the root of crime,⁵ were standard topics in these pamphlets and, perhaps needless to say, in presentments to grand juries, acts of parliament, and in countless sermons.

We may look more closely at one of these categories, gin-drinking. Fielding's strictures about the dangers of gin were fully anticipated in many pamphlets. He himself cites Thomas Wilson's *Distilled Spiritous Liquors the Bane of the Nation*,⁶ published in 1736, the year a radical and unsuccessful act to control gin-drinking was passed. Its argument is very close to Fielding's own in the *Enquiry*. Like Fielding, Wilson asserts that gin-drinking leads to

---

³ In *Social Pamphlets*. The discussion of the conventional aspects of Fielding's *Enquiry* that follows here is a summary of some parts of this earlier argument.

⁴ III. clxvii–clxxv. A full but not exhaustive bibliography of this literature is offered in Zirker, *Social Pamphlets*, pp. 161 ff.

⁵ *Enquiry*, pp. 77–98.   ⁶ *Enquiry*, p. 90 and n. 7.

crime, enfeebles the laboring class, and robs the nation of its future soldiers and sailors. Wilson wrote 'To [gin-drinking] is probably owing, That the Murders, and Robberies we have of late abounded with, are not only more *frequent*, but more *barbarous*, than ever: That those dismal Acts, the Perpetration of which were wont to be confined to the *dark* and *dead Night*, or to the *distant* and *private Road*, are now committed in *open day*, or *early Twilight*, and that in our very high Streets, both on Persons in *Coaches* and on Foot' (p. vi). As for its effects on the laboring class, he argued that 'the greatest Part of the Nation, that Part which is the Strength and Riches of every Country, the Laborious Hands, is intoxicated and enervated by a fatal Love of a slow but sure Poyson, which enters into the Blood and Marrow of its habitual Drinkers, and transmits its deadly Effects into the vitals of their miserable Posterity, on whom, in all Probability, it will have such terrible Consequences, that in a Generation or two we shall not have People able to do the Servile Offices, or to cultivate our Lands' (p. ix). And he pointed also to its decimation of the ranks of the military: 'Dreadful and visible are the Effects already on the Seafaring Men, as well as the Soldiers, of the Kingdom. It enervates them to so great a Degree, that in a little Time they will be fit for Nothing but a profound Peace, and will hardly be able to defend against a foreign Enemy the Blessings transmitted to us, through many Ages, by the Blood and Treasure of our worthy Predecessors' (p. 56). Isaac Maddox, Bishop of Worcester, to whom Fielding dedicates *Examples of Providence* and to whom he credits the passage of the Gin Act of 1751, had said much the same thing in his sermon 'The Expediency of Preventative Wisdom', delivered on Easter Monday, 1750.[7] But such opinions were so commonplace in the pamphlet literature on gin-drinking that the question of 'sources' does not arise, a point that is equally true of Fielding's comments on diversions and gambling.[8]

Fielding's concept of 'luxury' which, strangely for modern readers, subsumes such disparate activities as gin-drinking, gambling, and attendance at

---

[7] For Maddox, see *Examples of Providence*, p. 177.

[8] For example, the anonymous author of *The Vices of the Cities of London and Westminster*, which was published five days before Fielding's *Enquiry* (*General Advertiser*, 14 Jan. 1751), takes a position similar to Fielding's on both these issues and employs a rhetoric nearly indistinguishable from Fielding's. Of gambling he writes, 'I leave the Immorality of this Passion, to be settled and inculcated by Divines, I shall only here observe as a Politician, that the Public is mostly concerned to prevent this Passion from taking Possession of the trading, industrious and labouring Part of the Community; for as to the Nobility and Gentry, it is of very little Consequence what they do in this Respect, it being of very little Importance, whether five thousand a Year is in Possession of a Lord, or divided amongst a hundred Sharpers' (p. 38). He considers public diversions of no evil in themselves, but 'The Misery to be complain'd of is, that these Places are crowded by People, who are not able to bear the Expence either of Time or Money employ'd in them, in short, that they are resorted to by Tradesmen, their Wives, &c. of all Ranks, whose Business is neglected, and Credit ruin'd for the Sake of these polite Vanities'. He is annoyed too that 'the Quality is more crowded, and have no Choice left but either to stay Home, or submit to be jolted by every greasy Tradesman, that pushes into their Diversion' (pp. 47–8).

plays and pleasure gardens and the like, was itself the most common of commonplaces. John Sekora, in his ambitious and informative analysis of the history of this concept and its varied aspects in the eighteenth century, calls it 'the greatest single social issue and the greatest single commonplace'.[9] He sees the extension of the attack on luxury to include the habits of the laboring poor as a phenomenon peculiar to the 1750s, and this may be true within the larger picture of his study. But certainly earlier applications to the poor were common and contributed to Fielding's argument in the *Enquiry*. An anonymous pamphleteer writing in 1738, for instance, writes of luxury as a 'devouring torrent' that visits 'the Houses of our meanest Farmers and Tradesmen; nay, sometimes it humbly enters the lowly Cottages of the Poor themselves'. For this writer too luxury leads to desperate acts: 'hence it is, we see so many People, of all degrees, who having fooled away their solid Substance to gratify their vain Inclinations, sell their Religion and Country, and stick at no Methods, just or unjust, which lead to the gratifying a luxurious Appetite'.[1]

In pamphlets and books dealing in one way or another with the poor, the attack on luxury and idleness came in many guises. One common effect of such attacks, including Fielding's, was to establish or reaffirm a fixed place for the poor in the social structure. Many of the laws Fielding cites in the first three sections of the *Enquiry* clearly point up the legal distinction that existed between the extravagances of the rich and the debaucheries of the poor. Where legal distinctions were unclear, new laws could be passed. Gin, Fielding exclaims, should be placed 'beyond the Reach of the Vulgar!' What was foolish or sinful for the one was criminal for the other (the beggar of the *Beggar's Opera* points the moral: 'the lower sort of people have their vices in a degree as well as the rich: And . . . they are punished for them' [III. xvi.]). The laws of the land coincided with the concept of luxury in enforcing a stratified society, a point that Fielding's discussion of the rating of wages in Section IV and of the wandering of the poor in Section VI illustrates. Fielding believed that it was fitting and proper that justices of the peace should continue to set the price of the laborers' hire though he was aware that this still legally obligatory practice, dependent on a fourteenth-century law, was often ignored and was very difficult to enforce. He knew that the laws of settlement and removal, originating in the 13 & 14 Charles II, c. 12, had become incredibly complex and chaotic and were increasingly the subject of criticism, but he accepted the social principle embedded in them, namely that the poor man should remain in his fixed abode and contribute

---

[9] *Luxury: The Concept in Western Thought, Eden to Smollett* (Baltimore and London, 1977), p. 75. Sekora notes that 'the British Museum and London School of Economics possess more than 460 books and pamphlets in English that discuss luxury' (p. 67).

[1] *An Enquiry into the Causes of the Encrease and Miseries of the Poor of England*, p. 24.

his labor, the mite that he had to offer, to the social whole. The need, as Fielding saw it, was '*to hinder the Poor from wandering*', and if this desideratum proved impossible to obtain in practice, Fielding was right to argue that the law said it ought to be done.

The social and legal limitations of the rights and mobility of the poor that inform Fielding's arguments and attitudes in the *Enquiry* and the *Proposal* were strongly supported by conventional religious assumptions and by current economic thought. The fixed social role of the poor as described and celebrated in sermons of the day scarcely needs comment, though Swift's two sermons, 'On Mutual Subjection' and 'On the Poor Man's Contentment', may be cited as convenient examples; and Jacob Viner's chapter 'The Providential Origin of Social Inequality', in his *The Role of Providence in the Social Order*,[2] may be mentioned as a useful summary of the social implications of such sermons. Mercantile thought impinges too on the *Enquiry*. Fielding cites a good number of mercantilist writers in the *Enquiry* and the *Proposal*, writers like Petty, Graunt, Law, and Davenant. King's *British Merchant* (1713), a compendium of mercantile doctrine, was in his library. Like any literate man of his day, Fielding was familiar with that body of commonplaces which loosely may be called mercantile theory, a theory that centered on the shibboleth of the favorable balance of trade.[3] One of these commonplaces, what Smollett's Scots spokesman, Lishmahago, calls 'the hackneyed maxim, that . . . a supply of industrious people is a supply of wealth', figures frequently in this literature (Fielding employs it in the *Proposal*, p. 225). To maintain a favorable balance of trade, home products must be cheaply priced. The cost of labor then must be low. The low cost of labor depended on a large body of dependable and hard-working laborers—the industrious poor whose wages were fixed, whose abode was settled and whose way of life was marked by frugality and sobriety. The mercantilist saw the idle, extravagant, and criminal poor as a vast store of potential energy and whoever would harness this potential source of wealth and make these people 'sound and useful Members of the Commonwealth,

---

[2] Philadelphia: American Philosophical Society, 1972. According to Viner, the idea of providence as a defense or apology for the social status quo between 1660 and 1770 presents 'a unique case of a spontaneous union of theologians, philosophers, economists, and intellectuals in general' justifying 'an existing social structure and especially . . . its social and economic inequalities' (p. 95).

[3] The standard work on the theory of mercantilism is Eli Heckscher, *Mercantilism*, trans. Mendel Shapiro, 2nd edn., 2 vols. (New York, 1955). Also helpful are Edgar S. Furniss, *The Position of the Labourer in a System of Nationalism* (New York, 1920); and E. A. J. Johnson, *The Predecessors of Adam Smith* (New York, 1937). For revisionist discussion of the concept of mercantilism, often illuminating of Fielding's attitudes to the poor, see, for example, A. W. Coats, 'Changing Attitudes to Labour in the Mid-Eighteenth Century', *Economic History Review*, 2nd series, 11 (1958), 35–51 and 'Economic Thought and Poor Law Policy in the Eighteenth Century', *Economic History Review*, 2nd series, 13 (1960), 39–51; D. C. Coleman, 'Labour in the English Economy of the Seventeenth Century', *Economic History Review*, 2nd series, 8 (1956), 280–95; and Charles Wilson, 'The Other Face of Mercantilism', *Transactions of the Royal Historical Society*, 5th series, 9 (1959), 81–101.

would deserve so well of the Publick, as to have his Statue set up for a Preserver of the Nation'.[4] Consequently, schemes to employ the poor or to reform their idleness and criminality appeared in the context of economic writings as well as in primarily social, legal, or religious documents. As both the *Enquiry* and the *Proposal* show, however, there was no sharp line between these categories in eighteenth-century thought. Economic arguments appear in sermons, legal principles in social pamphlets. The precise shape of Fielding's assimilation in the *Enquiry* of these varied strands of argument is his own, but the impulse of combination itself was deeply embedded in the thought of his day.

The 'vision' of most of this literature on the poor was backward-looking. It sought to recapture a probably imaginary past when gin was unknown, beggars a rarity, 'Blest Paper Credit' a chimera, and the grand law of subordination, with its known relations, still obtained:

The law, proposals for the poor, economic attitudes, and religious doctrine agreed remarkably in supporting a static hierarchical society. From whichever point of view one considers the poor he reaches much the same conclusion concerning their place in society: the poor are servants to an endless train of masters, stretching from their immediate employer to the nation and to God. A frugal industrious laborer carrying out his tasks in a single area, accepting low wages in return for a feudalistic patronage from his social superiors, obeys the law, insures the continued strength of the nation, and serves his creator. His personal lot need not be unhappy. His place in society is assured, he is guaranteed assistance should some disaster strike, and he may enjoy the comfortable, patriarchal benevolence of his superiors.[5]

The *Enquiry* reflects this traditional and paternalistic view of society, but it also reveals Fielding's sometimes uneasy awareness of the radical changes that were transforming his society from a primarily agricultural and stationary one to a world dominated by trade and city finance. His ambiguous remarks on the benefits of trade, which, at the same time that it carries 'the Grandeur and Power of the Nation . . . to a Pitch that it could never otherwise have reached', necessarily introduces 'Luxury' and 'moral Evils',[6] are a case in point. Fielding's attempt to place his perception of social change in a historical framework, primarily in a theory of constitutional and legal history, is seen in his commentary on the constitution in the Preface to the Enquiry and in his celebration of Anglo-Saxon society, particularly the institutions of Alfred, throughout the *Enquiry* and the *Proposal*.

Fielding opens his Preface by observing that 'there is nothing so much talked of, and so little understood in this Country, as the *Constitution*', and then states that the concept of the constitution must include 'the original and

---

[4] Swift, *A Modest Proposal*. His deadly imitation of these writers catches their tone perfectly.
[5] Zirker, *Social Pamphlets*, p. 28.
[6] *Enquiry*, below, p. 70. See also the *Proposal*, p. 228.

fundamental Law of the Kingdom, from whence all Powers are derived . . . all legislative and executive Authority; all those municipal Provisions which are commonly called *The Laws*; and, *lastly*, the Customs, Manners, and Habits of the People'. In a perfect state each of these elements exists in balanced harmony. To detect the present imperfect balance of the English constitution, one must be a lawyer, who knows the statutes and the 'fundamental Law of the Kingdom', and a historian, who is versed in 'the Genius, Manners, and Habits of the People'. Then he will perceive that the laws, designed to apply to a traditional social structure, no longer harmonize with a change in the internal balance of power, a change which, viewed historically, has been wrought by an 'immense Addition' to the power of the commonalty through the introduction of trade which 'hath almost totally changed the Manners, Customs, and Habits of the People, more especially of the lower Sort'.

In making such an argument, Fielding is reshuffling in an interesting fashion some of the counters of a political controversy central to the 1730s, though of course discussion of a balanced constitution was a perennially lively political topic in the eighteenth century.[7] The opposition attack on Walpole in the 1730s was dominated by Bolingbroke, but Whig 'Patriots', including Fielding, joined the common cause. The opposition argument in part focused on the issue of a balanced constitution, the argument being that corruption and luxury fostered by Walpole had increased the power of the Ministry at the expense of both the Crown and Lords and Commons. Placemen, a standing army, septennial parliaments, the passage of power from landed to moneyed men, were the means by which Walpole had secured power and had upset the balance of the ancient constitution, the king himself being an innocent victim of the wily minister. Fielding's discussion of a balanced constitution in the *Enquiry* would have been reminiscent of this controversy. His inclusion of the 'Commonalty' as one of the weighted elements neatly expands the terms of the argument.

There is a historical dimension to the constitutional controversy of the 1730s that may also illuminate the *Enquiry*. Bolingbroke based his attack on a historical view which asserted that English liberties could be traced to an ancient Anglo-Saxon past. The original of the House of Commons was to be found in Alfred's England. The laws of the land had preceded and were unchanged by the Norman Conquest, for William had sworn to maintain the

---

[7] In *JJ* no. 7 (16 Jan. 1748), pp. 130 ff., Fielding quotes extensively and approvingly from Samuel Squire's *Historical Essay upon the Ballance of Civil Power in England* (1748), which argues that a true Whig always is 'for maintaining an equal Ballance of Power between the several Orders of the Legislature'. Fielding owned Squire's *An Enquiry into the Foundation of the English Constitution; or an Historical Essay upon the Anglo-Saxon Government* . . . (London, 1745; Baker, no. 209), which attributes English institutions to Anglo-Saxon originals. It also praises Alfred's efficient control of crime. Squire was chaplain to the Duke of Newcastle.

existing laws. Walpole's government was an assault on these ancient rights and institutions. His propagandists countered with a historical argument of their own which denied the existence of an ancient constitution. They argued instead that true English liberties arose in 1688 when the revolution overturned the absolutism of the Stuarts. The House of Commons had never been an Anglo-Saxon institution and William ruled by right of absolute conquest. The medieval past revealed a succession of absolute rulers.

Isaac Kramnick,[8] profiting from the work of J. G. A. Pocock,[9] has convincingly shown that these historical arguments of the 1730s were grounded in seventeenth-century constitutional controversy. Appeals to the antiquity of the House of Commons and to the immemorial past of the law were skillfully and learnedly made by such men as Coke, Petyt, Nathaniel Bacon, and a host of common-law lawyers whose intent was to curtail the power of the Crown and to assert the rights of the House of Commons. In so far as their arguments led to and justified the revolution of 1688, they were 'Whigs'. The 'Tory' answer to such arguments appeared notably in the historical writings of Robert Brady, who, taking advantage of the distinguished Anglo-Saxon scholarship of Spelman and others, accurately, if not effectively, denied the historical premises of the Whigs by showing that the Norman Conquest had radically altered English government and English law. Thus in the 1730s Walpole's writers used the arguments of the Tory Brady to counter the Whiggish theories of Bolingbroke.

Many of the seventeenth-century works in which this argument was conducted were in Fielding's library.[1] The issues, if no longer quite contemporary, must have been familiar to Fielding, and we can hear their echo, I think, in his frequent appeals to Anglo-Saxon institutions and in his praise of Alfred. What, he asks in the Preface, 'is become of the constitution of *Alfred*, which the Reader will find set forth at large in the following Treatise?' Both the *Enquiry* and the *Proposal* frequently hark back to that golden age when 'Travellers, as we are told, might pass through the whole Kingdom with Safety; [when] Bracelets of Gold might be hung up in the public Roads, and found at a distant Time by the Owner in the Place where they were left'. 'There is no part of our antient Constitution more admirable than that which was calculated to prevent the Concealment of Thieves and

[8] 'Augustan Politics and English Historiography: the Debate on the English Past, 1730–35', *History and Theory*, 6 (1967), 33–56; and *Bolingbroke and his Circle* (Cambridge, Mass. 1968), pp. 127 ff. H. T. Dickinson has also written instructively on this topic in his *Bolingbroke* (London, 1970) and *Liberty and Property* (New York, 1977).

[9] Pocock's *The Ancient Constitution and the Feudal Law* (Cambridge, 1957) is the seminal work on the 17th century context of the controversy over the history of the constitution.

[1] Including such central texts as Petyt's *Antient Right of the Commons of England* (Baker, no. 57), Nathaniel Bacon's *Historicall Discourse* (Baker, no. 277), and Brady's *History of England* (Baker, no. 294). Fielding cites Bacon in both the *Enquiry* (p. 132) and the *Proposal* (p. 261).

Robbers', he writes in the *Enquiry*, and proceeds to trace this 'Institution' to Alfred and to praise his division of the land into hundreds and his establishment of the frank-pledge system. In the *Charge*, Fielding had argued that the origin of trial by jury, the gem of English liberties, pre-dated even Anglo-Saxon times, for it 'very probably had some Existence even among the *Britons*' (below, p. 5).

A little more than a decade earlier, such praise of Alfred and the ancient constitution would inevitably have carried political connotations. 'A single jail, in Alfred's golden reign, / Could half the nation's criminals contain; / Fair justice then, without constraint ador'd, / Held high the steady scale, but drop'd the sword; / No spies were paid, no special juries known, / Blest age! but ah! how diff'rent from our own!' wrote Johnson when early tainted by the spirit of 'Patriot' opposition.[2] In 1735 'the Prince of Wales had ordered "a fine Statue of King Alfred to be made for his Gardens in *Pall-Mall*" with a Latin inscription stating that Alfred was *"the Founder of the* LIBERTIES *and* COMMONWEALTH *of England."* [3] Fielding, now an adherent of the party carrying on the Whig tradition of Walpole, would scarcely disparage English liberty under the Pelham Administration. He accepted the Whig dogma that the Glorious Revolution of 1688 ended decades of unconstitutional and arbitrary rule by the Stuarts. But as a trained lawyer he inherited the idea that the constitution and English law originated in a distant and immemorial past. As an ex-Patriot he was aware of the political connotations that praise of Alfred and his ancient constitution held, and he must have been sensitive to the polemical overtones carried by talk of a balanced constitution. Whatever Fielding's precise intentions may have been, the *Enquiry* reflects a view of history notably expressed in Bolingbroke's *Dissertation on Parties* and in legal and constitutional writings of the seventeenth century, now adjusted to the topic of the poor and the criminal law.

Two adverse responses to the *Enquiry*, both written by Tories, seem to answer Fielding's politically tendentious reflections. Early in March 1751 a Ben Sedgly[4] published a substantial pamphlet with the descriptive and leisurely title of *Observations on Mr. Fielding's Enquiry into the Causes of the late Increase of Robbers, &c. in which Not only the present reigning Vices among the Vulgar are more candidly and impartially considered; but the Follies and Vices of the Politer Part of the British Nation are freely represented; as also the pernicious Consequences of drinking Gin more particularly described: By Ben Sedgly, of*

---

[2] *London*, ll. 248–53.

[3] The *Craftsman*, 14 (6 Sept. 1735), 103–4 (cit. by Maynard Mack, *The Garden and the City* (Toronto, 1969, p. 140).

[4] Professor Bertrand Goldgar has pointed out to me that William Kenrick, in a note to his *Pasquinade* (1753), identifies 'Ben Sedgly' as the pseudonym used by Richard Rolt in his *A Reply to Mr. Fieldings Discourse on Robberies*. Rolt was a Jacobite sympathizer who lost his post in the Excise when he joined the revolt of 1745. Johnson wrote the Preface to Rolt's *Dictionary of Trade and Commerce* (1756).

Temple-Bar. To which are added, Considerations on the Nature of Government in general; and more particularly of the British Constitution; with a Vindication of the Rights and Privileges of the Commonalty of England, in Opposition to what has been advanced by the Author of the Enquiry, or to what may be promulgated by any Ministerial Artifices, against the Public Cause of Truth and Liberty: by Timothy Beck, The Happy Cobler of Portugal Street. This work is divided into three sections, the first of which comments on Fielding's discussion of luxury, the second on his eight 'preventative' recommendations. The third section, supposedly based on observations communicated to Sedgly by Timothy Beck, contains the vindication of the 'Commonalty' promised on the title-page. These first two sections, despite their antagonistic and sarcastic tone, rarely reveal sharp disagreement with Fielding's ideas, and one suspects that the writer's regard for Fielding's arguments grew as he proceeded in his examination of them. He places far more emphasis than Fielding on the notion that the vices of the rich lead the poor astray, asserting that no law can reach the 'fountain-head' of vice and that reformation must begin with 'the leaders of the herd' (p. 11). But he recognizes that luxury has increased alarmingly and explores the evils of gin-drinking vigorously, agreeing with Fielding that gin should be placed 'beyond the reach of the Vulgar'. Sedgly approves most of Fielding's suggestions in the last eight sections of the *Enquiry*. He rejects only two, that pardons be less frequently granted and that executions be swift and private. He is also unconvinced that wages should be rated or thief-takers honored.

The antagonism sharpens, however, in the last part. Here Fielding's aristocratic assumptions about the social place of the lower classes gave offence, particularly his apparent regret at the increased power of the commonalty: 'The author of the *Enquiry* seems particularly attentive for augmenting the power of the civil magistrate, so as to enable every justice of peace, to restrain the liberty "of every riotous independent butcher or baker, with two or three thousand pounds in his pocket;" for such blunt Englishmen are not to be intimidated at the tremendous frown of a petty tyrant, who, with a bashaw severity, can hold the rod of oppression over the head of poverty. If the commonalty have happily sprung from the chains of slavery, and interwoven themselves as so material a branch of the community, ought they to be deprived of that liberty for which their ancestors have so long and so gloriously, contended?' (pp. 71–2). The Happy Cobbler agrees that the English constitution has altered but, like Walpole's propagandists, celebrates the change, for it is from slavery to freedom: 'what were the liberties of our progenitors after the defeat of Harold? they were too precarious to be called a right: Englishmen were then a race of subjected vassals to their haughty insolent conquerers . . .' (p. 74). Herein sounds the perennial cry of the opposition, now issuing from

Portugal Street, near where Bosavern Penlez was captured, that the government was subverting English liberties.

The contributor of two essays to the *True Briton* lodged many of the same complaints against the *Enquiry*.[5] Like Timothy Beck, this writer took offence at Fielding's disparagement of the Commonalty ('How dare you write a book to abridge their Pleasures, and take away their natural Rights . . .') and couched his objections in an argument directed against Fielding's assumption of an ancient constitution and his celebration of a balanced constitution. He ridicules Fielding's description of this ancient constitution, rejecting particularly the idea of an Anglo-Saxon original for the House of Commons. He scornfully denies the existence of a happy past and argues instead that the Norman conquest effectively ended Alfred's institutions and left the Anglo-Saxons in a wretched condition. Significantly, his authority is the 'learned Dr. Brady', the historian who answered Coke and the common-law lawyers in the seventeenth century and whose arguments were adopted by the propagandists Walpole enlisted in the 1730s to answer Bolingbroke. Curiously, then, historical arguments first directed at 'Whiggish' seventeenth-century opponents of Stuart despotism and later employed to answer Tory and Opposition attacks on Walpole, are now adopted by Tory sympathizers with the rights and liberties of the lower orders in order to refute Fielding's lawyerly and conservative analysis of the English constitution and to challenge his call for an increase in the power of the Crown to balance the emerging power of the commonalty.[6]

Most responses to the *Enquiry*, however, were favorable.[7] The author of a *A Method Proposed to Prevent the many Robberies and Villanies Committed in . . .*

[5] 'Considerations *on Justice* Fielding's Inquiry' (*True Briton*, no. 9, 27 Feb. 1751) and '*Further* Considerations *on Justice* Fielding's Inquiry' (*True Briton*, no. 10, 6 Mar. 1751). The writer, Professor Battestin informs me, was George Osborne, a Jacobite sympathizer, who was encouraged by General Oglethorpe, also a Jacobite and a member of the Committee of 1751, to attack Fielding's *Proposal* (see BL Add. MSS 28236, fo. 23).

[6] That both Rolt and Osborne were Tories and yet were sympathetic to the rights of the 'Commonalty' and antagonistic to Fielding's bureaucratic solutions to the problems of the poor is not surprising. 'Tory democrats' (the phrase is Donald Greene's) might well dislike Fielding's kind of 'rational humanitarianism' (see Greene's *The Politics of Samuel Johnson* [New Haven, 1960], especially ch. 1). Charles Gray, who attacked plans to institutionalize the poor in a vast workhouse (see General Introduction, p. lxxv), was also a Tory. In the second *True Briton* article, Osborne, like Dr Johnson (see *Enquiry*, below, p. 166, n. 3), criticized Fielding's acceptance of the death penalty for minor offences and rejected his arguments against tender-hearted juries.

[7] See Cross, ii. 266–8. Ronald Paulson and Thomas Lockwood print excerpts from the favorable review of the *Enquiry* in the *Monthly Review* for January 1750/1 (in *Henry Fielding: The Critical Heritage* [London, 1969], pp. 239–45). However, a letter to the *London Magazine* in Mar. 1751 (signed by 'An Old Rake'), objected, like Sedgly, to Fielding's supposed indifference to the follies of the great: 'Does he think, that there is any pleasure or any vice, in which the *great* are allowed to indulge themselves, that can effectually by law be denied to the *little*? We know the contrary: Fashion has in all ages, and in all countries, triumphed over law. . . . Therefore, to prevent by law the enjoyment of any pleasure, or the indulgence of any vice, amongst those of inferior rank, whilst it is made fashionable by the practice

London observed midway in his argument that 'There is a worthy Magistrate of the [Cit]y of *Westminster* [*identified in a footnote as Fielding*], who has been, and is [stil]l indefatigable in having our Laws put [into] full Force, which are now subsisting, relating to the Poor, and are the best in the World, but the worst executed.—He has recommended it to the Publick in a Book lately published, concerning the preventing of Robberies committed in and about this great Metropolis, which if I could have my Wish, should be sent to every Parish in *London and Westminster*.'⁸ In 1751 Joshua Fitzsimmonds, a barrister, discussing 'frequent Robberies', confessed, 'I am in a great measure prevented in what I had to say, by Mr. *Fielding's* late Excellent Inquiry; which, tho' he seems to have too much Partiality for those who sit upon the Bench with him, is not only worth the Perusal of the Learned and Powerful, but also of those who would get an insight into the Parochial and Penal Laws of the Land'.⁹ In the Appendix to the third edition of 'The Expediency of Preventative Wisdom' Isaac Maddox wrote, 'While the foregoing Sheets were printing off, the Nation was much obliged . . . by a learned and seasonable Discourse, entitled *An Enquiry* . . .; it is much to be wished that the weighty Considerations therein offered, may effectually awaken Attention. . . . The Treatise itself has spread, and I hope will spread . . .' Arthur Murphy, Fielding's first biographer, remarked 'The Pamphlet on the *Encrease and Cause of Robberies* has been held in high estimation by some eminent persons who have administered justice in Westminster Hall',¹ and even Horace Walpole acknowledged that it was an 'admirable treatise'.² Its repute persisted strongly throughout the century, writers on the poor and criminal class invariably paying tribute to one suggestion or another Fielding had made.³ And of course it is today the best known of Fielding's social

---

of the great amongst us, I shall always look on as a chimerical project' (p. 130). 'Philo-Patria' was also mildly critical, insisting in *A Letter to Henry Fielding, Esq: Occasioned by his Enquiry* . . . (London, 1751) that not luxury but 'debauchery', i.e., 'infamous Women', is the cause of crime.

⁸ (London, 1752) p. 18.

⁹ *Free and Candid Disquisitions, on the Nature and Execution of the Laws of England Both in Civil and Criminal Affairs . . . With a postscript relating to Spirituous Licquors* . . . (London, 1751), p. 38. Josiah Tucker found similarly that Fielding had anticipated what he had to say about the diversions of the lower classes: 'Mr. Fielding hath so copiously set forth the evil Consequences attending the making Diversions cheap for People in common and middling Life, that I shall beg Leave to refer for fuller Information to his very seasonable and judicious Treatise concerning the *Causes of the late Encrease of Robberies*, &c' (*An Impartial Inquiry into the Benefits and Damages Arising to the Nation from Spirituous Liquors* [London, 1751], p. 4).

¹ 'An Essay on the Life and Genius of Henry Fielding, Esq.', prefixed to *The Works of Henry Fielding, Esq.*, ed. Arthur Murphy (London, 1762), i. 39. Despite Murphy's praise of the *Enquiry*, the decision to include it in his edition may have been made partly in order to 'bring the last volume to the size of the others' (Hugh Amory, 'Andrew Millar and the First Reeension of Fielding's *Works* [1762]', p. 58).

² *Memoirs of the Reign of George II* (1836), i. 44 (cit. Cross, ii. 267).

³ e.g. Thomas Ruggles, *The History of the Poor* (London, 1793), i. 220: 'In [1751], Mr. Henry Fielding, as well known to us in these days for his excellent novels, replete with nature, mirth, and

pamphlets, important to Fielding scholars but more often cited by social and legal historians.[4] Though the number of his own works in his library is admittedly few, that the *Enquiry* was the only one of his social writings so preserved is perhaps some measure of Fielding's sense of the intelligence, knowledge, and ambition that went into its making.

Strahan's ledger for January 1751 reveals a substantial printing of 1,500 copies of the *Enquiry*: 'Fielding on Robberies, 9 Sheets Nᵒ. 1500 @ £1:8: p. Sheet . . . . 12:12:–/Extraordinary Corrections in D.ᵒ and 5.ˢ to the Men . . . 1:12:–'.[5] A number of the Strahan entries for Fielding's works record a charge for 'Corrections and Alterations' or 'Extraordinary Corrections', but the additional charge here of '5.ˢ to the Men' perhaps suggests that Fielding made an unusual number of last minute changes in what certainly was a complex manuscript. Of the pamphlets printed in this volume (excluding *Elizabeth Canning*, which apparently was not printed by Strahan) only the *Proposal* and *Examples of Providence* had a larger run (in the case of *Examples of Providence*, there was a second printing of an additional 2,000 copies).[6] Patricia Hernlund finds in her study of Strahan's Ledgers that of 514 typical entries only 86 had initial runs as large as 1,500 copies.[7] Despite the considerable number of copies of this octavo first edition, a second edition, in 'twelves', was quickly called for, and in February Strahan entered the following charge: 'Fielding on Robberies, 2ᵈ Edit. 10 Sheets Nᵒ. 2000 @

---

pathos, as he was in those for his excellence as a magistrate, published "An inquiry into the Cause of the late Increase of Robbers, &c. with some Proposals for remedying the growing Evil." This treatise is full of observations, worthy a man of his abilities, and intimate knowledge, from extensive experience, as a Middlesex magistrate, of this important subject'; and Patrick Colquhoun, *A Treatise on the Police of the Metropolis* (London, 1797), p. 298: 'That able and excellent Magistrate, the late Henry Fielding, Esq. (to whose zeal and exertions in the exercise of the duties of a Justice of the Peace, in the Metropolis, the Public were under infinite obligations)—manifested, half a century ago, how much he was impressed with the injuries arising from frequent pardons.—Those who will contemplate the character and conduct of this valuable man, as well as that of his brother . . . will sincerely lament that their excellent ideas, and accurate and extensive knowledge upon every subject connected with the Police of the Metropolis, and of the means of preventing crimes were not rendered more useful to the Public.'

[4] The first edition of the *Enquiry* has been reprinted lithographically by the AMS Press for the *Foundations of Criminal Justice* series (New York, 1975).

[5] BL Add. MSS 48,800, fo. 78. The first newspaper notice for the *Enquiry*, announcing its publication '*In a few Days*', appeared in the *General Advertiser* of Friday 4 Jan. 1751. It was not until Thursday, 17 Jan., however, that this paper promised the *Enquiry* for 'Saturday next'. The 'This Day is published' notice appeared in the *General Advertiser* on Saturday and was repeated in each issue of the following week. These later advertisements added the information that the pamphlet was dedicated to the Lord High Chancellor.

[6] The largest printing of a Fielding pamphlet recorded by Strahan is 3,500 copies (*A Dialogue Between A Gentleman From London . . . And An Alderman*); the smallest is 500 (the *Dialogue between the Devil, The Pope, and the Pretender* and *A Proper Answer to a Late Scurrilous Libel*). Like the *Enquiry*, *Joseph Andrews* had a first edition of 1,500 copies and a second of 2,000.

[7] 'William Strahan's Ledgers: Standard Charges for Printing, 1738–85', *Studies in Bibliography*, 20 (1967), 104.

£1:13:p. Sheet 16:10:–'.[8] This second edition, published 6 March 1751,[9] reveals a good number of mainly minor revisions (see Textual Appendixes, below) and incorporates all but one of the corrections indicated in the *Errata* list appended to the first edition.[1]

5. The PROPOSAL

In his 'Dedication' of *A Proposal for Making an Effectual Provision for the Poor* to Henry Pelham, Fielding says, 'I here present you with that Plan which I had the Honour once to mention to you, and of which I have given a former Hint to the Public'. It was probably in November 1751 that Fielding enjoyed the opportunity to mention his 'plan', for the *London Daily Advertiser* of 25 November 1751 reported 'We are assured that Henry Fielding Esq.; has laid before the Right Hon. Henry Pelham Esq.; a scheme for employing the Poor much to the Advantage of the Nation and themselves; and also for putting an effectual Stop to the daring Outrages and Robberies we have lately been too much alarmed with; and it is hoped that it will meet with an Attention due its Importance.' Clearly more than employment of the poor was discussed on this occasion—probably Fielding also seized the opportunity to present his case for those funds necessary to maintain his troop of constables and honest thief-takers. The 'former Hint to the Public' undoubtedly refers to his discussion 'Of the Laws that relate to the Provision for the Poor', Section IV of the *Enquiry*, in which he remarked in summary, 'Thus have I endeavoured to give the Reader a general Idea of the Laws which relate to this single Point of employing the Poor; and, as well as I am able to discern, of their Defects, and the Reasons of those Defects. I have likewise given some Hints for the Cure, and have presumed to offer a Plan, which, in my humble Opinion, would effectually answer every purpose desired' (p. 124). This evidence suggests that the *Enquiry* and the *Proposal* comprise a consistent program for dealing with the causes underlying social disorders, the *Proposal* being the elaborated solution to the second cause of crime posited in the *Enquiry*, the failure to employ the poor (the first cause is 'luxury', leading to financial distress, leading to crime). There is other evidence, however, both internal and external, that casts doubt on the consistency of Fielding's 'program'

---

[8] Loc. cit.

[9] The first advertisement for the second edition was published in the *General Advertiser* on Wednesday, 6 Feb. 'Price 2s. 6d. sew'd'. This same notice was repeated on 7, 8, and 9 Feb. The 'This day is published' notice appeared in the *General Advertiser* for Friday, 8 Mar. 1751, and the advertisement is repeated several times in the following issues. This time the price is given as 2s. 6d. sewed, or 3s. bound, and the further information is added that the volume is 'In Twelves'. The second edition was still being advertised in Nov. 1751.

[1] A Dublin edition of no textual authority was published in 1751. Like the London second edition, it failed to make the correction of 'Town' to 'Tourn' indicated in the errata list of the first edition.

and suggests that he may not have envisaged his elaborate workhouse scheme when composing the *Enquiry* late in 1750.[1]

In Section IV of the *Enquiry*, Fielding does not in fact clearly hint at a workhouse scheme, but instead presents arguments that appear to advocate a reform of the parish system of poor-law administration either by increasing the efficiency of parish officers or by establishing a new set of parish administrators. Here, Fielding considers the three standard categories of the poor: the 'impotent' poor; the poor who are willing to work; and the able-bodied poor who 'refuse' to work. The number of poor who for reasons of age or physical incapacity are unemployable are so few that they may be left to the relief of voluntary charity and to the care of existing charitable 'hospitals', a position consistent with his remarks in the *Proposal* on this category of poor. He attributes the failure to find work for those willing to support themselves to 'one single Mistake, but a Mistake which must be fatal as it is an Error in the first Concoction. The Mistake I Point at is, that the Legislature have left the whole Work [of providing employment] to the Overseers.'[2] Fielding then remarks, 'I have myself thought of a Plan for this Purpose, which I am ready to produce, when I shall have any Reason to see the least Glimpse of Hope, that my Labour in drawing it out at length would not be absolutely and certainly thrown away' (p. 111). The *Proposal* certainly was to emphasize the importance of responsible and capable governors for the workhouse, but these strictures in the *Enquiry* on the inefficiency of parish officers do not necessarily prefigure a workhouse scheme, especially since such complaint was a staple item in arguments made by those who would retain but reform the parish system of poor-law administration.

There are other instances in the *Enquiry* where Fielding's commentary implies reform of the parish system rather than the extra-parish solution of a large workhouse. In considering how to employ the 'lazy and idle', for example, Fielding fixes on the rating of wages (a topic never mentioned in the *Proposal*) as a way to expose those unwilling to work, and strays into a long refutation of Josiah Child's argument in support of high wages. But his argument again concludes with a comment apparently emphasizing administrative inefficiency: 'the Case here is the same as with the Overseers before, the Trust is too great for the Persons on whom it devolves' (*Enquiry*, p. 122).

---

[1] Both Cross and Dudden (ii. 779 n. and 959) assume this consistency, though Cross was aware that Fielding's conclusion in the *Proposal* was 'somewhat at variance with that of the *Enquiry*' (ii. 271 and 273).

[2] *Enquiry*, p. 110. In the *Proposal* he subordinates the inefficiency of parish officers to the failure to consolidate the labor of the poor: '. . .the scattered State in which the Poor were left by the Statute of *Elizabeth*, is the principal Reason why this Law hath produced no better Effect. It is true indeed, the Management of the Poor was by that Statute intrusted to very improper Hands; but this will not universally account for the Evil . . . The true Reason therefore that the Poor have not yet been well provided for, and well employed is, that they have not yet been drawn together. Of this Opinion were [Hale, Child, and Petty]' (p. 260).

Puzzling too if Fielding had a large workhouse scheme in mind in the *Enquiry*, is his rejection of the arguments for such a workhouse in the pamphlets of Hale and Child. Neither of them, he concludes, 'seem to strike at the Root of the Evil' (*Enquiry*, p. 105). And he held back from their conclusion that the failure to employ the poor lay in defects in the laws ('I am not absolutely driven to this [conclusion] as the Fault may so fairly be imputed to the Non-execution of the Law' [*Enquiry*, p. 107]). In the *Proposal* Fielding was to assert 'upon the Whole it appears to me, that there are great Defects in [the laws relating to the poor], and that they are capable of being amended'.

Because of these ambiguities, it would have been very difficult for a reader in 1751 to infer from Section IV of the *Enquiry* that Fielding was in favor of a county workhouse which would house and employ over five thousand paupers and vagrants. One early reader, in fact, who was strongly opposed to such workhouses and who wished to retain the parish as the basic administrative unit of poor-relief, read the *Enquiry* as a document supporting his views. Some time after June 1751, Charles Gray published his *Considerations on Several Proposals Lately Made, for the Better Maintenance of the Poor*.[3] 'The great Question will be,' he wrote, 'Whether the Parochial maintenance established by Q. Elizabeth is the true way, or whether it may be better effected in the larger districts recommended by Judge Hale, Sir Josiah Child, the resolutions of the House of Commons in 1735, and the resolutions in 1751' (p. 2). His view was that the present laws, with 'small improvements and alterations' will suffice provided that 'persons of rank and substance' see that they are ably administered (p. vi). In the context of an argument that focuses on reform of parochial management, Gray read Fielding's remarks in the *Enquiry* as potential support for his position and looked forward to Fielding's publication of his plan: 'Mr. Fielding, in the excellent piece here alluded to, [the *Enquiry*] has shewn himself a most worthy labourer in the vineyard of the public: and 'tis a great pity that in a performance so masterly, the one thing needful (as to the present point) should be omitted. It is to be hoped, that he will soon oblige us with his plan, because at this time the thoughts of a Gentleman of so much ability and experience, could not but be extremely useful' (p. 6). Gray quotes several passages from the *Enquiry* on King Alfred's subdivision of the realm into hundreds, tithings, and decennaries, rightly noting Fielding's emphasis on the effectiveness of small administrative units. Gray must have been surprised and sharply disappointed when the *Proposal* was published.

Gray was a member of the Committee of 1751 which had been charged in

[3] Gray (1696–1782) was a Tory MP for Colchester (1742–55), aligned, in 1749, with the Opposition led by the Prince of Wales. A classical scholar and archaeologist as well as a reformer, he was one of the original trustees of the British Museum.

February to consider the criminal laws and whose responsibilities had been extended in March to include the laws relating to provision for the poor. As he indicates, his pamphlet was provoked by the report of this Committee in June, which included the two following resolutions:

Resolved, That it is the Opinion of this Committee, That many Parishes are too small separately to raise a Stock sufficient wherewith to employ the Poor to any Advantage.

Resolved, That it is the Opinion of this Committee, That it would, in all Probability, be a great Means of lessening to a considerable Degree, the Charge of the Poor, and of greatly decreasing their Number, in a very few Years, if some Method should be agreed on to maintain and employ the Poor by One common Fund in every county . . .[4]

The House agreed to all of the Committee's resolutions. Thus, at least by June 1751, it was clear that the House of Commons favored the large unit of the county by which to 'maintain and employ the Poor'. This Parliamentary interest prompted Gray's dissent, but it also led to public agitation for large workhouses. Two pamphleteers attacked Gray's essay in 1752, both vaguely arguing for large workhouses.[5] William Hay, who had actively supported the idea of a large workhouse in 1735, when Parliament had also appeared ready to adopt this idea, reissued his workhouse pamphlet in 1751.[6] In 1752, Thomas Alcock published *Observations on the Defects of the Poor Laws* recommending a large workhouse: 'Suppose then a Poor-House, Work-House, Hospital, or whatever you will please to call it, was erected in some convenient Place near the Middle of every Hundred. It should consist of three Parts, one for the Impotent, and the able and honest industrious Poor; one for the sick; and one for the Confinement, Labour, and Correction of Vagrants, Idlers, and Sturdy Beggars. It should be strong and plain: Grandeur here is absurd' (p. 55).[7]

The possibility that Fielding's *Proposal* represents an altered conception of how to deal with the unemployed and the unemployable appears all the more likely when considered in the context of this flurry of interest in workhouse schemes occurring after the publication of the *Enquiry*.[8] By the time Fielding

---

[4] *JHC* xxvi. 289.

[5] *A Letter to the Author of Considerations on Several Proposals for the better Maintenance of the Poor* (London, 1752); and *An Impartial Examination of a Pamphlet, intitled, Considerations* . . . (London, 1752).

[6] *Remarks on the Laws Relating to the Poor; with Proposals for the Better Relief and Employment.* I use the text reprinted from the edition of 1751 in *The Works of William Hay* (London, 1794), i. 106–70. Hay (1695–1755) sat for Seaford (1734–55), controlled by the Duke of Newcastle, Hay's cousin by marriage. Hay enjoyed a secret-service pension of £500 a year and, in 1754, was appointed keeper of the records in the Tower. See Sedgwick, ii. 119–20.

[7] Alcock (1709–98) was a clergyman, holding the livings of Runcorn, in Cheshire, and, later, St Budrock's, Plymouth. In addition to his pamphlets on the poor and some sermons, he published in 1796 *The Rise of Mahomet accounted for in Natural and Civil Principles*.

[8] The interest in poor-law legislation in 1751 is emphasized in *The Continuation of Mr. Rapin's History of England* (London, 1759), xxi. 448. Alcock remarked, 'The whole Nation, indeed, is now become so sensible of this growing Evil, that our Representatives in Parliament have taken the Matter

wrote his pamphlet, the active and prestigious Committee of 1751 had before it two Bills for the care of the poor (which he alludes to in the *Proposal*, below, pp. 263–4), and it seemed ready to recommend significant new legislation. Thus Fielding, like Alcock, Hay, and others, may well have been influenced by its deliberations. If so, Fielding, once again, was offering to the Pelham Administration as well as to the public his views on a topic of particular current interest.

The little that is known of the publishing history of the *Proposal* gives some support to these speculations. It was published on 29 January 1753, but not quite according to schedule. On 17 and 19 January (Wednesday and Friday), the *Publick Advertiser* announced that the *Proposal* would be published 'next week', but on the following Friday, 26 January, publication was advertised for the next Monday. On 29 January the 'This day is publish'd' notice did in fact appear. Strahan's ledger entry, with its recording of 'Extraordinary Corrections', perhaps suggests last minute revisions to the *Proposal*:

January [1753] Fielding on the Poor. N° 2000 @ £1:10
——9:–:–
        Extraordinary Corrections in D°
——— –:13:–[9]

In a 'Note' at the end of his pamphlet, Fielding asks the reader to 'excuse' the 'several little Mistakes in the foregoing Proposals . . . which escaped Correction in the Hurry in which this Pamphlet was printed'. The reason for this haste cannot be definitely known. It may have been domestic—a daughter, Louisa, who lived but a few months, was born early in December; or personal—Fielding's health had been declining rapidly in 1752 and he had resorted to various unlikely nostrums, especially for relief from the gout. But the last issue of the *Covent-Garden Journal* had appeared 25 November 1752 and it would be several months before he became caught up in the case of Elizabeth Canning. The 'Hurry' may well be owing simply to Fielding's eagerness to get his workhouse proposal before the public and Parliament.

Whether or not Fielding had determined on a workhouse scheme in 1750–1, his *Proposal* was timely beyond the immediate context of Parliamentary interest and free-lance pamphleteering. Workhouses and

into Consideration, and no doubt in a future Session will endeavour, either to reform the Errors and Abuses in the present Method, or contrive and establish some new and better Measures' (*Observations*, p. 5).. Interest in the workhouse remained strong throughout the decade, and Gray thought it necessary to reissue his *Considerations* in 1757. In 1760 he published *Further Considerations* . . . in which he quotes resolutions passed by the House of Commons on 30 May 1759. As described by Gray these resolutions bear striking resemblance to Fielding's *Proposal*, though I have not been able to find them in *JHC* for that date.

[9] BL Add. MSS 48800 fo. 84.

workhouse projectors had been familiar to Englishmen for over half a century, and the conviction that a solution to the problems posed by the poor lay in employing them in a workhouse had been steadily growing, especially since the Workhouse Act of 1722.[1] The impulse behind the earliest workhouses had been humanitarian and religious. The Bishopsgate Street workhouse which Fielding mentions[2] was as concerned to save men's souls as to relieve their bodily distress or to employ them. Thomas Firmin, whom Fielding praised in the *Covent-Garden Journal*,[3] published a workhouse proposal in 1678 that was as much philanthropic as economic in its emphasis. John Bellars, a Quaker friend of George Fox, published *Proposals for Raising a Colledge* [sic] *of Industry* in 1696 which projected self-supporting agricultural communities throughout England like 'little Colonies' in a foreign land.[4]

In later workhouse proposals, the impetus was more likely to be social and economic, but as early as 1700 one finds workhouse proposals which emphasize practical over humanitarian benefits. For instance, around that year an anonymous pamphleteer suggested that three large workhouses (each was to accommodate two thousand inhabitants) be erected to employ the poor of London and Westminster. These houses would be run by a governor and deputy-governor, chosen by 'Justices and Magistrates', whose duties and powers would have been much like the governors of Fielding's workhouse. He cites as authority for his project 'His Majesty's Wisdom, Care, and Goodness in recommending... in the last Sessions of Parliament... [that] *it would be happy if some effectual Expedient could be found for employing the Poor, which might tend to the Great Increase of our Manufactures, as well as remove a heavy Burden from the People*'.[5] Like Fielding, he connects poverty and unemployment with 'Robberies, House-breakings, Murders, and other Villainies': 'I am perswaded that a great many who are executed every Sessions and Assizes, would never have committed such Wickedness, if Poverty had not driven them to such abominable Actions'.[6] A workhouse would employ the poor, decrease crime, and protect the honest citizen from swarms of bold and importunate beggars, many of whom are imposters: 'The

---

[1] What follows is partially a summary of my discussion of Fielding and the workhouse in *Social Pamphlets*, especially pp. 117 ff.

[2] In the *Enquiry*, p. 104.

[3] *CGJ* (2 June 1752), ii. 9. Firmin (1632–97) was a London merchant. His workhouse was in Little Britain. He 'was particularly esteemed by the equally Learned, and Pious, Dr. *Wilkins*, Bishop of *Chester*; by the Honourable Mr. *Boyle*, the great Restorer of Natural, and Christian Philosophy; by that Eminent Oracle of the Law, Sir *Matthew Hale*, and (what will be the most lasting Elegy to our Friend, that I, or any other Hand can give him) he was happy in the Friendship of the most Excellent Prelate, that ever filled the Archepiscopal Chair, the Incomparable Dr. *Tillotson*' (*The Charitable Samaritan* [London, 1698], p. 5).

[4] Bellars reissued his *Proposals* in 1699 and again in 1723.

[5] [M.D.], *A Present Remedy for the Poor* (BL gives 'London, 1700'), p. 3.

[6] Ibid., p. 6.

number of Beggars increases daily, our Streets swarm with this kind of People, and their boldness and impudence is such, that they often beat at our Doors, stop Persons in the ways, and are ready to load us with Curses and Imprecations, if their Desires be not speedily answer'd. Besides, it is reported of the common Beggars, that they have their Meetings, and Rendevouz, where what they have got by their lazy Trade, they can spend freely in Debauchery, Drunkenness, and other sins.'[7]

After the Workhouse Act of 1722 (9 Geo. I, c. 7), which enabled parishes to combine in erecting joint workhouses, thus confirming in law what had already been common practice, the economic bias of workhouse proposals became dominant. The practical effect of this law was to establish the workhouse as a device to prevent the poor from applying for relief. Several parishes would erect a common workhouse, perhaps with good intentions, but inevitably it became so forbidding that only the most desperate sought relief in it. Those who refused to enter the workhouse forfeited their right to parish relief, and the poor-rate decreased.[8] The principle of combination fed the large workhouse scheme. The idea of employing, at low wages and in a circumscribed area, a large number of heretofore idle hands appealed mightily to a projector convinced that the riches and strength of the nation depended on a large body of industrious poor. One such, Lawrence Braddon, proposed that enormous 'Collegiate Cities', each holding twenty thousand people, 'be built very near the River of Thames, for encouraging Art, Industry, and Trade; In which Cities, all the capable, which are chargeable Poor, within the Bills of Mortality, from three years of age and upwards, should be employed. . . for the common Good of Great Britain'.[9] Braddon was extraordinarily sanguine about the theoretical earning power of nearly any human being: 'I could propose a way how any Person, past, [*sic*] Twelve Years of Age, that had neither Eye, nor Hand, and but one Foot, by the motion of that Foot, twelve Hours in a Day, and without much force, should get, six Pence per Day. . .'[1] One is grateful that not much force was required. Braddon's calculation of the value of a childbearing woman reminds us how firmly *A Modest Proposal* is grounded in such literature: 'For

[7] Ibid., pp. 6–7.
[8] The first edition (London, 1725) of *An Account of Several Work-Houses for Employing and Maintaining the Poor* contains over forty accounts of such workhouses; the second edition (London, 1732), over one hundred. Nearly all of the contributors confess failure to employ the poor profitably but claim their poor-rate has decreased.
[9] *Particular Answers to the Most Material Objections to the Proposal . . . for Relieving, Reforming, and Employing all the Poor of Great Britain* (London, 1722), pp. 12–13. Braddon (d. 1724), politician and lawyer, gained notoriety for his futile attempt to prove that the Earl of Essex had been murdered in the tower in 1683. As a result of his detective work, Braddon was fined £200 and imprisoned. He was released by William III, and in 1695 was appointed solicitor to the wine license office.
[1] *A Corporation Humbly Propos'd, For Relieving, Reforming, and Employing the Poor* (London, 1720), pp. 14–15.

every poor Woman, which bears a Child (under a probability of living) brings to her Native Country, a more valuable Treasure, than Ten Pounds Sterling. And were it possible for us to purchase, Ten Millions of Children, at Ten Pounds per Head, we should thereby purchase (what in Twenty Years) might put us in a Capacity, of giving Laws to all Europe'.[2] Yet Braddon considered himself an expert on the subject of employing the poor, saying, very much like Fielding (see below, p. 232), 'I have read, and for many Years consider'd, the many Proposals upon this Subject. . . . And I have also read and consider'd those numerous Laws, and some other Bills, which never past into Laws, concerning the Poor.'[3] He cites as his authorities Hale, Child, Davenant, Gregory King, Firmin, and Bellars.

That Fielding knew this pamphlet literature is reasonably certain. In reading about the poor and crime one could not miss workhouse proposals for they did not comprise a separate category: pamphlets on the poor usually included workhouse proposals. It is likely that most influential on Fielding were the writings of Hale,[4] Child,[5] John Cary,[6] and William Hay. I shall not repeat here my earlier argument for the broad similarities between their plans and Fielding's. It is worth pointing out, however, that by 1735, when Hay first published his pamphlet, the authority of Hale and Child had long been established: 'As to the Laws relating to the Relief and Employment of the Poor, I can only repeat what the Lord Chief Justice Hale, and Sir Josiah Child, have said on that Subject, whose Treatises deserve to be often read and considered by every Well-wisher to his Country',[7] an observation repeated by many writers before and after Hay. Hay reviews the arguments of Hale, Child, and Cary, and his summary of the points on which they (and he) agree confirms Fielding's place in the line of these writers.

This is the Substance of the three Schemes I mentioned; and it may be observed, that they all agree in these fundamental Points: I. That the Care of the Poor ought not to be left any longer to each Parish, but that every County shall be divided into larger Districts for that Purpose. II. That in each District proper Buildings should be provided for the Poor, at the common Charge of that District. III. That the Poor-Rates of every Parish in each District should be united into one common Fund. IV. That in each District there be established a Corporation with perpetual Succession, to whom the whole Care of the Poor shall be committed. V. That each Corporation shall be capable of taking Lands and Goods for the Benefit of the Poor.[8]

---

[2] Ibid., p. 16.   [3] Ibid., p. 23.

[4] *A Discourse Touching Provision for the Poor* (London, 1683). For Hale, see above, p. xxxii.

[5] *A Discourse about Trade* (London, 1690). For Child, see *Proposal*, below, p. 259 and n. 2.

[6] *An Account of the Proceedings of the Corporation of Bristol* (London, 1700) describes the Bristol workhouse established by an Act of Parliament in 1695. *A Discourse on Trade, and Other Matters Relative to it* (London, 1745) contains his plan for a large workhouse (this edition was in Fielding's library, Baker, no. 192). Cary (d. 1724) was a sugar merchant in the West Indies.

[7] *Remarks on the Laws Relating to the Poor*, p. 125.

[8] Ibid., pp. 139–40.

Hay's own proposals, more detailed than those of his predecessors, generally are consistent with Fielding's. The Resolutions of the House in 1735, which Hay's pamphlet was written to support, demonstrate the essential conventionality of Fielding's pamphlet:

Resolved,

1. That it is the Opinion of this Committee, that the Laws in being relating to the Maintenance of the Poor of this Kingdom are defective; and notwithstanding they impose heavy Burthens on Parishes, yet the Poor, in most of them, are ill taken care of.

Resolved,

2. That it is the Opinion of this Committee, that the Laws relating to the Settlement of the Poor, and concerning Vagrants, are very difficult to be executed, and chargeable in their Execution, vexatious to the Poor, and of little Advantage to the Public; and ineffectual to promote the good Ends for which they were intended.

Resolved,

3. That it is the Opinion of this Committee, that it is necessary for the better Relief and Employment of the Poor, that a public Work-house or Work-houses, Hospital or Hospitals, House or Houses of Correction, be established in proper Places, and under proper Regulations, in each County.

Resolved,

4. That it is the Opinion of this Committee, that in such Work-house or Work-houses, all Poor Persons able to labour be set to work, who shall either be sent thither, or come voluntarily for Employment.

Resolved,

5. That it is the Opinion of this Committee, that in such Hospital or Hospitals, Foundlings and other poor Children not having Parents able to provide for them, be taken Care of; as also, all poor Persons that are impotent or infirm.

Resolved,

6. That it is the Opinion of this Committee, that in such House or Houses of Correction, all idle and disorderly Persons, Vagrants, and such other Criminals, as shall be thought proper, be confined to hard Labour.

Resolved,

7. That it is the Opinion of this Committee, that towards the Charge of such Work-houses, Hospitals, and Houses of Correction, each Parish be assessed or rated; and that proper Persons be empowered to receive the Money so to be assessed or rated, when collected; and also all voluntary Contributions or Collections, either given or made for such Purposes.

Resolved,

8. That it is the Opinion of this Committee, that such Work-houses, Hospitals, and Houses of Correction, be under the Management of proper Persons, regard being had to such as shall be Benefactors to so good a Work.

Resolved,

9. That it is the Opinion of this Committee, that such Persons as shall be appointed for the Management of such Work-houses, Hospitals, and Houses of Correction, be one Body Politic in Law, capable to sue and be sued, and of taking and receiving charitable Contributions and Benefactions for the use of the same.

Resolved,

10. That it is the Opinion of this Commiteee, that for the better understanding and rendering more effectual the Laws relating to the Maintenance and Settlement of the Poor, it is very expedient, that they be reduced into one Act of Parliament.[9]

Thomas Alcock's workhouse plan in his *Observations on the Defects of the Poor Laws* (1752) is also similar to these earlier proposals. He became convinced that Fielding's *Proposal* borrowed from his pamphlet, and when he published a second pamphlet in 1753 he prefixed an 'Advertisement' in which he wrote, 'Since this Letter was put to the Press and almost printed off, the ingenious Mr. Fielding has obliged the Public with a Pamphlet, entitled, *A Proposal. . .*: Wherein, I have the Satisfaction to find, this Gentleman has adopted the General Plan for erecting public Work-houses for the better Management and Employment of the Poor, laid down in my Observations on the Poor Laws, &c. published towards the End of last Session of Parliament: Which I take this Occasion of mentioning, because I think it no small Recommendation of my Scheme to have the concurrent Testimony of so judicious a Writer in its Favour; tho' he has omitted to mention my Performance.[1] But his charge is unfounded. By the 1750s the idea of the large workhouse was in the public domain, and Alcock himself had little new to contribute (one could argue with more color that his *Observations* was indebted to the *Enquiry*). Fielding is more precise and detailed than any earlier proponent of a workhouse plan, especially in the specificity of his suggestions for its organization and administration, but it would be hard to point to an original idea in the *Proposal.*

The *Proposal* enjoyed a quiet but respectful reception. A paragraph in the *Gentleman's Magazine* for January 1753 recorded its publication and observed, 'Mr. *Fielding,* having made himself acquainted with all that has been hitherto done, and having by long experience gained some knowledge of the causes of [the] inefficacy [of the poor laws], has formed his plan: which appears to us, highly to deserve the attention of the public and legislature. And every man of influence about the metropolis would do well to give the

---

[9] Ibid., pp. 155–8. Unlike these Resolutions, Fielding does not propose to accommodate the infirm or children in his workhouse partly, as he says, because of two bills then before the House (*Proposal,* below, p. 264 and n. 7).

[1] *Remarks on Two Bills for the Better Maintenance of the Poor* (Oxford, 1753). Alcock dates his pamphlet 'February 10, 1753'.

whole an immediate perusal.' The next month a favorable longer review appeared, consisting mainly of excerpts. In February the *London Magazine* offered an 'Abstract' of the *Proposal* without comment. The *Monthly Review* said only that 'Mr. *Fielding's* method for answering the important purposes mentioned in the title page, is by the erection of a county work-house; the appointments and regulation of which he has also very judiciously sketched out. This performance is highly worthy the consideration of every well-wisher to the good order and posterity of our country.'[2] Richard Dircks has noted that the author of *A Plea for the Poor* (London, 1759) said 'This famous Plan, projected by Mr. Fielding was . . . approved by many Gentlemen of great Abilities in the House of Commons.'[3]

The first historian of the poor laws, the Reverend Richard Burn, accorded the *Proposal* an honorable place among the workhouse plans he reviewed and remarked that 'This discourse abounds with that strong sense and energy of expression, of which that author was happily possessed'.[4] Later, Thomas Ruggles, another poor-law historian, objected to Fielding's representation of the state of the poor, thought his workhouse would have been a grim place, and doubted the practicality of such a large workhouse. The observations that he 'ventured' on Fielding's ideas reflect a softening of attitude toward the poor increasingly common as the century drew to a close:

That they are collected from an intimate knowledge of the wretchedness and villainy which prevail among the lowest class of our fellow-creatures, in the purlieus of an over-grown metropolis; that the picture which he draws of them is too overcharged, the outline too hard, and, it is to be hoped, it is rather a caricature of the sink of wretchedness in London, than a natural representation of country manners, even in those families where laziness and debauchery are in league with poverty, to render human misery complete. His plan is also of a piece with his picture; therefore we read of dungeons, cells, iron grates, and fasting-rooms; although he indeed apologizes for the last, on the experience of their good effect in bridewells, and other houses of correction; but, besides all this, the expence attending building such large offices, together with houses for about half a dozen officers . . . is such an expence as would startle any county, although Middlesex should have set a successful example.[5]

Further scattered comments from late eighteenth-century writers on the poor show that the *Proposal* was remembered as an important poor-law document.[6] But relative to the *Enquiry*, its reputation was slight. Arthur

[2] 8 (Feb. 1753), 150.

[3] 'Henry Fielding's *A Proposal for Making an Effectual Provision for the Poor*: An Edition', unpublished doctoral dissertation, Fordham University (New York, 1961), p. x.

[4] *The History of the Poor Laws, with Observations* (London, 1764), p. 196.

[5] *The History of the Poor: their Rights, Duties, and the Laws Respecting Them* (London, 1793), i. 239–40.

[6] See, for example, John Scott, *Observations on the Present State of the Parochial and Vagrant Poor* (London, 1773), p. 99; R. Potter, *Observations on the Poor Laws, on the Present State of the Poor, and on*

Murphy chose not to include it in his edition of Fielding's Works, 'not being deemed of a colour with works of invention and genius'.[7] There was no second edition, though a Dublin edition of no textual authority was published in 1753. The *Proposal* was not reprinted until 1899 when Edmund Gosse included it in his edition of Fielding's *Works*.

6. EXAMPLES OF PROVIDENCE

Examples of the Interposition of Providence in the Detection and Punishment of Murder belongs to the tradition of religious writings mainly dating from the seventeenth and early eighteenth centuries which were concerned to assert, or to reassert against contemporary deistic or mechanistic views of the universe, the reality of God's presence in men's experience, his governance in the affairs of man, and his fitting distribution of rewards and punishments either here or in the hereafter. Tillotson's observation that 'Next to the acknowledgement of God's being nothing is more essential to Religion, than the Belief of his Providence',[1] reflects an emphasis on the centrality of the idea of providence to Christian doctrine common to many sermons of the time. But Fielding's *Examples of Providence* also has a more immediate context, one that is, broadly speaking, social, and before we consider its relationship to 'providential' literature and the sub-genre of exemplary providences, it will be useful to look closely at some of the special circumstances surrounding its composition and publication.

Examples of Providence forms a part of what Cross has aptly called Fielding's 'war against robbery and murder' (ii. 250 ff.) and as such it grows out of the same general impulse that produced the *Enquiry* and the *Proposal*, *Amelia*, and the *Covent-Garden Journal*, and which inspirits his energetic reforms of 'police' procedures in detecting crime and arresting and prosecuting criminals. It is most closely associated in point of time with the *Covent-Garden Journal*, the first number of which had appeared on 4 January 1752, just about two weeks after the publication of *Amelia* (18 December 1751) and a little more than three months before *Examples of Providence* (14 April). The reforming impulse of this, Fielding's fourth newspaper, was made apparent almost immediately. On 18 January the following notice, which was to appear regularly thereafter, first appeared: 'To the Public. All Persons who shall for the Future, suffer by Robbers, Burglars, &c. are desired immediately to bring, or send, the best Description they can of such Robbers, &c. with the Time, and Place, and Circumstances of the Fact, to

Houses of Industry (London, 1775), pp. 31–2; and Sir Frederick Morton Eden, *The State of the Poor* (London, 1797), i. 320–9.

[7] *The Works of Henry Fielding, Esq.* (London, 1762), i. 39.

[1] Sermon CXXXVIII, *Works* (1757), viii. 145.

Henry Fielding, Esq.; at his House in Bow-Street.'[2] The detailed account of crimes, arrests, and interrogations printed under the heading 'Covent Garden' which reported on Fielding's own activities as magistrate, was another regular feature of the paper. Many of the 'leaders' touch directly or indirectly on issues related to the law, crime, or social reform, and these topics often find their way into 'news items' or announcements 'To the Public' as well. In the context of such intense, even zealous reforming activity, the publication of a pamphlet intended to put the fear of God in the hearts of the poor concerning the 'most dreadful crime of Murder' need seem surprising only to those readers distressed or embarrassed by the primitive form Fielding employed for the sake of his audience.

The specific situation which prompted *Examples of Providence*, however, is the one Fielding refers to in his Dedication to the Bishop of Worcester when he reminds his Lordship of their conversation about 'the many flagrant instances of Murder that have lately alarmed the public'. Early in the pamphlet he remarks that if 'cruel and bloody actions' formerly appeared to Englishmen as 'prodigies', now murder 'is very lately begun . . . to be common among us'. As often with Fielding, what a casual reader takes to be the excess of rhetoric proves to be grounded in fact: there was an unusual and striking number of murders committed during the eight months preceding the publication of *Examples of Providence*. I make this statement on the evidence, statistically unsound but none the less persuasive, in *Select Trials . . . at the Sessions-House in the Old-Bailey* (four vols., London, 1764). This collection (Fielding owned an earlier edition: Baker, no. 552) prints the trials (abbreviated) of notable criminals with information about their crimes and lives gleaned from various sources. Its range of interest is reasonably complete: 'Murder, Robbery, Burglary, Rapes, Sodomy, Coining, Forging, Piracy and other Offences and Misdemeanours'.

Of eighteen cases reported from the sessions[3] of April 1750 through the July sessions of 1751, none is a murder case, a striking fact considering the impulse natural to such a collection to include cases as stimulating as possible. In choosing trials from the three sessions which follow this period and precede Fielding's pamphlet, however, the editor of *Select Trials* includes seven cases of murder (two of the four cases reported from the sessions of September 1751; three of the seven from February 1752; both of the cases selected from the January 1752 sessions were murder cases). Thus of the thirteen trials reported for this period, seven were for the crime of

---

[2] The Jensen edition of the *Covent-Garden Journal* includes only the leading essays for each issue. For 'announcements', accounts of crimes, etc., I quote from the original folio issues in the Burney Collection of newspapers in the British Library (cited as *Covent-Garden Journal*).

[3] Eight sessions were held at the Old Bailey during the course of each mayoral year (which began in Nov. when the new mayor took office). Each sessions covered four or five days of trials.

murder. When one adds the notorious murder committed by Mary Blandy (tried at Oxford, 29 February 1752; executed 6 April 1752), a case which particularly caught Fielding's attention; and the equally notable murder by Elizabeth Jefferys (tried at Chelmsford, March 1752; executed 28 March 1752),[4] one realizes that Fielding was reacting to a genuine upsurge in murders in *Examples of Providence*, and that his observations in his Dedication have their basis in sober truth.

The figures gathered from *Select Trials* are supported by the information contained in a broadsheet headed 'Guildhall 1st of June 1772. Steph. Theod. Janssen',[5] which prints 'three Tables *From 1749 to 1771 both Inclusive*'. The tables list (1) the number of persons sentenced to die each mayoral sessions and for what crimes; (2) the number of persons executed and for what crimes; and (3) the number of persons pardoned, transported, or 'died in Newgate', and for what crimes. For the period from September 1751 to February 1752 the broadsheet, like *Select Trials*, records seven murder trials at the Old Bailey and indicates that six of the seven murderers were executed and that one died in Newgate. The broadsheet also confirms Fielding's sense that the number of murders committed in 1751–2 was extraordinary. According to its figures, in a period of nearly three years preceding late 1751 only three persons had been convicted at the Old Bailey for the crime of murder, and one of them had been pardoned, his crime occurring in a duel, a matter of honor. For the whole period covered by Janssen's tables, the average number of murders per mayoral year is 3.4 (as many as four hundred felony trials might be heard at the Old Bailey over the course of the eight sessions held during a mayoral year). Murder was a surprisingly rare crime in mid-eighteenth-century London.[6]

The close connection between *Examples of Providence* and immediate public events is further emphasized when we regard it in the context of the Parliamentary activity, particularly with the passage of the Murder Act of 1752, nearly concurrent with its publication. The king's opening address to Parliament in November 1751 had renewed his earlier appeal for legislation to control crime and extravagance among the lower orders:

I cannot conclude without recommending to you, in the most earnest Manner, to consider seriously of some effectual provisions to suppress those audacious Crimes of Robbery and Violence, which are now become so frequent, especially about this great

---

[4] See *Examples of Providence*, below pp. 213 and 214. Both trials are printed in *State Trials* (xviii. 1118–94; and 1193–202).

[5] I am grateful to John H. Langbein for allowing me to use his copy of this broadsheet. It is reprinted as an appendix in John Howard, *An Account of the Principal Lazarettos in Europe*, 2nd edn. (London, 1791).

[6] This point has often been made. See, for instance, Radzinowicz, i. 30; Langbein, 'Shaping the Eighteenth-Century Criminal Trial: A View from the Ryder Sources', *University of Chicago Law Review*, 50 (1983), 44–5.

Capital, and which have proceeded in a great measure from that profligate Spirit of Irreligion, Idleness, Gaming, and Extravagance, which has of late extended itself, in an uncommon Degree, to the Dishonour of the Nation, and to the great Offence and Prejudice of the sober and industrious part of my People.[7]

Two pieces of legislation passed during this sessions seem to be a response to the king's address: 'An act for the better preventing thefts and robberies, and for regulating places of publick entertainment, and punishing persons keeping disorderly houses (25 Geo. II, c. 36); and 'An act for better preventing the horrid crime of murder' (25 Geo. II, c. 37). Although Cross does not see Fielding's hand in the Murder Act, he does assert that 'the lawyer who framed this statute had by him Fielding's "Examples of the Interposition of Providence," the first paragraph of which he condensed into his preamble' (ii. 280). The parliamentary sessions in which the Murder Act was passed, however, was prorogued 26 March 1752, more than two weeks before *Examples of Providence* was published and probably before it was written. Nor does the colorless and predictable language of the preamble support Cross's assertion.[8] The most striking provision in the Act, that the bodies of murderers, in Middlesex at least, be handed over to surgeons for dissection, is not mentioned by Fielding in his review of the terrors awaiting murderers, a curious omission had Fielding in fact worked with the framers of this legislation. Moreover, this provision, which was a harsh and, certainly in the eyes of the 'mob', a cruel one[9] (and which reflects the frequent impulse of eighteenth-century parliaments to pass repressive criminal legislation in response to current events), forms no part of the execution ritual proposed by Fielding in the *Enquiry*. As we have seen in considering the *Enquiry* and the *Proposal*, Fielding's relationship to legislation was puzzling—was he the 'man behind the scenes', or did he simply respond to contemporary interest? Some of the same puzzlement arises with regard to the Murder Act of 1752, but in this instance the evidence indicates that Fielding and Parliament were on a parallel course and that both were responding to the unusual number of recent murders.[1]

Fielding conducted a vigorous publicity campaign for his pamphlet in the

---

[7] *JHC* xxvi. 298.

[8] *Whereas the horrid crime of murder has of late been more frequently perpetrated than formerly, and particularly in and near the metropolis of this kingdom, contrary to the known humanity and natural genius of the* British *nation: and whereas it is thereby become necessary, that some further terror and peculiar mark of infamy be added to the punishment of death, now by law inflicted on such as shall be guilty of the said heinous offence: . . .'*

[9] For a fuller discussion of Fielding's relationship to legislation and further argument against his influence on the Murder Act, see Hugh Amory, 'A Preliminary Census of Henry Fielding's Legal Manuscripts', *PBSA* 62 (1968).

[1] For an account of the popular protests against dissection see Peter Linebaugh, 'The Tyburn Riot Against the Surgeons', pp. 65–117. The Murder Act formalized what had been a long-standing practice.

pages of the *Covent-Garden Journal*. The first notice of *Examples of Providence* appears in *Covent-Garden Journal* no. 27 (Saturday, 4 April 1752), where it is advertised for 'next week' with 'an Introduction and Conclusion, Both by Henry Fielding, Esq.' The advertisement affirms the timeliness of the topic and establishes the point frequently to be repeated that its proper readers are the 'inferior Kind of People': 'This Book (the Publication of which is occasioned by the many horrid Murders committed within this last Year) is calculated to raise just Sentiments of Horror at this most heinous Sin. It is very proper to be given to all the inferior Kind of People, and particularly to the Youth of both Sexes.' On the following Tuesday, *Examples of Providence* is announced for Monday, 13 April. This advertisement is repeated on Saturday. In the section entitled 'Covent-Garden April 13th' of the thirtieth number of the *Covent-Garden Journal*, the following notice appears:

This Day Mr. Fielding began to distribute Gratis, his little Book, just published, which contains a great Number of Instances of the Interposition of Providence, in the Detection and Punishment of Murder. An Example, which, it is hoped, will be followed by all who wish well to their Country, or who have indeed any Sentiment of Humanity.—No Family ought to be without this Book, and it is most particularly calculated for the Use of those Schools, in which Children are taught to read: For there is nothing of which children are more greedy, than Stories of the Tragical Kind; nor can their tender minds receive more wholesome Food, than that which unites the Idea of Horror with the worst of Crimes, at an Age when all their Impressions become in great Measure, a Part of their Nature; For *those Ideas which they then join together*, as Mr. Locke judiciously observes, *they are never after capable of separating.*[2]

In most of the issues of the *Covent-Garden Journal* after the thirtieth number, Fielding continued to remind the public of the book's social utility. Prominently placed half-column descriptions of *Examples of Providence* appeared on the second page of twenty-six of the final forty-two numbers. In *Covent-Garden Journal*, no. 36 it is reported that 'Last Week a certain Colonel of the Army bought a large Number of the Book called *Examples . . . Murder*, in order to distribute them amongst the private Soldiers of his Regiment. An Example well worthy of Imitation!' Fielding also cites

[2] A similar advertisement had appeared a few days earlier in the *General Advertiser* (Apr. 9): 'Monday next will be published . . . *God's Providence* . . . This Book (the Publication of which is occasioned by the many horrid Murders committed within this last Year) is calculated to raise just Sentiments of Horror at this most heinous Sin. It is very proper to be given to all the inferior Kind of People, and particularly the Youth of *Both* Sexes, whose natural Love of Stories will lead them to read with Attention what cannot fail of infusing into their tender Minds an early Dread and Abhorrence of staining their Hands with the Blood of their Fellow Creatures.' Cf. *Amelia*, IV. iii. 191: 'By which means [daily lessons in religion and morality] she had, in their tender minds, so strongly annexed the ideas of fear and shame to every idea of evil of which they were susceptible, that it must require great pains and length of habit to separate them'.

courtroom incidents confirming the powers of his 'little Book'. For instance, in *Covent-Garden Journal*, no. 31 appears an account of a man brought before Fielding charged with threatening his wife with a knife. He is rebuked by Fielding who none the less reconciles the couple and sends them off with 'the little Book against Murder, which the Man promised to read over before he slept'.

A second courtroom incident which Fielding relates is worth elaborating here for its dramatic illustration of the pathetic and bewildering social reality that led Fielding to the desperate act of compiling *Examples of Providence*. On 25 May a Thomas Wilford, who had confessed to cutting his wife's throat in a jealous rage, appeared before Fielding. He was repentant and begged Fielding to 'give him the little Book on the heinous Sin of Murder, lately published, which when he received, he shed a Shower of Tears, and wished he had read it before'.[3] The account of this murder in *Select Trials* (ii. 194–8) supplemented by Fielding's long report in the *Covent-Garden Journal* affords us ample detail about this sad story. Wilford, 'a quiet, inoffensive, honest lad', was the son of poor parents. Born with only one hand, he had been judged unfit for any trade. His parents sent him to the workhouse at Fulham (where Fielding proposed to erect his county workhouse) when he was six and he had worked there as errand boy and water carrier for eleven years. Sarah Williams came to this workhouse when she could no longer support herself as a prostitute, having contracted a venereal disease. She was twenty-two. They had been neighbors as children and in the workhouse had 'conceived a strong Fancy for each other' and resolved to marry. To this end they left the workhouse to return to London and seek their fortune. Wilford had saved twelve shillings during his eleven years in the workhouse, and the overseers, 'to encourage this young Couple', increased their capital with a gift of forty shillings to set them up as street vendors. They arrived in London on Wednesday, took lodgings, were married in the Fleet, and lived happily together for four days. On Sunday evening Sarah stayed out past midnight. A quarrel followed, then the murder. Wilford immediately confessed, crying 'I have murdered my poor Wife, whom I loved as dearly as my Life.' Early Monday morning he was brought before Fielding who committed him to Newgate where 'he spent his Time in reading such good Books as were put into his Hands' (*Select Trials*, ii. 198). Thomas Wilford was the first to suffer under the new Murder Act. After he was hanged, his body was carried to Surgeon's Hall where it was dissected and 'anatomized'.

What could Fielding (or what can we) make of such a story? Perhaps very little, but at least he didn't turn away from it as a correspondent to the *Covent-Garden Journal* turns away from 'all tragical and scandalous Stories'.

---

[3] *Covent-Garden Journal*, no. 42 (26 May 1752).

This writer—actually Fielding writing as a naïve optimist—rejoices that he 'was born in a Country where I can reflect with constant Pleasure on the Freedom, the Wealth, and indeed every political Happiness of the People', and wonders how 'our neighbouring Justice' (Fielding) bears 'the Sight of all those Wretches who are brought before him; but perhaps he hath sometimes Opportunities of doing Good, which makes him Amends'.[4] *Examples of Providence* seemed to Fielding a way of doing good and perhaps should be called naïve only by those who could have done better.[5]

Examples of Providence may also be placed in an ancient literary tradition stretching back to medieval exampla and beyond. Fielding's Example XXIV is a variant of the digression in the *Nun's Priest's Tale* demonstrating that 'mordre wol out', and finds analogues in Cicero and Valerius Maximus. The collection generally attests to the continuing vitality of that lore which lies behind Hamlet's 'For murder, though it have no tongue, will speak / With most miraculous organ' and Macbeth's 'they say, blood will have blood: / Stones have been known to move and trees to speak; / Augers and understood relations have / By magot-pies and choughs and rooks brought forth / The secret'st man of blood.' More particularly, its antecedents, as Fielding's notes indicate, are those seventeenth-century collections of providential stories and marvellous events that testify to the operation of God's special providence. John Reynolds,[6] for instance, in his Preface to the Reader, notes the 'iniquity of these last and worst daies of the World, in which the crying and scarlet-sin of Murther makes so ample, and so bloody a progression' and says that he has collected his 'bloody and mournful Tragedies' to remind the potential sinner of 'God's miraculous detection and severe punishment . . . in revenging blood for blood, and death for death'. With the exception of Wanley's *The Wonders of the Little World* (1678), which found its inspiration in a more scientific text, Bacon's *Advancement of Learning*, the works Fielding most often cites were similarly intended to illustrate this special providence.[7]

---

[4] *CGJ* i. 233 ff.

[5] Fielding encouraged the dissemination of his pamphlet by offering it at a bargain price: 'Ten Shillings a Dozen to those who give them away'. In his *Hogarth: His Life, Art, and Times* (New Haven and London, 1971), Ronald Paulson draws interesting parallels between Fielding's reforming pamphlets and Hogarth's 'popular prints' (e.g., *Industry and Idleness*, *Beer Street* and *Gin Lane*, and The *Four Stages of Cruelty*), and he notes that Hogarth offered some of these prints at bargain prices for similar reasons (see especially ii. 96 ff.).

[6] Brief biographical and bibliographical information for Fielding's sources is provided in the annotations to *Examples of Providence*.

[7] J. Paul Hunter provides a useful account of these largely ignored books in his *The Reluctant Pilgrim* (Baltimore, 1966), pp. 51–73. See also Perry Miller, *The New England Mind: The Seventeenth Century* (New York, 1939), pp. 228–31; Aubrey Williams, 'Interposition of Providence and the Design of Fielding's Novels', *South Atlantic Quarterly*, 70 (1971), 268–70; and James A. Levernier, Introduction to Increase Mather's *An Essay for the Recording of*

Fielding took eight of his thirty-three Examples from Reynolds's extraordinarily popular book, *The Triumphs of Gods Revenge Against . . . Murther*. Though he drastically abridges these stories (to about one-fifteenth their original length) they still make up nearly half the bulk of his examples. It is the only one of the strictly providential texts (Thomas Beard's *Theatre of God's Ivdgements* [1597] and William Turner's *A Compleat History of . . . Remarkable Providences* [1697] are the others) listed in the sale catalogue of Fielding's library, though the absence of Beard's and Turner's books does not preclude Fielding's ownership. *God's Revenge* is twice alluded to in *Jonathan Wild*,[8] and it may be the book lying beside the murdered girl in Hogarth's 'Cruelty in Perfection' from *The Four Stages of Cruelty* (1751).[9] According to J. Paul Hunter, earlier books in 'the "Providence" tradition', such as Beards's and Reynolds's, emphasized providential punishments; later ones (after *c.*1680), deliverances.[1] But this distinction is not reflected in Fielding's collection, which in its concentration on murder has set itself a narrow range.

There appears to be little design to his selection of stories. Five of them he had from 'gentlemen' or 'clergymen'; three were celebrated contemporary, or near contemporary, cases. Ten of the remainder were taken from Beard, Turner, or Wanley, and the two from Plutarch could easily have come from one of these writers as well. The story from Knolles (*General History of the Turks*, 1603) appears in Turner and Wanley. Thus these four central texts (Beard, Reynolds, Wanley, and Turner) account for all but four of the stories with printed sources: of the remaining four, two are from Defoe's *The Secrets of the Invisible World* (1729), which Fielding owned; one from Richard Baxter's *The Certainty of the Worlds of Spirits* (1691); and one is given no source by Fielding. My impression is that Fielding began with Reynolds and varied his stories with the far shorter ones in Beard, Wanley, and Turner (Wanley and Turner largely repeat Beard). Most of the rest easily came from memory. Whether or not the number of Fielding's stories, thirty-three, indicates a larger design, the reader may determine.

'Special providence' was a technical term which stood in distinction to 'general' or 'common providence', the latter terms denominating God's 'continued' creation of the world through the ordinary operation of secondary causes. Generally speaking, special providences also occurred

Illustrious Providences (1684; facsimile repr. Delman, New York: Scholars' Facsimiles and Reprints, 1977).

[8] III. iii. 104; and III. x. 127. In the latter passage the narrator calls it an 'excellent book'.

[9] There was, however, a later work with a similar title: John Tonge, *God's Revenge against Murther* (1680). Of the Hogarth print, Paulson aptly remarks, 'The third *Stage of Cruelty*, with the girl's wounds like "poor dumb mouthes" crying for justice, looks like an illustration for Fielding's . . . *God's Providence*; and this is exactly the sort of primitive strength Hogarth was trying to draw upon' (*Hogarth*, i. 109–10).

[1] *The Reluctant Pilgrim*, p. 66 n.

through possible means, but the sequence of events producing them was so extraordinary and arresting that the wise man perceived the 'interposing' hand of God. Barrow clearly indicates the nature of a special providence:

If that one thing should hit advantageously to the production of some considerable event, it may with some plausibility be attributed to fortune, or common providence: yet that divers things, having no dependence or coherence one with the other, in divers places, through several times, should all join their forces to compass it, cannot well otherwise than be ascribed to God's special care wisely directing, to his own hand powerfully wielding, those concurrent instruments to one good purpose. For it is beside the nature, it is beyond the reach of fortune, to range various causes in such order.[2]

Tillotson, in a sermon often quoted on this topic, says that if God usually works through general providence, he 'hath reserved to himself a power and liberty to interpose, and to cross as he pleases, the usual course of things; to awaken men to the consideration of him, and a continual dependance upon him; and to teach us to ascribe those things to his wise disposal, which, if we never saw any change, we should be apt to impute to blind necessity'.[3] Such clerical comments as these define the doctrinal context which informs Fielding's collection of 'particular instances in which God hath been pleased to demonstate his great abhorrence of this sin of Murder, by a supernatural and miraculous interposition of Providence, in the punishment, as well as detection, of this most abominable sin'.[4]

The books in this tradition from which Fielding draws his examples were intended for a 'popular' audience, one affected by the emotional appeal of a narrative and indifferent to theoretical formulations of the idea of God's providence. They were also largely of Puritan or Nonconformist origin. That Fielding was willing to employ the materials of this tradition with its sensational appeal and naïve intellectual content has been a minor embarrassment for some readers. Both Cross and Dudden hesitate to ascribe to Fielding the simplicity necessary to believe in his stories. Cross remarks 'Fielding, I fear, was rather credulous when it came to a supernatural story', and he clearly hopes that it was Sarah Fielding or William Young who compiled the narratives.[5] Dudden stiffly and circuitously observes 'It must be owned that, in recording instances of alleged

---

[2] Isaac Barrow, *Works* (New York, 1845), i. 118. Cited by Ralph W. Rader, 'Idea and Structure in Fielding's Novels', unpublished doctoral dissertation (Indiana University, 1958), p. 70.

[3] Sermon xxxvi, *Works* (1757), iii. 40. Cited by Martin Battestin, *The Providence of Wit* (Oxford, 1974), p. 153.

[4] *Examples of Providence*, p. 182. Usually a distinction was made between special providences, which fell within the range of possibility, and miracles. With one or two exceptions, Fielding's 'Examples' are not miraculous.

[5] ii. 269–70. There is no reason to doubt Fielding's authorship.

supernatural happenings, Fielding exhibits a degree of credulity which is rather surprising in a lawyer well practised in sifting evidence. No doubt his antecedent belief in a peculiarly "immediate interposition of the Divine Providence" for the detection and punishment of monstrous crimes inclined him to accept these strange stories rather easily'.[6] There really is no doubt, however, about Fielding's belief in special providences. The books he used may have appeared quaint to him and to many of his contemporaries—as Pope's jocular essay, *God's Revenge Against Punning, Shewing, the miserable Fates of Persons addicted to this Crying Sin, in Court and Town* (1716), suggests—but that does not call belief into question, as the *Essay on Man* abundantly shows.[7] *Examples of Providence* had a socially useful end, but it was natural for Fielding to seek its accomplishment partly by religious persuasion. In his gloss in the *Proposal* on his requirement of morning prayer and religious instruction in his projected workhouse, Fielding remarked 'Heaven and Hell when well rung in the Ears of those who have not yet learn't that there are no such Places, and who will give some Attention to what they hear, are by no Means Words of little or no Signification' (p. 271). This is compatible with the more abstract formulation in *Amelia* of Booth's doctrine of the passions as corrected by Dr Harrison: ' "if men act, as I believe they do, from their passions, it would be fair to conclude that religion to be true which applies immediately to the strongest of these passions, hope and fear; choosing rather to rely on its rewards and punishments than on that native beauty of virtue which some of the ancient philosophers thought proper to recommend to their disciples." '[8] In each case the underlying belief is that the appeal to hope and fear is both practical and Godly: he has so created us that these are our strongest passions, and his strongest appeal is naturally to them.

There are numerous instances in Fielding's writings that attest to his belief in a special providence. When Allworthy discovers Black George at Mr Nightingale's and by that means learns of his theft of Tom's bank bills, the incident is introduced with the observation 'Here an Accident happened of a very extraordinary Kind; one indeed of those strange Chances, whence very good and grave Men have concluded that Providence often interposes in the Discovery of the most secret Villany, in order to caution Men from quitting the Paths of Honesty, however warily they tread in those of Vice' (XVIII, iii. 920). The denouements of both *Tom Jones* and *Amelia* are attended

---

[6] ii. 958.

[7] One may also cite Boswell's comment on the 'extraordinary relief' from ill-health Johnson once enjoyed after prayer: 'I have no difficulty to avow that cast of thinking, which by many pretenders to wisdom, is called *superstitious*. But here I think even men of dry rationality may believe, that there was an intermediate [immediate?] interposition of divine Providence, and that "the fervent prayer of this righteous man" availed' (*Life*, iv. 272).

[8] *Amelia*, XII. v. 313.

by exclamations over God's 'Wonderful' providences. Providential readings of Fielding have now been long familiar,[9] and the skepticism which remains, and one suspects it is substantial, has been relatively silent.[1]

For the reader to whom *Examples of Providence* appears primarily as a religious document, it may seem to be one link in the chain of argument which characterizes the 'frame and architecture' of *Tom Jones* as 'the emblem of Design in the macrocosm' and which suggests that the 'narrative itself is the demonstration of Providence, the cause and agent of that Design.'[2] For those to whom it seems primarily a social document, it may be read as a timely and comprehensible footnote to the *Enquiry* and the *Proposal* and taken as another instance of Fielding's readiness to contribute quickly to topics claiming the attention of his superiors. The mixture of secular and religious impulses in Fielding's 'little Book' is much like that in *The Lives of the Most Remarkable Criminals*, whose compiler included early histories for two reasons, 'the first is, that the Wonders of Providence signified [*sic*] in these Transactions, might hereby be recorded, and preserved to Posterity; and the other, that the Wicked might from the Perusal be deterred from pursuing their vicious Courses, from the Prospect of those sudden, dreadful, and unexpected Strokes, which the best hid Criminal practices have met with, from the unsearchable Conduct of *divine justice*'.[3]

The printing of *Examples of Providence* is recorded in Strahan's 'Ledgers', f. 81: 'April [1752] Fielding on Murder 4 1/2 Sheets No. 2000 @ £1:12——— 7:4:–.' A further charge of £1:4 for 'Corrections and Alterations' is also recorded. This was a considerable number of copies.[4] Of the pamphlets in this volume printed by Strahan, only the *Proposal* had as large an initial printing. Together the two impressions of *Bosavern Penlez* only equal this first impression of *Examples of Providence*. And a second printing of

---

[9] Notably in the writings of Battestin, Rader, and Williams cited above. To these should be added Battestin's earlier book, *The Moral Basis of Fielding's Art*; Henry Knight Miller's 'Some Functions of Rhetoric in *Tom Jones*', *PQ* 45 (1966), 209–35; and Ralph W. Rader's 'The Form of *Tom Jones* and the Concept of Form in the Novel' (paper read at Indiana University, 1981). Further general discussions of the idea of providence may be found in Battestin's *The Providence of Wit*; Williams's *An Approach to Congreve* (New Haven and London, 1979); and Jacob Viner, *The Role of Providence in the Social Order* (Philadelphia, Pa, 1972).

[1] Dissent tends to be abrupt and commonsensical: the 'Christianizing of Fielding stresses an aspect of his work that is neither the most characteristic nor (I am sure readers of Fielding will agree) the most interesting one' (Fielding: *A Collection of Critical Essays*, ed. Ronald Paulson [Englewood Cliffs, NJ, 1962], p. 1). John Traugott's 'The Professor as Nibelung', *ECS* 3 (1970), 532–43, is a spirited rejoinder to history of ideas studies generally. Melvin New's ' "The Grease of God": The Form of Eighteenth-Century English Fiction', *PMLA* 91 (1976), 235–44, argues against the centrality of the idea of providence in the fiction of Fielding and others. Arthur Sherbo, 'The "Moral Basis" of *Joseph Andrews*', in *Studies in the Eighteenth Century English Novel* (East Lansing, 1969), p. 104–19, also strongly dissents.

[2] Battestin, *The Providence of Wit*, p. 151.   [3] (London, 1735), iii. 392–3.

[4] Patricia Hernlund's study shows that of 514 typical entries in Strahan's 'Ledgers', only 43 had runs of 2,000 or more copies ('William Strahan's Ledgers: Standard Charges for Printing, 1738–85', *Studies in Bibliography*, 20 [1967], 104).

a further thousand copies is recorded also for April: 'Printing off 1000 Copies more of Fielding on Murders—— 1:7–'. Fielding had apparently been successful in effecting a wide distribution of his pamphlet.

7. ELIZABETH CANNING

On 1 January 1753, Elizabeth Canning, a servant girl of Aldermanbury Postern, London Wall, failed to return to her master's house after spending the holiday evening with her aunt and uncle. She remained missing for twenty-eight days, until about ten o'clock on the night of 29 January, when she suddenly appeared at her mother's door, emaciated, in a 'very bad condition', wearing only a 'ragged bed-gown and a cap'. Elizabeth's story, as it took shape in the weeks that followed her return to her family, was dramatic. She claimed that two 'lusty' men had assaulted her on New Year's Day as she passed through Moorfield's by Bedlam Wall, had tied her hands and struck her, upon which she had fallen into one of the 'fits' to which she was subject. While she was unconscious the men had dragged her eight or nine miles north of London to a house of ill repute in Enfield Wash. The owner of the house was Susannah Wells, but it was another woman, the fearsome gypsy Mary Squires, who greeted Elizabeth on her arrival at Enfield Wash, cut off her stays, and locked her in an attic room or loft when she refused to become a prostitute. Elizabeth remained in that room for four weeks, subsisting on a pitcher of water and a quartern loaf of bread. Late in the afternoon of 29 January she escaped through a window and made her way back to her mother's house.

Her outraged friends were eager to prosecute Elizabeth's alleged assailants, and on the first of February Squires and Wells were arrested. On the 6 February Canning's solicitor, a lawyer named Salt, came to Bow Street for advice on how to proceed in the case. Fielding issued a warrant summoning the remaining inhabitants of Wells's house, and the following day Virtue Hall and Judith Natus, both lodgers, appeared before him. According to Elizabeth Canning, Virtue Hall had been present when Squires assaulted her. At first Hall denied the charge. But under Fielding's persistent examination, she changed her testimony to corroborate Elizabeth's. It was her evidence which ensured the conviction of Wells and Squires at their trial[1] (21 and 26 February, 1753), despite convincing testimony that Squires had been in Dorset on the day in question.

Doubts about Elizabeth's improbable story grew, however, and when Virtue Hall recanted her confession before Sir Crisp Gascoyne, Lord Mayor

---

[1] Squires was convicted of a felony, stealing Elizabeth's stays, value 10s., and was sentenced to death. Wells was convicted of abetting a felon and sent to Newgate. As part of her punishment, she was branded on her thumb immediately after conviction.

of London and presiding magistrate at the trial of Wells and Squires, public controversy between the 'Canningites', as Elizabeth's supporters came to be called, and the 'Egyptians' became intense. This rapidly growing controversy, which culminated but did not end in Elizabeth Canning's conviction of perjury early in May 1754, was the immediate provocation of Fielding's *A True State of the Case of Elizabeth Canning*, one of the earliest pamphlets published concerning this *cause célèbre*.

When in 1762 Churchill dismissed the furor over Elizabeth Canning in a couplet, 'And Betty Canning is at least, / With Gascoyne's help a six month's feast' (*The Ghost*, i. 403–4) he underrated both the inherent appeal of her story and its contemporary notoriety. Her case was considered and argued in newspapers and pamphlets continually from February 1753 until late in 1754.[2] Echoes of the controversy persisted during the remainder of the eighteenth century and in the nineteenth century. There have been three books on Elizabeth Canning in the twentieth century, one a work of substantial scholarship.[3] Josephine Tey based her mystery novel, *The Franchise Affair* (which became a film), on the story of Elizabeth Canning.[4] In writing about Canning one is in fact faced with a nearly overwhelming abundance of information. Her contemporaries pursued every detail connected with her story with a remarkable avidity and recorded their information with an equally remarkable scrupulosity. We know more than we want to know about the cleanliness of Elizabeth's shift on her return home, the workings of her bowels, the number of bread crusts that sustained her while she was purportedly held prisoner for twenty-seven days in the house of ill fame at Enfield Wash.[5] Partly it was this very abundance of evidence, much of it conflicting, that aroused so much controversy.[6] Here was God's

---

[2] At her trial, prosecuting counsel remarked, 'There have been accounts published, which have gone all over the kingdom; and, I believe, I may with truth say, all over Europe. I do not believe there is an individual in this great city that has not heard of this affair, nor hath a company met for one single evening, where this was not a subject-matter of conversation' (*State Trials*, xix. 463).

[3] Arthur Machan, *The Canning Wonder* (New York, 1926); Barrett R. Wellington, *The Mystery of Elizabeth Canning* (New York, 1940); and Lillian de la Torre [Lillian Bueno McCue], *Elizabeth is Missing* (New York, 1945). De la Torre presents the story of Elizabeth Canning as a mystery story, but her work is based on wide reading of contemporary documents and has been useful to this study.

[4] I am grateful to Ruth Watt for telling me of Tey's book.

[5] The prosecution's minute questioning of Elizabeth's uncle about her dinner the day of her disappearance provided Samuel Foote with useful material as late as 1762. London audiences found the line 'Pray, now let me ask you, was—the—toast buttered on both sides?' deliciously funny (see *State Trials*, xix. 475 n. 1; and Simon Trefman, *Sam. Foote, Comedian, 1727–1777* [New York, 1971], p. 126).

[6] Writing in 1897, Courtney Kenny remarked 'in this second trial [Canning's trial for perjury], there arose a still greater and more memorable difficulty, caused by the collision of the two greatest masses of direct testimony that ever were arrayed in positive contradiction to each other in any English Court except in the Tichborne case' (*Law Quarterly Review*, 13 [1897], 368–9). The recent adoption of the Gregorian calendar by Parliament, which required that the day after 2 September 1752 be designated 14 September 1752, left many witnesses uncertain as to the chronology of their testimony and tremendously complicated the unravelling of their contradictory statements.

plenty to exercise one's wit on, and it gave fresh point to the biblical phrase, 'cloud of witnesses'. In 1754 Canning was tried on the narrow charge of willful and corrupt perjury. The account of her trial runs to over four hundred pages.[7]

Although the lawyers were content to argue the question of whether Elizabeth Canning had actually been held captive for a month in Wells's house, ordinary mortals wanted to know more. Where, if her story was untrue, had she been during that time, and why had she lied? The answers to those questions have never emerged. Lillian de la Torre advances a complicated and finally unconvincing explanation based on the hypothesis that Elizabeth Canning suffered from 'hysterical amnesia', a hypothesis which allows her to confirm what appears likely in Elizabeth's story and to explain away what is impossible. Her theory grows out of the conviction that Elizabeth could not simply have been a liar, a conviction shared by Barrett R. Wellington, whose desperate solution posits a twin sister for Mary Squires to discount the testimony that placed her far from Enfield Wash on 1 January. Both writers want to believe in Elizabeth's veracity. So did Fielding. He has often been charged with naïvety for accepting Elizabeth's story, but it should be remembered in his defence that even disbelievers acknowledged her to be a most compelling witness. Though Josephine Tey radically changes the historical circumstances of the narrative, she retains the outward appeal of her Canning figure (Elizabeth Kane), who is 'a prosecuting counsel's dream of a victim'. The reader who wishes to recapture the richness of the case of Elizabeth Canning and to understand the appeal Elizabeth made to Fielding and others must return to the original documents.[8] For the student of Fielding, Cross and Dudden adequately recount the broad outline of events and sketch Fielding's role in them. What follows here is a more detailed account of the particulars of his involvement in the case and contemporary response to it.

Elizabeth Canning was a hard-working, dependable girl, and when she failed to return from her visit to her aunt and uncle her mother was sufficiently alarmed to put a notice in the *Daily Advertiser* offering a 'handsome reward' for information concerning her whereabouts. The first advertisement appeared on 4 January 1753. At least two more followed (6 and 20 January 1753). The third advertisement contains the fullest description of Elizabeth

---

[7] *State Trials*, xix. 283–692. This printed account of the trial is the most informative single document in the case of Elizabeth Canning.

[8] For a useful bibliography, see Lillian Bueno McCue, 'Elizabeth Canning in Print', *University of Colorado Studies*, series B (Boulder, Colorado, 1945), 2 (no. 4), 223–32. Documents are preserved at the Public Record Office, State Papers Domestic, Geo. II, 1747–59, Bundle 127, No. 25. Prints are described by Stephens and Hawkins in *Catalogue of Prints and Drawings in the British Museum: Political and Personal Satires*, III, pt. II.

Canning: 'a young woman upwards of eighteen years of age, pitted with the small pox, a high forehead, fresh coloured, light eyes and eye brows, dark hair, about five feet high [wearing] a masquerade purple stuff gown, a black quilted petticoat, a green under coat, blue stockings with red clocks, black leather shoes and clogs, a white shaving hat edged with green ribbon, and a white handkerchief and apron'. But by the time Elizabeth returned to her house late in the evening of 29 January (earlier that day Fielding's *Proposal for the Poor* had been published) her condition, according to every witness, was 'deplorable' and 'wretched', though as with nearly every 'fact' in her story, there were variations in the details of their descriptions.

Her unexpected and dramatic return attracted a succession of concerned and curious neighbors to whom she related, again with variations in detail, her unlikely misadventure. Fielding's account accurately if generally reflects the story her supporters accepted. He would not have been aware that one of these neighbors, a hartshorn rasper named Robert Scarrat, who had been a patron of Mother Wells's 'hedge bawdy-house', was probably largely responsible for fixing on Wells's house as the scene of Elizabeth's trial or that he had suggested details of the house that enabled her to make a convincing show of identifying it.[9] At any rate, Elizabeth's supporters quickly determined that Wells was her captor, for she was so proclaimed in the *London Daily Advertiser* on 31 January 1753, the day before her arrest. This announcement did not mention Mary Squires, the seventy-year-old gypsy woman of grotesque appearance whom Elizabeth accused the next day of cutting off her stays and attempting to terrify her into 'going their way', that is, becoming a prostitute.

Canning's friends had obtained a warrant from a London Alderman, Thomas Chitty, for 'the Body of a Person *that goes by the Name of Mother Wells, and lives at Enfield-Wash*' (dated 31 January 1753) and the next day had carried Elizabeth and her mother to Enfield Wash where she had identified not Wells but Squires as her assaulter. She also identified the loft or workroom in Wells's house as her prison though it was quite unlike the room she had earlier described. This room was reached by stairs leading from the kitchen, where Elizabeth and her friends had gathered, but she could not find it at first and had to be directed to it (a sketch of Wells's house is reproduced in the *Gentleman's Magazine* [July 1753], p. 307). Elizabeth could not make positive identification of any of the other inhabitants of the house (Wells's son-in-law, Richard Long; her daughter, Sal Howit; the gypsy's son, George, and her two daughters; Virtue Hall, and Judith Natus. Fortune Natus, Judith's husband, was at work.) Wells and Squires were taken to Justice Merry Tyshmaker, Elizabeth swore to them again, and they were sent

---

[9] *State Trials*, xix. 498 ff.

to prison. Three men among Elizabeth's retinue were disturbed enough by the variations in her story to drop quietly away as her supporters and later (23 March 1753) swore before Sir Crisp Gascoyne, Lord Mayor of London and the gypsy's champion, that 'although they had embarked in this affair at their own expence, as friends to public justice, and out of tenderness to a poor girl whom they believed was injured, yet from the satisfaction they received at the said Mrs. Wells's, from the appearance of things not at all answering the description that had been given, they concluded, that the story of the said *Elizabeth Canning* was impossible to be true, that they themselves had been imposed upon, and therefore they desisted to assist in the prosecution.'[1]

Most of her friends, however, were sufficiently satisfied with the day's work to consider the next step, prosecution of Squires and Wells. To this end they published (on 10 February 1753) *The Case of Elizabeth Canning* (see below, p. 293 n. 1), a single sheet signed by six substantial tradesmen, recounting her story, and characterizing it as one '*worthy the Compassion and charitable Contributions of all publick-spirited People, and every one who has any Regard for the Safety of their own Children and Relations*'. They hinted that '*a Subscription*, or Contribution, will soon be raised, to enable the Persons who have undertaken *to detect this notorious Gang, to prosecute* their good Intention with the utmost Vigour, as such a Nest of Villains is of the greatest Danger to the Safety of all his Majesty's good Subjects'.[2] They also informed the public where '*Cases*' might be had, gratis, and where donations would be accepted. The *Case* was advertised in the newspapers. The appeal for funds continued even after the trial of Wells and Squires (21 February 1753), for a later advertisement (24 February 1753) explains that 'Part of the Money which has hitherto been received, is designed for the *Benefit* of . . . Elizabeth Canning: And the *Expences* which have unavoidably attended this Affair having been very considerable, and likewise will be attended with still greater, before such a *desperate Gang* can be entirely rooted out, it is hoped that the Conviction of *Squires* and *Wells* will not be a Means of hindering further Donations for the apprehending the other Villains, who, if not detected, may commit more *enormous Acts* of *Violence* and *Cruelty*.'[3] According to one pamphleteer, Elizabeth's friends were so 'vehemently assiduous' in their prosecution as to distribute copies of the inflammatory *Case* in the court 'even on the Day of the Trial'.[4]

When Salt came to Bow Street on 6 February for advice on how to

---

[1] Sir Crisp Gascoyne, *An Address to the Liverymen of the City of London* (London, 1754), p. 21. Hereafter referred to as *Address*.

[2] Quoted from '*Canning's' Magazine* (London, 1753), p. 68. Not a magazine but a pamphlet. It reproduces in appendices a number of legal documents and newspaper announcements relating to Elizabeth Canning.

[3] '*Canning's' Magazine*, p. 79.   [4] Ibid., p. 61.

proceed with the prosecution, Fielding need not have been aware of the whirl of excitement probably still confined to the neighborhood of Aldermanbury Postern. Certainly he is careful in his description of his first meeting with Canning's solicitor to stress his indifference to the case and his reluctance to act. Only Salt's insistence on the need for haste lest Canning's persecutors escape persuaded Fielding to read Salt's brief, and then only after tea was concluded. His advice given, Fielding resisted for a time Salt's pleas that he take Canning's information and examine Hall, but he 'yielded ... at last, to the Importunities of Mr. Salt; and my only motives for so doing were, besides those Importunities, some Curiosity, occasioned by the extraordinary Nature of the Case, and a great Compassion for the dreadful Condition of the Girl, as it was represented to me by Mr. Salt' (*Elizabeth Canning*, below, p. 298). After Fielding examined Elizabeth the following day, his compassion and curiosity were even more powerfully aroused.

There is nothing more certain in this mysterious case than the extraordinary credibility of Elizabeth Canning. Many of her supporters never lost their faith. Well after Canning's trial in 1754, six of her supporters published a substantial tract arguing her innocence and publishing sixty-five depositions, most of them newly taken, to support their argument.[5] Her opponents rarely attacked Canning personally, and many of them were willing to allow that she somehow believed in her own testimony. Even the violently hostile John Hill was circumspect in his comments on her in his pamphlet, *The Story of Elizabeth Canning Considered* (see below, p. cxii), and only after she had been convicted of perjury and was in prison awaiting transportation did he descend to personal insult, implying in an 'inspector' column of 7 June 1754, that she was drunk with wine and Methodism in Newgate. His charges were immediately refuted.

Fielding's remark in the *Case of Bosavern Penlez* that he was a partaker of the milk of human kindness modestly lays claim to a quality he obviously possessed in abundance. Many instances in his reported cases at Bow Street, as well as the evidence of his imaginative writings, testify to his susceptibility to figures of pathos. As the author of *Tom Jones*, he was sharply aware that compassion and benevolence could be misdirected, but he was generally willing to run the risk. As man and magistrate Fielding's compassion tended to be excited by 'safe' objects—destitute widows of clergymen, the 'deserving' poor, a beautiful young girl bedded on her wedding night in a crowded room, a boy of twelve taken up for theft whose mother desperately pleaded for his release, a mother of three children charged with stealing a cap. Elizabeth Canning, hard-working, respectable, modest, and demure— 'a Child in Years, and yet more so in Understanding, with all the evident

---

[5] *A Refutation of Sir Crisp Gascoyne's Address* ... (London, 1754).

Marks of Simplicity that I ever discovered in a human Countenance' (*Elizabeth Canning*, below, p. 294—must have been irresistible.

As the proprietress of a suburban brothel of mean reputation, Susannah Wells appeared in a very different light; as prostitute in residence, Virtue Hall stood on the lowest rung of her profession. No one, as far as I know, spoke a good word for Hall or regretted Wells's branding or her months in Newgate. Mary Squires, whose grotesque appearance struck all observers ('The convict is so very remarkable, 'tis as impossible that any of the witnesses can be mistaken in her person, as that their different accounts can be true. She is at least 70, tall, and stoops; her face is long and meagre, her nose very large, her eyes very full and dark, her complexion remarkably swarthy, and her under-lip of a prodigious size'[6]), was a very Jewkes to frighten a Pamela with. Moreover, she was a gypsy and probably involved in smuggling. During the course of his campaign against smugglers, the Duke of Richmond had conferred with Fielding (see above, p. lvi) about the smuggling network in the south of England, and memory of the brutal murders committed by smugglers in 1749 was still fresh.[7] This connection may have further darkened Squires's aspect for Fielding. Canning's friends publicized the occult threats posed by gypsies and hinted that a larger plot remained to be discovered.[8] There was nothing about Wells, Squires, or Hall to attract Fielding's sympathies.

Rather, after the protracted examination of Virtue Hall the evening of 7 February—Fielding probably found considerable satisfaction in having brought her to a confession. He prided himself as a close examiner ('I can . . . declare, that I have never spared any Pains in endeavouring to detect Falsehood and Perjury, and have had some very notable Success that Way' [*Elizabeth Canning*, below, p. 310]), and there is a suggestion of triumph in the announcement in the *Publick Advertiser* (which printed Fielding's announcements from Bow Street[9]) of 10 Feb.:

On *Wednesday* last, at the earnest Desire of the Prosecutor, Mr. Justice *Fielding* undertook to examine into the Robbery of the Girl, who, in the Beginning of *January* last, after having been robbed in *Moorfield*, was carried by two Men to a House in *Enfield-Wash*, where she was stript of her Stays, and then confined in a miserable Room near a Month, with no other Sustenance than a Quartern Loaf and a Pitcher of Water. On *Thursday* Evening a Girl who lived in the House, and who was apprehended by a Warrant from the Justice, was brought before him, and was under Examination from Six 'till Twelve at Night; when, after many hard Struggles and stout Denials of the *Truth*, she, at length, confessed the Whole; by which Means it is

---

[6] Gascoyne, *Address*, pp. 4–5.

[7] See Cal Winslow, 'Sussex Smugglers', in *Albion's Fatal Tree* (New York, 1975), pp. 119–66; and *State Trials*, xviii. 1070–1116.

[8] See '*Canning's' Magazine*, appendices 10 and 12.

[9] For Fielding's connection with the *Publick Advertiser*, see Cross, ii. 428–9; and Dudden, ii. 927.

3. A T[ru]e Draught of Eliz. Canning

not doubted but that all the Actors of that cruel Scene will be brought to the Fate they deserve.

The allusion to 'hard Struggles' and 'stout Denials' was later to be cited by Gascoyne, Hill, and other pamphleteers as evidence of Fielding's misconduct of this examination.

Fielding's sense of satisfaction was undisturbed by any event until well after the trial of Wells and Squires. Whether the concourse of 'Noble Lords' as spectators at the second swearing of Canning and Hall's informations on 14 February (*Elizabeth Canning*, below, p. 306) was an annoyance or a pleasure to Fielding must remain uncertain. This event and the later request from 'some Gentlemen' for advice on the use of funds collected for Canning (*Elizabeth Canning*, below, p. 306) seemed at any rate to confirm that Fielding had played a wise and effective role in what was now a *cause célèbre*.

Sir Crisp Gascoyne, however, had been dissatisfied with the conviction of Squires. He thought the public, even the jury, prejudiced against the defendant ('surely no poor creature ever before appeared at the Bar, more perfectly deprived of the mercy of the law, which presumes guilt in no one before conviction'[1]). On the other hand, he found Canning's story improbable and was alarmed by the contradictory nature of the evidence. Particularly disturbing was the testimony of two witnesses from Abbotsbury which, if true, placed Mary Squires some one hundred and fifty miles away at the time Canning's testimony placed her at Enfield Wash. On 24 February Gascoyne instructed his solicitor, Thomas Ford, to write to the minister of Abbotsbury for confirmation of this testimony. James Harris, the vicar of Abbotsbury, responded on 5 March 1753 to the effect that several of his parishioners could swear that Mary Squires, her son, George, and her daughter, Lucy, stayed at the house of John Gibbons (one of the Abbotsbury witnesses) on 1 January 1753. Before Gascoyne received this letter, the clerk of Justice Gundry, one of the trial judges, had forwarded to him an earlier communication from Harris which contained other depositions to the same effect. Apparently Gundry had also been dissatisfied and had initiated inquiries. Gascoyne summoned Canning's 'espousers' and showed them these documents.

The rumors occasioned by Gascoyne's intervention reached John Hill, the wretched and unscrupulous hack best known to Fielding scholars for the bitter quarrel he and Fielding engaged in while the latter was conducting the *Covent-Garden Journal*.[2] Hill had discovered that Virtue Hall was being supported by Canningites at the Gatehouse prison in Westminster (to

---

[1] Gascoyne, *Address*, p. 3.
[2] On Hill and his relationship with Fielding see Jensen, Introduction to *CGJ* i. 35 ff. See also G. S. Rousseau, 'John Hill, Universal Genius Manqué', in *The Renaissance Man in the Eighteenth Century* (Los Angeles, 1978), pp. 49 ff.

identify George Squires should he reappear), and he had heard of the affidavits in Gascoyne's hands. Backed by the legal authority of the prominent Westminster magistrate, Thomas Lediard (who had been on the bench when Fielding delivered his *Charge to the Grand Jury*), Hill and Lediard gained access to Hall in prison and concluded that she was on the verge of another confession. That same evening (6 March) they repaired to the Lord Mayor's Mansion House with their information. Gascoyne, who had not known Hall's whereabouts, immediately summoned her. Elizabeth's friends also appeared at the Mansion House, but Hall's recantation, which she at first refused, was made in private to Gascoyne and Sir John Phillips, a prominent Jacobite who had been active in the election campaign of 1749 (see above, p. xlv ff.).

Fielding may have learned of these events nearly immediately, for solicitor Salt's brother was keeper of the Westminster gatehouse. Possibly, however, he first read of Hall's recantation in Hill's daily 'Inspector' column in the *London Daily Advertiser*. Hill's column of 9 March is full of Hall's confession and the evidence gathered by Gascoyne and also celebrates his own crucial role in detecting the 'truth'. He reprinted this column the next day, demand for it having exceeded the number printed. On 14 March Hill announced that Mary Squires was 'perfectly innocent' and that he intended to search out evidence to support an indictment against Elizabeth for willful and corrupt perjury. In other columns he kept the public informed about the succession of new affidavits coming in to Gascoyne.[3]

Hill's role in obtaining Hall's confession was a personal triumph. It may have seemed to Fielding a personal insult, and a particularly galling one considering that recent events had exacerbated their already bitter relationship. The 'paper-war' between Hill and Fielding, which had largely ended by February 1752, erupted again in November 1752, in the aftermath of a quarrel which broke out between Garrick's Drury Lane Theatre and Rich's Covent-Garden Theatre. At one point a party of Rich's supporters interrupted a performance at Drury Lane. The actor, Henry Woodward, a friend of Fielding's, was struck by an apple thrown by a 'gentleman' in the audience. According to the account in the *Gentleman's Magazine* (November 1752, p. 535), '*Woodward* resented the blow by some words, which by the gentleman's account implied a challenge, but by *Woodward's* no such thing'. The public took sides. Woodward swore to the truth of his version before Fielding; his assailant to the truth of his before Justice Lediard. Hill raucously assailed Woodward. The 'Court of Censorial Enquiry' in the final

---

[3] The anonymous author of *The Account of Canning and Squires Fairly Ballanc'd* (London, 1753) describes and rejects the arguments in Hill's 'Inspector' columns on Elizabeth Canning. This pamphlet must have been one of the first to appear, for it does not mention either Fielding's or Hill's pamphlet.

issue of the *Covent-Garden Journal* (25 November 1752, ii. 141) indicted Hill for licking up 'one large Mouthful of Dirt' from the kennel 'at the Parish of Billingsgate' and spitting it on 'his most serene Honour Alexander', but scornfully dismissed him as below the court's notice. As late as 6 December, Hill had observed that Fielding was 'contemptible'.

Whatever his precise motive, Fielding's response to the discoveries made by Hill and Gascoyne was quick. On 13 March, the same day that Gascoyne issued a warrant for Canning's arrest on a charge of perjury, the *Publick Advertiser* advised its readers 'to suspend their Judgment in the Case of the Gypsy Woman 'till a full State of the whole, which is now preparing by Mr. Fielding, is published'.[4] On Friday, 16 March, *A Clear State of the Case of Elizabeth Canning* was announced for 'Tues. next'; the following day the public was again told it must wait until Thursday for Fielding's pamphlet, 'especially since Mr. Inspector has entered so warmly into the Matter'. On Monday, 19 March, the following notice appeared: 'Notwithstanding the many Puffs on the other Side of the Question, the Friends of *Elizabeth Canning* flatter themselves, her Case will not be attended with that Intricacy as is insinuated; and the World in due Time will be acquainted with a true State of her Case, attested by Persons of undoubted Probity, Fortune, and Reputation; and they will likewise be *informed* who the *King* of the *Gipsies* is.'

A Clear State of the Case of Elizabeth Canning was published as announced on Tuesday, 20 March. *The Publick Advertiser* printed an approving two-column review the following day. Clearly, Fielding wrote *Elizabeth Canning* in a very short period of time. If it was 'preparing', as the *Publick Advertiser* states, by Tuesday, 13 March, it was nearly completed on Thursday, two days later, for writing near the end of his pamphlet, Fielding solemnly attests 'I am at this very Time, on this 15th day of *March*, 1753, as firmly persuaded as I am of any Fact in this World . . . that *Mary Squires* IS GUILTY . . . [and] that *Elizabeth Canning* is [innocent]'. His 'Postscript', which remarks on the 'extreme Hurry in which the foregoing Case was drawn up', was written on 18 March, a Sunday, and mentions new evidence gathered by Elizabeth's lawyer on 15 and 16 March (see *Elizabeth Canning*, below, p. 312 and n. 3). *Elizabeth Canning* is the only work in this volume for which there is no record in Strahan's 'Ledgers'. Presumably the haste of its publication obliged Millar to employ a different printer. On Thursday 22 March the *Publick Advertiser* announced the publication of the 'Second Edition' 'This Day at Noon'. Only signatures B–C⁴ (pages 1–16 of the text) were reset. Signatures D–I⁴ (which include the title-page, A1 having been printed as I4) were reprinted from standing type, 'THE SECOND EDITION' being squeezed in below Fielding's name on the first edition title-page. Except for one

---

[4] It must have been about this time that Fielding examined Canning for perhaps the last time. See *Elizabeth Canning*, below, pp. 306–7.

change in standing type (on E3ᵛ) and one variation in a catchword (on E1ᵛ), there are no textual differences between these two editions after page 16. Fielding, if indeed it is he who is responsible for the minor variations found, apparently had time only for a cursory revision of his text.[5]

Fielding's involvement in the case of Elizabeth Canning was not quite at an end. G. M. Godden discovered two letters to Newcastle (first printed in her *Henry Fielding, A Memoir* [London, 1910], pp. 273–5) which we now can understand more fully in the context of Gascoyne's activities to obtain a pardon for Squires. It was Gascoyne's duty as presiding magistrate at Squires's trial to submit a report to the king concerning those convicts condemned to death. To this end, he had continued during the last half of March and into April to collect evidence which concerned Squires's alibi. He submitted his report 10 April,[6] and Squires was immediately given a respite of six weeks. His Majesty's attorney and solicitor-general (Sir Dudley Ryder and William Murray, Lord Mansfield) were directed to consider the evidence on both sides.[7]

Gascoyne was convinced that Fielding was concealing evidence helpful to Squires. He asserted that attempts had been made to impugn the testimony of witnesses from Abbotsbury and that even the vicar had been slandered: 'the very clergyman, a gentleman of as fair and honourable a character as ever lived, was joined in the slander; and hardly the attestation of a nobleman of particular honour, who personally knew him, could rescue him from the censure'. A footnote indicates that this 'attestation' was made in 'A Letter from a noble lord to Mr. Fielding'[8] (Hill referred obscurely to Fielding's knowledge of this 'noble Personage's' testimony to the vicar's character[9]). Gascoyne also states that he is 'credibly assured' that Fielding had inquired of '*Mr. Arbuthnot* of *Weymouth* near *Abbotsbury*, a gentleman of fortune' concerning Squires's alibi and that Arbuthnot had transmitted sixty certificates confirming her alibi to Fielding. Of Fielding's supposed concealment of those documents, Gascoyne dryly remarked, 'I wish Mr. Fielding, who had before published so much on this subject, had now obliged the world with the publication of those certificates'.[1]

During this period Canning's second lawyer, John Miles, had been busy on her behalf. He advertised in the newspapers for witnesses who could place Squires at Enfield Wash between 1 and 10 January.[2] He also wrote to

---

[5] See Textual Appendixes I, II, and III, below.

[6] It is printed in Gascoyne, *Address*, p. 26.

[7] Squires was officially pardoned 21 May 1753. Wells was not released from Newgate until 21 Aug. 1753.

[8] Gascoyne, *Address*, p. 18. According to Gascoyne, Canning's friends asserted that all of the inhabitants of Abbotsbury were 'thieves and smugglers'.

[9] John Hill, *The Story of Elizabeth Canning Considered*, pp. 50–1.

[1] Gascoyne, *Address*, p. 24.   [2] See *Elizabeth Canning*, below, p. 312, n. 3.

the south-west seeking evidence to discredit witnesses supporting Squires. In at least one instance he received a reply confirming and adding to the evidence which supported Squires's story. He sunk this evidence and Gascoyne had learned of his duplicity.

On such evidence and with such suspicions, Gascoyne must have suggested to the king's officers that Fielding could provide information relevant to their inquiries. The two Fielding letters reprinted here are the result and reflect, especially the second, his chagrin at the implication he had behaved disingenuously.

My Lord Duke

I received an order from my Lord Chancellor immediately after the breaking up of the Council to lay before your Grace all the Affidavits I had taken since the Gipsey's Trial which related to that Affair. I then told the Messenger that I had taken none, as indeed the fact is the Affidavits of which I gave my Lord Chancellor an Abstract having been all sworn before Justices of the Peace in the Neighbourhood of Endfield, and remain I believe in the Possession of an Attorney in the City.

However in Consequence of the Commands with which your Grace was pleased to honour me yesterday, I sent my Clerk immediately to the Attorney to acquaint him with these Commands, which I doubt not he will instantly obey. This I did from my great Duty to your Grace for I have long had no Concern in this Affair, nor have I seen any of the Parties lately unless once when I was desired to send for the Girl (Canning) to my House that a great Number of Noblemen and Gentlemen might see her and ask her what Questions they pleased. I am, with the highest Duty,
    My Lord,
      Your Graces most obedient
        and most humble servant
          Henry Ffielding.

Ealing. April 14, 1753
His Grace the
    Duke of Newcastle.

My Lord Duke,

I am extremely concerned to see by a Letter which I have just received from Mr Jones by Command of your Grace that the Persons concerned for the Prosecution have not yet attended your Grace with the Affidavits in Canning's Affair. I do assure you upon my Honour that I sent to them the Moment I first received your Grace's Commands and having after three Messages prevailed with them to come to me I desired them to fetch the Affidavits that I might send them to your Grace being not able to wait upon you in Person. This they said they could not do, but would go to Mr Hume Campbell their Council, and prevail with him to attend your Grace with all their Affidavits many of which, I found were sworn after the Day mentioned in the order of Council. I told them I apprehended the latter could not be admitted, but insisted in the strongest terms on their laying the others immediately before your Grace, and they at last promised me they would, nor have I ever seen them since. I have now again ordered my Clerk to go to them to inform them of the last Commands

4. The Conjurers, 1753. Drawn from the Life by the Right Honourable the Lady Fa[nny] K[illigre]w

5. The Gypsy's Triumph. Published after the reprieve of Mary Squires

I have received, but as I have no Compulsory Power over them I can not answer for their Behaviour, which indeed I have long disliked, and have therefore long ago declined giving them any Advice, nor would I unless in Obedience to your Grace have anything to say to a set of the most obstinate Fools I ever saw; and who seem to me rather to act from a Spleen against my Lord Mayor, than from any Motive of protecting Innocence, tho' that was certainly their Motive at first. In Truth, if I am not deceived, I Suspect they desire that the Gipsey should be pardoned, and then to convince the World that she was guilty in order to cast the greater Reflection on him who was principally instrumental in obtaining such Pardon. I conclude with assuring your Grace that I have acted in this Affair, as I shall on all Occasions with the most dutiful Regard to your Commands, and that if my Life had been at Stake, as many know, I could have done no more.

> I am, with the highest Respect,
> My Lord Duke
> Y Grace's most obedient,
> and most humble servant,
> Henry Ffielding.

Ealing
April 27. 1753.
His Grace the Duke of
Newcastle.[3]

One notes that by 27 April Fielding is carefully silent as to his current view of Canning's guilt or innocence and that he is no longer critical of Gascoyne (*Elizabeth Canning*, below, p. 286 n. 8). He dissociates himself from Canning's supporters, whom he now sees as engaging in a campaign against the Lord Mayor. Gascoyne had implied throughout his *Address* that Canning's friends were his political enemies.[4] The mention of an exhibition of Canning to 'a great Number of Noblemen and Gentlemen' at the end of the letter of 14 April appears to refer to an incident that took place after the publication of *A Clear State of the Case of Elizabeth Canning*.

We may pass quickly over the subsequent events in Elizabeth Canning's story. Gascoyne presented a bill to the April sessions of the grand jury held at Hicks's Hall, charging Canning with perjury. Her supporters responded by filing a bill of perjury against the three countrymen who had testified for Squires. The grand jury threw out both bills 4 May. Each side persisted, and at the June sessions the grand jury found true bills against Canning and against John Gibbons, William Clarke, and Thomas Greville. The trials were set for the September sessions. Canning's supporters published (in a

---

[3] Printed from Cross, ii. 290–2. The letters are in the Public Record Office, State Papers Domestic, Geo. II, 1749–59, Bundle 127, No. 24.

[4] The authors of *A Refutation of Sir Crisp Gascoyne's Address* insistently reject this imputation, asserting instead that Gascoyne persisted in his defence of Squires because his ambition to sit in Parliament for London or Southwark had come to depend on his success in the Canning affair (see *Refutation*, Appendix, p. viii). Gascoyne was a Tory.

broadsheet and in the newspapers) their unwillingness that she should be tried until after 9 November, the date on which Gascoyne's mayoralty concluded and after which he would not preside over the court. Gascoyne said he would step down from the bench, but complicated legal maneuvering ensued which led to bitter charges of deception from both sides. Canning went into hiding and the process to proclaim her an outlaw was nearly perfected when she appeared at the February sessions in 1754, to give bail to stand her trial the following sessions.

The three countrymen meanwhile had appeared in September for their trial at the Old Bailey, but of the fifty witnesses who were to testify against them only one, an old woman who said she knew nothing of the matter, appeared. They were acquitted.[5]

On the 29 April 1754 Elizabeth Canning finally appeared at the bar and pleaded not guilty to the perjury charge preferred in June of the preceding year. A trial of unprecedented length ensued.[6] On 7 May, after two hours of deliberation, the jury brought in their verdict, 'Guilty of perjury, but not wilful or corrupt', a verdict too palpably agreeable to common sense to be allowed at the bar. They were instructed that this verdict could not be received and that they must find her guilty or innocent of the whole indictment. After brief further deliberation, they reached the verdict 'Guilty of Wilful and Corrupt Perjury'. Before sentencing, however, which had been scheduled for the following Monday, two jurors tried to retract their vote, since they did not believe her perjury wilful or corrupt. Thereupon Canning's counsel called for a new trial. A decision was deferred until 30 May. On that date Sir John Willes was the senior presiding judge. He rejected the argument for a new trial, observing that the two jurors were 'but weak men, first to consent and give in their verdict according to their oath, and then to recant'. Willes, who clearly was not a weak man, also spoke effectively against a motion for a sentence of six-months' imprisonment. He insisted on transportation. Eight aldermen[7] none the less voted for the lesser sentence. But all six professional judges, the Lord Mayor (by this time Thomas Rawlinson), and two aldermen (one of whom was Theodore Janssen) voted for transportation.

Elizabeth Canning left for America on 7 August 1754, the same day Fielding landed in Lisbon. She settled in Wethersfield, Connecticut, near Hartford. There, in 1756, she married a John Treat, to whom she bore a son (1758) and a daughter (1761), also named Elizabeth. While still in Newgate,

---

[5] Their trial is printed in *State Trials*, xix. 275–84.

[6] Courtney Kenny states that it was probably the first criminal trial to last more than a day and that it 'established the principle that in cases of misdemeanour the Court may adjourn and the jury may separate' ('The Mystery of Elizabeth Canning', p. 372).

[7] After 1742, London aldermen were enrolled on the Commission of Peace and were entitled to serve on the Bench.

Elizabeth had issued a statement to refute the rumor that she had 'squeaked' and, if pardoned, would confess her guilt. This statement concludes, 'I remain at this instant of time fully persuaded, and well assured, that Mary Squires was the person who robbed me; that the house of Susannah Wells was the place in which I was confined twenty-eight days; and that I did not, in my several informations or examinations before the different magistrates, or in my evidence on the trial of the said Mary Squires and Susannah Wells, knowingly, in any material, or even in the most minute circumstances, deviate from the truth.'[8] Elizabeth Canning died in 1773 without, as far as is known, ever having altered her story.[9]

Fielding's *A Clear State of the Case of Elizabeth Canning* was among the first of some forty pamphlets to appear in 1753 and 1754. It is a tribute to his moral authority and to the respect he commanded as magistrate that it was probably the best known of all the writings on the case. Well after the trial of Elizabeth Canning (he dates his pamphlet 8 July, 1754), Gascoyne still regarded Fielding as one of his major opponents. The several responses that Gascoyne's *Address* provoked defended and praised Fielding. For instance, the author of *A Refutation of Sir Crisp Gascoyne's Account of his Conduct, &c.* (London, 1754) observed that 'all the World knows the Character of Mr. *Justice Fielding*, his *Candor*, his *Integrity*, his *Impartiality* were never questioned' (p. 11). Fielding's was the only pamphlet alluded to at the trial, though it must be noted that the prosecution's allusions were for the purpose of rejecting Fielding's arguments. Allan Ramsay states that his attention was first drawn to the story of Elizabeth Canning when he saw 'a pamphlet advertised on the subject by Mr. Fielding.' He praises it generously ('perhaps there are none of his performances that more discover the ingenuity of the man of wit, the distinctness of the lawyer, or the politeness and candour of the gentleman'), but finally was left unconvinced: 'while I admired the stile and composition of this pamphlet, and the ingenious, and at the same time unadorned method, in which Mr. *Fielding* defended the cause of *Canning*, I could not help being surprised to find upon what slight grounds he and many other sensible men, had founded their belief of her veracity'.[1] He then presents a deductive argument which devastatingly exposes the improbabilities inherent in Canning' story.

---

[8] *A Refutation of Sir Crisp Gascoyne's Address*, [second] 'Appendix', p. 49.
[9] De la Torre gives a history of Elizabeth's life after her trial (*Elizabeth is Missing*, pp. 213–28).
[1] 'A Letter to the Right Honourable the Earl of —— Concerning the Affair of Elizabeth Canning', in *The Investigator* (London, 1762), pp. 2–3. Ramsay's pamphlet was first published as 'By a Clergyman' in 1753. He was the son of the Scotch poet and became portait painter to George III. His shrewd pamphlet confirms Johnson's judgement: 'I love Ramsay. You will not find a man in whose conversation there is more instruction, more information, and more elegance, than in Ramsay's' (*Life* iii. 336).

At least two pamphlets were written specifically to refute Fielding's account,[2] but only Hill, who describes himself as 'of all Men the least inclined to enter Disputes and Quarrels' (p. 11), treats Fielding scornfully.[3] Hill's *The Story of Elizabeth Canning Considered* appeared nine days after Fielding's pamphlet.[4] He wrote it, he says, for the sake of truth and to counteract the effects of Fielding's arguments, which had reawakened faith in Canning's story just when the public had begun to recognize her perjury:

I cannot see it [Fielding's *Elizabeth Canning*] aiming to overthrow that Justice and Compassion, which were growing up in the Minds of all Men, with Respect to the Object whom I had proposed to them as so worthy of those Emotions, without treating it with that Severity, and condemning it to that Ignominy which it deserves; without detecting its Misrepresentations, refuting its imagined Arguments, and pointing out to those, who have not already seen it, where they are to smile upon its Puerility (p. 7).

Insult runs throughout this shoddy performance (which Hill's hard facts nevertheless make effective) and it concludes with a reflection on Fielding's candor and integrity: 'For you, Mr. *Fielding*! I have no Right to call your Behaviour as a Magistrate in Question; nor have I Abilities to judge of it: I have, therefore, no where alluded to it: But certainly your private Treatment of this Subject, both before and in your Pamphlet, merits the strongest Censure' (p. 53).

Hill's assertion that Fielding's pamphlet renewed support for Canning is probably correct. The author of a later pamphlet adopted the Richardsonian tactic of writing to the moment in a series of letters designed to recapture the flow of public opinion. When he hears of Hall's recantation he writes, 'I cannot, as yet, altogether give up my former Opinion. Mr. *Fielding*, whose Capacity, as a *Writer*, we have often jointly admired, whose Knowledge of the human Heart is beyond Contradiction, and whose Abilities as a *Lawyer*, and Impartiality as a *Magistrate*, are indisputable, has undertaken the Defence of this unhappy Girl. The Publick are desired to suspend their Judgment of this Affair, till a *full State* of the *whole*, which is now preparing

---

[2] Hill's pamphlet and *The Truth of the Case, Or, Canning and Squires Fairly Opposed . . . with a full and rational Answer to all the Objections, Difficulties, Improbabilities and Impossibilities, raised and enforced . . . by Mr. 'Fielding' in his 'Clear State of the Case'* (London, 1753). This pamphleteer objects strenuously to Fielding's *hauteur* towards pamphleteers and coffee-house politicians.

[3] Another pamphleteer, however, was willing to publish a 'report' that Fielding coerced Hall's confession for monetary gain: 'if the report which is current should prove true, that a certain M———te and his C—k divided eighteen Pounds of the Money which was collected for the Girl for Service they did her, the Reader will not be much at a Loss to guess at the Reasons for the extraordinary Management [Fielding's supposed coercion of Hall] of this Affair.' He goes on to exclaim, 'What a Wretch then must that Person be, especially if he bears the King's Commission to do justice, if he perverted his Authority to such vile Purposes . . .' (*The Case of Elizabeth Canning Fairly Stated* [London, 1753], pp. 23, 24). The *Publick Advertiser* announced the publication of this pamphlet on 13 Mar., just a week before Fielding's *Elizabeth Canning* was published.

[4] The announcement of its publication appears in the *London Daily Advertiser* of 29 Mar.

by him, is published.'[5] When it appears, Fielding's 'performance' disappoints him—'Nay, I will go further, laugh as much as you please at me; I freely own, that nothing, I have either read or heard, relative to this Matter, has contributed more to the making me almost as great an Infidel as yourself, than the Perusal of this Performance' (p. 47)—but he notes, with some irony, that its effects have been extremely useful to the Canningites:

though this Pamphlet has had so contrary an Effect upon me, it has answered some other useful Purposes: Many Apostates have hereby been reclaimed, and Contributions, which began to droop, are plentifully revived. Where his Arguments could not prevail, it might be believed his Protestation would; for this Gentleman's Abilities and Integrity are justly so well established, that few will venture to contradict his Belief, especially as he 'appeals in the most solemn Manner to the Almighty for the Truth of what he asserts' (p. 83).

One point recurs in this pamphlet literature. Nearly all of the anti-Canningites criticize Fielding's procedure in taking Hall's testimony. Hill, Gascoyne, the prosecution at Canning's trial (see *Elizabeth Canning*, below, p. 308 n. 2), Ramsay, and the anonymous author of *'Canning's' Magazine* focus sharply on this point. Modern commentators agree that Fielding had been naïve to allow Salt to take Hall's testimony privately[6] (there is also the frequent but less compelling suggestion that he frightened or coerced Hall into making the statement he wished to hear). According to Courtney Kenny, 'The simple truth seems to be that if Fielding had taken the trouble to have Hall's information taken from her own lips in his own presence, the Canning mystery would have received its death-blow at once; and the *cause célèbre* would never have been tried'.[7] Kenny himself concludes that 'the principal lesson of this famous trial seems to me to be the importance of *a priori* considerations of credibility or incredibility as guides in forensic inquiries . . . . In Elizabeth Canning's case it is perhaps not unfair to say that, after the two vast masses of evidence for and against the alibi had . . . neutralized one another, the issue was decided, neither by direct nor by circumstantial evidence, but by the inherent incredibility of Canning's story.'[8] Kenny is obviously responding to the extraordinary fact that at the trial forty-one witnesses for Squires were in nearly direct contradiction with twenty-seven witnesses for Canning. But Kenny's principle of inherent probability as a deciding factor in resolving conflicting claims perhaps applies also to Fielding's response to the conflicting testimony of Canning and the motley inhabitants of Wells's house. He was faced in little with the kind of contradiction that the evidence at the trial had merely writ large. He

---

[5] *Genuine and Impartial Memoirs of Elizabeth Canning . . . From her Birth to the Present Time* (London, 1754), p. 44.
[6] Cross, ii. 298–9; Dudden, ii. 976–7; Jones, 232–3.
[7] 'The Mystery of Elizabeth Canning', p. 375.   [8] Ibid., p. 377.

impulsively resolved it in favor of the probability that the truth lay with an utterly compelling witness who told an improbable story. Of course in acting on this conclusion so forcefully he nearly exceeded the bounds of his commission—very much like Allworthy, whose judgements are often guided by '*a priori* considerations of credibility or incredibility'. It would be fitting to grant Fielding the defense he allows Allworthy, 'As his Intention was truly upright, he ought to be excused in *Foro Conscientiae*, since so many arbitrary Acts are daily committed by Magistrates, who have not this Excuse to plead for themselves' (IV. xi. 192). At any rate, it is some pleasure to record that on Friday, 21 April 1961, Elizabeth Canning was retried at the Bramshill Police College before a jury of twenty-six police officers who, after hearing the evidence, required only one minute's deliberation to find, by a majority of twenty-two members to four, Elizabeth Canning not guilty of perjury. On being informed of the decision reached two hundred and seven years earlier, this jury 'considered that the whole case had been grossly mismanaged and that there was, in the case of Elizabeth Canning, a great miscarriage of justice'.[9]

---

[9] Sergeant J. Archer *et al.*, 'The Case of Elizabeth Canning', *The Police College Magazine*, 7 (1961), 81. The occasion of this retrial was a meeting of the Henry Fielding Society under the direction of P. J. Stead, MA, FRSL, Director of Liberal Studies at the Police College, Bramshill. The writers of the article were all students of Course A/61/1.

TEXTUAL INTRODUCTION

THIS edition offers a critical unmodernized text of six of Fielding's social pamphlets written between 1749 and 1753: (1) *A Charge to the Grand Jury* (July 1749), (2) *A True State of the Case of Bosavern Penlez* (November 1749), (3) *An Enquiry into the Late Increase of Robbers* (January 1751), (4) *Examples of the Interposition of Providence* (April 1752), (5) *A Proposal for Making an Effectual Provision for the Poor* (January 1753), and (6) *A Clear State of the Case of Elizabeth Canning* (March 1753). The text is critical in that it has been established by the application of analytical criticism to the evidence of the various early documentary forms in which the materials appeared. It is unmodernized in that every effort has been made to present the text in as close a form to Fielding's own inscription and subsequent revision as the surviving documents permit, subject to normal editorial regulation.

I. THE COPY-TEXT AND ITS TREATMENT

No manuscript is known for any of the material in the present volume, nor is there any formal assignment of copyright from Fielding to the publisher extant that would permit us to assert flatly the authoritative nature of the manuscripts which were sent to the press. Nevertheless, all were issued by Fielding's regular publisher, A. Millar, and all but *Elizabeth Canning* were accounted for in Strahan's ledgers according to their titles. Given the nature of the material and the circumstances of publication, not a doubt can exist that these six pamphlets were set from Fielding's authoritative manuscripts, doubtless his holograph copies. Moreover, the special charges that Strahan made for extraordinary alterations, as in *An Enquiry*, attest to Fielding's care for revision in proof; and indeed the nature of the pamphlets suggests that Fielding saw each work through the press with some care. Further, in the *Enquiry*, not content with the revisions in proof for which Strahan charged, Fielding appended an errata list to correct misprints that had been overlooked, a sign of how seriously he took these texts.

For an unmodernized edition such as the Wesleyan–Clarendon Fielding, the most authentic form of what are known as the 'accidentals' of a text—the spelling, punctuation, capitalization, word-division, and such typographical matters as the use of italics—can be sought only in the document that lies closest to the lost holograph, that is, in the first printing of the first edition, the one printing that was set directly from manuscript. An editor will understand that the first edition by no means represents a diplomatic reprint of the manuscript and that in most respects the accidentals are a mixture of the author's and the compositors'. But whatever the relative impurity, the first edition stands nearest to the author's own characteristics and represents the only authority that has been preserved for the texture in which his words were originally clothed.

Problems may arise depending upon the extent, or existence, of an author's supervision when a work went into a second printing (from standing type completely or in great part) or into a true second edition in which all or most of the text is reset from a copy of the first edition. Fielding's *Charge to the Grand Jury* and his *Proposal* appear to have had only one printing and hence are without variation, no press-variants having been observed by Professor Zirker's textual collation of the copies he has listed under his bibliographical descriptions. (In passing it may be noted that Professor Zirker found no press-variation in any of the other works which he collated in multiple copies.) The *Examples of Providence* is recorded as having a second printing of 2,000 copies, but no external details identify the two printings. It is very likely, however, that the differences in the press figures which are recorded in the bibliographical description indicate copies of the second printing from standing type. Textually, collation reveals no variants and therefore the two printings can be treated as a single unit for the purpose of the text.

Elizabeth Canning went through what, as a matter of opinion, might be called either a second printing (with resetting) or a second edition. Because of the variant introduced into the identical title-page setting by which a rule and 'THE SECOND EDITION.' are squeezed in below Fielding's name in an otherwise reprinted sheet, the title A1 having been printed as I4, the latter term may seem preferable. In fact, sheets B–C, pp. 1–16, were completely reset but the rest of the sheets were reprinted from standing type. Clearly, demand developed beyond initial expectation when only the first two gatherings had been distributed, so that a second edition—consisting in large part of a second printing—was called for within a comparatively short time. Textual variation is wanting in the pages of standing type save for the addition to the title-page, but in reset pp. 1–16 not only is there a small amount of normal accidentals variation but several substantive variants occur, of which Professor Zirker thinks three have Fielding's authority. It is possible that Fielding read over copy for these pages when informed of the restricted number of pages that were to be reset; still, if so, it is odd that no attempt was made to alter readings in the standing type.[1] Unfortunately one

---

[1] In fact, professor Zirker's collation discloses that someone (presumably the printer) on sig. E3^v altered 'Gipsey's' in the standing type for the second printing to the more usual spelling 'Gipsy's' as found in this text. In the second printing, owing very likely to the problem of tying up and storing type-pages, on sig. E1^v the correct first-printing catchword 'In' (for 'In') in the direction-line has been carelessly restored as the error 'It'.

cannot entertain the plausible hypothesis that the standing-type pages are an over-run and not a second printing, and that the edition-sheet was enlarged beginning with sheet D or even E. If this had occurred the absence of authorial alterations would be readily explained; but the two minor variants observed contradict each other in the same forme. More important, the occasionally variable position of the pagination headlines indicates that the sheets are a true second printing and that the type-pages had been tied up between impressions. Whatever the reason, then, one may look for significant textual variation only in the first sixteen pages, and, of course, in the title-page.

Bosavern Penlez presents another textual problem. In his introduction Professor Zirker has shown that although the central part of the work could have been written in September, the early and late pages could not have been composed before Wilson's reprieval on October 17 and Penlez's execution on 18 October. Yet an entry in Strahan's ledger for September would imply that the first edition (or printing) was printed in that month: 'Sep.[r] [1749]: Fielding's account of Penlez 3 1/2 Sheets No. 1000 @ 18 p Sheet —— 3:3' (BL Add. MS 48890, fo. 71). On the same page a second entry appears as 'Nov.[r] [1749]: Fielding's account of Penlez. 2[d] Edit. No. 1000, deducting for 3 1/3 Sheets Stand[g]. — 2:11–'. As Professor Zirker shows, the work was actually published on 18 November 1749. The puzzle of these two entries and of this external evidence for two editions may be solved by consideration of Strahan's practice in making entires. Patricia Hernlund (*Studies in Bibliography*, 20 [1967], 89–93) explains the three different sets of books that Strahan kept, a so-called waste book for immediate entries, an intermediate recasting, and a final-form series of entries. Add. MS 48800, she states, is a ledger in final form. E. J. Duthie, of the British Library's Department of Manuscripts has kindly examined the original and confirmed that there are no indications from differences in ink or script that the whole of each entry was not made as a unit. She also points out that in this particular ledger there are twelve items for September, none for October, and five for November, and that the months of December 1749 and January 1750 have also been skipped as well as October. Professor William B. Todd, also in a private communication, points out the significance of the imbalance of entries for September in the light of the final, or summary form of this ledger, and of the fact that the first Penlez entry is the final one of the twelve listed in September and the second-edition entry is the second in the November listing. It would seem that in making up this summary of production Strahan merely failed to append in the margin the month of October. The month does not appear as an integral part of the individual entries but instead as an outset marginal heading applying to all entries thereafter listed.

It follows that there is no bar to the hypothesis that the first edition of

Penlez was printed toward the end of October, to be followed within a relatively short time by a second printing or edition that made use of standing type. As a consequence Strahan deducted the cost of resetting by allowing twelve shillings for the use of standing type and thus produced a second thousand copies for £2.11s. as against £3.3s. for the first printing. Very close line-for-line, page-for-page resetting may sometimes be difficult to identify with absolute positiveness, but examination of what can be identified as this second printing (not in any way formally differentiated from the first on the title-page as was *Elizabeth Canning*) by its variant press figures as well as the variant use of round and square brackets, reveals that all of sheet B (pp. 1–8), and then isolated signatures C3 (13), C4 (15), C4ˇ (16), E1ˇ (26), and E4 (31) were reset for a total of thirteen reset pages. The rest of the book, including the title-page, which had been printed as H4, was reimpressed from standing type. The gap between the distribution of C4ˇ and E1ˇ is readily enough explained by the evidence from the use of round or square brackets about the pagination that the first edition had been set in sections and that sheets D and E occur within different sections; thus they did not go through the presses in seriatim order. This second edition (to be distinguished from the first only by internal variation—the most obvious of which is the treatment of the pagination) was announced, as Professor Zirker notes, on 16 December.

Professor Zirker notes only one substantive variant (at 12.1) in the reset pages of the second edition and none in the pages of standing type. Two deliberate accidental changes were made in the standing type of E2ˇ (p. 28) and on E3 (p. 29) a type dropping out of 'In- | formant' led to a seeming error which was observed but miscorrected. In short, no evidence whatever exists to indicate that Fielding made any changes in the second edition. It follows that the first is the sole true authority for the text.

In contrast to the mixed nature of the *Canning* and *Penlez* second editions, the *Enquiry* went through a completely reset second edition in which Professor Zirker finds a sufficient number of substantive differences to warrant the belief that Fielding here and there made small revisions by marking up a copy of the first edition to serve the printer of the second.

Of the six pamphlets appearing in the present volume, therefore, three are found only in one edition as the sole authority; two in mixed editions of reset and standing type, in one of which, at least, Fielding made no alterations; and finally the *Enquiry*, which was somewhat casually and sporadically revised throughout. The lack of substantive thoroughness suggests the unlikelihood that Fielding in the *Enquiry* concerned himself in any appreciable manner with changes in the accidentals in the marked copy which was used to set the second edition. Moreover, if he did, there would be an insuperable difficulty in separating any such authoritative alterations (supposing them to exist beyond the stage of mere corrections) from the normal printing-house restyling that is inevitable in any reprint. Thus the copy-text for the *Enquiry*, as for the other five pamphlets, remains the first printing (or edition) according to W. W. Greg's classic rationale that the choice of copy-text is dictated by the authority of the accidentals (their relative closeness to the lost manuscript) and that altered substantives accepted from a revised edition as authoritative are taken in as emendations within the texture of the copy-text first printing.

In these circumstances Professor Zirker has been essentially conservative in his treatment of the texts in the present volume. Changes—even those that seem desirable as restoring Fielding's general stylistic habits—have been made cautiously in the accidentals because the lack of more than a single authority forces an editor to tread a tightrope between a too slavish adherence to inconsistency beyond normal conventions and a too free emendation that could approach a modernization repugnant to the standards of critical conservative old-spelling texts. Nevertheless, in some few cases Professor Zirker has been justified in improving the consistency (from compositorial randomness) of certain forms of capitalization or spelling and in supplying or correcting a small amount of necessary punctuation.

With few exceptions, all editorial accidental as well as all substantive alterations have been recorded in the textual apparatus so that the interested reader may reconstruct the copy-text in detail, as is often necessary for certain forms of scholarship. In a few purely formal matters, however, the following editorial changes have been made silently. (1) Typographical errors such as turned letters or wrong fount are not recorded, and (2) the heading capitals and small capitals which in the originals begin each pamphlet and some of the separate sections have been ignored. (3) Throughout, necessary opening or closing quotation marks have been supplied silently, as have closing parentheses. Moreover, running quotation marks in the left margin have been omitted and quotations have been indicated according to the modern custom. This necessary modernizing of an eighteenth-century text for a modern critical reading edition extends also to the silent removal of closing quotation marks at the end of the paragraph when the quotation, in fact, continues without interruption in the next paragraph, marked as usual by opening quotation marks. (4) Single quotes have been normalized to double, as is the common practice of the copy-texts, wherever quotation is primary and direct. (5) When the apostrophe and roman 's' follow an italicized name, the roman is retained only when it indicates the contraction for 'is' but is silently normalized to italic when the possessive case is required. (6) The fount of punctuation is normalized without regard for the variable practice of the original. Pointing within an italic passage is italicized; but pointing following an italicized word that is succeeded by roman text is silently placed in roman when it is syntactically related to the roman text. (7) The ampersand and other standard abbreviations (*e.g., viz., i.e., vid.*) have been placed in the fount opposite to that of the matter to which they pertain. (8) Speech assignments, wherever contracted, have been silently expanded. (9) Final periods have been additionally supplied between true independent sentences where Fielding's printer originally used only the long dash; periods thus supplied have been placed after the last word of the sentence and before the long dash, as is the common practice of the copy-text where both sorts of punctuation are present. (10) The highly variable and unsystematic treatment in the different texts of the long dash, principally in connection with Latin quotations, has been normalized. When such a quotation with its conventional following dash is itself a complete sentence and would be concluded in standard editions by a period, then the editor places the period before the dash. When the quotation itself is not syntactically complete, in headings or when used within Fielding's own prose which continues with the same sentence following the quotation, only the dash appears and any irrelevant periods are silently omitted. Finally, when a syntactically incomplete quotation ends a Fielding sentence, the period is placed after the dash silently, without regard for the copy-text positioning. (11) In the mottoes and in Latin and Greek quotations generally the ampersand is silently expanded to *et*; the contracted suffix *q* is expanded to *-que*; titles have been expanded and italicized; author's names have been expanded; the period customarily used after the author's name has been changed to a comma where there is following matter; designations of such things as book, epistle, and verse have been englished and expanded; pronunciation marks have been removed; and in the case of Greek diphthongs modern lettering has been adopted.

A few procedures for dealing with the text may be mentioned although they involve matters that are recorded. The texts in this volume are far from consistent in their method of dealing with interjections within quotation or directly quoted speech. Sometimes an inserted 'he says' will be treated in the modern manner, with closing quotes before it and opening quotes after it for the continuation; sometimes the 'he says' or its equivalent will be inserted between parentheses to mark its separate nature from the surrounding quotations. Sometimes, however, simple commas substitute for the parentheses, so that technically there is no indication that the 'he says' is not part of the quotation, and indeed ambiguities may occur. If any single system had been employed, the editor might have been content to follow it, as a feature of the period; but since the system varies even within individual texts, it has been thought convenient to normalize this textual situation by consistently adopting the compromise but acceptable method of the time, of enclosing all such interjected material in parentheses. However, each alteration of the text in this manner is recorded so that the exact reading of the copy-text can always be ascertained by those who wish to have this information.

2. THE APPARATUS

All the textual apparatus is placed in appendices where it may be consulted at leisure by those who wish to analyze the total evidence on which the present text has been established. In the first appendix appears the List of Substantive Emendations. All verbal variation has been recorded here. Since the purpose of this list is to present at a view the major editorial departures from the copy-text, only the earliest source of the approved variant is recorded, together with the history of the copy-text reading up to its accepted emendation in the earliest source. Certain emendations not found in the collated early texts have been assigned to W, that is, to the present edition, whether or not they actually originated here or with some preceding editor. By their nature they cannot be authoritative, even though they have proved to be necessary corrections, and hence a more precise record would serve little purpose, especially since minimal independent emendation has proved necessary in the substantives themselves. The basic note provides, first, the page–line reference and the precise form of the emended reading in the present text. Following the square bracket appears the identification of the earliest source of the emendation in the texts collated. A semicolon succeeds this notation, and following this appears the rejected copy-text reading with the sigla of the texts that provide its history up to the point of emendation. In these notations certain arbitrary symbols appear. When the variant to be noted is one of punctuation, a tilde (~) takes the place of the repeated word associated with the pointing. An inferior caret ($_\wedge$) calls attention to the absence of punctuation either in the copy-text or in the early text from which the alteration was drawn. Three dots indicate one or more omitted words in a series; *om.* means the matter in question was omitted.

   The List of Accidentals Emendations follows on the record of substantive and semi-substantive emendation, and conforms to the same rules. The list includes all changes made in the copy-text except for those described as silently normalized. A list of word-divisions holds information about hyphenated compounds that will lead to an accurate reconstruction of the copy-text from the modern print. The reader may take it that any word hyphenated at the end of a line in the present text had been broken by the modern printer and that the hyphenation was not present in the copy-text unless it is separately listed and confirmed here. Correspondingly, when a word is hyphenated at the end of a line in the copy-text, the editor has been charged with ascertaining whether it is a true hyphenated compound or else an unhyphenated word that has been broken; the facts are then recorded in this list. Although certain of the editorial decisions in the matter of these copy-text readings approach the level of emendation, no record has been made of their treatment in editions other than the copy-text.

In all entries in the accidentals list, the forms of the accidentals to the right as well as to the left of the bracket accord with the system of silent normalization adopted for the edited text. Moreover, no record is made of variation in the accidentals that is not the matter being recorded. That is, if a punctuation variant alone is the question, the lemma of the word to which the pointing refers will take the form of the accidentals of the Wesleyan text regardless of the spelling or capitalization of the word in the text from which the punctuation variant was drawn. In this respect, then, the tilde to the right of the bracket signifies only the substantive and not its accidentals form in any edition other than the copy-text.

The Historical Collation follows the same conventions of the List of Emendations save that the reading to the right of the bracket after the lemma is the rejected reading of editions or printing other than the copy-text. In this listing only the substantive variants are provided for reset portions of the text, but the few accidentals alterations made in the pages of standing type are recorded. The Historical Collation does not repeat the rejected readings noted in the List of Emendations; the Historical listing, therefore, is a complementary list to that of the Emendations and between the two will be found all substantive (and some accidentals) variants in the editions listed as collated.

FREDSON BOWERS

A
CHARGE
DELIVERED TO THE
GRAND JURY,
AT THE
SESSIONS of the PEACE
HELD FOR THE
City and Liberty of *Westminster*, &c.

On THURSDAY the 29th of JUNE, 1749.

By *HENRY FIELDING*, Esq;
CHAIRMAN of the said SESSIONS.

PUBLISHED

By Order of the COURT, and at the unanimous
Request of the Gentlemen of the GRAND JURY.

LONDON:
Printed for A. MILLAR, opposite *Catherine-Street*, in
the *Strand*. 1749.

City, Borough *and Town of* Westminster *in the County* *of* Middlesex.	*At the General Quarter Session of the Peace of our Lord the King,* *holden at the Town Court-House*[1] *near* Westminster-Hall, *in and for* *the Liberty of the Dean and Chapter of the Collegiate Church of St.* Peter,[2] Westminster, *the City, Borough and Town of* Westminster, *in the County of* Middlesex, *and* St. Martin le Grand,[3] London, *on* Thursday *the Twenty-ninth Day of* June, *in the Twenty-third Year of* *the Reign of our Sovereign Lord* George *the Second, King of* Great- Britain, &c. *before* Henry Fielding, *Esq; the Right Hon.* —— George *Lord* Carpenter, *Sir* John Crosse, *Baronet,* George Huddleston, James Crofts, Gabriel Fowace, John Upton, Thomas Ellys, Thomas Smith, George Payne, William Walmsley, William Young, Peter Elers, Martin Clare, Thomas Lediard, Henry Trent, Daniel Gach, James Fraser, *Esquires, and others their* *fellows, Justices of our said Lord the King, assigned to keep the Peace in* *the said Liberty, and also to hear and determine divers Felonies,* *Trespasses, and other Misdeeds done and committed within the said* *Liberty.*

His Majesty's Justices of the Peace for this City and Liberty of *Westminster*, now
assembled at this General Quarter Session of the Peace held for the said City and
Liberty, being of Opinion that the Charge this Day given by *Henry Fielding*. Esq; the
Chairman of this Session,[4] to the Grand Jury sworn to inquire for our Sovereign
Lord the King for the Body of this City and Liberty, and to the High and Petty
Constables of the same, is a very loyal, learned, ingenious, excellent and useful
Charge, highly tending to the Service of his Majesty and Administration and
Government, have unanimously agreed and resolved, That the Thanks of this Court
be, and the same are hereby given to the said *Henry Fielding*, Esq; for his said Charge.
And we do desire that he will be pleased to cause the same to be printed and
published, for the better Information of the Inhabitants and public Officers of this
City and Liberty in the Performance of their respective Duties.[5]   *By the Court.*

FORBES[6]

---

[1] In 1752 two petitions, one from the Westminster justices of the peace and one from 'several of the
Inhabitants of the City and Liberty of Westminster', were presented to the House of Commons
requesting a bill authorizing the construction of a new Town Court House to replace the present one
which 'is small, inconvenient, and dark; and, from the Heat thereof in the Summer, and the Stench of
a common Sewer under it, and the Dampness thereof in Winter, occasioned by the Lowness of its
Situation, as well as its being often affected by Spring Tides, is rendered very unwholesome at all
Seasons of the Year' (*JHC* xxvi. 355).

[2] Westminster Abbey 'is at present a collegiate Church; and the dean and 12 prebendaries were
incorporated by the name of *The Dean and Chapter of the collegiate church of* St. Peter Westminster, by
Queen Elizabeth' (John Entick, *A New and Accurate History and Survey of London, Westminster,
Southwark and Places Adjacent*, 4 vols. [London, 1766], iv. 411–13). Still the official title of
Westminster Abbey.

'Liberty': a district enjoying special privileges, generally freedom from the jurisdiction of the
customary administrative unit. Westminster 'fell under the dean and chapter of St. Peter's in civil as
well as ecclesiastical affairs, whose jurisdiction extends over the cities and liberties of Westminster, the
precinct of St. Martin's-le-grand in London . . . all which are exempt from the jurisdiction of the
bishop of London and of the archbishop of Canterbury; but the management of the civil power has

[*for notes 2 cont. to 6 see opposite*]

A
CHARGE

Delivered to the

GRAND JURY, &c.

Gentlemen of the Grand Jury,

There is no Part in all the excellent Frame of our Constitution which an *Englishman* can, I think, contemplate with such Delight and Admiration; nothing which must fill him with such Gratitude to our earliest Ancestors, as that Branch of *British* Liberty from which, Gentlemen, you derive your Authority of assembling here on this Day.

The Institution of Juries, Gentlemen, is a Privilege which distinguishes the Liberty of *Englishmen* from those of all other Nations: For as we find no Traces of this in the Antiquities of the *Jews*, or *Greeks*, or *Romans*; so it is an Advantage, which is at present solely confined to this Country;[7] not so much, I apprehend, from the Reasons assigned by FORTESCUE, in his Book *de Laudibus*, *cap.* 29. namely, *because there are more Husbandmen, and fewer Freeholders, in other Countries*;[8] as because, other Countries have less of

been, ever since the reformation, in lay hands, elected from time to time, and confirmed by the dean and chapter' (ibid. iv. 400).

The city and liberties of Westminster included nine parishes (St Anne in Westminster, St Clement Danes, St George Hanover-square, St James in Westminster, St Margaret in Westminster, St Martin in the Fields, St Mary-le-Strand, and St Paul in Covent Garden) and the Precinct of the Savoy (ibid. iii. 300).

[3] The liberty of St Martin-le-Grand, formerly a sanctuary with extraordinary privileges, was a small section within Aldersgate Ward (in the city of London). It 'is governed, and votes for parliament men, as a part of the city of Westminster' (ibid. iii. 355).

[4] Under the moribund ecclesiastical jurisdiction of St Peter's, Fielding's title as chairman of quarter sessions would have been 'Deputy Steward of Westminster' and he would have been chosen by the high steward of Westminster and confirmed by dean and chapter.

[5] Such complimentary requests for publication customarily prefixed printed *Charges*. Customary too is the identification of jurors.

[6] Court clerk.

[7] Sir William Blackstone calls the jury system 'the grand bulwark of [every Englishman's] liberties' (*Comm.* iv. 349); and 'the glory of the English Law' (iii. 379). He notes its absence in Rome, Sparta, and Carthage (ibid.) and its gradual disappearance from 'every country on the continent' (iii. 380).

[8] Sir John Fortescue, *De Laudibus Legum Angliae*, written *c.*1470; published 1537. Fielding seems to be using the translation of Robert Mulcaster, *A Learned Commendation of the Politique lawes of England* (London, 1573 [1st edn., 1567]). The italicized phrases here are Fielding's restatement of Fortescue's observation that England's wealth and abundance have created men of honor and substance who will not perjure themselves (ch. 29, 'Why inquests are not made by iuries of xii menne in other Realme, as well as in Englande'). But the two following italicized passages, except for modernization of orthography, are identical to Mulcaster's translation.

Fortescue (1394?–1476?), chief justice of the King's Bench and adherent to the Lancastrian cause,

Freedom than this; and being for the most Part subjected to the absolute Wills of their Governors, hold their Lives, Liberties, and Properties at the Discretion of those Governors, and not under the Protection of certain Laws. In such Countries it would be absurd to look for any Share of Power in the Hands of the People.

And if Juries in general be so very signal a Blessing to this Nation, as FORTESCUE, in the Book I have just cited, thinks it: *A Method*, says he, *much more available and effectual for the Trial of Truth, than is the Form of any other Laws of the World, as it is farther from the Danger of Corruption and Subornation;*[9] what, Gentlemen, shall we say of the Institution of Grand Juries,[1] by which an *Englishman*, so far from being convicted, cannot be even tried, not even put on his Trial in any Capital Case, at the Suit of the Crown; unless, perhaps, in one or two very special Instances, till Twelve Men at the least have said on their Oaths, that there is a probable Cause for his Accusation![2] Surely, we may in a kind of Rapture cry out with FORTESCUE, speaking of the Second Jury, *Who then can unjustly die in* England *for any criminal Offence, seeing he may have so many Helps for the Favour of his Life, and that none may condemn him, but his Neighbours, good and lawful Men, against whom he hath no Manner of Exception.*[3]

To trace the Original of this great and singular Privilege, or to say when and how it began, is not an easy Task; so obscure indeed are the Foot-steps of it through the first Ages of our History, that my Lord *Hale*,[4] and even my

---

followed Margaret of Anjou into exile. *De Laudibus* takes the form of a dialogue between Fortescue and Prince Edward, son of Margaret and Henry VI. It is in effect a comparative study of English and French forms of government and seems to have been written to instruct the layman in the elements of law. It is one of the 'books of authority' for English common law. *De Laudibus* is not listed in Baker.

[9] *De Laudibus*, trans. Mulcaster (London, 1573), p. 75. 'A Method' is Fielding's interpolation.

[1] The grand jury was eliminated from the English legal system in 1933. Its functions are now primarily performed by magistrates.

[2] 'For so tender is the law of England of the lives of the subjects, that no man can be convicted at the suit of the king of any capital offence, unless by an unanimous voice of twenty-four of his equals and neighbours: that is, by twelve at least of the grand jury, in the first place, assenting to the accusation: and afterwards, by the whole petit jury, of twelve more, finding him guilty, upon his trial' (Blackstone, *Comm.* iv. 306). Cf. Fielding's description in *Elizabeth Canning* (p. 283 ff.) of the two juries and legal process in capital cases generally.

For the 'one or two very special Instances', see William Hawkins (1673–1746), *A Treatise of the Pleas of the Crown*, 2nd edn. (London, 1724, 1726; 1st edn. 1716, 1724), ii. 211 ff.: 'where a man may be tried at the suit of the King for a capital Offence without any Indictment'. Fielding owned the second edition of Hawkins 'with a great number of MSS Notes by Mr. Fielding' (Baker, no. 102) and a four-vol. abridgement, 1728, 'interleaved with MSS. notes by Mr. Fielding' (Baker, no. 509). Fielding uses Hawkins's treatise throughout the *Charge*. I have used the second edition, citing it hereafter as 'Hawkins'. Percy H. Winfield says that 'Hawkins's work is deservedly of high authority and is still cited' (*The Chief Sources of English Legal History* [Cambridge, Mass., 1925], p. 326).

[3] *De Laudibus*, trans. Mulcaster, p. 63.

[4] Fielding's reference is to Sir Matthew Hale's *Historia Placitorum Coronae* (published posthumously; ed. Sollom Emlyn, 2 vols. [London, 1736]), which is a major legal authority throughout the *Charge*, *Bosavern Penlez*, and, especially, the *Enquiry*. Hale frequently discusses juries in *HPC*, but not from an historical point of view. The edition cited is no. 131 in the Baker catalogue and hereafter is cited as

Lord *Coke*, seem to have declined it. Nay, this latter in his Account of the Second or Petty Jury, is very succinct; and contents himself with *Co. Lit.* saying, that it is very antient and before the Conquest.[5] 155. *b.*

Spelman in his Life of *Alfred, lib.* 2. Pag. 71. will have that Prince to have been the first Founder of Juries;[6] but in Truth they are much older, and very probably had some Existence even among the *Britons*. The *Normans* likewise had antiently the Benefit of Juries, as appears in the *Custumier de Normandy*; and something like Grand Juries too we find in that Book under the Title *Suit de Murdyr*.[7]

Bracton, who wrote in the Reign of HENRY the Third, in his Book *de Corona, chap.* 1. gives a plain Account of this Matter:[8] And by him it appears,

'Hale'. In *The History of the Common Law of England* (published posthumously, 1713; ed. Charles M. Gray [Chicago and London, 1971]), however, Hale discusses the history of the jury system and cites *The Grand Contumier* [*sic*] *of Normandy* (see below, n. 7). For Hale see General Introduction, p. xxxii.

[5] 'This Trial of the Fact, per duodecim liberos & legales homines is very ancient. For hear what the Law was before the Conquest . . .' (*The First Part of the Institvtes of the Lawes of England, or, A Commentarie vpon Littelton* . . . [London, 1628], bk. II. ch. 12, fo. 156a). Coke also cites Fortescue: 'For the institution and right use of this triall by 12. men, and wherefore other Countries have them not, and this triall excels others. See Fortescue at large, cap. 25 & c. 29' (ibid.). For Coke see General Introduction. Coke's *Institutes* were in Fielding's library (Baker, no. 268) and are hereafter cited as *Inst.*

[6] Sir John Spelman (1594–1643) was the son of the famous antiquarian, Sir Henry Spelman. In his *Life of Alfred* (1678), as Fielding states, he ascribes the founding of the jury system to Alfred: 'from . . . this King [Alfred], many notable Parts of our Law . . . derive their first original. For Example: that Law, which . . . we gratulate to our Country, and prefer before the Laws of all our Neighbour-Nations, in point of Equality of Tryal, (I mean the Law of Tryal by the Verdict of 12 of our Peers or Equals) . . .' (*The Life of Alfred the Great, by Sir John Spelman, Kt. From the Original Manuscript in the Bodleian Library* . . . by the Publisher Thomas Hearne [Oxford, 1709], ii. 106).

[7] The allusions to juries and to grand juries both appear in ch. LXVIII, 'De Suyte de meurdre' (*Le grand coustumier du pays et duche de Normendie* [Rouen, 1539]). That to juries: 'Telle engste doibt estre faicte par vingt et quatre loyaulx hommes au moins / qui ne soient pas souspeconneux par amour ne par haine. Et la semonse doibt estre faicte par layal sergēt / qui ne soit corumpu par don / ne par loyer / par priere / par amour / ne par haine . . .' (fo. xcia); that to grand juries: 'Se enqueste doibt estre soustenue de larcī ou de roberie layaulx jureurs doibuent estre semons de la ou celuy qui est accuse a converse / et de la ou len dict q̄il fit le larcin, et quilz sachent la verite de ses faictz et de sa vie . . .' (fo. xciia).

Sir Frederick Pollock and Frederic William Maitland (*The History of English Law*, 2nd edn. [Cambridge, 1952], i. 65) say about this work only that it is one of the few Norman books on law and dates from the 13th century. Blackstone (*Comm.* i. 106) calls it 'an ancient book of very great authority' which describes the ducal customs of Normandy. In the 'Proeme' to the *Second Part of the Institutes*, Coke says that he has 'sometime in this and other Parts of the Institutes, cited the *Grand Custumier de Normandy* . . . being a Book compounded as well of the Laws of *England* . . . as of divers Customes of the Duchie of *Normandie*, which book was composed in the raign [*sic*] of King H. 3. viz. about 40 yeares after the Coronation of King Richard the first . . . about 138. yeares after the Conquest.'

[8] Henry of Bratton (d. 1268; generally known as Bracton), *De Legibus et consuetudinibus Angliae* (first published 1569; repr. 1640. The latter edition is listed in Baker, no. 86). *De Corona* is one of the 'tracts' into which Bracton's treatise is divided. His account of the formation and duties of juries may be found in *On the Laws and Customs of England*, ed. George E. Woodbine, trans., with revisions and notes, by Samuel E. Thorne (Cambridge, mass. [1968], ii. 327 ff. [fos. 116a ff.]).

'Bracton's book is the crown and flower of English mediaeval jurisprudence' (Pollock and Maitland, i. 206). Sir William Holdsworth states that 'Hale put the authority of Bracton's treatise on a level with that of the records of the courts, and Blackstone followed Hale in recognizing it as authoritative' (*Some*

that the Grand Juries before the Justices in *Eyre*,[9] differed very little at that time from what they now are, before Justices assigned to keep the Peace, Oyer, and Terminer, and Goal-Delivery,[1] unless in the Manner of chusing them, and unless in one other Respect; there being then a Grand Jury, sworn for every Hundred;[2] whereas at present one serves for the whole County, Liberty,[3] &c.

But before this Time, our Ancestors were sensible of the great Importance of this Privilege, and extremely jealous of it, as appears by the 29th Chapter of the Great Charter, granted by King JOHN, and confirmed by HENRY the Third.[4] For thus my Lord *Coke*, 2 *Instit.* 46. expounds that Chapter. *Nullus liber homo capiatur*,[5] &c. "No Man shall be taken, that is (says he) restrained of Liberty, by Petition or Suggestion to the King and his Council; unless it be by Indictment or Presentment of good and lawful Men, where such Deeds be done."

And so just a Value have our Ancestors always set on this great Branch of our Liberties, and so jealous have they been of any Attempt to diminish it,

---

Makers of English Law [Cambridge, 1938], p. 23). Current knowledge and opinion concerning Bracton are conveniently summarized in Theodore F. T. Plucknett, *A Concise History of the Common Law* (1929), 5th edn. (Boston, 1956), pp. 258 ff.

[9] 'In Eyre': *in itinere*, on a journey. The eyre system originated in the 12th century as an institution whereby the king could enquire into 'all matters of possible profit' due the crown. Visitations by the king's commissioned justices generally took place every seven years and represented the 'coming of royal power, . . . before [which] would appear the fullest assembly of the county' (S. F. C. Milsom, *Historical Foundations of the Common Law* [London, 1969], p. 17). According to Giles Jacob (*A New Law-Dictionary*, 10th edn. [London, 1782]), justices in eyre were commissioned to hear a wide variety of causes, but 'such causes especially, as were termed *pleas of the crown*'.

[1] The infrequency of visitation by justices in eyre meant long delays before accused could be tried. This problem was solved by the use of 'special commissions, known generally as *oyer* and *terminer* and jail delivery' (Milsom, *Historical Foundations*, p. 362). The former commission was 'directed to certain persons upon any great riot, insurrections, heinous misdemeanors, or trespasses committed'; the latter to those 'to hear and determine all causes appertaining to such, who for any offence are cast into gaol' (Jacob, *A New Law-Dictionary*). The functions of both commissions were gradually assumed by assize judges who, with the local justice of peace in his quarter sessions, administered all local justice in the 18th century.

[2] '*Hundreds* were so called because there was a Jurisdiction over Ten Tithings, or an Hundred Families dwelling in some neighbouring Towns' (Thomas Wood, *An Institute of the Laws of England*, 2 vols. [London, 1720], i. 4.). The jurisdiction of the hundred court had largely passed to that of the county by the 18th century.

Though Fielding seems scornful of Wood's *Institutes* in *Joseph Andrews* ('The Surgeon drew his Knowledge from those inestimable Fountains, called the *Attorney's Pocket-Companion*, and Mr. *Jacob's Law-Tables*; *Barnabas* trusted entirely to *Wood's Institutes*' [I. xv. 68–9]), Baker (no. 276) lists an undated three-vol. edn. '*interleaved with MSS. notes of Mr. Fielding*'.

[3] See above, p. 2 n. 2.

[4] Fielding refers to the 'fourth Great Charter' cited by 'old authors as the charter or statute of the ninth year of Henry III (1225), which reflects modifications in favor of the crown included in reissues of Magna Charta in 1216 and 1217' (Plucknett, *History of Common Law*, p. 23).

[5] The opening words of what is Ch. 39 in modern versions of Magna Charta: 'No free man shall be arrested or imprisoned or disseised or outlawed or exiled or in any way victimised, neither will we attack him or send anyone to attack him, except by the lawful judgment of his peers or by the law of the land' (*English Historical Documents*, ed. Mary Rothwell, in *English Historical Documents*, ed. David C. Douglas [New York, 1975], iii. 320).

that when a Commission to punish Rioters in a summary Way, was awarded in the Second Year of RICHARD the Second,[6] "it was," says Mr. *Lambard* in his *Eirenarcha*,[7] fol. 305. "even in the self-same Year of the same King, resumed, as a Thing over-hard (says that Writer) to be borne, that a Freeman should be imprisoned without an Indictment, or other Trial, by his Peers, as *Magna Charta* speaketh; until that the Experience of greater Evils had prepared and made the Stomach of the Commonwealth able and fit to digest it."

And a hard Morsel surely it must have been, when the Commonwealth could not digest it in that turbulent Reign, which of all others in our History, seems to have afforded the most proper Ingredients to make it palatable; in a Reign moreover when the Commonwealth seemed to have been capable of swallowing and digesting almost any thing; when Judges were so prostitute as to acknowledge the King to be above the Law;[8] and when a Parliament, which even *Echard* censures,[9] and for which Mr. *Rapin*, with a juster Indignation tells us, he knows no Name odious enough, made no scruple to sacrifice to the Passions of the King, and his Ministers, the Lives of the most distinguished Lords of the Kingdom, as well as the Liberties and Privileges of the People.[1] Even in that Reign, Gentlemen, our Ancestors could not, as

[6] 2 Rich. II, c. 6 (1378). The title of the act is 'Commissions shall be awarded to arrest rioters and other persons offensive to the peace, and to imprison them'. Repealed 2 Rich. II, st. 2. c. 2 (1379).

[7] William Lambarde (1536–1601), *Eirenarcha, or of the Office of the Justices in foure bookes* (1581; 12 editions by 1619. None listed in Baker). The passage quoted appears in III. i. 314–15 (London, 1610). 'The enormous success of the 'Eirenarcha' was both immediate and permanent. Lambard . . . [became] the basis for the later seventeenth-century treatises of which Michael Dalton's 'Countrey Ivstice' [1618] was the most famous' (B. H. Putnam, *Early Treatises on the Practice of the Justices of the Peace in the Fifteenth and Sixteenth Centuries*, in Oxford Studies in Social and Legal History, ed. Sir Paul Vinogradoff, vol. vii [Oxford, 1924], p. 218). Blackstone could still recommend *Eirenarcha* to the student as a book 'wherein he will find everything relative to [the office of the Justice of peace], both in ancient and modern practice, collected with great care and accuracy, and disposed in a most clear and judicious method' (*Comm.* i. 354).

[8] Planning to pack the Parliament of 1397, Richard II asked his assembled judges 'whether he had not power to turn out the fourteen commissioners appointed by Parliament, and annul such as were to his prejudice? They replied, The king was above the laws.' M. Rapin de Thoyras, *The History of England*, trans. N. Tindal, 4th edn. (London, 1757), iv. 44. Rapin's *Histoire d'Angleterre* (1723–5) was translated by Nicholas Tindal (1725–31) and there were several continuations. Though Voltaire thought it impartial, it was congenial to Whig readers and remained the standard history until Hume. Fielding's allusions to Rapin in *Joseph Andrews* (III. i. 185) and *Tom Jones* (VI. ii. 273) are satirical, but he found it useful, especially in the *Enquiry*, and owned a two-vol. edn. of 1732 (Baker, no. 308).

[9] Lawrence Echard (1670?–1730), *History of England*, 2 vols. (1707 and 1718), 3rd edn. (the edn. listed in Baker, no. 307), p. 169, 'censures' the Parliament of 1397 which 'revers'd every Thing of Moment enacted nine Years before by that which was called the *Unmerciful Parliament*' and condemned to death as traitors the lords Warwick, Arundel, and Glocester. 'Even' Echard, because of the strong Tory bias of his *History*. Partridge owns vol. ii of Echard's *Roman History* (*Tom Jones*, VIII. v. 421) and Sophia's aunt has read both volumes (VI. ii. 273). The *Roman History* is also cited contemptuously in *A Journey from This World to the Next*. In *Joseph Andrews* (III. i. 185) Echard is included among those historians who are romancers in disguise. His *History of England* is cited in the *Enquiry*, below, p. 85.

[1] 'If the parliament of 1386 [1388–9], deserved to be called the merciless, I know no name odious enough for this [parliament of 1397]. By a manifest prevarication, this assembly made no scruple to

Mr. *Lambard* remarks, be brought by any Necessity of the Times, to give up, in any single Instance, this their invaluable Privilege.

Another considerable Attempt to deprive the Subject of the Benefit of Grand Juries was made in the eleventh Year of HENRY the Seventh. The Pretence of this Act of Parliament, was the wilful Concealments of Grand Jurors, in their Inquests; and by it "Power was given to the Justices of Assize in their Sessions, and to the Justices of Peace in every County, upon Information for the King, to hear and determine all Offences and Contempts (saving Treason, Murder or Felony) by any Person against the Effect of any Statute."[2]

My Lord *Coke* in his 4th *Institute* fol. 40. sets forth this Act at large, not as a Law which in his time had any Force, but *in Terrorem*; and, as he himself says, that the like should never be attempted in any future Parliament.[3]

"This Act (says Lord COKE) had a fair flattering Preamble; but in the Execution, tended diametrically contrary; *viz.* to the high Displeasure of Almighty GOD; and to the great Let, nay, the utter Subversion of the Common Law; namely, by depriving the Subject of that great Privilege of being indicted and tryed by a Jury of their Countrymen."[4]

By Pretext of this Law, says the great Writer I have just cited, EMPSON and DUDLEY did commit upon the Subject insufferable Pressures and Oppressions.[5] And we read in History, that soon after the Act took place, Sir WILLIAM CAPEL, Alderman of *London*, who was made the first Object of its Tyranny, was fined Two thousand seven hundred Pounds, Sixteen hundred of which he actually paid to the King, by way of Composition. A vast Sum in those Days, to be imposed for a Crime so minute, that scarce any Notice is taken of it in History.[6]

Our Ancestors, however, bore not long this Invasion on their Liberties; for in the very first Year of K. HENRY VIII. this flagitious Act was repealed,[7] and

sacrifice to the passions of the king and his ministers, the most distinguished lords of the kingdom, as well as the liberties and privileges of the people' (Rapin, iv. 60).

[2] 11 Hen. VII, c. 3. A nearly verbatim quotation of the entire act.

[3] 'This statute of 11 H. 7. we have recited, and shewed the just inconveniences thereof, to the end, that the like should never hereafter be attempted in any Court of Parliament. And that others might avoid the fearfull end of those two time-servers, Empson and Dudley' (*IV Inst.* 41). *In Terrorem*: 'as a warning'.

[4] *IV Inst.* 39–40.

[5] Except for the interpolated 'says . . . cited', this sentence is verbatim from *IV Inst.* 41. Because they did not need indictments from a grand jury, Sir Richard Empson (d. 1510) and Edmund Dudley (1462?–1510) were able to fine and intimidate men dangerous to Henry VII. By 1509 they were 'the most hated men in England' (G. R. Elton, *Reform and Reformation: England, 1509–1557* [Cambridge, Mass., 1977], pp. 7, 17).

[6] In 1494 Henry VII 'extorted large sums from private persons, by forfeitures upon penal laws . . . The first he attacked in this manner was Sir William Capel, alderman of London, who was fined two thousand seven hundred pounds, and forced to compound with the king for sixteen hundred' (Rapin, v. 302). His 'minute' crime consisted of accepting false coin and not punishing the coiner (ibid., 358).

[7] I Hen. VIII, c. 6.

the Advisers of all the Extortions committed by it were deservedly sacrificed to the public Resentment.[8]

Gentlemen, I shall mention but two more Attacks on this most valuable of all our Liberties; the first of which was indeed the greatest of all, I mean that cursed Court of Star-Chamber, which was erected under the same King.[9]

I shall not before you, Gentlemen, enter into a Contest with my Lord COKE,[1] whether this Court had a much older Existence, or whether it first begun under the Statute of 3 HENRY VII.[2] For my Part I clearly think the latter.

1. Because the Statute which erects it mentions no such Court as then existing, and most manifestly speaks the Language of Creation, not of Confirmation.[3]

2. Because it was expresly so understood by the Judges, within Five Years after the Statute was made, as appears by the Year-Book of 8 HENRY VII. *Pasch. Fol.* 13. *Plac.* 7.[4]

Lastly, Because all our Historians and Law-writers before that Time are silent concerning any such Court; for as to the Records and Acts of Parliament cited by my Lord COKE, they are most evidently to be applied

---

[8] '[Empson and Dudley] were both indicted of high Treason both by the Common Law, and Act of Parliament, and in the [2.] yeare of H. 8. they lost both their heads' (*IV Inst.* 199).

[9] The Court of Star Chamber was a conciliar court to which complaints could be brought that common-law courts could not satisfy. Its name derives from the room at Westminster, 'camera stellata', in which it commonly sat. Its origins are obscure, but they date well before the reign of Henry VII. See Plucknett, *History of Common Law*, pp. 181 ff.; G. R. Elton, *Reform and Reformation*, p. 34; and *England under the Tudors* (London, 1955, repr. 1965), pp. 61–2; and J. H. Baker, *An Introduction to English Legal History* (London, 1971), p. 51. Its activities and powers radically increased under the direction of Cardinal Wolsey.

[1] Coke's account of Star Chamber appears in *IV Inst.* 60 ff.

[2] 3 Hen. VII, c. 1. To call the antiquity of the Court of Star Chamber into question by asserting that it had been created by this act of 1487 was central to 17th-century arguments for its abolition made by parliamentary statesmen opposed to prerogative government, common lawyers jealous of a rival judicature, and Puritans who had suffered its persecution. See Holdsworth, *History of English Law*, i. 492–516. The Court of Star Chamber was abolished in 1641.

[3] '. . . it is ordained . . . by the authority of the said parliament, That the chancellor and treasurer of *England* . . . and keeper of the King's privy seal . . . calling to them a bishop, and a temporal lord of the King's most honorable council, and the two chief justices of the King's bench . . . have authority to call before them . . . mis-doers . . . [and] punish them . . . as if they were thereof convict after the due order to the law' (3 Hen. VII, c. 1.).

Fielding's reading of this act is conventional and comprehensible, but mistaken. Plucknett states that 'Old writers took it [3 Hen. VII. c. 1.] as the statutory origin of the Court of Star Chamber, principally on the strength of a marginal title on the statute roll (repeated in the margin of *Statutes at Large*) which reads "*Pro camera stellata.*" So firm was this belief that when the court was abolished in 1641 the act of 1487 was repealed. It has now been shown that this act has no connection with the Star Chamber, and that the marginal title is an addition in a later handwriting' (*History of Common Law*, p. 182).

[4] '. . . the sudden opinion in 8 H. 7 and of others not observing the said distinction between Acts Declaratory of proceedings in an ancient Court, and Acts Introductory of a new law in raising of a new Court, is both contrary to law, and continuall experience' (*IV Inst.* 62).

Pasch[alis]: 'Easter Term'. *Plac*[ita]: 'plea'. For the Year Books see below, p. 127 n. 1.

only to the King and Council, to whom, in old Time, Complaints were, in very extraordinary Cases, preferred.[5]

This old Court, my Lord COKE himself confesses,[6] sat very rarely; so rarely indeed, that there are no Traces left of its Proceedings, at least of any such as were afterwards had under the Authority of the Statute. Had this Court had an original Existence in the Constitution, I do not see why the great Lawyer is so severe against the before-mentioned Act of the 11th of HENRY VII. or how he can, with any Propriety, call the Liberty of being accused and tried only by Juries, the Birth-right of an *English* Subject.[7]

The other Instance was that of the High Commission Court, instituted by Parliament in the first Year of Queen ELIZABETH.[8]

This Act likewise pretends to refer to an Authority in being. The Title of it is, An Act restoring to the Crown the antient Jurisdiction, &c.[9] By which, saith Lord COKE, 4 *Inst.* 325. the Nature of the Act doth appear; *viz.* that it is an Act of Restitution.

And hence the Court of Common-Pleas, in the Reign of JAMES I. well argued, that the Act being meant to restore to the Crown the antient ecclesiastical Jurisdiction, the Commissioners could derive no other Power from it than before belonged to that ecclesiastical Jurisdiction.[1]

But however necessary, as my Lord COKE says,[2] this act might have been
4 Inst. 326.   at its first Creation, or however the Intention of the Legislature might have been to restrain it, either as to Time or Persons, certain it is, that the Commissioners extended its Jurisdiction in many Cases, to the great Grievance of the Subject, and to the depriving them of that Privilege which I have just mentioned to be the Birth-right of an *Englishman*.

The Uses made of these Courts, and particularly under that unhappy Prince CHARLES I. need not be mentioned. They are but too well known. Let it suffice, that the Spirit of our Ancestors at last prevailed over these

---

[5] The hearing of special complaints by king and council was essentially the original function of Star Chamber.

[6] *IV Inst.* 61.

[7] See above, p. 8.

[8] I. Eliz., c. 1. The Court of High Commission 'consisted mainly of bishops and devoted itself largely to the criminal side of the ex-papal jurisdiction. Its proceedings were later likened (with some justice) to those of the continental inquisitions, so severely did it search for ecclesiastical offenders' (Plucknett, *History of Common Law*, p. 185; see also Holdsworth i. 605 ff.).

[9] The title in full is, 'An act to restore to the crown the ancient jurisdiction over the estate ecclesiastical and spiritual, and abolishing all sovereign powers repugnant to the same'.

[1] Coke states that 'the whole Court of Common pleas Pasch. 9 *Jacobi Regis*, upon often conference and mature deliberation' confirmed the many instances in which civil courts denied the jurisdiction of the ecclesiastical court (*IV Inst.* 335).

[2] Coke states that the 'necessity' leading to the establishment of the Court of High Commission was in reference to a past time when 'all the Bishops, and most of the Clergy of England, being then Popish, it was necessary to raise a Commission to deprive them, that would not deprive themselves'. Consequently, 'as necessity did cause this Commission, so it should be exercised but upon necessity, for it was never intended that it should be a continual standing Commission' (*IV Inst.* 326).

Invasions of their Liberties, and these Courts were for ever abolished.[3]

And, Gentlemen, if we have just Reason to admire the great Bravery and Steadiness of those our Ancestors, in defeating all the Attempts of Tyranny against this excellent Branch of our Constitution, we shall have no less Reason, I apprehend, to extol that great Wisdom, which they have from time to time demonstrated, in well ordering and regulating their Juries; so as to preserve them as clear as possible from all Danger of Corruption. In this Light, Gentlemen, we ought to consider the several Laws by which the Morals, the Character, the Substance, and good Demeanor of Jurors are regulated. These Jurors, Gentlemen, must be good and lawful Men, of Reputation and Substance in their Country, chosen at the Nomination of neither Party, absolutely disinterested and indifferent[4] in the Cause which they are to try.[5] Upon the whole, the Excellence of our Constitution, and the great Wisdom of our Laws, which FORTESCUE, my Lord COKE, and many other great Writers, have so highly extolled,[6] is in no one Instance so truly admirable as in this Institution of our Juries.

I hope, Gentlemen, I shall not be thought impertinent, in having taken up so much of your Time to shew you the great Dignity and Importance of that Office which you are now assembled here to execute; the Duties of which it is incumbent on me concisely to open to you; and this I shall endeavour in the best Manner I am able.

The Duty, Gentlemen, of a Grand Juror, is to enquire of all Crimes and Misdemeanors whatsoever, which have been committed in the County or Liberty for which he serves as a Grand Juror,[7] and which are anywise cognizable by the Court in which he is sworn to enquire.

And this Enquiry is in a twofold Manner, by way of Indictment, and by way of Presentment.

Which two Words, Mr. LAMBARD, *fol.* 461. thus explains:

A Presentment, says he, I take to be a meer Determination of the Jurors

---

[3] Opposition to the Court of High Commission had been growing since the last two decades of the 16th century. Laud's attempt to strengthen the court (1629–40) confirmed Puritan and Parliamentary opposition to the Court and ensured its downfall in 1641.

[4] 'Impartial'.

[5] Both Hale (ii. 152 ff.) and Hawkins (ii. 215 ff.) review the legal qualifications of a grand juror. Cf. *Elizabeth Canning*, below, p. 284.

[6] Coke's maxim, 'Lex est summa Ratio' (*I Inst.* 319b), or 'The Common Law is the Absolute Perfection of Reason', lies behind such enthusiastic encomiums as the following: '[The] Law of England is nothing else but an artificial Perfection of Reason; and therefore my Lord Coke tells us, If all the Reason that is dispersed into so many several Heads were united into one, yet he could not make such Law as the Law of England is, because by many successions of Ages it has been fined and refined, by an infinite number of Grave and Wise Men' (Sir Harebotle Grimston, 'Epistle Dedicatory' to Keble's *Reports* [see below, p. 15 n. 4]). Fielding quotes Coke on this topic, *Amelia*, I. ii. 15. For an acute commentary on the implications of such attitudes, see Daniel J. Boorstin, *The Mysterious Science of the Law* (1941; repr. Boston, 1958).

[7] 'The grand jury are sworn *ad inquirendum pro corpore comitatûs*, and therefore regularly they cannot inquire of a fact done out of that county' (Hale, ii. 163).

themselves; and an Indictment is the Verdict of the Jurors, grounded upon the Accusation of a third Person: So that a Presentment is but a Declaration of the Jurors, without any Bill offered before; and an Indictment is their finding of a Bill of Accusation to be true.[8]

The usual Method of Charge hath been to run over the several Articles, or Heads of Crimes, which might possibly become subject to the Enquiry of the Grand Jury.

This we find in BRACTON, who writ so long ago as the Reign of HENRY III. was the Practice of the Justices in Eyre, *l.* 3. *c.* 1.[9] And my Lord COKE says, 4 *Inst.* 183. That the Charge to be given at the Sessions of the Peace consisteth of two Parts; Laws Ecclesiastical for the Peace of the Church, and Laws Civil and Temporal for the Peace of the Land. And Mr. LAMBARD, in his *Eirenarcha*, gives the whole Form of the Charge at Length, in which he recapitulates every Article which was at that Time enquirable in the Sessions.[1]

But, Gentlemen, I think I may be excused at present from taking up so much of your Time; for tho' we are assembled to exercise the Jurisdiction of a very antient and honourable Liberty, yet, as there is another Sessions of Justices within that County of which this Liberty is a Part, before whom indictments for all Crimes of the deeper Dye are usually preferred,[2] it seems rather to savour of Ostentation than Utility, to run over those Articles which in great Probability will not come before you.

And indeed a perfect Knowledge of the Law in these Matters is not necessary to a Grand Juror; for in all Cases of Indictments, whether for a greater or lesser, a public or private Crime, the Business of a Grand Jury is only to attend to the Evidence for the King; and if on that Evidence there shall appear a probable Cause for the Accusation, they are to find the Bill true, without listening to any Circumstances of Defence, or to any Matter of Law.[3]

And therefore my Lord HALE, *vol.* 2. *fol.* 158. puts this Case. "If *A.* be killed by *B.* so that the Person of the Slayer and Slain be certain; and a Bill of Murder be presented to the Grand Jury, regularly they ought to find the Bill

---

[8] Lambarde, *Eirenarcha*, ed. cit., IV. v. 485.

[9] *De Legibus*, ii. 327 (fo. 115b) has as its heading 'How the justices ought to proceed in their eyre and in what order' and describes instructions justices ought to address to 'the greater men of the county' and to jurors.

[1] *Eirenarcha*, IV, iv. 406–84.

[2] In the *Charge*, Fielding is concerned only with misdemeanours against (to use his conventional division) 'the Divine Being', the crown, and against the individual. 'Crimes of the deeper Dye' would be 'preferred' before the Assembly of Justices in General Sessions at Hicks's Hall in St John Street, Clerkenwell (see E. G. Dowdell, *A Hundred Years of Quarter Sessions* [Cambridge, 1932], p. 1 and General Introduction, above, p. xxiii).

[3] 'But the grand inquest before justices of peace, gaol-delivery, or *oyer* and *terminer* ought only to hear the evidence for the king, and in case there be *probable* evidence (a), they ought to find the bill, because it is but an accusation, and the party is to be put upon his trial afterwards' (Hale, ii. 157).

for *Murder,* and not for *Manslaughter,* or *Se defendendo;*[4] because otherwise Offences may be smothered without due Trial; and when the Party comes on his Trial the whole Fact will be examined before the Court and the Petty Jury; for if a Man kills *B.* in his own Defence, or *Per Infortunium,*[5] or possibly in executing the Process of Law upon an Assault made upon him, or in his own Defence on the Highway, or in Defence of his House against those that come to rob him (in which three last Cases it is neither Felony nor Forfeiture, but upon Not Guilty pleaded he ought to be acquited) yet if the Grand Inquest find an *Ignoramus* upon the Bill, or find the Special Matter, whereby the Prisoner is dismissed and discharged, he may nevertheless be indicted for Murder seven Years after;"[6] whereas, if upon a proper Finding he had been acquitted, he could never afterwards be again arraigned without having the Plea of *Autrefoits acquit.*

This Doctrine of the learned Chief Justice you will apply to whatever Case may come before you: for wherever you shall find probable Cause, upon the Oaths of the King's Witnesses, you will not discharge your Office without finding the Bill to be true, shewing no Regard to the Nature of the Crime, or the Degree of the Guilt; which are Matters proper for the Cognizance and Determination of the Court only.

I must not, however, omit, on the Authority of the last-mentioned Judge, "that if, upon the hearing the King's Evidence, or upon your own Knowledge of the Incredibility of the Witnesses you shall be dissatisfied, you may then return the Bill *Ignoramus.*"[7]

H. P. C.
ii. 157.

It is true my Lord HALE confines this to Indictments for capital Offences; but I see no Reason why it may not be extended to any Indictment whatever.[8]

One Caution more occurs on this Head of Indictment; and it is the Duty of Secrecy. To have revealed the King's Counsel disclosed to the Grand Jurors was formerly taken to be Felony; nay, Justice SHARD, in the 27th Year of the *Book of Assises, Placit.* 63. doubted whether it was not Treason; and tho' at this Day the Law be not so severe, yet is this still a very great

---

[4] 'self-defence'.

[5] 'by misadventure'.

[6] In quoting Hale, Fielding omits a few details. The clause following the quoted passage summarizes what Hale says in his next paragraph: 'But if the grand jury had found the bill for murder, . . . and the party pleading not guilty the special matter is given in evidence, and the petty jury find the special matter, (or in the three last cases find him not guilty, as they may,) this acquittal upon this finding will be a good plea of *autrefoits aquit,* and he shall never be arraigned for it again' (ii. 158).

autrefois acquit ('previously acquitted'): one of the possible pleas to an indictment of felony based on the maxim that 'a Man shall not be brought into Danger of his Life for one and the same Offence, more than once' (Hawkins, ii. 368).

[7] Fielding adapts Hale's statement to the form of his direct address, changing 'they' to 'you'. Fielding's marginal citation 'H.P.C.', is to Hale's *Historia Placitorum Coronae.*

[8] Fielding recommends no more than common procedure: 'When the grand jury have heard the evidence, if they think it is a groundless accusation, they used formerly to indorse on the back of the bill, "*ignoramus;*" or, we know nothing of it: intimating, that though the facts might possibly be true, that truth did not appear to them' (Blackstone, *Comm.* iv. 305. See also Wood, *Institutes,* ii. 1066).

Misdemeanor, and fineable as such, and is moreover a manifest Breach of your Oath.[9]

I come now, Gentlemen, to the Second Branch of your Duty, namely, that of presenting all Offences which shall come to your Knowledge.

And this is much more painful, and of greater Difficulty than the former; for here you are obliged, without any direct Accusation, to inform yourselves as well as is possible of the Truth of the Fact, and in some measure likewise to be conusant[1] of those Laws which subject Offences to your Presentment.

Upon this Head therefore I shall beg Leave to remind you of those Articles which seem to be most worthy of your Enquiry, at this Time; for indeed it would be useless and tedious to enumerate the whole Catalogue of Misdemeanours that are to be found in our Statutes; many of which, though still in Force, are, by the Changes of Times and Fashions, become antiquated, and of little Use. *Cessante ratione Legis, cessat & ipsa Lex*;[2] and there are some accidental and temporary Evils which at particular Seasons have, like an epidemic Distemper, affected Society, but have afterwards disappeared, or at least made very faint Efforts to corrupt the public Morals. The Laws made to suppress such, tho' very wholesome and necessary at the Time of their Creation, become obsolete with the Evil which occasioned them, and which they were intended to cure. But, Gentlemen, there are Evils of a more durable Kind, which rather resemble chronical than epidemic Diseases; and which have so inveterated themselves in the Blood of the Body Politic, that they are perhaps never to be totally eradicated.[3] These it will be always the Duty of the Magistrate to palliate and keep down as much as possible. And these, Gentlemen, are the Misdemeanours of which you are to present as many as come to your Knowledge.

And first, Gentlemen, I will remind you of presenting all Offences committed immediately against the Divine Being; for tho' all Crimes do include in them some Degree of Sin, and may therefore be considered as Offences against the Almighty; yet there are some more directly levelled at his Honour, and which the Temporal Laws do punish as such.

And 1. all blasphemous Expressions against any one of the Sacred Persons in the Trinity, are severely punishable by the Common Law; for, as my Lord HALE says, in *Taylor's* Case, 1 VENT. 293. "Such Kind of wicked

---

[9] Fielding is probably following Hale: 'They [grand jurors] are sworn to keep the king's counsel undiscovered, the revealing or disclosing whereof was heretofore taken for felony, 27 *Ass.* 63 [27 *Lib. Ass.*, fo. 142, pl. 63.] but that law is antiquated, it is now only fineable' (ii. 161).

For the Year Book commonly known as *Liber Assisarum* and for Justice Shard[elowe] see below, *Enquiry*, p. 127.

[1] Still common legal form of cognizant.

[2] This maxim ('the reason of the law ceasing, the law itself ceases') is cited by Coke (*II Inst.* 11) and is listed in the 'Index of Maxims and Rules' appended to some later editions of the *Institutes*.

[3] Cf. *Enquiry*, p. 63.

A Charge Delivered to the Grand Jury 15

blasphemous Words are not only an Offence against GOD and Religion, but a Crime against the Laws, State, and Government;" and in that Case the Defendant for Blasphemy, too horrible indeed to be repeated, was sentenced to stand three Times in the Pillory, to pay a great Fine, and to find Security for his good Behaviour during Life.[5] 3 Keb. 607. 621. S. C.[4]

In like Manner, all scandalous and contemptuous Words spoken against our holy Religion, are by the Wisdom of the Common Law made liable to an Indictment; for "Christianity (says that excellent Chief-Justice, in the Case I have just cited) is Parcel of the Laws of *England*; therefore to reproach the Christian Religion is to speak in Subversion of the Law."[6] And to the same Purpose is *Attwood's* Case, in CRO. JAC. 421. where one was indicted before the Justices of Peace for saying, that the Religion now professed was a new Religion within fifty Years, &c. For as to the Doubt concerning the High Commissioners, started in that Case, and then, as it appears, over-ruled, that is now vanished.[7]

Nor are our Statutes silent concerning this dreadful Offence; particularly by 1 ELIZ. *c.* 2. *sect.* 9. a severe Punishment is enacted for any Person who shall in any Interludes, Plays, Songs, Rhimes, or by other open Words declare or speak any thing in derogation, depraving or despising the Book of Common-Prayer, &c.[8]

---

[4] Joseph Keble, *Reports in the Court of Kings Bench at Westminster from the XII to the XXX year [of] King Charles II*, 3 vols. (London, 1685), iii. 607, 621 (Baker, no. 275). Keble is the original reporter of Taylor's case, but for Fielding's probable source, see note following.
S.C.: *Scaccarium Computorum*, or Court of Exchequer.

[5] Taylor's Case: the case of Dominus Rex vs. Taylor was heard Hilary Term 27 & 28 Car. II. Taylor's offence was to say 'Christ is a Whoremaster, and Religion is a Cheat, and Profession a Cloak, and all Cheats, all are mine, and I am a King's Son, and fear neither God, Devil, nor man . . .' (Keble, iii. 607).
Fielding quotes the observations of Sir Matthew Hale, the presiding judge in the case, as he found them in *The . . . Reports of Sir Peyton Ventris Kt. Late One of the Justices of the Common-Pleas . . .* [two vols. in one] (London, 1701), i. 293 (Baker, no. 275). Ventris also cites Keble.

[6] Cit. Ventris, i. 293. The principle here enunciated that 'Christianity is Parcel of the Laws of *England*' made Taylor's case a famous one. See Blackstone, *Comm.* iv. 59.

[7] Fielding is referring to a case reported on by Sir George Croke: 'Error brought by him [Attwood] to reverse a Judgement upon an Endictment, before Justices of Peace for scandalous words; *That the Religion now professed was a New Religion within Fifty Years, Preaching was but prating, and hearing of Service more Edifying than two hours Preaching*: and being thereof Convicted, was fined 100 Marks. The error assigned was, that this was not any offence inquirable by Indictment, and before Justices of Peace, but only before the High Commissioners, and it was referred to the Kings Attorney to consider thereof; and Sir Henry Yelverton Attorney General certified, that it was not inquirable before them; and of that opinion was the Court, but they would advise' (*The Second Part of the Reports of Sir George Croke, Kt. . . . Justices of the Court of Kings Bench . . . Select Cases . . . during . . . Reign of the late King James. Revis'd and Published by Sir Harebotle Grimstone, Baronet. The Second Edition, Corrected* [London, 1669], p. 421). Thus as Fielding notes, the attorney-general refused to allow the jurisdiction of the Court of High Commission. The abolition of this court (see above, p. 11 n. 3) resolved any remaining doubt.
In a letter to John Nourse, a London bookseller, dated 9 July 1739, Fielding says 'I have got Cro: Eliz' (Godden, pp. 94–5). Croke's *Reports* is no. 271 in Baker.

[8] The offender forfeited 100 marks.

Mr. Lambard, I find, mentions this Act in his Charge,[9] though the Execution of it be in the Counties confined to the Justices of *Oyer* and *Terminer* and of Assize; but the 22d *Sect.* of the Statute seems to give a clear Jurisdiction to this Court, at two of our Quarter-Sessions.[1]

The last Offence of this Kind which the wicked Tongue of Man can commit, is by profane Cursing and Swearing. This is a Sin expresly against the Law delivered by God himself to the *Jews*,[2] and which is as expressly prohibited by our blessed Saviour in his Sermon on the Mount.[3]

Many Statutes have been made against this Offence; and by the last of these, which was enacted in the Nineteenth Year of the present King, every Day-labourer, common Soldier, common Sailor and common Seaman, forfeits One Shilling; Every other Person under the Degree of a Gentleman, Two Shillings; and every Person of or above that Degree, Five Shillings.[4]

And in case any Person shall after such Conviction offend again, he forfeits double; and for every Offence after a second Conviction, treble.[5]

Though the Execution of this Act be entrusted to one single Magistrate, and no Jurisdiction, unless by Appeal, given to the Sessions; yet I could not forbear mentioning it here, when I am speaking in the Presence of many Peace-Officers, who are to forfeit 40 Shillings for neglecting to put the Act in Execution.[6] And I mention it the rather to inform them, that whenever the Offender is unknown to any Constable, Petty Constable, Tithingman, or other Peace-Officer, such Constable, &c. is empowered by the Act, without any Warrant, to seize and detain any such Person, and forthwith to carry him before the next Magistrate.[7]

And if these Officers would faithfully discharge the Duty thus enjoined them, and which Religion as well as the Law requires of them, our Streets would soon cease to resound with this detestable Crime, so injurious to the Honour of God, so directly repugnant to his positive Commands, so highly offensive to the Ears of all good Men, and so very scandalous to the Nation in the Ears of Foreigners.

Having dispatched those Misdemeanors (the principal ones at least) which are immediately committed against God, I come now to speak of those which

---

[9] For Lambarde's 'Charge' see above, p. 12 and n. 8. In *Eirenarcha*, IV. iv. 417, Lambarde cites 1 Eliz., c. 2. and 23 Eliz., c. 1.

[1] Section 22 of 1 Eliz., c. 2. provides that 'the mayor of London, and all other . . . head officers . . . of . . . cities, boroughs and towns . . . to which justices of assize do not commonly repair . . .' shall have authority to 'hear and determine the offences abovesaid . . .' at Easter and Michaelmas terms.

[2] Exodus 20: 7.

[3] Matthew 6: 33–7.

[4] 19 Geo. II, c. 21. sect. 1. 'An act more effectually to prevent profane cursing and swearing'.

[5] Ibid.

[6] Sect. 7: 'any constable, petty constable, tythingman, or other peace-officer' who omits 'the performance of his duty in the execution of this act' shall forfeit 40 shillings.

[7] Sect. 3.

are committed against the Person of the King, which Person the Law wisely holds to be sacred.[8]

Besides those heinous Offences against this sacred Person which are punished *ultimo supplicio*,[9] there are many Articles, some of which involve the Criminal in the Guilt of Præmunire,[1] and others are considered in Law as Misprisions or Contempts. The former of these is by Mr. Serjeant HAWKINS, in his *Pleas of the Crown*, divided into two general Heads: *Viz.*

Into Offences against the Crown.

And Offences against the Authority of the King and Parliament.[2]

Under the former Head he enumerates nine several Articles; but as these chiefly relate to such Invasions of the Royal Prerogative as were either made in popish Ages in favour of the Bishops of *Rome*, or in those Times which bordered on the Reformation in favour of the Church of *Rome*, and are not practised, at least not openly practised in these Days, I shall have no Need to repeat them here.

Under the latter Head he mentions only one, which was enacted in the Reign of Queen ANNE, 6 *Ann. c.* 7.[3] If any Person shall maliciously and directly, by Preaching, Teaching, or advised Speaking, declare, maintain and affirm, that the pretended Prince of *Wales* hath any Right or Title to the Crown of these Realms, or that any other Person or Persons hath or have any Right or Title to the same, otherwise than according to the Acts of Settlement; or that the Kings or Queens of this Realm, with the Authority of Parliament, are not able to make Laws to limit the Crown and the Descent, &c. thereof, shall incur a Præmunire.

A most wholesome and necessary Law. And yet so mild hath been our

---

[8] '. . . by law the person of the king is sacred . . . for no jurisdiction upon earth has power to try him in a criminal way' (Blackstone, *Comm.* i. 242).

[9] With extreme (i.e. capital) punishment. A legal phrase. Hawkins (i. 34) distinguishes 'Offences more immediately against the King' as 'Capital or not Capital'. Capital offences are either high treason or felonies.

[1] 'A third species of offence more immediately affecting the king and his government, though not subject to capital punishment, is that of *praemunire*; so called from the words of the writ preparatory to the prosecution thereof: "*Praemunire facias A B*" cause A B to be forewarned that he appear before us to answer the contempt wherewith he stands charged: which contempt is particularly recited in the preamble to the writ. It took its original from the exorbitant power claimed and exercised in England by the pope, which even in the days of blind zeal was too heavy for our ancestors to bear' (Blackstone, *Comm.* iv. 103). 16 Rich. II, c. 5, known as the statute of *praemunire*, provides that he who is guilty of a *praemunire* suffers forfeiture of goods and must answer to the king and council for his offence. A *praemunire* generally involved some denial of the ecclesiastical supremacy of the crown.

[2] 'Offences more immediately against the King, not capital, come generally under the Titles of *Praemunire*, Misprision, and Contempts. . . . Offences coming under the Notion of *Praemunire*, seem to be reducible to the following general Heads:

1. Offences against the Prerogative of the Crown.

2. Offences against the Authority of the King and Parliament' (Hawkins, i. 48–9).

[3] The rest of the paragraph is an abridgement of section 2 of this act. It is nearly identical with the abridgement in Hawkins, i. 54–5.

Government, that I remember no one Instance of putting it in Execution.

Misprisions or Contempts[4] are against the King's Prerogative, against his Title, or against his sacred Person or Government.[5]

Under these Heads will fall any Act of public and avowed Disobedience; any denying his most just and lawful Title to the Crown; any overt Act which directly tends to encourage or promote Rebellion or Sedition; all false Rumours against his Majesty, or his Councils; all contemptuous Language concerning his sacred Person, by cursing, reviling him, &c. or by uttering any thing which manifests an Intention of lessening that Esteem, Awe and Reverence which Subjects ought to bear to the best of Princes.[6]

These are Offences, Gentlemen, which I must earnestly recommend to your Enquiry. This, Gentlemen, is your Duty as Grand Jurors; and it must be a most pleasing Task to you, as you are *Englishmen*; for in Proportion as you love and esteem your Liberties, you will be fired with Love and Reverence toward a Prince, under whose Administration you enjoy them in the fullest and amplest Manner.

Believe me, Gentlemen, notwithstanding all which the Malice of the Disappointed, the Madness of Republicans, or the Folly of Jacobites may insinuate,[7] there is but one Method to maintain the Liberties of the Country, and that is, to maintain the Crown on the Heads of that Family which now happily enjoys it.

If ever Subjects had Reason to admire the Justice of that Sentiment of the Poet *Claudian, That Liberty never flourishes so happily as under a good King*,[8] we have Reason at present for that Admiration.

I am afraid, Gentlemen, this Word *Liberty*, though so much talked of, is but little understood.[9] What other Idea can we have of Liberty, than that it is the Enjoyment of our Lives, our Persons, and our Properties in Security; to be free Masters of ourselves and our Possessions, as far as the known Laws of our Country will admit; to be liable to no Punishment, no Confinement, no Loss but what those Laws subject us to! Is there any Man ignorant

---

[4] According to Blackstone (*Comm.* iv. 119–21), misprisions are of two sorts: 'negative, which consist in the concealment of something which ought to be revealed; and positive, which consist in the commission of something which ought not to be done'. The former is called a misprision; the latter a contempt. Both are 'high offences . . . under the degree of capital'. For example, to conceal knowledge of a felony would be to commit a misprision of felony.

The paragraph following concerns positive misprisions, or *contempts*.

[5] 'Other positive Misprisions more immediately against the King seem reducible to the following Heads:

1. Contempts against his Palace or Courts of Justice.
2. Contempts against his Prerogative.
3. Contempts against his Person or Government.
4. Contempts against his Title' (Hawkins, i. 56–7).

[6] In this paragraph Fielding mentions only a few of the many offences cited in Hawkins, i. 59 ff.

[7] For a discussion of Fielding's association of Jacobites and republicans, see W. B. Coley, General Introduction to *JJ* pp. lxiii ff.

[8] *On Stilicho's Consulship*, iii. 114–15.   [9] Cf. *Enquiry*, p. 65 n. 7.

enough to deny that this is the Description of a free People; or base enough to accuse me of Panegyric, when I say this is our present happy Condition?[1]

But if the Blessing of Liberty, like that of Health, be not to be perceived by those who enjoy it, or at least must be illustrated by its Opposite, let us compare our own Condition with that of other Countries; of those whose Polity some among us pretend so much to admire, and whose Government they seem so ardently to affect. *Lettres de Cachet*,[2] Bastiles, and Inquisitions, may, perhaps, give us a livelier Sense of a just and mild Administration, than any of the Blessings we enjoy under it.

Again, Gentlemen, let us compare the present Times with the past. And here I need not resort back to those distant Ages, when our unhappy Forefathers petitioned their Conqueror *that he would not make them so miserable, nor be so severe to them, as to judge them by a Law they understood not.* These are the very Words, as we find them preserved in *Daniel*;[3] in Return to which, the Historian informs us, nothing was obtain'd but fair Promises.[4] I shall not dwell here on the Tyranny of his immediate Successor, of whom the same Historian records, that "seeking to establish absolute Power by Force, he made both himself and his People miserable."[5]

I need not, Gentlemen, here remind you of the Oppressions under which our Ancestors have groaned in many other Reigns, to shake off which the Sword of Civil War was first drawn in the Reign of King *John*, which was not entirely sheathed during many successive Generations.

I might, perhaps, have a fairer Title to your Patience, in laying open the tyrannical Proceedings of later Times, while the Crown was possessed by four successive Princes of the House of *Stuart*. But this, Gentlemen, would

---

[1] Fielding's conventional if rather restrictive view of liberty dominates his later social and political writings (see the Preface to the *Enquiry*, especially p. 73 and n. 9, and the *Proposal*, p. 267) but is probably consistent with the argument in his early poem 'Liberty', though a couplet such as 'Curse on all Laws which Liberty subdue, / And make the Many wretched for the Few' points up the effect on rhetoric of adherence to the 'Patriot' opposition to Walpole (see Henry Knight Miller's commentary on the poem, *Miscellanies* (1743), pp. xxx–xxxi).

[2] *Lettre de cachet*: 'a letter under the private seal of the French king, containing an order, often of exile or imprisonment' (*OED*). The oppressions of French arbitrary rule figure strongly in Fielding's political writings of 1745–8. See, for example, *TP* no. 3 (19 Nov. 1745); and *A Serious Address to the People of Great Britain* (1745).

[3] According to Samuel Daniel (*The Collection of the History of England, Revised, and by his last corrected Coppy Printed* [London, 1634], p. 43), 'the agreeed Lords, and sad people of England' petitioned William the Conqueror in 1089 'that he would not adde that misery, to deliver them up to be judged by a strange Law they understood not'. Daniel's *History* is not listed in Baker.

[4] Daniel says William 'was pleased to confirme that by his Charter, which he had twice fore-promised by his Oath . . . yet notwithstanding this confirmation . . . there followed a great innovation both in the Lawes and Governement in England' (ibid.).

[5] Summing up the reign of William II, Daniel says that he was 'A Prince, who for the first two yeares of his reigne . . . bare himselfe most worthily, and had been absolute for State; had he not after sought to be absolute in power, which (meeting with an exorbitant will) makes both prince and People miserable' (ibid., p. 60). The variance between quotations and cited authority suggests the existence of an intermediate text.

be to trespass on your Patience indeed: For to mention all their Acts of absolute Power, all their Attempts to subvert the Liberties of this Nation, would be to relate to you the History of their Reigns.

In a Word, Gentlemen, all the Struggles which our Ancestors have so bravely maintained with ambitious Princes, and particularly with the last-mentioned Family, was to maintain and preserve to themselves and their Posterity, that very Liberty which we now enjoy, under a Prince to whom I may truly apply what the Philosopher long ago said of Virtue, THAT ALL WHO TRULY KNOW HIM MUST LOVE HIM.[6]

The third general Head of Misdemeanours, Gentlemen, is of those which are committed against the Subject, and these may be divided into two Branches.

Into such as are committed against Individuals only:

And into such as affect the Public in general.[7]

The former of these will probably come before you by Way of Indictment; for Men are apt enough to revenge their own Quarrels; but Offences *in commune nocumentum*[8] do not so certainly find an Avenger; and thus those Crimes, which it is the Duty of every Man to punish, do often escape with Impunity.

Of these, Gentlemen, it may be therefore proper to awaken your Enquiry, and particularly of such as do in a more especial Manner infest the Public at this Time.

The first of this Kind is the Offence of profligate Lewdness; a Crime of a very pernicious Nature to Society, as it tends to corrupt the Morals of our Youth, and is expressly prohibited by the Law of God, under the Denunciation of the severest Judgment, in the New Testament.[9] Nay, we read in the 25th Chapter of *Numbers* the exceeding Wrath of God against the Children of *Israel* for their Fornication with the Daughters of *Moab*.[1] Nor did the Plague which on that Occasion was sent among them, and which destroyed Four and twenty thousand, cease, till *Phineas*, the Son of *Eleazar* and Grandson of *Aaron*, had slain the *Israelite* together with his Harlot.[2]

And this, Gentlemen, though a spiritual Offence, and of a very high

[6] 'You see her [virtue] . . . the very form and as it were the face of Moral Goodness; "and if," as Plato says, "it could be seen with the physical eye, it would awaken a marvellous love of wisdom".' Cicero, *De Officiis*, I. v ff. (Loeb). For a fuller gloss on the idea of 'naked virtue', which Fielding usually ascribes to Plato, see *Miscellanies* (1743), p. 173 n. 4; and *Tom Jones* (Dedication), I. 7 n.

[7] Hawkins (i. 197) categorizes 'Offences under the Degree of capital, more immediately against the Subject . . . [exclusions follow]' as '1. Such as more immediately affect the Publick. 2. Such as more immediately affect the Interests of particular Persons.'

[8] i.e. common nuisances.

[9] Fielding is probably thinking of I Corinthians 5, 6.

[1] '. . . and the people began to commit whoredom with the daughters of Moab' (Numbers 25: 1); 'And the Lord said unto Moses, Take all the heads of the people, and hang them up before the Lord against the sun . . .' (Numbers 25: 4).

[2] Numbers 25: 6–9.

Nature too, as appears from what I have mentioned, is likewise a temporal Crime, and, as Mr. LAMBARD (122) says, against the Peace.[3]

My Lord COKE, in his third *Institute*, 206, tells us, that in antient Times Adultery and Fornication were punished by Fine and Imprisonment, and were enquirable in Turns and Leets.[4] And in the Year-Book of *Henry* VII. we find the Custom of *London* pleaded for a Constable to seize a Woman taken in the Act of Adultery, and to carry her to Prison.[5]   1 *H*. 7. fol. 6. plac. 3.

And though later Times have given up this Matter in general to ecclesiastical Jurisdiction, yet there are two Species which remain at this Day cognizable by the Common Law.

The first is, any open Act of Lewdness and Indecency in public, to the Scandal of Good-manners.

And therefore in *Michaelmas* Term, 15 *Car.* 2 *B. R.*[6] Sir CHARLES SIDNEY was indicted for having exposed himself naked in a Balcony in *Covent-Garden*, to a great Multitude of People, with many indecent Words and Actions; and this was laid to be contrary to the King's Peace, and to the great Scandal of Christianity. He confessed the Indictment, and SIDERFIN, who reports the Case, tells us, that the Court, in Consideration of his   1 *Sid.* 168. embarrassed Fortune, fined him *only* 2000 Marks, with a short Imprisonment, and to be bound three Years to his good Behaviour.[7] An infamous Punishment for a Gentleman, but far less infamous than the Offence. If any Facts of this Nature shall come to your Knowledge, you will, I make no

---

[3] 'For Bawderie is not merely a spiritual offence, but mixed, and sounding somewhat against the Peace of the Land' (*Eirenarcha*, II. ii. 119).

[4] Fielding's reference is to ch. 98, 'de Lupanaribus et Fornicibus &c.' 'In antient Times . . . Imprisonment' are Coke's words.

Court-Leets and Sheriffs' Tourns were ancient local courts of record whose functions by Fielding's time had largely been assumed by justices of the peace at quarter sessions.

[5] In the Year-Book case cited, a constable charged with trespass pleaded the 'custom en Londres' for his arrest of a 'feme en avoutry' outside his jurisdiction. Coke (*III Inst.* 206) refers to this case and may have provided Fielding with the Year-Book reference.

[6] 15 Car. II. B[anco] R[egis], or King's Bench.

[7] Thomas Siderfin, *Les Reports des divers Special Cases arge & adjudge en le Court del Bank Le Roy . . . En les primier dix ans apres le Restauration . . . Charles II*, 2 vols. (London, 1633–4), i. 168 (Baker, no. 274). Siderfin reports the case of Sir Charles 'Sidley', i.e., the poet and wit Sedley (d. 1701) and all of Fielding's details appear in Siderfin's report including the legal point that Sedley's offence could be tried by common law.

Some of the flavor of the ingenious Sedley's infamous offence may be had from the account related to Pepys of the 'late triall of Sir Charles Sydly . . . for his debauchery a little while since at Oxford Kates; coming in open day into the Balcone and showed his nakedness—acting all the postures of lust and buggery that could be imagined, and abusing of scripture and, as it were, from thence preaching a Mountebanke sermon from that pulpitt, saying that there he hath to sell such a pouder as should make all the cunts in town run after him—a thousand people standing underneath to see and hear him.

'And that being done, he took a glass of wine and washed his prick in it and then drank it off; and then took another and drank the King's Health' (*The Diary of Samuel Pepys*, ed. Robert Latham and William Matthews, iv. [Berkeley and Los Angeles, 1971], p. 209). See also Johnson's 'Life of Dorset' in *Lives of English Poets*.

Doubt, present them, without any Respect to Persons. Sex or Quality may render the Crime more atrocious, and the Example more pernicious; but can give no Sanction to such infamous Offences, nor will, I hope, ever give Impunity.

The second Species which falls under this Head, is the Crime of keeping a Brothel or Bawdy-House. This is a Kind of common Nuisance, and is punishable by the Common Law.

It is true, that certain Houses of this Kind, under the Name of public Stews, have been sometimes tolerated in Christian Countries, to the great Scandal of our Religion, and in direct Contradiction to its positive Precepts: But in the thirty-seventh Year of HENRY the Eight, they were all suppressed by Proclamation. And those infamous Women who inhabited them were not, says Lord COKE, either buried in Christian Burial when they were dead, nor permitted to receive the Rites of the Church while they lived.[8]

And, Gentlemen, notwithstanding the Favour which the Law in many Cases extends to married Women,[9] yet in this Case the Wife is equally indictable, and may be found guilty with her Husband.[1]

Nor is it necessary that the Person be Master or Mistress of the whole House; for if he or she have only a single Room, and will therewith accomodate lewd People to perpetrate Acts of Uncleanness, they may be indicted for keeping a Bawdy-House. And this was the Resolution of the whole Court, in the *Queen* and PEIRSON. SALK. 332.[2]

Nor is the Guilt confined to those who keep such Houses; those who frequent them are no less liable to the Censure of the Law. Accordingly we find, in the select Cases printed at the End of Lord Ch. J. POPHAM'S *Reports*, that a Man was indicted in the Beginning of the Reign of CHARLES the First, at the Sessions of the Peace for the Town of *Northampton*, for frequenting a

---

[8] Coke, *III Inst.* 205, 'King H. 8. suppressed all the Stewes or Brothel-houses, which long had continued on the Bankside in Southwark, for that they were (as hath been said) prohibited by the law of God, and by the law of this land. And those infamous women were not buried in Christian buriall when they were dead, nor permitted to receive the rites of the Church whilest they lived.'

A marginal note in Coke supplies 'By proclamation . . . 37 H. 8.' It was within the king's prerogative to issue proclamations which 'have then a binding force, when, (as Sir Edward Coke observes,) they are grounded upon and enforce the laws of the realm' (Blackstone, *Comm.* i. 270).

[9] There were many crimes that a married woman, or *feme-covert* (*coverture*: 'under the protection, wing, or cover of her husband') could not be charged with when committed with or under the coercion of her husband.

[1] 'A Wife may be indicted together with her Husband, and condemned to the Pillory with him for keeping a Bawdy-House; for this is an Offence as to the Government of the House, in which the Wife has a principal Share; and also such an Offence as may generally be presumed to be managed by the Intrigues of her Sex' (Hawkins, i. 2–3).

[2] William Salkeld, *Reports of Cases Adjudg'd in the Court of King's Bench* . . . , 2 vols. in one (London, 1717), i. 382 (not 332): 'The Court agreed . . . That if a Lodger, who has only a single Room, will therewith accomodate lewd People to perpetrate Acts of Uncleanness, she may be indicted for keeping a Bawdy-House, as well as if she had the whole House.' Fielding owned this edition of Salkeld's *Reports* (Baker, no. 273).

suspected Bawdy-House. And the Indictment being removed into the *King's-Bench*, several Objections were taken to it, which were all over-ruled, Judgment was given upon it, and the Defendant fined.[3]

If you shall know, therefore, Gentlemen, of any such Crimes, it will be your Duty to present them to the Court.

For however lightly this Offence may be thought or spoken of by idle and dissolute Persons, it is a Matter of serious and weighty Consideration. It is the Cause, says my Lord COKE, of many Mischiefs, the fairest End whereof is Beggary; and tends directly to the Overthrow of Men's Bodies, to the wasting of their Livelihoods, and to the indangering of their Souls.[4]

To eradicate this Vice out of Society, however it may be the Wish of sober and good Men, is, perhaps, an impossible Attempt; but to check its Progress, and to suppress the open and more profligate Practice of it, is within the Power of the Magistrate, and it is his Duty.[5] And this is more immediately incumbent upon us, in an Age when Brothels are become in a Manner the Seminaries of Education, and that especially of those Youths, whose Birth makes their right Institution[6] of the utmost Consequence to the future Well-being of the Public: For whatever may be the Education of these Youths, however vitiated and enervated their Minds and Bodies may be with Vices and Diseases,[7] they are born to be the Governors of our Posterity. If, therefore, through the egregious Folly of their Parents, this Town is to be the School of such Youths, it behoves us, Gentlemen, to take as much Care as possible to correct the Morals of that School.

And, Gentlemen, there are other Houses, rather less scandalous, perhaps, but equally dangerous to the Society; in which Houses the Manners of Youth are greatly tainted and corrupted. These are those Places of public Rendezvous where idle Persons of both Sexes meet in a very disorderly

---

[3] Sir John Popham, *Reports and Cases Collected by the Learned Sir John Popham, Kt., late Lord Chief Justice of England. Written with his own Hand in French . . . now . . . translated . . .*, 2nd edn. (London, 1682), p. 208, as reprinted in *The English Reports*, ed. Max A. Robertson *et al.* (London, 1857), lxxix. 1297–8. The case, involving one Matthias Wheelhorse, is less clear than Fielding allows. The judgment of the King's Bench implies that one is indictable for frequenting bawdy-houses, but Wheelhorse was convicted only of being a noctivagus, or 'common night-walker', and fined 40*s*. Fielding owned the first edition (1656) of Popham's *Reports* (Baker, no. 269).

[4] This sentence conflates parts of two of Coke's sentences in *III Inst.* 205–6.

[5] The moderation of Fielding's strictures against bawdy-houses is worth calling attention to since he was attacked in *Old England* (15 July 1749), on the occasion of the Penlez riot, as a supporter of them: 'To him [Fielding] I [say], that the scandalous Connivance at, if not the Protection of, Brothel Houses, has been but too long the prevailing Practice among a certain *worshipful Order* of Men, *for divers valuable Considerations thereunto moving.* Whether he knows this by Experience, and if from a Customer he is become a Patron, is submitted to himself.' In the *Enquiry*, Fielding does not mention bawdy-houses as one of the causes of crime, for which he was criticized (by Philo-Patria, in *A Letter to Henry Fielding, Esq.* [London, 1751]), but in the *CGJ* for 1 Aug. 1752 (no. 57) he says as to 'any positive Good arising to a Society from the Encouragement of Prostitutes, this I own exceeds my Penetration' (ii. 72).

[6] 'Training, instruction, education, teaching' (*OED*).

[7] Cf. Fielding's portait of Beau Didapper in *Joseph Andrews* (IV. ix. 312–13).

Manner, often at improper Hours, and sometimes in disguised Habits. These Houses, which pretend to be the Scenes of innocent Diversion and Amusement, are in Reality the Temples of Iniquity.[8] Such Meetings are *contra bonos mores*;[9] they are considered in Law in the Nature of a Nuisance, and as such, the Keepers and Maintainers of them may be presented and punished.[1]

There is a great Difference, Gentlemen, between a morose and over-sanctified Spirit, which excludes all Kind of Diversion, and a profligate Disposition which hurries us into the most vicious Excesses of this Kind. "The Common Law," says Mr. PULTON in his excellent Treatise *de Pace, fol.* 25 *b.* "allows many Recreations, which be not with Intent to break or disturb the Peace, or to offer Violence, Force, or Hurt to the Person of any; but either to try Activity, or to increase Society, Amity, and neighbourly Friendship."[2] He there enumerates many Sorts of innocent Diversions of the rural Kind, and which for the most Part belong to the lower Sort of People. For the upper Part of Mankind, and in this Town, there are many lawful Amusements, abundantly sufficient for the Recreation of any temperate and sober Mind. But, Gentlemen, so immoderate are the Desires of many, so hungry is their Appetite for Pleasure, that they may be said to have a Fury after it; and Diversion is no longer the Recreation or Amusement, but the whole Business of their Lives. They are not content with three Theatres,[3] they must have a fourth;[4] where the Exhibitions are not only contrary to Law, but contrary to Good-Manners, and where the Stage is reduced back again to that Degree of Licentiousness[5] which was too

---

[8] Fielding's attack in this paragraph on masquerades and other 'places of public Rendezvous' anticipates his discussion of the evil social effects of 'luxury' on the poor in the *Enquiry* (see especially 'Section I: Of Too Frequent and Expensive Diversions Among the Lower Kind of People'). For a discussion of the context of these attacks, see Zirker, *Social Pamphlets*, especially ch. V.

[9] 'Against good manners'.

[1] By common law, 'The Offence of keeping a Bawdy-House . . . comes under the Cognizance of the Temporal Law, as a Common Nuisance [*sic*] . . . Offenders of this Kind are punishable . . . with Fine and Imprisonment' (Hawkins, i. 196).

[2] Ferdinando Pulton, *De Pace Regis et Regni* . . . (London, 1609), fo. 26a [not fo. 25b] as reprinted in the Classical English Law Texts series, ed. P. R. Glazebrook (London, 1973). Fielding's quotation marks should begin with 'be not'. He modernizes Pulton's orthography. Pulton's *De Pace* superseded earlier books on criminal law but was to be superseded by Coke. It is not listed in Baker.

[3] Fielding alludes to the two patent houses, Drury Lane and Covent Garden, and to the King's Opera House.

[4] The Little Theatre in the Haymarket, which Fielding had once managed (1735–7) and where several of his plays had been first performed. Traditionally the scene of irregular theatrical entertainment, this theater had been kept open after the Licensing Act (1737) by various subterfuges, most notably Foote's 'Dish of Tea' (for which one paid, the play being gratis).

[5] Perhaps Fielding is thinking of the riot of 16 Jan. 1749 following the non-appearance of the bottle conjuror (for details of this event see General Introduction, p. xxviii), but he must also have in mind Foote's mimicry of his own person (see General Introduction, p. xxvii, and W. B. Coley, General Introduction to *JJ* p. lviii). The Little Theatre in the Haymarket was to be the scene of the French Players riot in Nov. 1749, that figures in the uproar surrounding the execution of Bosavern Penlez and the contested Westminster election (see General Introduction, p. xlv).

enormous for the corrupt State of *Athens* to tolerate; and which, as the *Roman* Poet, rather, I think in the Spirit of a Censor than a Satyrist, tells us, those *Athenians*, who were not themselves abused, took Care to abolish, from their Concern for the Public.[6]

Gentlemen, our News-Papers, from the Top of the Page to the Bottom, the Corners of our Streets up to the very Eves of our Houses, present us with nothing but a View of Masquerades, Balls, and Assemblies of various Kinds, Fairs, Wells, Gardens, &c. tending to promote Idleness, Extravagance and Immorality, among all Sorts of People.[7]

This Fury after licentious and luxurious Pleasures is grown to so enormous a Height, that it may be called the Characteristic of the present Age. And it is an Evil, Gentlemen, of which it is neither easy nor pleasant to foresee all the Consequences. Many of them, however, are obvious; and these are so dreadful, that they will, I doubt not, induce you to use your best Endeavours to check the further Encrease of this growing Mischief; for the Rod of the Law, Gentlemen, must restrain those within the Bounds of Decency and Sobriety, who are deaf to the Voice of Reason, and superior to the Fear of Shame.

Gentlemen, there are another Sort of these Temples of Iniquity, and these are Gaming-Houses. This Vice, Gentlemen, is inseparable from a luxurious and idle Age; for while Luxury produces Want, Idleness forbids honest Labour to supply it. All such Houses are Nuisances in the Eye of the Common Law; and severe Punishments, as well on those who keep them, as on those who frequent and play at them, are inflicted by many Statutes.[8] Of these Houses, Gentlemen, you will, I doubt not, enquire with great Diligence; for though possibly there may be some Offenders out of your Reach, yet if those within it be well and strictly prosecuted, it may, perhaps, in Time have some Effect on the others. Example in this Case may, contrary to its general Course, move upwards; and Men may become ashamed of offending against those Laws with Impunity, by which they see their Inferiors brought to Punishment. But if this Effect should not be produced, yet, Gentlemen, there is no Reason why you should not exert your Duty as far as you are able, because you cannot extend it as far as you desire. And to say the Truth, to prevent Gaming among the lower Sort of People is

---

[6] Cf. *JJ* no. 22 (30 Apr. 1748), p. 264, where, addressing *Samuel Fut* [Foote], the court observes that persons 'have been formerly ridiculed under fictitious Fables and Characters; but surely since the Days of the Old Comedy, none, 'till your Time, have had the Audacity to bring real Facts and Persons upon the Stage: Nay, you have gone even beyond that Old Comedy, which was by Law banished from Athens, as an intolerable Evil.' The '*Roman* Poet' may be Horace, *Epistles*, II. iii ('The Art of Poetry'), 281–4: 'To these [writers of tragedy] succeeded Old Comedy, and won no little credit, but its freedom sank into excess and a violence deserving to be checked by law. The law was obeyed, and the chorus to its shame became mute, its right to injure being withdrawn' (Loeb).

[7] Cf. the *Enquiry*, p. 83.

[8] Fielding discusses the laws pertaining to gaming in the *Enquiry* (see below, pp. 95 ff.).

principally the Business of Society; and for this plain Reason, because they are the most useful Members of the Society; which by such Means will lose the Benefit of their Labour.[9] As for the Rich and Great, the Consequence is generally no other than the Exchange of Property from the Hands of a Fool into those of a Sharper, who is, perhaps, the more worthy of the two to enjoy it.

I will mention only one Article more, and that of a very high Nature indeed. It is, Gentlemen, the Offence of Libelling, which is punished by the Common Law, as it tends immediately to Quarrels and Breaches of the Peace, and very often to Bloodshed and Murder itself.[1]

The Punishment of this Offence, saith my Lord COKE, is Fine or Imprisonment; and if the Case be exorbitant, by Pillory and Loss of Ears.[2]

And, Gentlemen, even the last of these Judgments will appear extremely mild, if we consider in the first Place the atrocious Temper of Mind from which this proceeds.

Mr. PULTON, in the Beginning of his Treatise *de Pace*, says of a Libeller, "that he is a secret Canker, which concealeth his Name, hideth himself in a Corner, and privily stingeth his Neighbour in his Fame, Reputation, and Credit; who neither knows from whom, nor for what Cause he receiveth his Blows, nor hath any Means to defend himself:'[3] And my Lord COKE, in his 5th *Report* (125) compares him to a Poisoner, who is the meanest, the vilest, and most dangerous of all Murderers.[4] Nor can I help repeating to you a most beautiful Passage in the great Orator DEMOSTHENES, who compares this Wretch to a Viper, which Men ought to crush where-ever they find him; without staying 'till he bite them.[5]

In the second Place, if we consider the Injury done by these Libellers, it must raise the Indignation of every honest and good Man: For what is this, but, as Mr. PULTON says, "a Note of Infamy, intended to defame the Person at whom it is levelled, to tread his Honour and Estimation in the Dust, to extirpate and root out his Reputation from the Face of the Earth, to make

[9] For discussion of the economic implications of Fielding's statement here, see General Introduction, p. lxiii ff. and Zirker, *Social Pamphlets*, ch. VI.

[1] Fielding frequently commented on the evil of slander and libel, e.g., the *Champion*, 6 Mar. 1740; *Tom Jones*, XI. i; *CGJ* no. 14; *Joseph Andrews*, III. i. 189; and *Miscellanies* (1743), p. 14.

[2] Coke, *Fifth Report*, fo. 125a. Fielding owned two editions of Coke's *Reports* (Baker, nos. 1, 113).

[3] Pulton, *De Pace*, fo. 2a, who also cites Coke's *Fifth Report*, fo. 125.

[4] 'Poisoning may be done so secretly that none can defend himself against it; *for which cause the offence is the more dangerous, because the offender cannot easily be known*; and of such nature is libelling, it is secret, and robs a man of his good name, which ought to be more precious to him than his life' (*Fifth Report*, fo. 125b).

[5] *Against Aristogeiton*, i. 96: 'Perhaps none of you has ever been bitten by an adder or a tarantula, and I hope he never may be. All the same, whenever you see such creatures, you promptly kill them all. In just the same way, men of Athens, whenever you see a false accuser, a man with the venom of a viper in his nature, do not wait for him to bite one of you, but always let the man who come across him exact punishment' (Loeb). Fielding associates 'slander', 'viper', and 'poison' in the *Champion* (6 Mar. 1739/40), p. 232; *Jonathan Wild*, III. iii. 105; *JJ* (28 May 1748), p. 287; and *Tom Jones*, XI. i. 567–8.

him a Scorn to his Enemies, and to be derided and despised by his Neighbours."[6]

If Praise, and Honour, and Reputation, be so highly esteemed by the greatest and best of Men, that they are often the only Rewards which they propose to themselves from the noblest Actions: If there be nothing too difficult, too dangerous, or too disagreeable for Men to encounter, in order to acquire and preserve these Rewards; what a Degree of Wickedness and Barbarity must it be unjustly and wantonly to strip Men of that on which they place so high a Value.

Nor is Reputation to be considered as a chimerical Good, or as merely the Food of Vanity and Ambition. Our worldly Interests are closely connected with our Fame: By losing this, we are deprived of the chief Comforts of Society, particularly of that which is most dear to us, the Friendship and Love of all good and virtuous Men. Nay, the Common Law indulged so great a Privilege to Men of good Reputation in their Neighbourhood, that in many Actions the Defendant's Word was taken in his own Cause, if he could bring a certain Number of his Neighbours to vouch that they believed him.[7]

On the contrary, whoever robs us of our good Name, doth not only expose us to public Contempt and Avoidance, but even to Punishment: For by the Statute 34 EDW. III. *c.* 1. the Justices of the Peace are empowered and directed to bind all such as be not of good Fame to their good Behaviour, and if they cannot find sufficient Sureties, they may be committed to Prison.

Seeing, therefore, the execrable Mischiefs perpetrated by this secret Canker, this Viper, this Poisoner, in Society, we shall not wonder to hear him so severely condemned in Scripture;[8] nor that ARISTOTLE in his *Politics* should mention Slander as one of those great Evils which it is difficult for a Legislator to guard against;[9] that the *Athenians* punished it with a very severe and heavy Fine,[1] and the *Romans* with Death.[2]

[6] Fielding takes some minor liberties in quoting from *De Pace*, fo. 2a.

[7] One ancient mode of trial was *wager of law* whereby the defendant's word was taken as good if attested to by eleven 'neighbors' or 'compurgators' (Blackstone, *Comm.* iii. 341–3).

[8] In the *CGJ* no. 14 (18 Feb. 1752), i. 220, Fielding observes that the 'same sacred Table of Laws which forbids Murder, alike forbids us to bear false Witness against our Neighbour; and whoever reads and understands the [21st and] 22nd Verse[s] of the 5th Chap. of St. Matthew, will find equal Vengeance pronounced by the Divine Lawgiver of the New Testament against both these Crimes.' Both murderers and bearers of false witness are in danger of hell-fire.

[9] Fielding probably refers to Aristotle's observation that changes in the forms of democracy 'are chiefly due to the wanton licence of demagogues. This takes two forms. Sometimes they attack the rich individually, by bringing false accusations . . . sometimes they attack them as a class, by egging on the people against them' (*Politics*, bk. v, ch. V. sect. 1; 1304b; trans. Ernest Barker).

[1] The presidents of the games must banish any composer of comedies who ridicules a citizen; on failure to do so they incur a fine of 300 drachmas (Plato, *Laws*, bk. 11, 935–6; see above, p. 25 n. 6.

[2] 'The Law was this: If any one sing, or compose Verses injurious to the Reputation of another, let him be punished with Death. And it is remarkable, that this Law was introduced at a Time when the *Roman* Liberties were at the highest' (Fielding's note to verses from Horace quoted in *JJ* for 12 Mar. 1748 [no. 15], p. 199. For the law, W. B. Coley cites Cicero, *De Republica*, IV. x. 12, and Pliny, *Natural History*, XXVIII. iv.).

But tho' the Libeller of private Persons be so detestable a Vermin; yet is the Offence still capable of Aggravation, when the Poison is scattered upon public Persons and Magistrates.[3] All such Reflections are, as my Lord COKE observes, a Scandal on the Government itself: And such Scandal tends not only to the Breach of the Peace, but to raise Seditions and Insurrections among the whole Body of the People.[4]

And, Gentlemen, the higher and greater the Magistrates be against whom such Slanders are propagated, the greater is the Danger to the Society; and such we find to have been the Sense of the Legislature in the 2d Year of *R.* 2. For in the Statute of that Year, *chap.* 5. it is said, "that by such Means Discords may arise between the Lords and Commons, whereof great Peril and Mischief might come to all the Realm, and quick Subversion and Destruction of the said Realm."[5] And of such Consequence was this apprehended to be, that we find no less than four Statutes to prohibit and punish it; *viz. Westm.* 1. *c.* 33.[6] 2 *R.* 2 *c.* 5. 12 *R.* 2. *c.* 11.[7] and 2 and 3 *P. & M. c.* 12.[8] By this last Statute a Jurisdiction was given to the Justices of Peace to enquire of all such Offences; and if it was by Book, Ballad, Letter or Writing, the Offender's Right-hand was to be stricken off for the first Offence, and for the second he was to incur a Præmunire.[9]

This last Statute was afterwards prolonged in the last Year of Q. MARY,[1] and in the first of ELIZABETH, during the Life of that Princess, and of the Heirs of her Body.[2]

---

[3] Fielding refers to the libel technically known as *scandalum magnatum*: 'The honour of peers is . . . so highly tendered by the law, that it is much more penal to spread false reports of them and certain other great officers of the realm, than of other men: scandal against them being called by the peculiar name of *scandalum magnatum*, and subjected to peculiar punishments by divers ancient statues' (Blackstone, *Comm.* iii. 402. Blackstone cites Edw. I, c. 34; 2 Rich. II, st. 1. c. 5; and 12 Rich. II, c. 11 [see below, p. 33]). Fielding discusses *Scandalum Magnatum* in the *JJ* for 28 May 1748 (no. 26), pp. 288 ff.

[4] 'Every libel . . . is made either against a private man, or against a magistrate or public person. . . . *if it be against a magistrate, or other public person, it is a greater offence*; for it concerns not only the breach of the peace, but also the scandal of government' (*Fifth Report*, fo. 125a).

[5] 2 Rich. II, st. 1. c. 5 (entitled 'The penalty for telling slanderous lyes of the great men of the realm'). Fielding abridges part of the act's contents.

[6] The First Statute of Westminster was passed in the third year of the reign of Edward I (1275). The reference should be to c. 34.

[7] By 2 Rich. II, s. 1. c. 5 he who promulgated the libel was to be imprisoned until the 'mover' of the libel be found. 12 Rich. II, c. 11 provides that 'when any such is taken and imprisoned, and cannot find him by whom the speech be moved . . . that he be punished by the advice of the council . . .'.

[8] The citation should be to 1 & 2 Phil. & Mar., c. 3., an act confirming 3 Edw. I, c. 34. and 2 Rich. II, st. 1. c. 5.

[9] 'Justices of peace in every shire, city, &c. shall have authority to hear and determine the said offences, and to put the said two statutes in execution. . . . if he do it by book, rhime, ballad, letter or writing, he shall have his right hand stricken off. And if any person being once convicted of any of the offences aforesaid, do afterward offend, he shall be imprisoned during his life, and forfeit all his goods and cattels.'

[1] 4 & 5 Phil. & Mar., c. 9.

[2] 1 Eliz. I, c. 6.: 'The penalty mentioned in the statute of 1 & 2 P. & M. c. 3 for speaking false slanderous news of the King or Queen, or for committing any of the offences expressed in the said act, shall be expounded to extend to the Queen that now is, and to the heirs of her body.'

I have mentioned these Laws to you, Gentlemen, to shew you the Sense of our Ancestors of a Crime which, I believe, they never saw carried to so flagitious a Height as it is at present; when, to the Shame of the Age be it spoken, there are Men who make a Livelihood of Scandal. Most of these are Persons of the lowest Rank and Education, Men who lazily declining the Labour to which they were born and bred, save the Sweat of their Brows at the Expence of their Consciences; and in order to get a little better Livelihood, are content to get it, perhaps, in a less painful, but in a baser Way than the meanest Mechanic.[3]

Of these, Gentlemen, it is your Business to enquire; of the Devisers, of the Writers, of the Printers, and of the Publishers of all such Libels;[4] and I do heartily recommend this Enquiry to your Care.

To conclude, Gentlemen, you will consider yourselves as now summoned to the Execution of an Office, of the utmost Importance to the well-being of this Community: Nor will you, I am confident, suffer that Establishment, so wisely and carefully regulated, and so stoutly and zealously maintained by your wise and brave Ancestors, to degenerate into mere Form and Shadow. Grand Juries, Gentlemen, are in Reality the only Censors of this Nation. As such, the Manners of the People are in your Hands, and in yours only. You, therefore, are the only Correctors of them. If you neglect your Duty, the certain Consequences to the Public are too apparent: For as in a Garden, however well cultivated at first, if the Weeder's Care be omitted, the Whole must in Time be over-run with Weeds, and will resemble the Wildness and Rudeness of a Desert; so if those Immoralities of the People, which will sprout up in the best Constitution, be not from Time to Time corrected by the Hand of Justice, they will at length grow up to the most enormous Vices, will overspread the whole Nation, and in the End must produce a downright State of wild and savage Barbarism.

To this Censorial Office, Gentlemen, you are called by our excellent Constitution. To execute this Duty with Vigilance, you are obliged by the Duty you owe both to God and to your Country. You are invested with full Power for the Purpose. This you have promised to do, under the sacred

---

[3] With the charge that his fellow writers of newspapers were incompetent, ignorant, retailers of scandal, etc., Fielding often included the assertion that they were uneducated and low born, e.g.: 'it is manifest that the Writers of these Libels are not, nor cannot be Gentlemen; but must be sought after (if any one hath so mean a Curiosity) only among the lowest Dregs of the People, who are destitute of all Advantages of a liberal Education, and who can alone be supposed capable of transgressing all the Rules of Decency in so notorious a Degree' (*JJ* no. 26 [28 May 1748], pp. 290–1. Cf. *JJ* no. 20 [16 Apr. 1748]; *TP* no. 1 [5 Nov. 1745], p. 35; and *CGJ* no. 14 [18 Feb. 1752], i. 223).

[4] According to Laurence Hanson (*Government and the Press, 1695–1763* [Oxford, 1936], p. 47), customarily 'the printer and publisher, whose imprint is on the offending newspaper, are alone mentioned in the warrant, and only after their examination are further warrants issued for the arrest of those whom they incriminate' (cit. Coley, *JJ* p. 383 n. 1). Plucknett, in *History of the Common Law*, discusses the complicated laws concerning the press in the 18th century, pp. 498 ff.

Sanction of an Oath;[5] and you are all met, I doubt not, with a Disposition and Resolution to perform it, with that Zeal which I have endeavoured to recommend, and which the peculiar Licentiousness of the Age so strongly requires.

FINIS.

---

[5] The grand juror's oath was: 'You shall diligently inquire and true presentment make of all such matters and things as shall be given you in charge. The king's majesty's counsel, your fellows', and your own, you shall well and truly observe and keep secret. You shall present no man for envy, hatred, or malice; neither shall you leave any man unpresented for love, fear, favour, or affection, profit, lucre, gain, or any hope thereof; but in all things you shall present the truth, the whole truth, and nothing but the truth. So help you God' (J. H. Baker, 'Criminal Courts and Procedure at Common Law', in *Crime in England*, ed. J. S. Cockburn [Princeton, 1977], p. 33).

A

TRUE STATE

OF THE

CASE

OF

BOSAVERN PENLEZ,

Who fuffered on Account of the late Riot in the *STRAND.*

IN WHICH

The Law regarding thefe Offences, and the Statute of GEORGE the Firft, commonly called the Riot Act, are fully confidered.

By *HENRY FIELDING,* Efq;

Barrifter at Law, and one of his Majefty's Juftices of the Peace for the County of *Middlefex,* and for the City and Liberty of *Weftminfter.*

LONDON:

Printed for A. MILLAR, oppofite *Katherine-ftreet* in the *Strand.* 1749.

[Price One Shilling.]

A

TRUE STATE

OF THE

CASE

OF

BOSAVERN PENLEZ

It may easily be imagined, that a Man whose Character hath been so barbarously, even without the least Regard to Truth or Decency, aspersed, on account of his Endeavours to defend the present Government, might wish to decline any future Appearance as a political Writer;[1] and this, possibly, may be thought by some a sufficient Reason of that Reluctance with which I am drawn forth to do an Act of Justice to my King, and his Administration, by disabusing the Public, which hath been, in the grossest and wickedest Manner, imposed upon, with relation to the Case of *Bosavern Penlez*, who was executed for the late Riot in the *Strand*.

There is likewise another Reason of this Reluctance, with which those only who know me well can be certainly acquainted: and that is my own natural Disposition. Sure I am, that I greatly deceive myself, if I am not in some little Degree partaker of that Milk of human Kindness which *Shakespear* speaks of.[2] I was desirous that a Man who had suffered the

---

Title-page] 'State': 'statement'. Cf. *A Clear State of the Case of Elizabeth Canning*.

[1] Though Fielding was attacked frequently in the public press (see Coley, General Introduction to *JJ* pp. lxx–lxxi and lxxiv–lxxxii), he here doubtless alludes to the abuse that *The Jacobite's Journal* provoked. In the leader for Saturday, 16 Apr. 1748, he complains 'before my Paper . . . reached the 20th Number a heavier Load of Scandal [had] been cast upon me, than I believe ever fell to the Share of a single Man'. Several writers 'pursued me into private Life, *even to my boyish Years*; where they have given me almost every Vice in Human Nature. Again, they have followed me, with uncommon Inveteracy, into a Profession, in which they have very roundly asserted, that I have neither Business nor Knowledge: And, lastly as an Author, they have affected to treat me with more Contempt, than Mr. *Pope*, who had great Merit and no less Pride in the Character of a Writer, hath thought proper to bestow on the lowest Scribbler of his Time. All this, moreover, they have poured forth in a Vein of Scurrility, which hath disgraced the Press with every abusive Term in our Language' (pp. 235–6).

[2] Fielding's allusion to *Macbeth* (i. v. 17) caught the skeptical eye of the anonymous author of *The First Chapter of Terr'em the Son of Gore'am, in the Apocripha*, a satiric parable on the Westminster election of 1749 (see General Introduction, p. xlv ff.). He concludes abruptly, advising the reader that more about the election and scrutiny may be 'found written among the Chronicles of the Lords of Goat'am, by the Hand of the Man whose Heart aboundeth with the *Milk of Human Kindness*, even he that formerly followed the House of Jacob, who wrote the late lost Chronicle, called the Jacob-ite

Extremity of the Law should be permitted to rest quietly in his Grave. I was willing that his Punishment should end there; nay, that he should be generally esteemed the Object of Compassion, and consequently a more dreadful Example of one of the best of all our Laws.

But when this Malefactor is made an Object of Sedition, when he is transformed into a Hero, and the most merciful Prince who ever sat on any Throne is arraigned of blameable Severity, if not of downright Cruelty, for suffering Justice to take place; and the Sufferer, instead of remaining an Example to incite Terror, is recommended to our Honour and Admiration; I should then think myself worthy of much Censure, if having a full Justification in my Hands, I permitted it to sleep there, and did not lay it before the Public, especially as they are appealed to on this Occasion.[3]

Before I enter, however, into the Particulars of this Man's Case, and perform the disagreeable Task of raking up the Ashes of the Dead, though of the meanest Degree, to scatter Infamy among them, I will premise something concerning the Law of Riots in general. This I shall do, as well for the Justification of the Law itself, as for the Information of the People, who have been long too ignorant in this Respect; and who if they are now taught a little better to know the Law, are taught at the same Time to regard it as cruel and oppressive, and as an Innovation on our Constitution: For so the Statute of *George* the First, commonly call'd the *Riot Act*, hath lately been represented in a public News Paper.[4]

If this Doctrine had been first broached in this Paper, the Ignorance of it would not have been worth remarking; but it is in Truth a Repetition only of what hath been formerly said by Men who must have known better. Whoever remembers the political Writings published twenty Years ago, must remember that among the Articles exhibited against a former Administration, this of passing the Riot Act was one of the principal.[5]

Journal' 2nd edn. (London, 1750). Argus Centoculi also picked up Fielding's allusion, and it runs as a satiric refrain in the leaders of *Old England* for 25 Nov. and 9 and 16 Dec., 1749. After reading *Tom Jones*, 'Orbilius' feared Fielding's 'future Degeneracy from the *Milk of Human Kindness* to the Pap of infantile Insipidity' (*An Examen of the History of Tom Jones* [London, 1750], p. 119). This antagonistic pamphlet was announced for publication 9 Dec. 1749 during the fevered election contest of 1749.

[3] For discussion of the popular protests against Penlez's conviction and execution, see General Introduction, pp. xl ff.

[4] The *London Evening-Post* (2–4 Nov. 1749) quotes an attack on the Riot Act from 'The Fool', an essay series which appeared regularly in *The Daily Gazeteer*. According to the 'Fool' the Riot Act, originally passed to 'eradicate the Seeds of Rebellion', is now employed to punish the ignorant as readily as the rebellious. In *JJ* no. 12 (20 Feb. 1748), p. 172, Fielding calls the *London Evening-Post* a 'Grub-street Paper' and in no. 17 (26 Mar. 1748), p. 214, he lumps it together with *Old England* and the 'Fool' as a bad but harmless paper.

[5] The *Craftsman*, no. 214 (8 Aug. 1730) attacks the Riot Act as inconsistent with the nature of a government whose fundamental principle is liberty and associates it with Septennial Parliaments, both expressive of 'the Infamy of the Present Government'. Isaac Kramnick (*Bolingbroke and his Circle* [Cambridge, Mass., 1968], p. 172) and Archibald S. Foord (*His Majesty's Opposition: 1714–1830* [Oxford, 1964], p. 234) cite repeal of the Riot Act as part of the program of Walpole's opposition. Kramnick also notes that Lyttleton wrote against the Riot Act in 1739.

Surely these Persons mean to insinuate, that by this Statute Riots were erected into a greater Crime than they had ever before been esteemed, and that a more severe Punishment was enacted for them than had formerly been known among us.

Now the Falsehood of this must be abundantly apparent to every one who hath any competent Knowledge of our Laws. Indeed whoever knows any thing of the Nature of Mankind, or of the History of free Countries, must entertain a very indifferent Opinion of the Wisdom of our Ancestors, if he can imagine they had not taken the strongest Precautions to guard against so dangerous a political Disease, and which hath so often produced the most fatal Effects.

Riots are in our Law divided into those of a private and into those of a public Kind. The former of these are when a Number of People (three at the least) assemble themselves in a tumultuous Manner, and commit some Act of Violence amounting to a Breach of the Peace, where the Occasion of the Meeting is to redress some Grievance, or to revenge some Quarrel, of a private Nature; such as to remove the Inclosures of Lands in a particular Parish, or unlawfully and forcibly to gain the Possession of some Tenement, or to revenge some Injury done to one or a few Persons, or on some other such private Dispute, in which the Interest of the Public is no ways concerned. Such Riot is a very high Misdemeanor, and to be punished very severely by Fine and Imprisonment.

Mr. *Pulton* speaking of this Kind of Riot, writes thus: "Riots, Routs, unlawful and rebellious Assemblies, have been so many Times pernicious, and fatal Enemies to this Kingdom, the Peace, and Tranquility thereof, and have so often shaken the Foundation, and put in Hazard the very Form and State of Government of the same, that our Law-makers have been enforced to devise from Age to Age, one Law upon another, and one Statute after another for the repressing and punishing of them, and have endeavoured by all their Wits to snip the Sprouts, and quench the very first Sparks of them: As every Man may easily perceive there was Cause thereof, who will look back, and call to his Remembrance what that small Riot begun at *Dartmouth* in *Kent*, in the Reign of King *Richard* the Second, between the Collector of a Subsidy and a Tyler[6] and his Wife, about the Payment of one poor Groat, did come unto, which being not repressed in Time, did grow to so great a Rebellion, that after it put in Hazard the Life of the King, the burning of the City of *London*, the Overthrow of the whole Nobility, Gentlemen, and all the Learned of the Land, and the Subversion of this goodly Monarchy and Form of Government. Or if they will call to mind the small Riot, or Quarrel begun in the Reign of King *Henry* the Sixth, between a Yeoman of the Guard

[6] i.e., Wat Tyler.

and a Serving-man of *Richard Nevil's*, Earl of *Warwicke*, which so far increased for want of Restraint, that it was the Root of many woful Tragedies, and a Mean to bring untimely Death, first *Richard Plantagenet*, Duke of *York*, proclaimed Successor to the Crown, and the chief Pillar of the House of *York*, and after him King *Henry* the Sixth, and Prince *Edward* his Son, the Heirs of the House of *Lancaster*, and to ruinate with the one or the other of them, most of the Peers, great Men, and Gentlemen of the Realm, besides many Thousands of the common People. And therefore King *Edward* the First did well ordain, That no Sheriffs shall suffer Barretors[7] or Maintainers of Quarrels in their Counties: And that to all Parliaments, Treaties, and other Assemblies, each Man shall come peaceably, without any Armour; and that every Man shall have Armour in his House, according to his Ability, to keep the Peace. And King *Edward* the Third provided, That no Man shall come before the Justices, nor go or ride armed. And that suspected, lewd, and riotous Persons, shall be arrested, and safely kept until they be delivered by the Justices of Goal-Delivery. And that Justices of Peace shall restrain Offenders, Rioters, and all other Barretors, and pursue, take, and chasten them, according to their Trespass and Offence. King *Richard* the Second did prohibit Riots, Routs, and forcible Entries into Lands, that were made in divers Counties and Parts of the Realm. And that none from thenceforth should make any Riot, or Rumour. And that no Man shall ride armed, nor use Launcegaies.[8] And that no Labourer, Servant in Husbandry, or Artificer, or Victualler, shall wear any Buckler, Sword, or Dagger. And that all the King's Officers shall suppress and imprison such as make any Riots, Routs, or unlawful Assemblies against the Peace. King *Henry* the Fourth enacted, That the Justices of Peace and the Sheriff shall arrest those which commit any Riot, Rout, or unlawful Assembly, shall enquire of them, and record their Offences. King *Henry* the Fifth assigned Commissioners to enquire of the same Justices and Sheriffs Defaults in that Behalf, and also limited what Punishment Offenders attainted of Riot should sustain. King *Henry* the Seventh ordained, That such Persons as were returned to enquire of Riots should have sufficient Freehold or Copyhold Land within the same Shire. And that no Maintenance should hinder their Inquisition. And in the Reign of Queen *Mary* there was a necessary Statute established to restrain and punish unlawful and rebellious Assemblies raised by a Multitude of unruly Persons, to commit certain violent, forcible, and riotous Acts."[9]

---

[7] 'Brawlers' (*OED*).

[8] 'Lances'.

[9] Ferdinando Pulton, *De Pace Regis et Regni* . . . , fos. 24b–25a. Fielding corrects *King Henry the first* to *King Henry the Sixth* and changes *Treatises* to *Treaties*. For Pulton, see *Charge*, p. 24 n. 2.

The second Kind of Riot is of a public Kind; as where an indefinite* Number of Persons assemble themselves in a tumultuous Manner, in manner of War arrayed, and commit any open Violence with an avowed Design of redressing any public Grievance; as to remove certain Persons from the King, or to lay violent Hands on a Privy-Counsellor, or to revenge themselves of a Magistrate for executing his Office, or to bring down the Price of Victuals, or to reform the Law or Religion, or to pull down all Bawdy-houses, or to remove all Inclosures in general, &c.[†1] This Riot is High-Treason within the Words Levying War against the King, in the Statute of *Edward* III. "For here (says Lord *Coke*) the Pretence is public and general, and not private in particular[‡]. And this, (says he) tho' there be no great Number of Conspirators, is levying War within the Purview of the above Statute."[2]

In the Reign of King *Henry* VIII. it was resolved by all the Judges of *England*, that an Insurrection against the Statute of Labourers[4] for the inhancing of Salaries and Wages, was a levying of War against the King, because it was generally against the King's Law, and the Offenders took upon them the Reformation thereof, which Subjects, by gathering Power, ought not to do[‖].[5]

In the 20th of *Charles* II. a Special Verdict[6] was found at the *Old Bailey*, that *A, B, C,* &c. with divers others, to the Number of an Hundred, assembled themselves in Manner of War arrayed to pull down Bawdy-

---

* It may be gathered, perhaps, from Lord *Coke*, 3 Inst. 176. that the Number ought to be above 7 or at most 34, for such Number is, he says, called an Army. And a lesser Number cannot, I think, be well said to be *modo guerrino arraiati*.[3]

† *Hawk.* lib. 1. cap. 17. Sect. 25.

‡ 3 Inst. 9.

‖ 3 Inst. 10.

---

[1] Hawkins, i. 37. Fielding follows Hawkins closely: 'Those also who make an Insurrection in order to redress a publick Grievance . . . are said to levy War against the King . . . as where great Numbers by Force attempt to remove certain Persons from the King: or to lay violent Hands on a Privy Counsellor; or to revenge themselves against a Magistrate for executing his Office; or to bring down the Price of Victuals; or to reform the Law or Religion; or to pull down all Bawdy-Houses; or to remove all Inclosures in general, &c.' For Hawkins, see *Charge*, p. 4 n. 2.

[2] As Fielding indicates, Coke's comment on the Statute of Edward III (25 Ed. III, s. 5. c. 2) distinguishes treasonable from non-treasonable assemblies. An assembly is treasonable 'if they had risen of purpose to alter Religion established within the Realme, or Laws, or to go from Town to Town generally, and to cast down Inclosures, this is a levying of war (though there be no great number of the Conspirators) within the Purview of this Statute, because the pretence is publick and generall, and not private in particular' (III *Inst.* 9–10).

[3] 'in manner of war arrayed'.

[4] The famous Statute of Labourers passed in 1349 (23 Ed. III, c. 7) enjoined laborers to accept wages current before the Black Death.

[5] Except for minor changes in orthography and punctuation and a syntactical transposition (Coke wrote 'It was resolved by all the Judges of England in the reigne of King H. 8.'), Fielding follows Coke verbatim in this paragraph.

[6] In a case involving difficult matters of law, a jury may state the facts it considers proved and leave the decision to the court. This is called a *special verdict*.

houses, and that they marched with a Flag on a Staff, and Weapons, and pulled down Houses in Prosecution of their Conspiracies; which by all the Judges assembled, except one, was ruled to be High-Treason†.[7]

My Lord Chief Justice *Kelyng*, who tried the Cause, tells us, in his *Reports‡*, "that he directed the Jury, that he was well satisfied in his own Judgment, that such assembling together as was proved, and the pulling down of Houses upon pretence they were Bawdy-houses, was High-Treason, because they took upon them regal Power to reform that which belonged to the King by his Law and Justices to correct and reform; and it would be a strange Way and mischievous to all People to have such a rude Rabble without an Indictment to proceed in that Manner against all Persons Houses which they would call Bawdy-houses, for then no Man were safe, therefore as that way tore the Government out of the King's Hands, so it destroyed the great Privilege of the People, which is not to be proceeded against, but upon an Indictment first found by a Grand-Jury, and after upon a legal Trial by another Jury where the Party accused was heard to make his Defence; yet, says he, because the Kings of this Nation had oftentimes been so merciful as when such Outrages had been heretofore done not to proceed capitally against the Offenders, but to proceed against the Offenders in the Star-Chamber, being willing to reduce their People by milder Ways, if it were possible, to their Duty and Obedience; yet that Lenity of the King in some Cases did not hinder the King when he saw there was need to proceed in a severer Way, to take that Course which was warranted by Law, and to make greater Examples, that the People may know the Law, is not wanting so far to the Safety of the King and his People, as to let such Outrages go without capital Punishment, which is at this Time absolutely necessary, because we ourselves have seen a Rebellion raised by gathering People together upon fairer Pretences than this was, for no such Persons use at first to declare their wickedest Design, but when they see that they may effect their Design, then they will not stick to go further, and give the Law themselves, and destroy all that oppose them: But yet because there was no body of the Long Robe there but my Brother *Wylde*,[8] then Recorder of *London*, and my self, and that this Example might have the greater Authority,

† *Hale's* History of the Pleas of the Crown, vol. I. p. 134.
‡ Kel. 71.

---

[7] Hale, i. 134: 'There was a special verdict found at the Old Bailey anno 20 Car. II., that A. B. and C. with divers persons to the number of an hundred assembled themselves *modo guerrino* to pull down bawdy-houses and that they marched with a flag upon a staff and weapons, and pulled down certain houses in prosecution of their conspiracy; this by all the judges assembled, except one, was ruled to be levying of war, and so high treason within that statute; and accordingly they were executed.' Hale cites Kelyng (for whom see n. 9 following). The dissenting judge was Hale. For Hale, see *General Introductions*, p. xxxii.

[8] John Wilde or Wylde (1590–1669), chief baron of Exchequer. 'Long Robe': a member of the legal profession, here a judge.

I did resolve that the Jury should find the Matter Specially, and then I would procure a Meeting of all the Judges of *England*, and what was done should be by their Opinion, that so this Question might have such a Resolution as no Person afterwards should have Reason to doubt the Law, and *all Persons might be warned how they for the time to come mingle themselves with such Rabble on any kind of such Pretences."*[9]

And afterwards, out of Six against whom Special Verdicts were found, Four were executed.[1]

In the 13th Year of Queen *Elizabeth*, it was made Treason to compass, imagine, invent, devise, or intend to levy War gainst the Queen, &c.[2]

On this Statute *Richard Bradshaw*, a Miller, *Robert Burton*, a Mason, and others of *Oxfordshire*, were indicted and attainted. "This Case (says Lord *Coke*) was that they conspired and agreed to assemble themselves, with as many as they could procure, at *Enslowe-Hill*, in the said County, there to rise, and from thence to go from Gentleman's House to Gentleman's House, and to cast down Inclosures as well for Enlargement of Highways, as of arable Lands," &c. This was resolved to be a compassing to levy War against the Queen, and to be Treason, and the Offenders were executed at *Enslowe-Hill**.[3]

The last mentioned Case was in the 39th Year of Queen *Elizabeth*. And two Years before that, several Apprentices of *London* assembled themselves to the Number of Three Hundred and upwards, at *Bunhill* and *Tower-Hill*, in order to deliver some of their Fellows out of Prison, and threatned to burn

* Inst. 10.   2 *And* 66.   *Poph.* 122.[4]

---

[9] Sir John Kelyng (d. 1671; chief justice of King's Bench), *Reports of Crown Cases in the time of King Charles II*, 1708; 1739, 3rd edn., ed. Richard Loveland (London, 1873), pp. 71–2. Kelyng's *Reports* is no. 123 in Baker.

[1] Four of the assembled eleven judges shared Hale's doubt about the treasonable nature of the offence of two of the men convicted. Consequently, Kelyng, who was then Chief Justice of the King's Bench, recommended mercy and they were pardoned.

In this case and the two cases that follow, Fielding cites well-known precedents concerning treasonable riots. Hale's ch. XIV, 'Concerning levying of war *against the king*' (i. 130–58), refers to the same cases, cites the same statutes, and directs the reader to Coke, Anderson, Kelyng, and Popham. In his discussion of laws relating to treason, Sir William Holdsworth considers the same material and relies particularly on Hale (*History of English Law*, 2nd edn. (1937), viii. 310 ff.

[2] Eliz., c. 1.

[3] This passage from Coke follows immediately that quoted on p. 37 n. 2. Coke continues, 'And they agreed to get Armour and Artillery at the Lord Norrys his house, and to weare them in going from Gentlemans house to Gentlemans house for the purpose aforesaid, and to that purpose they perswaded divers others: and all this was a compassing and intention to levie war against the Queen, because the pretence was publick within the statute of 13 Eliz. cap. 1 . . . and the Offenders were attainted and executed at Enslowe-Hill' (III *Inst.* 10). Fielding omits detail that darkens the offence.

[4] Sir Edmund Anderson (1530–1605; chief justice of Common Pleas), *Les Reports du Treserudite Edmund Anderson . . . Chief Justice del Common-Bank*, two parts bound together, London, 1664, 1665. Anderson's *Reports* is no. 160 in Baker.

Sir John Popham (1531?–1607; chief justice of the King's Bench), *Reports and Cases Collected by . . . Popham*, London, 1656. Popham's *Reports* is no. 269 in Baker.

my Lord-Mayor's House, and to break open two Houses near the *Tower* where Arms were lodged. They had with them a Trumpet, and a Cloak upon a Pole was carried as their Colours; and being opposed by the Sheriff and Sword-Bearer of *London*, offered violence to their Persons—And for this Offence they were indicted of Treason, attainted and executed*.[5]

Now the Reason of the Judgment in all these Cases was because the Offenders had attempted by Force and Violence to redress Grievances of a public Nature: For, as *Anderson* in his Report of the last Case tells us, "When any Persons intend to levy War for any Matter which the King by his Law and Justice ought or can regulate in his Government, as King, this shall be intended a levying of War against the King; nor is it material whether they intend any Hurt to the Person of the King, if their Intent be against his Office and Authority."[6] This is within the Statute of the 13 *Eliz.* And wherever the Intent is within that Statute, the real levying War is within the Statute of *Edward* III.

I have set down these Cases only to shew the Light in which these Kinds of Riots have been always considered by our Ancestors, and how severely they have been punished in the most constitutional Reigns.

And yet extensive as this Branch of Treason on the Statute of *Edward* the Third may seem to have been, it was not held sufficient: For by the 3 and 4 of *Edward* VI. it was made High-Treason for twelve Persons, or above, being assembled together, *to attempt* to alter any Laws, &c. or to continue together above an Hour after they are commanded by a Justice of Peace, Mayor, Sheriff, &c. to return. And by the same Act it was made Felony for twelve Persons or above, *to practice* to destroy any Park, Pond, Conduit, or Dove-house, &c. or to pull down any Houses, Barns or Mills, or to abate the Rates of any Lands, or the Prices of any Victual, &c.[8]

This Statute was repealed in the first Year of Queen *Mary*, and then it was enacted that "if any Persons to the Number of twelve, or above, being assembled together, shall intend, go about, practice or put in use, with Force and Arms, unlawfully and of their own Authority, to change any Laws made for Religion by Authority of Parliament standing in Force, or any other Laws or Statutes of this Realm, or any of them, the same Number of twelve or above, being commanded or required by the Sheriff of the Shire, or by any Justice of Peace of the same Shire, or by any Mayor, Sheriff, Justices of Peace, or Bailiffs of any City, Borough or Town-corporate, where any such

---

* 2 *And* 2 *Hale's* Hist. vol. I. 125.[7]

---

[5] The prison rescue was attempted because 'divers apprentices of *London* and *Southwark* were committed to prison for riots, and for making proclamation concerning the prices of victuals, some whereof were sentenced in the star-chamber to be set in the pillory and whipt' (Hale, i. 144).

[6] Fielding's translation of Anderson's 'law-French'.

[7] The reference to Hale should be to pp. 144–5.

[8] 3 & 4 Ed. VI, c. 5.

Assemblies shall be lawfully had or made, by Proclamation in the Queen's Name to retire and repair to their Houses, Habitations or Places from whence they came, and they or any of them, notwithstanding such Proclamation, shall continue together by the Space of one whole Hour after such Commandment or Request made by Proclamation; or after that shall willingly in forcible and riotous Manner attempt to do or put in ure[9] any of the Things above specified, that then as well every such Abode together, as every such Act or Offence, shall be adjudged Felony, and the Offenders therein shall be adjudged Felons, and shall suffer only Execution of Death, as in Case of Felony. And if any Persons to the said Number of twelve or above, shall go about, &c. to overthrow, cut, cast down, or dig the Pales, Hedges, Ditches, or other Enclosure of any Park, or other Ground enclosed, or the Banks of any Fish-pond or Pool, or any Conduits for Water, Conduit-heads, or Conduit-pipes having Course of Water, to the Intent that the same, or any of them should from thenceforth lie open, or unlawfully to have Way or Common in the said Parks or other Grounds enclosed, or to destroy the Deer in any manner of Park, or any Warren of Conies, or any Dove-houses, or any Fish in any Fish-pond or Pool, or to pull or cut down any Houses, Barns, Mills or Bayes, or to burn any Stacks of Corn, or to abate or diminish the Rents of any Lands, or the Price of any Victual, Corn or Grain, or any other Thing usual for the Sustenance of Man; and being required or commanded by any Justice of Peace, &c. by Proclamation to be made, &c. to retire to their Habitations, &c. and they or any of them notwithstanding shall remain together by the Space of one whole Hour after such Commandment made by Proclamation, or shall in forcible Manner put in ure any the Things last before mentioned, &c. That then every of the said Offenders shall be judged a Felon, &c. And if any Person or Persons unlawfully, and without Authority, by ringing of any Bell or Bells, sounding of any Trumpet, Drum, Horn, or other Instrument, or by firing of any Beacon, or by malicious speaking of any Words, or making any Out-cry, or by setting up, or casting of any Bill or Writing, or by any other Deed or Act, shall raise or cause to be raised any Persons to the Number of twelve or above, to the Intent that the same Persons should do or put in ure any of the Acts above mentiond, and that the Persons so raised and assembled, after Commandment given in Form aforesaid, shall make their Abode together in Form as is aforesaid, or in forcible Manner put in ure any of the Acts aforesaid, That then all and singular Persons by whose Speaking, Deed, Act, or other the Means above specified, to the Number of twelve so raised, shall be adjudged Felons: And if the Wife, Servant, or other Persons shall any Way relieve them that be unlawfully assembled, as is aforesaid, with Victuals, Armors, Weapons, or

---

[9] 'Put into effect or operation' (a legal term).

any other Thing, that then they shall be adjudged Felons: And if any Persons above the Number of two, and under the Number of twelve, shall practise or put in ure any of the Things above mentioned, and being commanded by a Justice of Peace, &c. to retire, &c. and they make their abode by the Space of one Hour together, that then every of them shall suffer Imprisonment by the Space of one Year without Bail or Mainprise,[1] and every Person damnified shall or may recover his triple Damages against him; and every Person able, being requested by the King's Officers, shall be bound to resist them. If any Persons to the Number of forty or above, shall assemble together by forcible Manner, unlawfully, and of their own Authority, to the Intent to put in ure any of the Things above specified, or to do other Felonies or rebellious Act or Acts, and so shall continue together by the Space of three Hours after Proclamation shall be made at or nigh the Place where they shall be so assembled, or in some Market-town thereunto next adjoining, and after Notice thereof to them given, then every Person so willingly assembled in forcible Manner, and so continuing together by the Space of three Hours, shall be adjudged a Felon: And if any Copy-holder or Farmer being required by any of the King's Officers having Authority, to aid and assist them in repressing any of the said Offenders do refuse so to do, that then he shall forfeit his Copy-hold or Lease, only for Term of his Life."[2]

Some well-meaning honest *Jacobite* will perhaps object that this last Statute was enacted in a Popish Reign; but he will please to observe, that it is even less severe than that of *Edward* VI. to which I shall add that by the first of Queen *Elizabeth*, Chap. 16. this very Act of Queen *Mary* was continued during the Life of Queen *Elizabeth*, and to the End of the Parliament then next following.[3]

Having premised thus much, we will now examine the Statute of *George* I. commonly called the Riot Act;[4] which hath so often been represented either by the most profound Ignorance, or the most impudent Malice, as unconstitutional, unprecedented, as an oppressive Innovation, and dangerous to the Liberty of the Subject.

By this Statute all Persons to the Number of Twelve or more, being unlawfully, riotously, and tumultuously assembled together, to the Disturbance of the public Peace, and not dispersing themselves within an Hour after the Proclamation is read to them by a proper Magistrate, are made guilty of Felony without Benefit of Clergy.

---

[1] 'Securing the release of a prisoner by becoming surety for him' (*OED*).

[2] I Mar., c. 12.

[3] The 25 Ed. III (known as the Statute of Treasons) still provides the basic definition of treason in English law. Interpretation of its provisions varied, but there was agreement that it held that *overt* levying of war against the king was one of the conditions of an act of treason. The statutes of Ed. VI, Mary, and Eliz. I that Fielding cites differ, first, by making *conspiracy* to levy war against the king treasonable; and, second, in being acts in force only during the reign of the instituting monarch.

[4] I Geo. I, st. 2. c. 5.

2*dly*. The Statute gives a Power to all Magistrates and Peace-Officers, and to all Persons who are by such Magistrates and Peace-Officers commanded to assist them, to apprehend all such Persons so continuing together as above after the Proclamation read, and indemnifies the said Magistrates and Peace-Officers, and all their Assistants, if in Case of Resistance any of the Rioters should be hurt, maimed or killed.

3*dly*. It is enacted, That if any Persons unlawfully, riotously, and tumultuously assembled together, to the Disturbance of the Public Peace, shall unlawfully and with Force demolish or pull down, or begin to demolish or pull down any Church or Chapel, or any Building for religious Worship certified and registered, &c. or any Dwelling-House, Barn, Stable, or other Out-house, that then every such Demolishing or pulling down, or beginning to demolish or pull down, shall be adjudged Felony without Benefit of Clergy.

4*thly*. If any Persons obstruct the Magistrate in reading the Proclamation, so that it cannot be read, such Obstruction is made Felony without Clergy; and the continuing together, to the Number of Twelve, after such Let or Hindrance of reading the Proclamation, incurs the same Guilt as if the Proclamation had really been read.

These are all the penal Clauses in the Statute.

I observe then that this Law cannot be complained against as an Innovation: For as to that Part of the Statute by which Rioters who continue together for the Space of an Hour, after they are commanded by the Magistrate to disperse, are made guilty of Felony without Benefit of Clergy, what does it more than follow the Precedents of those Laws which were enacted in the Time of *Edward* the Sixth, Queen *Mary*, and Queen *Elizabeth*? And if the Law now under our Consideration be a little more severe than one of the former Acts, it must be allowed to be less severe than the other.[5]

Indeed this Power of the Magistates in suppressing all Kind of Riots hath been found so necessary, that from the second Year of *Edward* the Third even down to these Days, the Legislature hath from Time to Time more and more encreased it. Of such Consequence hath this Matter appeared, and so frequently hath it been under the Consideration of Parliament, that I think there are almost twenty Statutes concerning it.[6]

[5] Of the Riot Act, Leon Radzinowicz writes 'This Act neither curtailed nor altered any of the broad principles established under the common law and earlier statutes. It was indeed little more than a re-enactment of provisions made in the reigns of Edward VI and Mary' (Radzinowicz, iv. 131). Blackstone, however, considered that it significantly increased the power of the crown (*Comm.* iv. 441).

[6] Interpretive and statutory extensions of the Treasons Act were necessary in part because of the vagueness of its provisions and in part because laws had to match the broadening conception of what 'belonged' to the king. By 1714, when the Riot Act was passed, the ancillary statutes cited by Fielding had lapsed and the Court of Star Chamber no longer existed to perform their function. Thus the Riot Act, which in 1714 had been considered essential to secure the succession of the House of Hanover,

And upon the Statute of 13 *H.* 4 cap. 7. by which the Justices, Sheriff, &c. are empowered and ordered to suppress all Riots, it hath been holden, that not only the Justices, &c. but all who attend them, may take with them such Weapons as shall be necessary to enable them effectually to do it; and that they may justify the beating, wounding and even killing such Rioters as shall resist or refuse to surrender themselves*.[7]

As to that Branch of the Statute by which demolishing, &c. Houses, &c. is made Felony, the Offence, instead of being aggravated, seems to be lessened, namely, from Treason into Felony; according to the Opinion of Judge *Walmsley* in *Popham's Reports*, and of Lord Chief Justice *Hale* in his *Pleas of the Crown†*.[8]

It is true, as that learned Judge observes‡, that Statutes of *Edward* or *Mary* did not require (nor doth that of *George* I. require) that the Rioters should be in Manner of War arrayed. But how little of this Array of War was necessary upon the Head of the constructive Treason, must have appeared from the Cases I have mentioned; in one of which the *Insignia Belli* were a few Aprons carried on Staves§. In another they had a Trumpet, and a Cloke carried upon a Pole‖; and in others, as appears, there were no such *Insignia* at all.[9]

Again. Upon the Indictment of Treason any Overt-act would be sufficient; but here the Offence is restrained to such Acts as most manifestly threaten, not only the public Peace, but the Safety of every Individual.

* *Poph.* 121. 2 And. 67. *Hawk.* lib. 1. cap. 65. s. 21, &c.
† Vol. I. 134.
‡ Vol. I. 154.
§ *Kel.* 70.
‖ 2 *And.* 2.

---

provided the machinery necessary to control behavior dangerous to the state and made unnecessary conviction for treason by 'constructive extension', which was unpopular (Lord George Gordon was tried under the Treasons Act and Dr Johnson said 'he was glad Lord George Gordon had escaped, rather than a precedent should be established of hanging a man for constructive treason' [*Life*, iv. 87]). Also, since conviction under the Riot Act was a felony rather than treason, the harsh punishment of forfeit of property as well as of life was avoided. None the less it was not popular.

[7] Most of this paragraph comes directly from Hawkins (i, cap. 65, sect. 21, 161): 'Also it hath been holden, That those who attend the Justices in order to suppress a Riot, may take with them such Weapons as shall be necessary to enable them effectually to do it, and that they may justify the beating, wounding, and even the killing of such Rioters as shall resist, or refuse to surrender themselves.' Fielding omits Anderson's caution that killing should be avoided and Popham's observation that it is 'the more discreet way for every one in such a case to attend and be assistant to the justices, sheriffs, or other ministers of the King' (for Anderson and Popham, see above, p. 39 n. 4).

[8] Both Walmsley and Hale, in dissenting opinions to cases which Fielding has already cited for the majority opinion (see pp. 38 and 39, nn. 7 and 1 respectively), argued against conviction for treason partially on the ground that assemblies of twelve or more that demolished houses were guilty only of felony according to 1 Mar., c. 12. Walmsley is cited in Popham 121.

[9] Hale, reflecting on the effects of the notion of constructive treason embodied in the Acts of Edward VI and Mary, concludes that in not requiring that rioters be *mod guerrino arraiati* those Acts 'inflicted a new and farther punishment' (i. 154). Fielding's point is that the *insignia belli* of the Statute of Treasons were nominal anyway.

How then can this Statute be said, in the second Place, to be oppressive? Is it not rather the most necessary of all our Laws, for the Preservation and Protection of the People?

The Houses of Men are in Law considered as the Castles of their Defence;[1] and that in so ample a Manner, that no Officer of Justice is empowered by the Authority of any mesne civil Process to break them open.[2] Nay, the Defence of the House is by the Law so far privileged beyond that of the Person, that in the former Case a Man is allowed to assemble a Force, which is deny'd him in the latter;[3] and to kill a Man who attacked your House was strictly lawful, whereas some Degree of Guilt was by the Common Law incurred by killing him who attacked your Person.[4] To burn your House, (nay, at this Day to set Fire to it) is Felony without Benefit of Clergy.[5] To break it open by Night, either committing a Felony, or with Intent to commit it, is Burglary. To break it open by Day, and steal from it the Value of five shillings, or privately to steal from any Dwelling-House to the Value of forty Shillings, is Felony without Benefit of Clergy.[6] Is it then an unreasonable or oppressive Law, to prohibit the demolishing or pulling down your House, and that by Numbers riotously and tumultuously assembled, under as severe a Penalty? Is not breaking open your Doors and demolishing your House a more atrocious Crime in those who commit it, and much more injurious to the Person against whom it is committed, than the robbing it forcibly of Goods to the Value of five Shillings, or privately to the Value of forty? If the Law can here be said to be cruel, how much more so is it to inflict Death on a Man who robs you of a single Farthing on the Highway, or who privately picks your Pocket of thirteen Pence?[7]

But I dwell, I am afraid, too long on this Head: For surely no Statute had ever less the Marks of Oppression; nor is any more consistent with our Constitution, or more agreeable to the true Spirit of our Law.

And where is the Danger to Liberty which can arise from this Statute? Nothing in Reality was ever more fallacious or wicked than this Suggestion:

[1] The phrase derives from Coke, *Fifth Report*, 91.

[2] 'Mesne': 'Middle or intervening'. A mesne lord is one who holds property of a superior lord (ultimately the king) but who is lord to his tenant. A house could be entered in a criminal process but not in a civil one. Here mesne process simply means any legal order before final judgment.

[3] Hale, i. 547.

[4] Blackstone (*Comm.* iv. 177 ff.) puts homicide committed defending one's house in the category of 'justifiable homicide', which carries 'no share of guilt at all'; homicide committed in self-defense falls in his category of 'excusable homicide', which carries 'very little' guilt.

[5] 21 Hen. VIII, c. 1. and 9 Geo. I, c. 22.

[6] To break and enter a house at night with intent to commit a felony was burglary, punishable by death. The latter two crimes Fielding describes are larcenies but by statute also carried the death penalty without benefit of clergy (39 Eliz, c. 15. and 12 Ann., s. 1. c. 7. respectively). 'Privately': 'without breaking open; by stealth'.

[7] Stealing from the person by open and violent assault goods of any value was robbery, punishable by death; stealing privately from the person goods valued at more than 12 pence was grand larceny, punishable by death.

The public Peace, and the Safety of the Individual, are indeed much secured by this Law; but the Government itself, if their Interest must be or can be considered as distinct from, and indeed in Opposition to that of the People, acquires not by it the least Strength or Security. And this, I think, must sufficiently appear to every one who considers what I have said above: For surely there is no Lawyer who can doubt, even for a single Moment, whether any riotous and tumultuous Assembly, who shall avow any Design directly levelled against the Person of the King, or any of his Counsellors, be High-Treason or not, whether, as Lord *Hale* says, the Assembly were greater or less, or armed or not armed.[8] As to the Power of the Magistrate for suppressing such Kinds of Riots, and for securing the Bodies of the Offenders, it was altogether as strong before as it is now.

It seems, therefore, very difficult to see any evil Intention in the Makers of this Act, and I believe it will be as difficult to shew any ill Use that hath been made, or attempted to be made of it. In thirty-four Years I remember to have heard of no more than two Prosecutions upon it; in neither of which any distinct Interest of the Government, or rather, as I suppose is meant, of the Governors, was at all conerned.[9] And to evince how little any such evil Use is to be apprehended at present, I shall here repeat the Sentiments of our present excellent Lord Chief Justice,[1] as I myself heard them delivered in the *King's-Bench, viz.* That the Branch of the Statute which empowers Magistrates to read the Proclamation for the dispersing Rioters was made, as the Preamble declares, on very important Reasons, and intended to be applied only on very dangerous Occasions; and that he should always regard

---

[8] Hale, i. 151: 'But whether the assembly were greater or less, or armed or not armed, yet if the design were directly against the king, as to do him bodily harm, to imprison, to restrain him, or to offer any force or violence to him, it will be treason within the first clause of compassing the king's death . . .' Hale's observation concerns clear and specific acts of treason. Its relevance to Fielding's context is not clear.

[9] One instance Fielding must have in mind occurred 19 Feb. 1737, the opening night of his farce *Euridice, or the Devil Henpeck'd.* A group of footmen, angry at being driven from the gallery of the New Theatre in the Haymarket, forced their way back and created such a disturbance that the High Sheriff of Westminster was called, who read the Riot Act and made several arrests (Cross, i. 206–7; Dudden, i. 189). *Euridice* was hissed from the stage.

There were two violent protests against the Riot Act in 1738, both involving Sir Thomas De Veil. De Veil insisted that a leader of the protests against the unpopular Gin Act of 1736 be prosecuted under the Act. The offender, Roger Allen, was acquitted on 10 May 1738, to the delight of a 'prodigious mob' though the facts were proved against him. In Oct. 1738, 'the Town' prevented a performance by French players in the Haymarket (obnoxious particularly because of the Licensing Act of 1737). De Veil threatened to read the Riot Act and 'This affair made a prodigious noise, all the coffee-houses rung with it, the papers were filled with it, and the case of the *French* players became with some folks a point of law, and with others a point of state . . .'.(see *Memoirs of the Life and Times of Sir Thomas De Veil* [London, 1748], pp. 38–45; and Arthur H. Scouten, *The London Stage 1729–1747: A Critical Introduction* [Carbondale, 1968], pp. clxxvi–clxxvii).

[1] Sir William Lee succeeded Sir Philip Yorke (Lord Hardwicke) as chief justice of King's Bench in 1737 and so served until 1754. Fielding compliments Lee in 'Of True Greatness' (*Miscellanies* [1743], p. 29).

it as a very high Crime in any Magistrate, wantonly or officiously to attempt to read it on any other.

So much for this Law, on which I have dwelt perhaps longer than some may imagine to be necessary; but surely it is a Law well worthy of the fullest Justification, and is altogether as necessary to be publickly and indeed universally known; at a Time when so many wicked Arts are employed to infuse riotous Principles into the Mob, and when they themselves discover so great a Forwardness to put these Principles in Practice.

I will now proceed to the Fact of the late Riot, and to the Case which hath been so totally misrepresented. Both of which I shall give the Public from the Mouths of the Witnesses themselves.

Middlesex, ⎫ *The information of* Nathanael Munns, *one of the Beadles of the*
to wit.   ⎭ *Dutchy-Liberty of* Lancaster.[2]

This Informant on his Oath saith, That on *Saturday* the first Day of *July* last, this Informant was summoned to quell a Disturbance which was then in the *Strand* near the New Church,[3] where a large Mob was assembled about the House of one *Owen*, the Cause of which, this Informant was told, was, that a Sailor had been there robbed by a Woman. When this Informant first came up, the Populace were crying out, "Pull down the House, pull down the House!" and were so very outrageous, that all his Endeavours, and those of another Beadle of the same Liberty, to appease them, were vain. This Informant, however, attempted to seize one of the Ringleaders, but he was immediately rescued from him, and he himself threatned to be knocked down; upon which this Informant sent for the Constables, and soon after went to his own Home. And this Informant saith, that between Eleven and Twelve the same Evening two of the aforesaid Rioters being seized by the Constable, were delivered into the Custody of this Informant, who confined them in the Night-Prison[4] of the said Liberty, which Night-Prison is under this Informant's House.

And this Informant farther saith, That on the succeeding Night, being *Sunday* the 2d Day of *July*, about Twelve at Night, a great Number of the Mob came to this Informant's House, and broke open the Windows, and entered thereat, seized his Servant, and demanded the Keys of the Prison, threatning to murder her if she did not deliver them; but not being able to procure the same, they wrenched the Bars out of the Windows, with which,

---

[2] An irregularly shaped district along either side of the Strand between London and Westminster belonging to the Duchy or Dukedom of Lancaster reflecting the special legal jurisdiction granted originally to John of Gaunt in 1376. It lost its special status in 1873.

[3] St Mary-le-Strand, one of the new churches commissioned under an Act of Queen Anne, was erected in 1714–17. Its proximity to Owen's house authenticates Pope's lines 'Amid that area wide they took their stand, / Where the tall may-pole once o'erlooked the Strand; / But now (so Anne and Piety ordain) / A Church collects the saints of Drury-Lane' (*The Dunciad*, ii. 27–30).

[4] A secure house or room where a suspect could be held until he was brought before a magistrate.

as this Informant has been told, and verily believes, they broke open the Prison, and rescued the Prisoners. And this Informant further saith, That he was the same Evening at the Watch-house[5] of the said Liberty, where two other Prisoners were confined for the said Riot, and saith that a very great Mob came to the said Watch-house, broke the Windows of the same all to Pieces, demanding to have the Prisoners delivered to them, threatning to pull the Watch-house down if the said Prisoners were not set at Liberty immediately; after which they forced into the said Watch-house, and rescued the Prisoners. And this Informant farther saith, That he apprehends himself to have been in the most imminent Danger of his Life, from the Stones and Brickbats thrown into the Windows of the said Watch-house by the said Mob, before they forced the same.

Sworn before me,   *Nathanael Munns.*
    Henry Fielding.

Middlesex, } *The Information of* John Carter, *one of the Constables of the*
    to wit. } *Dutchy-Liberty of* Lancaster.

This Informant upon his Oath saith, That on *Saturday* the first of *July*, between the Hours of Seven and Eight in the Evening, he was present at the House of one *Owen* in the *Strand*, where there were a great Mob at that Time assembled, which filled up the whole Space of the Street for near two hundred Yards; and saith, that the said House was then broke open, and the Mob within it were demolishing and stripping the same; that the Windows of the said House were all broke to Pieces, and the Mob throwing out the Goods, which they soon after set Fire to, and consumed them in the Street; and saith, that he believes there were near two Waggon-Loads of Goods consumed, which caused so violent a Flame, that the Beams of the Houses adjoining were so heated thereby, that the Inhabitants were apprehensive of the utmost Danger from the Fire, and sent for the Parish-Engines upon that Occasion, which not being immediately to be procured, several Fire-men attended, by whose Assistance, as this Informant verily believes, the Fire was prevented from doing more Mischief. Upon this, this Informant not daring himself to oppose the Rage and Violence of the Mob, and not being able to find any Magistrate in Town, applied to General *Campbell*[6] at *Somerset-House*[7] for the Assistance of the Guards there, who presently detached a

---

[5] Headquarters for the watchmen and also a temporary prison. The octagon watchhouse on the Strand in front of St Mary-le-Strand is pictured in H. Phillips, *Mid-Georgian London* (London, 1964), p. 178.

[6] Probably General John Campbell (*c.*1693–1770) who was Groom of the Bedchamber to George II as Prince of Wales and King. His wife was keeper of Somerset House (Sedgwick, i. 523). He became the fourth Duke of Argyll in 1761.

[7] Somerset House (on the site of the present Somerset House) during Elizabeth's reign and most of the 17th century had been a palace where queens resided. In the 18th century it had become 'a

Corporal and twelve Men, upon the Approach of whom, the Word was given by the Mob to quit the House, which was immediately done by all except two, whom this Informant, by the Assistance of the Guards, seized upon, and presently conveyed them safe to the Night-Prison of the Liberty aforesaid. The Mob, however, without Doors, rather increased than diminished, and continued in a very riotous and tumultuous Manner, insomuch that it was thought necessary to apply for a further Guard, and accordingly an Officer and a considerable Body of Men, to the Number, as this Informant believes, of forty, was detached from the *Tilt-yard*;[8] but the Mob, far from being intimidated by this Reinforcement, began to attack a second House, namely, the House of one *Stanhope*,[9] throwing Stones, breaking the Windows, and pelting not only the Centinels who were posted before the Door, but the Civil as well as the Military Officers. And this Informant farther saith, that though by the Interposition of the Soldiers the Mob were prevented from doing further Mischief that Night, yet they continued together till he was relieved by another Peace-Officer, which was not till Twelve at Night; nor was the said Mob, as this Informant has heard, and verily believes, dispersed until between Two and Three in the Morning.

And this Informant further saith, That on *Sunday* the second of *July*, being the succeeding Day, he was called out of his Bed on account of the re-assembling of the Mob before the House of *Stanhope*, which they had attacked the Night before. That upon his Arrival there, he found a vast Mob got together, the House broke open and demolished, and all the Goods thereof thrown into the Street, and set on Fire; and saith, that the said Fire was larger than that the preceding Night. That he was then applied to by Mr. *Wilson*, Woollen-Draper, and principal Burgess of the said Liberty, and one Mr. *Acton*,[1] another Woollen-Draper, both of whom expressed the greatest Apprehension of Danger to the whole Neighbourhood, and desired this Informant immediately to apply to the *Tilt-yard* for a Number of Soldiers, which he accordingly did; but being sent by the Officer to a Magistrate, to obtain his Authority for the said Guard, before he could obtain the same,

---

mere lodging Pen, / A palace turn'd into a den, / To barracks turn'd, and soldiers tread / Where Dowagers have laid their head' (Churchill, *The Ghost*, iv. 1047–50).

[8] The Tilt-Yard (of Whitehall Palace) was an open space facing the Banqueting House. It is now part of the Parade in St James's Park.

[9] According to *The London Evening-Post* (1–4 July 1749) Stanhope's house was 'a few Doors lower' from Owen's. Its sign was the 'Bunch of Grapes'. When asked for a character witness (below, p. 56), Penlez gave the name of a barber 'who lived next to the *Bunch of Grapes* in the *Strand*'.

[1] William Wilson's shop was a few doors east of Somerset House on the south side of the Strand; Joseph Acton's a few doors west of Somerset House on the same side of the street (Phillips, *Mid-Georgian London*, pp. 173 and 176–7).

Mr. *Welch*,[2] High-Constable of *Holbourn* Division, procured the said Guard, by which means the aforesaid Rioters were soon after dispersed.

Sworn before me,   *John Carter.*
    H. *Fielding.*

Middlesex, ⎱ *The Information of* James Cecil, *one of the Constables of the*
    to wit. ⎰ *Parish of* St. George the Martyr, *in in the said County.*

This Informant upon Oath saith, That on the third of *July* last, he was ordered by Justice *Fielding* to attend the Prisoners to *Newgate*.[3] That though an Officer, with a very large Guard of Soldiers, attended upon the said Occasion, it was not without the utmost Difficulty that the said Prisoners[4] were conveyed in Coaches through the Street, the Mob frequently endeavouring to break in upon the Soldiers, and crowding towards the Coach Doors. And saith, that he seized one of the most active of the Mob, and carried him before the said Justice, who after having reprimanded, dismissed him. And further this Informant saith, that as he passed near the *Old Bailey* with the aforesaid Prisoners, he saw a great Mob assembled there, who, as this Informant was then acquainted, had been breaking the Windows of some House or Houses there;[5] and saith, that several of the said Mob were in Sailors Habits, but upon the Approach of the Soldiers they all ran away.

                                                              James Cecil.

Middlesex, ⎱ *The Information of* Saunders Welch, *Gentleman, High-Constable*
    to wit. ⎰ *of* Holbourn *Division, in the said County.*

This Informant saith, That on *Sunday* Morning about Ten of the Clock, on

[2] As High Constable, Welch occupied a position intermediate between the justices of the peace and the petty constables. For the most part he administered the executive orders of the justice of the peace and supervised the operations of the constables, but a wide variety of duties could be attached to this post, which was generally held by a substantial householder (see Sidney and Beatrice Webb, *English Local Government* [London, 1906], i. 489–502).

   Fielding expressed his warm regard for Welch ('Whom I never think or speak of but with love and esteem') in his *Voyage to Lisbon* (p. 44). He recommended his appointment as justice of the peace in Dec. 1753. Welch became justice of the peace for Middlesex and Westminster in Apr. 1755. Johnson also had great affection for Welch (*Life*, iii. 216, 219). For Welch, see John Thomas Smith, *Nollekens and his Times* (1828), *passim*; R. Leslie-Melville, *The Life and Work of Sir John Fielding* (London, 1934), *passim*; and Anthony Babington, *A House in Bow Street* (London, 1969), pp. 108 ff.

[3] The old prison of Newgate was opposite the Old Bailey Sessions House, a site now occupied by the Central Criminal Court. Both were destroyed in the Gordon Riots of 1780.

[4] *The London Evening-Post* (1–4 July 1749) records that Fielding committed nine prisoners to Newgate. Peter Linebaugh ('The Tyburn Riot Against the Surgeons', *Albion's Fatal Tree: Crime and Society in Eighteenth-Century England* (New York, 1975), p. 93) states that seven rioters were arrested.

[5] *The London Evening-Post* (1–4 July 1749) notes that rioters unsuccessfully attacked a house near the Old Bailey on Monday, 3 July.

the Second of *July* last, one *Stanhope*, who then kept a House in the *Strand*, near the New Church, came to this Informant and told him, that a House had been demolished the Night before in the *Strand*, by a great Mob, and that he had great Reason to fear that the said Mob would come and demolish his House, they having threatned that they would pull down all Bawdy-Houses. Upon which this Informant directed the said *Stanhope* to apply to a Magistrate, telling him, that he, this Informant, would conduct himself by the Magistrate's Directions. Upon which the said *Stanhope* departed, and returned no more to this Informant.

And this Informant saith, that as he was returning the same Evening between the Hours of Eleven and Twelve, from a Friend's House in the City, as he passed through *Fleet-Street* he perceived a great Fire in the *Strand*, upon which he proceeded on till he came to the House of one *Peter Wood*,[6] who told this Informant that the Mob had demolished the House of *Stanhope*, and were burning his Goods, and that they had threatned, as soon as they had finished their Business there, that they would come and demolish his House likewise, and prayed the Assistance of this Informant. Upon which, this Informant despairing of being able to quell the Mob by his own Authority, and well knowing the Impossibility of procuring any Magistrate at that Time who would act, applied to the *Tilt-yard* for a military Force, which with much Difficulty he obtained, having no Order from any Justice of Peace for the same. And this Informant saith, that having at last procured an Officer with about forty Men, he returned to the Place of the Riot; but saith, that when he came to *Cecil-street* End,[7] he prevailed upon the Officer to order his Drum to beat, in Hopes, if possible, of dispersing the Mob without any Mischief ensuing. And this Informant saith, that when he came up to the House of *Peter Wood*, he found that the Mob had in a great part demolished the said House, and thrown a vast Quantity of his Goods into the Street, but had not perfected their Design, a large Parcel of the Goods still remaining in the House, the said House having been very well furnished. And this Informant says, that he hath been told there was a Debate among the Mob concerning burning the Goods of that House likewise, as they had served those of two other Houses. And this Informant says, that had the Goods of the said House been set on Fire, it must infallibly have set on Fire the Houses on both Sides, the Street being there extremely narrow, and saith, that the House of Mess. *Snow* and *Denne*, the Bankers,[8] is

[6] For Peter Wood's part in the riot and subsequent involvement in the Westminster Election, see General Introduction, p. xxxix ff. His house was 'the tenth east of St. Clement Danes, on the north side of the Strand, facing Devereux Court' (Phillips, *Mid-Georgian London*, p. 182).

[7] No longer in existence. It ran into the south side of the Strand, nearly opposite Southampton Street. Fielding's Registrar office was 'opposite Cecil Street in the Strand'.

[8] Snow's banking house was at no. 217 The Strand, near Devereux Court (E. Beresford Chancellor, *The Annals of the Strand* [London, 1912]), p. 157).

almost opposite to that of *Peter Wood*. And this Informant saith, that at his coming up, the Mob had deserted the House of the said *Peter*, occasioned, as he verily believes, and hath been informed, by the Terror spread among them from beating the Drum as aforesaid, so that this Informant found no Person in the aforesaid House save only *Peter Wood*, his Wife, and Man-Servant, and two or three Women who appeared to belong to it, and one *Lander*, who was taken by a Soldier in the upper Part of the said House, and who, it afterward appeared at his Trial, to the Satisfaction of the Jury, came along with the Guard.[9]

And this Informant farther says, that the said Rioters not immediately dispersing, several of them were apprehended by the Soldiers, who being produced to *Peter Wood*, were by him charged as principally concerned in the Demolition of his House, upon which they were delivered by this Informant to a Constable of the Dutchy Liberty, and were by that Constable conveyed, under a Guard of Soldiers, to *New-Prison*.[1] And this Informant farther saith, that he remained on the Spot, together with Part of the Guards, till about Three of the Clock the next Morning, before which Time the Mob were all dispersed, and Peace again restored.

And this Informant further saith, that on the *Monday* Morning, about Twelve of the Clock, he attended *H. Fielding*, Esq; one of his Majesty's Justices of the Peace for the County of *Middlesex*, who had been out of Town during all the preceding Riot, and acquainted him with it. That immediately the said Justice sent an Order for a Party of the Guards to conduct the aforesaid Prisoners to his House, the Streets being at that Time full of Mob, assembled in a riotous and tumultuous Manner, and Danger of a Rescue being apprehended. And saith, that the above mentioned Prisoners, together with *Bosavern Penlez*, who was apprehended by the Watch in *Carey-street*,[2] were brought before the said Justice, who, after hearing the Evidence against them, and taking the Depositions thereof, committed them to *Newgate*. And this Informant saith, that whilst he attended before the said Justice, and while the Prisoners were under Examination there was a vast Mob assembled, not only in *Bow-street*, but many of the adjacent Streets, so that it was difficult either to pass or repass. And further saith, that he, this Informant, received several Informations that the Mob had declared that, notwithstanding what had been done, they intended to carry on the same

---

[9] Benjamin Lander was able to prove that when the mob was in Wood's house he had been drinking with one of the soldiers sent from the Tilt Yard. He entered the house after the soldiers had arrived but was arrested when Wood accused him of damaging his house and Mrs Wood swore that he had knocked her down (*The Case of the Unfortunate Bosavern Penlez*, pp. 31 ff.).

[1] According to Defoe (*A Tour Through the Whole Island of Great Britain* [London, 1962], i. 368), the bridewell at Clerkenwell, 'the particular Bridewell for the county of Middlesex', was called the New Prison.

[2] Carey Street runs nearly parallel and north of the Strand between Portugal Street and Chancery Lane. It now forms the northern perimeter of the Royal Courts of Justice.

Work again at Night. Upon which, this Informant was, by the said Justice, dispatched to the Secretary at War,[3] to desire a Reinforcement of the Guard.

And this Informant farther saith, that he was present when the said Justice, from his Window, spoke to the Mob, informed them of their Danger, and exhorted them to depart to their own Habitations: For which Purpose, this Informant likewise went among them, and entreated them to disperse, but all such Exhortations were ineffectual. And this Informant further saith, that he was present at the House of the said Justice, when several Informations were given, that a Body of Sailors, to the Number of four Thousand, were assembling themselves at *Tower-hill*, and had declared a Resolution of marching to *Temple-Bar* in the Evening.[4] And so riotous did the Disposition of the Mob appear that whole Day, to wit, *Monday*, that Numbers of Persons, as this Informant hath been told, removed their Goods from their own Houses, from Apprehensions of sharing the Fate of *Owen*, *Stanhope* and *Wood*. To obviate which Danger, the aforesaid Justice, the Officer of the Guard and this Informant, sat up the whole Night, while a large Party of Soldiers were kept ready under Arms, who with the Peace-Officers patroled the Streets where the chief Danger was apprehended; by means of all which Care the public Peace was again restored.[5]

Sworn before me,   *Saunders Welch.*
    Henry Fielding.

Middlesex, } *The Information of* Samuel Marsh, Edward Fritter, Robert
    to wit. } Oliver, *and* John Hoar.

Samuel Marsh, of St. *Clement-Danes*, in the said County, Labourer, one of

---

[3] Henry Fox, first Baron Holland (1705–74), a supporter of Walpole and, later, of Pelham. A subscriber to the *Miscellanies* and, perhaps, an acquaintance of Fielding at Eton.

[4] A letter from Fielding to Bedford (3 July 1749) recently discovered by the Battestins ('Fielding, Bedford, and the Westminster Election of 1749', *ECS* 11 (1977–8), 153, confirms Welch's testimony here and attests to the seriousness with which Fielding regarded the possibility of renewed rioting: 'I think it my Duty to acquaint your Grace that I have read repeated Informations of upwards of 3000 Sailors now in Arms abt. Wapping and that they threaten to march to this End of the Town this Night, under Pretence of demolishing all Bawdy Houses. I have an Officer and 50 Men and submit to yr Grace what more Assistance may be necessary. I sent a Messenger five Hours ago to the Secretary at War but have yet no Answer.'

In a letter to Bedford probably written earlier the same day asking for the place of Solicitor to the Excise, Fielding had closed, 'I am at this Moment busied in endeavoring to suppress a dangerous Riot, or I wd have personally waited on your Grace to solicite [*sic*] a Favour which will make me and my Family completely Happy' (Cross, ii. 242).

[5] Some years later Welch described the Strand riots and claimed the major role in quelling them: '. . . a sailor going to one of these dens of lust in the Strand, was there beat in a cruel manner and robbed; instead of applying to a magistrate, he carried his grievance, and applied for redress to his brother tars at Wapping, and they came in numbers and gutted the houses of three of the bawds in the Strand, and made a bonfire of the goods before their doors. This occasioned a just, though unpopular execution: and the riot was with great difficulty and danger quelled by the then high-constable of Holborn division' (*A Proposal . . . to remove . . . Prostitutes from the Streets of this Metropolis* [London, 1758], pp. 8–9).

the Watchmen of St. *Dunstan's* in the West, in the City of *London*, maketh Oath, That on the Third of *July* last, as he was going his Rounds, a little after One in the Morning, one Mr. *Philip Warwick*, an Engraver by Trade, who then lived at *Pimlico* near *Buckingham*-House,[6] from whence he is since removed, came to this Informant in *Bell-yard*, opposite the *Apollo* Passage,[7] and said, there was a Man above who had a great Bundle of Linnen, which he (*Warwick*) thought the said Man had stolen, and desired this Informant to take Care of him: And farther acquainted this Informant, that the said Man told him, that the Linnen which he then had in the Bundle was his Wife's, which said *Warwick* did not believe to be true. And this Informant farther saith, that when he had received this Account, he went directly to the Place where the said Man was; and saith, that the said Man, before this Informant came up to him, had thrust most of the abovesaid Linnen into his Bosom and Pockets; and saith, that just as this Informant came up to him, and called out to him, saying, *Friend, here, come and take the Cap you have dropt*, the said Man scrambled up the rest of the Things, and ran away as fast as he could all up *Bell-yard*; upon which this Informant ran after him, and called to *Edward Fritter*, another Watchman, to stop him. And this Informant farther saith, that the said Man being afterwards taken by *Fritter*, and in Custody of him and this Informant, being asked by them, to whom the said Linnen belonged, declared, that they belonged to the Bitch his Wife, who had pawned all his Cloaths; and that he had taken away these that she might not pawn them likewise. To which this Informant answered, that Answer would not do; for that he was resolved to have a better Answer before he left him. And this Informant saith, that he and the said *Fritter* then carried the said Man to the Watch-house, where he sat down on a Bench; and this Informant saith, that whilst the said Man sat there, several Persons came into the Watch-house unknown to this Informant, one of whom said to the Prisoner, "You Son of a Bitch, pull the Things out of your Bosom and out of your Pockets, and don't let the Constable find them upon you, unless you have a Mind to hang yourself." Upon which the Prisoner pulled out the Linnen from his Bosom and his Pocket, and laid it upon the Bench; and saith that the said Linnen was afterwards delivered to Mr. *Hoare* the Constable. And further saith, that the aforesaid Man, who was apprehended as abovesaid, was the same *Bosavern Penlez* who was afterwards convicted of the Riot at the *Old Bailey*, and executed for the same. And further saith, that he believes the said *Penlez* was then a little in Liquor, but by no means dead drunk; for that

[6] Buckingham House was on what is now the site of Buckingham Palace. 17th- and 18th-century maps designate a small field in this area Pimlico.

[7] Apollo Passage has disappeared, but Bell Yard still leads north off the Strand to Carey Street. In 1749 one entered Bell Yard, a 'filthy old place' according to Pope (cit. Phillips, *Mid-Georgian London*, p. 187), through Apollo Passage, a narrow passage between and under houses just within Temple Bar.

he talked and behaved very rationally all the Time he was in the said Watch-house. And further saith, that *Penlez*, when he was in the Watch-house, said, that the Woman to whom the Linnen belonged was not his Wife; for that he was an unfortunate young Fellow, and had kept Company with bad Women, and that he had been robbed by one of them of fifteen Shillings, and had taken away her Linnen out of Revenge.

Edward Fritter, of the Precinct of *White-friars*, in the City of *London*, Shoemaker, one of the Watchmen of the Liberty of the Rolls,[8] maketh Oath, That upon the Third of *July* last, a little after One in the Morning, as he was at his Stand at the upper End of *Bell-yard*, *Samuel Marsh*, another Watchman, called out to him, "Stop that Man before you, stop that Man before you:" And this Informant saith, that when he heard these Words, the said Man had just pass'd by him, making off as fast as he could; upon which this Informant ran after him, and at about an hundred Yards Distance overtook him, and pushed him up against the Rails in *Carey-street*. And this Informant then said to him, "So, Brother, what is all this you have got here?" To which the Man answered, "I am an unfortunate young Man, and have married one of the Women of the Town, who hath pawned all my Cloaths, and I have got all her Linnen for it." And this Informant saith, that the said Man had at that Time some Linnen under his Arm. Soon after which, the said Man, who, as this Informant saith was *Bosavern Penlez*, was carried to the Watch-house, where this Informant was present when all passed that Informant *Marsh* hath sworn. And this Informant hearing the Information of *Marsh* read, declares, that all which is there related to have passed, is true.

Robert Oliver, of the Liberty of the Rolls, Shoemaker, and Beadle of that Liberty, maketh Oath, and saith, That he was present when *Bosavern Penlez* was brought into the Watch-house belonging to the said Liberty, on the Third of *July* last, between One and Two in the Morning; and saith, that he was present in the said Watch-house upon his Duty all the Time that the said *Penlez* staid there; and upon hearing the Information of *Marsh* read to him this Informant, he this Informant upon his Oath confirms the same in every Particular.

John Hoare, of the Liberty of the Rolls aforesaid, Victualler, then one of the Constables of the Liberty of the Rolls, maketh Oath, and saith, that at Two in the Morning, on the 3d of *July*, he was called by one of the Watchmen of that Liberty, and informed that a Thief was apprehended and confined in the Watch-house; upon which this Informant went directly thither, and found *Bosavern Penlez* and the Linen lying on the Bench, as mentioned in *Marsh's* Information. And this Informant further saith, that he

---

[8] The Rolls Liberty was a parish of its own because of Rolls House and Chapel, Chancery Lane, where the rolls and records of the Court of Chancery were kept until mid-19th century. Rolls House was the official residence of the Master of the Rolls, who also kept his court here.

then examined the said *Penlez* how he came by that Linnen, to which the said *Penlez* answered, that he had taken up the said Linnen in the Street, to which this Informant answered, that if he (*Penlez*) could give no better Account, he must secure him till the Morning. Then this Informant asked him, if he could send to any one who would give him a Character.—Upon which *Penlez*, after some Hesitation, mentioned the Name of a Barber who lived next to the *Bunch of Grapes* in the *Strand*, who was sent to, and refused to come. And this Informant saith, that he then proposed to *Penlez* to send for some other Person; but that the said *Penlez* mentioned no other Person. Upon which this Informant carried the said *Penlez* to *New-Prison*, and there delivered him into Custody.—And this Informant further saith, that he attended the next Day before *H. Fielding*, Esq; one of his Majesty's Justices of the Peace for the said County, when the said *Penlez* was examined, and the aforesaid Linnen was produced by this Informant. *To wit*, Ten lac'd Caps, four lac'd Handkerchiefs, three Pair of lac'd Ruffles, two lac'd Clouts, five plain Handkerchiefs, five plain Aprons, and one lac'd Apron; all which the Wife of *Peter Wood* swore to be her Property. And this Informant saith, that *Penlez* being asked by the Justice, how he came by the said Linen, answered, he had found them; and could not, or would not give any other Account.

The Mark of	*Sam. Marsh.*
	Ed. Fritter.
Sworn before me	*Rob. Oliver.*
H. Fielding.	*John Hoare.*

Middlesex. To wit.

Robert Oliver aforesaid further on his Oath says, That when *Penlez* was examined before the Justice, he solemnly denied that he was in the House of *Peter Wood*, or near it.

Rob. Oliver.

Sworn before me
  H. Fielding.

Now upon the whole of this Evidence, which I have taken the Pains to lay before the Public, and which is the Evidence of Persons entirely disinterested and of undoubted Credit, I think it must be granted by every impartial and sensible Person;

1. That the Riot here under Consideration, was of a very high and dangerous Nature, and far from deserving those light or ludicrous Colours which have been cast upon it.[9]

---

[9] As, for instance, in the *Unfortunate Penlez*, see General Introduction, above, p. xliii.

2. That the Outrages actually committed by the Mob, by demolishing the Houses of several People, by cruelly and barbarously misusing their Persons, by openly and audaciously burning their Goods, by breaking open Prisons and rescuing Offenders, and by resisting the Peace-Officers, and those who came to their Assistance, were such as no Government could justify passing over without some Censure and Example.

3. That had not Mr. *Welch* (one of the best Officers who was ever concerned in the Execution of Justice, and to whose Care, Integrity and Bravery the Public hath, to my Knowledge, the highest Obligations) been greatly active in the Discharge of his Duty; and had he not arrived Time enough to prevent the Burning of that Pile of Goods which was heaped up before *Wood's* House, the most dreadful Consequences must have ensued from this Riot. For not to mention the Mischiefs which must necessarily have happened from the Fire in that narrow Part of the Town, what must have been the Consequence of exposing a Banker's Shop to the Greediness of the Rabble? Or what might we have reasonably apprehended from a Mob encouraged by such a Booty, and made desperate by such atrocious Guilt?

4. I think it may very fairly be inferred, that the Mob, which had already carried on their riotous Proceedings during two successive Nights, and who during the whole Day on *Monday*, were in Motion all over the Town, had they not been alarmed and intimidated by the Care of the Magistrate, would have again repeated their Outrage, as they had threatned on *Monday* Night. And had such a Riot continued a little longer, no Man can, I think, foresee what it might have produced. The Cry against Bawdy-Houses might have been easily converted into an Out-cry of a very different Nature, and Goldsmiths might have been considered to be as great a Nuisance to the Public as Whores.

5. The only remaining Conclusion which I shall draw, is, That nothing can be more unjust, or indeed more absurd, than the Complaint of Severity which hath been made on this Occasion. If one could derive this silly Clamour from Malevolence to the Government, it might be easily converted into the most delicate of Compliments: For surely those must afford very little Cause of Complaint, whose Enemies can find no better Object of their Censure than this. To say the Truth, the Government is here injudiciously attacked in its most defensible Part. If it be necessary, as some seem to think, to find Fault with their Superiors, our Administration is more liable to the very opposite Censure. If I durst presume to look into the Royal Breast, I might with Certainty affirm, that Mercy is there the Characteristic. So truly is this benign Prince the Father of his People, that he is never brought, without paternal Reluctance, to suffer the Extremity of Justice to take Place.

A most amiable Excess, and yet an Excess by which, I am afraid, Subjects may be as liable to be spoiled as Children![1]

But I am willing to see these Clamours in a less culpable Light, and to derive them from a much better Motive: I mean from a Zeal gainst lewd and disorderly Houses. But Zeal in this Case, as well as in all others, may hurry Men too far, and may plunge them headlong into the greater Evils, in order to redress the lesser.

And surely this appears to be the Case at present, when an Animosity against these Houses hath made Men blind to the clearest Light of Evidence; and impelled them to fly in the Face of Truth, of Common Sense, I might say yet more, and all in the Behalf of a licentious, outrageous Mob, who in open Defiance of Law, Justice or Mercy, committed the most notorious Offences against the Persons and Properties of their Fellow-Subjects, and who had undoubtedly incurred the last and highest Degree of Guilt, had they not been happily and timely prevented.

When I mention this Zeal as some kind of Excuse or Mitigation, I would be understood to apply it only to those Persons who have been so weak (at least) to espouse the Cause of these Malefactors: as to the Rioters themselves, I am satisfy'd they had no such Excuse. The Clamour against Bawdy-Houses was in them a bare Pretence only. Wantonness and Cruelty were the Motives of most, and some, as it plainly appeared, converted the inhuman Disposition of the Mob to the very worst of Purposes, and became Thieves under the Pretence of Reformation.

How then is it possible for any Man in his Senses to express a Compassion for such Offenders, as for Men, who while they are doing an illegal Act, may yet be supposed to act from a laudable Motive? I would ask such Men this Question. By whom are these Houses frequented and supported? Is it not by the Young, the Idle, and the Dissolute?—This is, I hope, true; no grave Zealot will, I am convinced, assert the contrary. Are these then the People to redress the Evil? Play-houses have been in a former Age reputed a Grievance; but did the Players rise in a Body to demolish them? Gaming-houses are still thought a Nuisance; but no Man, I believe, hath ever seen a Body of Gamesters assembled to break them open, and burn their Goods. It is indeed possible, that after a bad Run of Luck they might be very well pleased with an Opportunity of stealing them.

The Nuisance which Bawdy-houses are to the Public, and how far it is interested in suppressing them, is not our present Consideration. The Law clearly considers them as a Nuisance, and hath appointed a Remedy against

---

[1] Cf. Fielding's remarks on too frequent pardons in the *Enquiry*, p. 163 ff. The author of *The Case of the Unfortunate Bosavern Penlez*, on the other hand, suggests that since the king withheld his pardon in this case, juries in the future will refuse to convict offenders for whom they have sympathy. Fielding lavishly praises George II's clemency in *TP* no. 27, p. 217.

them; and this Remedy it is in the Power of every Man, who desires it, to apply.[2] But surely it will not be wished by any sober Man, that open illegal Force and Violence should be with Impunity used to remove this Nuisance; and that the Mob should have an uncontrolled Jurisdiction in this Case. When by our excellent Constitution the greatest Subject, no not even the King himself, can, without a lawful Trial and Conviction divest the meanest Man of his Property, deprive him of his Liberty, or attack him in his Person;[3] shall we suffer a licentious Rabble to be Accuser, Judge, Jury, and Executioner; to inflict corporal Punishment, break open Men's Doors, plunder their Houses, and burn their Goods? I am ashamed to proceed further in a Case so plain, where the Absurdity is so monstrous, and where the Consequences are so obvious and terrible.

As to the Case of the Sufferer, I shall make no Remarks. Whatever was the Man's Guilt, he hath made all the Atonement which the Law requires, or could be exacted of him; and tho' the popular Clamour made it necessary to publish the above Depositions, nothing shall come from me to add to, or to aggravate them.

If, after perusing the Evidence which I have here produced, there should remain any private Compassion in the Breast of the Reader, far be it from me to endeavour to remove it. I hope I have said enough to prove that this was such a Riot as called for some Example, and that the Man who was made that Example, deserved his Fate. Which, if he did, I think it will follow, that more hath been said* and done in his Favour than ought to have been; and that the Clamour of Severity against the Government hath been in the highest Degree injustifiable.

To say Truth (as I have before hinted) it would be more difficult to justify the Lenity used on this Occasion. The first and second Day of this Riot, no Magistrate, nor any other higher Peace-Officer than a Petty-Constable (save only Mr. *Welch*) interfered with it. On the third Day, only one Magistrate took upon him to act. When the Prisoners were committed to *Newgate*, no public Prosecution was for some time ordered against them;[4] and when it

---

* He was buried by a private Subscription, but not at the public Expence of the Parish of St. *Clement Danes*, as hath been falsely asserted.[5]

---

[2] As Fielding had pointed out in his *Charge*, p. 22.

[3] Cf. Fielding's commentary on an Englishman's right to a trial by jury in his *Charge* (p. 4) and in *Elizabeth Canning* (p. 283).

[4] The 'Historical Chronicle' in *GM* for July 1749 notes that 'A bill of indictment was found at Hicks's-Hall, against 4 persons, for feloniously and riotously beginning to demolish the Star tavern in the *Strand*, laid on the statute of 1 Geo. I. Cap. 5. But the evidence not being ready, the tryal was deferr'd to the next session, on the motion of the attorney general.'

[5] The false assertion appears in *The London Evening-Post* (17–19 Oct. 1749). *The Penny London Post* (27–30 Oct. 1749) states that Penlez was buried at the 'Expence of some gentlemen of the Parish of St. Clements, where the Riot happened, who, to testify their respect to his Memory, accompany'd his Corpse to the Grave'.

was ordered, it was carried on so mildly, that one of the Prisoners (*Wilson*) being sick in Prison, was (tho' contary to Law) at the Desire of a noble Person[6] in great Power, bailed out, when a Capital Indictment was then found against him.[7] At the Trial, neither the Attorney nor Solicitor-General, nor even one of the King's Council appeared against the Prisoners. Lastly, when two were convicted, one only was executed; and I doubt very much whether even he would have suffered, had it not appeared that a capital Indictment[†] for Burglary was likewise found by the Grand Jury against him, and upon such Evidence as I think every impartial Man must allow would have convicted him (had he been tried) of Felony at least.

Thus I have finished this ungrateful Task which I thought it the more incumbent on me to undertake, as the real Truth of this Case, from the Circumstances mentioned at the Bottom of this Page, was known only to myself, and a very few more. This I thought it my Duty to lay before some very noble Persons,[8] in order to make some Distinction between the two condemned Prisoners, in Favour of *Wilson*, whose Case to me seemed to be the Object of true Compassion. And I flatter myself that it might be a little owing to my Representation, that the Distinction between an Object of Mercy, and an Object of Justice at last prevailed, to my Satisfaction, I own entirely, and I hope, now at last, to that of the Public.

FINIS

[†] Upon this Indictment he was arraigned, but the Judge said,[9] as he was already capitally convicted for the same Fact, tho' of a different Offence, there was no Occasion of trying him again. By which Means the Evidence which I have above produced, and which the Prosecutor reserved to give on this Indictment, was never heard at the *Old-Bailey*, nor in the least known to the Public.

---

[6] Unidentified.

[7] Bail for one under capital indictment was less irregular than Fielding indicates. The Court of King's Bench, for instance, could bail a prisoner accused of treason or murder.

[8] Both Newcastle and Bedford, as Secretaries of State, had effective power to obtain a pardon.

[9] John Willes, chief justice of Common Pleas. According to B. Maelor Jones (*Henry Fielding: Novelist and Magistrate* [London, 1933], p. 141), Willes wanted to hang both Wilson and Penlez.

AN

ENQUIRY

Into the CAUSES of the late

Increafe of Robbers, &c.

WITH SOME

PROPOSALS for Remedying this
GROWING EVIL.

IN WHICH

The Prefent Reigning VICES are impartially
expofed; and the Laws that relate to the
Provifion for the POOR, and to the Punifhment of FELONS are largely and freely examined.

*Non jam funt mediocres hominum libidines, non humanæ auda-
ciæ ac tolerandæ. Nihil cogitant nifi cædem, nifi incendia,
nifi rapinas.* CIC. in Catil. 2ᵈᵃ.

By HENRY FIELDING, Efq;

Barrifter at Law, and One of His Majefty's Juftices
of the Peace for the County of *Middlefex,* and for
the City and Liberty of *Weftminfter.*

LONDON:

Printed for A. MILLAR, oppofite to *Katharine-Street,*
in the *Strand.* M. DCC. LI.

[Price 2 *s.* 6 *d.*]

AN
ENQUIRY

Into the CAUSES of the late

Increafe of Robbers, &c.

WITH SOME

PROPOSALS for Remedying this
GROWING EVIL.

IN WHICH

The Prefent Reigning VICES are impartially
expofed ; and the LAWS that relate to
the Provifion for the Poor, and to the
Punifhment of FELONS are largely and
freely examined.

Non jam funt mediocres hominum libidines, non humanæ
audaciæ ac tolerandæ. Nihil cogitant nifi cædem, nifi
incendia, nifi rapinas. CIC. in Catil. 2ᵈᵃ.

By HENRY FIELDING, Efq;

Barrifter at Law, and one of His Majefty's
Juftices of the Peace for the County of *Middle-*
fex, and for the City and Liberty of *Weftminfter*.

The SECOND EDITION.

LONDON:

Printed for A. MILLAR, oppofite to Katharine-
Street, in the Strand. MDCCLI.

TO THE
RIGHT HONOURABLE
Philip Lord Hardwick,
Lord High Chancellor of *Great Britain*.[1]

MY LORD,

As the Reformation of any Part of our Civil Polity requires as much the Knowledge of the Statesman as of the Lawyer, the following Sheets are, with the strictest Propriety, addressed to a Person of the highest Eminence in both these Capacities.

The Subject of this Treatise cannot be thought unworthy of such a Protection, because it touches only those Evils which have arisen in the lower Branches of our Constitution. This Consideration will account for their having hitherto escaped your Lordship's Notice; and that alone will account for their having so long prevailed: But your Lordship will not, for this Reason, think it below your Regard;[2] since, however ignoble the Parts may be in which the Disease is first engendered, it will in time be sure to affect the whole Body.[3]

Title-page] *In Catilinam*, II. v. 10. 'For the lusts of these men are no longer moderate, and their wantonness is inhuman and unbearable, they think of nothing but murder, arson, and rape' (Loeb). Cicero refers to the 'criminal gangs of desperate men' whom he hopes will follow Catiline out of Rome. *Non enim iam . . . humanae et tolerandae audaciae* in the received text.

[1] Philip Yorke (1690–1764), cr. Baron Hardwicke 1733; 1st Earl of Hardwicke, 1754. Hardwicke was a loyal supporter of Walpole and later was a central figure of the Pelham Administration. His abilities as lawyer and politician brought him the positions of solicitor-general (1720–4), attorney-general (1724–33), Chief Justice of King's Bench (1733–7), and lord chancellor (1737–56). Fielding complimented him handsomely in *Tom Jones* by comparing the principle of conscience, which 'doth certainly inhabit some human Breasts' to the 'LORD HIGH CHANCELLOR of this Kingdom in his Court', who 'presides, governs, directs, judges, acquits and condemns according to Merit and Justice; with a Knowledge which nothing escapes, a Penetration which nothing can deceive, and an Integrity which nothing can corrupt' (IV. vi. 172). In *TP* no. 33, p. 255, Fielding had characterized Hardwicke as a 'great and glorious Man . . . whose Goodness of Heart is no less conspicuous than those great Parts, which, both in the Character of a Statesman and a Lawyer, are at once the Honour and the Protection of his Country.' He paid other tributes to Hardwicke in *TP* (no. 16) and *JJ* (nos. 8, 11, and 15), and sent him a copy of his *Charge* (see above, p. xxxiii).

[2] In the *Voyage to Lisbon*, Fielding comments bitterly on 'that political oeconomy of this nation, which, as it concerns only the regulation of the mob, is below the notice of our great men; tho', in the due regulation of this order depend many emoluments which the great men themselves, or, at least, many who tread close on their heels, may enjoy, as well as some dangers, which may some time or other arise from introducing a pure state of anarchy among them' (p. 82).

[3] The familiar body/state/disease metaphor is ubiquitous in writings dealing with the lower class. To give one of many possible examples, the anonymous author of *The Vices of the Cities of London and Westminster* (Dublin, 1751), complaining of the general profligacy of the poor, writes, 'All are sensible

The Subject, indeed, is of such Importance, that we may truly apply to it those Words of *Cicero*, in his First Book of Laws: *Ad Reipublicæ formandas & stabiliendas vires, & ad sanandos Populos omnis pergit Oratio.*[4] How far I have been able to succeed in the Execution, must be submitted to your Lordship's Candour. I hope I have no immodest Opinion of my own Abilities; but, in truth, I have much less Confidence in my Authority. Indeed the highest Authority is necessary to any Degree of Success in an Attempt of this Kind. Permit me, therefore, my Lord, to fly to the Protection of the Highest which doth now exist, or which perhaps ever did exist, in this Kingdom.[5]

This great Sanction is, I am convinced, always ready to support what really tends to the Public Utility: If I fail, therefore, of obtaining the Honour of it, I shall be fully satisfied that I do not deserve it, and shall sit down contented with the Merit of a good Intent: for surely there is some Praise due to the bare Design of doing a Service to the Public. Nor can my Enemies, I think, deny that I am entirely disinterested in my Endeavour, unless they should discover the Gratification which my Ambition finds in the Opportunity of this Address.

I am with the most profound Respect,

My Lord,

Your Lordship's most obedient,

most devoted humble Servant,

Henry Fielding.

---

of the Evil that threaten [*sic*] us, every Individual confesses the dangerous Malady that preys upon the Vitals of the Body politic, and all with one Voice cry out for Redress, and a speedy Reformation of these glaring abuses' (pp. 1–2). The image recurs throughout Fielding's work, e.g. *TP* no. 2, p. 47; *JJ* nos. 23 (p. 271) and 47 (p. 414); *Charge*, p. 14; *Bosavern Penlez*, p. 35; *Proposal*, p. 229 and 231; *Examples of Providence*, p. 179; and *Amelia*, XI. ii. 249.

[4] *Laws*, I. xiii. 37. *Ad res publicas firmandas et ad stabiliendas urbes sanandosque populos omnis nostra pergit oratio*: 'Our whole discourse is intended to promote the firm foundation of states, the strengthening of cities, and the curing of the ills of the peoples' (Loeb). Fielding's substantive changes are to make *states* singular and to change *cities* to *powers*.

[5] As Lord High Chancellor, Hardwicke held the highest legal office in England. Fielding also seems to be appealing to The Law as superior to political or royal authority.

THE
PREFACE.

There is nothing so much talked of, and so little understood in this Country, as the *Constitution*.[6] It is a Word in the Mouth of every Man;[7] and yet when we come to discourse of the Matter, there is no Subject on which our Ideas are more confused and perplexed.[8] Some, when they speak of the Constitution, confine their Notions to the Law; others to the Legislature; others, again, to the governing or executive Part; and many there are, who jumble all these together in one Idea. One Error, however, is common to them all: for all seem to have the Conception of something uniform and permanent, as if the Constitution of *England* partook rather of the Nature of the Soil than of the Climate, and was as fixed and constant as the former, not as changing and variable as the latter.[9]

Now in this Word, *The Constitution*, are included the original and fundamental Law of the Kingdom, from whence all Powers are derived, and by which they are circumscribed; all legislative and executive Authority; all those municipal Provisions which are commonly called *The Laws*; and, *lastly*, the Customs, Manners, and Habits of the People. These, joined together, do, I apprehend, form the Political, as the several Members of the Body, the animal Oeconomy, with the Humours and Habit, compose that which is called the Natural Constitution.

[6] The constitution was a constant topic in *The Craftsman* and other opposition as well as ministerial journals and pamphlets especially in the 1730s (see General Introduction, pp. lxiv ff.). But here Fielding may be thinking particularly of Montesquieu's *Esprit des Lois* (1748) which was translated into English in 1750. Extracts dealing with the English constitution had appeared in the *Monthly Review* for July and Oct. 1749 (see F. T. H. Fletcher, *Montesquieu and English Politics* [London, 1939], pp. 17 ff.). Or, he may be harking back to the period 1745–7 when, in *The True Patriot*, *The Jacobite's Journal*, and related writings, he campaigned vigorously against the 'Jacobite' conception of an 'old constitution': 'that is, the Constitution as it existed under . . . James the Second' ('A Proper Answer', *JJ* p. 88). Fielding also mentions Montesquieu in *CGJ* no. 15 (i. 224) and the *Voyage to Lisbon*, p. 49.

[7] e.g. the bailiff in *Amelia* (VIII. ii. 70) who defines 'liberty' for Booth: ' "Oh, 'tis a fine thing, 'tis a very fine thing, and the constitution of England." '

[8] Fielding echoes III. x. 2, 3 ('Of the abuse of words'), of Locke's *Essay Concerning Human Understanding* (*Works*, 5th edn. [London, 1751], i. 228: Baker, no. 456). He quotes from these sections at length in *CGJ* no. 4 (i. 153). Cf. *The Champion* for 17 Jan. 1739/40 and 27 Mar. 1740.

[9] The idea that climate affects a nation's culture is old (e.g. Aristotle, *Politics*, VII. vii. 1.) but that it affects political constitutions was particularly topical because of Montesquieu's comments in Bk. XIV of *Esprit des Lois*, 'Of Laws in Relation to the Nature of the Climate'. Bolingbroke too had remarked, 'Now, tho the true interest of several states may be the same in many respects, yet is there always some difference to be perceived, by a discerning eye, both in these interests, and in the manner of pursuing them; a difference that arises from the situation of countries, from the character of people, from the nature of government, and even from that of climate and soil (*The Idea of a Patriot King*, ed. Sydney W. Jackman [Indianapolis, 1965], p. 64). *The Idea of a Patriot King* was first published by Bolingbroke (with *A Letter on the Spirit of Patriotism*) in 1749 (Baker, no. 243). Cf. *The Champion*, 15 Dec. 1739.

The *Greek* Philosophy will, perhaps, help us to a better Idea: for neither will the several constituent Parts, nor the Contexture of the whole, given an adequate Notion of the Word. By the *Constitution* is, indeed, rather meant something which results from the Order and Disposition of the whole; something resembling that Harmony for which the *Theban* in *Plato's Phædo* contends; which he calls ἀόρατόν τι καὶ ἀσώματον, *something invisible and incorporeal.*[1] For many of the *Greeks* imagined the Soul to result from the κρασις or Composition of the Parts of the Body,[2] when these were properly tempered together, as Harmony doth from the proper Composition of the several Parts in a well tuned musical Instrument: In the same manner, from the Disposition of the several Parts in a State, arises that which we call the *Constitution.*

In this Disposition the Laws have so considerable a Share, that, as no Man can perfectly understand the whole, without knowing the Parts of which it is composed, it follows, that, to have a just Notion of our Constitution, without a competent Knowledge of the Laws, is impossible. Without this, the reading over our Historians may afford Amusement, but will very little instruct us in the true Essentials of our Constitution. Nor will this Knowledge alone serve our Purpose. The mere Lawyer, however skilful in his Profession, who is not versed in the Genius, Manners, and Habits of the People, makes but a wretched Politician. Hence the Historian, who is ignorant of our Law, and the Lawyer who is ignorant of our History, have agreed in that common Error, remarked above, of considering our Constitution as something fixed and permanent: for the exterior Form of Government (however the People are changed) still, in a great Degree, remains what it was; and the same, notwithstanding all its Alterations, may be said of the Law.

To explain this a little farther: From the Original of the Lower House of Parliament to this Day, the Supreme Power hath been vested in the King and the Two Houses of Parliament. These Two Houses have, each at different Times, carried very different Weights in the Balance, and yet the Form of Government remained still one and the same: So hath it happened to the Law; the same Courts of Justice, the same Form of Trials, &c. have preserved the Notion of Identity, tho', in real Truth, the present Governing Powers, and the present legal Provisions, bear so little Resemblance to those of our Ancestors in the Reign of King *John*, or indeed in later Times, that could any Lawyer or Statesman of those Days be recalled to Life, he would

---

[1] *Phaedo*, sect. 36. Socrates refutes the idea of the soul as a harmony and Simmias the Theban, who had advanced it in opposition to Socrates' argument for the soul's immortality, recants.

[2] e.g. Phaedo's auditor, Echecrates of Philius, who says, 'the doctrine that the soul is a kind of harmony has always had . . . a wonderful hold upon me' (*Phaedo*, sect. 38 [Loeb]).

make, I believe, a very indifferent Figure in *Westminster-hall*,[3] or in any of the Parts there adjacent.

To perceive the Alterations in our Constitution doth, in fact, require a pretty just Knowledge both of the People and of the Laws: for either of these may be greatly changed, without producing any immediate Effect on the other. The Alterations in the great Wheels of State abovementioned, which are so visible in our Historians, are not noticed in our Laws, as very few of the great Changes in the Law have fallen under the Eye of our Historians.

Many of both Kinds have appeared in our Constitution; but I shall at present confine myself to one only, as being that which principally relates to the Subject of the following Treatise.

If the Constitution, as I above asserted, be the Result of the Disposition of the several Parts before mentioned, it follows, that this Disposition can never be altered, without producing a proportional Change in the Constitution. "If the Soul (says *Simmias* in *Plato*) be a Harmony resulting from the Disposition of the corporeal Parts, it follows, that when this Disposition is confounded, and the Body is torn by Diseases or other Evils, the Soul immediately (whatever be her Divinity) must perish."[4] This will be apparent, if we cast our Eyes a Moment towards the animal Oeconomy; and it is no less true in the political.

The Customs, Manners, and Habits of the People, do, as I have said, form one Part of the Political Constitution; if these are altered therefore, this must be changed likewise; and here, as in the Natural Body, the Disorder of any Part will, in its Consequence, affect the whole.[5]

One known Division of the People in this Nation is into the Nobility, the Gentry, and the Commonalty. What Alterations have happened among the two former of these, I shall not at present enquire; but that the last, in their Customs, Manners, and Habits, are greatly changed from what they were, I think to make appear.

If we look into the earliest Ages, we shall find the Condition of this Third Part to have been very low and mean. The highest Order of this Rank, before the Conquest, were those Tenants in Socage, who held their Lands by the Service of the Plough; who, as *Lyttleton* tells us, "were to come with

---

[3] Where the three common-law courts of King's Bench, Common Pleas, and Exchequer sat during term time.

[4] *Phaedo*, sect. 36.

[5] That the constitution or state was a harmony or organism arising from the balanced arrangement of its parts which disproportion (or unnatural growth) destroyed, was a commonplace: e.g. 'The *disproportionate increase of a part* of the state is also an occasion which leads to constitutional changes. The analogy of the body is instructive. The body is composed of parts, and it must grow proportionately if symmetry is to be maintained. Otherwise it perishes . . . or again it may sometimes change into the form of some other animal . . . The same is true of a state' (Aristotle, *Politics*, v. iii. 6). Cf. Cicero, *De republica*, II. xlii; Locke, *The Second Treatise of Government*, XIII, sects. 157–8; Pope, *An Essay on Man*, iii. 283 ff.; and Bolingbroke (who follows Machiavelli), *The Idea of a Patriot King*, p. 35.

their Plough for certain Days in the Year, to plow and sow the Demesne of the Lords;"[6] as the Villains, saith the same Author, "were to carry and recarry the Dung of his Lord, spread it upon his Land, and to perform such like Services."[7]

This latter was rightly accounted a slavish Tenure. The Villains were indeed considered in Law as a Kind of Chattle belonging to their Masters: for though these had not the Power of Life and Death over them, nor even of maiming them with Impunity,[8] yet these Villains had not even the Capacity of purchasing Lands or Goods; but the Lord, on such Purchase, might enter into the one, and seize the other for his own Use. And as for the Land which they held in Villenage, tho' Lord *Coke* says, it was not only held at the Will of the Lord, but according to the Custom of the Manor; yet, in antient Times, if the Lord ejected them, they were manifestly without Remedy.[9]

And as to the former, tho' they were accounted Freemen, yet were they obliged to swear Fealty to their Lord; and tho' Mr. *Rapin* be mistaken, when he says they could not alienate their Land, (for before the Statute of *Magna Charta, Chap.* 32. they could have given or sold the whole, but without any Alteration of the Tenure)[1] yet was the Estate of these but very mean. "Tho' they are called Freemen (says Lord *Coke*), yet they ploughed, harrowed, reaped, and mowed, &c. for the lord;" and *Bracton, Dicuntur Socmanni eo quod deputati sunt tantummodo ad culturam.*[2]

Besides such as were bound by their Tenures to the Service of Agriculture, the Number of Freemen below the Degree of Gentry, and who got their Livelihood in the Mercantile or Mechanical Way, was very inconsiderable. As to the Servants, they were chiefly bound by Tenure, and those of the lower Sort differed very little from Slaves.

That this Estate of the Commonalty is greatly changed, is apparent; and to this Alteration many Causes in subsequent Ages have contributed.

First, The Oath of Fealty, or Fidelity, which of old Time was administered with great Ceremony, became afterwards to be omitted; and though this Fealty still remained incident to every Socage Tenure, yet the Omission of

---

[6] Sir Edward Coke, *I Inst.*, fo. 87a.

[7] Ibid., fo. 116b.

[8] Cf. Rapin, 'Among the Anglo-Saxons, the lords had not the power of life and death over their slaves. Nay, the laws provided, they should not cripple or maim them without incurring a penalty' ii. 14.

[9] Coke, *I Inst.*, fo. 119b.

[1] By ch. 32 of the Magna Charta a freeman was enabled to sell part of his land, the buyer assuming an appropriate obligation to the lord of the fee. Previously, as Fielding indicates, he could alienate only the whole. Rapin had stated that tenants in socage 'were possessed only of what they called socland, or lands of the plough, which they could not alienate, because they were properly but farmers' (ii. 13).

[2] *I Inst.*, fo. 86b: 'And sometimes they are called liberi homines, qui tamen arabant, herciabant, falcabant, and metebant, &c.' Coke cites the same passage from Bracton (*De Legibus*, ed. Thorne, p. 226): '[The term socage is derived from *socus*, a plough, and thus tenants who hold in socage] may be called sokemen because, so it seems, they are deputed to agricultural work only.'

the Form was not without its Consequences; for, as Lord *Coke* says, speaking of Homage, *Prudent Antiquity did, for the more Solemnity and better Memory and Observation of that which is to be done, express Substances under Ceremonies.*[3]

2*dly*, Whereas in the antient Tenures the principal Reservation was of personal Services from the inferior Tenants, the Rent being generally trifling, such as Hens, Capons, Roses, Spurs, Hawks, &*c.* afterwards the Avarice or Necessity of the Lords incited them to convert these for the most part into Money, which tended greatly to weaken the Power of the Lord, and to raise the Freedom and Independency of the Tenant.

3*dly*, The dismembering Manors by Leases for Years, as it flowed from the same Sources, so it produced the same Effects. These were probably very rare before the Reign of *Edward* I. at which time the Statute of *Glocester* secured the Estate of this Tenant.[4]

4*thly*, The Estate of the Villain or Copyholder seems clearly, as I have said, to have originally been holden only at the Will of the Lord; but the Law was afterwards altered, and in the Reign of *Edward* IV. some of the best Judges were of Opinion, that if the Copyholder was unlawfully ejected by his Lord, he should have an Action of Trespass against him at the Common Law.[5]

From this Time the Estate of the Copyholder (which, as *Briton* tells us, was formerly a base Tenure) began to grow into Repute, and, though still distinguished in some Privileges from a Freehold, became the Possession of many opulent and powerful Persons.[6]

By these and such like Means the Commonalty, by Degrees, shook off their Vassalage, and became more and more independent on their Superiors. Even Servants, in Process of Time, acquired a State of Freedom and Independency, unknown to this Rank in any other Nation; and which, as the Law now stands, is inconsistent with a servile Condition.

But nothing hath wrought such an Alteration in this Order of People, as the Introduction of Trade.[7] This hath indeed given a new Face to the whole

[3] *I Inst.*, fo. 65b.

[4] 'The Statute of Glocester [6 Edw. I; 1278] gave the Lessee for yeares some remedy by Way of receipt, and a triall Whether the Demandant did move the plea by good right or collusion, and if it were found by collusion then the termor should injoy his tearme . . .' *I Inst.*, fo. 46b.

[5] Fielding follows Coke, *I Inst.* I. ix ('Tenant by Coppie'), sect. 77.

[6] Coke (*I Inst.*, fo. 58b) notes that both Bracton and Littleton use the phrase 'base tenure' to describe the estate of the copyholder. The relevant part of *Britton* (ed. Nichols, ii. 13–14) does not use this phrase but his description of the estate agrees with the others. On the limitation of a copyhold estate, Rapin notes 'For as of old villains were not reckoned as members of the commonwealth, but part and parcel of their owner's substance, so were they therefore excluded from any share in the legislature, and their successors still continue without any right to vote at elections, by virtue of their copyholds' (ii. 15 n. u). *Britton*: a late 13th-century legal work (authorship unknown) based on Bracton. That it was in Law French instead of Latin contributed to its influence.

[7] Fielding generally shared his contemporaries' respect for the industrious merchant though, considering the hapless Heartfree, he ought to have agreed with Johnson's blunt observation, 'trade could not be managed by those who manage it, if it had much difficulty' (*Life*, ed. Hill and Powell, iii.

Nation, hath in a great measure subverted the former State of Affairs, and hath almost totally changed the Manners, Customs, and Habits of the People, more especially of the lower Sort. The Narrowness of their Fortune is changed into Wealth; the Simplicity of their Manners into Craft; their Frugality into Luxury; their Humility into Pride, and their Subjection into Equality.[8]

The Philosopher, perhaps, will think this a bad Exchange, and may be inclined to cry out with the Poet,

> —— *Sævior armis*
> *Luxuria incubuit.*'——
> *Nullum crimen abest, facinusque libidinis, ex quo*
> *Paupertas Romana perit.*[9]

Again,

> *Prima peregrinos obscœna pecunia mores*
> *Intulit, & turpi fregerunt sæcula luxu*
> *Divitiæ molles.*————[1]

But the Politician finds many Emoluments to compensate all the moral Evils introduced by Trade, by which the Grandeur and Power of the Nation is carried to a Pitch that it could never otherwise have reached; Arts and Sciences are improved, and human Life is embellished with every Ornament, and furnished with every Comfort which it is capable of tasting.[2]

382). Fielding's most enthusiastic encomium on trade appears in the *Voyage to Lisbon*: 'There is . . . nothing so useful to man in general, nor so beneficial to particular societies and individuals, as trade. This is that *alma mater*, at whose plentiful breast all mankind are nourished. It is true, like other parents, she is not always equally indulgent to all her children; but tho' she gives to her favourites a vast proportion of redundancy and superfluity, there are very few whom she refuses to supply with the conveniencies, and none with the necessaries of life' (p. 60). But it is clear from the present context that he was not at ease with an institution that could produce a 'riotous independent Butcher or Baker, with two or three thousand Pounds in his Pocket'. For a fuller discussion of the contradictions in Fielding's social attitudes, see Zirker, *Social Pamphlets, passim.*

[8] Fielding's treatment of the 'commonalty' provoked some angry response. See General Introduction, p. lxvii ff.

[9] Juvenal, *Satires*, vi. 291–4: 'Luxury, more deadly than any foe had laid his hand upon us . . . Since the day when Roman poverty perished, no deed of crime or lust has been wanting to us' (Loeb).

[1] Ibid., 298–300: 'Filthy lucre first brought in amongst us foreign ways; wealth enervated and corrupted the ages with foul indulgences' (Loeb). Fielding's burlesque translation of Juvenal's lines may be found in *Miscellanies* (1743), pp. 115–17, ll. 440–3 and 448–51. He quotes these lines in a similar context in *A Dialogue between a Gentleman from London . . . and an Honest Alderman*: 'Indeed, to speak a bold political Truth, some Degree of Corruption always hath attended, and always will attend a rich and flourishing Nation. The virtuous Principles on which the *Roman* Commonwealth was founded, excluded this no longer than 'till Wealth flowed in upon them. Their Satyrist, you remember, introduces his Complaints of their Corruption by these Words . . .' (*JJ* p. 31).

[2] Although the emphasis in Mandeville is on 'luxury' as a spur to trade ('Luxury/employed a Million of the Poor,/And odious Pride a Million more', and see, especially, 'Remark L' of *The Fable of the Bees*) rather than as an effect of trade, he undoubtedly provides the best gloss on Fielding's acknowledgement of the benefits of commerce. Moreover, arguing against national frugality, Mandeville anticipates closely Fielding's point here: '. . . promote Navigation, cherish the Merchant,

In all these Assertions he is right; but surely he forgets himself a little, when he joins the Philosopher in lamenting the Introduction of Luxury as a casual Evil; for as Riches are the *certain* Consequence of Trade, so is Luxury the no less *certain* Consequence of Riches; Nay, Trade and Luxury do indeed support each other; and this latter, in its turn, becomes as useful to Trade, as Trade had been before to the Support of Luxury.[3]

To prevent this Consequence therefore of a flourishing Commerce is totally to change the Nature of Things, and to separate the Effect from the Cause. A Matter as impossible in the Political Body as in the Natural. Vices and Diseases, with like Physical Necessity, arise from certain Habits in both; and to restrain and palliate the evil Consequences, is all that lies within the Reach of Art. How far it is the Business of the Politician to interfere in the Case of Luxury, we have attempted to shew in the following Treatise.

Now, to conceive that so great a Change as this in the People should produce no Change in the Constitution, is to discover, I think, as great Ignorance as would appear in the Physician, who should assert, that the whole State of the Blood may be entirely altered from poor to rich, from cool to inflamed, without producing any Alteration in the Constitution of the Man.

To put this in the clearest Light: There appear to me to be Four Sorts of Political Power; that of Bodily Strength, that of the Mind, the Power of the Purse, and the Power of the Sword. Under the Second of these Divisions may be ranged all the Art of the Legislator and Politician, all the Power of Laws and Government. These do constitute the Civil Power; and a State may then be said to be in good Order, when all the other Powers are subservient to this; when they own its superior Excellence and Energy, pay it a ready Obedience, and all unite in Support of its Rule.

But so far are these Powers from paying such voluntary Submission, that they are all extremely apt to rebel, and to assert their own Superiority; but none is more rebellious in its Nature, or more difficult to be governed, than that of the Purse or Money. Self-opinion, Arrogance, Insolence, and Impatience of Rule, are its almost inseparable Companions.

Now if these Assertions are true, what an immense Accession of this

and encourage Trade in every Branch of it; this will bring Riches, and where they are, Arts and Sciences will soon follow, and by the Help of what I have named and good Management, it is that Politicians can make a People potent, renown'd and flourishing' (*Fable*, ed. F. B. Kaye [Oxford, 1924], i. 184–5). Though Fielding's few allusions, explicit or implicit, to Mandeville are uniformly hostile, he echoes many of Mandeville's social attitudes in the pamphlets reprinted in this volume. See, for example, the *Proposal*, p. 228.

[3] Cf. Mandeville, *Fable*, i. 185: 'Great Wealth and Foreign Treasure will ever scorn to come among Men, unless you'll admit their inseparable Companions, Avarice and Luxury: Where Trade is considerable Fraud will intrude. . . . and . . . while Man advances in Knowledge, and his Manners are polish'd, we must expect to see at the same time his desires enlarg'd, his Appetites refin'd, and his Vices increas'd.'

Power hath accrued to the Commonalty by the Increase of Trade? for tho' the other Orders have acquired an Addition by the same Means, this is not in the same Proportion, as every Reader, who will revolve the Proposition but a Moment in his own Mind, must be satisfied.

And what may we hence conclude? Is that Civil Power, which was adapted to the Government of this Order of People in that State in which they were at the Conquest, capable of ruling them in their present Situation? Hath this Civil Power kept equal Pace with them in the Increase of its Force, or hath it not rather, by the Remissness of the Magistrate, lost much of its antient Energy? Where is now that Power of the Sheriff, which could formerly awaken and arm a whole County in an Instant? Where is that *Posse Comitatus*, which attended at his Beck?[4] What is become of the Constitutions of *Alfred*, which the Reader will find set forth at large in the following Treatise? What of the antient Conservators of the Peace?[5] Have the Justices, on whom this whole Power devolves, an Authority sufficient for the Purpose? In some Counties, perhaps, you may find an overgrown Tyrant, who lords it over his Neighbours and Tenants with despotic Sway, and who is as regardless of the Law as he is ignorant of it;[6] but as to the Magistrate of a less Fortune, and more Knowledge, every riotous independent Butcher or Baker, with two or three thousand Pounds in his Pocket, laughs at his Power, and every Pettyfogger makes him tremble.[7]

It is a common and popular Complaint, that the Justices of Peace have already too much Power. Indeed a very little is too much, if it be abused; but, in truth, this Complaint proceeds from a Mistake of Business for Power: The Business of the Justice is indeed multiplied by a great Number of Statutes; but I know not of any (the Riot Act perhaps excepted) which hath at all enlarged his Power. And what the Force of that Act is, and how able the Magistrate is, by means of the Civil Power alone, to execute it in any popular Commotion, I have myself experienced.[8] But when a Mob of Chairmen or

[4] The decline of the power of the office of sheriff (and his court) began in the 13th century and continued through the 19th until 'All that remains of his once extensive powers over the military and police forces of the shire is his power to call out the posse comitatus [power of the county]' (Holdsworth, i. 68). This decline reflects in part the crown's desire to see its law administered by its own appointees, i.e., justices of the peace, whose powers, especially since the 16th century, increased until 'lawyers abandoned all hope of describing [their] duties in any methodic fashion, and the alphabet [became] the one possible connecting thread' (ibid., i. 286).

[5] I. Edw. III, st. 2. c. 16 (1327) established provisions for the appointment of conservators of the peace in each county who, as Fielding indicates, were replaced by justices of the peace (*c.*1363).

[6] Epitomized among Fielding's representations of the type by Squire Western, whose excesses had produced 'two informations exhibited against him in the King's Bench' and whose clerk prevents him from sending Honour Blackwell to Bridewell 'only for Ill-breeding' (*Tom Jones*, VII. ix. 357).

[7] Cf. the 'vile Petty-fogger' in *Tom Jones* (VIII. viii. 431–2) who was 'without Sense or Knowledge of any Kind; one of those who may be termed Train-bearers to the Law; a Sort of Supernumeraries in the Profession, who are the Hackneys of Attornies, and will ride more Miles for half a Crown, than a Post-boy'.

[8] Referring to the riots described in *Bosavern Penlez*. See especially Fielding's discussion of the Riot Act, ibid., p. 42 ff.

Servants, or a Gang of Thieves and Sharpers, are almost too big for the Civil Authority to suppress, what must be the Case in a seditious Tumult, or general Riot of the People?

From what hath been said, I may, I think, conclude, that the Constitution of this Country is altered from its antient State.

2*dly*, That the Power of the Commonalty hath received an immense Addition; and that the Civil Power having not increased, but decreased, in the same Proportion, is not able to govern them.

What may and must be the Consequences of this, as well as what Remedy can be applied to it, I leave to the Consideration of others: I have proceeded far enough already on the Subject, to draw sufficient Ill-will on myself, from unmeaning or ill-meaning People, who either do not foresee the mischievous Tendency of a total Relaxation of Government, or who have some private wicked Purpose to effect from public Confusion.

In plain Truth, the principal Design of this whole Work, is to rouse the CIVIL Power from its present lethargic State. A Design which alike opposes those wild Notions of Liberty that are inconsistent with all Government, and those pernicious Schemes of Government, which are destructive of true Liberty. However contrary indeed these Principles may seem to each other, they have both the same common Interest; or, rather, the former are the wretched Tools of the latter: for Anarchy is almost sure to end in some kind of Tyranny.[9]

Dr. *Middleton*, in his Life of *Cicero*, hath a fine Observation to my present Purpose, with which I will conclude this Preface.

"From the Railleries of the *Romans* (says he) on the *Barbarity and Misery of our Island*, one cannot help reflecting on the surprising Fate and Revolutions of Kingdoms: how *Rome*, once the Mistress of the World, the Seat of Arts,

---

[9] For a description of the progress of excessive liberty to anarchy to tyranny, see Plato, *Republic*, viii. 562–4. Fielding's comments on abuses and misconceptions of liberty are especially frequent in the last ten years of his career. Recurrent are (1) the insistence that vulgar conceptions of liberty are vague or quite empty of meaning, e.g. in the *Voyage to Lisbon* where he condemns 'the vague and uncertain use of a word called Liberty, of which, as scarce any two men with whom I have ever conversed, seem to have one and the same idea, I am inclined to doubt whether there be any simple universal notion represented by this word, or whether it conveys any [clear] or . . . determinate idea' (p. 82; cf. *Amelia*, VII. ii. 70, and note the duplication of Lockean rhetoric here and on p. 65 of the *Enquiry* and p. 15 of *A Dialogue between a Gentleman from London . . . and an Honest Alderman*); (2) the conviction that the lower classes (and writers of newspapers) demand and exercise a license that will lead to anarchy and tyranny (e.g. *A Dialogue*, p. 15; *Covent-Garden Journal* no. 47; the *Proposal*, p. 267; and the *Charge*, *passim*; and (3) the negative definition of liberty as 'the Enjoyment of all those Privileges which the Law allows' (*A Dialogue*, p. 15, and cf. *JJ* no. 46, the *Voyage to Lisbon*, p. 83, and the *Charge*, p. 18. Fielding's definition of liberty is essentially in accord with Locke's in the *Second Treatise of Government*: 'Freedom then is not what Sir Robert Filmer tells us "a liberty for every one to do what he lists, to live as he pleases, and not to be tied by any laws"; but freedom of men under government is to have a standing rule to live by, common to every one of that society and made by the legislative power erected in it, a liberty to follow my own will in all things where the rule prescribes not . . .' (iv. 22; and see vi. 57 and vii. 94). Fielding's emphasis, however, is on fear of revolution and license, presumably because of the revolt of 1745 and his experience as magistrate.

Empire and Glory, now lies sunk in Sloth, Ignorance and Poverty; enslaved to the most cruel, as well as to the most contemptible of Tyrants, *Superstition and Religious Imposture*: while this remote Country, anciently the Jest and Contempt of *the polite Romans*, is become the happy Seat of Liberty, Plenty, and Letters; flourishing in all the Arts and Refinements of Civil Life; yet running perhaps the same Course, which *Rome* itself had run before it; from virtuous Industry to Wealth; from Wealth to Luxury; from Luxury to an Impatience of Discipline and Corruption of Morals; till by a total Degeneracy and Loss of Virtue, being grown ripe for Destruction, it falls a Prey at last to some hardy Oppressor, and, with the Loss of Liberty, losing every thing else, that is valuable, sinks gradually again into its original Barbarism."[1]

---

[1] *The Life of Marcus Tullius Cicer.* (1741; London, 1810), ii. 110–11. In *Shamela*, Fielding had mocked Conyers Middleton's dedication of his *Cicero* to Hervey, but in *Joseph Andrews* (III. vi. 239), he implies respect for the *Life* itself by invoking the muse 'who hadst no Hand in that Dedication, and Preface, or the Translations which thou wouldst willingly have struck out of the Life of *Cicero*'.

AN

ENQUIRY

INTO THE

CAUSES of the late Increase of ROBBERS, &c.

INTRODUCTION.

The great Increase of Robberies within these few Years, is an Evil which to me appears to deserve some attention; and the rather as it seems (tho' already become so flagrant) not yet to have arrived to that Height of which it is capable, and which it is likely to attain: For Diseases in the Political, as in the Natural Body, seldom fail going on to their Crisis, especially when nourished and encouraged by Faults in the Constitution. In Fact, I make no Doubt, but that the Streets of this Town, and the Roads leading to it, will shortly be impassable without the utmost Hazard; nor are we threatned with seeing less dangerous Gangs of Rogues among us, than those which the *Italians* call the Banditi.[2]

Should this ever happen to be the Case, we shall have sufficient Reason to lament that Remissness by which this Evil was suffered to grow to so great a Height. All Distempers, if I may once more resume the Allusion, the sooner they are opposed, admit of the easier and the safer Cure.[3] The great

[2] For Fielding's pursuit of these gangs, see General Introduction, p. lv ff. Though complaints about increasing crime are common throughout the 18th century, they were particularly shrill in the years following the Peace of Aix-la-Chapelle when 34,000 men were discharged from the navy and 20,000 from the army: 'the reduction of the army and navy had thrown on society, a vast body of men, unfitted for the habits and pursuits of ordinary life; and the transition from war to peace, had been attended by a considerable increase of crime' (William Coxe, *Memoirs of the Administration of the right Honourable Henry Pelham* [London, 1829], ii. 112). There is abundant supporting evidence, e.g. Rapin, *History of England* (1759), xxi. 398 ff. and 420; Smollett, *History of England*, 3rd edn. (London, 1760), x. 368. The extent of the government's concern over the disbanded military is marked by its offer of land grants and other benefits to those who would emigrate to Nova Scotia. According to Rapin (xxi. 400–1), '3,750 persons and families entered themselves for Nova Scotia'.

[3] Doctors in both *Joseph Andrews* (I. xiv. 63) and *Tom Jones* (v. vii. 240) cite the appropriate tag from Persius (*Satires*, iii. 64). From *Tom Jones*: 'Surely the Gentlemen of the *Æsculapian* Art are in the Right in advising, that the Moment the Disease is entered at one Door, the Physician should be introduced at the other; what else is meant by that old Adage: *Venienti occurrite Morbo?* "Oppose a Distemper at its first Approach." '

Difficulty of extirpating desperate Gangs of Robbers, when once collected into a Body, appears from our own History in former Times.[4] *France* hath given us a later Example in the long Reign of *Cartouche*,[5] and his Banditi; and this under an absolute Monarchy, which affords much more speedy and efficacious Remedies against these political Disorders, than can be administred in a free State, whose Forms of Correction are extremely slow and incertain, and whose Punishments are the mildest and the most void of Terror of any other in the known World.

For my own Part, I cannot help regarding these Depredations in a most serious Light: Nor can I help wondering that a Nation so jealous of her Liberties, that from the slightest Cause, and often without any Cause at all, we are always murmuring at our Superiors, should tamely and quietly support the Invasion of her Properties by a few of the lowest and vilest among us: Doth not this Situation in reality level us with the most enslaved Countries? If I am to be assaulted and pillaged, and plundered; if I can neither sleep in my own House, nor walk the Streets, nor travel in safety; is not my Condition almost equally bad whether a licenced or unlicenced Rogue, a Dragoon or a Robber, be the Person who assaults and plunders me? The only Difference which I can perceive is, that the latter Evil appears to be more easy to remove.

If this be, as I clearly think it is, the Case, surely there are few Matters of more general Concern than to put an immediate End to these Outrages, which are already become so notorious, and which, as I have observed, do seem to threaten us with such a dangerous Increase. What indeed may not the Public apprehend, when they are informed as an unquestionable Fact, that there is at this Time a great Gang of Rogues, whose Number falls little short of a Hundred, who are incorporated in one Body, have Officers and a Treasury; and have reduced Theft and Robbery into a regular System. There are of this Society of Men who appear in all Disguises, and mix in most Companies. Nor are they better versed in every Art of Cheating, Thieving, and Robbing, than they are armed with every Method of evading the Law, if they should ever be discovered, and an Attempt made to bring them to Justice. Here, if they fail in rescuing the Prisoner, or (which seldom happens) in bribing or deterring the Prosecutor, they have for their last

---

[4] Probably a reference to the 'Gang of Rogues then called *Roberdsmen*' cited in Section VI, below, p. 136.

[5] Cartouche's career is described in the anonymous *Life and Actions of Lewis Dominique Cartouche: Who was broke Alive upon the Wheel at Paris Nov. 28, 1721 N.S., Trans. from the French* (London, 1722). Cartouche, like Sheppard, Turpin, and Wild, captured the public imagination and his exploits, according to the translator, were described regularly in the *Gazette*. Fielding's allusion to him is apposite because his gang had been established shortly after the Peace of Utrecht and was composed largely of disbanded soldiers and officers. Cartouche had been in the army himself. He terrorized Paris from the Peace of Utrecht to 1719: 'The Highways were as unsafe as the City, and daily Attacks were made upon Coaches' (p. 36).

Resource some rotten Members of the Law to forge a Defence for them, and a great Number of false Witnesses ready to support it.[6]

Having seen the most convincing Proofs of all this, I cannot help thinking it high Time to put some stop to the further Progress of such impudent and audacious Insults, not only on the Properties of the Subject, but on the National Justice, and on the Laws themselves. The Means of accomplishing this (the best which suggest themselves to me) I shall submit to the public Consideration, after having first enquired into the Causes of the present Growth of this Evil, and whence we have great Reason to apprehend its further Increase. Some of these I am too well versed in the Affairs of this World to expect to see removed; but there are others, which without being over sanguine, we may hope to remedy; and thus perhaps one ill Consequence, at least, of the more stubborn political Diseases, may cease.

SECT. I.

Of too frequent and expensive Diversions among the Lower Kind of People.

First then, I think, that the vast Torrent of Luxury which of late Years hath poured itself into this Nation, hath greatly contributed to produce, among many others, the Mischief I here complain of. I aim not here to satirize the Great, among whom Luxury is probably rather a moral than a political Evil. But Vices no more than Diseases will stop with them; for bad Habits are as infectious by Example, as the Plague itself by Contact. In free Countries, at least, it is a Branch of Liberty claimed by the People to be as wicked and as profligate as their Superiors. Thus while the Nobleman will emulate the Grandeur of a Prince; and the Gentleman will aspire to the proper State of the Nobleman; the Tradesman steps from behind his Counter into the vacant Place of the Gentleman. Nor doth the Confusion end here: It reaches the very Dregs of the People, who aspiring still to a Degree beyond that which belongs to them, and not being able by the Fruits of honest Labour to support the State which they affect, they disdain the Wages to which their Industry would intitle them; and abandoning themselves to Idleness, the more simple and poor-spirited betake themselves to a State of Starving and Beggary, while those of more Art and Courage become Thieves, Sharpers and Robbers.[7]

---

[6] I have not found any evidence to confirm Fielding's description in this paragraph of such a highly organized gang of criminals. He may be alluding to thieves associated with the organization of receivers of stolen goods he describes in Section V, below, p. 126.

[7] Fielding frequently observed tht the vices of the rich corrupt the manners of the poor (e.g., the maid's defense of her slip with the Merry Andrew on the Puppet-show stage in *Tom Jones* [XII. vi. 641]: 'If I am a Wh—e . . . my Betters are so as well as I. What was the fine Lady in the Puppet-show just now? I suppose she did not lie all Night out from her Husband for nothing'). The rhetorical 'train' which traces the progress of luxury or vice downward through the social ranks was commonplace in writings on the poor (for instances, see Zirker, *Social Pamphlets*, pp. 74–5).

Could Luxury be confined to the Palaces of the Great, the Society would not perhaps be much affected with it; at least, the Mischiefs which I am now intending to obviate can never be the Consequence. For tho', perhaps, there is not more of real Virtue in the higher State, yet the Sense of Honour is there more general and prevalent.[8] But there is a much stronger Reason. The Means bear no Proportion to the End: For the Loss of Thousands, or of a great Estate, is not to be relieved or supplied by any Means of common Theft or Robbery.—With regard to such Evils therefore the Legislature might be justified in leaving the Punishment, as well as the pernicious Consequence, to end in the Misery, Distress, and sometimes utter Ruin of a private Family. But when this Vice descends downward to the Tradesman, the Mechanic, and the Labourer, it is certain to engender many political Mischiefs, and among the rest is most evidently the Parent of Theft and Robbery, to which not only the Motive of Want but of Shame conduces: For there is no greater Degree of Shame than the Tradesman generally feels at the first Inability to make his regular Payments; nor is there any Difficulty which he would not undergo to avoid it. Here then the Highway promises, and hath, I doubt not, often given Relief. Nay I remember very lately a Highwayman who confessed several Robberies before me, his Motive to which, he assured me, (and so it appeared) was to pay a Bill that was shortly to become due.[9] In this Case therefore the Public becomes interested, and consequently the Legislature is obliged to interpose.

To give a final Blow to·Luxury by any general Prohibition, if it would be adviseable, is by no Means possible. To say the Truth, bad Habits in the Body Politic, especially if of any Duration, are seldom to be wholly eradicated. Palliatives alone are to be applied; and these too in a free Constitution must be of the gentlest Kind, and as much as possible adapted to the Taste and Genius of the People.

The gentlest Method which I know, and at the same Time perhaps one of the most effectual, of stopping the Progress of Vice, is by removing the Temptation. Now the two great Motives to Luxury, in the Mind of Man, are Vanity and Voluptuousness. The former of these operates but little in this

---

[8] The faintness of this qualification is underlined by the narrator's ironical statement in *Tom Jones* (xviii. xi. 964) that Lord Fellamar was 'strictly a Man of Honour, and would by no Means have been guilty of an Action which the World in general would have condemned'.

[9] *Select Trials* reports on thirteen trials 'for the Highway' held at the Old Bailey Sessions between Sept. 1748 and Sept. 1750. The thirteen accused (an inaccurate number in so far as the trial accounts make clear that many of these highwaymen had accomplices still at large) were all found guilty and hanged. They were for the most part young, poor, and menially employed, if employed at all. Five were seamen, six, Irishmen. Two were women (a barmaid and a prostitute). Only James Macleane, known as the 'Gentleman Highwayman', even approximately fits the figure of bourgeois pathos Fielding sketches here. After a varied career, Macleane had married an industrious woman who kept their grocer and chandler shop afloat. After her death, he wasted their funds and took to the highway (*Select Trials*, ii. 36 ff.). Gentleman-like highwaymen may still be found in *Moll Flanders*, *Tom Jones*, and *Humphry Clinker*, but they could rarely be seen in 18th-century London.

Regard with the lower Order of People. I do not mean that they have less of this Passion than their Betters; but the apparent Impossibility of gratifying it this Way deters them, and diverts at least this Passion into another Channel; for we find it puts them rather on vying with each other in the Reputation of Wealth, than in the outward Appearance of Show and Grandeur. Voluptuousness or the Love of Pleasure is that alone which leads them into Luxury. Here then the Temptation is with all possible Care to be withdrawn from them.

Now what greater Temptation can there be to Voluptuousness, than a Place where every Sense and Appetite of which it is compounded, are fed and delighted; where the Eyes are feasted with Show, and the Ears with Music, and where Gluttony and Drunkenness are allured by every Kind of Dainty; nay where the finest Women are exposed to View, and where the meanest Person who can dress himself clean, may in some Degree mix with his Betters, and thus perhaps satisfy his Vanity as well as his Love of Pleasure?

It may possibly be said that these Diversions are cheap: I answer, that is one Objection I have to them: Was the Price as high as that of a Ridotto,[1] or an Opera,[2] it would, like these Diversions, be confined to the higher People only; besides the Cheapness is really a Delusion. Unthinking Men are often deceived into Expence, as I once knew an honest Gentleman who carried his Wife and two Daughters to a Masquerade,[3] being told that he could have four Tickets for four Guineas; but found afterwards, that in Dresses, Masques, Chairs, &c. the Night's Entertainment cost him almost Twelve. I am convinced that many thousands of honest Tradesmen have found their Expences exceed their Computation in a much greater Proportion. And the Sum of seven or eight Shillings (which is a very moderate Allowance for the Entertainment of the smallest Family) repeated once or twice a Week through a Summer, will make too large a Deduction from the reasonable Profits of any low Mechanic.

---

[1] 'An entertainment or social assembly consisting of music and dancing. Introduced into England in the year 1722, at the Opera House in the Haymarket' (*OED*).

[2] The customary price of a theater ticket was five shillings for a box seat, two and six for the pit; for the opera in the 1740s, either seat was half a guinea, though prices varied. See Arthur H. Scouten, *The London Stage, 1729–1747*, pp. lxv and lxix. In *Evelina* Mr Branghton is amazed at the high price of opera tickets.

[3] By the 1720s the Masquerade, which was essentially a costume ball, had been established at the Opera House by 'Count' Heidegger, and by 1751 masquerades had long been the object of rebuke such as Dr Harrison makes in *Amelia*: 'though perhaps they may not be as some represent them, such brothels of vice and debauchery as would impeach the character of every virtuous woman who was seen at them, [they] are certainly . . . scenes of riot, disorder, and intemperance, very improper to be frequented by a chaste and sober Christian matron' (x. iv. 200–1). Battestin (*Tom Jones*, XIII. vi. 708 n.) notes Fielding's attacks on masquerades in *The Masquerade* (1728), *The Champion* (19 Feb. 1739/40), *Miss Lucy in Town* (1742), and the *Charge*. Pat Rogers also provides useful information about masquerades in *Henry Fielding, a Biography* (New York, 1979), pp. 21–2.

Besides the actual Expence in attending these Places of Pleasure, the Loss of Time and Neglect of Business are Consequences which the inferior Tradesman can by no Means support. To be born for no other Purpose than to consume the Fruits of the Earth is the Privilege (if it may be called a Privilege) of very few.[4] The greater Part of Mankind must sweat hard to produce them, or Society will no longer answer the Purposes for which it was ordained. *Six Days shalt thou labour*, was the positive Command of God in his own Republic. A Severity, however, which the Divine Wisdom was pleased somewhat to relax; and appointed certain Times of Rest and Recreation for his People. Such were the *Feast of the unleavened Bread*, the *Feast of the Weeks*, and the *Feast of the Tabernacles*. On which Occasions it is written, *Thou shall rejoice before the Lord thy God, thou and thy Son and thy Daughter, and thy Servant, and thy Maid, and the Levite that is within thy Gates, and the Stranger, and the Fatherless, and the Widow**.

All other Nations have imitated this divine Institution. It is true among the *Greeks*, arising from the Nature of their Superstition, there were many Festivals; yet scarce any of these were universal, and few attended with any other than religious Ceremonies[†]. The *Roman* Calendar is thinner strewed with these Seasons of Idleness. Indeed there seems to have been one only Kind of universal Sport and Revelling amongst them, which they called the *Saturnalia*, when much too great Indulgence was given to all Kinds of Licentiousness. Public Scenes of Rendezvous they had none. As to the *Grecian* Women, it is well known they were almost intirely confined to their own Houses;[5] where the very Entertainment of their finest Ladies was only Works of the finer Sort. And the *Romans*, by the *Orchian* Law, which was made among many others for the Suppression of Luxury, and was published in the third Year of *Cato's* Censorship, thought proper to limit the Number

---

* *Exod.* Chap. xxxiv. *Deut.* Chap. xvi.

† The Gods, says *Plato*, pitying the laborious Condition to which Men were born, appointed holy Rites to themselves, as Seasons of Rest to Men; and gave them the Muses, with *Apollo* their Leader and *Bacchus*, to assist in the Celebrations, &c. *De Leg.* I. ii. p. 787. *Edit Ficini.*[6]

---

[4] Horace's phrase, '*Fruges consumere nati*' (*Epistles*, I. ii. 27) is cited playfully in *Tom Jones* (III. ii. 120). Jonathan Wild, justifying his right to booty he has not won, remarks, 'It is well said of us, the higher Order of Mortals, that we are born only to devour the Fruits of the Earth; and it may be as well said of the lower Class, they are born only to produce them for us' (I. viii. 26).

[5] As was noted, for example, in Charles Rollin, *Ancient History*: '[Grecian] ladies were very reserved, seldom appeared in public, had separate apartments, called *Gynaecea*, and never ate at table with the men when strangers were present' (Philadelphia, 1825; English trans. London, 1732), i. 53.

[6] *De Legibus*, II. iii. 653 in the received text: 'The gods, however, took pity on the human race, born to suffer as it was, and gave it relief in the form of religious festivals to serve as periods of rest from its labours. They gave us the Muses, with Apollo their leader, and Dionysus; by having these gods to share their holidays, men were to be made whole again, and thanks to them, we find refreshment in the celebration of these festivals.' Plato was skeptical, however, of this traditional view, and argued that drinking parties (a synecdoche for recreation generally) should inculcate virtue or be abolished.

of Persons who were to assemble even at any private Feast*. Nay the Exhibitions of the Theatre were suffered only at particular Seasons, and on Holydays.

Nor are our own Laws silent on this Head, with Regard at least to the lower Sort of People, whose Diversions have been confined to certain stated Times. Mr. *Pulton*† speaking of those Games and Assemblies of the People which are lawful, says, that they are lawful at certain Places and Seasons of the Year, allowed by old and ancient Customs.[7] The Statute of *Hen.* VIII.‡ goes farther, and expresly enacts, that no Manner of Artificer or Craftsman of any Handicraft or Occupation, Husbandman, Apprentice, &c. shall play at the Tables, Tennis, Dice, Cards, Bowls, &c. out of *Christmas* under the Penalty of 20s.

Thus we find that by divine as well as human Institution, as well by our own Laws as those of other Countries, the Diversions of the People have been limited and restrained to certain Seasons: Under which Limitations, *Seneca* calls these Diversions the necessary Temperament of Labour. "Some Remission (says he) must be given to our Minds, which will spring up the better, and more brisk from Rest. It is with the Mind as with a fruitful Field, whose Fertility will be exhausted if we give it no Intermission. The same will accrue to the Mind by incessant Labours, whereas both from gentle Remission will acquire Strength. From constant Labour arises a certain Dulness and Languor of the Spirits; nor would Men with such Eagerness affect them, if Sport and Merriment had not a natural Sweetness inherent in themselves; the frequent Use of which however will destroy all Gravity and Force in our Minds. Sleep is necessary to our Refreshment, but if this be continued Night and Day, it will become Death. There is a great Difference between the Remission of any Thing and its Dissolution. Lawgivers, therefore, instituted certain Holydays, that the People might be compelled by Law to Merriment, interposing this as a necessary Temperament to their Labours.‖"[9]

Thus the *Greek* and *Latin* Philosopher, tho' they derive the Institution

---

* *Macrob. Saturnalia.* lib. 2. c. xiii. *Note,* This RIOT ACT passed in one of the freest Ages of the *Roman* Republic.[8]

† *De Pace,* fol. 25.

‡ 33 *Hen.* VIII. c. ix.   ‖ Sen. *De Tranquill. Animi.* p. 167. *Edit. Lips.*

---

[7] Ferdinando Pulton also lists a number of common games and pastimes that are always legally enjoyed, 'for these assemblies be not made with the intent to break or disturbe the Peace' (*de Pace,* fo. 25a). He cites 33 Hen. VIII, c. 8 & 9. For Pulton, see *Charge,* p. 24.

[8] Macrobius, *Saturnalia,* iii. 17 (trans. Percival Vaughn Davies [New York, 1969], p. 241): 'The Orchian Law [was] proposed . . . in the third year after the appointment of Cato as censor. . . . its main provisions prescribed the permissible number of guests at a meal'.

[9] Apparently Fielding's translation from Seneca's 'The Tranqvilitie and Peace of the Minde' (see *Works,* trans. T. Lodge [London, 1614], p. 653). Fielding owned a 1615 edition, ed. Justus Lipsius (Baker, no. 476).

differently, the one alledging a divine and the other a human Original, both agree that a necessary Relaxation from Labour was the only End for which Diversion was invented and allowed to the People. This Institution, as the former of these great Writers tells us, was grosly perverted even in his Time; but surely neither then, nor in any Age or Nation, until now, was this Perversion carried to so scandalous an Excess as it is at present in this Kingdom, and especially in and near the Metropolis, where the Places of Pleasure are almost become numberless: for besides those great Scenes of Rendezvous, where the Nobleman and his Taylor, the Lady of Quality and her Tirewoman, meet together and form one common Assembly, what an immense Variety of Places have this Town and its Neighbourhood set apart for the Amusement of the lowest Order of the People; and where the Master of the House, or Wells, or Garden, may be said to angle only in the Kennels, where baiting with the vilest Materials, he catches only the thoughtless and tasteless Rabble? And these are carried on, not on a single Day, or in a single Week; but all of them during half, and some during the whole Year.[1]

If a Computation was made of the Money expended in these Temples of Idleness by the Artificer, the Handicraft, the Apprentice, and even the common Labourer, the Sum would appear excessive; but without putting myself to that Trouble, I believe the Reader will permit me to conclude that it is much greater than such Persons can or ought to afford; especially as Idleness, its necessary Attendant, adds greatly to the Debtor's Side in the Account; and that the necessary Consequence must be Ruin to many, who from being useful Members of the Society will become a heavy Burden or absolute Nuisance to the Public. It being indeed a certain Method to fill the Streets with Beggars, and the Goals with Debtors and Thieves.

That this Branch of Luxury hath grown to its present Height, is owing partly to a Defect in the Laws; and this Defect may, with great Decency and Respect to the Legislature, be very truly imputed to the Recency of the Evil; for as our Ancestors knew it not, they may be well excused for not having foreseen and guarded against it. If therefore it should seem now necessary to be retrenched, a new Law will, I apprehend, be necessary for that Purpose;

---

[1] *Humphry Clinker* (1771) provides a useful gloss on this passage. In his tirade against London (letter dated 29 May) Matthew Bramble complains that the 'hod-keeper, the low mechanic, the tapster, the publican, the shop-keeper, the pettifogger, the citizen, the courtier, *all tread upon the kibes of one another*' and that 'the gayest places of public entertainment are filled with fashionable figures; which, upon inquiry, will be found to be journeymen taylors, serving-men, and abigails, disguised like their betters'. He cites Ranelagh and Vauxhall, 'the court, the opera, the theatre, and the masquerade', and 'other public gardens of inferior note'. For the proliferation of these latter, see Sir Walter Besant, *London in the Eighteenth Century* (London, 1925), pp. 412 ff.; and M. Dorothy George, 'London and the Life of the Town', in *Johnson's England*, ed. A. S. Turberville (London, 1933), i. 189 ff. Both Warwick Wroth, *The London Pleasure Gardens* (London, 1896) and E. Beresford Chancellor, *The Pleasure Haunts of London* (London, 1925) contain abundant information on public places of entertainment.

the Powers of the Magistrate being scarce extensive enough, under any Provision extant, to destroy a Hydra now become so pregnant and dangerous. And it would be too dangerous as well as too invidious a Task to oppose the mad Humours of the Populace, by the Force of any doubtful obsolete Law; which, as I have hinted before, could not have been directly levelled at a Vice which did not exist at a Time when the Law was made.

But while I am recommending some Restraint of this Branch of Luxury, which surely appears to be necessary, I would be understood to aim at the Retrenchment only, not at the Extirpation of Diversion; nay, and in this Restraint, I confine myself entirely to the lower Order of People. Pleasure always hath been, and always will be, the principal Business of Persons of Fashion and Fortune, and more especially of the Ladies, for whom I have infinitely too great an Honour and Respect to rob them of any their least Amusement. Let them have their Plays, Operas, and Oratorios, their Masquerades and Ridottos; their Assemblies, Drums, Routs, Riots, and Hurricanes;[2] their *Ranelagh* and *Vauxhall*, their *Bath, Tunbridge, Bristol, Scarborough*, and *Cheltenham*;[3] and let them have their Beaus and Danglers to attend them at all these; it is the only Use for which such Beaus are fit; and I have seen in the Course of my Life, that it is the only one to which by sensible Women they are applied.[4]

In Diversion, as in many other Particulars, the upper Part of Life is distinguished from the Lower. Let the Great therefore answer for the Employment of their Time, to themselves, or to their spiritual Governors. The Society will receive some temporal Advantage from their Luxury. The more Toys which Children of all Ages consume, the brisker will be the Circulation of Money, and the greater the Increase of Trade.[5]

The Business of the Politician is only to prevent the Contagion from

[2] In *Tom Jones* (XVII. vi. 898) Fielding defines a drum as 'an Assembly of well dressed Persons of both Sexes, most of whom play at Cards, and the rest do nothing at all; while the Mistress of the House performs the Part of the Landlady at an Inn'. Besant quotes an 18th-century definition of a drum: 'a riotous assembly of fashionable people of both sexes at a private house; not unaptly styled a drum, from the noise and emptiness of the entertainment. There are also drum-major, rout, tempest, and hurricane, differing only in degrees of multitude and uproar, as the significant name of each declares' (*London in the Eighteenth Century*, p. 404).

[3] In a paper contributed to the *Rambler* (no. 97, 19 Feb. 1751) just about a month after the publication of the *Enquiry*, Samuel Richardson bemoans the extravagance of country town assemblies at 'Tunbridge, Bath, Cheltenham, Scarborough!' Like Fielding, he connects 'places of open resort, and general entertainment, which fill every quarter of the metropolis, . . . Breakfasting-places, dining-places; routs, drums, concerts, balls, plays, operas, masquerades' with 'public sales of the goods of broken housekeepers, which the general dissoluteness of manners has contributed to make very frequent'.

[4] Fielding's persistent scorn for fashionable life is perhaps summed up by his comment in 'An Essay on Conversation' (*Miscellanies* [1743], p. 140): 'If Men were to be rightly estimated, and divided into subordinate Classes, according to the superior Excellence of their several Natures, perhaps the lowest class of either Sex would be properly assigned to those two Disgracers of the human Species, commonly called a Beau, and a fine Lady.' Cf. *A Proposal*, below, p. 272.

[5] Cf. *A Proposal*, p.228.

spreading to the useful Part of Mankind, the *ΕΠΙΠΟΝΟΝ ΠΕΦΥΚΟΣ ΓΕΝΟΣ**;[6] and this is the Business of Persons of Fashion and Fortune too, in order that the Labour and Industry of the rest may administer to their Pleasures, and furnish them with the Means of Luxury. To the upper Part of Mankind Time is an Enemy, and (as they themselves often confess) their chief Labour is to kill it; whereas, with the others, Time and Money are almost synonymous; and as they have very little of each to spare, it becomes the Legislature, as much as possible, to suppress all Temptations whereby they may be induced too profusely to squander either the one or the other; since all such Profusion must be repaired at the Cost of the Public.

Such Places of Pleasure, therefore, as are totally set apart for the Use of the Great World, I meddle not with. And though *Ranelagh* and *Vauxhall*, by reason of their Price,[7] are not entirely appropriated to the People of Fashion, yet they are seldom frequented by any below the middle Rank; and a strict Regard to Decency is preserved in them both. But surely two such Places are sufficient to contain all those who have any Title to spend their Time in this idle, though otherwise innocent Way. Nor should such a Fashion be allowed to spread into every Village round *London*, and by degrees all over the Kingdom; by which means, not only Idleness, but all Kinds of Immorality, will be encouraged.

I cannot dismiss this Head, without mentioning a notorious Nuisance which hath lately arisen in this Town; I mean, those Balls where Men and Women of loose Reputation meet in disguised Habits. As to the Masquerade in the *Hay-market*,[8] I have nothing to say; I really think it a silly rather than a vicious Entertainment: But the Case is very different with these inferiour Masquerades; for these are indeed no other than the Temples of Drunkenness, Lewdness, and all Kind of Debauchery.

SECT. II.

Of DRUNKENNESS, *a second Consequence of Luxury among the Vulgar.*

But the Expence of Money, and Loss of Time, with their certain Consequences, are not the only Evils which attend the Luxury of the Vulgar. Drunkenness is almost inseparably annexed to the Pleasures of such People. A Vice by no means to be construed as a spiritual Offence alone, since so

---

* Plato.

[6] *De Legibus*, II. iii. 653: [mankind] 'born to misery'. Fielding quotes from the same passage he cites above, p. 80 n. 6.

[7] In the 1730s the price of admission to Vauxhall was one shilling. The admission price to Ranelagh, first opened in 1742, varied from one shilling to a guinea, depending on the entertainment offered.

[8] Alluding to 'Count' Heidegger's masquerade at the Opera House in the Haymarket (see above, p. 79 n. 3).

many temporal Mischiefs arise from it; amongst which are very frequently Robbery and Murder itself.

I do not know a more excellent Institution than that of *Pittacus*, mentioned by *Aristotle* in his *Politics**; by which a Blow given by a drunken Man, was more severely punished than if it had been given by one that was sober; *for Pittacus, says Aristotle, considered the Utility of the Public, (as drunken men are more apt to strike) and not the Excuse, which might otherwise be allowed to their Drunkenness.*[9] And so far both the Civil Law and our own have followed this Institution, that neither have admitted Drunkenness to be an Excuse for any Crime.[1]

This odious Vice (indeed the Parent of all others) as History informs us, was first introduced into this Kingdom by the *Danes*, and with very mischievous Effects. Wherefore that excellent Prince *Edgar* the *Peaceable*, when he set about reforming the Manners of his People, applied himself very particularly to the Remedy of this great Evil, and ordered Silver or Gold Pins to be fixed to the Sides of their Pots and Cups, beyond which it was not lawful for any Person to drink[†].[2]

What Penalty was affixed to the Breach of this Institution, I know not; nor do I find any Punishment in our Books for the Crime of Drunkenness, till the Time of *Jac.* I. in the fourth Year of whose Reign it was enacted, "That every Person lawfully convicted of Drunkenness, shall, for every such Offence, forfeit the Sum of Five Shillings, to be paid within a Week next after his, her, or their Conviction, to the Hands of the Churchwardens of the Parish where, &c. to the Use of the Poor. In Default of Payment, the Sum to be levied by Distress, and, in Default of Distress, the Offender is to be commited to the Stocks, there to remain for the Space of six Hours[‡]".[3]

For the second Offence they are to be bound to their good Behaviour, with two Sureties, in a Recognizance of Ten Pounds[||].

Nor is only that Degree of Drunkenness forbidden, which Mr. *Dalton* describes, "so as to stagger and reel to and fro, and where the same Legs which carry him into a House, cannot carry him out again[§];"[4] for, by the

---

* L. 2. c. 10.   ‡ *Jac.* I. chap. 5.   § *Dalt.* chap. 7. sect 5.
† *Eächard*, p. 88. || Ib. sect. 6.

[9] *Politics*, II. 12. 13. Henry Knight Miller (*Essays on Fielding's Miscellanies* [Princeton, NJ, 1961], p. 84 n.) points out that in *Tom Jones* (v. x. 257) Fielding uses Aristotle's comment on Pittacus to soften our judgement of Tom's drunken celebrations.

[1] Hawkins, i. 6: 'and he who is guilty of any Crime whatever, thro' his voluntary Drunkenness, shall be punished for it as much as if he had been sober'.

[2] 'But . . . King *Edgar* was very diligent in suppressing these Vices; and particularly that of Drunkenness, which the Danes had introduc'd with such mischievous Effects; upon the Account of which he order'd Silver or Gold Pins to be fix'd to the Sides of their Pots or Cups, beyond which it was unlawful to drink themselves, or cause others to do the same' (Lawrence Echard, *The History of England*, 3rd edn, [London, 1720], p. 88). For Echard, see *Charge*, above, p. 7 n. 9.

[3] Fielding paraphrases 4 Jac. I, c. 5. sect. 2.

[4] Michael Dalton, *The Country Justice* . . . (London, 1727), ch. 7, sect. 5, p. 29: 'Now, to know a

same Act of Parliament, all Persons who continue drinking or tipling in any Inn, Victualling-house, or Ale-house, in their own City, Town or Parish (unless such as being invited by a traveller, shall accompany him during his necessary Abode there; or except Labouring and Handicraftsmen in Cities, and Corporate and Market Towns, upon a working Day, for an Hour at Dinner-time, in Ale-houses, where they take their Diet; and except Labourers and Workmen, who, during their Continuance in any Work, shall lodge or victual in any Inn, &c. or except for some urgent and necessary Occasion, to be allowed by two Justices of the Peace) shall forfeit the Sum of Three Shillings and Sixpence, for the Use of the Poor; to be levied as before, and, for Want of Distress, to be put in the Stocks for four Hours||.

This Act hath been still farther enforced by another in the same Reign§. By the latter Act, the Tipler is liable, whether his Habitation be within the same or any other Parish. 2*dly*, The Proof by one Witness is made sufficient; and, 3*dly*, A very extraordinary Clause is added, by which the Oath of the Party offending, after having confessed his own Crime, is made Evidence against any other Offender, though at the same Time.

Thus we see the Legislature have taken the utmost Care not only to punish, but even to prevent this Vice of Drunkenness, which the Preamble of one of the foregoing Statutes calls a *loathsome* and *odious Sin*, and the Root and Foundation of many other enormous Sins, as Murder, &c.[5] Nor doth the Wisdom of our Law stop here. Our cautious Ancestors have endeavoured to remove the Temptation, and, in a great measure, to take away from the People their very Power of offending this way. And this by going to the Fountain-head, and endeavouring to regulate and restrain the Scenes of these Disorders, and to confine them to those Uses for which they were at first designed; namely, for the Rest, Refreshment and Convenience of Travellers.

A cursory View of the Statutes on this Head will demonstrate of what Consequence to Society the Suppression of this Vice was in the Opinion of our Ancestors.

By the Common Law, Inns and Ale-houses might be kept *ad libitum*;[6] but

---

|| 4 *Jac.* I. chap. 4. sect. 4 & 1 *Jac.* I. chap. 9.   § 21 *Jac.* I. chap. 7.

drunken Man the better, the Scripture describeth them *to stagger and reel to and fro, Job 12. 25 Isa. 24. 20.* And so where the same Legs which carry a Man into the House cannot bring him out again, it is a sufficient Sign of Drunkenness.' Dalton's *Country Justice* (1618), based on Lambarde's *Eirenarcha*, was the most popular of such handbooks in the 17th and early 18th centuries. Fielding owned 1705 and 1715 editions (Baker, nos. 107 & 157) and he could have found much of the material for his résumé of laws concerning drunkenness in Dalton. Unlike all later treatises on justices of the peace, Dalton's *Country Justice* could be cited in court as an authority.

[5] 4 Jac. I, c. 5: 'An acte for repressinge the odious and loathsome synne of Drunckenness'.

[6] Salkeld (see below, p. 88 n. 4) states that before 5 & 6 Edw. VI, c. 25 anyone could keep an alehouse without a license 'for it was a means of Livelihood which anyone was free to follow'. *ad libitum*: 'for the purpose of pleasure'.

if any Disorders were suffered in them, they were indictable as a common Nuisance.

The first Reform which I find to have been made by Parliament, was in the Reign of *Henry* VII.* when two Justices were empowered to suppress an Ale-house.

The Statute of *Edward* VI.† is the first which requires a precedent Licence. By this Act no Man can keep an Ale-house, without being licensed by the Sessions, or by two Justices; but now, by a late Statute, all Licences granted by Justices out of their Sessions are void‡.

By the Statute of *Charles* I.‖ which alters the Penalties of that of *Edward* VI. the Punishment for keeping an Ale-house, or commonly selling Ale, Beer, Cyder and Perry,⁸ without a Licence, is to pay Twenty Shillings to the Use of the Poor, to be levied by Distress; which, if Satisfaction be not made within three Days, is to be sold. And if there be no Goods whereon to distrain, and the Money be not paid within six Days after Conviction, the Offender is to be delivered to the Constable, or some inferiour Officer, to be whipped. For the second Offence, he is to be committed to the House of Correction for a Month; and for the third, he is to be committed to the said House, till by Order of the Justices, at their General Sessions, he be discharged.

The Conviction is to be on the View of the Justice, Confession of the Party, or by the Oath of two Witnesses.

And by this Statute, if the Constable or Officer to whom the Party is committed to be whipt, &c. do not execute his Warrant, the Justice shall commit him to Prison, there to remain till he shall procure some one to execute the said Warrant, nor until he shall pay Forty Shillings to the Use of the Poor.

The Justices, at the Time of granting the Licence, shall take a Recognizance from the Party, not to suffer any unlawful Games, nor other Disorders, in his House; which is to be certified to the Sessions, and the Justices there have a Power to proceed for the Forfeiture§.

By the Statute of *Jac.* I.** Alehouse-keepers, who suffer Townsmen to sit tipling (unless in the Cases abovementioned*) forfeit Ten Shillings to the Poor; the Distress to be sold within six Days; and if no Distress can be had, the Party is to be committed till the Forfeiture is paid.

---

* II *H.* VII.
† 5 *Edw.* VI. c. 25.⁷
‡ 2 *G.* II. c. 28. sect. 11.

‖ 3 *Car.* I. cap. 4.
§ 5 *E.* VI. *ubi sup.*
** Cap. 9. *ubi sup.*⁹
* *Supra*, p. 14. in the Case of *Tiplers*.

---

⁷ 5 & 6 Edw. VI, c. 25. sect. 1.
⁹ 1 Jac. I, c. 9. sect. 2.

⁸ A Cider-like beverage made from pears.

Vintners, who keep Inns or Victualling-houses, are within this Act*.

And by two several Statutes†, Alehouse-keepers, convicted of this Offence, are prohibited from keeping an Ale-house for the Space of three Years.

Justices of Peace likewise, for any Disorders committed in Ale-houses contrary to the Condition of the Recognizance, may suppress such Houses‡; but then the Proceeding must be on the Recognizance, and the Breach of the Condition proved‖.

Now, on the concise View of these several Laws, it appears, that the Legislature have been abundantly careful on this Head; and that the only Blame lies on the Remissness with which these wholesome Provisions have been executed.

But though I will not undertake to defend the Magistrates of former Times, who have surely been guilty of some Neglect of their Duty; yet, on behalf of the present Commissioners of the Peace, I must observe, their Case is very different.[1] What Physicians tell us of the animal Functions, will hold true when applied to Laws; Both, by long Disuse, lose all their Elasticity and Force. Froward Habits grow on Men, as they do on Children, by long Indulgence; nor will either submit easily to Correction in Matters where they have been accustomed to act at their Pleasure. They are very different Offices to execute a new or a well known Law, and to revive one which is obsolete.[2] In the Case of a known Law, Custom brings Men to Submission; and in all new Provisions, the Ill-will, if any, is levelled at the Legislature, who are much more able to support it than a few, or a single Magistrate. If therefore it be thought proper to suppress this Vice, the Legislature must once more take the Matter into their Hands; and to this, perhaps, they will be the more inclined, when it comes to their Knowledge, that a new Kind of Drunkenness, unknown to our Ancestors, is lately sprung up amongst us, and which, if not put a stop to, will infallibly destroy a great Part of the inferiour People.[5]

---

* 1 *Car.* I. cap. 4.   ‡ 5 *E.* VI. *ubi sup.*[5]

† 7 *Jac.* I. cap. 10. 21 *Jac.* I. cap. 7.   ‖ *Salk.* 45.[4]

---

[1] In the lengthy debate on the Gin Act of 1743 (16 Geo. II, c. 8) in the House of Lords, the bishops and the Opposition argued that the stringent Act of 1736 failed only because justices of the peace had not enforced its provisions.

[2] In discussing the rating of wages (*Enquiry*, below, p. 115), Fielding is willing to enforce a law 'grown into utter Neglect and Disuse'.

[3] 5 & 6 Edw. VI, c. 25 sect. 3.

[4] *Salk*: William Salkeld, *Reports of Cases . . . King's Bench*, 2 vols. (London, 1717 [Baker, no. 273]). The purport of Salkeld's report is that justices can suppress unlicensed houses at will but licensed houses 'are not punishable without a breach of the recognizance [i.e., unless there has been some breech of a recorded obligation]' (i. 45). Fielding also cites Salkeld in the *Charge*, above, p. 22.

[5] In 1689 the distillery trade was opened to British subjects at the same time that the importation of foreign spirits was prohibited. As early as 1695 Charles Davenant warned of the dangers of brandy

The Drunkenness I here intend, is that acquired by the strongest intoxicating Liquors, and particularly by that Poison called *Gin*; which, I have great reason to think, is the principal Sustenance (if it may be so called) of more than an hundred thousand People in this Metropolis. Many of these Wretches there are, who swallow Pints of this Poison within the Twenty-four Hours; the dreadful Effects of which I have the Misfortune every Day to see, and to smell too. But I have no need to insist on my own Credit, or on that of my Informers; the great Revenue arising from the Tax on this Liquor (the Consumption of which is almost wholly confined to the lowest Order of People) will prove the Quantity consumed better than any other Evidence.[6]

Now, besides the moral ill Consequences occasioned by this Drunkenness, with which, in this Treatise, I profess not to deal; how greatly must this be supposed to contribute to those political Mischiefs which this Essay proposes to remedy? This will appear from considering, that however cheap this vile Potion may be, the poorer Sort will not easily be able to supply themselves with the Quantities they desire; for the intoxicating Draught itself disqualifies them from using any honest Means to acquire it, at the same time that it removes all Sense of Fear and Shame, and emboldens them to commit every wicked and desperate Enterprize. Many Instances of this I see daily: Wretches are often brought before me, charged with Theft and Robbery, whom I am forced to confine before they are in a Condition to be examined; and when they have afterwards become sober, I have plainly perceived, from the State of the Case, that the *Gin* alone was the Cause of the Transgression, and have been sometimes sorry that I was obliged to commit them to Prison.

But beyond all this, there is a political ill Consequence of this Drunkenness, which, though it doth not strictly fall within my present Purpose, I shall be excused for mentioning, it being indeed the greatest Evil of all, and which must, I think, awaken our Legislature to put a final Period to so destructive a Practice. And this is that dreadful Consequence which must attend the poisonous Quality of this pernicious Liquor to the Health, the Strength, and the very Being of Numbers of his Majesty's most useful Subjects. I have not enough of physical Knowledge, to display the ill Effects

and spirits to the poor and recommended that they be taxed so that 'it may be worth no Man's while to take it, but for Medicine' (*An Essay upon Ways and Means of Supplying the War*, p. 138). By the 1720s attacks on gin-drinking essentially identical with Fielding's were commonplace and continued to increase in the next two decades. Major legislation to control this 'new kind of drunkenness' had been passed in 1729, 1736, and 1743. See Sidney and Beatrice Webb, *The History of Liquor Licensing* (London, 1903); and M. Dorothy George, *London Life in the XVIII Century* (London, 1925), pp. 27 ff.

[6] The production and sale of spirits was profitable to corn growers and distillers as well as to the government, and acts to control the consumption and sale of gin met both respectable and unrespectable opposition. The restrictive Act of 1736, opponents predicted, would cost the government £70,000 in revenues (George, *London Life in the XVIII Century*, p. 35). In 1751 over seven million gallons of spirits were legally distilled.

which such poisonous Liquors produce in the Constitution: For these I shall refer the Reader to *The Physical Account of the Nature of all distilled spirituous Liquors, and the Effect they have on human Bodies**. And tho', perhaps, the Consequence of this Poison, as it operates slowly, may not so visibly appear in the Diminution of the Strength, Health and Lives of the present Generation; yet let a Man cast his Eyes but a Moment towards our Posterity, and there the dreadful Consequences must strike on the meanest Capacity, and must alarm, I think, the most sluggish Degree of Public Spirit. What must become of the Infant who is conceived in *Gin?* with the poisonous Distillations of which it is nourished both in the Womb and at the Breast.[8] Are these wretched Infants (if such can be supposed capable of arriving at the Age of Maturity) to become our future Sailors, and our future Grenadiers? Is it by the Labour of such as these, that all the Emoluments of Peace are to be procured us, and all the Dangers of War averted from us? What could an *Edward* or a *Henry*, a *Marlborough* or a *Cumberland*,[9] effect with an Army of such Wretches? Doth not this polluted Source, instead of producing Servants for the Husbandman, or Artificer; instead of providing Recruits for the Sea or the Field, promise only to fill Alms-houses and Hospitals, and to infect the Streets with Stench and Diseases?

In solemn Truth, there is nothing of more serious Consideration, nor which more loudly calls for a Remedy, than the Evil now complained against. For what can be more worthy the Care of the Legislature, than to preserve the Morals, the Innocence, the Health, Strength and Lives of a great Part (I will repeat, the most useful Part) of the People? So far am I, in my own Opinion, from representing this in too serious or too strong a Light, that I can find no Words, or Metaphor, adequate to my Ideas on this Subject. The first Inventer of this diabolical Liquor may be compared to the Poisoner of a Fountain, whence a large City was to derive its Waters; the highest Crime, as

---

* This was composed by a very learned Divine, with the Assistance of several Physicians, and published in the Year 1736. The Title is, *Distilled Spirituous Liquors the Bane of the Nation.*[7]

---

[7] Thomas Wilson (1703–84), the son of Thomas Wilson, Bishop of Sodor and Man. In 1737 he was made one of the king's chaplains and given the rectory of St Stephen's, Walbrook; in 1743 he became prebendary of Westminster; in 1753 he obtained the rectory of St Margaret's, Westminster. All of Fielding's argument is present in Wilson's pamphlet. Wilson argues that gin-drinking leads to crime, enfeebles the laboring classes, and consequently undermines England's military strength. See Introduction, p. lx ff. and Zirker, *Social Pamphlets*, pp. 88 ff.

[8] The central figure in Hogarth's *Gin Lane*, published nearly simultaneously with the *Enquiry*, is a drunken nursing mother whose child is falling helplessly down a stairwell. Off to the right another mother is administering a quieting draught of gin to her child.

[9] 'The glorious Duke of *Cumberland*' (*Tom Jones*, VII. xi. 367) once more receives Fielding's praise by being ranked with England's most notable generals (Edward: the Black Prince; Henry: Henry V). Cumberland, George II's youngest son, had defeated the Pretender's army at Culloden. John Churchill, first Duke of Marlborough, often received Fielding's praise (see *Miscellanies* [1743], p. 23 and n.; and *JJ* p. 65 and n.).

it hath been thought, of which Human Nature is capable.[1] A Degree of Villainy, indeed, of which I cannot recollect any Example: But surely if such was ever practised, the Governors of that City could not be thought blameless, did they not endeavour, to the utmost, to with-hold the Citizens from drinking the poisonous Draught; and if such a general Thirst after it prevailed, as, we are told, possessed the People of *Athens* at the Time of the Plague*, what could justify the not effectually cutting off all Aqueducts, by which the Poison was dispersed among the People?

Nor will any thing less than absolute Deletion serve on the present Occasion. It is not making Men pay 50 *l.* or 500 *l.* for a Licence to poison; nor enlarging the Quantity from two Gallons to ten, which will extirpate so stubborn an Evil.[2] Here may, perhaps, be no little Difficulty. To lay the Axe to the Still-head, and prohibit all Distillery in general, would destroy the Chymist. If distilling this or that Spirit was forbidden, we know how easily all partial Prohibitions are evaded; nay the Chymist (was the Matter confined to him) would soon probably become a common Distiller, and his Shop no better than a Gin-shop;[3] since what is more common than for Men to adopt the Morals of a Thief at a Fire, and to work their own private Emolument out of a public Mischief.[4] Suppose all spirituous Liquors were, together with other Poison, to be locked up in the Chymists or Apothecaries Shops, thence never to be drawn, till some excellent Physician calls them forth for the Cure of nervous Distempers! Or suppose the Price was to be raised so high, by a severe Import, that Gin would be placed entirely beyond the Reach of the Vulgar! Or perhaps the Wisdom of the Legislature may devise a better and more effectual Way.[5]

But if the Difficulty be really insuperable, or if there be any political

---

* ᾿Εδρασαν ἐς φρέατα ἀπαύστω τῇ δίψη ξυνεχόμενοι. They ran into the Wells, being constantly possessed by an inexhausted Thirst. *Thucydid.* p. 112. *Edit. Hudsoni.*[6]

---

[1] A traditional villainy contemplated by such as Barabas (*The Jew of Malta*, II. iii. 177). Cf. *The Historical Register*, ed. William W. Appleton (Lincoln, Nebr., 1967), p. 5.

[2] Fielding alludes to provisions in the Act of 1736 (9 Geo. II, c. 23) which required that anyone selling spirituous liquors in quantities less than two gallons pay a tax of £50 per year. Three licenses were purchased between 1736 and 1743 (George, *London Life*, p. 35). This act, Pope says, '[hurled] the Thunder of the Laws on Gin' [*Epilogue to the Satires, Dialogue I*, l. 140).

[3] In 1747 the compound distillers 'were given leave to retail on taking out a £5 licence. Under cover of this Act the old evils came back again and the consumption went up' (George, *London Life*, p. 36).

[4] Perhaps justifying again the execution of Bosavern Penlez.

[5] Considering the vagueness of Fielding's proposals in this and the following paragraph, it is difficult to understand why he should be credited with the specific reforms of 1751 (24 Geo. II, c. 40) and 1753 (26 Geo. II, c. 13). See, for example, George, *London Life*, p. 36; Jones, p. 173; Dudden, ii. 794.

[6] John Hudson (1662–1719). His edition (1696) of Thucydides' *History of the Peloponnesian War* is no. 616 in Baker. 'What they would have liked best would have been to throw themselves into cold water; as indeed was done by some of the neglected sick, who plunged into the rain-tanks in their agonies of unquenchable thirst; though it made no difference whether they drank little or much' (II. xlix).

Reason against the total Demolition of this Poison, so strong as to countervail the Preservation of the Morals, Health and Beings of such Numbers of his Majesty's Subjects, let us, however, in some measure, palliate the Evil, and lessen its immediate ill Consequences, by a more effectual provision against Drunkenness than any we have at present, in which the Method of Conviction is too tedious and dilatory. Some little Care on this Head is surely necessary: For tho' the Encrease of Thieves, and the Destruction of Morality; though the Loss of our Labourers, our Sailors, and our Soldiers, should not be sufficient Reasons, there is one which seems to be unanswerable, and that is, the Loss of our Gin-drinkers: Since, should the drinking this Poison be continued in its present Height during the next twenty Years, there will, by that Time, be very few of the common People left to drink it.

SECT. III.

Of Gaming *among the Vulgar; a third Consequence of their Luxury.*

I come now to the last great Evil which arises from the Luxury of the Vulgar; and this is Gaming: A School in which most Highwaymen of great Eminence have been bred. This Vice is the more dangerous, as it is deceitful, and, contrary to every other Species of Luxury, flatters its Votaries with the Hopes of increasing their Wealth; so that Avarice itself is so far from securing us against its Temptations, that it often betrays the more thoughtless and giddy Part of Mankind into them; promising Riches without Bounds, and those to be acquired by the most sudden as well as easy and indeed pleasant Means.

And here I must again remind the Reader, that I have only the inferiour Part of Mankind under my Consideration. I am not so ill-bred as to disturb the Company at a polite Assembly; nor so ignorant of our Constitution, as to imagine, that there is a sufficient Energy in the executive Part to controul the Oeconomy of the Great, who are beyond the Reach of any, unless capital Laws.[7] Fashion, under whose Guidance they are, and which created the Evil, can alone cure it. With Patience therefore must we wait, till this notable Mistress of the Few shall, in her good time, accomplish so desirable a Change: In fact, till Great Men become wiser or better; till the Prevalence of some laudable Taste shall teach them a worthier Manner of employing their Time; till they have Sense enough to be reasoned, Modesty enough to be laughed, or Conscience enough to be frightened out of a silly, a shameful and a sinful Profligacy, attended with horrid Waste of Time, and the cruel Destruction of the Families of others, or of their own.

[7] The summaries of statutes that Fielding provides below make clear the economic and class bias of laws against gaming.

In the mean time we may, I think, reasonably desire of these great Personages, that they would keep their favorite Vice to themselves, and not suffer others, whose Birth or Fortune gives them no Title to be above the Terrour of the Laws, or the Censure of their Betters, to share with them in this Privilege. Surely we may give Great Men the same Advice, which *Archer*, in the Play, gives to the Officers of the Army; *To kick out all——in Red but their own.*[8] What Temptations can Gamesters of Fashion have, to admit *inferiour* Sharpers into their Society? Common Sense, surely, will not suffer a Man to risque a Fortune against one who hath none of his own to stake against it.

I am well apprized that this is not much the Case with Persons of the first Figure; but to Gentlemen (and especially the younger Sort) of the second Degree, these Fellows have found much too easy an Access. Particularly at the several public Places (I might have said Gaming Places) in this Kingdom, too little Care is taken to prevent the promiscuous Union of Company; and Sharpers of the lowest Kind have frequently there found Admission to their Superiours, upon no other Pretence or Merit than that of a laced Coat, and with no other Stock than that of Assurance.

Some few of these Fellows, by luckily falling in with an egregious Bubble,[9] some thoughtless young Heir, or more commonly Heiress, have succeeded in a manner, which, if it may give some Encouragement to others to imitate them, should, at the same time, as strongly admonish all Gentlemen and Ladies to be cautious with whom they mix in public Places, and to avoid the Sharper as they would a Pest.[1] But much the greater Part of such Adventurers have met with a more probable and more deserved Fate; and having exhausted their little Fund in their Attempts, have been reduced to a Dilemma, in which it required more Judgment and Resolution than are the Property of many Men, and more true Sense of Honour than belongs to any debauched Mind, to extricate themselves by honest Means. The only Means, indeed, of this Kind, are to quit their assumed Station, and to return to that Calling, however mean and laborious, to which they were born and bred.

But besides that the Way to this is often obstructed with almost insuperable Difficulties; and false Shame, at its very Entrance, dashes them in the Face, how easily are they dissuaded from such disagreeable Thoughts by the Temptations with which Fortune allures them, of a Possibility, at least, of still supporting their false Appearances, and of retrieving all their former Hopes? How greedily, may we imagine, this enchanting Alternative

---

[8] Farquhar, *The Beaux' Stratagem* (1707), II. ii. When Boniface calls the highwayman Gibbet 'Captain', Archer exclaims in an aside, 'Captain your servant.—Captain! a pretty fellow! 'Sdeath, I wonder that the officers of the army don't conspire to beat all scoundrels in red but their own.'

[9] A gull.   [1] The plague.

will be embraced by every bold Mind, in such Circumstances? for what but the Danger of the Undertaking can deter one, who hath nothing of a Gentleman but his Dress, to attain which he hath already divested himself of all Sense of Honesty? How easy is the Transition from Fraud to Force? from a Gamester to a Rogue? Perhaps, indeed, it is civil to suppose it any Transition at all.

From this Source, therefore, several of our most notable Highwaymen have proceeded; and this hath likewise been the Source of many other Depredations on the honest Part of Mankind. So mischievous have been this Kind of Sharpers in Society, that they have fallen under the particular Notice of the Legislature: for a Statute in the Reign of Queen *Anne*, reciting, "That divers lewd and dissolute Persons live at great Expences, having no visible Estate, Profession or Calling, to maintain themselves, but support those Expences by Gaming only;" enacts, "That any two Justices of the Peace may cause to be brought before them all Persons within their respective Limits, whom they shall have just Cause to suspect to have no visible Estate, profession or Calling, to maintain themselves by, but do, for the most part, support themselves by Gaming; and if such Persons shall not make the contrary appear to such Justices, they are to be bound to their good Behaviour for a Twelve-month; and, in Default of sufficient Security, to be committed till they can find such Security; which Security (in case they give it) is to be forfeited on their playing or betting at any one Time for more than the Value of 20 Shillings*."

As to Gaming in the lower Classes of Life, so plainly tending to the Ruin of Tradesmen, the Destruction of Youth, and to the Multiplication of every Kind of Fraud and Violence, the Legislature hath provided very wholesome Laws†.

---

* 9 *Annæ*, chap. 14. sect. 6, 7. It would be of great Service to the Public, to extend this Statute to idle Persons and Sharpers in general; for many support themselves by Frauds, and cheating Practices, even worse than Gaming; and have the Impudence to appear in the Dress of Gentlemen, and at public Places, without having any Pretensions of Birth or Fortune, or without any honest or visible Means of Livelihood whatever. Such a Law would not be without a Precedent; for such is the excellent Institution mentioned by *Herodotus*, in his *Euterpe*.[2]——"*Amasis* (says that Historian) established a Law in *Egypt*, that every *Egyptian* should annually declare before the Governor of the Province, by what Means he maintained himself; and all those who did not appear, or who could not prove that they had some lawful Livelihood, were punished by Death. This Law *Solon* introduced into *Athens*, where it was long inviolably preserved as a most just and equitable Provision." *Herod. Edit. Hudsoni*, p. 158.[3] This Punishment is surely too severe; but the Law, under a milder Penalty, is well worthy to be adopted.

† By a Statute made in the Reign of *Edward* IV, now repealed,[4] Playing at several Games therein mentioned, was punished by two Years Imprisonment, and the Forfeiture of 10 *l.* and the Master of the House was to be imprisoned for three Years, and to forfeit 20 *l.* A great Sum in those Days!

[2] Alexandrian scholars divided Herodotus' *History* into nine books and assigned a muse to each. Bk. II was known as 'Euterpe' (the muse of flute-playing).

[3] The story is in Herodotus, ii. 177 (Loeb). According to the *DNB*, John Hudson (see above, p. 91 n. 6) completed an edition of Herodotus which he 'neglected to publish'. I have found no record of such an edition. Item no. 645 in Baker is 'Herodotus, Gr. & Lat. Galei [Thomas Gale (1635?–1702)] . . . London. 1679'; no. 64 is 'Herodiani Historia, Gr. & Lat. . . . Oxon. 1678'.

[4] 17 Edw. IV, c. 3. 33 Hen. VIII, c. 9 repealed all former acts restraining unlawful games.

By the 33d of *Henry* VIII. "Every Artificer, Craftsman of any Handycraft or Occupation, Husbandman, Labourer, Servant at Husbandry, Journeyman or Servant of Artificer, Mariners, Fishermen, Watermen, or any Serving Men, are prohibited from playing at Tables, Dice, Cards, &c. out of *Christmas*, and in *Christmas* are permitted to play only in their Masters Houses, or in his Presence, under the Penalty of 20 *s*. And all Manner of Persons are prohibited from playing at any Bowl or Bowls, in any open Place out of their Garden or Orchard, under the Penalty of 6 *s*. 8 *d*.

"The Conviction to be by Action, Information, Bill, or otherwise, in any of the King's Courts; one Half of the Penalty to the Informer.

"Provided that Servants may play at any Times with their Masters, or by their Licence; and all Persons, who have 100 *l. per Annum*, Freehold, may give their Servants, or others, resorting to their Houses, a licence to play within the Precinct of their Houses, Gardens, or Orchard."

By this Statute likewise, "No Person whatever, by himself, Factor, Deputy, Servant, or other Person, shall, for Gain, keep, &c. any Common, House, Alley, or Place of Bowling, Coyting, Clash-Coyls, Half-Bowl, Tennis, Dicing-Table, or Carding,[5] or any other Manner of Game, prohibited by any Statute heretofore made, or any unlawful Game invented or made, or any other new unlawful Game hereafter to be invented or made: the Penalty is 40 *s. per* Day, for keeping the House, &c. and 6 *s*. 8 *d*. for every Person haunting and playing at such House. These Penalties to be recovered, &c. as above.

"And all Leases of Gaming-houses, Alleys, &c. are made void at the Election of the Lessee."

Farther by the said Statute, "Power is given to all Justices of Peace, Mayors, or other Head-Officers, in every City, &c. to enter suspected Houses and Places, and to commit the Keepers of the said Houses, and the Persons there haunting, resorting, and playing, to Prison; and to keep them in Prison, till the Keepers have found sureties to enter into a Recognizance to the King's Use, no longer to keep such House, &c. and the Persons there found, to be bound by themselves, or with Sureties, &c. at the Discretion of the Justice, &c. no more to haunt the said Places, or play at any of the said Games."[6]

And now by the Statute of *George* II.[7] this last Clause is enforced, by giving the Justice the same Power on the Information of two Persons, as he had before on View; and, by a more explicit Power, to take Sureties or not of the Party, at his Discretion.

---

[5] 'Coyting': similar to horseshoes; 'Clash-Coyles' or 'Kayles': a kind of skittles or ninepins; 'Half-Bowl': a variety of bowling; 'Carding': card games.

[6] Fielding summarizes and loosely quotes from 33 Hen. VIII, c. 9. sect. 10–17.

[7] 2 Geo. II, c. 28.

Lastly, The Statute of *Henry* VIII. enjoins the Justices, &c. to make due Search weekly, or once *per* Month, at the farthest, under the Penalty of forfeiting 40 s. for every Month, during their Neglect.

Thus stands the Law, by which it may appear, that the Magistrate is armed with sufficient Authority to destroy all Gaming among the inferiour People; and that, without his Neglect or Connivance, no such Nuisance can possibly exist.

And yet, perhaps, the Fault may not so totally lie at his Door; for the Recognizance is a mere Bugbear, unless the Party who breaks it, should be sued thereon; which, as it is attended with great Expence, is never done; so that though many have forfeited it, not a single Example of an Estreat hath been made within my Remembrance.[8]

Again, it were to be wished, that the Statute of *George* II. had required no more than one Witness to the Information: for even one Witness, as I have found by Experience, is very difficult to be procured.

However, as the Law now is, seeing that the general Bent of the People opposes itself to this Vice, it is certainly in a great measure within the Magistrate's Power to suppress it, and so to harass such as propose to find their Account in it, that these would soon be discouraged from the Undertaking; nor can I conclude without observing, that this hath been lately executed with great Vigour within the Liberty of *Westminster*.[9]

There are, besides, several other Provisions in our Statute Books against this destructive Vice. By the Statute of Queen *Anne**, whoever cheats at Play, forfeits five Times the Sum won by such Cheating, shall be deemed infamous, and suffer such corporal Punishment as in Case of Perjury. And whoever wins above 10 *l*. at any one Sitting, shall likewise forfeit five Times the Sum won. Going Shares with the Winner, and Betting on his Side, are in both Instances, within the Act.

By the same Act, all Securities for Money won at Play, are made void; and if a Mortgage be made on such Account, the Mortgagee doth not only lose

---

* 9 *Annæ*, chap. 14. by which the Statute of 16 *C.* II. is enlarged and made more severe.[1]

---

[8] After a recognizance (a bond or obligation recorded before a court or magistrate) has been broken, a justice of the peace must enter an estreat (a true copy of the recognizance) on the rolls of a court preliminary to further legal proceedings.

[9] *GM* of Feb. 1751 (p. 87), reports an instance of Fielding's vigor in suppressing gaming houses: 'Justice *Fielding* having receiv'd information of a rendevous of gamesters in the *Strand*, procured a strong party of guards, who seized 45 at the tables, which they broke to pieces and carried the gamesters before the justice, who committed 39 of them to the gatehouse, and admitted the other 6 to bail. . . . there were 3 tables broken to pieces, which cost near 60£ a piece, under each of them were observed 2 iron rollers, and 2 private springs, which those who were in the secret could touch, and stop the turning whenever they had any youngsters to deal with, and so cheated them of their money' (see General Introduction, p. lv).

[1] 16 Car. II, c. 7. had provided that a cheater forfeit treble his winnings.

all Benefit of it, but the Mortgage immediately enures[2] to the Use of the next Heir*.

By this Law Persons who have lost above 10 *l.* and have actually paid it, may recover the same by Action within three Months; and if they do not sue for it within that Time, any other Person may†. And the Defendant shall be liable to answer a Bill for discovering such Sum lost, upon Oath.

By 18 *George* II.‡ whoever wins or loses 10 *l.* at Play, or by Betting at any one Time, or 20 *l.* within 24 Hours, is liable to be indicted, and shall be fined five Times the Value of the Money lost.

By 12 *George* II.‖ the Games of Pharaoh, the Ace of Hearts, Basset, and Hazard,[3] are declared to be Lotteries; and all Persons who set up, maintain, and keep them, forfeit 200 *l.* and all who play at them, forfeit 50 *l.* The Conviction to be before one Justice of Peace, by the Oath of one Witness, or Confession of the party. And the Justice neglecting his Duty, forfeits 10 *l.* *Note*, The Prosecution against the Keeper, &*c.* may be for a Lottery, on the 8 *George* I. where the Penalty is 500 *l.*[4]

The Act of 18 *George* II. includes the Game of Roly Poly,[5] or other prohibited Game at Cards or Dice, within the Penalties of the abovementioned.

I have given this short Sketch of these several Acts, partly for the Use and Encouragement of Informers, and partly to insinuate to certain Persons with what Decency they can openly offend against such plain, such solemn Laws, the severest of which many of themselves have, perhaps, been the Makers of. How can they seriously answer either to their Honour or Conscience giving the pernicious Example of a Vice, from which, as the Legislature justly says in the Preamble to the 16th of *Charles* II. "Many Mischiefs and Inconveniences do arise, and are daily found in the encouraging of sundry idle and disorderly Persons in their dishonest, lewd, and dissolute Course of Life; and to the circumventing, deceiving, cousening, and debauching of many of the younger Sort, both of the Nobility and Gentry and others, to the Loss of their precious Time, and the utter Ruin of their Estates and Fortunes, and withdrawing them from noble and laudable Employments and Exercises!"[6] Will a Nobleman, I ask, confess that he can employ his Time in no better Amusement; or will he frankly own that he plays with any other View than that of Amusement? Lastly, What can a Man who sins in open Defiance of the Laws of his Country, answer to the *Vir bonus est Quis*? Can he say,

---

* Ibid. sect. 1. † Ibid. sect. 2. ‡ Chap. 34. ‖ Chap. 28.

---

2 Takes effect.
3 Pharaoh, Ace of Hearts, and Basset are card games; Hazard is a game of dice.
4 12 Geo. II, c. 28 includes the 'Note' to the provision of 8 Geo. I, c. 2.
5 Roulette.
6 Loosely quoted from 16 Car. II, c. 7.

Qui consulta Patrum, Qui Leges Juraque servat?[7]

Or can he apply that celebrated Line,

Oderunt peccare boni Virtutis Honore

to himself, who owes to his Greatness, and not to his Innocence, that he is not deterred from such Vices—*Formidine Pœnæ?*[8]

SECT. IV.

Of the Laws that relate to the PROVISION *for the Poor.*

Having now run through the several immediate Consequences of a general Luxury among the lower People, all which, as they tend to promote their Distresses, may be reasonably supposed to put many of them of the bolder Kind upon unlawful and violent Means of relieving the Mischief which such Vices have brought upon them; I come now to a second Cause of the Evil, in the improper Regulation of what is called the Poor in this Kingdom, arising, I think, partly from the Abuse of some Laws, and partly from the total Neglect of others; and (if I may presume to say it) somewhat perhaps from a Defect in the Laws themselves.

It must be Matter of Astonishment to any Man to reflect that in a Country where the Poor are, beyond all Comparison, more liberally provided for than in any other Part of the habitable Globe, there should be found more Beggars, more distrest and miserable Objects than are to be seen throughout all the States of *Europe*.

And yet undoubted as this Fact is, I am far from agreeing with Mr. *Shaw**, who says, "There are few, if any, Nations or Countries where the Poor are more neglected, or are in a more scandalous nasty Condition than in *England*. Whether (says he) this is owing to that natural inbred Cruelty for which *Englishmen* are so much noted among Foreigners, or to that Medley of Religions which are so plentifully sown, and so carefully cherished among us; who think it enough to take Care of themselves, and take a secret Pride and Pleasure in the Poverty and Distresses of those of another Persuasion, &*c.*"[9]

---

* Vol. II. p. 1.

[7] Horace, *Epistles*, I. xvi. 40–1. 'Who is the good man? He who observes the Senate's decrees, the statutes and laws' (Loeb). Partridge quotes these lines (*Tom Jones*, XII. iv. 630–1).

[8] Ibid., 52–3: *Oderunt peccare boni virtutis amore. / Tu nihil admittes in te formidine poenae:* 'The good hate vice because they love virtue; you [the slave] will commit no crime because you dread punishment' (Loeb).

[9] Joseph Shaw, *The Practical Justice of the Peace*, 3rd edn. (London, 1736), i. 1. A 1733 edition is listed in Baker (no. 10). After 'cherished among us' Fielding omits 'who throwing of [*sic*] the common ties of Humanity, Christianity, and of *Englishmen*'.

That the Poor are in a very nasty and scandalous Condition is, perhaps too true; but sure the general Charge against the People of *England*, as well as the invidious Aspersion on particular Bodies of them, is highly unjust and groundless. Nor do I know that any Nation hath ventured to fix this Character of Cruelty on us. Indeed our Inhospitality to Foreigners hath been sometimes remarked; but that we are cruel to one another is not, I believe, the common, I am sure it is not the true Opinion. Can a general Neglect of the Poor be justly charged on a Nation in which the Poor are provided for by a Tax frequently equal to what is called the Land-Tax,[1] and where there are such numerous Instances of private Donations, such Numbers of Hospitals,[2] Alms-houses, and charitable Provisions of all Kinds?[3]

Nor can any such Neglect be charged on the Legislature; under whose Inspection this Branch of Polity hath been almost continually from the Days of Queen *Elizabeth* to the present Time. Insomuch that Mr. *Shaw* himself enumerates no less than thirteen Acts of Parliament relating to the indigent and helpless Poor.[4]

If therefore there be still any Deficiency in this Respect, it must, I think, arise from one of the three Causes abovementioned; that is, from some Defect in the Laws themselves, or from the Perversion of these Laws; or, lastly, from the Neglect in their Execution.

I will consider all these with some Attention.

The 43d of *Eliz.** enacts:

First, That the Churchwardens of every Parish, and two substantial

* Chap. iii.[5]

---

[1] The land tax was a tax on landed property levied by the central government. The poor-rate was a tax levied at the parish level for the relief of the poor. In 1776 the House of Commons calculated the amount raised by the poor-rate was £1,720,316. Estimates in the 1750s ranged from £1,000,000 (Fielding's in the *Proposal*) to £3,500,000 (W. A. Speck, *Stability and Strife: England, 1714–1760* [Cambridge, Mass., 1977], p. 77). Cf. *JJ* no. 31, p. 330 n. Peter Pounce complains in *Joseph Andrews* (p. 275) ' "the greatest Fault in our Constitution is the Provision made for the Poor . . . Sir, I have not an Estate which does not contribute almost as much again to the Poor as to the Land-Tax." '

[2] Usually not a medical hospital but a charitable institution for the care of the poor, aged, and infirm.

[3] After describing the principal hospitals in London, Defoe states that 'this age has produced some of the most eminent acts of publick charity, and of the greatest value, I mean from private persons that can be found in any age within the reach of our English History' (*Tour*, i. 373). He goes on to observe that 'These, added to the innumerable number of alms-houses which are to be seen in almost every part of the city, make it certain, that there is no city in the world can shew the like number of charities from private hands, there being, as I am told, not less than twenty thousand people maintained of charity, besides the charities of schooling for children, and besides the collections yearly at the annual feasts of several kinds, where money is given for putting out children apprentices &c.' (ibid., 374). George Rudé briefly describes eight charitable hospitals existing in 1751 (*Hanoverian London, 1714–1808* [Berkeley and Los Angeles, 1971], p. 84). Cf. the *Champion* 21 Feb. 1739/40 and the *Jacobite's Journal*, 2 July 1748.

[4] Shaw, *Practical Justice*, ii. 4. The complexity of the poor laws was notorious. Holdsworth points out that by far the longest section in Burn's *The Justices of the Peace and Parish Officer*, 8th edn. (1764) is that devoted to the poor laws (x. 162 n.).

[5] Ch. 2.

Householders at least, shall be yearly appointed to be Overseers of the Poor.

Secondly, That these Overseers shall, with the Consent of two Justices of the Peace, put out Apprentices the Children of poor People. And all married or unmarried Persons who have no Means or Trade to maintain themselves shall be put to work.

Thirdly, That they shall raise by a Parochial Tax a convenient Stock of Flax, Hemp, Wool, Thread, Iron, and other Ware and Stuff, to set the Poor to work.

Fourthly, That they shall from the same Tax provide towards the necessary Relief of the Lame, Impotent, Old, Blind, and others, being poor and not able to work.

Fifthly, That they shall out of the same Tax put the Children of poor Persons Apprentices.

That these Provisions may all be executed, that Act vested the Overseers with the following Powers; and enforced the executing them by the following Penalties.

I. The Overseers are appointed to meet once at least every Month in the Church after Divine Service; there, says the Act, to consider of some good Course to be taken, and some meet Order to be set down *in the Premises*. And to do this they are enjoined by a Penalty: For every one absenting himself from such Meeting without a just Excuse to be allowed by two Justices of the Peace, or being negligent in his Office, or in the Execution of the Orders aforesaid, forfeits 20 s.

And after the End of their year, and after other Overseers nominated, they are within four Days to make and yield up to two Justices of the Peace a true and perfect Account of all Sums of Money by them received or assessed, and of such Stores as shall be in their Hands, or in the Hands of the Poor to work, and of all other Things concerning their Office, &c. And if the Churchwardens and Overseers refuse to account, they are to be committed by two Justices till they shall have made a true Account.

II. The Overseers and Churchwardens, both present and subsequent, are empowered by Warrant from two Justices to levy all the Monies assessed, and all Arrearages of those who refuse to pay, by Distress and Sale of the Refusers Goods; and the subsequent Overseers may, in the same Manner, levy the Money and Stock in the Hands of the Precedent: And for want of Distress the Party is to be committed by two Justices, without Bail, till the same be paid.

III. They have a Power to compel the Poor to work; and such as refuse or neglect the Justice may commit to the House of Correction or common Goal.

IV. The Overseers may compel Children to be Apprentices, and may bind them where they shall see convenient; 'till the Man-child shall attain the Age of 24, or the Woman-child the Age of 21, or till the Time of her Marriage; the Indenture to be as effectual to all Purposes as the Covenant of one of full Age.

V. They have a Power to contract with the Lord of the Manor*, and on any Parcel of Ground on the Waste,[6] to erect at the general Charge of the Parish convenient Houses of Dwelling for the impotent Poor; and to place several Inmates in the same Cottage, notwithstanding the Statute[†] of Cottages.[7]

VI. They can compel the Father and Grandfather, Mother and Grandmother, and Children of every poor, old, blind, and impotent Person, or of any other Person not being able to work (provided such Father, &c. be of sufficient Ability) at their own Charges to relieve and maintain such poor Person in such Manner and after such Rate, as shall be assessed by the Sessions, under the Penalty of 20 s. for every Month's Omission.

VII. If no Overseers be named, every Justice within the Division forfeits *5 l.*

So far this Statute of *Elizabeth*, by which the Legislature may seem very fully to have provided, *First*, For the absolute Relief of such Poor as are by Age or Infirmity rendered unable to work; and *Secondly*, For the Employment of such as are able.[8]

The former of these, says Lord *Hale* in his Discourse on this Subject, "seems to be a Charity of more immediate Exigence; but the latter (*viz.* the Employment of the Poor) is a Charity of greater Extent, and of very great and important Consequence to the public Wealth and Peace of the Kingdom, as also to the Benefit and Advantage of the Poor."[9] And this, as Mr. *Shaw* observes, "Would prevent the Children of our Poor being brought up in Laziness and Beggary, whereby Beggary is entailed from Generation to Generation: This is certainly the greatest Charity; for though he who gives to any in Want, does well, yet he who employs and educates the Poor, so as to render them useful to the Public, does better; for that would be many hundred thousand Pounds *per Ann.* Benefit to this Kingdom."[1]

Now the former of these Provisions hath, perhaps, though in a very slovenly and inadequate Manner, been partly carried into Execution; but the

---

* This must be done by Consent and Order of Sessions.

† These Cottages are never after to be applied to any other Use.

[6] 'An uncultivated piece of land not in any man's occupation but lying common' (*OED*).

[7] 31 Eliz., c. 7. This Act prohibits, with exceptions, building cottages housing more than one family on less than four acres of land.

[8] Fielding summarizes accurately the chief provisions of the 43 Eliz., frequently incorporating the language of the Act in his account. He does not present the provisions of the Act in their original order.

[9] Sir Matthew Hale, *A Discourse Touching Provision for the Poor* (London, 1683), pp. 7–8. Writers on the poor frequently quote this passage from Hale's well-known pamphlet.

[1] Shaw, *Practical Justice*, i. 3.

latter, I am afraid I may too boldly assert, hath been utterly neglected and disregarded. Surely this is a most scandalous Perversion of the Design of the Legislature, which through the whole Statute seems to have had the Employment of the able Poor chiefly under their Consideration: For to this Purpose only almost every Power in it is established, and every Clause very manifestly directed. To say the Truth, as this Law hath been perverted in the Execution, it were, perhaps, to be wished it had never been made. Not because it is not our Duty to relieve real Objects of Distress; but because it is so much the Duty of every Man, and I may add, so much the Inclination of most *Englishmen*, that it might have been safely left to private Charity; or a public Provision might surely have been made for it in a much cheaper and more effectual Manner.

To prove the Abuse of this Law, my Lord *Hale* appeals to all the populous Parishes in *England*, (he might, I believe, have included some which are not over populous) "Indeed (says he) there are Rates made for the Relief of the impotent Poor; and it may be the same Relief is also given in a narrow Measure unto some others that have great Families, and upon this they live miserably, and at best from Hand to Mouth; and if they cannot get Work to make out their Livelihood, they and their Children set up a Trade of Begging at best; but it is rare to see any Provision of a Stock in any Parish for the Relief of the Poor; and the Reasons are principally these: 1. The generality of People that are able, and yet unwilling, to exceed the present necessary Charge; they do choose to live for an Hour rather than project for the future; and although possibly trebling their Exhibition in one gross Sum at the Beginning of the Year, to raise a Stock, might in all probability render their future yearly Payments, for seven Years together, less by half, or two thirds, than what must be without it; yet they had rather continue on their yearly Payments, Year after Year, though it exhaust them in time, and make the Poor nothing the better at the Year's end. 2. Because those Places, where there are most Poor, consist for the most Part of Tradesmen whose Estates lie principally in their Stocks, which they will not endure to be searched into to make them contributary to raise any considerable Stock for the Poor, nor indeed so much as to the ordinary Contributions: But they lay all the Rates to the Poor upon the Rents of Lands and Houses, which alone, without the Help of the Stocks, are not able to raise a Stock for the Poor, although it is very plain that Stocks are as well by Law rateable as Lands, both to the Relief and raising a Stock for the Poor. 3. Because the Churchwardens and Overseers, to whom this Power is given, are Inhabitants of the same Parish, and are either unwilling to charge themselves or to displease their Neighbours in charging more than they needs must towards the Poor: And although it were to be wished and hoped that the Justices of the Peace would be forward to enforce them if they might, though it may concern them also in point of present Profit; yet if they would do any thing herein, they are not empowered to compel the Churchwardens and Overseers to do it, who most certainly will never go about it to burden, as they think, themselves, and displease their Neighbours, unless some compulsory Power were not only lodged by Law, but also executed by some that may have a Power over them to enforce it; or to do it, if they do it either partially or too sparingly. 4. Because People do not consider the Inconvenience that will in Time grow to themselves by this Neglect, and the Benefit that would in a little Time accrue to them by putting it in Practice, if they would have but a little Patience."[2]

To these I will add a fifth Reason: Because the Churchwardens and Overseers are too apt to consider their Office as a Matter of private Emolument; To waste Part of the Money raised for the Use of the Poor in Feasting and Riot, and too often to pervert the Power given them by the Statute to foreign, and sometimes to the very worst of Purposes.[3]

The above Considerations bring my Lord *Hale* to complain of some Defects in the Law itself; "in which (says he) there is no Power from the Justices of the Peace, nor any superintendent Power, to compel the raising of a Stock where the Churchwardens and Overseers neglect it.

"The Act chargeth every Parish apart, where it may be they are liable to do little towards it; neither would it be so effectual as if three, four, five, or more contiguous Parishes did contribute towards the raising of a Stock proportionably to their Poor respectively.

"There is no Power for hiring or erecting a common House, or Place, for their Common Workhouse; which may be, in some Respects, and upon some Occasions, useful and necessary."[4]

As to the first of these, I do not find any Alteration hath been made, nor if there was, might it possibly produce any desired Effect. The Consequence, as it appears, would be only making Churchwardens of the Justices of Peace, which many of them are already, not highly to the Satisfaction of their Parishes; too much Power vested in one Man being too apt perhaps to beget Envy.

The second and third do pretty near amount to one and the same Defect; And this, I think, is at present totally removed. Indeed, in my Lord *Hale's* own Time, though probably after he had written this Treatise, a Workhouse

---

[2] Hale, *Discourse*, pp. 18–23.

[3] Complaints against the inefficiency and corruption of parish officers were frequent. See, for instance, [John Marriot], *A Representation of Some Mismanagements by Parish-Officers in the Method at present followed for Maintaining the Poor* . . . (London, 1726); the anonymous *A Short View of the Frauds, Abuses, and Impositions of Parish Officers, with some Considerations on the Laws relating to the Poor* . . . (London, 1744); and Dorothy Marshall, *The English Poor in the Eighteenth Century* (London, 1926), pp. 57 ff. A parish wake in honor of a pauper despised and ignored while alive was a painful sight to those paying the poor rate.

[4] Hale, *Discourse*, pp. 23–4.

was erected in *London* under the Powers given by the Statute made in the 13 and 14 of *Charles II. and I believe with very good Success.[5]

Since that Time other Corporations have followed the Example, as the City of *Bristol* in the Reign of King *William*†,[6] and that of *Worcester* in the Reign of Queen *Anne*‡, and in other Places.[7]

And now by a late Statute, made in the Reign of King ‖*George* I. the Power of erecting Workhouses is made general over the Kingdom.[8]

Now either this Method, proposed by Lord *Hale*, is inadequate to the Purpose; or this Act of Parliament hath been grosly perverted: For certain it is that the Evil is not removed, if indeed it be lessened, by the Erection of Workhouses. Perhaps, indeed, one Objection which my Lord *Hale* makes to the Statute of *Eliz.* may here recur, seeing that there is nothing compulsory, but all left to the Will and Direction of the Inhabitants.

But in Truth the Method itself will never produce the desired Effect, as the excellent Sir *Josiah Child* well observes§—"It may be objected (says he) that this Work (the Provision for the Poor) may as well be done in distinct Parishes, if all Parishes were obliged to build Workhouses, and employ their Poor therein, as *Dorchester* and some others have done with good Success. I answer, that such Attempts have been made in many Places to my Knowledge, with very good Intents and strenuous Endeavours; but all that I ever heard of proved vain and ineffectual."[9] For the Truth of which, I believe, we may appeal to common Experience.

And, perhaps, no less ineffctual would be the Scheme proposed by this

---

* Chap. xii.	† 8 & 9 *W.* III. c. xxx[1]	‡ 2 *Annæ*, c. viii.
‖ 9 *George* I. chap. i.	§ *Essay on Trade*, c. ii.	

[5] The 14 Car. II, c. 12. authorized workhouses 'within [the] cities of London and Westminster and within . . . the County of Middlesex and Surrey'. The workhouse Fielding refers to is the London Workhouse in Bishopsgate Street, enthusiastically described by Tillotson's friend, the High-Church, non-juring divine, Robert Nelson in *An Address to Persons of Quality and Estate* (London, 1715), pp. 180 ff. See also George, *London Life*, pp. 218–19. The workhouse was not in fact established until 1698. Hale died in 1676, his *Discourse* being published posthumously.

[6] The workhouse at Bristol was well known because of two pamphlets published close to the time of its erection by John Cary, a Bristol merchant. They were reprinted together as *A Discourse on Trade, and Other Matters Relative to it* in 1719 and 1745. Fielding owned the 1745 edition (Baker, no. 192). The workhouse was still in operation when Fielding rode the Western Circuit. For Cary's probable influence on Fielding, see General Introduction, p. lxxix.

[7] For instance, at least seven private acts establishing workhouses were passed during the 9 and 10 Wil. III.

[8] The 9 Geo. I, c. 7 [not c. 1] enabled several parishes to combine in erecting a workhouse and to refuse relief to those poor who refused to enter it, and consequently is known as 'The Workhouse Test Act'. Its effects are described in *An Account of several Work-Houses for Employing and Maintaining the Poor* . . . (London, 1725; 2nd edn., 1732). Over one hundred reports appear in the second edition, nearly all acknowledging failure to employ the poor but claiming success in reducing the number of applicants for poor-relief.

[9] Sir Josiah Child, *A New Discourse about Trade* (London, 1690), pp. 77–8 (Baker, no. 27). For Child, see below, p. 259, n. 2.

[1] 7 & 8 Wil. III, *32*. A private act.

worthy Gentleman,[2] tho' it seems to promise fairer than that of the learned Chief Justice; yet neither of them seem to strike at the Root of the Evil. Before I deliver any Sentiments of my own, I shall briefly take a View of the many subsequent Provisions with which the Legislature have from Time to Time enforced and strengthened the foregoing Statute of *Elizabeth*.

The Power of putting out Children *Apprentices is enforced by the 3d of †*Charles* I. which enacts, "that all Persons to whom the Overseers shall bind Children by Virtue of the Statute of *Eliz*. may receive and keep them as Apprentices." But there yet wanted, as Lord *Hale* says, a *sufficient Compulsory for Persons to take them;*[3] wherefore it is enacted, by 8 and 9 ‡*Will*. III. "That all Persons to whom Apprentices are appointed to be bound by the Overseers with the Consent of the Justices, shall receive them, and execute the other Part of the Indenture, under the Penalty of 10 *l.* for refusing, to be recovered before two Justices, on the Oath of one of the Churchwardens or Overseers."[4]

The Power of setting the Poor to Work is enlarged by 3 ‖*Charles* I. This Act gives the Churchwardens and Overseers of the Poor a Power, with the Consent of two Justices, or of one, if no more Justices shall be within their Limits, to set up and occupy any Trade for the setting the Poor to work.

The Power of relieving the impotent Poor (*i.e.* of distributing the public Money) the only one which hath much exercised the Minds of the Parish Officers, the Legislature seems to think rather wanted restraining than enlarging; accordingly, in the Reign of King §*William* they made an Act to limit the Power of the Officers in this Respect. As the Act contains the Sense of Parliament of the horrid Abuse of the Statute of *Elizabeth*, I will transcribe Part of a Paragraph from it *verbatim*.

"And whereas many Inconveniences do daily arise in Cities, Towns Corporate, and Parishes, where the Inhabitants are very numerous by Reason of the unlimited Power of the Churchwardens and Overseers of the Poor, who do frequently upon frivolous Pretences (but chiefly for their own private Ends) give Relief to what Persons and Number they think fit, and such Persons being entered into the Collection Bill, do become after that a great Charge to the Parish, notwithstanding the Occasion or Pretence of

---

* See 7 *Jac*. I. c. iii. which directs the Manner of putting out Apprentices, in Pursuance of any Gifts made to Corporations, &c. for that Purpose.

† Chap. iv. sect. 22. p. 8. the same Clause is in 21 *Jac*. c. xxviii. par. 33.

‡ Chap. xxx. sect. 6.[5]

‖ Chap. iv. sect. 22. *ubi supra*.

§ 3 and 4 *W*. and *M*. c. xi. sect. 11.

---

[2] Child proposes a workhouse serving the cities of London and Westminster and all boroughs included in the Bills of Mortality. The passage Fielding has just quoted is directed against the small parish workhouse.

[3] Hale, *Discourse*, p. 7. The italics are Fielding's.

[4] Fielding summarizes the Act.   [5] 8 and 9 Will. III, c. 30. sect. 5.

their Collection oftentimes ceases, by which Means the Rates for the Poor are daily increased, contrary to the true Intent of a Statute made in the 43d Year of the Reign of her Majesty Queen *Elizabeth*, intituled, *An Act for the Relief of the Poor*, for remedying of which, the Statute enacts, that for the future, a Book shall be provided and kept in every Parish (at the Charge of the same Parish) wherein the Names of all Persons receiving Collection, &c. shall be registered, with the Day and Year of their first receiving it. This Book to be yearly, or oftener, viewed by the Parishioners, and the Names of the Persons who receive Collection shall be called over, and the Reason of the receiving it examined, and a new List made; and no other Person is allowed to receive Collection but by Order of a Justice of Peace, &c. except in case of pestilential Diseases or Small Pox*."

The 8th and 9th of the same King, reciting the Fear of the Legislature, *that the Money raised only for the Relief of such as are as well impotent as poor, should be misapplied and consumed by the idle, sturdy, and disorderly Beggars,* "enacts that every Person, his Wife, Children, &c. who shall receive Relief from the Parish shall wear a Badge marked with the Letter *P*, &c. in Default of which, a Justice of Peace may order the Relief of such Persons to be abridged, suspended, or withdrawn, or may commit them for 21 Days to the House of Correction, there to be kept to hard Labour. And every Churchwarden or Overseer who relieves any one without such a Badge, being convicted before one Justice, forfeits 20 *s*."

Whether the Justices made an ill Use of the Power given them by the Statute of the 3d and 4th of King *William*, I will not determine; but the Parliament thought proper afterwards to abridge it, for by the 9th of †*George* I, the Justices are forbidden "to make any Order for the Relief of a poor Person, 'till Oath is first made of a reasonable Cause; and that Application hath been made to the Parishioners at the Vestry, or to two Officers, and that Relief hath been refused. Nor can the Justice then give his Order, 'till he hath summoned the Overseers to shew cause why Relief should not be given."

By the same Statute, "Those Persons to whom the Justices order Relief, are to be registered in the Parish Books, as long only as the Cause of the Relief continues. Nor shall any Parish Officer be allowed any Money given to the unregistered Poor, unless on the most emergent Occasion. The Penalty for charging such Money to the Parish Account is 5 *l*. The Conviction is to be before two Justices."[7]

Lastly, That the Parish may in all possible Cases be relieved from the

---

* The same Statute in another Part[6] charges the Overseers, &c. with applying the Poors Money to their own Use.

† Chap. 30. sect. 2.

[6] Sect. 12.   [7] 9 Geo. I, c. 7. sect. 1.

Burden of the Poor, whereas the Statute of *Elizabeth* obliges the Father, Mother, &c. and Children, if able, to relieve their poor Children and Parents; so, by the 5th of *George* I.[†] it is provided, "That where any Wife or Child shall be left by the Husband or Parents a Charge to any Parish, the Churchwardens or Overseers may, by the Order of two Justices, seize so much of the Goods and Chattles, and receive so much of the annual Rents and Profits of the Lands and Tenements of such Husband and Parent, as the Justices shall order, towards the Discharge of the Parish; and the Sessions may empower the Churchwardens and Overseers, to dispose thereof, for the providing for the Wife and bringing up the Children, &c."

Such is the Law that relates immediately to the Maintenance of the impotent Poor; a Law so very ample in its Provision, so strongly fortified with enforcing Powers, and so cautiously limited with all proper Restraints, that, at first Sight, it appears sufficiently adequate to every Purpose for which it was intended, but Experience hath convinced us of the contrary.

And here I am well aware of the delicate Dilemma to which I may seem reduced; since how shall I presume to suppose any Defects in a Law, which the Legislature seems to have laboured with such incessant Diligence? But I am not absolutely driven to this disagreeable Necessity, as the Fault may so fairly be imputed to the Non-execution of the Law; and indeed to the ill Execution of the Statute of *Elizabeth*, my Lord Chief Justice *Hale* chiefly imputes the imperfect Provision for the Poor in his Time.

Sir *Josiah Child*, it is true, speaks more boldly, and charges the Defects on the Laws themselves: One general Position, however, which he lays down, *That there never was a good Law made, that was not well executed*, is surely very questionable.[8] So therefore must be his Opinion, if founded on that Maxim; and this Opinion, perhaps, he would have changed, had he lived to see the later Constitutions on this Head.

But whatever Defects there may be in the Laws, or in the Execution of them, I much doubt whether either of these Great Men hath found the Means of curing them. And this I am the more forward to say, as the Legislature, by a total Neglect of *both* their Schemes, seem to give sufficient Countenance to my Assertion.

In a Matter then of so much Difficulty, as well as so great Importance, how shall I venture to deliver my own Opinion? Such, indeed, is the Difficulty and Importance of this Question, that Sir *Josiah Child* thinks, *if a whole Session of Parliament were employed on this single Concern, it would be Time*

[†] Chap. 8.

---

[8] Child, *A New Discourse*, p. 63. Cf. *Amelia*, I. ii. 15: 'It will probably be objected, that the small imperfections which I am about to produce do not lie in the laws themselves, but in the ill execution of them; but, with submission, this appears to me to be no less an absurdity than to say of any machine that it is excellently made, though incapable of performing its functions. Good laws should execute themselves in a well-regulated state.'

spent as much to the Glory of God, and Good of this Nation, as in any thing that
noble and worthy Patriots of their Country can be engaged in.[9]

However, under the Protection of the candid, and with Deference to the
learned Reader, I will enter on this Subject, in which, I think, I may with
Modesty say, I have had some Experience; and in which I can with Truth
declare, I have employed no little Time. If any Gentleman, who hath had
more Experience, hath more duly considered the Matter, or whose superior
Abilities enable him to form a better Judgment, shall think proper to improve
my Endeavours, he hath my ready Consent. Provided the End be effected, I
shall be contented with the Honour of my Share (however inconsiderable) in
the Means. Nay, should my Labours be attended only with Neglect and
Contempt, I think I have learned (for I am a pretty good Historian) to bear
such Misfortunes without much Repining.

By THE POOR, then, I understand such Persons as have no Estate of their
own to support them, without Industry; nor any Profession or Trade, by
which, with Industry, they may be capable of gaining a comfortable
Subsistence.

This Class of the People may be considered under these three Divisions:

First, Such Poor as are unable to work.

2*dly*, Such as are able and willing to work.

3*dly*, Such as are able to work, but not willing.

As to the *First* of these, they are but few.[1] An utter Incapacity to work must
arise from some Defect, occasioned either by Nature or Accident. Natural
Incapacities are greatly the most, (perhaps the only) considerable ones; for as
to accidental Maims, how very rarely do they happen, and, I must add, how
very nobly are they provided for, when they do happen! Again, as to natural
Incapacities, they are but few, unless those two general Circumstances, one
of which must, and the other may befal all Men; I mean, the Extremes of
Youth and Age: for, besides these, the Number of Persons who really labour
under an utter Incapacity of Work, will, on a just Inspection, be found so
trifling, that two of the *London* Hospitals might contain them all. The Reader
will be pleased to observe, I say of those who *really labour*, &c. for he is much
deceived, who computes the Number of Objects in the Nation, from the
great Number which he daily sees in the Streets of *London*. Among whom I
myself have discovered some notorious Cheats, and my good Friend
Mr. *Welch*,[2] the worthy High Constable of *Holborn* Division, many more.
Nothing, as I have been well informed, is more common among these
Wretches, than for the Lame, when provoked, to use their Crutches as

---

[9] Child, *A New Discourse*, p. 65. Fielding changes 'singular' to 'single'. Child's remark is quoted by
many contemporary and later commentators on laws relating to the poor.

[1] A view Fielding repeats in the *Proposal*, below, p. 263.

[2] For Welch, see *Bosavern Penlez*, above, p. 50.

Weapons instead of Supporters; and for the Blind, if they should hear the Beadle at their Heels, to outrun the Dogs which guided them before.[3] As to Diseases to which Human Nature is universally liable, they sometimes (though very rarely; for Health is the happy Portion of Poverty)[4] befal the Poor; and at all such Times they are certainly Objects of Charity, and entitled by the Law of God to Relief from the Rich.

Upon the whole, this first Class of the Poor is so truly inconsiderable in Number, and to provide for them in the most ample and liberal Manner would be so very easy to the Public; to support and cherish them, and to relieve their Wants, is a Duty so positively commanded by Our Saviour, and is withal so agreeable and delightful in itself, affording the most desirable Object to the strong Passion of Pity; nay, and in the Opinion of some, to Pride and Vanity also; that I am firmly persuaded it might be safely left to voluntary Charity, unenforced by any compulsive Law.[5] And if any Man will profess so little Knowledge of Human Nature, and so mean and unjust an Opinion of the Christianity, I might say the Humanity, of his Country, as to affect a contrary Opinion, notwithstanding all I have said, let him answer the following Instance, which may be called an Argument *à posteriori*, for the Truth of my Assertion. Such, I think, is the present Bounty to Beggars; for, at a Time when every Man knows the vast Tax which is raised for the Support of the Poor, and when all Men of Property must feel their Contributions to this Tax, Mankind are so forward to relieve the Appearance of Distress in their Fellow-creatures, that every Beggar, who can but moderately well personate Misery, is sure to find Relief and Encouragement; and this, though the Giver must have great Reason to doubt the Reality of the Distress, and when he can scarce be ignorant that his Bounty is illegal*, and that he is encouraging a Nuisance. What then must be the Case, when there should be no such Tax, nor any such Contribution; and when, by relieving a known and certain Object of Charity, every good Man must be

---

* This was forbidden by many Statutes, and by the Act of 27 *Henry* VIII. every Person giving any Money in Alms, but to the common Boxes and common Gatherings in every Parish, forfeits twelve Times as much as he gives.[6]

---

[3] 'I shall . . . show what persons I apprehend to be the greatest objects of charity among us; which are certainly not to be met with in our streets; whose begging inhabitants deserve punishment more than relief, and are a shame not to the legislative but the executive power of our laws' (the *Champion*, Feb. 16, 1739/40, p. 205). See also the account of Julian's 'life' as fraudulent beggar in ch. xx of *A Journey from this World to the Next*. Johnson gleaned different information from Welch: 'Saunders Welch, the Justice, who was once High-Constable of Holborn, and had the best opportunities of knowing the state of the poor, told me, that I under-rated the number, when I computed that twenty a week, that is, above a thousand a year, died of hunger; not absolutely of immediate hunger; but of the wasting and other diseases which are the consequences of hunger. This happens only in so large a place as London, where people are not known. What we are told about the great sums got by begging is not true: the trade is overstocked' (*Life*, iii. 401).

[4] An unfortunate commonplace. Cf. the *Proposal*, p. 227.

[5] Cf. *Proposal*, p. 263.

[6] 27 Hen. VIII c. 25. sect. 13. The forfeit was ten times the alms.

assured, that he is not only doing an Act which the Law allows, but which Christianity and Humanity too exact of him?

However, if there be any Person who is yet unwilling to trust the Poor to voluntary Charity, or if it should be objected, that there is no Reason to lay the whole Burden on the worthier Part of Mankind, and to excuse the covetous Rich; and that a Tax is therefore necessary to force open the Purses of these latter; let there be a Tax then, and a very inconsiderable one would effectually supply the Purpose*.

I come now to consider the *second* Class. These are in Reason, tho' not in Fact, equally Objects of the Regard of the compassionate Man, and much more worthy the Care of the Politician; and yet, without his Care, they will be in a much worse Condition than the others: for they have none of those Incitements of Pity which fill the Pockets of the artful Beggar, and procure Relief for the Blind, the Lame, and other visible Objects of Compassion: Such therefore, without a Law, and without an honest and sensible Execution of that Law, must languish under, and often perish with Want. A melancholy and dreadful Reflection! and the more so, as they are capable of being made not only happy in themselves, but highly useful to the Service of the Community.

To provide for these, seems, as I have said, to have been the chief Design of the Statute of *Elizabeth*, as well as of several Laws enacted since; and that this Design hath hitherto failed, may possibly have arisen from one single Mistake, but a Mistake which must be fatal, as it is an Error in the first Concoction. The Mistake I point at is, that the Legislature have left the whole Work to the Overseers. They have rather told them what they are to do (*viz.* to employ the industrious Poor) than how they shall do it. It is true, the original Act directs them, by a parochial Tax, to raise a convenient Stock of Flax, Hemp, Wool, Thread, Iron, and other Ware and Stuff, to set the Poor to Work. A Direction so general and imperfect, that it can be no Wonder, considering what sort of Men the Overseers of the Poor have been, that it should never have been carried into Execution.

To say the Truth, this Affair of finding an universal Employment for the industrious Poor, is of great Difficulty, and requires Talents not very bountifully scattered by Nature among the whole human Species. And yet difficult as it is, it is not I hope impracticable, seeing that it is of such infinite Concern to the Good of the Community. Hands for the Work are already supposed, and surely Trade and Manufacture are not come to so low an Ebb, that we should not be able to find Work for the Hands. The Method of adapting only seems to be wanting. And though this may not be easy to

---

* The Reader is desired to consider the Author here as speaking only of the impotent Poor, and as hoping that some effectual Means may be found out of procuring Work, and consequently Maintenance for the able and industrious.

discover, it is a Task surely not above the Reach of the *British* Parliament, when they shall think proper to apply themselves to it. Nor will it, I hope, be construed Presumption in me to say, that I have myself thought of a Plan for this Purpose, which I am ready to produce, when I shall have any Reason to see the least Glimpse of Hope, that my Labour in drawing it out at length would not be absolutely and certainly thrown away.[7]

The last, and much the most numerous Class of Poor, are those who are able to work, and not willing. This likewise hath fallen under the Eye of the Legislature, and Provisions have been made concerning it; which, if in themselves efficacious, have at least failed of producing any good Effect, from a total Neglect in the Execution.

By the 43 *Eliz.* the Churchwardens and Overseers, or greater Part of them, with the Consent of two Justices, shall take Order for the setting to Work the Children of all such Parents as they shall think not able to maintain them; as also, all such married or unmarried Persons, as shall have no Means to maintain themselves, nor any ordinary Trade or Calling whereby to get their Living.

Besides this Power of compelling the Poor to work, the Legislature hath likewise compelled them to become, 1. Apprentices, and, 2. Servants. We have already seen the Power of the Overseers, with the Assistance of the Justices, to put poor Children Apprentices; and likewise to oblige their Masters to receive them. And long before, a Compulsion was enacted* on poor Persons to become Apprentices; so that any Housholder, having and using Half a Ploughland in Tillage, may compel any poor Person under Twenty-one and unmarried,[8] to serve as an Apprentice in Husbandry, or in any other Kind of Art, Mystery, or Science (before expressed in the Act†:) and if such Person, being so required, refuse to become an Apprentice, one Justice of Peace may compel him, or commit him to Prison, there to remain till he will be bound.

2dly, The Poor are obliged to become Servants.

By the 5th of Eliz.‡ it is enacted, "That every Person being unmarried, and every other Person under the Age of 30, who hath been brought up in any of the Sciences, &c. of Clothiers, Woollen Cloth Weavers, Tuckers, Fullers, Clothworkers, Shearmen, Dyers, Hosiers, Taylors, Shoemakers, Tanners, Pewterers, Bakers, Brewers, Glovers, Cutlers, Smiths, Farriers, Curriers, Sadlers, Spurriers, Turners, Tappers, Hatmakers or Feltmakers, Butchers, Cooks, or Millers, or who hath exercised any of these Trades by the Space of three Years or more; and not having in Lands, Rents, &c. an Estate of 40 s.

* 5 *Eliz.* c. 4. § 35.   † *Viz.* Every Trade then used.   ‡ Chap. 4. § 4.

[7] Presumably what was to become the *Proposal.* For an argument that Fielding's solution to the problem of employing the poor changed between 1751 and 1753, see General Introduction, p. lxxii ff.
[8] The Act does not stipulate that he be unmarried.

clear yearly Value, Freehold, nor being worth in Goods 10 *l.* and so allowed by two Justices of the County, where he hath most commonly inhabited, or by the Mayor, &c. nor being retained with any Person in Husbandry, nor retained in any of the above Sciences, or in any other Art or Science; nor lawfully retained in Houshold, or in any Office, with any Nobleman, Gentleman, or others; nor having a convenient Farm, or other Holding, in Tillage, whereupon he may lawfully employ his Labour, during the Time that he shall continue unmarried, or under the Age of Thirty, upon Request made by any Person using the Art or Mystery, wherein the Person so required hath been exercised as aforesaid, shall be retained.

"And every Person between the Age of Twelve and Sixty, not being lawfully retained in the several Services mentioned in the Statute**, nor being a Gentleman born, or a Scholar in either University or in any School, nor having an Estate of Freehold, of 40 *s. per Annum* Value, nor being worth in Goods 10 *l.* nor being Heir to 10 *l. per Annum*, or 40 *l.* in Goods; nor being a necessary or convenient Servant lawfully retained; nor having a convenient Farm or Holding, nor otherwise lawfully retained, shall be compelled to be retained to serve in Husbandry, by the Year, with any Person using Husbandry within the same Shire.

"Every such Person refusing to serve upon Request, or covenanting to serve, and not serving; or departing from his Service before the End of his Term, unless for some reasonable Cause to be allowed before a Justice of the Peace, Mayor, &c. or departing at the End of his Term without a Quarter's Warning given before two Witnesses, may be committed by two Justices of the Peace to Prison, there to remain without Bail or Mainprize, till he shall become bound to his Master, &c. to serve, &c*."

"Nor shall any Master in any of the Arts and Sciences aforesaid, retain a Servant for less than a Year[†]; nor shall any Master put away a Servant retained by this Act within his Term, nor at the End of the Term without a Quarter's Warning, under the Penalty of 40 *s.*[‡]"

"Artificers, &c. are compellable by a Justice of the Peace, or the Constable or other Head-Officer of a Township, to serve in the Time of Hay or Corn Harvest. The Penalty of Disobedience is Imprisonment in the Stocks by the Space of two Days and one Night[‖]."

"Women between the Age of 12 and 40, may be obliged, by two Justices, to enter into Service by the Year, Week, or Day; or may be committed *quousque*[§]."[9]

The Legislature having thus appointed what Persons shall serve, have gone farther, and have directed a Method of ascertaining how they shall

---

** Ibid. § 7.   * Ib. sect. 5, 6, 9.   † Ib. sect. 3.   ‡ Ib. sect. 5, 6, 8.
‖ Ib. sect. 28.[1]   § Ib. sect. 24.

9 'As long as [required]'.   1 Sect. 22.

serve: for which Use principally is that excellent Constitution of 5 *Elizabeth***, "That the Justices of the Peace, with the Sheriff of the County, if he conveniently may, the Mayor, &c. in Towns Corporate, shall yearly within six Weeks of *Easter*, assemble together, and, with the Assistance of such discreet Persons as they shall think proper to call to them, and respecting the Plenty or Scarcity of the Time, and other Circumstances, shall, within the Limits of their Commission, rate and appoint the Wages of Artificers, Labourers, &c. by the Year, Month, Week, or Day, with or without Meat and Drink." Then the Statute enumerates several Particulars,[2] in the most explicit Manner, and concludes with these general Words: "and for any other kind of reasonable Labour and Service.

"These Rates are appointed to be engrossed in Parchment, and certified into Chancery, before the 12th Day of *July*; and before the first Day of *September*, several printed Proclamations, containing the Rates, and a Command to all Persons to observe them, are to be sent to the Sheriff and Justices, and to the Mayor, &c. These Proclamations are to be entered of Record with the Clerk of the Peace, to be fixed up in the Market-Towns, and to be publickly proclaimed in all the Markets till *Michaelmas**."

"And if any Person, after the said Proclamations shall be so sent down and published, shall, by any secret Ways or Means, directly or indirectly retain or keep any Servant, Workman, or Labourer, or shall give any greater Wages, or other Commodity, contrary to the true Intent of the Statute, or contrary to the Rates assessed, he shall forfeit 5 *l.* and be imprisoned by the Space of ten Days†."

"And every Person who is retained, or takes any Wages contrary to the Statute, shall be imprisoned 21 Days: And every such Retainer, Promise, Gift and Payment, or Writing and Bond for that Purpose, are made absolutely void.‡"

"Every Justice of Peace, or Chief Officer, who shall be absent at the Rating of Wages, unless the Justices shall allow the reasonable Cause of his Absence, forfeits 10 *l.*‖"

That this Statute may from time to time be carefully and diligently put in Execution, "The Justices are appointed to meet twice a Year, to make a special and diligent Enquiry of the Branches and Articles of this Statute, and of the good Execution of the same, and severely to correct and punish any Defaults: for which Service they are allowed 5 *s. per* Day§." No inconsiderable Allowance at that Time!

But all this Care of the Legislature proved, it seems, ineffectual; for 40

** Ib. sect. 15.   * Ib. sect. 16.[3]   † Ib. sect. 18.   ‡ Ib. sect. 19, 20.
‖ Ib. sect. 17.   § Ib. sect. 37, 38.

---

[2] i.e., particularizes many labors for which wages can be set.
[3] Sects. 15 and 16.

Years after the making this Statute, we find the Parliament complaining, "That the said Act had not, according to the true Meaning thereof, been duly put in Execution; and that the Rates of Wages for poor Artificers, Labourers, and other Persons, had not been rated and proportioned according to the politic Intention of the said Act*." A Neglect which seems to have been occasioned by some Doubts raised in *Westminster-hall*, concerning the Persons who were the Subjects of this Law. For the clearing therefore any such Doubt, this subsequent Statute gives the Justices an express Power "to rate the Wages of any Labourers, Weavers, Spinsters, and Workmen or Workwomen whatsoever, either working by the Day, Week, Month, Year, or taking any Work at any Person's Hands whatsoever, to be done by the Great,⁴ or otherwise†."

And to render the Execution of this Law the more easy, the Statute of *James* I. enacts, 1. "That in all Counties where General Sessions are kept in several Divisions, the Rating Wages at such respective General Sessions, shall be as effectual within the Division, as if they had been rated at the Grand General Session‡."

2. The Method of certifying the Rates in Chancery appearing, I apprehend, too troublesome and tedious, "such Certificate is made no longer necessary, but the Rates being assessed and engrossed in Parchment, under the Hands and Seals of the Justices, the Sheriff, or Chief Officer of Towns Corporate, may immediately proclaim the same‖."⁵

And whereas Wool is the great Staple Commodity of this Kingdom, and the Woollen Trade its principal Manufacture, the Parliament have given particular Attention to the Wages of Artificers in this Trade.

For, 1. By the Statute of *James* I.§, "No Clothier, being a Justice of Peace in any Precinct or Liberty, shall be a Rater of Wages for any Artizan depending upon the making of Cloth."

2. "Clothiers not paying so much Wages to their Workmen or Workwomen, as are rated by the Justices, fofeit 10 *s*. for every Offence**."

3. By a late Statute***, "All Persons anywise concerned in employing any Labourers in the Woollen Manufactory, are required to pay the full Wages or Price agreed on, in Money, and not in Goods, Truck, or otherwise; nor shall they make any Deduction from such Wages or Price, on account of any Goods sold or delivered previous to such Agreement. And all such Wages are to be levied, on Conviction, before two Justices, by Distress; and, for Want of Distress, the Party is to be committed for six Months, or until full

---

* Preamble to 1 *Jac.* c. 6.   † Ib: sect. 3.   ‡ Ib. sect 5.   ‖ Ib. sect. 6.
§ Ib. sect. 7.⁶   ** Ib. sect. 7.   *** 12 *Geo.* I. c. 34. sect. 3.

⁴ 'Work . . . done by the Great': 'piecework' (*OED*).
⁵ The phrase 'such Certificate is made no longer necessary' is not in the Act but its sense is implied.
⁶ Sect. 9.

Satisfaction is made to the Party complaining. Besides which the Clothier forfeits the Sum of 100 *l.***"

4. By the same Statute, "All Contracts, By-laws, &c. made in unlawful Clubs, by Persons brought up in, or exercising the Art of a Woollcomber or Weaver, for regulating the said Trade, settling the Prices of Goods, advancing Wages, or lessening the Hours of Work, are declared to be illegal and void; and any Person concerned in the Woollen Manufactures, who shall knowingly be concerned in such Contract, By-law, &c. or shall attempt to put it in Execution, shall, upon Conviction before two Justices, suffer three Months Imprisonment*."

But long before this Act, a general Law was made†, to punish all Conspiracies for raising Wages, limiting Hours of Work, &c. among Artificers, Workmen, and Labourers; and if such Conspiracy was to extend to a general Advance of Wages all over the Kingdom, any Insurrection of a Number of Persons, in Consequence of it, would be an overt Act of High Treason.[8]

From this cursory View it appears, I think, that no Blame lies at the Door of the Legislature, which hath not only given the Magistrate, but even private Persons, with his Assistance, a Power of compelling the Poor to work; and, 2*dly*, hath allotted the fullest Powers, and prescribed the most effectual means for ascertaining and limiting the Price of their Labour.

But so very faulty and remiss hath been the Execution of these Laws, that an incredulous Reader may almost doubt whether there are really any such existing. Particularly as to that which relates to the rating the Wages of Labourers; a Law which at first, it seems, was too carelessly executed, and which hath since grown into utter Neglect and Disuse.[9]

Hath this total Disuse arisen, in common with the Neglect of other wholesome Provisions, from Want of due Attention to the Public Good? or is the Execution of this Law attended with any extraordinary Difficulty? or, lastly, are we really grown, as Sir *Josiah Child* says, wiser than our Forefathers, and have discovered any Fault in the Constitution itself; and that to retrench the Price of Labour by a Law is an Error in Policy?

This last seems to me, I own, to be very strange Doctrine, and somewhat of a Paradox in Politics; however, as it is the Sentiment of a truly wise and

---

** Ib. sect. 4.[7]   * Ib. sect. 1.   † 2 & 3 *E.* VI. c. 15.

[7] The citation applies only to the last sentence of the paragraph. The forfeit was £10.

[8] This Act does not mention insurrections or high treason.

[9] For a discussion of the various attempts in the 18th century to fix wages, see Holdsworth, xi. 469–75; and x. 166–7. See also Ashton, *An Economic History* (London, 1955), p. 218; William Lecky, *A History of England in the Eighteenth Century* (New York, 1887), vi. 233–5; and Edgar S. Furniss, *The Position of the Laborer in a System of Nationalism* (New York, 1920), pp. 158–9. In the *Voyage to Lisbon*, Fielding acknowledges that this power is little known to justices of the peace and says, 'It is a great pity then that this power, or rather this practice, was not revived; but this having been so long omitted, that it is become obsolete, will be best done by a new law' (p. 84).

great Man, it deserves a fair Discussion. Such I will endeavour to give it; since no Man is more inclined to respect the Opinions of such Persons, and as the Revival of the Law, which he opposes, is, I think, absolutely necessary to the Purpose I am contending for.

I will give the Passage from Sir *Josiah* at length. It is in Answer to this Position, *That the Dearness of Wages spoils the* English *Trade*.[1] "Here (says he) the Author propounds the making a Law to retrench the Hire of poor Mens Labour, (an honest charitable Project, and well becoming an Usurer!) The Answer to this is easy. *First*, I affirm, and can prove, he is mistaken in Fact; for the *Dutch*, with whom we principally contend in Trade, give generally more Wages to all their Manufacturers, by at least Twopence in the Shilling, than the *English*. *Secondly*, Wherever Wages are high, universally throughout the whole World, 'tis an infallible Evidence of the Riches of that Country; and wherever Wages for Labour run low, it is a Proof of the Poverty of that Place. *Thirdly*, It is Multitudes of People, and good Laws, such as cause an Encrease of People, which principally enrich any Country; and if we retrench by Law the Labour of our People, we drive them from us to other Countries that give better Rates; and so the *Dutch* have drained us of our Seamen and Woollen Manufacturers, and we the *French* of their Artificers and Silk-manufacturers; and many more we should, if our Laws otherwise gave them fitting Encouragement; of which more in due Place. *Fourthly*, If any particular Trades exact more here than in *Holland*, they are only such as do it by virtue of Incorporations, Privileges, and Charters, of which the Cure is easy, by an Act of Naturalization,[2] and without compulsory Laws. It is true, our Great Grandfathers did exercise such Policy, of endeavouring to retrench the Price of Labour by a Law (altho' they could never effect it;) but that was before Trade was introduced into this Kingdom; we are since, with the rest of the Trading World, grown wiser in this Matter, and I hope shall so continue.*"[3]

To this I reply, 1. That the making such a Law is not only an honest, but a charitable Project; as it proposes, by retrenching the Price of poor Mens Labour, to provide Labour, and consequently Hire for all the Poor who are capable of Labour. In all Manufactures whatever, the lower the Price of Labour is, the cheaper will be the Price to the Consumer; and the cheaper this Price is, the greater will be the Consumption, and consequently the

---

* Preface to his Discourse on Trade.

---

[1] Child is answering *Interest of Money Mistaken* (London, 1668), a pamphlet written in support of usury and against high wages.

[2] Child advocates an act such as that of 1709 which made naturalized subjects of foreign immigrants who took the statutory oaths and received the sacrament in *any* Protestant church.

[3] Except for changes in accidentals, Fielding quotes accurately from the unpaginated Preface to Child's *A New Discourse*.

more Hands employed.[4] This is likewise a very charitable Law to the poor Farmer, and never more necessary than at this Day, when the Rents of Lands are rated to the highest Degree.[5] The great Hopes which the Farmer hath, (indeed his common Relief from Ruin) is of an Exportation of Corn. This Exportation can not be by Law, unless when the Corn is under such a particular Price. How necessary then is it to him, that the Price of Labour should be confined within moderate Bounds, that the Exportation of Corn, which is of such general Advantage to the Kingdom, should turn, in any considerable manner, to his private Profit?[6] And what Reason is there to imagine, that this Power of limiting Wages should be executed in any dishonest or uncharitable Manner? Is it not a Power entrusted to all the Justices of the County; or Division, and to the Sheriff, with the Assistance of grave, sober, and substantial Persons, who must be sufficient Judges of the Matter, and who are directed to have Regard to the Plenty and Scarcity of the Times? Is it to be suspected, that many Persons of this Kind should unite in a cruel and flagitious Act, by which they would be liable to the Condemnation of their own Consciences, to the Curses of the Poor, and to be reproached by the Example of all their neighbouring Counties? Are not much grosser Exorbitancies to be feared on the other Side, when the lowest Artificers, Husbandmen, and Labourers, are made Judges in their own Cause; and when it is left to their own Discretion, to exact what Price they please for their Labour, of the poor Farmer or Clothier; of whom if they cannot exact an extravagant Price, they will fly to that Alternative which Idleness often prefers, of Begging or Stealing? *Lastly*, Such a Restraint is very wholesome to the poor Labourers themselves; of whom Sir *Josiah* observes*, "that they live better in the dearest Countries for Provisions, than in the cheapest, and better in a dear Year than in a cheap, especially in relation to the public Good; for, in a cheap Year, they will not work above two Days in a Week; their Humour being such that they will not provide for a hard Time, but just work so much, and no more, as may maintain them in that mean Condition to which they have been accustomed."[7] Is it not

* Discourse on Trade, p. 17.

---

[4] For a discussion of the economic assumptions of this statement, see General Introduction, p. lxiii.

[5] By 1749 the land-tax had dropped from its wartime high of four shillings in the pound to three, still a relatively high rate.

[6] An Act of 1689 (I Wil. & Mar., c. 12) authorized payment of a government bounty on exported corn when prices on the home market fell below a certain figure. The bounty became a controversial issue after 1750. Defenders of exportation and of the bounty (Henry Pelham among them) argued, as Fielding does here, that exportation of corn was beneficial to all classes, for it encouraged larger crops, hence cheaper provisions for the poor, hence cheaper wages. See Donald Grove Barnes, *A History of the English Corn Laws from 1660–1846* (New York, 1930), chs. II and III).

[7] Child, *A New Discourse*, Preface. Many observed that only necessity kept a poor man at labor. Arthur Young's remark is typical: 'Every one but an idiot knows that the lower classes must be kept poor or they will never be industrious . . . they must (like all mankind) be in poverty or they will not

therefore, upon this Concession, demonstrable, that the poor Man himself will live much better (his Family certainly will) by these Means? Again, many of the Poor, and those the more honest and industrious, will probably gain by such a Law: for, at the same time that the impudent and idle, if left to themselves, will certainly exact on their Masters; the modest, the humble, and truly laborious, may often (and so I doubt not but the Case is) be oppressed by them, and forced to accept a lower Price for their Labour, than the Liberality of Gentlemen would allow them.

2*dly*, The two Assertions contained in the next Paragraph both seem to me suspicious. First, That the *Dutch* and other Nations have done all that in them lies, to draw from us our Seamen, and some of our Manufacturers, is certainly true; and this they would do at any Price: but that the *Dutch* do in general give more Wages to their Manufacturers than the *English*, is, I believe, not the Fact. Of the Manufactures of *Holland*, the only considerable Article which we ourselves take of them, except Linen, are Toys; and to this we are induced, not because the *Dutch* are superior to our Workmen in Genius and Dexterity, (Points in which they are not greatly celebrated) but because they work much cheaper. Nor is, 2*dly*, The immediate Transition from Trade to Manufacture altogether so fair. The *Dutch*, it is true, are principally our Rivals in Trade in general, and chiefly as Carriers; but not so in Manufacture, particularly in the Woollen Manufacture. Here our chief Rivals are the *French*, amongst whom the Price of Labour is known to be considerably lower than with us. To this, among other Causes, (for I know there are others, and some very scandalous ones) they owe their Success over us in the *Levant*.[8] It is indeed a Truth which needs no Comment nor Proof, that where Goods are of equal Value, the Man who sells cheapest will have the most Custom; and it is as certainly true, that he who makes up his Goods in the cheapest Manner, can sell them so.

3*dly*, Sir *Josiah* asserts, "That wherever Wages are high universally throughout the World, 'tis an infallible Evidence of the Riches of that Country; and wherever Wages for Labour run low, it is a Proof of the

work' (*The Farmer's Tour through the East of England* [London, 1771], iv. 361). Against this truth may be set one infrequently observed: 'I [Francis Place] know not how to describe the sickening aversion which at times steals over the working man, and utterly disables him for a longer or shorter period from following his usual occupation, and compels him to indulge in *idleness*. I have felt it, resisted it to the utmost of my power, but have been completely subdued by it that, in spite of very pressing circumstances, I have been obliged to submit and run away from my work. This is the case with every workman I have ever known . . .' (cit. George, *London Life*, p. 208).

[8] There were frequent complaints against the Levant Company in the 18th century, mainly by clothiers who charged that the monopolistic practices of the Company raised the price of British woollen goods above that of other countries (E. Lipson, *The Economic History of England*, 6th edn. [London, 1956], ii. 351–2). In *Reflections on the Expediency of opening the Trade to Turkey* ('A New Edition', London, 1755 [1st edn. 1750?]), Josiah Tucker writes 'the prodigious Encrease of their [the French] Levant Trade cannot possibly be ascribed to any other Cause but to the Monopolies and Exclusions of the English against their own Countrymen, in Favour of the French' (p. 9).

Poverty of that Place."—If this be true, the Concession will do him no Service; for it will not prove, that to give high Wages is the Way to grow rich; since it is much more probable, that Riches should cause the Advance of Wages, than that high Wages should produce Riches.[9] This latter, I am sure, would appear a high Solecism in private Life, and I believe it is no less so in public.

4*thly*, His next Assertion, *That to retrench by Law the Labour of our People, is to drive them from us*, hath partly received an Answer already. To give this Argument any Force, our Wages must be reduced at least below the Standard of other Countries; which is, I think, very little to be apprehended; but, on the contrary, if the Labourer should carry his Demands ever so little higher, as may be reasonably expected, the Consumption of many Manufactures will not only be confined to our own People, but to a very few of those People.

Thus, I hope, I have given a full Answer to this great Man, whom I cannot dismiss, without observing a manifest Mistake of the Question, which runs thro' all his Arguments; all that he advances concluding indeed only to the *Quantum* of Wages which shall be given for Labour. He seems rather to argue against giving too little, than against regulating what is to be given; so that his Arguments are more proper for the Consideration of the Justices at their Meeting for settling the Rates of Wages, than for the Consideration of the Legislature, in a Debate concerning the Expediency of the above Law. To evince the Expediency of which, I appeal to the concurrent Sense of Parliament in so many different Ages; for this is not only testified expressly in the above Statutes of *Elizabeth* and *James*, but may be fairly implied from those of *Edward* VI. and *George* I. above recited.

I have moreover, I think, demonstrated, 1. The Equity of this Law; and that it is as much for the Service of the Labourer as of his Master. 2. The Utility of it to Trade: I shall only add, the Necessity of it, in order to execute the Intention of the Legislature, in compelling the Idle to work; for is it not the same Thing to have the Liberty of working or not at your own Pleasure, and to have the absolute Nomination of the Price at which you will work? The Idleness of the common People in this Town is, indeed, greatly to be attributed to this Liberty; most of these, if they cannot exact an exorbitant Price for their Labour, will remain idle. The Habit of exacting on their Superiors is grown universal, and the very Porters expect to receive more for their Work than the Salaries of above Half the Officers of the Army amount to.

I conclude then, that this Law is necessary to be revived, (perhaps with some Enlargements) and that still upon one Account more; which is, to

---

[9] Child argues that riches are an effect, not a cause, of national prosperity.

enable the Magistrate clearly to distinguish the Corrigible from the Incorrigible in Idleness: for when the Price of Labour is once established, all those Poor who shall refuse to labour at that Price, even at the Command of a Magistrate, may properly be deemed incorrigibly idle.

For these the Legislature have, by several Acts of Parliament, provided a Punishment, by Commitment to *Bridewell* either for more or less Time: And a very severe Punishment this is, if being confirmed in Habits of Idleness, and in every other vicious Habit, may be esteemed so.[1]

These Houses are commonly called Houses of Correction, and the Legislature intended them certainly for Places of Correction of Idleness at least: for in many Acts, where Persons are ordered to be committed to *Bridewell*, it is added, *There to be kept to hard Labour,* nay, in the Statute of *Jac.* I.* these Houses of Correction are directed "to be built with a convenient Backside adjoining, together with Mills, Turns, Cards,[2] and such like necessary Implements, to set Rogues and other idle People on Work." Again, in the same Statute,[3] Authority is given to the Master or Governor, "to set to work such Rogues, Vagabonds, idle and disorderly Persons, as shall be brought or sent unto the said House, (being able) while they shall continue in the said House; and to punish them, by putting Fetters on them and by Whipping; nor are the said Rogues, &c. to have any other Provision than what they shall earn by their Labour."

The Erection of these Houses, as is usual with new Institutions, did at first greatly answer the good Purposes for which they were designed, insomuch that my Lord *Coke* observes, "that upon the making of the Statute 39 *Eliz.* for the Erection of Houses of Correction, and a good Space after, whilst Justices of Peace and other Officers were diligent and industrious, there was not a Rogue to be seen in any Part of *England.*"[4] And again he prophecies, that "from the Erection of these Houses we shall have neither Beggar nor idle Person in the Commonwealth†."[5]

---

* Chap. 4. These Houses were first begun to be erected *Ann.* 13 *Eliz.*[6] the Prison for Idleness being, before that Time the Stocks. In the 11th Year of *Henry* VII. Vagabonds, Beggars, &c. are ordered to be set three Days and three Nights in the Stocks.[7]   † 2 Inst. 729.

---

[1] Bridewell was originally a palace (for Henry VIII) then (by 1556) a prison. It was to provide the generic term for houses of correction, which were to punish wrongdoers and put vagrants and beggars to work. Fielding insisted on the corruptive nature of bridewells. In the *Covent-Garden Journal* no. 59 (14 Aug. 1752) he records his decision not to proceed against the performers of an unlicensed *Venice Preserved* since he would have had to commit them to Bridewell 'which must have proved their ruin'. Allworthy refuses to send Jenny Jones to a bridewell where she would have been 'sacrificed to Ruin and Infamy by a shameful Correction' (*Tom Jones*, I. ix. 59. Cf. ibid., IV. xi. 192; and *CGJ* no. 57, ii. 70).

[2] The machinery of traditional prison occupations. Mills were used to beat hemp; cards and turns were employed in the manufacture of cloth.

[3] 7 Jac. I, c. 4. sect. 3.

[4] *II Inst.* 729, 'An Exposition of the Statute of 7 Jac. Regis, cap. 4.'

[5] Ibid. 728–9. Coke actually says that if more houses of correction were erected 'we shall . . .'.

[6] 13 Eliz., c. 25.   [7] 11 Hen. VII, c. 2.

But this great Man was a much better Lawyer than he was a Prophet; for whatever these Houses were designed to be, or whatever they at first were, the Fact is, that they are at present in general, no other than Schools of Vice, Seminaries of Idleness, and Common-shores of Nastiness and Disease. As to the Power of Whipping, which the Act of *James* I. vests in the Governor, that, I believe, is very seldom used, and perhaps when it is, not properly applied. And the Justice in very few Instances (in none of Idleness) hath any Power of ordering such Punishment*.

And with Regard to Work, the Intention of the Law is, I apprehend, as totally frustrated. Insomuch that they must be very lazy Persons indeed who can esteem the Labour imposed in any of these Houses as a Punishment. In some, I am told, there is not any Provision made for Work. In that of *Middlesex* in particular,[8] the Governor hath confessed to me that he hath had no Work to employ his Prisoners, and hath urged as a Reason, that having generally great Numbers of most desperate Felons under his Charge, who, notwithstanding his utmost Care, will sometimes get access to his other Prisoners, he dares not trust those who are committed to hard Labour with any heavy or sharp Instruments of Work, lest they should be converted into Weapons by the Felons.[9]

What good Consequence then can arise from sending idle and disorderly Persons to a Place where they are neither to be corrected nor employed; and where with the Conversation of many as bad, and sometimes worse than themselves, they are sure to be improved in the Knowledge, and confirmed in the Practice of Iniquity? Can it be conceived that such Persons will not come out of these Houses much more idle and disorderly than they went in? The Truth of this I have often experienced in the Behaviour of the Wretches brought before me; the most impudent and flagitious of whom, have always been such as have been before acquainted with the Discipline of *Bridewell*: A Commitment to which Place, tho' it often causes great Horror and

---

* By the last Vagabond Act, which repeals all the former, Rogues and Vagabonds are to be whipt, OR sent to the House of Correction.[1]

---

[8] The Clerkenwell bridewell was the Middlesex county House of Correction. Tothill Fields bridewell primarily served the city of Westminster but apparently served the county as well. See Defoe, *Tour*, i. 368; and Henry Mayhew and John Binny, *The Criminal Prisons of London* (London, 1862; repr. New York, 1968), p. 362. Fielding committed offenders to either bridewell. Four days before the publication of the *Enquiry*, Fielding wrote to the Duke of Newcastle recommending William Pentlow, one of his constables, to the post of 'Keeper' of the Clerkenwell bridewell (BM Add. Mss, 32685, fo. 59). Pentlow got the appointment (Cross, ii. 253).

[9] The horrors and abuses of the Clerkenwell House of Correction are described in two pamphlets by Jacob Ilive, *Reasons Offered for the Reformation of the House of Correction in Clerkenwell* (London, 1757); and *A Scheme for the Employment of all Persons sent as Disorderly to the House of Correction in Clerkenwell* (London, 1759). Ilive charges that the governor, for the sake of the fees involved, contrived to receive felons. When Ilive entered Clerkenwell 20 July 1756, the governor was a Henry Wallbank.

[1] 17 Geo: II, c. 5.

Lamentation in the Novice, is usually treated with Ridicule and Contempt by those who have already been there.

For this Reason, I believe, many of the worthiest Magistrates have, to the utmost of their Power, declined a rigorous Execution of the Laws for the Punishment of Idleness, thinking that a severe Reprimand might more probably work the Conversion of such Persons than the committing them to *Bridewell*. This I am sure may with great Certainty be concluded, that the milder Method is less liable to render what is bad worse, and to complete the Destruction of the Offender.

But this is a Way of acting, however worthy be the Motive, which is sometimes more justifiable to a Man's own Conscience, than it would be in the *Court of King's Bench*, which requires the Magistrate to execute the Laws entrusted to his Care, and in the Manner which those Laws prescribe. And besides the Indecency of shewing a Disregard to the Laws in being, nothing surely can be more improper than to suffer the Idleness of the Poor, the Cause of so much Evil to the Society, to go entirely unpunished.

And yet should the Magistrate do his Duty as he is required, will the Intent and Purpose of the Legislature be answered? The Parliament was, indeed, too wise to punish Idleness barely by Confinement. Labour is the true and proper Punishment of Idleness, for the same Reason which the excellent Dr. *Swift* gives why Death is the proper Punishment of Cowardice.[2] Where then is the Remedy? Is it to enforce the Execution of the Law as it now stands, and to reform the present Conduct of the several *Bridewells*? This would I believe be as difficult a Work as the cleansing the *Augean* Stables of old; and would require as extraordinary a Degree of Political, as that did of Natural Strength, to accomplish it. In Truth, the Case here is the same as with the Overseers before, the Trust is too great for the Persons on whom it devolves: And tho' these Houses are, in some Measure, under the Inspection of the Justices of Peace, yet this in the Statute is recommended in too general a Manner to their Care, to expect any good Fruits from it. As "to the true and faithful Account, which they are to yield to the Justices, at the Sessions, of the Persons in their Custody," this is at present little more than Matter of Form; nor can it be expected to be any other in the Hurry of a public Sessions, and when the Stench arising from the Prisoners is so intolerable that it is difficult to get any Gentlemen to attend the Court at that Time.[3] In the last Vagrant Act indeed two Justices

---

[2] 'It is unwise to punish Cowards with Ignominy; for if they had regarded that, they would not have been Cowards: Death is their proper Punishment, because they fear it most' ('Thoughts on Various Subjects', *The Prose Writings of Jonathan Swift*, ed. Herbert Davis [Oxford, 1957], i. 242). Fielding cites another 'Thought' from this work in *JJ* no. 20, p. 237.

[3] Fielding might also have mentioned fear of 'gaol fever'. 'In May 1750, at the famous Black Sessions at the Old Bailey, about 100 prisoners from Newgate came for trial. The trials took place in a hall 30 feet square, packed with spectators, and the prisoners not in the dock were kept in two small

are appointed twice, or oftener, every Year to examine into the State and Nature of Houses of Correction, &c. yet as it gives them no Power but of reporting to the Sessions, I believe it hath not produced any good Effect: For the Business of the Sessions is so complicated and various, that it happens, as in all Cases where Men have too much to do, that they do little or nothing effectually.[4] Perhaps, indeed if two or more Justices of the Peace were appointed to meet once every Month at some convenient Place, as near as possible to the *Bridewell*, there to summon the Governor before them, to examine the Accounts of his Stock and Implements for Work, and to make such Orders (under what Restrictions the Parliament shall think proper) as to such Justices shall seem requisite; this might afford a Palliative at least. In short, the great Cure for Idleness is Labour; and this is its only proper punishment; nor should it ever be in the Power of the idle Person to commute this Punishment for any other.

In the Reign of *Edward* VI. a most severe Law, indeed, was made for the Punishment of Idleness.—"If any Person (says the Statute) shall bring to two Justices of Peace any runagate Servant, or any other, which liveth idly and loiteringly by the Space of three Days, the said Justices shall cause the said idle and loitering Servant or Vagabond to be marked with an hot Iron on the Breast with the Letter V, and adjudge him to be Slave to the same Person that brought and presented him, to have to him, his Executors and Assigns for two Years, who shall take the said Slave and give him Bread, Water, or small Drink, and refuse Meat, and cause him to work by beating, chaining, or otherwise, in such Work and Labour as he shall put him, be it never so vile. And if such Slave absent himself from his Master within the Term, by the Space of fourteen Days, he shall be adjudged by two Justices of the Peace to be marked on the Forehead or the Ball of the Cheek, with a Hot Iron, with the Sign of an S, and shall be adjudged to be Slave to his said Master for ever; and if the said Slave shall run away a second Time he shall be adjudged a Felon."

This Statute lived no longer than two Years, indeed it deserved no longer a Date; for it was cruel, unconstitutional, and rather resembling the cruel Temper of a *Draco*,[5] than the mild Spirit of the *English* Law. But, *est Modus*;[6] there is a Difference between making Men Slaves, and Felons, and

---

* 1. *Ed.* VI. 13 Rep.[7]

rooms which had not been cleaned for many years. Of the six judges on the bench four died; of the jury and minor officials some forty died' (J. J. Hammond and Barbara Hammond, 'Poverty, Crime, Philanthropy', in *Johnson's England*, ed. A. S. Turberville [Oxford, 1952], i. 319).

[4] 'Bridewells were technically under the justices . . . but the whole question of administration was complicated and confused, and as a matter of practice the jailer usually reigned supreme', ibid. 317.

[5] 7th-century BC Athenian legislator whose codification of the laws became proverbial for severity.

[6] Horace, *Sermonum*, I. i. 106. *est modus in rebus*: 'there is measure in all things' (Loeb).

[7] I Edw. VI, c. 3. Rep[ealed].

compelling them to be Subjects; in short, between throwing the Reins on the Neck of Idleness, and riding it with Spurs of Iron.

Thus have I endeavoured to give the Reader a general Idea of the Laws which relate to this single Point of employing the Poor; and, as well as I am able to discern, of their Defects, and the Reasons of those Defects. I have likewise given some Hints for the Cure, and have presumed to offer a Plan, which, in my humble Opinion, would effectually answer every Purpose desired.

But 'till this Plan shall be produced; or (which is more to be expected) 'till some Man of greater Abilities, as well as of greater Authority, shall offer some new Regulation for this Purpose; something, at least, ought to be done to strengthen the Laws already made, and to enforce their Execution. The Matter is of the highest Concern; and imports us not only as we are good Men and good *Christians*; but as we are good *Englishmen*. Since not only preserving the Poor from the highest Degrees of Wretchedness, but the making them useful Subjects, is the Thing proposed; *a Work*, says Sir *Josiah Child**, *which would redound some hundreds of thousands per Ann. to the public Advantage.*[8] Lastly, it is of the utmost Importance to that Point which is the Subject Matter of this Treatise, for which Reason I have thought myself obliged to give it a full Consideration. "The Want of a due Provision (says Lord [†]*Hale*) for Education and Relief of the Poor in a Way of Industry, is that which fills the Goals with Malefactors, and fills the Kingdom with idle and unprofitable Persons that consume the Stock of the Kingdom without improving it, and that will daily increase, even to a Desolation in Time. And this Error in the first Concoction is never remediable but by Gibbets and whipping."[9]

In serious Truth, if proper Care should be taken to provide for the present Poor, and to prevent their Encrease by laying some effectual Restraints on the Extravagance of the lower Sort of People, the remaining Part of this Treatise would be rendered of little Consequence; since few Persons, I believe, have made their Exit at *Tyburn*, who have not owed their Fate to some of the Causes before mentioned. But as I am not too sanguine in my Expectations on this Head, I shall now proceed to consider of some Methods to obviate the Frequency of Robbers, which if less efficacious, are perhaps much easier than those already proposed. And if we will not remove the Temptation, at least we ought to take away all Encouragment to Robbery.

* Page 88.
[†] At the End of his Discourse touching the Relief of the Poor.

---

[8] *A New Discourse*, p. 56.
[9] Hale, *Discourse*, pp. 79–80. Fielding omits Hale's last sentence: 'But there must be a sound, prudent and resolved Method for an Industrious Education of the Poor, and that will give better remedy against these corruptions than the after gain of penalties can.'

SECT. V.

Of the Punishment of RECEIVERS OF STOLEN GOODS

Now one great Encouragement to Theft of all Kinds is the Ease and Safety with which stolen Goods may be disposed of. It is a very old and vulgar, but a very true Saying, "that if there were no Receivers, there would be no Thieves."[1] Indeed could not the Thief find a Market for his Goods, there would be an absolute End of several Kinds of Theft; such as Shop-lifting, Burglary, &c. the Objects of which are generally Goods and not Money. Nay Robberies on the Highway would so seldom answer the Purpose of the Adventurer that very few would think it worth their while to risque so much with such small Expectations.

But at present, instead of meeting with any such Discouragement, the Thief disposes of his Goods with almost as much Safety as the honestest Tradesman: For first, if he hath made a Booty of any Value, he is almost sure of seeing it advertised within a Day or two, directing him *to bring the Goods to a certain Place where he is to receive a Reward* (sometimes the full Value of the Booty) *and no Questions asked.*[2] This Method of recovering stolen Goods by the Owner, a very learned Judge formerly declared to have been, in his Opinion, a Composition of Felony.[3] And surely if this be proved to be carried into Execution, I think it must amount to a full Conviction of that Crime. But, indeed, such Advertisements are in themselves so very scandalous, and of such pernicious Consequence, that if Men are not ashamed to own they prefer an old Watch or a Diamond Ring to the Good of the Society, it is pity some effectual Law was not contrived to prevent their giving this public Countenance to Robbery for the future.[4]

But if the Person robbed should prove either too honest, or too obstinate, to take this Method of recovering his Goods, the Thief is under no Difficulty

---

[1] 'The shops of these fellows [pawnbrokers] may indeed be called the fountains of theft; for it is in reality the encouragement which they meet with from these receivers of their goods that induces men very often to become thieves, so that these deserve equal if not severer punishment than the thieves themselves' (*Amelia*, XI. vii. 277).

[2] According to Mandeville, when Jonathan Wild flourished one first applied to him to regain stolen goods. If the thief were an 'irregular Practitioner', 'we immediately put an Advertisement in some News-Paper or other, with a Promise that such a Reward will be given, and no Questions asked' (*An Enquiry into the Causes of the Frequent Executions at Tyburn* [London, 1725], p. 4 [Augustan Reprint Society publication, 105]). In the *Covent-Garden Journal*, no. 3 (11 Jan. 1752), Fielding tells of a thief appearing before him who had kept his booty in expectation of a reward being advertised (cit. Jones, p. 187). Examples of such advertisements are printed in Appendix G of Radzinowicz, ii. 440–1.

[3] Sir Thomas Parker, 1st Earl of Macclesfield (d. 1732), lord chief justice (1710), lord chancellor (1718–25). 'The practice of advertising a reward for bringing goods stolen, and no questions asked . . . I have heard lord chancellor Macclesfield declare to be highly criminal, as being a sort of compounding of felony' (cited in Hale, i. 546 n.).

[4] By 25 Geo. II. (1751) c. 36. sect. 1, 'any person publickly advertising a reward with no questions asked, for the return of things which have been stolen or lost . . . shall . . . forfeit the sum of fifty pounds for every such offence, to any person who will sue for the same.'

in turning them into Money. Among the great Number of Brokers and Pawnbrokers several are to be found, who are always ready to receive a gold Watch at an easy Rate, and where no Questions are asked, or, at least, where no Answer is expected but such as the Thief can very readily make.

Besides the clandestine Dealers this Way who satisfy their Consciences with telling a ragged Fellow, or Wench, that *they hope* they came honestly by Silver, and Gold, and Diamonds; there are others who scorn such pitiful Subterfuges, who engage openly with the Thieves, and who have Warehouses filled with stolen Goods only. Among the *Jews* who live in a certain Place in the City, there have been, and still are, some notable Dealers this Way, who in an almost public Manner have carried on a Trade for many Years with *Rotterdam*, where they have their Warehouses and Factors, and whither they export their Goods with prodigious Profit, and as prodigious Impunity. And all this appeared very plainly last Winter in the Examination of one *Cadosa* a *Jew*, in the Presence of the late excellent Duke of *Richmond*, and many other Noblemen and Magistrates.[5]

What then shall we say? Is not this Mischief worthy of some Remedy, or is it not capable of it? The noble Duke (one of the worthiest of Magistrates as well as of the best of Men) thought otherwise, as would have appeared, had his valuable Life, for the Good of Mankind, been prolonged.[6]

Certain it is, that the Law as it now stands is ineffectual to cure the Evil. Let us see therefore, if possible, where the Defect lies.

At the Common Law, any one might lawfully (says Lord *Hale*) have received his own Goods from the Felon who stole them*. But if he had received them upon Agreement not to prosecute, or to prosecute faintly, this would have been Theftbote punishable by Imprisonment and Ransom.[7]

But in neither of the foregoing Cases would the Receiver of the Goods have become an Accessary to the Felon. So if one Man had bought another's Goods of the Thief, though he had known them to be stolen, if he had given the just Value for them, he would not have become an Accessary†.[8] But if he

---

* Hist. P. C. vol. 1. p. 546. 619. *ib.*
† Hist. P. C. *ubi supra.*

---

[5] See General Introduction, p. lv. For smugglers' warehouses and illegal traffic to Holland under Wild's leadership, see Gerald Howson, *Thief-Taker General: the Rise and Fall of Jonathan Wild* (New York, 1970), pp. 141 ff. and 227 ff.

[6] Charles Lennox (1701–50), 2nd Duke of Richmond, a supporter of Walpole and friend of Newcastle. Richmond died 8 Aug. Fielding had dedicated *The Miser* (1735) and 'Of Good-Nature' to him (see *Miscellanies* [1743], p. 30 n). Murphy states that Richmond was Fielding's patron (*Works*, 1762, i. 27). See also General Introduction, p. lvi.

[7] 'A. hath his goods stolen by B. if A. receives his goods again simply without any contract to favour him in his prosecution, or to forbear prosecution, this is lawful; but if he receive them upon agreement not to prosecute or to prosecute faintly, this is theft-bote punishable by imprisonment and ransom' (Hale, i. 619). Hawkins (i. 125) and Giles Jacob (*A New Law-Dictionary* [London, 1782]), define theftbote by citing this passage.

[8] Hale, i. 619. The rest of Fielding's paragraph is drawn from this page.

had bought them at an Undervalue, this, Sir *Richard Hyde*[9] held, would have made him an Accessary. My Lord *Hale* differs from his Opinion, and his Reason to some Readers may seem a pleasant one; *for if there be any odds* (says he) *he that gives more, benefits the Felon more than he that gives less than Value.* However this, his Lordship thinks, may be a Misdemeanor punishable by Fine and Imprisonment; but that the bare receiving of Goods knowing them to be stolen makes not an Accessary.

So says the great Lord *Hale*, and so indeed was the Law; though the Judges seem not to have been unanimous in their Opinion. In the Book of *Assizes**, [1]*Scrope* is said to have held otherwise; and though *Shard*[2] there quashed an Appeal of Felony for receiving stolen Goods only, yet I cannot help observing, that the Reporter of the Case hath left a Note of Astonishment at the Judgment of the Court. This, says he, was wonderful![3] and wonderful surely it is, if he who receives, relieves, comforts, or assists a Felon, shall be an Accessary, that he shall not be so, who knowingly buys the Goods of the Felon; which is generally, I believe, the strongest Relief, Comfort and Assistance, which can be given him, and without the Hope and Expectation of which, he would never have committed the Theft or Robbery.

It is unnecessary, however, to enter further into this Controversy; since it is now expressly declared by Statute†, "That the Receivers of stolen Goods, knowing them to be stolen, shall be deemed Accessaries after the Fact."

But this Statute, though it removed the former Absurdity of the Law, was not sufficient to remedy the Evil; there yet remaining many Difficulties in bringing these pernicious Miscreants to Justice, consistent with legal Rules. For,

1. As the Offence of the Accessary is dependent on that of the Principal, he could not be tried or out-lawed, till after the Conviction or Attainder of the Principal; so that however strong Evidence there might be against the Receiver, he was still safe, unless the Thief could be apprehended.

2. If the Thief on his Trial should be acquitted, as often happens through some Defect of Evidence in the most notorious Cases, the Receiver, being only an Accessary, tho' he hath confessed his Crime, or though the most

---

* 27 Assiz. 69.   † 3 & 4 *W.* and *M.* c. 9.

[9] Hale cites 'Sir Nich. Hyde', and Fielding probably read 'Rich.' for 'Nich.' Sir Nicholas Hyde (d. 1631) was chief justice of England 1627–31.

[1] The standard edition of the Year Books for the 18th century was that of 1679 in eleven folio parts (Winfield, *Sources*, pp. 175 ff). Part V is known as *Liber Assisarum* because it contains mainly reports of cases heard before justices of assize 1–50 Edw. III. Item no. 105 in Baker is 'Year Books, 7 vol. *compleat & best edit*' (no date).

[2] Sir Geoffrey le Scrope (d. 1340), judge of Common Pleas 1323, chief justice 1324 and 1328–38. The 'Shard' Fielding found cited in the Year Book is an abbreviation for Sir John de Shardelowe (d. 1344?), judge of Court of Common Pleas 1332–42.

[3] '*Quod mirum*'. 27 *Lib. Ass.*, fo. 143, p. 69. Hale cites this report, i. 620.

undeniable Evidence could be brought against him, must be acquitted likewise.

3. In Petit Larceny there can be no such Accessary*: for tho' the Statute says,[4] that a Receiver of stolen Goods, knowing, &c. shall be an Accessary after the Fact, that is, legally understood to mean only in Cases where such Accessary may be by Law; and that is confined to such Felonies as are to receive Judgment of Death, or to have the Benefit of Clergy. Now, for Petit Larceny, which is the Stealing of Goods of less Value than a Shilling, the Punishment at Common Law is Whipping; and this was properly enough considered as too trifling an Offence to extend the Guilt to Criminals in a second Degree. But since Juries have taken upon them to consider the Value of Goods as immaterial, and to find upon their Oaths, that what is proved to be worth several Shillings, and sometimes several pounds, is of the Value of Tenpence, this is become a Matter of more Consequence.[5] For Instance; If a Pickpocket steal several Handkerchiefs, or other Things, to the Value of Twenty Shillings, and the Receiver of these, knowing them to be stolen, is discovered, and both are indicted, the one as Principal, the other as Accessary, as they must be; if the Jury convict the Principal, and find the Goods to be of as high Value as a Shilling, he must receive Judgment of Death; whereas, by finding the Goods (which they do upon their Oaths) to be of the Value of Tenpence, the Thief is ordinarily sentenced to be whipt, and returns immediately to his Trade of picking Pockets, and the Accessary is of course discharged, and of course returns to his Trade of receiving the Booty. Thus the Jury are perjured, the Public highly injured, and two excellent Acts of Parliament defeated, that two Miscreants may laugh at their Prosecutors, and at the Law.

The two former of these Defects are indeed remedied by a later Statute[†], which enacts, "That the Buyers and Receivers of stolen Goods, knowing them to be stolen, may be prosecuted for a Misdemeanour, and punished by

---

* *Cro.* Eliz. 750.[6] *Hale*, Hist. Vol. 1. p. 530, 618.
† 3 and 4 *W.* and *M.* c. 9.

---

[4] 3 & 4 Wil. & Mar., c. 9. sect. 4.

[5] Hale suggests that juries who undervalued goods stolen were recognizing the effect of inflation: 'This law [of 1109] still remains at this day; but considering the alteration of the value of money, the severity of it is much greater now than then . . . yet a theft above the value of 12d. is still liable to the same punishment, upon which Sir Hen. Spelman justly observes, that while all things else have rose in their value and grown dearer, the life of man is become much cheaper' (i. 12, n. f).

[6] *The First Part of the Reports of S*ᵣ *George Croke . . . from the 24th to the 44th of the late Queen Elizabeth . . . Revised and published in English, by Sir Harbottle Grimston . . .* (London, 1669). Croke's *Reports* is no. 271 in Baker. Croke (1560–1642) reports on the case of Ann Lasington who 'was Endicted of Petit Larceny, and another was Endicted as accessary. And because one cannot be accessary in the Case, no more then in Trespass, the accessary was . . . discharged.'

'But in this case of petit larceny there can be no accessaries neither before nor after' (Hale, i. 530).

Fine and Imprisonment, though the principal Felon be not before convicted of Felony."[7]

This last Statute is again repeated in the 5th of Queen *Anne*[†]; and there the Power of the Court to punish in the Case of the Misdemeanour, is farther encreased to any other corporal Punishment, which the Court shall think fit to inflict, instead of Fine and Imprisonment; and, in the Case of the Felony, the Accessary is to receive Judgment of Death; but the Benefit of Clergy is not taken away. Lastly, By the Statute of *George* II.[‡] the Receivers of stolen Goods, knowing, &c. are to be transported for 14 Years.[8] And by the same Statute, every Person taking Money or Reward, directly or indirectly, under Pretence or upon Account of helping any to stolen Goods, unless such Person apprehend and bring to his Trial the Felon, and give Evidence against him, is made guilty of Felony without Benefit of Clergy.[9]

And thus stands the Law at this Day; which, notwithstanding the repeated Endeavours of the Legislature, Experience shews us, is incapable of removing this deplorable Evil from the Society.

The principal Defect seems, to me, to lie in the extreme Difficulty of convicting the Offender; for,

1. Where the Thief can be taken, you are not at Liberty to prosecute for the Misdemeanour.[1]

2. The Thief himself, who must be convicted before the Accessary is to be tried, cannot be a Witness.[2]

3. Without such Evidence it is very difficult to convict of the Knowledge, that the Goods were stolen; which, in this Case, can appear from Circumstances only. Such are principally, 1. Buying Goods of Value, of Persons very unlikely to be the lawful Proprietors. 2*dly*, Buying them for much less than their real Value. 3*dly*, Buying them, or selling them again, in a clandestine Manner, concealing them, &c. None of these are commonly liable to be proved; and I have known a Man acquitted, where most of these Circumstances have appeared against him.

What then is to be done, to extirpate this stubborn Mischief? to prove the

[†] Chap. 31.
[‡] Chap. 11.

[7] Fielding does not quote from but summarizes 1 Annae, st. 2. c. 9. sect. 2. Fielding's footnote citing 3 & 4 Wil. & Mar., is in error.

[8] 4 Geo. I, c. 11. sect. 1 [not 'Geo. II'].

[9] Sect. 4. Because of this section, the Act became known as 'The Jonathan Wild Act' (see Howson, *Thief-Taker General*, pp. 92 ff.). Sir William Thomson (see *Enquiry*, below p. 163 and n. 5) reportedly wrote those parts of the Act directed at Wild. In *Jonathan Wild* (IV. i. 48) Fielding remarks 'By this law it was made capital in a prig to steal with the hands of other people'.

[1] In 1719 Wild was prosecuted for a misdemeanor because the thieves from whom he had received stolen goods had been convicted and executed and consequently could not testify against him on a felony charge. But the court ruled that he could not be tried for a misdemeanor either, since the thieves had been taken.

[2] See *Enquiry*, below, p. 160.

pernicious Consequence of which, I need, I think, only appeal to the Sense of Parliament, testified in so many repeated Acts, and very strongly expressed in their Preambles.

First, Might it not be proper to put an effectual Stop to the present scandalous Method of compounding Felony, by public Advertisements in the News Papers? Might not the inserting such Advertisements be rendered highly criminal in the Authors of them, and in the Printers themselves, unless they discover such Authors?[3]

2dly, Is it impossible to find any Means of regulating Brokers and Pawnbrokers?[4] If so, What Arguments are there against extirpating entirely a Set of Miscreants, which, like other Vermin, harbour only about the Poor, and grow fat by sucking their Blood?

3dly, Why should not the receiving stolen Goods, knowing them to be stolen, be made an original Offence? by which means the Thief, who is often a paultry Offender in Comparison of the Receiver, and sometimes his Pupil, might, in little Felonies, be made a Witness against him: for thus the Trial of the Receiver would in no Case depend on the Trial or Conviction of the Thief.

4thly, Why may not the bare buying or taking to Pawn stolen Goods, above a certain Value, be made Evidence of receiving with Knowledge, &c. unless the Goods were bought in Market overt,[5] (no Broker's or Pawnbroker's Shop to be reputed such Market overt) or unless the Defendant could prove, by a credible Witness to the Transaction, that he had good Cause to regard the Seller or Pawner of the Goods to be the real Owner. If 20 s. was the Value limited, it would answer all the Purposes contended for; and would in nowise interfere with the honest Trade (if indeed it ever be so) between the Pawnbroker and the Poor.

If none of these Methods be thought possible or proper, I hope better will be found out. Something ought to be done, to put an End to the present Practice, of which I see daily the most pernicious Consequences; many of the younger Thieves appearing plainly to be taught, encouraged and employed by the Receivers.

SECT. VI.

Of Laws relating to VAGABONDS.

The other great Encouragement to Robbery, beside the certain Means of finding a Market for the Booty, is the Probability of escaping Punishment.

---

[3] See *Enquiry*, above, p. 125 and n. 2.

[4] Two of Sir John Fielding's pamphlets (*A Plan for Preventing Robberies* [1755] and *An Account of the Origin and Effects of a Police* [1758]) contain 'rules' and 'advice' for pawnbrokers.

[5] i.e., an open or public market. Any shop in London was a *market overt* except on Sunday. In the country, *market overt* was only on market day in market places established by custom.

First, then, The Robber hath great Hopes of being undiscovered: And this is one principal Reason, why Robberies are more frequent in this Town, and in its Neighbourhood, than in the remoter Parts of the Kingdom.

Whoever indeed considers the Cities of *London* and *Westminster*, with the late vast Addition of their Suburbs; the great Irregularity of their Buildings, the immense Number of Lanes, Alleys, Courts and Bye-places; must think, that, had they been intended for the very Purpose of Concealment, they could scarce have been better contrived. Upon such a View, the whole appears as a vast Wood or Forest, in which a Thief may harbour with as great Security, as wild Beasts do in the Desarts[6] of *Africa* or *Arabia*. For by *wandering* from one Part to another, and often shifting his quarters, he may almost avoid the Possibility of being discovered.

Here, according to the Method I have hitherto pursued, I will consider, what Remedy our Laws have applied to this Evil, namely the *wandring* of the Poor, and whether, and wherein these Remedies appear defective.

There is no Part of our antient Constitution more admirable than that which was calculated to prevent the Concealment of Thieves and Robbers. The Original of this Institution is given to *Alfred*, at the End of his Wars with the *Danes*, when the *English* were very much debauched by the Example of those Barbarians, and betook themselves to all Manner of Licentiousness and Rapine. These Evils were encouraged, as the Historians say, by the vagabond State of the Offenders, who, having no settled Place of Abode, upon committing any Offence, shifted their Quarters, and went where it was difficult to discover them. To remedy this Mischief, therefore, *Alfred* having limited the Shires or Counties in a better Manner than before, divided them into Hundreds, and these again into Tithings, Decennaries, or ten Families.*.[7]

Over every one of these Tithings or Decennaries, there was a Chief, called the Tithingman or Burghholder, who had a Power to call a Court, and to try small Offences; the greater being referred to that Court, which was in like manner established over every Hundred.

* "By these ten Families (says the Annotator to *Rapin*) we are not to understand ten House-keepers, but ten Lords of Manors, with all their Vassals, Tenants, Labourers, and Slaves; who, though they did not all live under their Lord's Roof, were all counted Part of his Family. As there were no little Freeholders in those Times, nor for long after, ten such Families must occupy a large Space of Ground, and might well constitute a rural Tithing."[8] But this rural Tithing would be larger than the Hundred itself; and the very Name and Office of a Tithingman continued in Parishes to this Day, shews that Lords of Manors could not be here meant.

[6] Wildernesses.

[7] Rapin, i. 330: 'As they had no settled abode, upon committing any offence, they shifted their quarters, and went where it was difficult to discover them. Alfred beholding with indignation honest men thus exposed to the insults of villains, was extremely desirous to put a stop to so great mischief. . . . He divided all England into shires, or counties, the counties into hundreds, and the hundreds into tythings.'

[8] Rapin, ii. 16–17, n. y. The annotator is presumably Nicholas Tindal.

Every one of these Heads of Families were Pledges to each other for the Behaviour of all their Family; and were likewise reciprocally Pledges for each other to the Hundred.

If any Person was suspected of a Crime, he was obliged to find Security for his good Behaviour out of the same Hundred and Tithing. This if he could not find, he had Reason to apprehend being treated with great Severity; and if any accused Person, either before or after his finding Bail, had fled from Justice, the whole Tithing and Hundred should pay a Fine to the King.[9]

In Case of the Default of Appearance in a Decenner, his nine Pledges had one and thirty Days to bring the Delinquent forth to Justice. If this failed, then the Chief of those Decenners, by the Vote of that and the Neighbour Decennaries, was to purge himself both of the Guilt of the Fact, and of being Parties to the Flight of the Delinquent. And if they could not do this, then they were by their own Oaths to acquit themselves, and to bind themselves to bring the Delinquent to Justice as soon as they could; and, in the mean time to pay the Damage out of the Estate of the Delinquent; and if that were not sufficient, then out of their own Estate*.[1]

Every Subject in the Kingdom was registred in some Tithing; only Persons of the first Rank had the Privilege (says Mr. *Rapin*†) that their single Family should make a Tithing, for which they were responsible.[2] "All Archbishops, Bishops, Earls, Barons, and all (says *Bracton*) who have Sok and Sah, Tol and Team, and these Kinds of Liberties, ought to have under their FRIDHBURGH, all their Knights, Servants, Esquires; and if any of them prove delinquent, the Lord shall bring him to Justice, or pay his Fine‡."[3]

The Master of the Family was answerable for all who fed at his Board, and were of his Livery, and for all his Servants of every Kind, even for those who served him for their Food only, without Wages. These were said to be of his Manupast;[4] so were his Guests; and if a Man abode at any House but two Nights, the Master of that House was answerable for him‖.[5]

---

* *Bacon's* Histor. Disc. p. 43.   † Dissertation on the Government of the *Anglo-Saxons.*
‡ *Bract.* L. 3. De Corona, chap. 10.   ‖ *Bract.* ubi sup. *Brit.* 19 b.

[9] The substance of this and the two preceding paragraphs may be found in Rapin, i. 330 and ii. 16–17.

[1] This paragraph is taken nearly verbatim from Nathaniel Bacon's *An Historicall Discourse of the Uniformity of the Government of England. The First Part* (London, 1647), p. 70 (ch. XXVI, 'Of the Division of the Hundreds into Decennaries'). A 1739 edition is listed in Baker (no. 277).

[2] This sentence comes nearly verbatim from Rapin, ii. 16–17. Vol. ii of Rapin is entitled 'A Dissertation on the Government, Laws, Manners, Customs, and Language of the Anglo-Saxons.'

[3] Bracton, lib. 3, fo. 124b (ii. 351, ed. cit.). *Fridburgh*: lit. 'Peace-pledge'; mistranslated by Normans as 'frankpledge'. 'Sok and Sah, Tol and Team': a formulaic expression in Anglo-Saxon legal documents granting jurisdictional rights.

[4] 'Of his household'.

[5] Bracton, lib. 3. fo. 124b (ii. 351, ed. cit.); Britton, fo. 19b.

In a word, says *Bracton*, every Man, as well Freemen as others, ought to belong to some Frankpledge, (*i.e.* to some Decenna) unless he be a Traveller, or belong to the *Manupast* of some other; or unless he gives some countervailing Security to the Public, as Dignity, (*viz.* Nobility) Order, (Knighthood, or of the Clergy) or Estate, (*viz.* either Freehold in Land, or personal Effects) (*res immobiles*)) if he be a Citizen.[6]

By the Laws of *Edward the Confessor*, every Person, of the Age of 12 Years, ought to be sworn in a View of Frankpledge, *That he will neither become a Thief himself, nor be anywise accessary to Theft.*[7]

This Court, *Briton** tells us, was to be holden twice a Year,[8] which was afterwards reduced to once a Year by *Magna Charta*;[9] and no Man, says the *Mirror*, was, by an ancient Ordinance, suffered to remain in the Kingdom, who was not enrolled *in Decenna*, and had Freemen for his Pledges†.[1]

Such was this excellent Constitution, which even in *Alfred's* Time, when it was in its Infancy, wrought so admirable an Effect, that *Ingulphus* says,[2] a Traveller might have openly left a Sum of Money safely in the Fields and Highways, and have found it safe and untouched a Month afterwards‡.[3] Nay, *William* of *Malmsbury* tells us, the King ordered Bracelets of Gold to be hung up in the cross-ways, as a Proof of the Honesty of his People, none ever offering to meddle with them‖.[4]

But this Constitution would have been deficient, if it had only provided for the incorporting the Subjects, unless it had confined them to the Places where they were thus incorporated.

---

* *Brit.* 36 b.   † *Mirr.* chap. 1. sect. 17. & chap. 5. sect. 1.
‡ Script. post *Bedam*, p. 870.   ‖ Ib. p. 44.

---

[6] Bracton, loc. cit. *Res immobiles*: 'immovables'.

[7] Bracton, loc. cit.

[8] 'Further let inquiry be made concerning sheriffs who have held their tourn oftener than twice a year; and of their hundreders and others who have held their views of frankpledge oftener than twice a year . . .' (fo. 36b).

[9] Magna Charta, ch. 35, limits the sheriff's tourn to 'accustomed times' twice a year and the view of frankpledge to Michaelmas. It requires the sheriff 'to be content with as much as [he] was wont to have for his View-making in the times of King Henry our Grandfather'.

[1] Andrew Horne, *The Mirrour of Justices* (first published 1642; MSS from the 13th century), trans. William Hughes (London, 1646), pp. 53 and 226. Fielding owned this translation from law-French (Baker, no. 548). The authorship, date, and purpose of the *Mirrour* are uncertain (see Winfield, pp. 266–8). Holdsworth, ii. 32) calls it a 'legal romance'. Among its heterogeneous matter is an idealized account of Alfred's England. Coke (and many others) accepted the *Mirrour* and through him it affected English law. For its influence on Puritan radical politics in the 17th century, see Christopher Hill, *Puritanism and Revolution* (New York, 1964 [first pub. London, 1958]), pp. 58 ff.

[2] Ingulf (d. 1109), abbot of Crowland or Croyland. His *History of the Abbey of Croyland* (first pub. in [Sir Henry Saville's] *Rerum Anglicarum Scriptores post Bedam* [London, 1596]) is probably a 15th-century forgery, of which some 17th-century scholars were suspicious and which some 19th-century scholars accepted as genuine.

[3] Familiar lore in the 18th century about Alfred's England.

[4] Book V of 'De Gestis Regum Anglorum' in [Saville] *Scriptores post Bedam* (Frankfurt, 1601), p. 44. Fielding owned this edition (Baker, no. 320).

And therefore by the Laws of *Alured* or *Canute*, it was rendered unlawful for any of the Decenners to depart from their Dwelling, without the Consent of their Fellow-Pledges; nor were they at Liberty to leave the Country, without the Licence of the Sheriff or Governor of the same§.[5]

And if a Person, who fled from one Tithing, was received in another, the Tithing receiving him should answer for his Deed (*i. e.* by Amercement[6]) if he was there found**.[7]

"Before this Order was established (says *Rapin*) the meaner Sort of People might shift their Quarters, by reason of their Obscurity, which prevented them from being taken Notice of. But it was impossible for them to change their Habitation, after they were obliged to bring a Testimonial from their Tithing, to enable them to settle and be registred in another*."[8]

Whilst this antient Constitution remained entire, "Such Peace (says Lord *Coke*) was preserved within the Realm, as no Injuries, Homicides, Robberies, Thefts, Riots, Tumults, or other Offences, were committed; so as a Man, with a white Wand, might safely have ridden, before the Conquest, with much Money about him, without any Weapon, through *England*†." Nay even in the tumultuous Times of *William the Conqueror*, the Historians tell us, there was scarce a Robber to be found in the Kingdom.

This View of Frankpledge[9] remained long after the Conquest: for we find it twice repeated in one Chapter of *Magna Charta*‡; and there particularly it is said, *Fiat autem visus de Frankpleg' sic videlicet QUOD PAX NOSTRA TENEATUR.*[1] Nay, *Bracton*, who wrote after that Time, and *Fleta* after him, speak of Frankpledge as then subsisting.[2]

The Statute of *Marlborough* likewise, which was made the 52d of *Henry* III. mentions the same Court;[3] as doth *Briton*, who wrote still later, in many

§ *Bacon*, p. 44.   ** *Brit.* ubi supra.
* *Rapin*, ubi sup.
† 2 Instit. 73.
‡ Chap. 33.

[5] Nathaniel Bacon, *An Historicall Discourse* (London, 1647), p. 71: '. . . none of them might depart from their dwelling without the consent of his fellow pledges, nor out of the County without allowance of the Sheriffe, or other Governour of the Same'. Bacon cites the laws of Alured (i.e. Alfred) and Canute in the margin of his text.

[6] A Fine.   [7] *Britton*, fo. 19b.   [8] Rapin, ii. 17.

[9] 'Frankpledge has been defined as "a system of compulsory collective bail fixed for individuals, not after their arrest for crime, but as a safeguard in anticipation of it" ' (Holdsworth, i. 13). The 'view' (or official inquiry into the operation of the tithing system) of frankpledge was made twice a year in a full meeting of the hundred court held by the sheriff. In the 13th century the view of frankpledge was taken in the sheriff's tourn which was held twice a year (Holdsworth, i. 76).

[1] 'The View of Frankpledge shall be so done, that our Peace may be kept.' Coke cites the Latin quotation (*II Inst.* 69).

[2] Bracton, fo. 124b (ii. 351, ed. cit.); *Fleta*, bk. I, ch. xxvii. *Fleta* is largely an epitome of Bracton written about 1290 (Winfield, p. 262). It has been translated for the Selden Society (vol. ii, 1955; vol. iii, 1972) by H. G. Richardson and G. O. Sayles.

[3] 52 Hen. III, c. 10 (1367).

Places.[4] And in the 17th of *Edward* II. an Act was made, called, *The Statute for the View of Frankpledge*.[5]

Nay, in the Reign of *Henry* IV. we find an Amercement for not coming to a View of Frankpledge; and there the whole Court of King's Bench were of Opinion, that every Man, as well Masters as Servants, were obliged to repair to this Court[§]; tho' then possibly it was degenerated, and become little more than Form.

But in Process of Time, this Institution dwindled to nothing; so that Lord *Coke* might truly say, *Quod vera institutio illius curiæ evanuit & velut umbra ejusdem adhuc remanet*;[7] and a little after, speaking of the Frankpledge, the *Decennarii*, and the *Decenna*, he says, "They are Names continued only as Shadows of Antiquity*."[8] Nay, this great Man himself (if, after a most careful and painful Perusal of all he hath writ, as well here as in his 4th *Institute*, and other Places on the Subject, I may be allowed to say so) seems to have no very clear Idea concerning them; and might have fairly owned, of the Original of the Leet and Frankpledge, what one of the Sages doth of an Hundred, in the Book of *Henry* VII. "That a Hundred had existed above a hundred Years; and therefore, as to the true Definition of a Hundred, and whether it was composed of a hundred Towns, or a hundred Lordships, and whether it had antiently more or less Jurisdiction, he frankly owned that he knew nothing of the Matter[†]."[9]

The Statute of *Marlborough*[‡] had perhaps given a fatal Blow to the true and ancient Use of the View of Frankpledge; of which, as Lord *Coke* says[∥], the Sheriffs had made an ill Use:[1] for, in the 3d Year of the succeeding King[§], we find the Legislature providing against notorious Felons, and such as be openly of evil Fame, that they shall not be admitted to Bail;[2] and, in the 13th,

∥ But this Matter was before that transferred from the Decennary Court to the Leets and Sheriff's Tourn.

§ Hil. 3 *H.* IV. Pl. 19.[6]   * 2 Inst. 72, 73.   † 8 *H.* VII. 3 b.

‡ Chap. 24. By which Justices in Eyre are forbidden to amerce Townships, because all of twelve Years old were not sworn.

∥ 2 Instit. 147.   § *Westminster*, 1. chap. 15.

---

[4] e.g. fos. 3b and 10a (i. 7 and 23, ed. cit.).

[5] The statute of this title is 18 [not 17] Ed. II (1325).

[6] The reference to the Year Book should be Hil[ary] 2 Hen. IV, pl. 19.

[7] 'But this institution has vanished and only its shadow remains' (*II Inst.* 72).

[8] *II Inst.* 73.

[9] Apparently Fielding's translation of the Year Book Trin[ity]. 8 Hen. VII, pl. 1 (fo. 3b). 'b' is the marginal 'B' in the 1678–70 editions of the Year Books signalling folio b of earlier editions.

[1] The practice had been that the chief pledge represent his tithing at the view of frankpledge. Coke (*II Inst.* 147) says that sheriffs amerced townships that failed to send all their members and summoned twelve or more townships at a time, for the sake of the amercement. The Statute of Marlborough (52 Hen. III, c. 10) exempted many from attendance at the sheriff's tourn and 'did much to fix its character as a court which was concerned with petty offences and with the smaller details of local government' (Holdsworth, i. 79). Ch. 24 states that sheriffs shall not amerce townships 'because all being twelve Years came not afore the Sheriffs and Coroners . . . so that there came sufficient'.

[2] St. Westminster I (3 Edw. I, c. 15).

the Statute of *Winchester* entirely altered the Law, and gave us a new Constitution on this Head.[3]

1. By this Act the whole Hundred is made answerable in Case of Robberies.

2. In order to prevent the Concealment of Robbers in Towns, it is enacted, 1. That the Gates of all walled Towns shall be shut from Sun-setting to Sun-rising. 2. A Watch is appointed, who are to arrest all Strangers. 3. No Person is to lodge in the Suburbs, nor in any Place out of the Town, unless his Host will answer for him. 4. The Bailiffs of Towns shall make Enquiry once within 15 Days at the farthest, of all Persons lodged in the Suburbs, &c. and of those who have received any suspicious Persons.

3. To prevent the Concealment of Robbers without the Towns, it is enacted, That the Highways leading from one Market-Town to another, shall be enlarged, and no Bushes, Woods, or Dykes, in which Felons may be concealed, shall be suffered therein.

4. Felons are to be pursued by Hue and Cry.

This Statute, says Lord *Coke*, was made against a Gang of Rogues then called *Roberdsmen*, that took their Denomination of one *Robin Hood*, who lived in *Yorkshire* in the Reign of *Richard* I. and who, with his Companions, harbouring in Woods and Desarts, committed a great Number of Robberies and other Outrages on the Subject. From this Arch-thief a great Number of idle and dissolute Fellows, who were called *Drawlatches, Ribauds,* and *Roberdsmen,* took their Rise, and infested this Kingdom for above a Century, notwithstanding the many Endeavours of the Legislature from time to time to suppress them.[4]

In all these Laws, the principal Aim visibly was, to prevent idle Persons wandering from Place to Place, which, as we have before seen, was one great Point of the Decennary Constitution.

Thus by a Law made in the 34th Year of *Edward* III. A Labourer departing from his Service into another County was to be burned in the Forehead with the Letter F. And by the same Statute, if a Labourer or Servant do fly into a City or Borough, the Chief Officer, on Request, was to deliver him up.[5]

Again, in the 7th Year of *Richard* II. the Justies of Peace are ordered to examine Vagabonds; and, if they have no Sureties for their good Behaviour, to commit them to Prison.[6]

---

[3] 13 Edw. I, st. 2 (1285). Fielding's four points following appear in order in chs. 2, 4, 5, and 6. This statute opens, by the way, by noting that 'Robberies, Murthers, Burnings, and Theft, be more often used than they have been before'.

[4] Coke, *III Inst.* 197. Essentially the same account of Robin Hood appears on p. 345 of *A Treatise on the Office of Constable* (see *Enquiry*, below, p. 145 n. 3) as printed in Sir John Fielding's *Extracts from such of the Penal Laws* . . . (a new edition, London, 1762). Fielding also cites Coke on 'Roberdsmen' in the *Champion*, 7 June 1740, p. 321.

[5] 34 Edw. III, cc. 10 & 11.   [6] 7 Rich. II, c. 5.

In the 11th Year of *Henry* VII. it was enacted, That Vagabonds and idle Persons should be set on the Stocks three Days and three Nights, and have no other Sustenance but Bread and Water, and then shall be put out of the Town; and whosoever gave such idle Persons Relief, forfeited 12 *d.*[7]

By 22 *Henry* VIII. Persons calling themselves *Egyptians*[8] shall not come into the Realm, under Penalty of forfeiting their Goods; and, if they do not depart within 15 Days after they are commanded, shall be imprisoned.[9]

By the 1 and 2 *Philip* and *Mary*†, *Egyptians* coming into the Kingdom, and remaining here a Month, are made guilty of Felony without Benefit of Clergy.

And those who bring them into the Realm, forfeit 40 *l.*[1]

By the 5 *Eliz.* the Crime of Felony without Clergy is extended to all who are found in the Company of *Egyptians*, or who shall conterfeit, transform, or disguise themselves as such.[2]

By 22 *Henry* VIII. A Vagabond taken begging shall be whipped, and then sworn to return to the Place of his Birth, or last Abode for three Years, there to put himself to Labour.[3]

By 27 *Henry* VIII. A valiant Beggar, or sturdy Vagabond, shall be whipped for the first Offence, and sent to the Place of his Birth, &c. for the second, the upper Part of the Gristle of his right Ear cut off; and if after that he be taken wandering in Idleness, &c. he shall be adjudged and executed as a Felon.[4]

I shall mention no more Acts (for several were made) between this and the 39th *Elizabeth*, when the former Acts concerning Vagabonds were all repealed, and the several Provisions against them were reduced to one Law.[5]

This Act, which contained many wholesome Provisions, remained in Force a long time, but at length was totally repealed by the 12th of Queen *Anne*; as this was again by the 13 *George* II. which last mentioned Statute stands now repealed by another made about six Years ago*.[6]

I have taken this short View of these repealed Laws, in order to enforce two Considerations. First, That the Removal of an Evil, which the Legislature have so often endeavoured to redress, is of great Importance to the Society. 2*dly*, That an Evil which so many subsequent Laws have failed of removing, is of a very stubborn Nature, and extremely difficult to be cured.

† Chap. 4.   * 17 *George* II. c. 5.

---

[7] 11 Hen. VII, c. 2.   [8] Gypsies.   [9] 22 Hen. VIII, c. 10. sect. 2.
[1] 1 & 2 Phil. & Mar., c. 4. sects. 3 & 2.   [2] 5 Eliz., c. 20. sect. 3.
[3] 22 Hen. VIII, c. 12.   [4] 27 Hen. VIII, c. 25.   [5] 39 Eliz., c. 4.
[6] The 13 Geo. II, c. 24. repealed 12 Annae, st. 2. c. 23, and was in turn repealed by the 17 Geo. II, c. 5 (the famous Vagrant Act of 1744, entitled 'An act to amend and make more effective the laws relating to rogues, vagabonds, and other idle and disorderly persons, and to houses of correction' (see *Enquiry*, below, p. 141 n. 5.

Here I hope to be forgiven, when I suggest, that the Law hath probably failed in this Instance, from Want of sufficient Direction to a single Point. As on a former Head, the Disease seems to be no other than *Idleness*, so here *Wandering* is the Cause of the Mischief, and that alone to which the Remedy should be applied. This, one would imagine, should be the chief, if not sole Intent of all Laws against Vagabonds, which might, in a synonymous Phrase, be called Laws against Wanderers. But as the Word itself hath obtained by vulgar Use a more complex Signification, so have the Laws on this Head had a more general View than to extirpate this Mischief; and by that means, perhaps, have failed of producing such an Effect.

I will therefore confine myself, as I have hitherto done on this Head, to the single Point of preventing the Poor from Wandering, one principal Cause of the Increase of Robbers; as it is the chief Means of preserving them from the Pursuit of Justice. It being impossible for any Thief to carry on his Trade long with Impunity among his Neighbours, and where not only his Person, but his Way of Life, must be well known.

Now to obviate this Evil, the Law, as it now stands, hath provided in a twofold Manner. 1. By way of Prevention; and, 2*dly*, By way of Remedy.

As to the first, the Statute of *Elizabeth* declares*, That no Person retained in Husbandry, or in any Art or Science in the Act mentioned†, after the Time of his Retainer is expired, shall depart out of any City, Parish, &c. nor out of the County, &c. to serve in any other, unless he have a Testimonial under the Seal of the City or Town Corporate, or of the Constable or other Head-Officer, and two other honest Housholders of the City, Town or Parish, where he last served, declaring his lawful Departure, and the Name of the Shire and Place where he served last. This Certificate is to be delivered to the Servant, and registred by the Parson for 2 *d*. and the Form of it is given in the Act.

And no Person is to be retained in any other Service, without shewing such Testimonial to the Chief Officer of the Town Corporate, and in every other Place to the Constable, Curate, &c. on Pain of Imprisonment, till he procure a Testimonial; and, if he cannot procure such Testimonial within 21 Days, he shall be whipped and treated like a Vagabond; so shall he be if found with a forged Testimonial. And those who receive him without shewing such Testimonial as aforesaid, forfeit 5 *l*.[7]

As to the 2d, the Law hath been extremely liberal in its Provisions. These are of two Sorts; 1. Simply compulsory; and, 2. Compulsory with Punishment. Under the former Head may be ranged the several Acts of

---

* 5 *Eliz*. c. 4. sect. 10. in Force though not in Use.
† *i. e.* in almost every Trade.

---

[7] 5 Eliz., c. 4. sect. 11.

Parliament relating to the Settlement, or rather Removal of the Poor.[8]

As these Statutes, tho' very imperfectly executed, are pretty generally known, (the Nation having paid some Millions to *Westminster-Hall* for their Knowledge of them) I shall mention them very slightly in this Place.[9]

The Statute of *Elizabeth*, together with the wise Execution of it, having made the Poor an intolerable Burden to the Public, Disputes began to arise between Parishes to whose Lot it fell to provide for certain Individuals: for the Laws for confining the Poor to their own Homes, being totally disregarded, these used to ramble wherever Whim or Conveniency invited them. The Overseers of one Parish were perhaps more liberal of the Parochial Fund than in another; or sometimes probably the Overseer of the Parish A was a Friend or Relation of a poor Person of the Parish of B, who did not choose to work. From some such Reason, the Poor of one Parish began to bring a Charge on another.

To remedy such Inconveniences, immediately after the Restoration*, a Statute was made, by which if any poor Man, likely to be chargeable, came to inhabit in a foreign Parish, unless in a Tenement of 10 *l.* a Year, the Overseers might complain to one Justice within 40 Days, and then two Justices were to remove the poor Person to the Place of his last legal Settlement.[1]

By a second Act†, the 40 Days are to be reckoned after Notice given in Writing to the Church-warden or Overseer by the poor Person, containing the Place of his Abode, Number of his Family, &c.

But by the same Statute, the executing a public annual Office during a Year, or being charged with, and paying to the public Taxes, &c. or (if unmarried and not having a Child) being lawfully hired into any Parish, and serving for

---

* 13 and 14 *Car.* II. c. 12.
† 3 and 4 *W.* and *M.* c. 11. See 1 *Jac.* II. c. 17.

[8] Fielding accurately suggests that the tendency of these laws in operation was to prevent people likely to need parish relief from gaining a legal settlement. Hence the machinery of 'removal' of a pauper to the parish where he had a legal settlement received much attention. Richard Burn (*The History of the Poor Laws* [London, 1764], p. 211) says that the laws concerning settlement and removal caused parish officers 'To keep an extraordinary look-out, to prevent persons coming to inhabit without certificates, and to fly to the justices to remove them; and if a man brings a certificate, then to caution all the inhabitants not to let him a farm of 10£ a year, and to take care to keep him out of all parish offices, to warn them, if they will hire *servants*, to hire them half yearly, or by the month, by the week, or by the day, rather than by any way that shall give them a settlement; or if they do hire them for a year, then to endeavour to pick a quarrel with them before the year's end, and so get rid of them.'

[9] A full account of the disastrous consequences, including costly lawsuits at Westminster Hall, of the laws concerning settlement and removal may be found in Marshall, *The English Poor*, pp. 161 ff. (see also Zirker, *Social Pamphlets*, pp. 15 ff.). Robert Foley's *Laws Relating to the Poor*, 2nd edn., (London, 1743) devotes 150 of its 280 pages to laws concerning settlement and removal. In *Joseph Andrews* (IV. iii. 284–5) Lawyer Scout's jargon indicates the incomprehensibility of these laws for the layman.

[1] A brief summary of 13 & 14 Car. II, c. 12. sect. 1 (1662).

one Year, or being bound Apprentice by Indenture, and inhabiting, &c. are all made good Settlements without Notice.[2]

By a third Statute[†], Persons bringing a Certificate signed by the Overseers, &c. and allowed by two Justices, cannot be removed till they become chargeable.

By a fourth[‡], no such Certificate Person shall gain a Settlement by any other Act, than by *bona fide*[3] taking a Lease of a Tenement of 10 *l. per Annum*, or by executing an annual Office.

By a fifth[||], no Apprentice or hired Servant of Certificate Person shall, by such Service or Apprenticeship, gain any Settlement.

By a sixth[§], no Person by any Purchase, of which the Consideration doth not *bona fide* amount to 30 *l.* shall gain any Settlement longer than while he dwells on such Purchase.

So much for these Laws of Removal, concerning which there are several other Acts of Parliament and Law Cases innumerable.[4]

And yet the Law itself is, as I have said, very imperfectly executed at this Day, and that for several Reasons.

1. It is attended with great Trouble: for as the Act of *Ch.* 2d *very wisely* requires two Justices, and the Court of King's Bench requires them both to be present together, (tho' they seldom are so) the Order of Removal is sometimes difficult to be obtained, and more difficult to be executed; for the Parish to which the Party is to be removed (perhaps with a Family) is often in a distant County; nay, sometimes they are to be carried from one End of the Kingdom to another.

2. It is often attended with great Expence, as well for the Reason aforesaid, as because the Parish removing is liable to an Appeal from the Parish to which the Poor is removed. This Appeal is sometimes brought by a wealthy and litigious Parish against a poor one, without any Colour of Right whatever.

3. The Removal is often ineffectual: for as the Appeal is almost certain to be brought, if an Attorney lives in the Neighbourhood; so is it almost as sure to succeed, if a Justice lives in the Parish. And as for Relief in the King's Bench, if the Justices of Peace will allow you to go thither, (for that they will not always do) the delay as well as the Cost is such, that the Remedy is often worse than the Disease.

For these Reasons, it can be no wonder that Parishes are not very forward

---

[†] 8 and 9 *W.* III. c. 30. [sect. 1].   [‡] 9 and 10 *W.* III. c. 11.
[||] 12 *Anne.* c. 18. [sect 2].   [§] *Geo.* I. c. 7. [9 *Geo.* I. c. 7. sect. 5.]

[2] Sects. 3, 6, 7, & 8. Section 2 of 1 Jac. II, c. 17 continues 13 & 14 Car. II, c. 12 for seven years. Sect. 3 stipulates 40 days after notice in writing.
[3] 'In or with good faith'.
[4] Fielding owned a book on such cases: *Cases and Resolutions in the King's Bench, on Settlements and Removals* (1732) (Baker, no. 13).

to put this Law in Execution. Indeed, in all Cases of Removal, the Good of the Parish, and not of the Public, is consulted; nay, sometimes the Good of an Individual only; and therefore the poor Man, who is capable of getting his Livelihood by his Dexterity at any Handicraft, and likely to do it by his Industry, is sure to be removed with his Family; especially if the Overseer, or any of his Relations, should be of the same Occupation; but the idle Poor, who threaten to rival no Man in his Business, are never taken any notice of, till they become actually chargeable; and if by Begging or Robbing they avoid this, as it is no Man's Interest, so no Man thinks it his Duty to apprehend them.

It cannot therefore be expected, that any Good of the Kind I am contending for, should be effected by this Branch of the Law; let us therefore, in the second Place, take a view of that which is expressly levelled at Vagrants, and calculated, as it appears, for the very Purpose of suppressing Wanderers.

To survey this Branch will be easy, as all the Laws concerning Vagrants are now reduced into one Act of Parliament; and it is the easier still, as this Act is very clearly penned, and (which is not always the Case) reduced to a regular and intelligible Method.[5]

By this Act then three Degrees of Offences are constituted:

First, Persons become idle and disorderly within the Act, by, 1. Threatning to run away and leave their Wives or Children to the Parish. 2. Unlawfully returning to the Place from whence they have been legally removed by the Order of two Justices, without bringing a Certificate, &c. 3. Living idle without Employment, and refusing to work for usual and common Wages. 4. By begging in their own Parishes.

Secondly, Persons by, 1. Going about as Patent-Gatherers, or Gatherers of Alms under Pretence of Loss by fire, or other Casualty; or, 2. Going about as Collectors for Prisons, Goals, or Hospitals. 3. Being Fencers and Bear-wards. 4. Or common Players of Interludes, &c. 5. Or Minstrels, Jugglers. 6. Pretending to be Gypsies, or wandering in such Habit. 7. Pretending to Physiognomy, or like crafty Science, &c. 8. Using any subtle Craft to deceive and impose on any of his Majesty's Subjects. 9. Playing or sitting at unlawful Games. 10. Running away, and leaving Wives or Children, whereby they become chargeable to any Parish. 11. Wandering abroad as petty Chapmen or Pedlars, not authorized by Law. 12. Wandering abroad and lodging in Ale-houses,[6] Barns, Out-houses, or in the open Air, not giving a good

---

[5] 17 Geo. II, c. 5 (see above, p. 137 n. 6). This Act is unusually precise and detailed (there are 34 sections). It distinguishes three categories of offenders ('idle and disorderly', 'rogues and vagabonds', and 'incorrigible rogues'), the members of which Fielding enumerates fully in the paragraphs following (sections 1, 2, and 4 of the Act). This Act was not amended until 1783.

[6] 'As the wind appeared still immoveable, my wife proposed my lying on shore. I presently agreed, tho' in defiance of an act of parliament, by which persons wandering abroad, and lodging in alehouses,

Account of themselves. 13. Wandering abroad and begging, pretending to be Soldiers, Mariners, seafaring Men, or pretending to go to work at Harvest. 14. Wandering abroad and begging, are to be deemed Rogues and Vagabonds.

Thirdly, 1. End-gatherers[7] offending against the 13 *George* I. entitled, *An Act for the better Regulation of the Woollen Manufactures*, &c. being convicted of such Offence; 2. Persons apprehended as Rogues and Vagabonds escaping, or, 3. refusing to go before a Justice, or, 4. refusing to be examined on Oath, or, 5. refusing to be conveyed by a Pass, or, 6. on Examination giving a false Account of themselves after Warning of the Punishment. 7. Rogues and Vagabonds escaping out of the House of Correction, &c. or, 8. those who having been punished as Rogues and Vagabonds, shall offend again as such, are made incorrigible Rogues.

Now as to the *first* of these three Divisions, it were to be wished, that Persons who are found in Ale-houses, Night-houses, &c. after a certain Hour at Night, had been included; for many such, tho' of very suspicious Characters, taken up at Privy Searches, fall not under any of the above Descriptions. Some of these I have known discharged, against whom capital Complaints have appeared, when it hath been too late. Why might not the Justice be entrusted with a Power of detaining any suspicious Person, who could produce no known Housekeeper, or one of Credit, to his Character, for three Days, within which Time he might, by Means of an Advertisement, be viewed by Numbers who have been lately robbed?[8] Some such have been, I know, confined upon an old Statute as Persons of evil Fame, with great Emolument to the Public.

But I come to the *second* Head, namely, of Vagabonds: And here I must observe, that *Wandering* is of itself made no Offence: so that unless such Wanderer be either a petty Chapman, or a Beggar or Lodger in Ale-houses, &c. he is not within the Act of Parliament.

Now, however useful this excellent Law may be in the Country, it will by no means serve the Purpose in this Town: for tho' most of the Rogues who infest the Public Roads and Streets, indeed almost all the Thieves in general, are Vagabonds in the true Sense of the Word, being Wanderers from their

---

are decreed to be rogues and vagabonds; and this too after having been very singularly officious in putting that law in execution' (*Voyage to Lisbon*, p. 84).

[7] Collectors of refuse wool.

[8] A notice in the *Covent-Garden Journal* for 12 June 1752 (no. 47) shows that such advertisements were made when possible: 'On Tuesday last the three Persons taken up on Suspicion of robbery on the Highway, were brought before the Justices to be re-examined; when, after all the *Pains* which the Justices had taken, and the Expence which they had been at in advertising, not one Prosecutor thought fit to appear. In a Nation where there is such Zeal for the Public in every Man's Bosom, it is wonderful there are no more Robbers.' A notice addressed 'To the Public' regularly appeared in the *Covent-Garden Journal* inviting victims of thieves to come to Fielding with 'the best Description they can of . . . Robbers, &c. with the Time and Place, and Circumstances of the Fact'.

lawful Place of Abode, very few of them will be proved Vagabonds within the Words of this Act of Parliament. These Vagabonds do indeed get their Livelihood by Thieving, and not as petty Beggars or petty Chapmen; and have their Lodging not in Ale-houses, &c. but in private Houses, where many of them resort together, and unite in Gangs, paying each 2 *d. per* Night for their Beds.

The following Account I have had from Mr. *Welch*, the High Constable of *Holbourn*; and none who know that Gentleman, will want any Confirmation of the Truth of it.

"That in the Parish of St. *Giles's* there are great Numbers of Houses set apart for the Reception of idle Persons and Vagabonds, who have their Lodgings there for Twopence a Night: That in the above Parish, and in St. *George, Bloomsbury,* one Woman alone occupies seven of these Houses, all properly accommodated with miserable Beds from the Cellar to the Garret, for such Twopenny Lodgers: That in these Beds, several of which are in the same Room, Men and Women, often Strangers to each other, lie promiscuously, the Price of a double Bed being no more than Threepence, as an Encouragement to them to lie together: That as these Places are thus adapted to Whoredom, so are they no less provided for Drunkenness, Gin being sold in them all at a Penny a Quartern; so that the smallest Sum of Money serves for Intoxication: That in the Execution of Search-Warrants, Mr. *Welch* rarely finds less than Twenty of these Houses open for the Receipt of all Comers at the latest Hours: That in one of these Houses, and that not a large one, he hath numbered 58 Persons of both Sexes, the Stench of whom was so intolerable, that it compelled him in a very short time to quit the Place."[9] Nay, I can add, what I myself once saw in the Parish of *Shoreditch,* where two little Houses were emptied of near seventy Men and Women; amongst whom was one of the prettiest Girls I had ever seen, who had been carried off by an *Irishman,* to consummate her Marriage on her Wedding-night, in a Room where several others were in Bed at the same time.[1]

If one considers the Destruction of all Morality, Decency and Modesty; the Swearing, Whoredom; and Drunkenness, which is eternally carrying on in these Houses, on the one hand, and the excessive Poverty and Misery of most of the Inhabitants on the other, it seems doubtful whether they are more the Objects of Detestation, or Compassion: for such is the Poverty of these Wretches, that, upon searching all the above Number, the Money

---

[9] The account from Welch which Fielding prints here is very close to what Welch wrote in a letter to the Duke of Newcastle in 1753 and appended to his pamphlet *A Proposal . . . to remove . . . Common Prostitutes from the Streets of this Metropolis* (London, 1758). The relevant pages are 52–3.

[1] 'Shoreditch has also numbers of them [cheap lodging houses]. A few years ago I assisted Mr. Henry Fielding in taking from under one roof upwards of seventy lodgers of both sexes' (Welch, ibid., p. 53).

found upon all of them (except the Bride, who, as I afterwards heard, had robbed her Mistress) did not amount to One Shilling; and I have been credibly informed, that a single Loaf hath supplied a whole Family with their Provisions for a Week. Lastly, if any of these miserable Creatures fall sick (and it is almost a Miracle, that Stench, Vermin, and Want should ever suffer them to be well) they are turned out in the Streets by their merciless Host or Hostess, where, unless some Parish Officer of extraordinary Charity relieves them, they are sure miserably to perish, with the Addition of Hunger and Cold to their Disease.

This Picture, which is taken from the Life, will appear strange to many; for the Evil here described, is, I am confident, very little known, especially to those of the better Sort. Indeed this is the only Excuse, and I believe the only Reason, that it hath been so long tolerated: for when we consider the Number of these Wretches, which, in the Out-skirts of the Town, amounts to a great many Thousands*, it is a Nuisance which will appear to be big with every moral and political Mischief. Of these the excessive Misery of the Wretches themselves, oppressed with Want, and sunk in every Species of Debauchery, and the Loss of so many Lives to the Public, are obvious and immediate Consequences. There are some more remote, which, however, need not be mentioned to the Discerning.

Among other Mischiefs attending this wretched Nuisance, the great Increase of Thieves must necessarily be one. The Wonder in fact is, that we have not a thousand more Robbers than we have; indeed, that all these Wretches are not Thieves, must give us either a very high Idea of their Honesty, or a very mean one of their Capacity and Courage.

Where then is the Redress? Is it not *to hinder the Poor from wandering*, and this by compelling the Parish and Peace Officers to apprehend such Wanderers or Vagabonds, and by empowering the Magistrate effectually to punish and send them to their Habitations? Thus if we cannot discover, or will not encourage any Cure for Idleness, we shall at least compel the Poor to starve or beg at home: for there it will be impossible for them to steal or rob, without being presently hanged or transported out of the way.

---

* Most of these are *Irish*, against the Importation of whom a severe Law was made in the Reign of *Hen.* VI. and many of the repealed Vagrant Acts contained a Clause for the same Purpose.[2]

[2] According to Welch, '*The unlimited wandering of the Poor of our own kingdom, and the uncontrouled importation of Irish vagabonds, are two great causes of the supply of rogues to this town*' (ibid., p. 48). The 'severe Law' is 1 Hen. VI, c. 3., which provides that all people born in Ireland (with specified exceptions) leave England within a month or forfeit goods and suffer imprisonment.

SECT. VII.

Of apprehending the Persons of Felons.[3]

I come now to a third Encouragement which the Thief flatters himself with, *viz.* in his Hopes of escaping from being apprehended.

Nor is this Hope without Foundation: How long have we known Highwaymen reign in this Kingdom after they have been publicly known for such? Have not some of these committed Robberies in open Day-light, in the Sight of many people, and have afterward rode solemnly and triumphantly through the neighbouring Towns without any Danger or Molestation. This happens to every Rogue who is become eminent for his Audaciousness, and is thought to be desperate; and is in a more particular Manner the Case of great and numerous Gangs, many of which have for a long time committed the most open Outrages in Defiance of the Law. Officers of Justice have owned to me that they have passed by such with Warrants in their Pockets against them without daring to apprehend them; and indeed they could not be blamed for not exposing themselves to sure Destruction: For it is a melancholy Truth, that at this very Day, a Rogue no sooner gives the Alarm, within certain Purlieus, than twenty or thirty armed Villains are found ready to come to his Assistance.[4]

On this Head the Law may seem not to have been very defective in its Cautions; *First*, by vesting not only the Officers of Justice, but every private Man, with Authority for securing these Miscreants, of which Authority it may be of Service to the Officers, as well as to the Public in general, to be more particularly informed.

---

[3] The unusually specific and detailed account in Section VII of laws pertaining to arrest and to the institution of hue and cry reflects Fielding's immediate and practical concerns as a Bow Street magistrate who, without a police force, was to effect the arrest of violent and often organized criminals. The account of these laws here is close to that in *A Treatise on the Office of Constable*, of which Sir John Fielding says, 'The late Henry Fielding . . . observing from daily Experience the great Difficulties and Dangers to which the Peace Officers were exposed in the Execution of their Office . . . resolved to draw up and publish a plain and complete Account of the Office of Constable, which he begun; but by a lingering Illness which put a Period to his valuable Life, he was prevented from perfecting this useful Work . . . I have carefully collected and revised the Observations found among my Brother's Manuscripts on this Subject, and have made such Additions as may possibly render the Work more useful' (*Extracts from . . . the Penal Laws*, a new edition [London, 1762], pp. 321–2).

As the preponderance of footnotes indicates, both accounts are reorderings of Hale who cites most of the Year Book reports and legal treatises Fielding cites. Consequently my annotations focus on clarifying Fielding's use of Hale. The citations to Dalton's *Country Justice* are from 'Warrants' and 'Arrest and Imprisonment' (chs. 169 and 170 in the 1727 edition).

[4] Both Cross (ii. 250 ff.) and Dudden (ii. 758 ff.) provide useful contemporary evidence of lawlessness at mid-century, and evidence is abundant. My impression is, however, that similar evidence might be marshalled for any period in the 18th century. Defoe remarked in 1729, for instance, that if crime continued to increase 'we shall not dare to stir out of our habitations; nay it will be well if they arrive not to the impudence of plundering our houses at noonday' ('Second Thoughts are Best', *Works* [London, 1841], xviii. 12).

First, By * *Westminster* I. Persons of evil Fame are to be imprisoned without Bail.[5] By the Statute of *Winchester†*, suspicious Night-walkers are to be arrested and detained by the Watch.[6] A Statute made in ‡5 *Ed*. III. reciting that many Manslaughters, Felonies, and Robberies had been done in Times past, enacts, That if any Person have an evil Suspicion of such Offenders, they shall be incontinently arrested by the Constable, and shall be delivered to the Bailiff of the Franchise, or to the Sheriff, to be kept in Prison till the coming of the Justices.[7] The 34 ‖*Edw*. III. gives Power to the Justices of Peace, *inter alia*, to enquire of Wanderers, and such as will not labour, and to arrest and imprison suspicious Persons, and to take Sureties of the good Behaviour of Persons of evil Fame, "to the Intent (says the Statute) that the People be not by such Rioters, &c. troubled nor endamaged, nor the Peace blemished, nor Merchants nor others passing by the Highways of the Realm disturbed, nor put in Peril by such Offenders."[8]

Secondly, By the Common law every Person who hath committed a Felony may be arrested and secured by any private Man present at the said Fact, though he hath no general nor particular Authority, *i. e.* though he be no Officer of Justice, nor have any Writ or Warrant for so doing; and such private Man may either deliver the Felon to the Constable, secure him in a Goal, or carry him before a Magistrate§. And if he refuses to yield, those who arrest may justify beating *him;[9] or, in case of absolute Necessity, killing him†.[1]

Nor is this Arrest merely allowed; it is enjoyned by Law, and the Omission without some good Excuse is a Misdemeanor punishable by Amercement or Fine and Imprisonment‡.[2]

Again every private Man may arrest another on Suspicion of Felony,

---

* *Westm.* I. chap. xv.	† *Winton.* chap. iv.	‡ *5 Edw.* III. c. xiv.
‖ 34 *Edw.* III. c. i.	§ *Hale's* Hist. P. C. vol. I. 587. v. II. 77.	* *Pult.* 10 a.
† *Hale's Hist. v. 1. 588.*	‡ *Hale*, vol. I. 588. v. II. 77, 76.	

[5] 3 Edw. I, c. 15.

[6] 3 Edw. I, st. 2.

[7] The preamble to this statute reads in part, 'And because there have been diverse Man-slaughters, Felonies, and Robberies done in time past, by People that be called Roberdsmen, Wastors, and Draw-latches . . .'.
'Incontinently': 'immediately' ('meintenant').

[8] A nearly verbatim quotation from the statute.

[9] Pulton, *de Pace*, 10b (not 10a): 'for when a felonie is committed, the Constable, or any others may arrest suspicious [*sic*] persons: and if any that is arrested will not yeeld, but assault him or them that do arrest him, they may justifie the beating of him, for that he doth resist the peace . . .'.

[1] Hale, i. 587–8. 'If A. commit a felony, B. who is a private person, may arrest him for that felony without any warrant, nay farther, if A. will not suffer himself to be taken, but either resists or flies so that he cannot be taken unless he be slain, if B. or any in assistance in that case of necessity kill him, it is no felony.'

[2] Hale, ii. 76: 'the apprehending of a felon is in many cases a duty and not arbitrary, even in cases of a private person without any other warrant, than what the law gives, and that the omission thereof is a misdemeanor, and punishable by fine or amercement.'

though he was not present at the Fact[†].[3] But then if the Party arrested should prove innocent, two Circumstances are necessary to justify the Arrest. 1st, A Felony must be actually committed; and 2dly, there must be a reasonable Cause of Suspicion[‡];[4] and common Fame hath been adjudged to be such Cause[‖].[5]

But in this latter Case my Lord *Hale* advises the private Person, if possible, to have recourse to the Magistrate and obtain his Warrant, and the Assistance of the [§]Constable; for this Arrest is not required by Law, nor is the Party punishable for neglecting it; and should the Person arrested, or endeavoured to be arrested, prove innocent, the Party arresting him, &c. will, in a great Measure, be answerable for the ill Consequence; which if it be the Death of the innocent Person occasioned by Force or Resistance, this will, at least, be Manslaughter; and if the other should be killed in the Attempt, this likewise will amount to Manslaughter only[*].

Again, any private Person may justify arresting a Felon pursued by Hue and Cry. This, as the Word imports, is a public Alarm raised all over the Country, in which the Constable is first to search his own Vill[6] or Division, and then to raise all the neighbouring Vills about who are to pursue the Felon with Horse and [†]Foot. And this Hue and Cry may either be after a Person certain, or on a Robbery committed where the Person is not known; and in the latter case, those who pursue it may take such Persons as they have probable Cause to suspect, [‡]Vagrants, &c.

This Method of Pursuit lies at the Common Law, and is mentioned by *Bracton*[‖];[7] and it is enforced by many Statutes, as by [§]*Westm*. 1. "All are to be ready at the Summons of the Sheriff, and at the Cry of the County, to arrest Felons as well within Franchises as without."[8] By 4 *Edw*. I. "Hue and Cry is

---

[†] *Lamb*. I. 2. c. 3. *Dalt*. 403. *Hale's* Hist. v. 1. 588.3 *Hen*. VII. c. 1.
[‡] *Hale's* Hist. v. 2. 80. [‖] *Dalt*. 407. 5 *H*. VII. 4, 5. [§] *Hale's* Hist. v. 2. 76.
[*] *Hale's* Hist. v. 2. 82.–3–4. [†] *Hale's* Hist. v. 2. 101.
[‡] *Hale's* Hist. v. 2. 103. [‖] *Lib*. 3. c. 1. [§] *Cap*. 9.

---

[3] Lambarde, *Eirenarcha* (see *Charge*, above, p. 7), bk. 2, ch. 3, contains much of what Fielding says concerning arrest but does not say that a private person may arrest another on suspicion of felony. 3 Hen. VII, c. 1. is concerned with arrest of murderers, but does not cover the case in point. Fielding's other citations here are apposite. When making a citizen's arrest, Dr Harrison insists, over the protest of an ignorant bailiff, that 'any man may arrest a felon without any warrant whatever' (*Amelia*, XII. vi. 324).
[4] Hale, ii. 78: 'But to make good such a justification of imprisonment, 1. There must be in fact a felony committed by some person . . . 2. The party, (if a private person,) that arrests, must suspect B. to be the felon. 3. He must have reasonable causes of such suspicion . . .'
[5] Hale, ii. 81: 'The third thing to be observed in this arrest by a private person upon suspicion is, that he hath a probable cause of suspicion.'
'And these probable causes are very many, as for instance common fame.' Hale cites the Year Book reports 5 Hen. VII, fo. 4b and 5 Hen. VII, fo. 5a.
[6] A feudal designation of a territorial unit roughly corresponding to the Anglo-Saxon tithing.
[7] Hale (i. 99) cites and quotes the pertinent passage in Bracton.
[8] 3 Edw. I, c. 9. Cited and quoted by Hale, ii. 98.

ordered to be levied for all Murders, Burglaries, Men slain, or in Peril to be slain, and all are to follow it."⁹ And lastly, the Statute of *Winton* enacts as we have seen before.¹

And this Pursuit may be raised, 1. By a private Person. 2. By the Country without an Officer. 3. By an Officer without a Warrant. 4. By the Warrant of a Magistrate.² And this last, if it can be obtained, is the safest Way: for then all who assist are enabled by the Statutes 7 and 21 *Jac.* to plead the general Issue‖.³

The Common Law so strictly enjoined this Pursuit, that if any Defect in raising it lay in the Lord of the Franchise, the Franchise should be seized into the King's Hands; and if the Neglect lay in the Bailiff, he should have a heavy Fine, and a Year's Imprisonment, or suffer two Years Imprisonment without a Fine§. And now by a very late** Statute, "if any Constable, Headborough, &c. of the Hundred where any Robberies shall happen, shall refuse or *neglect* to make Hue and Cry after the Felons with the utmost Expedition, as soon as he shall receive Notice thereof, he shall for every such Refusal and Neglect forfeit 5*l.* half to the King and half to the Informer."⁴

Now Hue and Cry is of three different Kinds: 1. Against a Person certain by Name. 2. Against a Person certain by Description. 3. On a Robbery, Burglary, &c. where the Person is neither known, nor capable of being described.⁶

When a Hue and Cry is raised, every private Man is not only justified in pursuing; but may be obliged by Command of the Constable to pursue the Felon, and is punishable, if he disobey, by Fine and Imprisonment*. And in this Case whether a Felony was committed or not, or whether the Person arrested (provided he be the Person named or described by the Hue and Cry) be guilty or innocent, or of evil or good Fame, the Arrest is lawful and justifiable, and he who raised the Hue and Cry is alone to answer for the Justice of it†.

In this Pursuit likewise the Constable may search suspected Houses, if the

---

‖ *Hale's* Hist. v. 1. 465. v. 2. 99, 100.   § *Fleta*, I. 1. c. 24. *ad Init.*⁵
** 8 *Geo.* II. c. 16.   * *Hale's* Hist. v. 1. 588. v. 2. 104.
† 29 *Ed.* III. 39. 35 *Hen.* IV. Pl. 24.⁷ *Hale's* Hist. v. 2. 101–2.

---

⁹ 4 Edw. I, stat. 2. Cited and quoted by Hale, ii. 98.

¹ See above, p. 136 n. 3. Cited and quoted by Hale, ii. 98–9.

² Each of these points is pursued in the pages following.

³ Hale (ii. 100) cites the statutes of 7 & 21 Jac. I. 'To plead the general Issue': to enter a plea of not guilty rather than a special plea in response to some part of the indictment.

⁴ Sollom Emlyn, Hale's editor, quotes 8 Geo. II, c. 16 (ii. 99, n. b.). Fielding's quotation appears to be an abridgment of Emlyn's. This Act attempts to make hue and cry, which has 'been so much neglected and delayed that felons have had time to make their escape', more effective.

⁵ For Fleta see above, p. 134 n. 2. *ad Init.*: 'toward the beginning'.

⁶ These categories are used in *A Treatise on the Office of Constable*, p. 348. They derive from Hale, ii. 102–3.

⁷ Trin. 29 Edw. III, fo. 39 (cit. Hale, ii. 102). Henry IV reigned 14 years: '35 Hen. IV' is an error.

Doors be open; but breaking the Door will not be justifiable, unless the Felon be actually in the House; nor even then unless Admittance hath been first demanded and denied[‡]. And what the Constable may do himself will be justifiable by any other in his Assistance, at least, by his Command[‖]. Indeed a private Person may justify the Arrest of an Offender by the Command of a Peace Officer; for he is bound to be aiding and assisting to such Officer, is punishable for his Refusal, and is consequently under the Protection of the Law[§].

Lastly, a private Person may arrest a Felon by Virtue of a Warrant directed to him: for though he is not bound to execute such Warrant, yet if he doth, it is good and justifiable[**].

Thirdly, Officers of public Justice may justify the Arrest of a Felon by Virtue of their Office, without any Warrant. Whatever therefore a private Person may do as above, will certainly be justifiable in them.

And as the arresting Felons, &c. is more particularly their Duty, and their Fine will be heavier for the Neglect, so will their Protection by the Law be the greater: For if, in arresting those that are *probably suspected*, the Constable should be killed, it is Murder; on the other Hand, if Persons pursued by these Officers for Felony, or *justifiable Suspicion* thereof, shall resist or fly from them; or being apprehended shall rescue themselves, resist, or fly; so that they cannot *otherwise* be apprehended or re-apprehended, and are *of Necessity* slain, it is no Felony in the Officers, or in their Assistants, tho' possibly the Parties killed are innocent; for by resisting the King's Authority in his Officers; they draw their own Blood on themselves[*].

Again, To take a Felon or suspected Felon, the Constable without any Warrant may break open the Door. But to justify this, he must shew; 1. That the Felon, &c. was in the House. 2. That his Entry was denied. 3. That it was denied after Demand and Notice that he was Constable[†].

Lastly, A Felon may be apprehended by Virtue of a Warrant issuing from a Magistrate lawfully authorized; in the Execution of which the Officer hath the same Power, and will, at least, have the same Protection by Law as in the Arrest *Virtute Officii*. And this Warrant, if it be specially directed to him, the Constable may execute in any Part within the Jurisdiction of the Magistrate; but he is only obliged to execute it within the Division for which he is Constable, &c.[1]

[‡] Ib. 102, 103.   [‖] Ib. 104.   [§] Pult. 6. 15.[8] Hale's Hist. v. 2. 86.
[**] Dalt. 408. Hale's Hist. v. 2. 86.[9]
[*] Dalt. 409. 13 Ed. IV. 4, & 9. 5 to 92.[2] Hale's Hist. v. 2. 86. 90, 91.
[†] Ib. v. 1. 581. v. 2. 110.[3]

[8] Pulton, *de Pace*, fo. 6. sect. 15.
[9] The reference to Hale should be to i. 581; and ii. 86 & 110.   [1] Hale, i. 582; ii. 110–11.
[2] Hale (i. 581 and ii. 91) cites the Year Book report 13 Edw. IV, fo. 9a. '5 to 92': unidentified; an unlikely citation.
[3] The reference should be to Hale, ii. 90.

In the Execution of a Warrant for Felony, the Officer may break open the Doors of the Felon or of any Person where he is concealed; and the breaking the Doors of the Felon is lawful at all Events, but in breaking those of a Stranger the Officer acts at his Peril: for he will be a Trespasser if the Felon should not be there*.

Such are the Powers which the Law gives for the apprehending Felons (for as to the particular Power of Sheriffs and Coroners, and the Process of superior Courts, they may well be passed by in this Place.) Again, these Powers we see are enforced with Penalties; so that not only every Officer of Justice, but every private Person is obliged to arrest a known Felon, and may be punished for the Omission.

Nor doth the Law stop here. The apprehending such Felons is not only authorized and enjoined, but even encouraged, with Impunity to Persons guilty themselves of Felony, and with Reward to others.

By 3 and 4 of †*William* and *Mary*, Persons guilty of Robbery in the Highway, Fields, &c. who, being out of Prison, shall discover any two Offenders to be convicted of such Robbery, are entitled to his Majesty's Pardon of such Robberies, &c. as they shall have then committed.[4]

By 10 and 11 of ‡*William* III. this is extended to Burglary, and such Felonies as are mentioned in the Act.

By the same Act all Persons who shall apprehend a Felon for privately stealing Goods to the Value of 5 s. out of Shop, Warehouse, Coach-house, or Stable, by Night or by Day (provided the Felon be convicted thereof) shall be entitled to a Certificate which may be assigned once, discharging such Apprehender or his Assignee from all Parochial Offices in the Parish of Ward where such Felony was committed. This Certificate is to be enrolled by the Clerk of the Peace, and cannot be assigned after it hath been used.[6]

If any Man be killed by such House-breaker, &c. in the Attempt to apprehend him, his Executors or Administrators shall be entitled to such Certificate.[7]

By the 3 and 4 of *W*. and *M*. whoever shall apprehend and prosecute to Conviction any Robber on the Highway, shall receive of the Sheriff 40 *l*. within a Month after the Conviction for every Offender; and in case of the Death or Removal of the Sheriff, the Money to be paid by the succeeding Sheriff within a Month after the Demand and Certificate brought. The Sheriff on default forfeits double the Sum, to be recovered of him by the Party, his Executors, &c.

---

* *Hale's* Hist. v. 1. 582. v. 2. 117. 5 Co. 91 b.[5]   † Chap. 8.
‡ Chap. 23.   * Chap. 8. *ubi supra.*

---

[4] The citation should be to 4 & 5 Wil. & Mar., c. 8. sect. 7.
[5] Hale (ii. 117) cites Coke's Fifth Report, 91b.
[6] 10 & 11 Wil. III, c. 23. sect. 2.   [7] 10 & 11 Wil. III, c. 23. sect. 4.

And if the Person be killed in this Attempt by any such Robber, the Executors of such Person, &c. are entitled to the Reward, under the like Penalty.

Again, by the same Act the Horse, Furniture, Arms, Money, or other Goods, taken with such Highwaymen, are given to the Apprehender who shall prosecute to Conviction, notwithstanding the Right or Title of his Majesty, any Body Politic or Lord of Franchise, or of those who lent or let the same to hire to such Robber, with a saving only of the Right of such Persons from whom such Horses, &c. were feloniously taken.[8]

By a Statute of Queen *Anne*, the 40 *l.* Reward is extended to Burglary and House-breaking.[9]

But tho' the Law seems to have been sufficiently provident on this Head; there is still great Difficulty in carrying its Purpose into Execution, arising from the following Causes.

First, With Regard to private Persons, there is no Country, I believe, in the World, where that vulgar Maxim so generally prevails, that what is the Business of every Man is the Business of no Man;[1] and for this plain Reason, that there is no Country in which less Honour is gained by serving the Public. He therefore who commits no Crime against the Public, is very well satisfied with his own Virtue; far from thinking himself obliged to undergo any Labour, expend any Money, or encounter any Danger on such Account.

2dly, The People are not entirely without Excuse from their Ignorance of the Law: For so far is the Power of apprehending Felons, which I have above set forth, from being universally known, that many of the Peace Officers themselves do not know that they have any such Power, and often from Ignorance refuse to arrest a known Felon 'till they are authorized by a Warrant from a Justice of Peace. Much less then can the compulsory Part to the private Persons carry any Terror of a Penalty of which the Generality of Mankind are totally ignorant; and of inflicting which they see no Example.

Thirdly, So far are Men from being animated with the Hopes of public Praise to apprehend a Felon, that they are even discouraged by the Fear of Shame. The Person of the Informer is in Fact more odious than that of the Felon himself; and the Thief-catcher is in Danger of worse Treatment from the Populace than the Thief.[2]

Lastly, As to the Reward, I am afraid that the Intention of the Legislature is very little answered: For not to mention that the Prosecutor's Title to it is

---

[8] 4 & 5 Wil. & Mar., c. 8. sects. 2 & 6.   [9] 5 Annae, c. 31. sects. 1 & 2.

[1] Cf. Defoe's *Everybody's Business is Nobody's Business* (London, 1725).

[2] The notoriety of Jonathan Wild, who in 1720 publicly proclaimed himself 'Thief-taker general of Great Britain and Ireland', intensified public hatred of informers. John Fielding (in *A Plan for Preventing Robberies within Twenty Miles of London* [London, 1755]) attempted to distinguish between the legitimate thief-takers whom Henry and he employed and criminals like McDaniel who informed on innocent parties for the sake of the reward. See General Introduction, p. lvii.

too often defeated by the foolish Lenity of Juries, who by acquitting the Prisoner of the Burglary and finding him guilty of the simple Felony only, or by finding the Goods to be less than the Value of 5 s. both often directly contrary to Evidence, take the Case entirely out of the Act of Parliament; and sometimes even when the Felon is properly convicted, I have been told that the Money does not come so easily and fully to the Pockets of those who are entitled to it as it ought.[3]

With Regard to the first and fourth of these Objections, I chuse to be silent: To prescribe any Cure for the former, I must enter into Disquisitions very foreign to my present Purpose; and for the Cure of the latter, when I consider in whose Power it is to remedy it, a bare Hint will, I doubt not, suffice.

The second Objection, namely, the Excuse of Ignorance, I have here endeavoured to remove by setting forth the Law at large.

The third therefore only remains, and to that I shall speak more fully, as the Opinion on which it is founded is of the most pernicious Consequence to the Society; for what avail the best of Laws, if it be a Matter of Infamy to contribute towards their Execution? The Force of this Opinion may be seen in the following Instance. We have a Law by which every Person who drives more than six Horses in a Waggon forfeits as many Horses as are found to exceed that Number.[4] This Law is broken every Day, and generally with Impunity: For though many Men yearly venture and lose their Lives by stealing Horses, yet there are very few who dare seize a Horse, where the Law allows and encourages it, when by such Seizure he is to acquire the Name of an Informer: So much worse is this Appellation in the Opinion of the Vulgar than that of Thief; and so much more prevalent is the Fear of popular Shame than of Death.

This absurd Opinion seems to have first arisen from the Statute of 18* *Eliz.* entitled, *An Act to redress Disorders in common Informers.* By this Statute it appears, that very wicked Uses had been made of penal Statutes by these Informers, whom my Lord *Coke* calls[†] *Turbidum Hominum Genus*; and says, "That they converted many penal Laws which were obsolete, and in time grown impossible or inconvenient to be performed, into Snares to vex and intangle the Subject."[5]

By the Statute itself it appears, that it was usual at that Time among these Persons to extort Money of ignorant and fearful People by the Terror of

---

* Chap. 5.   † 3 Inst. c. 87.

[3] In 1754 Fielding supported the petition (which was rejected) of 'his six mirmidons' for proper disbursement of a reward for capturing highwaymen (State Papers 36/125, letters 4, 22 [cit. Radzinowicz, iii. 25]).

[4] 5 Geo. I, c. 12. sect. 1.

[5] *III Inst.* 192. *Turbidum Hominum Genus*: 'a race of disorderly men'.

some penal Law; for the Breach of which the Informer either instituted a Process, or pretended to institute a Process, and then brought the timorous Party to a Composition.[6]

This Offence therefore was by this Act made a high Misdemeanour, and punished with the Pillory.

Now who that knows any thing of the Nature or History of Mankind, doth not easily perceive here a sufficient Foundation for that Odium to all Informers which hath since become so general: For what is more common than from the Abuse of any thing to argue against the Use of it, or to extend obloquy from Particulars to Universals?

For this the common Aptitude of Men to Scandal will sufficiently account; but there is still another and stronger Motive in this Case, and that is the Interest of all those who have broken or who intend to break the Laws. Thus the general Cry being once raised against Prosecutors on penal Laws, the Thieves themselves have had the Art and Impudence to join it, and have put their Prosecutors on the Footing of all others: Nay I much question whether in the Acceptation of the Vulgar, a Thief-catcher be not a more odious and contemptible Name than even that of Informer.

Nothing, I am sensible, is more vain than to encounter popular Opinion with Reason; nor more liable to Ridicule than to oppose general Contempt, and yet I will venture to say, that if to do Good to Society be laudable, so is the Office of a Thief-catcher; and if to do this Good at the extreme Hazard of your Life be honourable, then is this Office honourable. True, it may be said; but he doth this with a View to a Reward. And doth not the Soldier and the Sailor venture his Life with the same View? For who, as a Great Man lately said, serves the Public for nothing?[7]

I know what is to be my Fate in this Place, or what would happen to one who should endeavour to prove that the Hangman was a great and an honourable Employment.[8] And yet I have read in *Tournefort*,[9] of an Island in

---

[6] 18 Eliz., c. 5. sect. 3.

[7] Cf. *TP* no. 17, p. 153, 'It was the Saying of a great Man, *That no one served the Public for nothing.*' The 'great Man' presumably is Walpole. However, in a note to *The Vernoniad* (Henley, xv. 51), Fielding relates a story from Aulus Gellius, the sense of which is nearly apposite.

[8] The argument would have been particularly unconvincing in 1751. The public executioner was John Thrift, who in 1750 had been imprisoned in Newgate for killing a man in a quarrel. He was pardoned. See Phillips, *Mid-Georgian London*, pp. 260 and 104. From a similar point of view, Fielding praises the gallows as 'a certain wooden Edifice' which 'is, or at least might be, of more Benefit to Society than almost any other public erection' (*Tom Jones*, VII. xv. 391).

[9] Joseph Pitton de Tournefort (1656–1708), French botanist whose system of classification was superseded by Linnaeus. His *A Voyage into the Levant* was translated into English (London, 1718) in two volumes. The description of the islands of the Greek Archipelago is in vol. i. Fielding is remembering a passage from ii. 232: 'The Executioner in *Georgia* is very rich, and People of Quality exercise the Office: it is so far from being counted infamous, as in all other parts of the World, that here it reflects Glory upon a whole Family. They will boast what a number of Hang-men they have had among their Ancestors; and they build upon this Principle that nothing is so noble as executing Justice, without which no man could live safe. A Maxim worthy the Georgians!' Fielding cites this

the *Archipelago*, where the Hangman is the first and highest Officer in the State. Nay in this Kingdom the Sheriff himself (who was one of the most considerable Persons in his County) is in Law the Hangman, and Mr. *Ketch*[1] is only his Deputy.

If to bring Thieves to Justice be a scandalous Office, what becomes of all those who are concerned in this Business, some of whom are rightly thought to be among the most honourable Officers in Government? If on the contrary this be, as it surely is, very truly honourable, why should the Post of Danger in this Warfare alone be excluded from all Share of Honour?

To conclude a Matter, in which tho' serious, I will not be too tedious: What was the great *Pompey* in the Piratic War*? What were *Hercules*, *Theseus*,[2] and other the Heroes of old, *Deorum in Templa recepti*[4]—Were they not the most eminent of Thief-catchers?

SECT. VIII.

Of the Difficulties which attend Prosecutions.

I now come to a fourth Encouragemant which greatly holds up the Spirits of Robbers, and which they often find to afford no deceitful Consolation; and this is drawn from the Remissness of Prosecutors, who are often,

  1. Fearful, and to be intimidated by the Threats of the Gang; or,

  2. Delicate, and cannot appear in a public Court; or,

  3. Indolent, and will not give themselves the Trouble of a Prosecution; or,

  4. Avaricious, and will not undergo the Expence of it; nay perhaps find their Account in compounding the Matter; or,

  5. Tender-hearted, and cannot take away the Life of a Man; or,

Lastly, Necessitous, and cannot really afford the Cost, however small, together with the Loss of Time which attends it.

The first and second of these are too absurd, and the third and fourth too infamous to be reasoned with. But the two last deserve more particular

---

* *Cicero* in his Oration *pro Lege Manilia* calls this, if I remember rightly, *Bellum Turpe*; but speaks of the Extirpation of these Robbers as of the greatest of all *Pompey's* Exploits.[3]

---

passage more fully and accurately in the *True Patriot* (no. 20), p. 173. Tournefort's book is not in Baker.

  [1] A generic term for the hangman, after the executioner of that name (d. 1686). In *TP* no. 20 (p. 173), justifying the execution of Jacobite rebels, Fielding argues for the dignity and importance of the office of hangman, cites Tournefort, and mentions Jack Ketch. He also praises the office of hangman in the *Champion* for 27 Mar. 1740, pp. 258–9.

  [2] Hercules recovered his stolen cattle and executed the thief, Cacus (who elicits Wild's sympathy in *Jonathan Wild*, I. iii. 10); Theseus slew the highwayman Periphetes of Epidaurus, whose custom was to kill all travelers with his iron club.

  [3] Cicero, *On the Manilian Law*, xi. 31. Pompey's defeat of the pirates is the climactic item in a series of his victories celebrated by Cicero.

  [4] Horace, *Epistles*, ii. 1. 6: 'Welcomed into the temples of the gods' (Loeb). Spoken of heroes whose earthly rewards matched not their desert.

Notice, as the fifth is an Error springing originally out of a good Principle in the Mind, and the sixth is a Fault in the Constitution very easily to be remedied.

With Regard to the former of these, it is certain, that a tender-hearted and compassionate Disposition, which inclines Men to pity and feel the Misfortunes of others, and which is, even for its own Sake, incapable of involving any Man in Ruin and Misery, is of all Tempers of Mind the most amiable; and tho' it seldom receives much Honour, is worthy of the highest.⁵ The natural Energies of this Temper are indeed the very Virtues principally inculcated in our excellent Religion; and those, who because they are natural, have denied them the Name of Virtues, seem not, I think, to be aware of the direct and impious Tendency of a Doctrine that denies all Merit to a Mind which is naturally, I may say necessarily, good.⁶

Indeed the Passion of Love or Benevolence whence this admirable Disposition arises, seems to be the only human Passion that is in itself simply and absolutely good; and in *Plato's* Commonwealth⁷ or (which is more) in a Society acting up to the Rules of *Christianity*, no Danger could arise from the highest Excess of this Virtue; nay the more liberally it was indulged, and the more extensively it was expanded, the more would it contribute to the Honour of the Individual, and to the Happiness of the whole.

But as it hath pleased God to permit human Societies to be constituted in a different Manner, and Knaves to form a Part, (a very considerable one, I am afraid) of every Community, who are ever lying in wait to destroy and ensnare the honest Part of Mankind, and to betray them by means of their own Goodness, it becomes the good-natured and tender-hearted Man to be watchful over his own Temper; to restrain the Impetuosity of his Benevolence, carefully to select the Objects of this Passion, and not by too unbounded and indiscriminate an Indulgence to give the Reins to a Courser, which will infallibly carry him into the Ambuscade of the Enemy.⁸

---

⁵ For benevolence, good-nature, and related 'doctrine' in Fielding, see Martin Battestin, *The Moral Basis of Fielding's Art* (Middletown, Conn., 1959); Henry Knight Miller, *Essays on Fielding's 'Miscellanies'* (Princeton, NJ, 1961), pp. 54–88; *Tom Jones*, I. iii. 39 n. 1; and R. S. Crane, 'Suggestions toward a Genealogy of the "Man of Feeling"', *ELH* 1 (1934), 205–30.

⁶ Fielding most often associates the 'rigoristic' ethic (see F. B. Kaye, Introduction to the *Fable of the Bees* [I. xlvii ff.]) that denies the name of virtue to instinctive goodness with Mandeville. Booth, though not a Mandevillian, seems to confess this error: 'Indeed, I never was a rash disbeliever; my chief doubt was founded on this—that, as men appeared to me to act entirely from their passions, their actions could have neither merit nor demerit' (*Amelia*, XII. v. 313). Dr Harrison's brief response implies that the validity of Christian ethics is confirmed by its congruence with our passional nature. Cf. *Tom Jones*, VI. i. 268–9 & n. 2.

⁷ The nobleman whom Dr Harrison asks to support Booth's merited claim to a commission cynically accepts the lapsed society Fielding regrets here and in the following paragraph: ' "This [to reward merit] is all mere Utopia," cries his lordship; "the chimerical system of Plato's commonwealth, with which we amused ourselves at the university; politics which are inconsistent with the state of human affairs" ' (*Amelia*, XI. ii. 248).

⁸ For the necessity of prudence, or practical wisdom ('the great, useful and uncommon Doctrine' of

Our Saviour himself inculcates this Prudence among his Disciples, telling them, that he *sent them forth like Sheep among Wolves: Be ye therefore*, says he, *wise as Serpents, but innocent as Doves.*[9]

For Want of this Wisdom, a benevolent and tender-hearted Temper very often betrays Men into Errors not only hurtful to themselves, but highly prejudicial to the Society. Hence Men of invincible Courage, and incorruptible Integrity, have sometimes falsified their Trust; and those, whom no other Temptation could sway, have paid too little Regard to the Sanction of an Oath, from this Inducement alone. Hence likewise the Mischief which I here endeavour to obviate, hath often arisen; and notorious Robbers have lived to perpetrate future Acts of Violence, through the ill-judging Tenderness and Compassion of those who could and ought to have prosecuted them.[1]

To such a Person I would suggest these Considerations:

First, As he is a good Man, he should consider, that the principal Duty which every Man owes, is to his Country, for the Safety and Good of which all Laws are established; and therefore his Country requires of him to contribute all that in him lies to the Execution of those Laws. Robbery is an Offence not only against the Party robbed, but against the Public, who are therefore entitled to Prosecution; and he who prevents or stifles such the Prosecution, is no longer an innocent Man, but guilty of a high Offence against the Public Good.

Secondly, As he is a good-natured Man, he will behold all Injuries done by one Man to another with Indignation. What *Cicero* says of a Pirate, is as true of a Robber, that he is *hostis humani generis*;[2] and if so, I am sure every good-natured Man must be an Enemy to him. To desire to save these Wolves in Society, may arise from Benevolence; but it must be the Benevolence of a Child or a Fool, who, from Want of sufficient Reason, mistakes the true Objects of his Passion, as a Child doth when a Bugbear appears to him to be the Object of Fear. Such Tenderheartedness is indeed Barbarity, and

---

Tom Jones [XII. viii 652]), especially for the good-natured man, see Battestin, 'Fielding's Definition of Wisdom: Some Functions of Ambiguity and Emblem in *Tom Jones*', *ELH* 35 (1968), 118–217; and *Tom Jones*, I. iii. 39 & n. 1.

[9] Matthew 10: 16.

[1] This passage exemplifies the moral simplifications that distinguish Fielding's social pamphlets from his fiction. In the latter judgement of behavior is influenced by comprehension of motive. Consequently, Tom releases the highwayman Enderson. Allworthy, condemning Tom's mercy to Black George as 'Weakness' and 'Pernicious to Society', has none the less 'applied to the Judge on the Behalf of such [highwaymen] as have had any mitigating Circumstance in their Case' unless 'Dishonesty is attended with any blacker Crime, such as *Cruelty*, Murder, *Ingratitude*, or the like' (XVIII. xi. 969; my italics).

[2] An enemy to the human race. The phrase is found in Coke, *III Inst.* 113, and may derive from Cicero, *De Officiis*, III. xxix. 107: 'pirata . . . est . . . communis hostis omnium'. In *JJ* no. 20 (p. 237), Fielding quotes the phrase, attributing it to Hale, who did in fact use it (in *Historia Plactitorum Coronae*, i. 455).

resembles the meek Spirit of him who would not assist in blowing up his Neighbour's House, to save a whole City from the Flames.[3] "It is true," said a late learned Chief Justice*, in a Trial for Treason, "here is the Life of a Man in the Case, but then you (speaking to the Jury) must consider likewise the Misery and Desolation, the Blood and Confusion, that must have happened, had this taken Effect; and put one against the other, I believe that Consideration which is on Behalf of the King will be much the stronger."[4] Here likewise is the Life of a Man concerned; but of what Man? Why, of one who being too lazy to get his Bread by Labour, or too voluptuous to content himself with the Produce of that Labour, declares War against the Properties, and often against the Persons of his Fellow Subjects; who deprives his Countrymen of the Pleasure of travelling with Safety, and of the Liberty of carrying their Money or their ordinary Conveniencies with them; by whom the Innocent are put in Terror, affronted and alarmed with Threats and Execrations, endangered with loaded Pistols, beat with Bludgeons and hacked with Cutlasses, of which the Loss of Health, of Limbs, and often of Life, is the Consequence; and all this without any Respect to Age, or Dignity, or Sex. Let the good-natured Man, who hath any Understanding, place this Picture before his Eyes, and then see what Figure in it will be the Object of his Compassion.

I come now to the last Difficulty which obstructs the Prosecution of Offenders; namely, the extreme Poverty of the Prosecutor. This I have known to be so absolutely the Case, that the poor Wretch who hath been bound to prosecute, was under more Concern than the Prisoner himself. It is true that the necessary Cost on these Occasions is extremely small; two Shillings, which are appointed by Act of Parliament for drawing the Indictment, being, I think, the whole which the Law requires; but when the Expence of Attendance, generally with several Witnesses, sometimes during several Days together, and often at a great Distance from the Prosecutor's

---

* Lord Chief Justice *Pratt*.

[3] With considerable point, J. L. and B. Hammond set beside this passage from Fielding ('To desire to save these Wolves . . . from the Flames') the following passage from *Rambler*, no. 114: 'He who knows not [answered Dr Johnson] how often rigorous laws produce total impunity, and how many crimes are concealed and forgotten for fear of hurrying the offender to that state in which there is no repentance, has conversed very little with mankind. And whatever epithets of reproach or contempt this compassion may incur from those who confound cruelty with firmness, I know not whether any wise man would wish it less powerful, or less extensive' ('Poverty, Crime, Philanthropy' in *Johnson's England*, i. 316).

[4] Sir John Pratt (1657–1725) summing up for the crown in the trial of Christopher Layer for high treason in Nov. 1722 (the comment is preserved in *State Trials*, xvi. 299). Layer was convicted, executed, and his head set on Temple Bar. A well-known trial because of its connection with the Jacobite conspiracy of Bishop Atterbury and because of the notorious harshness of the Bench to Layer (he was kept loaded with chains though painfully ill). For Layer see R. W. Ketton-Cremer, *A Norfolk Gallery* (London, 1948), pp. 125–48. Pratt's son, Charles, the first Earl Camden, was with Fielding at Eton and later on the Western circuit. He was a subscriber to the *Miscellanies*.

Home; I say, when these Articles are summed up, and the Loss of Time added to the Account, the whole amounts to an Expence which a very poor Person, already plundered by the Thief, must look on with such Horrour (if he should not be absolutely incapable of the Expence) that he must be a Miracle of Public Spirit, if he doth not rather choose to conceal the Felony, and sit down satisfied with his present Loss; but what shall we say, when (as is very common in this Town) he may not only receive his own again, but be farther rewarded, if he will agree to compound it?

Now how very inconsiderable would be the whole Cost of this Suit either to the County or the Nation; If the Public, to whom the Justice of Peace gives his whole Labour on this Head *gratis*, was to defray the Cost of such Trials (by a kind of *forma pauperis* Admission) the Sum would be so trivial, that nothing would be felt but the good Consequences arising from such a Regulation?[5]

I shall conclude this Head with the Words of my Lord *Hale*: "It is (says he) a great Defect in the Law, to give Courts of Justice no Power to allow Witnesses against Criminals their Charges; whereby," says he, "many poor Persons grow weary of their Attendance, or bear their own Charges therein, to their great Hindrance and Loss."[6]

SECT. IX.

Of the TRIAL *and* CONVICTION *of* FELONS.

But if notwithstanding all the Rubs which we have seen to lie in the Way, the Indictment is found, and the Thief brought to his Trial, still he hath sufficient Hopes of escaping, either from the Caution of the Prosecutor's Evidence, or from the Hardiness of his own.

In Street Robberies the Difficulty of convicting a Criminal is extremely great. The Method of discovering these is generally by means of one of the Gang, who being taken up, perhaps for some other Offence, and, thinking himself in Danger of Punishment, chooses to make his Peace at the Expence of his Companions.

But when, by means of his Information, you are made acquainted with the whole Gang, and have, with great Trouble, and often with great Danger, apprehended them, how are you to bring them to Justice? for though the Evidence of the Accomplice be ever so positive and explicit, nay ever so connected and probable, still, unless it be corroborated by some other Evidence, it is not sufficient.[7]

---

[5] The 25 Geo. II, c. 36. sect. 11 (1752) empowered the court, after conviction of the defendant, to reimburse the expences of the prosecutor. [*in*]*forma pauperis*: 'in the character or manner of a papuer' (a legal term).

[6] Hale, ii. 282.

[7] 'I have often spent whole days, nay sometimes whole nights, especially when there was any

Now how is this corroborating Evidence to be obtained in this Case? Street Robberies are generally committed in the dark, the Persons on whom they are committed are often in Chairs and Coaches, and if on Foot, the Attack is usually begun by knocking the Party down, and for the Time depriving him of his Senses. But if the Thief should be less barbarous, he is seldom so incautious as to omit taking every Method to prevent his being known, by flapping the Party's Hat over his Face, and by every other Method which he can invent to avoid Discovery.

But indeed any such Methods are hardly necessary: for when we consider the Circumstance of Darkness, mentioned before, the extreme Hurry of the Action, and the Terror and Consternation in which most Persons are in at such a Time, how shall we imagine it possible, that they should afterwards be able, with any (the least) Degree of Certainty, to swear to the Identity of the Thief, whose Countenance is, perhaps, not a little altered by his subsequent Situation, and who takes care as much as possible he can, by every Alteration of Dress, and otherwise, to disguise himself.

And if the Evidence of the Accomplice be so unlikely to be confirmed by the Oath of the Prosecutor, what other Means of Confirmation can be found? for as to his Character, if he himself doth not call Witnesses to support it (which in this Instance is not incumbent on him to do)[8] you are not at Liberty to impeach it. The greatest and most known Villain in *England*, standing at the Bar equally *rectus in curia* with the Man of the highest Estimation, if they should be both accused of the same Crime.[9]

Unless therefore the Robbers should be so unfortunate as to be apprehended in the Fact, (a Circumstance which their Numbers, Arms, &c. renders ordinarily impossible) no such Corroboration can possibly be had; but the Evidence of the Accomplice standing alone and unsupported, the Villain, contrary to the Opinion, and almost direct Knowledge of all present, is triumphantly acquitted, laughs at the Court, scorns the Law, vows Revenge against his Prosecutors, and returns to his Trade with a great Increase of Confidence, and commonly of Cruelty.

---

difficulty in procuring sufficient evidence to convict them [gangs of villains]; which is a very common case in street-robberies, even when the guilt of the party is sufficiently apparent to satisfy the most tender conscience' (*Voyage to Lisbon*, p. 33).

[8] 'The prosecutor cannot enter into the defendant's character, unless the defendant enable him to do so, by his calling witnesses to support it.' William Hawkins, *Pleas of the Crown* (London, 1824), ch. 46 ('Of Evidence'), sect. 193. This point is not in the first or second edition of Hawkins (Fielding owned the second edition).

[9] 'Courts of justice know nothing of a cause more than what is told them on oath by a witness; and the most flagitious villain upon earth is tried in the same manner as a man of the best character, who is accused of the same crime' (*Voyage to Lisbon*, p. 33).

Rectus in Curia: 'Right in court, is he who stands at the bar, and no man objects any offence against him. . . . And when a person *outlawed* hath reversed the outlawry, so that he can participate of the benefit of the law, he is said to be *Rectus in curia*' (Jacob, *Dictionary*).

In a Matter therefore of so much Concern to the Public, I shall be forgiven, if I venture to offer my Sentiments.

The Words of my Lord *Hale* are these: "Tho' a *particeps criminis* be admissible as a Witness in Law, yet the Credibility of his Testimony is to be left to the Jury; and truly it would be hard to take away the Life of any Person upon such a Witness that swears to save his own, and yet confesseth hmself guilty of so great a Crime, unless there be also very considerable Circumstances, which may give the greater Credit to what he swears*."[1]

Here I must observe, that this great Man seems rather to complain of the Hardship of the Law, in taking away the Life of a Criminal on the Testimony of an Accomplice, than to deny that the Law was so. This indeed he could not well do; for not only the Case of an Approver,[2] as he himself seems to acknowledge,[3] but many later Resolutions would have contradicted that Opinion.

2*dly*, He allows that the Credibility of his Testimony is to be left to the Jury: and so is the Credibility of all other Testimonies. They are absolute Judges of the Fact; and God forbid that they should in all Cases be tied down by positive Evidence against a Prisoner, though it was not delivered by an Accomplice.

But surely, if the Evidence of an Accomplice be not sufficient to put the Prisoner on his Defence, but the Jury are directed to acquit him, though he can produce no Evidence on his Behalf, either to prove an *Alibi*, or to his Character, the Credibility of such Testimony cannot well be said to be left to a Jury. This is virtually to reject the Competency of the Witness: For to say the Law allows him to be sworn, and yet gives no Weight to his Evidence is, I apprehend, a mere Play of Words, and conveys no Idea.

In the third Place, This great Man asserts the Hardship of such Conviction—Now if the Evidence of a supposed Accomplice should convict a Man of fair and honest Character: It would, I confess, be hard; and it is a Hardship of which, I believe, no Experience can produce any Instance. But if on the other Hand, the Testimony of an Accomplice with every Circumstance of Probability attending it against a Vagabond of the vilest Character, and who can produce no single Person to his Reputation, is to be absolutely rejected, because there is no positive Proof to support it; this I think, is in the highest Degree hard (I think I have proved how hard) to the Society.

---

* *Hale's* Hist. v. 1. 305.

[1] Hale, i. 304, 305.

[2] 'There is another species of confession, which we read much of in our ancient books . . . which is called *approvement*. And that is when a person indicted of treason or felony, and arraigned for the same, doth confess the fact before plea pleaded; and appeals or accuses others, his accomplices, of the same crime, in order to obtain his pardon' (Blackstone, *Comm.* iv. 328–9).

[3] e.g., Hale, ii. 67 and 226 ff.

I shall not enter here into a Disquisition concerning the Nature of Evidence in general; this being much too large a Field; nor shall I examine the Utility of those Rules which our Law prescribes on this Head. Some of these Rules might perhaps be opened a little wider than they are, without either Mischief or Inconvenience;[4] and I am the bolder in the Assertion, as I know a very learned Judge[5] who concurs with this Opinion. There is no Branch of the Law more bulky, more full of Confusion and Contradiction, I had almost said of Absurdity, than the Law of Evidence as it now stands.

One Rule of this Law is, that no Man interested shall be sworn as a Witness. By this is meant pecuniary Interest; but are Mankind governed by no other Passion than Avarice? Is not Revenge the sweetest Morsel, as a Divine calls it, which the Devil ever dropped into the Mouth of a Sinner?[6] Are not Pride, Hatred, and the other Passions, as powerful Tyrants in the Mind of Man; and is not the Interest which these Passions propose to themselves by the Enjoyment of their Object, as prevalent a Motive to Evil as the Hope of any pecuniary Interest whatever.

But to keep more closely to the Point—Why shall not any Credit be given to the Evidence of an Accomplice?—My Lord *Hale* tells us, that he hath been guilty of a great Crime: and yet if he had been convicted and burnt in the Hand, all the Authorities tell us, that his Credit had been restored;[7] a more miraculous Power of Fire than any which the *Royal Society*[8] can produce. The same happens, if he be pardoned.[9]

Again, says Lord *Hale*, he swears to save his own Life. This is not altogether so: For when once a Felon hath impeached his Companions, and is admitted an Evidence against them, whatever be the Fate of his Evidence, the Impeacher always goes free. To this, it is true, he hath no positive Title, no more hath he, if a single Felon be convicted on his Oath. But the Practice is as I mention, and I do not remember any Instance to the contrary.[1]

---

[4] Cf. Hale, ii. 289: 'In some cases presumptive evidences go far to prove a person guilty, tho there be no express proof of the fact to be committed by him, but then it must be very warily pressed, for it is better five guilty persons should escape unpunished, than one innocent person should die.'

[5] Unidentified.

[6] Robert South (1634–1716), 'Prevention of Sin an unvaluable Mercy', in *Sermons . . . upon Several Occasions*, 7 vols. (Oxford, 1823), ii. 155: 'Revenge is certainly the most luscious morsel that the devil can put into the sinner's mouth.' Allan Wendt ('Fielding and South's "Luscious Morsel"' *N & Q* 202 [1957], 256–7) cites four other instances of Fielding's allusion to South's observation (*The Mock Doctor, The Champion, Shamela,* and *Amelia*). Fielding greatly admired South.

[7] 'If a man be convict of felony, and prays his clergy, and is burnt in the hand, he is now a competent witness . . .' (Hale, ii. 278).

[8] For Fielding's conventionally scornful attitude toward the Royal Society, see 'Some Papers Proper to be Read before the R——L Society' (*Miscellanies* [1743], 191 ff.); and Miller's *Fielding's 'Miscellanies'*, pp. 315–31.

[9] 'If the king pardon these offenders, they are thereby rendered competent witnesses, tho their credit is to be still left to the jury . . .' (Hale, ii. 278).

[1] 'It hath also been usual for the justices of the peace, by whom any persons charged with felony are committed to gaol, to admit some one of their accomplices to become a witness . . . against his fellows; upon an implied confidence . . . that if such accomplice makes a full and complete discovery of that

But what Inducement hath the Accomplice to perjure himself, or what Reason can be assigned why he should be suspected of it? That he himself was one of the Robbers appears to a Demonstration; that he had Accomplices in the Robbery is as certain. Why then should he be induced to impeach A and B, who are innocent, and not C and D, who are guilty? Must he not think that he hath a better Chance of convicting the Guilty than the Innocent. Is he not liable if he gives a false Information, to be detected in it? One of his Companions may be discovered and give a true Information, what will then become of him and his Evidence? And why should he do this? From a Motive of Friendship? Do the worst of Men carry this Passion so much higher than is common with the best? But he must not only run the Risk of his Life but of his Soul too. The very Mention of this latter Risque may appear ridiculous, when it is considered of what Sort of Persons I am talking. But even these Persons can scarce be thought so very void of Understanding as to lose their Souls for nothing, and to commit the horrid Sins of Perjury and Murder without any Temptation, or Prospect of Interest, nay even against their Interest. Such Characters are not to be found in History,[2] nor do they exist any where but in distempered Brains, and are always rejected as Monsters, when they are produced in Works of Fiction: for surely we spoil the Verse rather than the Sense by saying, *Nemo* gratis *fuit Turpissimus.*[3] Under such Circumstances, and under the Caution of a good Judge, and the Tenderness of an *English* Jury, it will be the highest Improbability that any Man should be wrongfully convicted; and utterly impossible to convict an honest Man: For I intend no more than that such Evidence shall put the Prisoner on his Defence, and oblige him either to controvert the Fact by proving an *Alibi*, or by some other Circumstance; or to produce some reputable Person his Character. And this brings me to consider the second Fortress of the Criminal in the Hardiness of his own Evidence.

The usual Defence of a Thief, especially at the *Old Bailey*, is an *Alibi**: To prove this by Perjury is a common Act of *Newgate* Friendship; and there seldom is any Difficulty in procuring such Witnesses. I remember a Felon

---

* I. e. *That he was at another Place at the Time.*

and of all other felonies to which he is examined by the magistrate, and afterwards gives his evidence without prevarication or fraud, he shall not himself be prosecuted for that or any other previous offence of the same degree' (Blackstone, *Comm.* iv. 331). As Fielding and Blackstone indicate, an accomplice admitted as a crown witness had no title by law to go free. The practice of the courts, of dubious legality, was simply not to prosecute an accused who had been admitted as an 'evidence'. Fielding accurately describes a practice which has long confused legal historians. See John H. Langbein, 'Shaping the Eighteenth-Century Criminal Trial', *University of Chicago Law Review*, 50 (1983), 84 ff.

[2] They were to be found in London, however. See *Voyage to Lisbon*, p. 36, and Introduction, p. lvii and n. 1.

[3] 'No one reaches the depths of villainy as a favor.' Fielding alters Juvenal's *nemo repente fuit turpissimus* (*Satires*, ii. 83), a line which he quotes in *Tom Jones* (VII. xiii. 381) and *Amelia* (VI. i. 279).

within this Twelvemonth to have been proved to be in *Ireland* at the Time when the Robbery was sworn to have been done in *London*, and acquitted; but he was scarce gone from the Bar, when the Witness was himself arrested for a Robbery committed in *London* at that very Time when he swore both he and his Friend were in *Dublin*: For which Robbery, I think, he was tried and executed.[4] This kind of Defence was in a great Measure defeated by the late Baron *Thompson*,[5] when he was Recorder of *London*, whose Memory deserves great Honour for the Services he did the Public in that Post. These Witnesses should always be examined with the utmost Care and Strictness, by which Means the Truth (especially if there be more Witnesses than one to the pretended Fact) will generally be found out. And as to Character, tho' I allow it to have great Weight, if opposed to the single Evidence of an Accomplice, it should surely have but little where there is good and strong Proof of the Fact; and none at all, unless it comes from the Mouths of Persons, who have themselves some Reputation and Credit.

SECT. X.

Of the Encouragement given to Robbers by frequent Pardons.

I come now to the sixth Encouragement to Felons, from the Hopes of a Pardon, at least with the Condition of Transportation.

This I am aware, is too tender a Subject to speak to. To pardon all Crimes where the Prosecution is in his Name,[6] is an undoubted Prerogative of the King. I may add, it is his most amiable Prerogative, and that which as *Livy* observes*, renders Kingly Government most dear to the People: For in a

---

* Dec. 1. I. 2. cap. 3. Esse Gratiæ Locum esse Beneficii; & irasci et ignoscere posse (*Regem scilicet*) inter amicum atque inimicum Discrimen nosse, Legem rem surdam inexorabilem esse, &c.[7]

[4] In Dec. 1749 Lawrence Savage testified that Garret Lawler was in prison in Ireland at the time Lawler was accused of housebreaking and he was acquitted ('The Evidence against him was an Accomplice, and no strengthening Circumstance appearing to corroborate his Testimony, the Jury acquitted [Lawler], on the Evidence of this *Lawrence Savage*, and others, of his being at another Place'). While giving his testimony, the unlucky Savage, who was in fact Lawler's brother, was recognized by a pawnbroker as the one who had attempted to sell him a stolen watch at the very time his testimony placed him in Ireland (Fielding had issued a warrant for Savage's arrest in Oct.). Savage was arrested, convicted, and sentenced to death in Jan. 1750. See *Select Trials*, i. 280 ff.

[5] Sir William Thompson or Thomson (1678–1739) was recorder of London, solicitor-general, MP for Ipswich and baron of the Exchequer (1729). He was instrumental in Wild's arrest (he is the 'learned judge' alluded to in *Jonathan Wild* who 'procured a clause in an Act of Parliament as a trap for Wild' [IV. i. 148]) and was one of the judges at his trial in 1725. Pursuant to his office, it was he who pronounced sentence of death on Wild.

[6] The king's power to pardon is largely for 'all offences merely against the crown, or the public'. Therefore, for example, 'in appeals of all kinds (which are the suit, not of the king, but of the party injured) the prosecutor may release, but the king cannot pardon' (Blackstone, *Comm.* iv. 398).

[7] Livy, *History of Rome*, II. iii. 'There was room for countenance and favour; a king could be angry, could forgive, could distinguish between friend and enemy. The law was a thing without ears,

Republic there is no such Power. I may add farther, that it seems to our excellent Sovereign to be the most favourite Part of his Prerogative, as it is the only one which hath been carried to its utmost Extent in the present Reign.

Here therefore I beg to direct myself only to those Persons who are within the Reach of his Majesty's sacred Ear. Such Persons will, I hope, weigh well what I have said already on the Subject of false Compassion, all which is applicable on the present Occasion: And since our King (as was with less Truth said of another*) *is of all Men the truest Image of his Maker in Mercy*, I hope too much Good-nature will transport no Nobleman so far as it once did a Clergyman in *Scotland*, who in the Fervour of his Benevolence prayed to God that he would graciously be pleased to pardon the poor Devil.[8]

To speak out fairly and honestly, tho' Mercy may appear more amiable in a Magistrate, Severity is a more wholesome Virtue; nay Severity to an Individual may, perhaps, be in the End the greatest Mercy, not only to the Public in general, for the Reason given above; but to many Individuals for the Reasons to be presently assigned.

To consider a human Being in the Dread of a sudden and violent Death; to consider that his Life or Death depend on your Will; to reject the Arguments which a good Mind will officiously[9] advance to itself; that violent Temptations, Necessity, Youth, Inadvertency have hurried him to the Commission of a Crime which hath been attended with no Inhumanity; to resist the Importunities, Cries, and Tears of a tender Wife, and affectionate Children, who, though innocent, are to be reduced to Misery and Ruin by a strict adherence to Justice. These altogether form an Object which whoever can look upon without Emotion, must have a very bad Mind; and whoever by the Force of Reason can conquer that Emotion must have a very strong one.[1]

And what can Reason suggest on this Occasion? First, that by saving this Individual, I shall bring many others into the same dreadful Situation. That the Passions of the Man are to give Way to the Principles of the Magistrate. Those may lament the Criminal, but these must condemn him. It was nobly

---

* By *Dryden* of *Charles* II.[2]

inexorable . . .' (Loeb). These are the reflections of disaffected young men on their loss of privilege after Tarquin was banished and a republic established.

Beneficio and *leges* in the received text.

Dec. I: early editions followed the ancient custom of dividing the work into decads of ten books.

[8] Perhaps the same sermon that inspired Uncle Toby's regret on hearing that the devil was damned to all eternity (*Tristram Shandy*, III. xi).

[9] Eager to do kind offices.

[1] Cf. the *Voyage to Lisbon*, p. 66: 'Here we past that cliff of Dover, which makes so tremendous a figure in Shakespear, and which whoever reads without being giddy, must, according to Mr. Addison's observation, have either a very good head, or a very bad one' (echoing *Tatler*, no. 17).

[2] *Absalom and Achitophel*, ll. 7–10: 'Then *Israel's* Monarch, after Heaven's own heart, / His vigorous warmth did, variously, impart / To Wives and Slaves: And, wide as his Command, / Scatter'd his Maker's Image through the Land.'

said by *Bias* to one who admired at his shedding Tears whilst he past Sentence of Death, "Nature exacts my Tenderness, but the Law my Rigour."[3] The elder *Brutus**, is a worthy Pattern of this Maxim; an Example, says *Machiavel***, most worthy of being transmitted to Posterity.[4] And *Dionysius Halicarnasseus*[†] calls it a *great and wonderful Action, of which the* Romans *were proud in the most extraordinary Degree.*[5] Whoever derives it therefore from the Want of humane and paternal Affections is unjust; no Instances of his Inhumanity are recorded. "But the Severity (says *Machiavel*) was not only profitable but necessary;"[6] and why? Because a single Pardon granted *ex mera Gratia & Favore*,[7] is a Link broken in the Chain of Justice, and takes away the Concatenation and Strength of the whole. The Danger and Certainty of Destruction are very different Objects, and strike the Mind with different Degrees of Force. It is of the very Nature of Hope to be sanguine, and it will derive more Encouragement from one Pardon, than Diffidence from twenty Executions.

It is finely observed by *Thucydides*[‡], "that though civil Societies have allotted the Punishment of Death to many Crimes, and to some of the inferior Sort, yet Hope inspires Men to face the Danger; and no Man ever came to a dreadful End, who had not a lively Expectation of surviving his wicked Machinations."[8]—Nothing certainly can more contribute to the

---

* He put his two Sons to Death for conspiring with *Tarquin*.[9]

Neither *Livy* nor *Dionysius* give any Character of Cruelty to *Brutus*; indeed the latter tells us, *that he was superior to all those Passions which disturb Human Reason.* Τῶν ἐπιταραττόντων τοὺς λογισμοὺς παθῶν κάρτερος.[1]

** Disc. l. 3. c. 3.   [†] Page 272. Edit. *Hudson*.   [‡] P. 174. Edit. *Hudson*.

[3] Bias of Prienê, one of the seven sages of Greece, to whom ancient writers (e.g. Diodorus Siculus, Diogenes Laertius) attributed various epigrams.

[4] Discourses of Nicholas Machiavel upon the First Decade of Titus Livius', in *Works*, 3rd edn. (London, 1720 [this edition is in Baker, no. 447]), III. iii: ''Tis an Example well worthy to be transmitted to Posterity, to see a Father sitting in Judgment upon his Sons, and not only Sentence them to Death, but be present, and a Spectator of their Execution.'

[5] *The Roman Antiquities of Dionysius of Halicarnassus*, v. 8. He decribes 'the ... noble and astonishing behaviour of Brutus ... in which the Romans take the greatest pride', but goes on to add that 'it will appear cruel and incredible to the Greeks' (Loeb). Fielding owned John Hudson's 2-vol. edition of *Dionysius Halicarnassus* (Oxford, 1704), Baker, no. 479.

[6] Loc. cit. 'The severity of Brutus in maintaining that Liberty which he had procured in *Rome*, was no less necessary than profitable.'

[7] 'Purely out of grace and favor'. A legal term and still a common expression.

[8] Thucydides, *History*, III. xlv. The quotation, from a speech by Diodotus, is not clearly apposite since it is part of an argument against capital punishment as an effective deterrent. Diodotus concludes, 'In a word, it is impossible, and a mark of extreme simplicity, for anyone to imagine that when human nature is whole heartedly bent on any undertaking it can be diverted from it by rigorous laws or by any other terror' (Loeb). Fielding quotes earlier from John Hudson's *Thucydides* (*Enquiry*, p. 91).

[9] According to tradition, Junius Brutus (*fl.* 510 BC) led the rising against the Tarquins after the rape of Lucrece and executed his sons when they attempted to restore the Tarquins. Brutus is also praised in *JJ* (26 Mar. 1748), p. 210; and *Tom Jones* (IV. iv. 162).

[1] Dionysius Halicarnassus, v. 8. Livy's account of Junius Brutus and his sons is in *History of Rome*, II. iv–v.

raising this Hope than repeated Examples of ill grounded Clemency: For as *Seneca* says, *Ex Clementia omnes idem sperant**.[2]

Now what is the principal End of all Punishment: Is it not as Lord[†] *Hale* expresses it, "to deter Men from the Breach of Laws, so that they may not offend, and so not suffer at all? And is not the inflicting of Punishment more for Example, and to prevent Evil, than to punish?" And therefore, says he, presently afterwards, "Death itself is necessary to be annexed to Laws in many Cases by the Prudence of Law-givers, though possibly beyond the single Merit of the Offence simply considered." No Man indeed of common Humanity or common Sense can think the Life of a Man and a few Shillings to be of an equal Consideration, or that the Law in punishing Theft with Death proceeds (as perhaps a private Person sometimes may) with any View to Vengeance. The Terror of the Example is the only Thing proposed, and one Man is sacrificed to the Preservation of Thousands.[3]

If therefore the Terror of this Example is removed (as it certainly is by frequent Pardons) the Design of the Law is rendered totally ineffectual; The Lives of the Persons executed are thrown away, and sacrificed rather to the Vengeance than to the Good of the Public, which receives no other Advantage than by getting rid of a Thief, whose Place will immediately be supplied by another. Here then we may cry out with the [‡]Poet:

$$\text{——— } Sævior \ Ense$$
$$Parcendi \ Rabies. \text{ ———}^4$$

This I am confident may be asserted, that Pardons have brought many more Men to the Gallows than they have saved from it. So true is that

---

* De Clementia, lib. i. c. i.
[†] *Hale's* Hist. v. i. p. 13.   [‡] *Claudian.*

[2] *On Mercy*, i. i. 9. 'From mercy men all hope to have the same' (Loeb).
[3] Cf. Fielding's anecdote in the *Voyage to Lisbon*: ' "For it is very hard, my Lord," said a convicted felon at the bar to the late excellent Judge Burnet, "to hang a poor man for stealing a horse." "You are not to be hanged, Sir," answered my ever-honoured and beloved friend, "for stealing a horse, but you are to be hanged that horses may not be stolen" ' (p. 36).
Blackstone defends the death penalty for theft on similar grounds ('the *public* mischief is the thing, for the prevention of which our laws have made it [robbery] a capital offence'), but he is generally more cautious ('For, though the end of punishment is to deter men from offending, it can never follow from thence that it is lawful to deter them at any rate and by any means'); and he is openly scornful that 'in the eighteenth century it could ever have been made a capital crime, to break down (however maliciously) the mound of a fish pond . . . or to cut down a cherry tree in an orchard' (*Comm.* iv. 6, 10, 4). In *Rambler*, no. 114 (20 Apr. 1751) Johnson seems to be responding directly to this paragraph in Fielding: 'To equal robbery with murder is to reduce murder to robbery, to confound in common minds the gradations of iniquity, and incite the commission of a greater crime to prevent the detection of a less.' See J. L. and B. Hammond, 'Poverty, Crime, Philanthropy', *Johnson's England*, i. 314.
[4] Claudian, *The First Book Against Rufinus*, i. 234 ff. Again the context is not clearly appropriate. Claudian is attacking Rufinus' sadistic cruelty. 'Nor does he even slay with a swift death; ere that he enjoys the infliction of cruel torture, the rack, the chain, the lightless cell, these he sets before the final blow. Why, *this remission is more savage, more madly cruel, than the sword*—this grant of life that agony may accompany it! Is death not enough for him?' (Loeb.)

Sentiment of *Machiavel*, That Examples of Justice are more merciful than the unbounded Exercise of Pity[§].

SECT. XI.

Of the Manner of Execution.

But if every Hope which I have mentioned fails the Thief: If he should be discovered, apprehended, prosecuted, convicted, and refused a Pardon; what is his Situation then? Surely most gloomy and dreadful, without any Hope, and without any Comfort. This is, perhaps, the Case with the less practised, less spirited, and less dangerous Rogues; but with those of a different Constitution it is far otherwise. No Hero sees Death as the Alternative which may attend his Undertaking with less Terror, nor meets it in the Field with more imaginary Glory. Pride, which is commonly the uppermost Passion in both, is in both treated with equal Satisfaction. The Day appointed by Law for the Thief's Shame is the Day of Glory in his own Opinion. His Procession to *Tyburn*, and his last Moments there, are all triumphant; attended with the Compassion of the meek and tender-hearted, and with the Applause, Admiration, and Envy of all the bold and hardened. His Behaviour in his present Condition, not the Crimes, how atrocious soever, which brought him to it, are the Subject of Contemplation. And if he hath Sense enough to temper his Boldness with any Degree of Decency, his Death is spoke of by many with Honour, by most with Pity, and by all with Approbation.[6]

How far such an Example is from being an Object of Terror, especially to those for whose Use it is principally intended, I leave to the Consideration of every rational Man; whether such Examples as I have described are proper to be exhibited must be submitted to our Superiors.

The great Cause of this Evil is the Frequency of Executions:[7] The

[§] In his Prince.[5]

---

[5] Ch. XVII ('Of Cruelty, and Clemency, and whether it is best for a Prince to be beloved, or feared') of *The Prince* (London, 1720, p. 221). 'A Prince therefore is not to regard the scandal of being cruel, if thereby he keeps his Subjects in their Allegiance, and united, seeing by some few examples of Justice you may be more merciful, than they who by an universal exercise of pity, permit several disorders to follow, which occasion Rapine and Murder; and the reason is, because that exhorbitant mercy has an ill effect upon the whole universality, whereas particular Executions extend only to particular persons.'

[6] An excellent and full account of the procession to Tyburn and the ceremonies of execution may be found in Radzinowicz, i. 168 ff. The scene may still be perceived visually in Plate XI of Hogarth's *Industrious and Idle Apprentice* (1747), and Fielding provides a brief description at the end of *Jonathan Wild* (IV. xiv. 199 ff.). Swift's poem, '*Clever* Tom Clinch *going to be hanged*' (*The Poems of Jonathan Swift*, ed. Harold Williams [Oxford, 1958], ii. 399–400), and Polly's vision of Macheath on execution day (*Beggar's Opera*, I. xii) confirm Fielding's complaints here of the public's sympathy for those about to be hanged.

[7] As Fielding points out at the end of this section, criminals were executed every six weeks. Radzinowicz (i. 147) cites figures showing that of 389 capital convictions in London and Middlesex

Knowledge of Human Nature will prove this from Reason; and the different Effects which Executions produce in the Minds of the Spectators in the Country where they are rare, and in *London* where they are common, will convince us by Experience. The Thief who is hanged to Day hath learnt his Intrepidity from the Example of his hanged Predecessors, as others are now taught to despise Death, and to bear it hereafter with Boldness from what they see to Day.

One Way of preventing the Frequency of Executions is by removing the Evil I am complaining of: For this Effect in Time becomes a Cause; and greatly increases that very Evil from which it first arose. The Design of those who first appointed Executions to be public, was to add the Punishment of Shame to that of Death; in order to make the Example an Object of greater Terror. But Experience hath shewn us that the Event is directly contrary to this Intention. Indeed a competent Knowledge of Human Nature might have foreseen the Consequence. To unite the Ideas of Death and Shame is not so easy as may be imagined.[8] All Ideas of the Latter being absorbed by the Former. To prove this, I will appeal to any Man who hath seen an Execution, or a Procession to an Execution; let him tell me when he hath beheld a poor Wretch, bound in a Cart, just on the Verge of Eternity, all pale and trembling with his approaching Fate, whether the Idea of Shame hath ever intruded on his Mind? Much less will the bold daring Rogue who glories in his present Condition, inspire the Beholder with any such Sensation.[9]

The Difficulty here will be easily explained, if we have Recourse to the Poets; (for the good Poet and the good Politician do not differ so much as some who know nothing of either Art affirm; nor would *Homer* or *Milton* have made the worst Legislators of their Times:)[1] The great Business is to

during the years 1749 through 1754, 285 offenders were executed, that is, 5 or 6 executions every six weeks.

[8] The *Covent-Garden Journal* for 14 Apr. 1752 recommends Fielding's *Examples of Providence* to tender minds as 'wholesome Food' for it 'unites the Idea of Horror with the worst of crimes at an Age when all their Impressions become in great Measure, a Part of their Nature: *For those Ideas which they then join together,* as Mr. Locke judiciously observes, *they are never after capable of separating.'*

[9] There is an angry comment in the *Covent-Garden Journal* (28 Mar. 1752) concerning a recent execution at which the 'Criminals . . . behaved with the wonted Affectation of Mock-Heroism'. 'It is not my Intention to raise my good Reader's Mirth, but his Indignation, and by that Means to prevail with those in whose Power it is, to prevent for the future the exhibiting of these horrid Farces.' Fielding refers the reader to this section of the *Enquiry* and then says, 'I wish some greater Man *would alter a few Words in it, and make it his own'.* There is a similar protest against the 'ridiculous Drama' at Tyburn in *Covent-Garden Journal,* no. 55 (18 July 1752) which concludes with the wish that, if his advice in the *Enquiry* is unacceptable, we would 'no longer proceed to string up hundreds of our Fellow-Creatures every year, a matter as shocking to all Men of Humanity, as it is entertaining to a dissolute Rabble, who (I repeat it again) instead of being terrified, are hardened and encouraged by the sight.' Cf. the *Champion* for 3 Jan. 1739/40, pp. 134–5.

[1] Fielding pays similar tribute in *Tom Jones:* '*Homer* and *Milton*, who, though they added the Ornament of Numbers to their Works, were both Historians of our Order, were Masters of all the Learning of their Times' (IX. i. 492).

raise Terror, and the Poet[2] will tell you, that Admiration or Pity, or both, are very apt to attend whatever is the Object of Terror in the human Mind. This is very useful to the Poet, but very hurtful on the present Occasion to the Politician, whose Art is to be here employed to raise an Object of Terror, and, at the same time, as much as possible, to strip it of all Pity and all Admiration.

To effect this, it seems that the Execution should be as soon as possible after the Commission and Conviction of the Crime;[3] for if this be of an atrocious Kind, the Resentment of Mankind being warm, would pursue the Criminal to his last End, and all Pity for the Offender would be lost in Detestation of the Offence. Whereas, when Executions are delayed so long as they sometimes are, the Punishment and not the Crime is considered; and no good Mind can avoid compassionating a Set of Wretches, who are put to Death we know not why, unless, as it almost appears, to make a Holiday for, and to entertain the Mob.

Secondly, It should be in some degree private. And here the Poets will again assist us. Foreigners have found fault with the Cruelty of the *English* Drama, in representing frequent Murders upon the Stage.[4] In fact, this is not only cruel, but highly injudicious: A Murder behind the Scenes, if the Poet knows how to manage it, will affect the Audience with greater Terror than if it was acted before their Eyes.[5] Of this we have an Instance in the Murder of the King in *Macbeth*, at which, when *Garrick* acts the Part, it is scarce an Hyperbole to say, I have seen the Hair of the Audience stand an End.[6] Terror hath, I believe, been carried higher by this single Instance, than

---

[2] After Aristotle, *Poetics*, 6 ff.

[3] The 25 Geo. II, c. 37 ('An act for better preventing the horrid crime of Murder') provides for speedy, solemn, and sober execution of murderers. Fielding notes in the *Covent-Garden Journal* for 28 Mar. 1752 that a report of three felons being executed in Newgate struck 'horror' in the 'lower People'.

[4] For example, Voltaire in 'Discours sur la tragédie' (1730; the 'Dedication' of his *Brutus* to Bolingbroke). In Dryden's *An Essay of Dramatick Poesie* Lisideius objects to violence on the English stage and Neander agrees with him: 'But for death, that it ought not to be represented, I have besides the Arguments alledg'd by *Lisideius* the authority of *Ben. Johnson*, who has forborn it in his Tragedies.'

[5] Horace, *Ars Poetica*, 179–88. In *Eurydice Hissed* Sourwit asks Spatter if he won't 'let us see the farce fairly damned before us'. Spatter replies, 'No, sir. It is a thing of too horrible a nature, for which reason I shall follow Horace's rule and only introduce a description of it.' Cf. Trapwit in *Pasquin*, III. i: 'What, would you have every thing brought upon the stage? I intend to bring ours to the dignity of the French stage; and I have Horace's advice on my side; we have many things both said and done in our comedies which might be better performed behind the scenes: the French you know, banish all cruelty from the stage; and I don't see why we should bring on a lady in ours, practising all manner of cruelty upon her lover.'

[6] Garrick first played Macbeth in 1744, removing some of the accretions that had rendered it more opera than drama (Thomas Davies, *Memoires of the Life of David Garrick*, a new edition [London, 1780], i. 116). The performance was sensationally successful in 1747 with Mrs Pritchard as Lady Macbeth: 'The beginning of the scene after the commission of the murder was conducted in terrifying whispers. . . . The dark colouring, given by the actor to these abrupt speeches, makes the scene awful and tremendous to the auditors! The wonderful expression of heartful horror, which Garrick felt when he shewed his bloody hands, can only be conceived and described by those who saw him!'

by all the Blood which hath been spilt on the Stage.—To the Poets I may add the Priests, whose Politics have never been doubted. Those of *Egypt* in particular, where the sacred Mysteries were first devised, well knew the Use of hiding from the Eyes of the Vulgar, what they intended should inspire them with the greatest Awe and Dread.[7] The Mind of Man is so much more capable of magnifying than his Eye, that I question whether every Object is not lessened by being looked upon; and this more especially when the Passions are concerned: for these are ever apt to fancy much more Satisfaction in those Objects which they affect, and much more of Mischief in those which they abhor, than are really to be found in either.

If Executions therefore were so contrived, that few could be present at them, they would be much more shocking and terrible to the Crowd without Doors than at present, as well much more dreadful to the Criminals themselves, who would thus die in the Presence only of their Enemies; and where the boldest of them would find no Cordial to keep up his Spirits, nor any Breath to flatter his Ambition.

3*dly*, The Execution should be in the highest degree solemn. It is not the Essence of the Thing itself, but the Dress and Apparatus of it, which make an Impression on the Mind, especially on the Minds of the Multitude to whom Beauty in Rags[8] is never a desirable, nor Deformity in Embroidery a disagreeable Object.

Montagne, who, of all men, except only *Aristotle*, seems best to have understood Human Nature, enquiring into the Causes why Death appears more terrible to the better Sort of People than to the meaner, expresses himself thus: "I do verily believe, that it is those terrible Ceremonies and Preparations wherewith we set it out, that more terrify us than the Thing itself; a new and contrary Way of Living, the Cries of Mothers, Wives and Children, the Visits of astonished and afflicted Friends, the Attendance of pale and blubbered Servants, a dark Room set round with burning Tapers, our Beds environed with Physicians and Divines; in fine, nothing but Ghastliness and Horror round about us, render it so formidable, that a Man almost fancies himself dead and buried already*."[9]

* *Montagne*, Essay 19.

(Davies, *Dramatic Miscellanies*, a new edition [London, 1785], ii. 149–50). Fielding dramatizes his regard for Garrick in Partridge's response to his Hamlet (*Tom Jones*, XVI. v. 853 ff.; and see p. 853 n. 2).

[7] I have not found a specific source for this sentence, but that the 'mysteries' originated in Egypt and were maintained by priests is a commonplace in commentators both ancient (e.g. Herodotus, Diodorus Siculus) and contemporary (e.g. the Abbé Banier's *Mythology and Fables of the Ancients* [no. 219 of the sale catalogue], vol. i [London, 1739]; Charles Rollin's *Ancient History of the Egyptians . . . and Grecians*, vol. i [Paris, 1730–8]; Shaftesbury's *Characteristics*, ed. John M. Robertson [London, 1900], i. 181 ff.; and William Warburton, *The Divine Legation of Moses* [1738–41], bk. II, sect. iv).

[8] Cf. *Tom Jones*, IV. vi. 174: '*Congreve* well says, *There is in true Beauty something which vulgar Souls cannot admire*; so can no Dirt or Rags hide this Something from those Souls which are not of the vulgar Stamp.'

[9] Nearly verbatim with Charles Cotton's translation of Montaigne's ch. XIX 'That to study

"If the Image of Death" (says the same Author) "was to appear thus dreadful to an Army, they would be an Army of whining Milk-sops; and where is the Difference but in the Apparatus? Thus in the Field" (I may add, at the Gallows) "what is encountered with Gaiety and Unconcern, in a Sickbed becomes the most dreadful of all Objects."[1]

In *Holland*, the Executions (which are very rare) are incredibly solemn. They are performed in the Area before the Stadthouse, and attended by all the Magistrates. The Effect of this Solemnity is inconceivable to those who have not observed it in others, or felt it in themselves; and to this, perhaps more than to any other Cause, the Rareness of Executions in that Country is owing.[2]

Now the following Method, which I shall venture to prescribe, as it would include all the three Particulars of Celerity, Privacy, and Solemnity, so would it, I think, effectually remove all the Evils complained of, and which at present attend the manner of inflicting capital Punishment.

Suppose then, that the Court at the *Old Bailey*[3] was, at the End of the Trials, to be adjourned during four Days; that, against the Adjournment-day, a Gallows was erected in the Area before the Court; that the Criminals were all brought down on that Day to receive Sentence; and that this was executed the very Moment after it was pronounced, in the Sight and Presence of the Judges.

Nothing can, I think, be imagined (not even Torture, which I am an Enemy to the very Thought of admitting) more terrible than such an Execution; and I leave it to any Man to resolve himself upon Reflection, whether such a Day at the *Old Bailey*, or a Holiday at *Tyburn*, would make the strongest Impression on the Minds of every one.

Thus I have, as well as I am able, finished the Task which I proposed, have endeavoured to trace the Evil from the very Fountain-head, and to shew whence it originally springs, as well as all the Supplies it receives, till it becomes a Torrent, which at present threatens to bear down all before it.

And here I must again observe, that if the former Part of this Treatise should raise any Attention in the Legislature, so as effectually to put a Stop to the Luxury of the lower People, to force the Poor to Industry, and to provide for them when industrious, the latter Part of my Labour would be of

Philosophy, is to learn to die' (*Essays*; 4th edn. [London, 1711]). Fielding owned a 1743 edition of Montaigne (Baker, no. 510).

[1] Loc. cit.

[2] Cross (i. 70) lists the many instances of allusions to Holland in Fielding's works and, probably on the basis of this paragraph in the *Enquiry*, states that Fielding saw an execution in Holland. Sir William Temple remarks that in Holland the people were 'Terrified with severe Executions' (*Observations upon the United Provinces of the Netherlands* [London, 1673], p. 114).

[3] The Old Bailey Sessions House, next to Newgate, was an open-air court until 1735 (see Gerald Howson, *Thief-Taker General*, appendix IV). Here the 'Black Sessions' of 1750 took place. Public executions were transferred from Tyburn to the Sessions Yard before the Old Bailey in 1783.

very little Use; and indeed all the Pains which can be taken in this latter Part, and all the Remedies which can be devised, without applying a Cure to the former, will be only of the palliative Kind, which may patch up the Disease, and lessen the bad Effects, but never can totally remove it.

Nor, in plain Truth, will the utmost Severity to Offenders be justifiable, unless we take every possible Method of preventing the Offence. *Nemo ad supplicia exigenda provenit, nisi qui remedia consumpsit*, says *Seneca**,[4] where he represents the Governors of Kingdoms in the amiable Light of Parents. The Subject, as well as the Child, should be left without Excuse before he is punished: for, in that Case alone, the Rod becomes the Hand either of the Parent or the Magistrate.

All Temptations therefore are to be carefully removed out of the Way; much less is the Plea of Necessity to be left in the Mouth of any. This Plea of Necessity is never admitted in our Law; but the Reason of that is, says Lord *Hale*,[5] because it is so difficult to discover the Truth. Indeed that it is not always certainly false, is a sufficient Scandal to our Polity; for what can be more shocking than to see an industrious poor Creature, who is able and willing to labour, forced by mere Want into Dishonesty, and that in a Nation of such Trade and Opulence.

Upon the whole, something should be, nay must be done, or much worse Consequences than have hitherto happened, are very soon to be apprehended. Nay, as the Matter now stands, not only Care for the Public Safety, but common Humanity, exacts our Concern on this Occasion; for that many Cart-loads of our Fellow-creatures are once in six Weeks carried to Slaughter, is a dreadful Consideration; and this is greatly heightened by reflecting, that, with proper Care and Regulations, much the greater Part of these Wretches might have been made not only happy in themselves, but very useful Members of the Society, which they now so greatly dishonour in the Sight of all Christendom.

FINIS.

---

* De Clementia, Lib. 2. Fragm.

[4] *On Mercy*, I. xiv. 1. 'No one resorts to the exaction of punishment until he has exhausted all the means of correction' (Loeb). *pervenit* in the received text.

[5] Hale, i. 54: 'Mens properties would be under a strange insecurity, being laid open to other mens necessities, whereof no man can possibly judge, but the party himself.' In the Preface to his *Discourse*, however, Hale lists 'necessity' as one of the causes for the increase of crime, concluding 'doubtless as the multitude of poor, and necessitious, and uneducated persons, increase, the multitude of malefactors will increase, notwithstanding the examples of severity'.

To the PUBLIC.

The rude Behaviour and insolence of Servants of all Kinds is become a general Complaint: for which Insolence the Law has given no other Power of punishing than by turning them away; and this would be often Punishment enough, if the Servant could not easily provide himself with another Place: But here they find no Manner of Difficulty; for many Persons are weak enough to take Servants without any Character; and if this be insisted on, there is an ingenious Method in this Town of obtaining a false Character from one who personates the former Master or Mistress: To obviate all this, an Office is erected in the *Strand*, opposite *Cecil-Street*, where the best Servants in every Capacity are to be heard of; and where the Public may be assured, that no Servant shall ever be register'd, who cannot produce a real good Character from the last Place in which he or she actually lived; the Method of ascertaining which may be seen at the said Office; where Estates, Houses, Lodgings, and every thing else to be sold or lett, are carefully register'd; and where consequently they may be heard of, by those who desire to hire or purchase the same.

Note, This Office is established by a Society of Gentlemen on the Principles recommended by *Montagne* in the Thirty-fourth of his *Essays*, and must soon become of the highest Utility to the Public. Nay, that great Author laments the Want of such an Office, as a great Defect in the *French* Government. We have thought it therefore not improper to recommend this Office at the End of a Work, in which the Public Utility is sincerely intended, as it seems to deserve the Encouragement of all, who think the Public Utility worthy of their Regard.[6]

N.B. Books containing a full Account of the Office, are now to be had at it.

---

[6] For the Register Office see Cross, ii. 226; and Dudden, ii. 737–8. John Fielding's *A Plan of the Universal Register Office* was published 21 Feb. 1751 (Cross and Dudden attribute the signed introduction to John; the text to Henry). M. Dorothy George's 'The Early History of Registry Offices', *The Economic Journal* (supplement), 4 (1929), 570–91, has a useful history of the institution and discusses the Fieldings' version. She points out that Montaigne's 'Chapter XXXIV, "Of one Defect in Government"' was widely known.

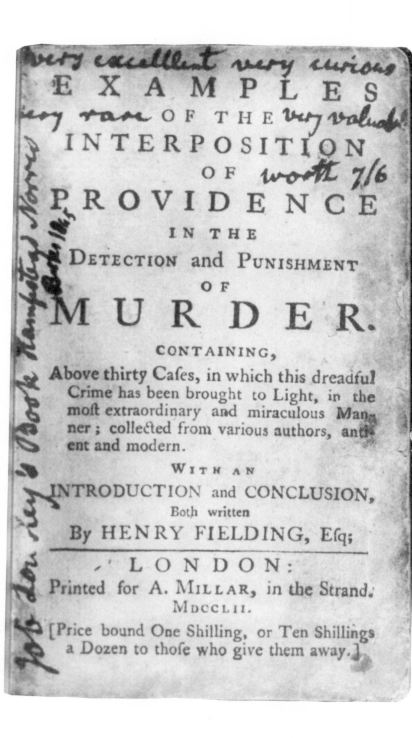

EXAMPLES

OF THE

INTERPOSITION

OF

PROVIDENCE

IN THE

DETECTION and PUNISHMENT

OF

MURDER.

CONTAINING,

Above thirty Cafes, in which this dreadful Crime has been brought to Light, in the moft extraordinary and miraculous Manner; collected from various authors, antient and modern.

WITH AN

INTRODUCTION and CONCLUSION,

Both written

By HENRY FIELDING, Efq;

LONDON:

Printed for A. MILLAR, in the Strand.

MDCCLII.

[Price bound One Shilling, or Ten Shillings a Dozen to thofe who give them away.]

TO THE

Right Rev. Father in God,

ISAAC

Lord Bishop of

WORCESTER.[1]

My Lord,

In a conversation to which I had some time since the honour to be admitted with your Lordship, you was pleased to lament, among other great and growing evils, the many flagrant instances of Murder that have lately alarmed the public.[2] I then took occasion to mention the plan of such a book as I now present to your Lordship; this immediately received your encouragement, and, I hope, will now receive your protection.

To give an attempt of this kind its full force, the sanction of some great name is necessary; and where, my Lord, could I find one so proper, as that of a prelate of so distinguished a character; whose zeal for the good of his country is so universally known and acknowledged, and who hath, with such vigour and success, employed the most eminent talents, and the most unwearied industry, in the cause of the public?[3]

[1] Isaac Maddox (1697–1759), Bishop of Worcester (1743), philanthropist, and specialist in charity sermons. Actively campaigned (in parliament and pulpit) against gin-drinking. See above, p. lxi, n. 8.

[2] In the *Covent-Garden Journal* for 1 Feb. 1752 the report of a murder is followed by the comment, '*More shocking Murders have been committed within this last Year, than for many Years before. To what can this be so justly imputed, as to the manifest Decline of Religion among the lower People. A Matter which even in a civil Sense, demands the Attention of the Government.*' For a discussion of the recent rash of Murders, see General Introduction, p. lxxxiv.

[3] Fielding must have particularly admired Maddox's sermon (which went through several editions) 'The Expediency of Preventative Wisdom', delivered on Easter Monday, 1750, to the lord mayor, aldermen, and common council of the city of London and to the governors 'of the several hospitals'. Maddox praised the various hospitals and charitable organizations of London but emphasized that 'this Benevolent and Godlike Temper, excellent and praiseworthy as it is, must . . . be regulated by the Rules of Prudence'. Anticipating Fielding's arguments in the *Enquiry*, he stressed the need to employ the poor, to curtail idleness and extravagance and, especially, to stop gin-drinking. In an appendix to the third edition of this sermon (London, 1751) Maddox says 'While the foregoing Sheets were printing off, the Nation was much obliged . . . by a learned and seasonable Discourse, entitled *An Enquiry* . . . It is much to be wished that the weighty Considerations therein offered, may effectually awaken attention. . . . The treatise itself has spread, and I hope will spread . . .', and he quotes two passages from Fielding's discussion of the dangers of gin.

In the *Covent-Garden Journal* for 10 Mar. 1752 the following comment accompanies notice of another sermon by Maddox: '*This worthy Prelate is a true Labourer in the Vineyard. To his great Care and Diligence, the late Act against Spiritous Liquors was chiefly owing.*'

To this consideration, my Lord, I hope you will impute my present desire of your Lordship's patronage; and not to that pride which I shall always have in telling the world, that I am, with the greatest respect,

my Lord,

your Lordship's

most obliged,

and most dutiful,

humble servant,

Bow-Street, April
1752.

HENRY FIELDING.

EXAMPLES

OF THE

Interposition of PROVIDENCE in the Detection and Punishment of Murder.

That the most dreadful crime of Murder hath of late encreased in a very deplorable degree in this kingdom, is a fact which every man must confess, and which every good man must very bitterly lament. Till this age, indeed, cruel and bloody actions were so seldom heard of in England, that when they happened, they appeared as prodigies, and raised not only the detestation, but the astonishment of the people. In all the arts of fraud, knavery and theft, we have long since been equal to any of our neighbours; but Murder is very lately begun, perhaps is even now beginning to be common among us.

In the politic, as in the natural body, no disorders ever spring up without a cause; much less do any diseases become epidemical by mere accident.[4] These must all have their causes, and such causes must be adequate to the effects which they produce.

For my part, I sincerely declare I can discover no more than one cause of the horrid evil of which I am complaining: ONE indeed most perfectly adequate to the production of every political mischief; and which I am convinced hath more than all others, contributed to the production, and to the encrease of all those moral evils with which the public is at present so extremely afflicted.

My sensible reader will presently guess, that I mean that general neglect (I wish I could not say contempt) of religion,[5] which hath within these few years so fatally overspread this whole nation; hath grown to be a kind of fashion among us, and like other fashions, having begun among the higher ranks of people, hath descended gradually through all orders, till it hath reached the very lowest in the society.[6]

This is a matter too clear, I think, and too self-evident to require any proof: for when we reflect on those solemn denunciations, of the most

---

[4] For the body/state/disese metaphor, see *Enquiry*, p. 63.

[5] On Fielding's concern for this topic, see James A. Work, 'Henry Fielding, Christian Censor,' in *The Age of Johnson, Essays presented to Chauncey Brewster Tinker* (New Haven, 1949), pp. 139–48; and Martin C. Battestin, *The Moral Basis of Fielding's Art* (Middletown, Conn., 1959), *passim*.

[6] For the effects of bad example and the descent of vice through the ranks of society, see the *Enquiry*, p. 77.

grievous judgments against this crime by Almighty God, how is it possible to conceive that a creature who believes that this God is, and that these denunciations of vengeance came from him, should, unless he were a downright fool or madman, thus audaciously fly in the face of a being, in whose words we must be assured there is all truth, and in whose right hand is all power?[7]

But besides the frequent declarations of God's most bitter wrath against this deadly sin in the Old Testament; besides the fearful and tremendous sentence of eternal punishment against it in the New Testament;[8] the Almighty hath been pleased to distinguish the atrociousness of the Murderer's guilt, by levelling his thunder directly at his head, in this world. The Divine providence hath been pleased to interpose in a more immediate manner in the detection of this crime than of any other. Of which interpositions not only the holy scriptures, but the histories and traditions of all ages, and of all countries, do give us many and unquestionable examples. To this truth, the horrors with which the minds of Murderers are particularly haunted; and the most unaccountable, indeed miraculous means, by which the most secret and cunning Murders have often been detected, do abundantly bear testimony: not to mention the many stories of apparitions on this dreadful occasion; some of which have been so well and faithfully attested, that to reject them with a hasty disbelief, seems to argue more of an obstinate and stubborn infidelity, than of a sound and sober reason.

Here then I shall present the reader, with a few examples of this immediate interposition of the Divine providence on this occasion. To transcribe the whole, would fill a large volume; and though perhaps, I may have omitted many more worthy of being inserted, than some of those which I have chosen, yet I trust, that what I shall here present the serious and attentive reader, will be sufficient to convince him of that awful truth, abovementioned; of which, if we may venture to assert any thing on such a subject, the motive seems to have been to deter men, by such manifest preternatural interpositions of Divine providence, from the commission of this dreadful, this execrable, this unpardonable sin.

The first Murder we hear of, is in the sacred history. It is that committed by Cain on the body of his brother Abel.

In this we find the Almighty personally interposing, and calling the offender to the severest account. This was discovered by God himself, and how discovered? Why, as the sacred text tells us, by the "Crying of the blood of the slain for vengeance against the Murderer."[9]

[7] Exodus 15: 6.
[8] In the *Covent-Garden Journal*, no. 14 (18 Feb. 1752) Fielding cites Matthew 5: 22. for the 'tremendous sentence' against murderers in the New Testament (i. 220).
[9] Genesis 4: 10. Cf. Tom Jones, II. iv. 90.

And this vengeance was accordingly executed by the all-righteous judge, in a curse pronounced by himself against Cain; who, in pursuance of his sentence, wandered thro' the earth, groaning and trembling, according to the translation of the LXX.[1] Haunted, says a commentator on Eusebius,[2] with his brother's ghost whithersoever he went; for it was a notion which prevailed among the Jews, as well as all other nations, that the ghosts of those who were murdered, persecuted their Murderers, continually terrifying them, and requiring their punishment at the hands of justice. And of the truth of this opinion, the most authentic histories, as well as the traditions of all ages and countries, afford us very positive assurance.

That Cain was not put to death by God for his offence, seems an instance rather of the Divine severity, than of any mercy intended towards him. The design was possibly to make him a living and lasting example of the Almighty wrath, against this heinous crime. Cain himself, when he cried out that his punishment was greater than he could bear, would have considered death as a mitigation of his sentence.[3] How much more dreadful indeed was the alternative of being banished from the face of God, of being driven as a vagabond and a runagate out of the holy land; and being compelled to wander about with a mark of infamy,[4] set by God's own hand upon him; afraid of all whom he should meet, haunted by his brother's incensed and injured spirit; and much more haunted, perhaps, by his own conscience; the ground, as the Jewish rabbies say, shaking under him, so that all who met him, ran away from him, crying, "This is the cruel man that killed his brother."[5]

There is, perhaps, no truth whatever, which can be supported by so many authorities from history, as this of the divine vengeance against Murder. The example of Herod is extremely affecting to this purpose. "The fate of Herod (says Eusebius)[6] is well worthy our consideration; divine justice pursued him immediately after those cruel murders which he had committed; and his sufferings in this life seemed to exhibit a kind of prelude of those torments

---

[1] The Septuagint, translation of the Old Testament into Greek between 250 BC and *c.*100 BC supposedly by 72 translators in 72 days. The text used by St Paul. Fielding owned a Septuagint (Baker, no. 59). 'Groaning and trembling' is the translation in the Septuagint of what is rendered in the King James version as 'a fugitive and a vagabond'.

[2] Eusebius Pamphili (*c.*263–339?), Bishop (of Caesarea, Palestine), chronicler, and church historian. Fielding owned his *Ecclesiastical History* (Baker, no. 618).

[3] Genesis 4: 13. Cf. Fielding's comment in *Covent-Garden Journal*, no. 20 (10 Mar. 1752) on the fugitive lover and accomplice of Mary Blandy (see Example XXXIII below): 'Let us for a Moment only cast our eyes on the Wretch, who hath caused all this, who hath hitherto escaped the Hands of Justice; perhaps to be more exquisitely punished in the State of a profligate abandoned fugitive; sent like the first Murderer, to wander over the Earth, till he shall cry with Cain, *My Punishment is greater than I can bear*' (i. 255).

[4] Genesis 4: 15.

[5] Such extra-scriptural legends are part of the 'Haggadah'. See *Encylopaedia Judaica, s.v.* Cain.

[6] Fielding quotes from the *Ecclesiastical History* (I. viii) describing the punishment of Herod the Great for his crime 'against Christ and the children of his age'.

which were prepared for him after his death. The former happiness of his reign was on a sudden obscured by a succession of the most terrible calamities, by the murders of his wife, his children, and of the nearest of his relations and friends. Josephus[7] hath drawn the picture at length, and it surpasses all the tragical stories which poets have ever invented."—He then relates from that historian the manner of Herod's death, which he says, was by a rod sent from heaven. By this the king was afflicted with a disease of a very exemplary kind; and which did manifest the immediate interposition of providence, as well by the singularity, as by the extremity of those excruciating torments, in which by a slow tedious wasting (being indeed devoured alive by vermin) he was dragged to his miserable end.[8]

A like account the same historian gives us of the dreadful catastrophe of Maximinus, a great murderer of the Christians, by the same extraordinary and miraculous means.[9]

Indeed, not only the ecclesiastical writers, but prophane historians abundantly furnish us with examples of the wrath of God against the great tyrants and murderers of mankind, whose deaths have been, for the most part, as violent as their lives, and the former have been as wretched, as the latter detestable. Of this the latter part of the Roman history is almost one continued record. Tiberius, Caligula, Claudius, Nero, Vitellius, Domitian, Commodus, Caracalla, and Heliogabalus, were not greater instances of cruelty while they lived, than of misery when they died.[1]

I will proceed to particular instances in which God hath been pleased to demonstrate his great abhorrence of this sin of Murder, by a supernatural and miraculous interposition of Providence, in the punishment, as well as detection, of this most abominable sin.

Of this sin, which is committed not only in defiance of the positive revealed laws of God, and all the punishments which in these laws are denounced against it; but in manifest opposition to those secret institutions,[2] which God hath written in the heart and conscience of every man, where there is no principle so deeply engraved, none written in such legible characters as this divine Command, THOU SHALT DO NO MURDER.

---

[7] Josephus' (AD 37–95?) famous work, *The Jewish War*, was one of Eusebius' major sources in Bk. I of his *Ecclesiastical History*.

[8] Among Herod's exemplary afflictions was 'gangrene of the genitals, breeding worms'.

[9] Eusebius, *Ecclesiastical History*, IX. x. Galerius Valerius Maximinus (d. 313) was emperor of Rome 308–13.

[1] For similar lists of evil emperors, see the *Jacobite's Journal*, no. 16 (19 Mar. 1748), p. 205; and the *Covent-Garden Journal*, no. 19 (7 Mar. 1752), i. 251; and compare Gibbon's statement that 'The dark unrelenting Tiberius, the furious Caligula, and the feeble Claudius, the Profligate and cruel Nero, the beastly Vitellius, and the timid, inhuman Domitian, are condemned to everlasting infamy' (*Decline and Fall*, ch. 3).

[2] 'First principles' (*OED*). Cf. *Charge*, p. 23.

EXAMPLE I.

We read in Plutarch, that a soldier of king Pyrrhus being slain, his faithful dog would by no means be inticed from the dead body; and the king coming by, the dog fawn'd on him, as seeming to supplicate his vengeance on his master's murderers. The king thereupon ordered his whole army to march by in order before him, and as soon as the murderers appeared, the dog flew fiercely on them, and would have torn them in pieces, had he not been with-held. The two soldiers terrified with so uncommon an attack, together with the accusation, and so faithful a witness directed by heaven for their accuser, fell on their knees, and confess'd the fact, for which they were both immediately executed.   [*Plutarch*: de serâ numinis vind.][3]

EXAMPLE II.

The same author relates a story of one Bessus, who having murdered his father, was so pursued with a guilty conscience, that he thought the swallows, when they chatter'd, were saying, "Bessus has kill'd his father." Whereupon, being unable to conceal his guilt, he confess'd the fact, and received condign punishment.   [*Plutarch's* Morals, *Solin.*[4]]

Many have been the instances, where the murderer, from the racking torments of his mind, hath been driven to distraction, and by that means, in his raving fits, hath confess'd his crime; and tho' such a confession in sleep, or in madness, cannot well be deem'd sufficient evidence against a man, yet never was such confession made, but it either led so strongly to the finding circumstantial evidence of the fact, as was sufficient to convict the guilty person; or else struck by the terror of a discovery being made, the murderer hath, when returned to his senses, confessed the fact: In both which cases is very plainly seen, the immediate interposition of Providence, in order to bring the offender to public justice, as may be illustrated also by the following facts.

---

[3] Examples I and II both appear in Plutarch, *The Philosophy Commonlie called the Morals*, trans. 'by Several Hands' in 5 vols. (London, 1694). Fielding owned this edition (Baker, no. 49), but his redactions are much shorter than the stories in Plutarch and omit significant detail. His source is doubtless Beard, Wanley, or Turner (for whom see below) who also include both tales and whose versions are closer to Fielding's. Fielding has confused the citations to Plutarch. The story of Bessus appears in 'de sera numinis vinditia' ('Concerning such whom God is slow to Punish'), iv. 181; that of Pyrrhus in the essay entitled 'Which are the most crafty, Water-Animals, or the Creatures that breed upon the Land' (v. 202).

[4] Another authority, Julius Solinus (3rd century AD) whose *Polyhistor* epitomizes Pliny's *Natural History*.

EXAMPLE III.

Alphonso, of the city of Veruli was the only son of his mother Sophia, and knowing himself to be heir to her great jointure, when she died, he regarded not the precepts or examples of that excellent and wise lady his mother, but gave a loose to all his vicious inclinations, which gave the lady Sophia the greatest uneasiness imaginable.

Cassino, brother to Sophia, having lost his wife, intreated this his sister to take the care of his only daughter Eleonora, who was now fifteen years old; and this charge Sophia performed so well, that when Eleonora became of the age of fourteen years, she was esteemed one of the best educated, as well as one of the most beautiful young ladies of that city.

Alphonso, charm'd with his cousin's beauty, but more with the great fortune to which she was heiress, resolved to endeavour at gaining her; but as this could not be done with the character he bore of extravagance and debauchery, he feign'd a most sudden and thorough reformation; and though for some time his mother gave little credit to his sincerity, and could not be prevailed on to ask the alliance of her brother, yet, after seeing in her son a whole year's continuance in the most regular and decent course of life, she was induced from her maternal fondness, and hopes of the truth of this pretended reformation, to intercede with her brother Cassino, that a match might be made between Alphonso and Eleonora. But as Cassino had not the same motives for partiality to Alphonso as his mother had, he saw through his disguise, and absolutely refused his consent, and as his sister was still importunate with him to grant her request, he took his daughter home to his own house, and begged to be troubled no more about the matter. Alphonso soon returned to his old courses, and the good virtuous Sophia, though her grief was very great, to see her son such a reprobate, rejoiced that her intercession did not prevail to the ruin of her amable niece. Alphonso in some time again wanted to renew his address to Eleonora, and asked his mother once more to propose it to her brother Cassino, but Sophia not only refused his request, but in pretty sharp terms, remonstrated against the debauchery of his life. So little was he moved with her discourse, that he now began to consider her as keeping him out of a large fortune by her life, and as being a disagreeable monitor, whose lectures were of force enough to make him feel the sting, from his riotous living, but not sufficient to make him forsake his excesses; he therefore, without the least gratitude for her repeated indulgences towards him, (for she had been the kindest of mothers) determined to free himself from her lectures, and to possess himself of her fortune. For this purpose he bought a quantity of poison, which he carried in his pocket, in order to wait for a convenient opportunity of giving it, which too soon offered; for in a few days, his mother was taken extremely ill as she was walking with her son and a maid-servant, in her own garden, and leaning on her maid's arm, she begged her son to run in and fetch such a particular bottle, in which was a cordial, that was ordered her by a physician to take, whenever she was seized with these kind of complaints. Alphonso ran with all the haste of apparent filial duty and tenderness, but fraught with all the inhuman cruelty of a fiend; and bringing back the cordial into which he had conveyed the poison, his mother drank it down, and finding herself rather worse than better, she was put to bed, and in a few hours expired. Alphonso made so grand a funeral for his mother, and bewailed her in such pathetic terms, that no one in the least suspected her being poisoned, and her death was imputed to her sudden seizure in the garden. But it was not long before Alphonso again asked the consent of Cassino to marry his daughter, which being refused, he resolved (having hardened himself by one Murder) that Cassino should not live; and then he doubted not of carrying his point with Eleonora. One evening therefore in the dusk he rode to Cassino's house, tied his horse to the gate, and seeing Cassino walking in his garden, his usual custom in the evening, he with a carbine loaden with a brace of bullets shot him through the head; when, instead of untying his horse and riding away, the vengeance of God followed him so as to turn his brain, and he ran into the next house, crying out he was very ill and must go to bed. The people of the house, out of compassion, took him in and put him to bed, sending, at the same time, for a physician, who found him perfectly delirious, raving and crying out that he had just shot Cassino, and a year before had poisoned his mother Sophia. By blisters and other applications his senses in a few hours returned to him, and being told what he had said in his raving fit, he with great confidence denied the truth of it, and said it would be unjust, as well as silly to believe a madman. But by this time the dead body of Cassino was found shot in his garden; Alphonso's horse was found tied by the pallisadoes that looked into the garden, where Cassino lay dead, and a carbine that had been fired off was found by the bedside of Alphonso; and which the people of the house, declared they saw him bring in with him in his hand. These circumstances were deemed sufficient to try and convict him, and he was executed for the murder of Cassino; and on the scaffold again confessed the poisoning of his mother Sophia.

[God's Revenge, &c. p. 473.]⁵

[5] John Reynolds (*fl.* 1620–40) or Reinolds, merchant of Exeter, compiled *The Triumphs of Gods Revenge against the Crying and Execrable Sin of Murther*. The first collection of five tales appeared *c.* 1621. Five more collections were published, all being issued in a single volume in 1635 containing thirty 'tragical histories'. There were at least 10 editions before 1719. I have compared Fielding's abridgements with the 1679 sixth edition. Fielding owned the 1635 edition (Baker, no. 450).

Fielding has radically abridged Reynolds's stories, omitting many details and complications, eliminating the many letters in the originals, and of course not reproducing the illustrative woodcuts. Even so, the Examples based on Reynolds are the longest in *Examples of Providence*. Fielding's Example III is Reynolds's 'History XXIII'.

EXAMPLE IV.

Parthenius, treasurer to Theodobert king of France, having killed his dear friend Ausanius and his wife, of which he was never in the least suspected, detected himself, by crying out in his sleep for help against Ausanius and his wife, who he said, were dragging him to the great tribunal of God, to answer for his Murder. On this confession in his sleep, he was apprehended; his restless conscience soon made him repeat and confirm such his confession, and he was accordingly condemned and executed.

[*Wanly's* Wonders of the little World, l. 1. c. 41. p. 89. *Beard's* Theatre of Wonders, l. 2 ch. 10, p. 285.][6]

EXAMPLE V.

A soldier in colonel Venables regiment that came out of Ireland, looked melancholy and pin'd, and grew so pale and thin, that he was worn almost to a skeleton. His officer, thinking the poor fellow might have some cause for grief which it might be in his power to remove, kindly urged him to declare what it was that made him so wretched; and at last, the soldier, unable longer to indure the racking torments of his own mind, made a confession to his captain, that he formerly had been a servant to a man that carried about stockings and such ware to sell; and that for his money he had murdered his master, and buried him in such a place; that he had immediately fled into Ireland, and inlisted himself for a soldier; that he had never enjoyed any happy hours, but particularly from the time he had landed in England; that he had every night been haunted with the ghost of his master; who said to him, "Wilt thou not yet confess thy wicked Murder." He added, that he was now glad to suffer death at once, in order to avoid the lingering punishment of wasting by degrees under excessive tortures. He afterwards made a proper confession before a magistrate: the body was searched for and found, and

---

[6] Thomas Beard's *Theatre of God's Ivdgements* was first published in 1597, reprinted 1612, 1631, 1648. I have compared Fielding's versions with the 1631 edition ('revised and augmented') to which Fielding's book, chapter, and page references are accurate. Beard was a puritan divine, Oliver Cromwell's schoolmaster. His *Theatre* collects instances of God's judgements against a wide variety of sinners. Several chapters in Bk. II describe punishments of murderers, and it is from these chapters that Fielding draws his examples.

William Wanley (1634–80) published *The Wonders of the Little World, or A General History of Man. In six Books*, in 1678. As its title suggests, it is something of an early 'Believe it or not' with religious leanings. Ch. 41 of the first Book, 'Of the strange ways by which Murthers have been discovered', is a very small part of the whole work. Wanley was an Anglican divine with strong nonconformist connections. The antiquarian, Humfrey Wanley, was his son.

Fielding's version is roughly the same length as those in Beard and Wanley, but he modernizes style and familiarizes detail. For instance, Wanley's 'stoned to death' becomes 'condemned and executed'. Wanley cites Beard.

the man was hanged in chains where the Murder was committed.   [*Baxter's Hist. Disc. of Apparitions*, p. 58.][7]

EXAMPLE VI.

A traveller was found murthered near Itzhow in Denmark; and because the Murderer was unknown, the magistates caused the hand of the slain to be cut off, and hung up by a string to the top of a room in the town-prison. Ten years after, the Murderer came into that room, having been taken up for some very slight offence, and the hand immediately began to drop blood upon the table that stood underneath it. The goaler on that, accused the prisoner with the murder, who struck with the apparent judgment of God, in the discovery of it, confessed the fact, and submitted to the punishment so justly due to his crime.

[*Turner* 28.][8] From *Beard's* Theatre. L. 2. c. 11.

EXAMPLE VII.

Smith and Gurney, two watermen of Gravesend, were hired by a grasier to carry him down to Tilbury-Hope, for he intended to buy cattle at a Fair in Essex. These villains finding he had money, robbed him, and threw him over-board. This Murder was concealed many years; at last, in the summer 1656. the two fellows, as they were drinking at an alehouse, had a quarrel, and Gurney in his passion, accused Smith with the Murder, which Smith soon retorted upon him. Being apprehended, and separately examined, they confessed the fact, were condemned at Maidstone assizes, and hanged in chains at Gravesend.   [*Turner* 29.][9]

---

[7] Richard Baxter, *The Certainty of the Worlds of Spirits. Fully evinced by unquestionable Histories of Apparitions and Witchcrafts, Operations, Voices, &c.* . . . (London, 1691), pp. 57–8. This work by the famous and prolific Presbyterian divine (1615–91) does not appear in Baker, though there is an abridgement of *Reliquiae Baxterianae* listed (no. 51). Fielding modernizes Baxter's style and avoids the ambiguity of his conclusion: 'And as I remember, his going to Hispaniola was his punishment, in stead of Death, where vengeance followed him'.

[8] William Turner (1653–1701), vicar of Walberton, Sussex, published in 1697 *A Compleat History of the most Remarkable Providences, both of Judgment and Mercy, Which have Hapned [sic] in this Present Age.* Turner's work has four separate paginations, or 'Alphabets'. Fielding's Example VI is from ch. CXIII on the page cited. Turner cites Beard.

Turner recommends his book 'as useful to Ministers in Furnishing Topicks of Reproof and exhortation, and to Private Christians for their Closets and Families'. Part one ('History of Divine Providences') contains 150 chapters, each illustrating the operation of providence in a special category, e.g. good angels, bad angels, premonitions, faith, prudence, charity.

[9] Ch. CXIII, p. 29.

EXAMPLE VIII.

In the Northern part of England (I think in Lancashire: for I had the story from a clergyman of that country) the minister before he began to read prayers at church, saw a paper lying in his book, which he supposed to be the banns of marriage. He opened it, and saw written in a fair and distinct hand, words to the following purpose, "That John P. and James D. had murdered a travelling man, had robbed him of his effects, and buried him in such an orchard." The minister was extremely startled, and asked his clerk hastily, if he had placed any paper in the prayer-book. The clerk declared he had not; but the minister prudently concealed the contents of the paper, for the two names therein contained were those of the clerk, and the sexton of the church.

The minister then went directly to a magistrate, told him what had happened, and took the paper out of his pocket to read it, when to his great surprize nothing appeared thereon, but it was a plain piece of white paper! The justice on that accused the minister of whim and fancy, and said that his head must certainly have been distempered, when he imagined such strange contents on a blank piece of paper. The good clergyman, plainly saw the hand of God in this matter, and by earnest intreaties, prevailed on the justice, to grant his warrant against the clerk and sexton; who were taken up on suspicion, and separately confined and examined; when so many contradictions appeared in their examination, for the sexton, who kept an alehouse, owned the having lodged such a man at his house, and the clerk said, he was that evening at the sexton's, but no such man was there, that it was thought proper to search their houses, in which were found several pieces of gold, and some goods belonging to men that travel the country; yet they gave so tolerable an account of these, that no positive proof could be made out, till the clergyman, recollecting, that the paper mentioned the dead body to be buried in such an orchard, a circumstance which had before slipped his memory, the place was searched, and the body was found: on hearing which, the sexton confessed the fact, accusing the clerk as his accomplice, and they were both accordingly executed.

EXAMPLE IX.

At a country village called Sprease, in the Venetian territories, fifteen miles from the city of Brescia, lived a farmer whose name was Alibius, who in his youth married a country girl called Merilla, by whom he had one daughter. But when he was about fifty years old, he was so displeased to find that his wife should also advance in years, and not continue in that youth and bloom in which she was when he married her, that he began to dislike and hate her: he left her, and went into a gentleman's service in Brescia, where after some years, he was made a macebearer to the chief magistrate, and by his outward behaviour acquired great reputation for an honest, sober and discreet man. At length a young widow called Philatea, to whom, by her husband, Alibius was left a trustee, favoured him so much, that he soon found his poor unhappy wife Merilla was the only obstacle to his enjoying both a fine young woman, and an ample fortune. He therefore, without the least remorse, resolved to dispatch her, and for that purpose bought some poison at Brescia, and riding to Sprease, he feigned great love and affection to his old wife Merilla, and treating her with milk and apples, he mixt in them some of the poison, enough as he imagined to destroy her, and the next morning early again returned to Brescia. Hearing no news of his wife's death, which he hourly expected from the doses he had given her, but which were only sufficient to make her extremely ill, but not to take away her life, he once more set out on the same design; but finding his daughter there, he was afraid to repeat his potions, as she dwelt very strongly on her poor mother's late illness, and Alibius's conscience made him imagine, that she at least half intimated, that his milk and apples had been the occasion of her disorder. Yet did not these checks of conscience work strongly enough with him, to prevent his guilt and shameful exit, or to save a poor innocent women from the cruelty of a man that ought to have been her protector. For in his third attempt, he came to Sprease in the middle of the night, and was let in by a little grand-daughter about ten years old. He went directly into his wife's chamber, with another dose of poison, prepared for her, but finding her asleep, he with a billet[1] out of the chimney, dashed out her brains, and riding back with all speed to Brescia, he appeared in his publick office by six of the clock in the morning, and no one suspected his having been out of the town. The poor child who let him in, knew him not, for he had never taken any notice either of her or her mother, since her marriage, and could give no other account, but that a ruffian had rushed into the house, and killed her grand-mother.

Alibius made great pretended lamentations for his wife, but soon after was married to the young and wealthy Philatea, and expected quietly to enjoy the fruits of his inhuman barbarity. But Providence designed otherwise, and he was made a public example of the folly, as well as wickedness, of expecting, that happiness will ever be the fruit of iniquity, or that so detestable a sin as Murder will go unpunished.

He had not lived long with his new wife, before an old companion of his coming to Brescia, in his drunken cups, declared, that Alibius and his daughter Amelia were the murderers of Merilla; and this report began to be

---

[1] 'A thick piece of firewood' (*OED*).

current in the mouth of every one. On which the magistrates of the town of Brescia, who are extremely diligent in their offices, sent for Alibius, and examined him on this report, and sent also for the man who first set it on foot. Alibius boldly denied the fact, and the man declared he knew not what had induced him to utter such a scandal, which was only done in his liquor, for now being sober, he was far from accusing Alibius or his daughter, nor so much as remembered, his having done so when drunk. Although this affair seemed pretty well cleared up, yet one of the magistrates said, that since Merilla was certainly murdered, and as it could not be for her wealth, she being a very poor woman, he thought there needed a further examination, for as the old Proverb says, "there is no smoak without some fire," so is there seldom any report without some foundation for it. Alibius on this, thinking at once to exculpate himself, and shew his innocence, and depending on the fair character he had acquired, cried out, that nothing could be more true than what was last spoken; and then seeming to shed tears for the loss of his wife, he said, he owned that he himself had some suspicions of his daughter Amelia, but his tenderness as a father, had restrained him from seeking justice where it appeared due, for a murdered wife. This had the desired effect; every one praised both his speech and his conduct; and Amelia his daughter was immediately taken up, and adjudged to the rack. As poor Amelia was perfectly innocent, she was greatly shocked and astonished at the accusation. She bore the torment with patience and resignation, nor once reproached or complained of her cruel accusers.

Alibius, infatuated with his success, and urged on by his hatred to his daughter, depending also most cruelly and basely on her affection for him, urged them once more to put her to the torment; hoping, that by the grief of her mind, and pains of her body, she could not long survive her second tryal; when quite overcome with this repeated insult of inhumanity from her father, she begged a patient hearing of the judge, and declared to him her suspicions of his being her mother's murderer, as also of his former attempt to poison her with milk and apples. This was at first looked upon as a malicious retort, in hopes to save her own life; but luckily for her, the apothecary's servant who had sold the poison to Alibius, was then present; and recollecting the time, it exactly answered to Amelia's information. This man also declared, that he had sold Alibius another dose of poison, just about the time that Merilla was murthered; but as her death was from a blow, and as Alibius was not known to be absent that night from Brescia, there was no suspicion at that time in this man, but that the poison was, as he professed, bought to kill his rats. Another circumstance was now related, which concurred with the rest to prove his guilt; namely, that his horse, with the hard riding that night, had slipped his shoulder; which the farrier, who cured the beast declared in court. This farrier had before no suspicion from that circumstance; for Alibius had told the man, that he had lent his horse to a boy, who had, through the giddiness of youth, slipped his shoulder in riding, and the farrier never thought any more of the matter. These concurring circumstances, together with the evidence of the whole village of Sprease, to his ill treatment of his wife Merilla, and his neglect and hatred both of her and her daughter, were deemed sufficient to acquit Amelia; especially as her father, who was her only accuser, gave no reasons but his bare word for his suspicions. And it was thought proper immediately to put Alibius to the rack. He indured only one torment, before he confessed the whole truth, but declared his wife Philotea innocent of the knowledge. He was condemned, and accordingly executed in the 73d year of his age: a most miserable example of cruelty and hypocrisy; punished by the very means that he took, to add the death of an innocent daughter, to that of an injured wife.

[God's Revenge, p. 65.][2]

EXAMPLE X.

Victorina, a Venetian lady was married by her parents, not much with her own liking, to an old man; and soon after falling into the company of a gay young gentleman called Sypontus, she not only intrigued with him, but soon weary of the restraint of a husband's jealous eye, they agreed to murder the old gentleman. This wicked purpose Sypontus undertook, and executed in this manner. The old gentleman used to divert himself every evening in his gondola, on the water. Sypontus leapt from his own boat well armed, into that of the old gentleman. He first dispatched him, then his two watermen, and threw them into the sea; and returning into his own boat, he stabbed his own waterman also, and threw him overboard. Having thus secured every witness to his guilt, by adding murder to murder, he landed after it was dark, and that night waited on the wicked contriver of all this mischief, and acquainted her with his success. They agreed not to see each other for some time, for fear of suspicion; and it was generally believed, that the old gentleman was drowned. But in about eight days, his body was found by some fishermen; and as he plainly appeared to have been murdered, many were the conjectures, but no certainty could be obtained concerning the murderer. In a short time, a brother to the murdered old gentleman came to Venice, and suspecting that his sister-in-law Victorina, bore no real affection to her deceased husband, and had been but too familiar with Sypontus, he feared there had been foul play towards his poor brother: He therefore with large gifts prevailed on Victorina's maid Felicia, to declare what she knew of her lady's intrigues with Sypontus; and also to steal from her lady's cabinet a

[2] Reynolds, 'History V'.

letter from Sypontus, in which he gave some distinct hints of the dangers he had run, and the acts he had performed for her sake. This letter being laid before a magistrate, he immediately took up Victorina and Sypontus, and separately confined them. Sypontus hearing that his accusation arose from a letter under his own hand, imagined that Victorina had accused and betrayed him, but finding means privately to correspond with her, and being assured of her innocence towards him, and that Felicia had stolen the letter and exposed it, he resolved at the expence of his own life to preserve hers; so great did the merit of her ill-placed affection to him appear in his eyes, that he consider'd not that he was preserving both a Murderer and adulteress, who was indeed only reserved for future punishment. Being put to the torture, he readily confessed the fact, but, at his execution, he with his dying breath declared Victorina ignorant of the knowledge of his crime, on which, at the earnest intreaty of her father, she was released.

Victorina soon forgot both her old husband, and her lover Sypontus, and was married, much against her father's consent, to a debauch'd profligate young fellow, called Fassino, who soon repaid her for her disloyalty to her first husband, by leaving her for the company of the most abandon'd and profligate part of woman-kind, on whom he lavish'd all his health and fortune; while he bestowed on his wife only diseases, ill humour, and distressed circumstances. She soon came to a thorough hatred of her husband, and having once stained her mind with Murder, she, without hesitation, determined to dispatch Fassino. She sent secretly for an apothecary called Augustino, who lived at Naples, but at that time happen'd to be in Venice, and offer'd him a very large reward, if he would undertake to poison her husband Fassino. He not only refused the money, or to undertake the business, but intreated her to lay aside such wicked purposes, and she appear'd to be very much moved with his discourse, and promised to take his advice. Soon after he was departed from Venice, she privately bought some arsenic, and resolved to wait for a convenient opportunity of giving it to her husband.

It was not long before Fassino came home from a debauch, very ill, and desired to have some broth made for him. Victorina ordered her own maid Felicia to make the broth, and, whilst her back happen'd to be turned to the fire, Victorina slip'd into the broth, as it was boiling, half the arsenic she had bought, and conveyed the other half privately into Felicia's trunk. Fassino died of the poison. Victorina and the maid were both taken up, but it appeared so strong against Felicia, as the remainder of the poison was found in her trunk, that she was condemn'd to be hang'd; and as she did not, for she could not positively, accuse her mistress, Victorina was again released, and exulted extremely in her double mischief, of getting rid of her husband, and being revenged on Felicia for what she had formerly done. But on the day that Felicia was to be executed, after she was ascended the scaffold, Augustino, the Neopolitan apothecary, landing at St. Mark's bridge, and seeing a great croud of people, enquired the occasion, and being told what it was, he hasten'd to the judges *who are there present at such executions*,[3] and begg'd them to delay, for a few minutes, the fate of the girl, 'till he had informed them of something that might save an innocent person, and bring the guilty to punishment. He then acquainted them with what had formerly pass'd between himself and Victorina; and, after they had thoroughly examined into the matter, Victorina was again taken up, and being confronted with Augustino the apothecary, she trembled, and was near fainting away. On the first mention of the rack, she declared the whole truth, and confessed also the Murder of her former husband, and her intentions, so near succeeding, of taking away the life of Felicia. The whole court was shock'd with the blackness of her crimes. Felicia was released, and Victorina was executed with all the rigour of the law.

[God's Revenge, &c. p. 37.][4]

EXAMPLE XI.

In Metz, a city of Lorrain, lived a merchant who was very wealthy, but of a most covetous and cruel disposition. One of his servants having given him some slight offence, he beat him with his own hands, in so severe a manner that the poor lad expired at his feet; yet, as there was no witness to this piece of cruelty, he for some time, escaped punishment; for, carrying down the dead body into the cellar, he there buried it himself, and, when the boy was missed, it was generally believed that he had run away from his master, and no further inquiry was made concerning him. In less than a year after this cruel murder had been committed, the executioner of the city stole one night into the merchant's house, and got privately down into the cellar, where he first slew the maid who was sent for some wine, and then her mistress who came thither in order to see what was become of her maid. He then took off the lady's cloaths, and rifling them both of all they had in their pockets, as also taking some pieces of plate from the sideboard, stole off unperceived by any one. The merchant, on his return home, finding the Murder of his wife and servant, and the plunder of the house, complain'd to the senate, and they promised to take all proper means to discover both the thief, and the murderer; but it being well known, that the merchant had lived in a most brawling and unhappy manner with his wife, and had also been known to strike her, and use her with much cruelty, the man who really had committed

---

[3] Fielding's italics recall his recommendation in the *Enquiry* that judges be present at executions.
[4] Reynolds, 'History VI'.

the theft and murder, on that hint, whisper'd amongst the crowd, "that 'twas very likely that the merchant himself, on finding his house robb'd, might take that opportunity to murder his wife, (and the maid too, perhaps, for helping her mistress) that by such means he might avoid the suspicion which must attend every cruel husband whose wife is found to have died by violence." This rumor so strongly prevail'd, that the merchant was taken up, and put to the rack. The torture was so great, that he soon cry'd out that he prefer'd death to such torments, and if they would release him, he would confess the truth. He then, being deeply struck in his conscience, own'd the murder of his servant, but strongly denied that of his wife and maid. They search'd the cellar, and found the dead body of the boy, and the merchant was accordingly executed for the same. But with his last breath he so strongly denied the murder of his wife and maid, that 'twas not doubted, but the thief who had plunder'd the house, and the murderer was the same; nor was it long before the wicked fellow the executioner, who had been the means of bringing the merchant to justice, was punish'd for his complicated crimes of theft, murder, and false accusation. For, wanting money, he pawn'd a silver bowl to a Jew, on which was the merchant's arms. The Jew took it, but carried it directly before a magistrate, who immediately seized on the executioner, search'd his house, where he found many more things belonging to the merchant, as also the watch, and several baubles and trinkets, belonging to his wife, which must have been taken from her pocket when she was murdered. These proofs were so strong against him, both of the Murder and theft, that he was condemn'd and executed with all the rigor of the law.

[*Turner's* Divine Judgments, 30.][5]

EXAMPLE XII.

Some highwaymen in Germany, after having robb'd a gentleman in a wood, agreed to murder him, to prevent discovery. He begg'd hard for his life, but could not prevail; and as they were endeavouring to cut his throat, seeing a flight of cranes over his head, he cried out, "O ye cranes, as you are the witnesses to my Murder, I adjure ye to detect these Murderers, and bring them to justice."

Not long after, as these thieves and murderers were drinking at an inn, and dividing their spoil, a great flight of cranes came, and settled on the house, and made a most dreadful noise and clamour; on which they fell a laughing, and one said to the rest, "There are the cranes come, to discover the murder of the gentleman whom we killed in the wood, but I believe no

---

[5] *Remarkable Providences*, ch. CXIII, p. 30.

one will understand their language, and they will lose their labour." A person overhearing this speech, and, from their locking themselves into their room, suspecting they were not very honest men, went to a magistrate and got a warrant to take them up. On searching them, many things of value were found on them; and on taxing them with the Murder, (without telling them the grounds for such accusation) they separately gave such contradictory answers, that the suspicion against them was strong enough to induce a narrower search.

The dead body was afterwards found; and, as the thieves in their hurry had taken but one of his shoe buckles, that which was found in the dead man's shoe was compared with the buckle found in the possession of the thieves. This circumstance was deem'd strong enough to convict them both of the robbery and Murder, for which they were all three executed, and which, with many other things, they confess'd at the gallows.

[Wonders of the little World. L. 1. c. 41. p. 90. *Beard's* Theatre, l. 2 c. 11. p. 299.][6]

EXAMPLE XIII.

Monsieur de Laurier, a very rich jeweller of the city of Dijon, in the province of Burgundy, had been at Francfort, where he had sold a considerable quantity of goods, for which he received 1700 crowns. Returning home with the aforesaid sum, and also with the value of as much more in jewels, he was taken very ill at the town of Salines, and obliged to take up his lodging at an inn, the keeper of which was named Adrian, and his wife Isabella.

The jeweller's companions being men of business, and not related to him, left him, and his fever increased so much, that he gave himself over for a dead man, and sent for a physician of that place. The doctor attended him some time, but finding his patient at last on the mending hand, though not yet able to travel, he left off his visits. On his return after a few days absence, Adrian acquainted the physician, that Monsieur de Laurier was well, and set out for his own house at Dijon. But the truth was far otherwise; for this wicked host Adrian, imagining that De Laurier had great riches about him, resolved that he should not go alive from his house: he communicated his cruel purpose to his wife Isabella, who, with tears and prayers, besought him to lay aside his horrid design; but when he found she was not to be moved to be an assistant in his guilt, he sent her many leagues off, under pretence of visiting her aged father, who, he said, as he had heard, was very near his

[6] In both Wanley and Beard the providential fowls are crows, and their accounts are about half the length of Fielding's, suggesting perhaps another unnamed source. The story is also in Turner, *Remarkable Providences*, ch. CXIII, p. 28, and the fowls are crows. Turner cites Beard.

death. He after, one night, sent away both his man and maid-servant, on some pretence, and then, with another bloody-minded villain, to whom he promised half the booty, he strangled the old man in his bed, and buried his body in the orchard. In ten days his wife return'd, and to her, as well as his servants, he declared that De Laurier had left his house; and as to his horse, Adrian's accomplice carried that into a wood, about four leagues from Salines, hoping that the beast would find his way to Dijon, and that De Laurier's son would suppose his father had been robb'd and murdered on the road.

Just that day month, after the Murder had been committed, a wolf came into Adrian's orchard, and digging at the place where De Laurier was buried, tore up the carcase, and began to devour it; when some gentlemen with dogs, leaping the hedge, came into the same orchard, the wolf fled; but the gentlemen, seeing the body, had it taken up, and carried into the midst of the city, where many people came to look at it, and amongst the rest, the physician La Motte, who knew it to be the face of De Laurier, whom he had attended at Adrian's house. The officers of justice immediately surrounded Adrian's house, and took up his servants, and his wife Isabella; but, for Adrian himself, he was that night rioting at the house of his wicked accomplice in the Murder, and on hearing the report that De Laurier's body was found, they both fled, hoping to escape out of the reach of that jurisdiction; but being fearful of appearing in daylight, they hid themselves in a large wood, about two leagues from Salines, and lying concealed all day, they only travelled after it was dark. After wandering the whole night, they constantly, as soon as it was day, found themselves on that side of the wood from whence they could see the city of Salines; and though they lay for nine days concealed, and for nine nights travelled with all the speed and care imaginable, yet never could they find themselves advanced beyond the same side of the wood at which they entered. Weakened with fasting and extreme hunger, they at last became so faint, that they were hardly able to support themselves any longer: By this time, De Laurier's son being come from Dijon, and having buried his father, was returning home, and in company with him was La Motte the physician. These two on break of day entered the wood, and there discovered Adrian and his companion, lying under the shade of a tree. They were at first afraid, being but two in number, to attack such desperate villains; but more people coming up, they soon laid hands on the murderers, whom they found very little able to make resistance. They were first tortured, and afterwards executed for the inhospitable and cruel act.   [God's Revenge, &c. p. 369.][7]

---

[7] Reynolds, 'History XXVII'.

EXAMPLE XIV.

Signior Thomasi Vituri, a nobleman of the city of Pavia, had one only daughter named Christinetta; to whom most of the young gentlemen of that neighbourhood made their addresses. Amongst these was Signior Gasperino, a noble young gentleman of Cremona; who desired his friend Loduvicus Pisani, to accompany him in his visits to Christinetta. But unhappily for him, Christinetta fell most desperately in love with Pisani, and therefore gave Gasperino an absolute refusal. As soon as Gasperino was departed, she by letter made Pisani acquainted with her passion, and he returning to Pavia, was, with the consent of her parents, married to her.

Gasperino thinking himself ill used by Pisani, sends him a challenge, which he accepts: They met, attended by seconds, and Pisani was killed; but as it was allowed to be a fair and honourable duel, Gasperino easily obtained his pardon.

Gasperino's passion for Christinetta was so great, that he again made his addresses to her, and she smothering her resentment for the death of her husband, gave him great encouragement; and one evening appointed to meet him, in a garden adjoining to the nun's garden, in Pavia. Hither she brought with her, two ruffians Brindoli and Bianco; who fell on Gasperino at his arrival, and although he for some time defended himself, the ruffians overpowered and with repeated stabs slew him; and to prevent him from groaning, so as to be heard by the nuns, Christinetta herself stuffed her handkerchief into his mouth, and being dead, they carried his body to the other side of the garden, and threw it into a well.

The nuns, hearing the clashing of swords, sent speedily to the place, from whence the sound came, and though the murderers were fled, yet much blood remained in the place. Hence believing that there had been mischief, the nuns sent to all the surgeons in the city, to enquire what wounded persons they had under their care, and by that means they soon discovered Brindoli and Bianco, to have been wounded that very evening. Gasperino also being missed, there was a strong suspicion that they were his murderers; but they firmly denied it, and declared, that they received their wounds from each other, having had a quarrel, which they decided by the sword.

Even the rack, which they both endured, could force no confession from them; and Christinetta, hearing that they had suffered torments, without betraying her, greatly hoped and believed, that she should go unpunished to her grave.

But the magistrates being yet unsatisfied, in not hearing any news of Gasperino, and being informed by his servant, that he went out that evening towards the nun's garden, ordered a stricter search to be made for his body, which at length was found in the well; but still they were at a loss for the murderers; as neither by proof, or their own confession, could they convict Bianco or Brindoli of having been in his company: But on farther examining the dead body, they perceived the corner of a white handkerchief, to hang out of the deceased's mouth; and, pulling it from thence, they saw on one corner of it, the name of Christinetta. This was sufficient to have her taken up, and on the very first torment, she not only confessed the fact, but accused her two accomplices Bianco and Brindoli; and they were all three publickly executed. The bodies of the two ruffians after being hanged, were thrown into the river Po; and the inhuman Christinetta, who with a pretence of kindness betrayed, and then assisted in the murder of Gasperino, was first hanged, then her body was burnt, and her ashes scattered into the air.

[God's Revenge, &c. p. 16.][8]

EXAMPLE XV.

In those countries abroad, where it is no uncommon thing to hire ruffians to kill for them, there is one circumstance which shews the folly as well as wickedness of employing such bloody agents; namely, that it never, or very seldom ever happened, but these men, either for their repeated villanies or some robbery come to publick execution, and then they surely publish every hired fact they were ever employed in. By which means, the principal mover of a Murder, is daily at the mercy of the breath of a wretch whom he knows to be a villain and a murderer. Innumerable are the instances abroad of these kind of discoveries, among which is the following.

In a village, near the town of Sens in Burgundy, lived two brothers, the eldest was called Vimorie, and the name of the younger was Harcourt. Vimorie married a very plain woman called Masserina, for the sake of her wealth; and Harcourt married for love a beautiful young girl, whose personal perfections were her only dowry. In less than a year, Harcourt growing weary of his amiable wife, began to wish that he had made wealth and not beauty his choice; and being a wretch without natural affection to his brother, and possessing every ill quality that human nature is capable of, he determined, within himself, to rob his brother both of his fortune and his wife, and this in a way that the law could not possibly reach him. This was no other than by making use of the personal advantages in which he excelled in a very eminent degree, and of that rhetoric which he had from experience found was seldom ineffectual with women. Every art that could possibly be made use of for that purpose he employed, and by these base means he prevailed with the unfortunate Masserina to forsake her husband, and to fly with him. She (being a widow when she married Vimorie) had her whole fortune in her own

---

[8] Reynolds, 'History II'.

power; this she bestowed on Harcourt, and without the least shame or compunction, they lived publicly together at Genoa. Vimorie and the disconsolate wife of Harcourt seeing there was no redress, endeavoured to console themselves with their lot; which being innocence of mind, though devoid of affluence of fortune, was greatly preferable to the guilty hours of Harcourt and Masserina.

It was not long before a very large estate of inheritance came to Masserina by the death of her brother; but as she was absent, her injured husband, Vimorie, was soon put in possession of it by law.

Harcourt, by his riot and extravagance, soon spent all the fortune that Masserina had in her own power, and hearing of this large acquisition kept from him, as he called it, by his brother, he soon came to the bloody resolution of taking away his life. He first tampered with his own servant Noel, to undertake the murder of Vimorie; but, on his refusal, he put on a disguise, and going himself to the village where his brother lived, shot him in the dusk of the evening, as he was going into his own house; and then posted back with such speed to Geneva, that he was never missed, nor was the least suspicion cast on him for the murder. There was still one bar remained to his enjoyment of this fortune, which the fond deluded Masserina wished to bestow on him by marriage, and that was the life of his own deserted wife: but as those who commit one cruel act, never hesitate at a second, he hires a mountebank, named Tivoly, to go to Sens, and there to poison her, which was soon effected; after which he and Masserina both returned to Sens, were publickly married, and, for a short time, seemed to enjoy the highest worldly success from their most diabolical cruelty. But Tivoly the mountebank, being taken up and condemned for a robbery, he confessed the poisoning of Harcourt's wife, and declared himself hired by him and Masserina to perform it. Noel also, Harcourt's man, being ill of a fever, declared (thinking himself on his death-bed) the offer of money his master had made him to murder his brother Vimorie. These two accusations, and other circumstances considered, Harcourt and Masserina were taken up and put to the torture, where they soon confessed the crimes for which they were both publickly executed.

[God's Rev. &c. p. 325.][9]

EXAMPLE XVI.

Signior Albemare, a young gentleman of Millan, courted a beautiful young lady called Clara. He had obtain'd her parents consent, but could not gain hers, as she frankly told him, that her heart and honour were both

---

[9] Reynolds, 'History XVI'. There is no authority for Fielding's first paragraph.

engaged to signior Baretano. After a fruitless attendance on Clara for six months, he found her so fixed in her affection to Baretano, that he could have no hope, but in the death of his rival. This he soon effected, by hiring two ruffians, Leonardo and Pedro, to murder him, for which he gave them two hundred ducats; and taking care himself to be far from Millan when this cruel Murder was committed, he escaped suspicion, nor could the magistrates, at that time, gain the least insight into this bloody business.

After a year's lamentation for the death of her beloved Baretano, Clara consented to marry Albemare. But it was not long before he grew tired of this jewel, for which he had paid so large a price *as his own eternal damnation*, and he returned to his old way of living, which was associating with the most debauch'd and profligate part of the human kind. Pedro, one of his wicked agents in the Murder of Baretano, having lavish'd away all the money he had earn'd by his villainy, had recourse to a robbery, for which he was taken. Whilst in prison, he wrote a letter to Albemare, that if he did not procure for him his pardon for this robbery, he would, at the gallows, confess the Murder of Baretano, and also at whose instigation it was committed. Albemare return'd him a civil answer, and promised to grant his request, and the next night sent his own servant Valerio to him, to acquaint him, that his pardon was obtained, and would be sent him the next morning. But this was no other than a falshood, invented for the present to stop his mouth, 'till he could effectually prevent his discovery of the Murder. This he did by giving him poison in a bottle of wine, which his servant carried to him in prison, for that purpose; and the next morning, Pedro being found dead in his bed, 'twas supposed that he had poison'd himself to prevent his public execution.

Not long after, Leonardo, the other assassin, who was at Pavia, wrote a letter to Albemare, saying he was very poor, and begging him to give, or lend him, fifty ducats. Albemare took no notice of this letter, on which Leonardo, very much enraged, wrote him a second, and said, that he would full as soon be hang'd as starv'd; and therefore if Albemare would not supply him with money to support him in a comfortable way of life, he would confess the Murder of Baretano, and impeach him. This letter came when Albemare was abroad, and his servant Valerio being obliged to go out, laid it on a cupboard in his master's room, in order to be in his sight as soon as he came in. But a natural fool that Albemare kept in his house, seeing where the letter was put, climb'd up upon a stool, took it down, and ran with it into the court yard, jumping about, and crying out, *that God Almighty had sent him a letter.* Clara, at this time, coming in from church, and seeing the fool with this letter, took it out of his hand, and observing 'twas directed to her husband, put it in her pocket, in order to give it him when he came home, and ask'd his servant, (who was just return'd) from whence it came, to which the servant answer'd, he could not tell; but the fool following Clara, kept crying out, "the letter is sent from God Almighty, I tell you, 'tis God's own letter to me, and not to my master Albemare." The strangeness of the idiot's words, and his urgency in repeating them, gave Clara so strong a curiosity to open the letter, that she could not resist; when, seeing the contents, she was, for some time, like one turn'd into stone with horror, nor knew which way to act, for she was extremely shock'd at the thought of being her husband's accuser. But the knowledge of a Murder bore too near a resemblance to the having committed one, for an honest mind to undergo, and reflecting also on the speech of the idiot, *no doubt divinely dictated*, she consider'd herself as bound in duty to God and her conscience, to discover all she knew. She gave the letter, therefore, into the hands of a magistrate, relating the manner in which she came by it. Upon this, her husband Albemare was taken up, Leonardo also was brought from Pavia, and seeing his own letter, he soon confessed the fact, and accused Albemare of hiring him to undertake it. They were both accordingly executed for the same. Leonardo died penitent, but Albemare impiously cursed both his wife, the fool, and his servant Valerio, whom he accused of being his instrument to poison Pedro, in prison, the night before his intended execution. Valerio, also, on that, was arraigned, and condemned to the rack, where he soon confessed the fact, but declared his innocence with regard to the Murder of Baretano. Leonardo and Valerio were both gibbetted, and the body of Albemare, after being hang'd, was burnt, and his ashes thrown into the air.   [God's Revenge against Murder p. 213][1]

EXAMPLE XVII.

Laurietta, a beautiful young heiress, of Avignon in France, was of so dissolute and debauch'd a mind, that although she had youth, beauty, and fortune sufficient to have match'd her with a man of the first rank and fortune in the kingdom, yet she gave herself up to all manner of extravagance and wantonness, and led the life of a common courtezan. One of her chief favourites was count Poligny, a very brave and worthy young gentleman, but who, for the fault of incontinency with this fair seducer, lost his life in the flower of his youth, for he was stabb'd one evening, as he went from her apartment. The person suspected of this cruel action, was Monsieur de Belvile, a younger gentleman who had been greatly favour'd by Laurietta; but was discarded when she received into her service the unhappy Poligny.

As no proofs appeared to justify the suspicion of Belvile's being the Murderer of Poligny, he was never openly accused of it, but Laurietta

---

[1] Reynolds, 'History XII'.

believing in her own mind, that it was Belvile who had deprived her of her favourite lover, resolved to be revenged on him, and for that purpose sent him a kind letter, wondering it had been so long since she had been bless'd with his company.

Belvile, with all the ardor of a lover, answered her epistle, and appointed the next evening to wait on her at her own house. She prepared herself, and maid-servant Lucetta, with poignards, hid under their garments, ready to receive him, but he saved them that trouble, by bringing with him a brace of pistols, which they, as in play, took out of his hands, and Laurietta, after many feigned caresses of welcome, desired him to look out at the window, at something she pretended to shew him, and then fired a brace of balls, directly through his back. He fell dead at her feet, but yet she could not refrain from giving him several stabs with her poignard, and she and Lucetta carried down the body into the cellar, and buried it under a heap of billets.

On Belvile's being missed, his valet declared, that he attended him to the lady Laurietta's gate, and saw him enter there, on which she was strictly examined, and she confess'd that Belvile had made her a visit, but that his stay was extremely short, nor did she know what was become of him. Although no positive proof could be brought against her, yet they thought proper to give her the torment, but no confession did they force from her lips. Her maid Lucetta on hearing that her mistress was put to the torture, fear'd that she would confess, and betray her, and therefore fled; but in passing the fenny lakes that are between Avignon and Orange, she was drown'd. The flight of Lucetta made them more strongly suspect Laurietta, and they again gave her the torture, which she indured in the same manner as the first. On which they intended in a week's time to release her, and she shewed the highest marks of joy, on the thought of her enlargement. But her wickedness was not, even in this world, to escape unpunish'd.

She was of a most extravagant temper, and had well nigh lavish'd away her whole fortune on her licentious pleasures. She lived in a large hired house, in the finest street in Avignon, but, for the last three years, had paid no rent. Her landlord Monsieur de Richcourt, willing to secure his money, seized for his rent, and sold not only the furniture, but even all the liquor in the cellar, and the very fuel which was left in the house; and, on removing the billets, which he had sold, they found the earth under them had been newly dug up, and, on further search, they found the dead body of Belvile. This put the matter quite out of doubt, and, on the day that Laurietta expected to have been released, they brought the mangled corpse of Belvile into the prison to her, the sight of which had a stronger effect than all their torments, and she immediately fell on her knees, and confess'd the fact; which was indeed too plain to be denied, and she was executed for the same before the gates of her own house. She was first hang'd, and then her body was burnt, together with that of her maid Lucetta, which was consumed by the same fire, and their mingled ashes were scatter'd into the air.

[*God's Revenge*, &c. 127.][2]

EXAMPLE XVIII.

A man was taken up on suspicion of Murder, but when brought to the bar, the evidence appeared not strong enough to convict him. He behaved with great apparent boldness, for he knew there were no witnesses to the fact; and he had also taken all necessary caution to prevent a discovery. But the judge observed in the man's countenance, a terror and confusion, which his pretended boldness could not hide, and therefore kept his eye steadily fixt on him the whole time. As soon as the last witness was dismissed, the man asked, if they had any more evidence against him; when the judge looking sternly at him, asked him if he did not himself know of one more that could appear against him, whose presence would put the matter out of doubt. On which the man started and cried out, "My lord, he is not a legal witness, no man can speak in his own cause, nor was the wound I gave him half so large, as what he shews against me." The judge presently perceived by the man's starting, and the wildness and terror of his look, that he either saw the ghost of the murdered man, or that his imagination had from his guilty conscience formed such an appearance; and therefore making the proper answers from such a supposition, he soon brought the murderer to confess the fact, for which he was condemned, and hanged in chains, at the place where he declared the murder was committed. At his death he averred, that the ghost of the murdered person had appeared before his eyes at his trial.   [*Moretus*, p. 101.][3]

EXAMPLE XIX.

A gentleman in good circumstances about the year 1640, murdered his friend, a man in business, near Bow-church in Cheapside; and with such circumstances of malice, revenge and cruelty, as made it impossible for him to expect any mercy. He therefore made his escape into France, where he lived for some years: But from the horrors of his guilty conscience, which almost every night presented before his eyes, whether sleeping or waking, his murthered friend, he felt ten-fold the punishment, which, by flight, he vainly

---

[2] Reynolds, 'History VIII'.

[3] Moretus: Andrew Moreton, pseudonym for Daniel Defoe, *The Secrets of the Invisible World Disclos'd; or an Universal History of Apparitions* (London, 1729), pp. 101–4. There is considerably more detail in Defoe's account. Fielding owned a copy of this work (Baker, no. 242), which was first published in 1727 as *An Essay on the History and Reality of Apparitions*.

hoped to escape. After twenty years residence, or rather wandering abroad, through most part of Europe, he resolved to venture back into England. He changed his name; and as time, and the change of climates had altered his person, he doubted not but he might in some retired part of his own country, wear out the remainder of his days; and perhaps, recover that peace of mind, which he had there left behind him. But publick justice, though slow, at last overtook him: For the very evening that he landed in a wherry at Queen-hithe-stairs, walking up to Cheapside, in order to get into a coach, just in the dusk, and by the very door of his murdered friend, he heard a voice cry out, "Stop him, stop him, there he is." On this he ran as fast as he was able, and soon found himself followed by a large mob. He was soon overtaken and seized, on which he cried out, "I confess the fact, I am the man that did it." The mob on that said, as he had confessed the crime, they would proceed to execution; and, after making him refund the stolen goods, would give him the discipline of pumping, kenneling[4] and the like: on which he said he had stolen nothing, for though he had murdered Mr. L——, yet he had no intention of robbing his house. By this answer, the mob found themselves mistaken, for they were pursuing a pickpocket, and seeing this man run hard, believed him to be the pickpocket; but now were for letting him go as a person distracted, that knew not what he said. One man however who lived in that neighbourhood, and had heard of the murder of Mr. L——, desired that this gentleman might be examined before a magistrate, and he was accordingly carried before the Lord-Mayor, who took his confession of the fact, for which he was soon after hanged: and he declared at the gallows, that the day of his execution, was the happiest day he had known since he had committed that horrid, treacherous, inhuman act, the murder of a friend, who loved him, and to whom he lay under the highest obligations. [*Moretus's secrets of the invisible world disclosed.* p. 105.][5]

EXAMPLE XX.

In the reign of king James I. one Ann Waters having an unlawful and wanton intercourse with a young man in the neighbourhood; and finding her husband some embarrassment to their wicked pleasures, determined to put

[4] 'pumping': holding someone under a pump; 'kenneling': holding someone in the kennel or gutter. Traditional punishments inflicted by the 'mob' on minor offenders, such as pickpockets.

[5] Ibid., pp. 105–10. Defoe's account is shaped to reveal the psychology of guilt, not the operation of providence. A passage in *Moll Flanders* reflects this distinction between Fielding and Defoe. It concludes, '[a guilty conscience] works sometimes with such vehemency in the minds of those who are guilty of any atrocious villany such as a secret murther in particular, that they have been oblig'd to discover it, tho' the consequence has been their own destruction. Now, tho' it may be true that the divine justice ought to have the glory of all those discoveries and confessions, yet 'tis as certain that Providence, which ordinarily works by the hand of nature, makes use here of the same natural causes to produce those extraordinary effects' (Boston, 1959), p. 282.

him out of the way; and accordingly one night, assisted by her paramour, she strangled her husband, and they buried his body under a dunghill in the cow-house. The man was missing, and his wife made such a lamentation about him, that the people greatly pitied her, and gave her all the assistance in their power in searching for her husband; but as she knew where she had laid him, she took care to direct their search, far from the place where her barbarity would have been discovered.

After the search was at an end, and 'twas imagined, that the man might be gone away for debt, without acquainting his wife with his intentions; a woman in the neighbourhood dreamt that a stranger told her, that Ann Waters had strangled her husband, and hid him under the dunghill. She at first disregarded the dream, but it being repeated several nights, it began publickly to be talk'd of; and at length they got authority to search the dunghill, where the dead body was found; and other concurrent circumstances appearing, the wife was apprehended and convicted of the murder, which before her execution she confessed, and impeached the young fellow her accomplice: He, on her being apprehended, immediately fled, but was pursued and taken, and on his own confession was also executed for the murder. Ann Waters was burnt, and her paramour was hang'd in chains.

[*Turner* 29. *Wanly's* wonders, &c. l. 1. c. 41. p. 90. *Baker's* Chron. p. 614.][6]

EXAMPLE XXI.

In Leicestershire, not far from Lutterworth, a miller had murdered a man in his mill, and privately buried him in his garden; and soon after leaving the place, he settled in a county far off, and lived a long time, believing that his villainy would never be discovered. But after twenty years, he returned to visit some friends in the village where he formerly lived; and just at that time, the miller who had the mill, having occasion to dig deep in his garden, found the body or rather bones of the murdered man. The neighbours then recollected that about twenty years ago, a man who had been missing in the parish, and was never heard of after; some likewise recollected who was then possessor of the mill; and that very miller being now in the parish, they ran to the house where he was, and surrounding it, unanimously called on him as the murderer of that man. The miller was so shocked with the sudden and general accusation, and so stung in conscience for the crime, that he soon confessed the fact, and was accordingly executed.

[*Wanly's* Wonders, &c. l. 1. c. 41. p. 90. *Beard's* Theatre, &c. l. 2. c. 11. p. 299.][7]

---

[6] Turner (ch. XCIII, p. 29) takes his account verbatim from Wanley and cites Wanley and [Sir Richard] Baker's *Chronicle*. Wanley also cites Baker. Baker places the event in the second year of James's reign. Fielding slightly elaborates the account as found in Turner and Wanley.

[7] Wanley correctly cites Beard (II. xi. 302).

EXAMPLE XXII.

In the year 1690. a man in Ireland, dreamed that he was riding out with a relation of his, who lived at Amesbury, in Wiltshire, on the downs near that town; and that his relation was robbed and murdered by two men, whose persons and dress he perfectly remembered. His dream was so strong, that he wrote to his cousin at Amesbury, begging him not to ride late, and then related the dream he had had concerning him. The man received the letter, but laughed at the caution; and the next night on the very spot therein mentioned, he was both robbed and murthered. His wife extremely afflicted for his loss, shewed this letter to her friends, and from the exact description of the murderers they were taken up, separately confined, and by their equivocal and contradictory answers, some of the murdered man's things being also found upon them, they were convicted, and hanged in chains on the spot where the murder was committed. [*Turner*, p. 54.][8]

EXAMPLE XXIII.

In the same year, in the month of April, William Barwick, who lived near York, murdered his wife, by drowning her in a pond, and buried her body in a bank covered by a quickset hedge, near to the pond.

He gave it out amongst his neighbours that his wife was gone to Selby, to an uncle, who had sent to her, in order to make her his heir. A month after, one John Lofthouse, whose wife was sister to the deceased, having occasion to water the quickset-hedge before-mentioned, saw a woman pass hastily from the pond to the hedge, and then disappear. He thought it looked very like Barwick's wife, but believing her far off, he thought no more of the matter. The next day going to the same place, he again saw the same apparition walk from the pond to the hedge, and then he saw her sit down on the bank, and plainly perceived it to be the face of his wife's sister, but looking much paler than she used to do. He ran home in a great fright, and told his wife what he had seen, who advised him to declare it to the minister of the parish. He did so, and the minister bid him be for some time very secret, till he had sent to Selby, to enquire if Barwick's wife was at the place, to which he pretended he had sent her. But finding neither any news of the woman, or any such uncle as her husband had talked of, Barwick was immediately taken up, and being stung in conscience, confessed the fact. He was condemned at York assizes the September following, by judge Powel, and was hanged in chains. [*Turner*, p. 31.][9]

[8] Turner, ch. VIII, p. 54.
[9] Turner, ch. CXIII, p. 31.

EXAMPLE XXIV.

Two Arcadians of intimate acquaintance, lodged at Mægara. One at a friend's house, the other at an inn. He that lodged with his friend, saw in his sleep, his companion supplicating his host not to kill him; and heard his voice begging him to come to his assistance. Suddenly awaking, he started from his bed, and was hastily running out of the room; but recollecting his senses, he found he had only been in a dream, he therefore returned to his bed, and composed himself again to sleep. His friend again appeared to him with several wounds in his body, and said, "Since you could not prevent my murther, yet I conjure you to revenge it. My host has killed me, and has laid my body at the bottom of a dung-cart, and is now carrying it out of the west gate of the city." The man at this suddenly awaked again, and putting on his clothes, ran hastily to the western gate, where he overtook a cart, and under a heap of dung, found the mangled body of his murdered friend. The inn-keeper was seized, and suffered the punishment he so well deserved. [*Turner* 49. Valer. Maxim. 1. c. 7. Dr. *More* Immort. of the soul. l. 2. c. 16.][1]

EXAMPLE XXV.

It is very common abroad, when a murder has been committed, for the survivors, if there are any, to describe the face and person of the murderer to some painter, who having drawn the likeness, prints are taken of it, and dispersed about, whereby many a murder has been discovered. One very remarkable instance happened of a discovery from these prints, where a common thief who had been guilty of many robberies, and some murders, had clapped a patch over one of his eyes, by which he designed to mislead any description that might be given of him in case he should be observed. His plot took, a print of him was published as having been guilty of a most cruel and inhuman murder, and, as he thought himself safe by this stratagem, he bought one of the prints, carried it about with him, declared his great zeal to find out the murderer, and with much earnestness bid every one remark, that the villain had but one eye. His noisy assiduity was observed by a sagacious person, who suspected there was something more than common in his behaviour; the gentleman therefore begged, that this voluntary avenger of murder, might be taken up, and the person who had described the murderer sent for to look at him. It was a maid-servant to the murdered lady, who had recovered it, although she was also left for dead

---

[1] Turner (ch. VIII, p. 49) cites Val[erius] Max[imus] and Dr [Henry] More. Booth cites Valerius Maximus in *Amelia* (VI. vii. 310), and Fielding owned a copy of his *Facta et Dicta Memorabilia* (Baker, no. 373).

when the house was robbed. She immediately said, that the accused person was not the man, for the villain had but one eye. The gentleman then asked her in what manner his eye seemed lost, whether it was sunk in his head, or appeared dead and wanting sight; the maid answered, that it was covered with a black patch, and she therefore could not answer his question. The gentleman immediately ordered a black eye patch to be put over the eye of the suspected man; when the maid positively swore to him, and he was executed, confessing when on the rack that he was guilty of the crime.[2]

EXAMPLE XXVI.

In the west of England a man had been murdered, but four years had passed, and the murderer had not been discovered. In a large company of men met together at an ordinary, one of them looking earnestly at a grazier, cry'd out, "You are the man, sir, that four years ago killed farmer W——" The grazier turn'd as pale as death, and staggered so, that he was forced to sit down in a chair. The cumpany gathered round him, and asked him if the accusation was just. He fell on his knees, and with great contrition and tears, confessed the fact, and was condemned and executed for the same. The person who taxed the grazier with the murder, being asked on what foundation he had accused him, declared, that it was no other than a strong and sudden impulse, which he could not resist, although his life might have paid the forfeit for his speech.

This Story was given me by a reverend clergyman of Wiltshire.

EXAMPLE XXVII.

A gentleman of high rank and fortune abroad, had invited several officers to dine with him, (amongst which was the father of the gentleman who told me the story) and just as they set down to the table, one of the officers looking up, cried out "Good God! I am a dead man, take her away, for pity's sake take her away, for I cannot bear that look." And immediately he fell from his chair in a fit upon the floor. They gave him all proper assistance, and recovered him enough to place him again on his seat, when looking to the same side of the room, he again cried out, "There she is still, take her away, or I shall confess all, and suffer the punishment I so well deserve." He then fell into a stronger fit than before; and the gentleman of the house having great compassion for the poor man, and thinking he was seized with a frenzy fever, ordered him to be carried up stairs, and put to bed, and sent to the next town, which was six miles off, for a surgeon to let him blood.

---

[2] I have not found a source for this Example, nor for Examples XXVI, XXVII, and XXVIII.

One of the company observing, that his agonies came on, by his looking up at a picture which hung in the room, asked the gentleman of the house, whose picture it was; to which he answered, that it was the picture of a young lady, who about two years before had been found murdered in her bed, and her house robbed of all the most valuable effects in it; that there never had yet been the least trace to find out the murderer; that all the remainder of her furniture had been publickly sold, and that he had bought that portrait as being well drawn, and the representation of a fine woman. The gentleman of the house then asked the other officers, what they knew of the man who was gone to bed in a fit, for he had only invited him out of civility to the rest of the gentlemen of the regiment. They declared they knew nothing of his family, but that he had lately bought a pair of colours.[3]

As soon as the surgeon arrived, he blooded the sick man, who again came to his senses; and being asked what had given him so much uneasiness, he look'd wildly, would give no answer, and only muttered that he was subject to such fits; but looking up earnestly in the surgeon's face, he seem'd in great confusion, and they apprehended, was again falling into a fit. The gentleman of the house taking the surgeon apart, asked him, if he knew the person he had blooded. The surgeon answered, that he believed he did not know him, for he heard he was an officer in the army; whereas he should otherwise have taken him for a strolling idle fellow, that he once remembered to have seen, who was not likely, either by his birth or fortune, to bear the king's commission. The gentleman desired the surgeon to go to him again, and to accost him by the name of that vagabond, to see what effect it would have on him, and if it was a mistake, 'twas easy to ask his pardon, and it would soon be made up. The surgeon returning into the room, came familiarly up to the officer, who was still in bed, took him by the hand and said, "How is it, Pedro? I little thought to have seen you here, nor knew you just now while you was in your fit." On which he cried out, "Well since I find I am discovered, I will confess all, if you will not let me look on that face in the parlour any more." He accordingly, before the gentleman of the house, made a full confession of his having entered the house of the lady, whose picture had so terrified him, and by the help of one of her servants, whom he killed and buried in the cellar, and who, it was supposed, was fled for the robbery and murder, had rifled the house, and murdered the lady. That he found five hundred pound in gold in her bureau, with which he equipped himself for the army; but all her jewels, plate, &c. he had bury'd for fear of a discovery, in a place, where by his direction, they were all found; as was also the bones of the murdered servant in the cellar. He was accordingly executed for the same.

[3] i.e., purchased a commission.

EXAMPLE XXVIII.

In the north of France, a most barbarous and cruel Murder had been committed on a young gentleman of fortune; and, with all the care and vigilance of the magistrates, not the least trace of the Murderer could be found. Seven years after this had happen'd there was a current report all over the town where he had lived, that now the Murderer of this young gentleman was found, for it was Monsieur De —— that had done it, who was his most intimate friend, and lived, at that time, in great credit and reputation in the town. After this report had prevailed one whole day, it began to be wonder'd at, that Monsieur De —— was not taken up, and on that, by endeavouring to trace the foundation of such an accusation, 'twas found to be only a general rumor, and no one could be fix'd on as the first inventor; on which the report soon died, and every one wish'd to find the author of so base a calumny.

Just that day twelvemonth the same rumor again prevail'd all over the town, with this addition, that Monsieur De —— had confessed the fact, and had shewn to the magistrates a place in his garden where he had buried in a box the hanger with which he had kill'd his friend, and all his own bloody cloaths in which he had committed the Murder. This report made a crowd gather about the gentleman's house, saying they would come in to look at things that had been discover'd in the garden. The gentleman, seeing a mob at his door, ask'd from his window the cause of the riot, and hearing what they said, with many imprecations also on him for his cruelty, and some sticks and stones flung at his head, he really believed himself discover'd, and slipping down a pair of back stairs, he hastened to his stable, which was behind the house, took his best horse, and fled as fast as possible to get out of the French territories. The magistrates of the town, knowing the report of the gentleman's confession to be false, sent proper officers to quiet and disperse the mob, and to prevent the gentleman from being kill'd by their ill-founded rage. But on finding he was privately fled, they began to reflect seriously on the matter, and to think that this strange rumor, the author of which again could not be found, was sent by Providence to detect this Murder; they therefore order'd some men to dig in the garden, in the spot where the bloody cloaths, &c. were reported to be hid, and there they found all the things which had before been described, and tho' they had been buried eight years, the blood was as fresh on them as ever. Messengers were immediately sent in pursuit of Monsieur De —— whom they overtook about two leagues from the city, for his horse having thrown him, he was lying on the ground, with his leg broke short off. As soon as he was brought back, he presently confess'd the fact, and was executed accordingly.

The two last preceding stories were told me by a gentleman whose father was an officer in the Irish regiments, in the French service, and who, he said, was an eye-witness to the former; and had the relation of the latter from a French officer whom he knew to be a man of great honour and veracity.

EXAMPLE XXIX.

In the year 1611, Sir Thomas Glover, then being our ambassador at Constantinople, some of his servants were one day diverting themselves with throwing snow-balls, when one of the ambassador's servants threw a ball, which hit a Turk such a blow on the eye, that it struck him instantly dead.

The aga of the janisaries complain'd to the grand visier, and the grand visier demanded the servant of the ambassador to be given up to public justice.

It was in vain that the ambassador urged that the blow was given by accident, and not by design; for the grand visier insisted that he would have blood for blood, which is a law never dispensed with amongst the Turks. The ambassador then declared, that he knew not which of his servants to deliver up, for he could not discover by whose hand the ball had been thrown; but to prevent a tumult which seemed beginning to arise, (and the end of which might have reached even to the throne) he order'd all his servants to appear, and promised to give up the man that should be pronounced guilty. Five or six Turks instantly seized on one Simon Dibbins, a man newly come from Candia, and the rest of the janisaries, with one voice, declared him to be the guilty man.

The ambassador, knowing this man to have been absent from the place when the snow-ball was thrown, again protested with great vehemence against his execution: but finding that neither intreaties, nor great sums of money which were offered, could prevail for his enlargement, after they had once seized on him, he thought it was better that one man (innocent as he thought him) should suffer, than by any farther opposition, to run the risque of losing many lives by a general insurrection.

The day of his execution being fixed, the ambassador sent his chaplain to him in prison, and Dibbins then confessed, that he had, some years before, killed a man in England, and, for fear of detection, had fled to Candia; but, he said, he was now convinced, that the general outcry against him was the voice of God, by that means to bring him to justice, for a most bloody and premeditated Murder.

He was accordingly executed before the gate of the ambassador's house, who, from the account given by his chaplain, was very well satisfied to find, that, by the death of Dibbins, a Murderer was punish'd, and an innocent man who was only the accidental cause of a Turk's death, was saved from a sentence which would have been as hard on him, as it was just on the wretch who suffer'd no more than he really deserved.   [*Knowle's* Turkish History, p. 134.][4]

EXAMPLE XXX.

The following fact was told me by a gentleman whose great-grand-father was an Irish judge, and before whom the thing happen'd. The particulars have been preserved in the family by tradition ever since, but the name of the person that was executed is purposely omitted, as being of no inconsiderable family in that nation.

A gentleman was tried in Ireland for killing his friend in a duel, and the circumstances appearing very favourable on his side, the verdict was brought in manslaughter. This crime being within benefit of clergy, the prisoner had the book offered him to read; on which he started and hesitated in such a manner, that those who stood near him asked him why he did not proceed. He answered, he could not see the words, they were so stained with blood. He added, that he wonder'd they should use him in such a manner, and desired they would give him a fair book. Several people standing by look'd on the book, and all declared, that not the least drop of blood appear'd on it, but the words were perfectly legible. The prisoner, on that, fetch'd a deep sigh, and said, "I plainly perceive the vengeance of God is pursuing me; for although I declare myself innocent of the death of my friend, any otherwise than by being forced into it for self-defence, yet I confess myself worthy of public punishment; for some years ago I barbarously murdered my own father."

He then related all the particulars of the Murder, and his confession was so full, that he must have been condemn'd on that account, had he taken his tryal: but his incapacity for reading in any book they offered him, by the appearance of blood before his eyes, still continuing, no other tryal was necessary, and he was executed by virtue of his first conviction.

He died very penitent, persisting in his confession of the Murder of his father, allowing the justice of his punishment, and acknowledging the hand of God, in forcing him to a confession of his horrid crime.

EXAMPLE XXXI.

I cannot omit a very extraordinary instance of the power of imagination in a guilty conscience, shewn at the tryal of Catherine Hayes,[5] which was told

---

[4] Richard Knolles, *General History of the Turks* (London, 1603). Fielding shortens and simplifies the account in Knolles (as it appars in the 6th edn. [London, 1687, i. 906]) to increase its exemplary power. Both Wanley and Turner print versions of this story and cite Knolles, p. 1311.

[5] Catherine Hayes was executed 9 May 1726. She was assisted in the murder and dismemberment of her husband by her reputed son and another man. She never confessed her guilt. See *The Complete*

me by a person of high rank and character, who was present at her tryal.

Catherine Hayes, near thirty years ago, was tried, convicted, and burnt, for the Murder of her husband, which (assisted by her own son and some others) she effected by cutting off his head, and throwing it into a river. On examining the evidence against her, there was a coat produced in court that formerly belonged to her husband, and had been given by her, as part of the reward, to one of her wicked accomplices in the Murder. This coat was held up in order to be view'd, and, by the manner of its being lifted up, (the under parts of the skirts being hid by the crowd) its appearance was very much like that of a man without his head. This struck such a horror into the heart of the prisoner at the bar, especially as it was the very coat of her husband, that she fell dead upon the floor, and though she afterwards returned to life, yet she made no farther defence, but hung her head, and sullenly submitted to the sentence that was past upon her; whereas it had been observed, before this circumstance, that she was exceedingly bold in her denial of the facts alledged by the witnesses; made many pertinent observations on the evidence, and seemed under no kind of confusion or disorder. But whatever it pleased God to represent to her mind at that time, the consequence, as many must remember at this day, was as I have here related it; and all who were present were struck with amazement and horror.

EXAMPLE XXXII.

In the late instance of miss Jeffries,[6] may certainly be seen the secret hand of providence in bringing her to justice. 'Tis well known, that, some time before the Murder of Mr. Jeffries, Swan, who also suffered for it, and Mathews the evidence,[7] were in London; and, at a public house, engaged in a riotous quarrel with some of their drunken companions. One of them challenging a fellow to fight, stripp'd off his cloaths, and gave his coat to a man to hold for him, 'till the battle should be decided, when out of his coat pocket dropp'd a brace of pistols. On this he was taken up, on suspicion of being a highwayman, and, to procure his liberty, miss Jeffries herself appear'd, and declared that some jewels which were found on him were hers,

---

Newgate Calendar, ed. G. T. Crook (London, 1926), iii. 30 ff. Her crime excited all the interest due a dismemberment. Fielding alludes to her in *Amelia* (i. vi. 40); Thackerary's *Catherine* is based on the story of Catherine Hayes.

[6] Elizabeth Jefferys and John Swan were tried 11 Mar. 1752 and executed 28 Mar. 1752 (about two weeks before the publication of *Examples of Providence*). Jefferys had 'enticed and persuaded' John Swan and Thomas Mathews to murder her uncle, but Swan alone committed the crime and was convicted of petty treason, he being the victim's servant. Martin Wright, whom Fielding compliments in *Elizabeth Canning*, was one of the trial judges, and Fielding's clerk, Joshua Brogden, was among the spectators (see the report on this trial in the *Covent-Garden Journal* for 14 Mar. 1752).

[7] In return for his testimony on behalf of the crown, Mathews was admitted an 'evidence' and was not prosecuted. Fielding comments on this use of crown witnesses in the *Enquiry*, p. 161.

and that she sent them by him to be pawn'd, and that the pistols were her uncle's, which she too had order'd him to get clean'd. This, for the present, got the man off; but when the Murder was committed, and with one of those very pistols, Swan or Mathews, or both, were too strongly pointed out not to come under great suspicion of having a hand in the Murder. Yet still miss Jeffries, being of that sex of which nothing but gentleness should be presumed, being neice to the murder'd man, and having been bred up under his care, could never have been suspected of being either a principal, or an accessary, in a crime so horrid and repugnant to every breast not divested of humanity, had she not, by the accident before-mention'd, so far departed from her character, as publickly to appear in vindication of a man, who now might pretty strongly be presumed to be a Murderer, and who was then (most likely with her knowledge) preparing the pistols for the cruel purpose to which they were applied. May it not, therefore, be said, that the drunken quarrel in London was the clue by which this Murder was unravell'd? It was certainly by that means that miss Jeffries was suspected of having, by the Murder of her uncle, taken out of the hands of God the punishment of a man, who, it must be confess'd, (if her own account of the murder be true) was very highly culpable.[8] Yet, *vengeance is mine*, saith the Lord;[9] and so it manifestly appears in this instance.

EXAMPLE XXXIII.

In miss Mary Blandy[1] is seen the strong infatuation which often attends those who commit Murder, and which seldom fails of leading them to justice.

As this unhappy lady is acknowledged to have had an exceeding good understanding, and great quickness of parts and invention, what but infatuation could make her go on in that horrid fact of poisoning her father, in so public and bare-fac'd a manner? For, according to the evidence of several witnesses, she had frequently utter'd speeches very unbecoming in a

---

[8] According to Jefferys, her uncle 'took her from her father when she was five yers old . . . when she was sixteen . . . debauched her . . . she lived in a continued state of incest with him (having had two miscarriages by him), till about a year before his death, when he slighted her in favour of another woman' (*State Trials*, xviii. 1196).

[9] Romans 12: 19.

[1] Mary Blandy, the daughter of a respectable attorney of Henley upon Thames, was tried in Oxford 29 Feb. 1752 for the murder of her father by arsenic poisoning. Her defence was that she administered the arsenic (over a period of many months) innocently, believing it a potion that would win her father's affection for her lover, Cranstoun (who had provided her with the arsenic). The record of the trial (*State Trials*, xviii. 1117–94) supports Fielding's statements of fact except his suggestion that she might have escaped when she walked to Henley (she was followed by 'the mob' and forced to take shelter in a public house). Fielding comments on this case several times in the *Covent-Garden Journal* and writes with particular sympathy for Mary Blandy in no. 20 (10 Mar. 1752; i. 253 ff.).

daughter, and such as must give but too just cause for suspicion: and her repeated doses to her father made even him to suspect that she intended to poison him, as appear'd also from what he said to her; yet his affection for this unhappy girl was so great, that he could not force himself into a belief of her intentions strong enough to prevent them.

What, but the same infatuation, could have prevented her from making use of the money, and things of value in her hands, for her escape? And this she might easily have effected, when she walked to Henley, had she gone on in a post-chaise to London, instead of returning back to her father's house, which she must know, from what had before passed, would lead to her being taken up, and tried; and that she had little reason, from her first unguarded manner of proceeding, to hope for an acquittal at her trial.

And now, my good countrymen, let me seriously exhort you, to weigh well with yourselves the following considerations, which must, I think, sufficiently deter you from this most deadly crime: A crime, which, though perhaps not considered by law as the highest,[2] is in truth and in fact, the blackest sin, which can contaminate the hands, or pollute the soul of man.

First, this is the greatest injury which one human being can do to another.

Secondly, it is always irreparable. There is scarce any other mischief which we can bring on our neighbour, but it will be afterwards in our power to undo again. If by force or fraud we take away the property of another, it will be in our power to restore them; but here no future penitence will avail. Here can be no restitution: no reparation!

Nor is the injury done solely to the murdered person. It often involves a whole family in its consequences. A disconsolate widow, a number of distressed wretched orphans are left to deplore the loss of a husband and a father; a parent is deprived of a beloved wife or child, a loss sometimes more bitter than would have been that of their own lives.

Besides the violently robbing a man of his life, and of all the blessings and enjoyments of it; there is one consideration of so dreadful a nature, that the bare hint of it, is sufficient to chill every heart with horror. We know not in what state of mind we find the person whom we destroy; nor with what load of fresh contracted unrepented guilt, we send him to his final account.—We surprize the unhappy wretch unawares, preparing himself perhaps for that repentance which might have obtained his pardon, and by preventing which, we may be guilty of destroying both his body and soul.

It is no wonder, that a crime in itself so execrable, in its consequence so dreadful, should be stamped with every mark of human abhorrence and divine vengeance.

The laws of every civilized people, punish it with death; in many countries

---

[2] High treason is the 'highest' crime (Blackstone, *Comm.* iv. 75).

the most exquisite torments are inflicted on a Murderer; nay, even in this, where tortures are held in a just abhorrence, and where punishments are in so eminent a manner mild and gentle; the law is not barely satisfied with taking away the Murderer's life; he is denied even the burial of a christian; and his body is exposed a prey to the ravenous birds of the air. His infamy is preserved as long as nature will admit, a gibbet exposes him as a terrible example to others, and he becomes the monument of his own shame, and of that of all his relations.[3]

In other crimes, it is usual for the criminal to find protection, and the sufferer to be regarded with pity by the tender-hearted; but in murder there is scarce a single person so profligate and abandoned, as to afford the fugitive a refuge. Every man is ready to discover and yield him up, to pursue and to take him; every man is desirous to bring him to justice, views him with detestation when in chains; and sees him on the gallows with pleasure.

In robbery, theft, and such like transgressions, an offender sometimes remains many years in impunity; for on such occasions, he hath scarce any person, unless those who are immediately injured, or the officers of justice themselves, to apprehend and avoid: but with murder, all mankind are alarmed. All the human passions are roused against him; and it presently becomes a common cause to bring him to justice. Hence it very rarely happens that this criminal long escapes the punishment which is his due. Never, indeed, unless he exchanges it for what is, perhaps, much worse, to linger out a miserable life with the loss of country, friends, fortune, and fame; to be shunned, despised, detested, and cursed, by all mankind.

Nor is this wretch, in all probability, a greater object of horror to others, than he is to himself. If his conscience be not seared, as it were with a hot iron, if his heart be not shut to all the compunctions of remorse, and of shame, his own mind is his worst tormentor; and the horrors which attend all his reflections appear more dreadful, when he casts his eyes behind him, than even the sight of his pursuers would be.

And, if he casts his eyes forwards, what comfort can even hope afford him? That very justice from which he hath so eagerly run, seems often the only friend to whose arms he can fly. This, many of those Murderers who have been brought, at last, tho' late, to their deserved punishment, have honestly confessed; have owned that the day of their execution was much the happiest which they had experienced since the day of their guilt.

And this must surely be, in general, the case, had we any certain assurance that our punishment for so enormous, so execrable a sin, was to end in this world; but, alas! how just reason have we to apprehend that this will not be

---

[3] Oddly, Fielding does not mention that the 'Act for better preventing the horrid crime of murder' (25 Geo. II, c. xxxii), already in effect when *Examples of Providence* was published, provides that a murderer's body shall be 'dissected and anatomized'.

the case. In every other crime the offender who hath paid the price of his life, may flatter himself that he hath fully expiated his offence: but, in Murder, it is far otherwise; and that, especially, from the last causes which I have assigned above, where I have endeavoured to set forth the extreme heinousness of this crime.

Here, then, is a thought which must shake the firmest mind; and make the boldest heart to tremble. *Fear not him*, saith our Saviour, *who can kill the body; but fear him who can destroy both body and soul.*[4]

What are the terrors of earthly judgment, compared to this tremendous tribunal? Great courage may, perhaps, bear up a bad mind (for it is sometimes the property of such) against the most severe sentence which can be pronounced by the mouth of a human judge; but where is the fortitude which can look an offended Almighty in the face? Who can bear the dreadful thought of being confronted with the spirit of one whom we have murdered, in the presence of all the Host of Heaven, and to have justice demanded against our guilty soul, before that most awful judgment-seat, where there is infinite justice, as well as infinite power? A most dreadful situation indeed! from which may God, of his infinite mercy, deliver us all.

FINIS.

[4] Matthew 10: 28.

A
PROPOSAL
FOR
Making an Effectual Provision
FOR THE
POOR,
FOR
Amending their MORALS,
AND FOR
Rendering them useful MEMBERS of the
SOCIETY.

To which is added,

A PLAN of the BUILDINGS proposed, with
proper Elevations.

Drawn by an Eminent Hand.

By HENRY FIELDING, Esq;

Barrister at Law, and one of his Majesty's Justices of the
Peace for the County of Middlesex.

Ista sententia maximè et fallit imperitos, et obest sæpissime
Reipublicæ, cùm aliquid verum et rectum esse dicitur, sed
obtineri, id est obsisti posse populo, negatur.
Cic. de Leg. lib. 3.

LONDON:
Printed for A. MILLAR, in the Strand.
MDCCLIII.

EXPLANATION OF THE PLAN.

A Mens Courts, containing 3000 Persons.
B Womens Courts, containing 2000 Persons.
C Chapel.
D Prison Court, containing 1000 Persons.
E Justice Hall.
F Governor's House.
G Deputy Governor's.
H Chaplain's Houses.
I Treasurer's House.
K Receiver's House.
L Sutleries.
M Burying-grounds.
N Womens Airing-ground.
O Mens Airing-ground.
P Sutlery-grounds.
Q Front Grounds.
R Elevation of the Governor's House.
S Front of the Deputy Governor's.
T Ditto of the Chaplains.
a Principal Gate.
b Place of the Steeple.
c Mens Way to the Chapel.
d Prisoners Chapel.
e Prisoners Way to their Chapel.
g Gates.
h Prisons, or Fasting-Rooms.
i Cells.
k Whipping Post.
l Keepers Houses.
m Lodges for the Assistants.
n Womens Infirmary.
p Matron's House.
r Officers Houses.
s Stairs.
t Mens Infirmary.
y u Privies.
w Workrooms, above which are the Lodging-wards, 160 in Number.
x Lodges for the Watchmen and Assistants.
y Storehouses.

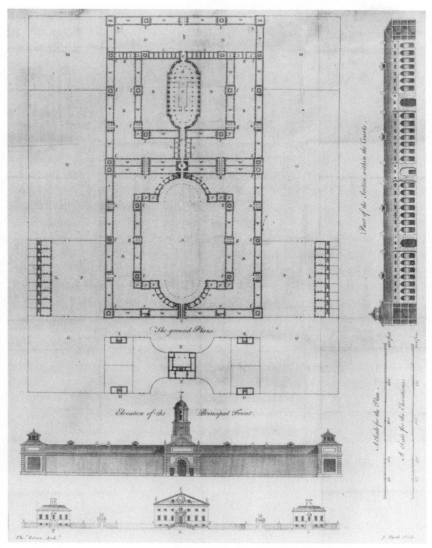

6. Architect's Plan for Workhouse. Signed 'Tho.ˢ Gibson Arch.ᵗ J. Mynde Sculp.'

TO THE RIGHT HONOURABLE
HENRY PELHAM,[1]
Chancellor of his Majesty's Exchequer.

S I R,

In addressing to you the following Sheets, I only embrace an Opportunity of expressing the deep Sense I have of the Obligations you have conferred on me: For it would be unreasonable to expect, that one in your Station should find sufficient Leisure to weigh and consider duly the Subject here treated of. While your Attention is so much engaged in Matters of higher Moment, it would seem hard, that no other should be willing to undertake this inferior Province of Government, or should indeed be equal to it; but that one Man should be obliged to support the whole.

And yet, if ever there was a Time when a Minister of State might find such Leisure, I think it may be the present. It is true, indeed, that when a skilful Governor of a Ship hath brought his Vessel through Rocks, Quicksands and Storms, to ride safely before the Wind, he hath a Right to enjoy that Safety which he hath procured, and to indulge his own Ease;[2] and yet even then, if he is informed that his Vessel is leaky, or some of the minutest Tackling in Disorder, should not he give some Attention to those

---

Title-page] Cicero, *de Legibus*, III. xv. 34: 'This is a view which, more than any other, both leads the inexperienced astray, and is very frequently a hindrance in public affairs; the belief, I mean, that certain measures are wise and good, but are impracticable; that is, that the people cannot be opposed' (Loeb).

Sketch] The English almshouse from the 14th to the 18th century is characterized by an open court, or courts, enclosed by a rectangular building in which there are dormitories, a chapel, an infirmary, and staff quarters. The plan of Fielding's workhouse contains these features and adds workrooms. His proposed building would have been larger and more complex than the typical almshouse, but not radically different. See W. H. Godfrey, *The English Almshouse* (London, n.d.).

Sketch] Thomas Gibson and J. Mynde: unidentified. Cross (ii. 273) doubts that Gibson could be the portrait painter of that name. Richard J. Dircks accepts this identification, points out that Gibson died in Apr. 1753 and argues that Fielding must have had the *Proposal* under way early in 1751 ('Some Notes on Fielding's Proposal for the Poor', *N & Q* 207 [1962], 457–8).

[1] The dedication of the *Proposal* to Pelham (1695?–1754; first lord of the Treasury and chancellor of the Exchequer, 1743), now clearly the successor to Walpole as first minister, balances that of the *Enquiry* to Hardwicke, Fielding paying tribute to the two men in power he had praised most frequently in the *Jacobite's Journal* (see *JJ* pp. xlviii–xlix and *passim*). Pelham may have financed the *Jacobite's Journal* (ibid., pp. lv and lxxv). It was Pelham's Administration, of course, which Fielding supported in his political writings of the late 1740s. He is complimented in *Tom Jones* (XI. ix. 612).

[2] Perhaps Fielding's metaphor combines Horace's 'ship of state' (*Odes*, I. xiv) with the opening lines of bk. ii of Lucretius' *De Rerum Natura* (quoted in *Jonathan Wild*, IV. xiv. 200).

inferior Matters which others neglect, which retard the Vessel in her Course, and may perhaps, however slowly, at last produce her Destruction?[3]

There is, perhaps, Sir, something above the Stile of Prose in this Allusion, but there is nothing in it beyond that of Truth.

To return, however, to the plainest Stile: I here present you with that Plan which I had the Honour once to mention to you, and of which I have given a former Hint to the Public.[4] If this be carried into Execution, it will in its Consequence, I am convinced, remove almost every Evil from the Society of which honest Men at present complain; will complete the Obligations which Posterity shall owe to the present Age; and will heap Praises on that Name which shall be then as much loved and honoured by Mankind, as it is now by,

S I R,

Your Most Obliged,

Most Humble,

And Most Obedient Servant,

HENRY FIELDING.

Jan. 19. 1753.

---

[3] Pelham's Administration was in fact solidly established. Recriminations against the Peace of Aix-la-Chapelle had quieted; the rumblings of Jacobite disaffection had nearly ceased; Pelham's quarrel with Newcastle had happily ended with the departure from the administration of the Duke of Bedford and Lord Sandwich; effective opposition disappeared on the death of the Prince of Wales; and relations with the king were excellent. The king's speeches opening Parliament 14 Nov. 1751 and 11 Jan. 1753 had both urged attention to domestic issues.

[4] See General Introduction, pp. lxxii ff.

A

PROPOSAL

For making an effectual Provision for the POOR, &c.

INTRODUCTION.

That the Strength and Riches of a Society consist in the Numbers of the People, is an Assertion which hath obtained the Force of an Axiom in Politics.[5] This, however, supposes the Society to be so constituted, that those Numbers may contribute to the Good of the Whole: for could the contrary be imagined; could we figure to ourselves a State in which a great Part of the People, instead of contributing to the Good of the Public, should lie as a useless and heavy Burden on the rest of their Countrymen, the very Reverse of the above Maxim would be true; and the Numbers of such a People would be so far from giving any Strength to the Society, that they would weaken and oppress it; so that it would, in a merely civil Sense, be the Interest of such a Society to lessen its Numbers, and by some means or other to shake or lop off the useless and burthensome Part.

    Numbers of Men, says Mr. *Locke, are to be preferred to Largeness of Dominions*;[6] and the Reason, as he well observes, is *for that Labour puts the Difference of the Value on every thing.*[7] "Let any one consider (says he) what the

[5] The following references, all to a context concerning primarily employment for the poor, suggest the ubiquity of this 'Axiom': *Bread for the Poor* . . . (London, 1678), p. 3; Charles Davenant, *An Essay upon the Probable Methods of making a People Gainers in the Ballance of Trade* . . . , 2nd edn. (London, 1700), p. 33; Roger North, *A Discourse of the Poor* (London, 1753), p. 47; [Lawrence Braddon], *A Corporation Humbly propos'd, For Relieving, Reforming, and Employing the Poor* (London, 1720), p. 8; Daniel Defoe, 'Giving Alms no Charity' (London, 1704), reprinted in *A Select Collection of Scarce and Valuable Economical Tracts*, ed. J. R. McCulloch (London, 1859), p. 38; *Observations upon the Vagrant Laws* . . . (London, 1742), p. 12; Sir John Fielding, *An Account of the Origin and Effects of a Police* (London, 1758), p. viii; R. Potter, *Observations on the Poor Laws* (London, 1775), p. 1.

    The part this maxim plays in *A Modest Proposal* is discussed by Louis A. Landa in '*A Modest Proposal* and Populousness', in *Eighteenth Century English Literature*, ed. James L. Clifford (New York, 1959), pp. 102–11. For similar 'insinuations' of mercantile doctrine into Houyhnhnmland, see L. A. Landa's 'The Dismal Science in Houyhnhnmland', *Novel*, 13 (1979–80), 38–49.

[6] John Locke, *The Second Treatise of Government* (1690), ed. Thomas P. Peardon (New York, 1952), sect. 42.

[7] Ibid., sect. 40.

Difference is between an Acre of Land, planted with Tobacco or Sugar, sown with Wheat or Barley; and an Acre of the same Land lying in common, without any Husbandry upon it; and he will find, that the Improvement of Labour makes the far greater Part of the Value. I think it will be but a very modest Computation to say, that of the Products of the Earth, useful to the Life of Man, 9/10 are the Effects of Labour: Nay, if we will rightly estimate things, as they come to our Use, and cast up the several Expences about them, what in them is purely owing to Nature, and what to Labour, we shall find in most of them 99/100 are wholly to be put on the Account of Labour."[8] In this alone, as he demonstrates, lies the Difference between us and the *Americans*, "who are furnished by Nature as liberally as ourselves with all the Materials of Plenty, yet have not the one hundredth part of the Conveniencies we enjoy; and among whom a King of a large and fruitful Territory feeds, lodges, and is clad worse than a Day-Labourer in *England**."[9]

It is not barely, therefore, in the Numbers of People, but in Numbers of People well and properly disposed, that we can truly place the Strength and Riches of a Society.

From the Universality of the Maxim which I have mentioned, qualified (I mean) as above, it seems to follow, that a State is capable of this Perfection, and that some States have actually been so constituted. Of this Kind particularly seem to me the *Ægyptian* Policy of old, and that of *Holland* in modern Times.[1] I do not mean to say that any Human Society is so absolutely capable of this Perfection, that every Individual shall contribute some Share to the Strength of the Whole. Nature hath denied us this, by laying certain Individuals, in every Society, under a natural Incapacity not only of administring to the Good of others; but even of providing for, and protecting themselves. Such are the Incapacities of Infancy, and of old Age, and of Impotency either of Mind or Body, natural or accidental.

Of all these, Policy, perhaps, would dictate to us only to preserve the first, and accordingly we read of Nations, among whom those Numbers who were either by Age, or any incurable Infirmity rendered useless and burthensome to the Public, were without Mercy cut off by their Laws. But this neither Religion or Humanity will allow; and therefore to this Burthen, which is imposed on us by God and Nature, we must submit; nor will the Evil, while confined to such absolute Incapacity, be very grievous or much to be lamented.

From what I have here advanced, it seems, I think, apparent, that among a

---

* Essay on Civil Government, IId. Vol. of *Locke's* Works, page 178, 179.

[8] Loc. cit.

[9] Ibid., sect. 41. *Americans*: American Indians.

[1] Holland was often praised for effecient management of its economy. See Sir William Temple's *Observations upon the United Provinces of the Netherlands* (1673), especially ch. VI, and see *Enquiry*, p. 118.

civilized People that Polity is the best established in which all the Members, except such only as labour under any utter Incapacity, are obliged to contribute a Share to the Strength and Wealth of the Public. 2dly, That a State is capable of this Degree of Perfection, and, consequently, that to effect this is the Business of every wise and good Legislature.

And this seems to have been the great Aim of the first Founders of the *English* Constitution; by the Laws of which no Man whatsoever is exempted from performing such Duties to the Public as befit his Rank; according to the Observation of that most wonderful young Prince, *Quem tantum terris fata ostenderunt.*[2] "As there is no Part (says he) admitted in the Body that doth not work and take Pains, so ought there no Part of the Commonwealth to be, but laboursome in his Vocation. The Gentleman ought to labour in the Service of his Country; the Serving-man ought to wait diligently on his Master; the Artificer ought to labour in his Work; the Husbandman in tilling the Ground; the Merchant in passing the Tempests; but the Vagabonds ought clearly to be banished, as is the superfluous Humour of the Body; that is to say, the Spittle and Filth; which, because it is for no Use, is put out by the Strength of Human Nature*." Thus far this *incomparable* young Prince, as the excellent Historian of the Reformation calls him; who was, says the Bishop, the *Wonder of his Time*,[3] and indeed will be so of all succeeding Ages.

To divide the same kind of Labours equally among all the Members of Society, is so far from being necessary, that it is not even convenient; nor could it indeed be possible in any State, without such a perfect Equality in all its Branches as is inconsistent with all Government, and which befits only that which is sometimes called the State of Nature, but may more properly be called a State of Barbarism and Wildness.

Those Duties, however, which fall to the higher Ranks of Men, even in this Commonwealth, are by no Means of the lightest or easiest Kind. The Watchings and Fatigues, the Anxieties and Cares which attend the highest Stations, render their Possessors, in real Truth, no proper Objects of Envy to those in the lowest, whose Labours are much less likely to impair the Health of their Bodies, or to destroy the Peace of their Minds; are not less consistent with their Happiness, and much more consistent with their Safety.[4]

---

* King *Edward's* Remains preserved at the End of the IId. Vol. of Bishop *Burnet's* History of the Reformation, page 70.

[2] *Aeneid*, vi. 869. 'Whom the fates shall but show to earth'.

[3] Of Edward VI (who established Bridewell as a workhouse), Burnet remarks, 'Thus died King Edward the sixth, that incomparable young Prince. He was then in the sixteenth Year of his Age, and was counted the wonder of that Time' (Gilbert Burnet, *The History of the Reformation of the Church of England* [London, 1679, 1681], ii. 224). The 'Observation of . . . [the] most wonderful young Prince' is, as Fielding's note indicates, from the separately paginated 'Collection of Records' at the end of vol. ii which includes 'King Edwards *Journal and Remains*'. Burnet's *History* is in Baker, no. 438.

[4] Cf. *Enquiry*, p. 109. That the poor were really better off than the rich is the least persuasive

It is true, indeed, that in every Society where Property is established and secured by Law, there will be some among the Rich whose Indolence is superior to the Love of Wealth and Honour, and who will therefore avoid these Public Duties, for which Avarice and Ambition will always furnish out a sufficient Number of Candidates; yet however idle the Lives of such may be, it must be observed, First, That they are by no Means burthensome to the Public, but do support themselves on what the Law calls their own; a Property acquired by the Labour of their Ancestors, and often the Rewards, or Fruits at least of Public Services. 2dly, That while they dispose what is their own for the Purposes of Idleness, (and more especially, perhaps, if for the Purposes of Luxury,) they may be well called useful Members of trading Commonwealths, and truly said to contribute to the Good of the Public.[5]

But with the Poor (and such must be in any Nation where Property is, that is to say, where there are any Rich) this is not the Case: For having nothing but their Labour to bestow on the Society, if they withhold this from it, they become useless Members; and having nothing but their Labour to procure a Support for themselves, they must of Necessity become burthensome.

On this Labour the Public hath a Right to insist, since this is the only Service which the Poor can do that Society, which in some Way or other hath a Right to the Service of all its Members; and as this is the only Means by which they can avoid laying that Burthen on the Public which in case of absolute Incapacity alone it is obliged to support.

Here then seems to arise a twofold Duty to the Legislature; First, To procure to such the Means of Labour; and, 2dly, To compel them to undertake it. The former, indeed, naturally precedes the latter, and is presupposed by it: For if the Means of employing them be not to be found, the ablest Hands will be in the same Condition with the weakest, and will alike become a necessary Burthen on the Community; which is so far from being at Liberty to punish a Man for involuntary Idleness, that it is obliged to support him under it.

Both these, therefore, are the proper Business of every Legislature, and both for above a hundred Years together have been very much the Business of ours. If they have succeeded, I am sure I shall egregiously throw away my Time in composing the following Sheets; in which, however, I shall have the Consolation of much good Company to keep me in Countenance.[6] To say

commonplace of the time. On the question whether there was inequality of happiness between rich and poor, one cannot better La Bruyère's remark, 'He who is powerful and rich, and to whom nothing is lacking, may well formulate the question; its answer, however, should be left to a poor man' (cit. Jacob Viner, *The Role of Providence in the Social Order* (Philadelphia, Pa, 1972), p. 99).

[5] Cf. *Enquiry*, p. 70 and n. 2.

[6] For example, by far the longest section in Richard Burn's *The Justices of the Peace and Parish Officer* (8th edn., 1764) is that on the poor laws. Fielding owned two copies (Baker, nos. 16 & 569) of Samuel Carter's *Legal Provisions for the Poor* (London, 1725). For the substantial pamphlet literature on the poor, see General Introduction, p. lx.

Truth, if the Errors in our present Provisions are not very great and fatal, or if the Remedies proposed do not seem perfectly adequate to the Removal of them, I would not, by no Means, advise any great Alteration: For, as the *Greek* Historian* observes of Laws in general, "That City which is governed by the worse Laws, but those firm and stable, is in a safer Condition than the City where the Laws are better and more eligible in their original Institution, but where they are administered in a loose and fluctuating Manner."[7]

Which Fluctuation in our own Laws hath been, I find, an old Complaint in this Kingdom. *Holingshed* tells us long ago, "that our great Number of Laws was said to breed a general Negligence and Contempt of all good Order; because we have so many, says he, that no Subject can live without the Transgression of some of them; and in this respect the *often Alteration of our Ordinances doth much Harm.*"[8]

But if there was any Occasion of this Complaint in his Time, I am sure there is much more now; for as to our Statutes, they are increased much more than tenfold since the Reign of *Henry* the VIII. with such Variety of Alterations, Explanations, and Amendments, that in many Cases no good Lawyer will pretend readily to say what the Law at present is. Even in Queen *Anne's* Time there was a Cause determined in the Queen's Bench, expresly against the Letter of an Act of Parliament; which, as *Carthew*, who reports it, tells us, was not once mentioned, either at the Bar, or on the Bench; the Reason of which must have been, because it was unknown.[9]

Nor is there any Walk in all this Wilderness of Laws more intersected or more perplexed with Mazes and Confusion, than this which leads to the Provision for the Poor; and hence it is, that through no other Way a more plentiful Harvest hath of late Years been brought into Westminster-Hall.

Sensible as I am of this Mischief, I should not venture to propose any further Experiments, if I was not also sensible, that the Disease is become absolutely intolerable; and had not at the same Time very sanguine Hopes that the Remedy, which I shall propose, will prove in the highest Degree effectual.[1]

---

* *Thucydides.*

[7] *A History of the Peloponnesian War*, III. ix. Fielding quotes the speech of Cleon, whom Thucydides characterizes as 'the most violent man at Athens', against altering an earlier decision to execute the Mitlenians.

[8] W[illiam] H[arrison], 'An Historicall description of the Iland of Britaine . . .', in Holinshed's *The Chronicles of England, Scotland and Ireland* (London, 1587), ch. 18, p. 111.

[9] Thomas Carthew's *Reports of Cases adjudged in the Court of King's Bench from the Third Year of King James the Second, to the Twelfth Year of King William the Third* (London, 1728), p. 152: 'And in debating the case . . . another Case . . . was mentioned which was adjudged in B.R. when Hale was chief justice; and the Copy of the Prohibition was now produced, which was concerning the same matter in the same Place; . . . But the Court held that Case to pass *sub silentio* . . . for it was not remembered by any.' Fielding owned a 1741 edition of Carthew's *Reports* (Baker, no. 142) which, however, does not cover cases from Queen Anne's time.

[1] For Fielding's metaphor see *Enquiry*, p. 63.

That the Poor are a very great Burthen, and even a Nusance to this Kingdom; that the Laws for relieving their Distresses, and restraining their Vices, have not answered those Purposes; and that they are at present very ill provided for, and much worse governed, are Truths which every Man, I believe, will acknowledge. Such have been the unanimous Complaints of all the Writers who have considered this Matter down from the Days of Queen *Elizabeth*; such is apparently the Sense of our present Legislature, and such is the universal Voice of the Nation.[2]

The Facts must be very glaring that can produce this unanimous Concurrence in Opinion; and so in Truth they are. Every Man who hath any Property, must feel the Weight of that Tax which is levied for the Use of the Poor; and every Man who hath any Understanding, must see how absurdly it is applied. So very useless indeed is this heavy Tax, and so wretched its Disposition, that it is a Question whether the Poor or the Rich are actually more dissatisfied, or have indeed greater Reason to be dissatisfied; since the Plunder of the one serves so little to the real Advantage of the other: for while a Million yearly is raised among the former, many of the latter are starved; many more languish in Want and Misery; of the rest, Numbers are found begging or pilfering in the Streets To-day, and To-morrow are locked up in Goals and Bridewells.[3]

Of all these deplorable Evils we have constant Evidence before our Eyes. The Sufferings of the Poor are indeed less observed than their Misdeeds; not from any Want of Compassion, but because they are less known; and this is the true Reason why we so often hear them mentioned with Abhorrence, and so seldom with Pity. But if we were to make a Progress through the Outskirts of this Town, and look into the Habitations of the Poor, we should there behold such Pictures of human Misery as must move the Compassion of every Heart that deserves the Name of human. What indeed must be his Composition who could see whole Families in Want of every Necessary of Life, oppressed with Hunger, Cold, Nakedness, and Filth, and with Diseases, the certain Consequence of all these; what, I say, must be his Composition, who could look into such a Scene as this, and be affected only in his Nostrils*?

That such Wretchedness as this is so little lamented, arises therefore from its being so little known; but if this be the Case with the Sufferings of the

---

* Some Members of Parliament actually made this Progress in Company with Mr. *Welch*, and owned the Truth exceeded their Imagination.[4]

[2] For current interest in poor-law legislation, see General Introduction, pp. lxxv ff.

[3] The best modern account of the poor in this period is Dorothy Marshall, *The English Poor in the Eighteenth Century* (London, 1926).

[4] For Welch's account of such a 'Progress' and Fielding's first-hand knowledge of such suffering, see *Enquiry*, pp. 143–44.

Poor, it is not so with their Misdeeds. They starve, and freeze, and rot among themselves; but they beg, and steal, and rob among their Betters. There is not a Parish in the Liberty of *Westminster* which doth not raise Thousands annually for the Poor, and there is not a Street in that Liberty which doth not swarm all Day with Beggars, and all Night with Thieves. Stop your Coach at what Shop you will, however expeditious the Tradesman is to attend you, a Beggar is commonly beforehand with him; and if you should not directly face his Door, the Tradesman must often turn his Head while you are talking to him, or the same Beggar, or some other Thief at hand, will pay a Visit to his Shop! I omit to speak of the more open and violent Insults which are every Day committed on his Majesty's Subjects in the Streets and Highways. They are enough known, and enough spoken of. The Depredations on Property are less noticed, particularly those in the Parishes within ten Miles of *London*. To these every Man is not obnoxious;[5] and therefore it is not every Man's Business to suppress them. These are however grown to the most deplorable Height, insomuch that the Gentleman is daily, or rather nightly, plundered of his Pleasure, and the Farmer of his Livelihood.

But tho' some of these Articles are more universally notorious than others, they are in general enough known to raise an universal Indignation at a very heavy Tax[6] levied for the Use of those who are no less a Nusance than a Burthen to the Public; and by which, as woful Experience hath taught us, neither the Poor themselves, nor the Public are relieved.

With regard to the Evil, Men will agree almost unanimously; but with regard to the Remedy, I shall expect no such general Concurrence: Nay, the more deplorable and desperate the Case is, the more backward may we presume Men will be to allow the Possibility of any Cure, or the Efficacy of any Remedy for that Purpose.

It may very reasonably be presumed, that so national and atrocious a Grievance, and which it is the Interest of all Men of great Property to redress, would not have subsisted so long, had it been capable of being redressed. And this Presumption may very fairly be confirmed by the many Endeavours which our Parliament have used, and the indefatigable Pains they have taken in this Matter.

If, after all these Endeavours, the Evil should not be removed or even abated; on the contrary, if it should be even increased, surely no Man can be blamed who shall conclude it to be irremediable; and shall compare it to some inveterate Defect in our animal Constitution, to which, however grievous, an honest Physician will advise us to submit, there being no Cure for it in the Art of Physic.

---

[5] 'Exposed or liable to the evil of [something]' (*OED*).

[6] For estimates of the amount, see *Enquiry*, p. 99.

This is indeed so rational, and at the same Time so decent a Conclusion, that, far from blaming it, I am almost overborne with it. I am almost deterred from prosecuting the Attempt any farther, and in some degree conscious of the Immodesty of my Undertaking. For tho' some few of Tempers perhaps equally sanguine with those who still hope to see the Longitude discovered,[7] may not despair of seeing this great Evil one Day redressed, how little can a Man as I am, without Authority, hope to gain even their Attention on this Subject?

Let it be remembered however in my Favour, that some of the noblest and most useful Discoveries have been made by Men of little Note or Authority in the World; for which perhaps a handsomer Reason than the bare Intervention of Chance might be assigned. Men of the greatest Abilities are not always the forwardest to push themselves into the Public Notice. If eminent Fortune, or eminent Friends do not throw open to us the first Gates which lead to Fame and Greatness, a thousand mean Tricks and Arts must be submitted to, to procure us an Admittance. These are easily known, and as easily practised by Persons of small Parts and much Cunning, while they are overlooked and despised by real Genius, which is generally attended by a sullen Pride, that disdaining to seek after the World, expects to be sought out by it. Such are the Men who, as *Horace* expresses it, deceive Mankind, and pass through the World without being known by it. A Temper of Mind which may be as happy for the Possessor, as *Horace* and *Epicurus* seem to think it, but which very unhappily for the Public, is bestowed by Nature on the wrong Persons.[8]

But there is a second Reason less refined, and consequently more obvious; this is the Force of a long and constant Application to any one Subject: Very moderate Parts, with this Assistance, will carry us a great Way, indeed may in Time perform Wonders; and to this I can, with great Truth, and I hope, with equal Modesty, assert the strongest Pretensions; having read over and considered all the Laws in any wise relating to the Poor, with the utmost Care and Attention, and having been many years very particularly concerned in the Execution of them. To these I have likewise added a careful Perusal of every thing which I could find that hath been written on this Subject, from the Original Institution in the 43d of *Elizabeth* to this Day; and upon the Whole it appears to me, that there are great Defects in these Laws, and that they are capable of being amended.

Whether I have discovered what these Defects are, and have been yet

---

[7] An Act of 1714 offered a prize of up to £20,000 (amount dependent upon accuracy) for a method to determine longitude at sea. John Harrison was the first successful claimant, receiving £7,500 in 1765.

[8] Perhaps an allusion to Horace, *Epistles*, I. xvii. 10: *nec vixit male, qui natus moriensque fefellit*: 'and he has not lived amiss who from birth to death has passed unknown'. An 'Epicurean precept', according to the Loeb editor.

farther so fortunate as to find out the Method of removing them, I now submit to the Public, after this Preface, and this short Apology for an Undertaking which I allow to be of very great Difficulty, and to which I shall, of consequence, neither be surprized or offended, if I am thought unequal. The Attempt, indeed, is such, that the Want of Success can scarce be called a Disappointment, tho' I shall have lost much Time, and misemployed much Pains; and what is above all, shall miss the Pleasure of thinking that in the Decline of my Health and Life, I have conferred a great and lasting Benefit on my Country.[9]

[9] In the Introduction to the *Voyage to Lisbon*, Fielding movingly describes his physical decline while serving his country.

PROPOSALS

FOR ERECTING

A County Work-house, &c.

PROPOSALS

FOR ERECTING

A County Work-house, &c.

PAR. I.   That there shall be erected, for the County of *Middlesex*, at some
convenient Place within the said County, a large Building, County-house,
consisting of three several Courts, according to the annexed Plan. The two and
outermost of the said Courts to be called the County-house, and the County-House of Correction
innermost Court to be called the County-House of Correction; with a to be erected.
Chapel and Offices, according to the said Plan.

II. That the said County-house shall be large enough to contain Five
Thousand Persons, and upwards; and the said County-House of Correction What Poor they
large enough to contain Six Hundred Persons, and upwards. shall contain.

III. That both the said Houses shall be so contrived, that the Men and Men and
Women may be kept entirely separate from each other. Women to be
kept separate.

IV. That the said County-house shall consist, 1. Of Lodgings for the Of what
Officers. 2. Of Lodging-rooms for the Labourers. 3. Of Working-rooms for Buildings the
the same. 4. Of an Infirmary. 5. Of a Chapel. 6. Of several large Store- County-house
rooms, with Cellarage. is to consist.

V. That the said County-House of Correction shall consist, 1. Of Of what the
Lodgings for the Officers. 2. Of Lodging-rooms for the Prisoners. 3. Of County-House
Working-rooms for the same. 4. Of an Infirmary. 5. Of a Fasting-room. 6. of Correction.
Of several Cells or Dungeons. 7. Of a large Room with Iron Grates, which
shall be contiguous to and look into the End of the Chapel.

VI. There shall be likewise built one House for the Governor, one for the Additional
Deputy Governors, one for the Chaplains, one for the Treasurer, and one Buildings.
other for the Receiver General of the said House. There shall be likewise Suttling-
built on each Side of the said County-house, Nine Houses for the providing houses.
the Labourers and Prisoners with the Necessaries of Life.

VII. That the said Eighteen Houses shall be leased to proper Persons, by How to be
the Governor for the Time being, for the Term of Seven Years, subject to a leased.
Condition of Forfeiture and Re-entry on the Breach of certain Rules and
Statutes of the said House, herein after particularly mentioned.

Note, the Arguments in support of these Proposals are printed at the End of them, to which the
Reader is desired to refer as he proceeds.

VIII. That the Lodging-rooms of the County-house shall be furnished with Beds, allowing one Bed to two Persons; one large Joint-stool, and two small ones, for each Bed. And that the Working-rooms of the said House shall be provided with all Kinds of Implements and Tools, for carrying on such Manufactures as shall from Time to Time be introduced into the said House.

IX. That the Lodging-rooms of the County-House of Correction shall be furnished with a Coverlet and Blankets, for the Prisoners, and Matting to lie on; and the Working-rooms shall be provided with Implements for beating Hemp, chopping Rags, and for other of the hardest and vilest Labour.

X. That *A, B, &c.* shall be Commissioners for carrying this Act into Execution. That the said Commissioners, or three of them, shall meet once a Week, at such Places within the said County as they shall think most proper, from *Lady-day* 1753, to *Michaelmas* 1753;[1] and once a Fortnight from *Michaelmas* 1753, to *Lady-day* 1755; then to make up their Accounts before a Committee of the House of Commons, if then sitting; if not, at the next Sessions, after which the said Commission to cease and be determined.

XI. That, in order to defray the Expence of the aforesaid Building, and provide the same with all necessary Furniture, as well as to provide Implements and Materials for setting the Poor to work, and for other Expences during the first Year, a Sum not exceeding ____ shall be immediately raised.[2]

XII. That the following Officers shall be appointed for the Government and Care of the said Houses; and these Officers shall be allowed the following Salaries:

COUNTY-HOUSE.

One Governor
Two Clerks
Two Deputies
One Clerk each
Treasurer
Receiver
Three Clerks
Store-keeper
Three Clerks
Two Chaplains

Marginal notes:
County-house how furnished.
How County-House of Correction.
Sum to be raised.

---

[1] Lady-day: the Annunciation, 25 Mar; Michaelmas: 29 Sept. (two of the four quarter-days of the English business year).
[2] Fielding leaves the amount to be spent blank.

Six Keepers
Six Assistants
One Superintendent to every Room
Four Watchmen
Clerk
Sexton

HOUSE OF CORRECTION.

One Keeper
Three Under-keepers
Six Assistants
Superintendent to every Room
Two Watchmen

INFIRMARY.

Surgeon
Apothecary
Matron
Nurses

XIII. That the Governor shall sue and be sued by the Name of the Governor of the County-house of *Middlesex*. And that besides all other Powers to be given him, he shall have Power, as Governor of the said House, to make Contracts with all Persons whatever, and to draw on the Treasurer for any Sums of Money so contracted for, in Payment for any Implements or Materials of any Kind of Manufacture, Trade, or Mystery.[3] He shall likewise have full Power to exercise and carry on, in either of the said House, any such Manufacture, Trade, or Mystery, as may be lawfully exercised and carried on within this Kingdom; and may once every Month hold a grand Market at the County-house, or in some convenient Place near adjoining thereto, for the Disposal of such Wares and Manufactures as shall be wrought by the Labourers in the said Houses. And that every particular Article of such Sale, with the Price for which it was sold, shall be entered in two Books; one of which shall be kept in the Receiver, the other in the Store-keeper's Office, as hereafter is more particularly expressed.

XIV. That when any Person shall be brought before a Justice of Peace for the County of *Middlesex*, and shall be convicted before him, on the Oath of one credible Witness, of any Offence by which he is made a disorderly Person, or a Rogue and Vagabond, by a certain Act passed in the 17th of his present Majesty, called the Vagrant Act;[4] or shall be so convicted of any

Who shall be committed to the County-house, &c.

1. Persons within the Vagrant Act.

[3] 'Mystery': 'craft, trade'.
[4] The Vagrancy Act of 1744 (17 Geo. II, c. 5) consolidated earlier acts and remained the leading act until 1822. It distinguished three categories of offenders: the 'idle and disorderly'; 'rogues and

2. Or those liable to be sent to the House of Correction.

other Crime, for which he is liable to be committed to the House of Correction for any fixed Time, or at the Discretion of one or more Justices, by any Law now in being, it shall be lawful for the said Justice to commit such Person to the County-house, or the County-House of Correction, at his Discretion; which Commitment shall be in the following Form:

> Receive into your Custody the Body of *J. S.* herewith sent you, convicted before me, on the Oath of *J. N.* a credible Witness, of an Offence within the Statute of   commonly called
> and him safely keep in your said Custody until the next general or Quarter-Sessions.—(or for any shorter Time, to be specified in the Commitment.) Given, &c.

And this Mittimus, if to the County-house, shall be directed to the Governor of the County-house, his Deputy, &c. if to the County-House of Correction, to the Keeper of, &c. And whereas it will happen, that such Prisoners will be frequently conveyed to the said Houses from distant Parts of the County, the Justice shall endorse on the Back of his Commitment the Sum to be paid by the Receiver of the County-house, as an Allowance for the Charges of conveying the said Prisoner or Prisoners, such Allowance not to exceed 6 d. by the Mile; and if Need be, 6 d. more for the necessary Refreshment of such Prisoner.

3. Or Persons appointed to be committed to the County Goal in Execution.

XV. That it shall be likewise lawful for the Justices to commit to either of the said Houses, all Persons convicted before them of any Crimes, of which, by the Laws now in being, any one or more Justices of Peace have Cognizance in a summary Way, out of their Sessions, and when the Offenders, being so convicted, are appointed to be committed to the County Goal by way of Punishment for their said Offences.

4. Or Persons accused of small Thefts.

XVI. That where any Person shall be accused on Oath of Petit-larceny[5] before any Justice of Peace, and it shall appear to him that it was the Party's first Offence, and that the Theft was not exaggerated by any heinous Circumstances, the Justice may at his Discretion commit the Offender to either of the aforesaid Houses till the next Sessions, or for a less Time; or if he sees proper, may proceed to commit the Person to the County Goal, and bind over all the necessary Parties to prosecute, as he may lawfully do at this Time.

5. Or Wanderers without a Pass.

XVII. That it shall be lawful for any of his Majesty's Subjects to seize all suspicious Persons who shall be found wandering on foot about the Fields, Lanes, or Highways, or in the Streets of any of the Towns, or Parishes of the

vagabonds'; and the 'incorrigible' (those who had once been apprehended as rogues and vagabonds); and enabled the legal procedures Fielding proposes here.

[5] Theft of goods valued at less than 12*d.*

said County, or within the Liberty[6] of *Westminster*, and all Labourers or Servants, or Persons of low Degree, who, after the Hour of Ten in the Evening shall be found harbouring in any Alehouse or Victualling-house; and if such Persons shall not give reasonable Satisfaction to him or them, by whom he or she is apprehended, that he or she belongs to the said County, and is going on some lawful Errand or Business, or if he or she belongs to any other County, or is then six Miles distant from his own Habitation, and shall not produce a Pass or Certificate[7] signed by some Magistrate, Minister, or Churchwarden, expressing whither or on what Account he or she is then travelling, it shall be lawful for the Party apprehending, to confine such Person till he or she can be delivered to the Constable, or other Peace Officer, or shall be carried by the Party himself so apprehending such Person before some Justice of the Peace, who shall examine the said Person; and if he or she shall appear to be a Wanderer or idle Person, and shall have no legal Pass as aforesaid, such Justice may commit him or her to the County-house, or County-House of Correction, as he shall think proper, there to remain till the next General or Quarter-Sessions, or for any less Time, at his Discretion. And all Constables, Headboroughs,[8] *&c.* are hereby ordered to apprehend all such Persons of whom they shall have Notice, and to receive all such Persons into their Custody as shall be delivered to them, and to convey them before some Justice, under the Penalty of Five Pounds to be levied by Warrant from the said Justices, one Half to the Use of the Person complaining, the other Half to the Use of the said County-house. Provided nevertheless, that whoever shall presume maliciously to detain any Person contrary to the plain Intent of this Law, shall forfeit to the Person so aggrieved the Sum of ten Pounds, to be recovered by Action, *&c.*

XVIII. And whereas it may often happen, that poor Persons have lawful Occasions to travel above six Miles from Home, and into a foreign County, on Errands of Business for themselves or others, or to procure Work, or sometimes to visit their near Relations, who live at a Distance from them—That any Magistrate of the County or Place, or Minister, or Churchwarden of the Parish being applied to, and properly informed of the Truth of such lawful Occasion, shall deliver to such Persons a Pass in the following Words, *Mutatis mutandis.*[9]

Parish of   Permit *A. B.* the Bearer hereof, to pass to the Town of *Middlesex* *Shaftesbury* in the County of *Dorset*, and there to remain during

Pass when and how to be obtained by the Party.

---

[6] See *Charge*, p. 2.

[7] According to the settlement laws, a laborer could not travel from his parish without an authorizing pass.

[8] Originally the head of a tithing or frankpledge; here a petty constable.

[9] 'With the necessary changes'.

the Time limited in this Pass, he behaving himself orderly and according to Law.

Given under my Hand this 10th of *Nov.* 1752.[1]

C. D. Minister of the said Parish.

This Pass to continue in Force one Month from the Date hereof inclusive, and no longer.

—or by any other.

XIX. That it shall be lawful for any Gentleman, Farmer, Artificer, or Tradesman, to employ any Journeyman, Servant, or Labourer, of any other Parish or County besides his own, he having first obtained from such Magistrate, Minister, or Churchwarden as aforesaid, such Pass as aforesaid, which the said Magistrate, *&c.* are hereby required to grant, at the Desire of such Gentleman, Farmer, *&c.* Such Pass to be appointed to continue in Force for so long Time as such Gentleman, *&c.* shall require, during the Continuance of which Pass it shall not be lawful for any Person whatever, to molest or remove the said Journeyman or Labourer from his said Service, unless for some Crime cognizable before a Magistrate, any Law to the contrary notwithstanding.

Who may go voluntarily to the County-house and how.

XX. And whereas many able and industrious Persons, who are willing to get a Livelihood by honest Labour, are often, for want of such Labour, reduced to great Distress, and forced against their Will to become chargeable to the Parishes to which they belong: That when any poor Person shall apply to the Minister, or Churchwarden of any Parish, and shew to either of them such their Inability to procure a Livelihood in their own Parish, or in any other Parish in that Neighbourhood, the said Minister or Churchwarden shall deliver to such poor Person a Certificate in the Words following:

To the Governor of the County-house of the said County.

Parish of *Middlesex.*   I recommend to your Care *C. D.* the Bearer hereof, to be provided for in your County-house, he being an honest industrious Person, but incapable, at present, of procuring Work in this Neighbourhood.

Given under my Hand this 10th. *Nov.* 1752.

A. B. Churchwarden of the said Parish.

Which said Pass being produced and sworn to, before any Justice of Peace of the said County, shall be countersigned by him. Provided that it shall

---

[1] The impulse to infer date of composition from the date used here must be curbed by the unuseful date Fielding offers below, p. 248.

Shaftesbury is on the road to London about five miles east of East Stour.

appear to the Justice, that such Pass was obtained, at the Desire of the Party obtaining it, and that from absolute Want of Labour in the said Parish.

XXI. That whoever shall presume to counterfeit any such Pass or Certificate as aforesaid, or to personate him or her, to whom such Pass or Certificate was originally granted, is hereby declared to be guilty of a very high Misdeameanor, of which being convicted upon the Oath of one Witness, or by his own Confession, before one Justice of the County where he shall be apprehended, he shall be committed by the said Justice to the County-House of Correction, if within the County of *Middlesex*, or to the House of Correction in any other County, there to be severely whipt and put to hard Labour for any Time not exceeding twelve, or less than six Calendar Months. Penalty on counterfeit Passes.

XXII. That if any Person shall be absent from his Parish with a Pass, either obtained by himself, or at the Request of any other, and shall not return to his said Parish at the Expiration thereof, (Sickness or other Inability excepted) such Person being lawfully convicted thereof by Confession or Oath of one Witness, shall be sent to the County-House of Correction, if found in *Middlesex*, or being apprehended in any other County, to the House of Correction there, by any Justice of the said County, there to be whipt and to remain to hard Labour till the next Sessions; and then to be continued or discharged, at the Discretion of the Justices. —or on not returning at the Expiration of the Passes.

XXIII. That when any Person shall come to the County-house with a Certificate as above, the Governor or his Deputy shall examine the said Person as to his Age, Ability, and Skill in any Work or Manufacture, and shall then order the Receiver to enter in a Book, to be kept for that Purpose, the Name and Age of the said Person, the Parish to which he belongs, and the Day of his Admission into the County-house, together with the Kind of Labour to which he is appointed; and a Duplicate thereof shall likewise be entered in another Book, to be kept by the Store-keeper, after which the said Person shall be set to work, according to his Abilities, *&c.* In the said Book shall likewise be entered, an Account of the Moneys advanced to him by the Receiver, and of the Repayments to be made by him as hereafter is ordered and appointed. Manner of Admission of Volunteers into the County-house.

XXIV. And if any such Person shall depart from the said House more than the Space of one Mile, or shall absent himself above one Hour from the said House, without the Leave of the Governor or Deputy Governor, such Person being thereof convicted upon the Oath of one Witness, or on his own Confession, before the Governor, his Deputy, or any one Justice of the Peace, shall be committed to the County-House of Correction, there to remain till the next Sessions, or for any less Time: Provided nevertheless that the Governor, or his Deputy, are hereby required to grant a Licence of How Volunteers to be detained.

Departure to all such Persons, whenever the same shall be demanded; unless such Persons shall not then have finished the particular Piece of Work in which he shall be employed, or unless he shall then remain indebted to the Receiver of the said House; such Licence of Departure to be in the following Words:

County-house   *A. B.* The Bearer hereof, who came voluntarily to the
of *Middlesex.*   County-house aforesaid, is at his own Request discharged
                from the same, and at Liberty to return to his lawful
                Habitation in the Parish of   in the said County.

                                            C. D. Governor.

To which the Governor may, at his Discretion, add a Clause, signifying the Industry or good Behaviour of the said Party.

Manner of Admission of those committed to the County-house.   XXV. That every Person who shall be brought by Mittimus to the County-house, shall be examined, entered, and set to work as above; a Badge with these Words, *County-house,* in large Letters, shall likewise be sewed on the left Shoulder of the said Person, who shall be confined within the said House, till he is discharged in Manner as hereafter is expressed; and whoever shall presume to tear off, or otherwise destroy the said Badge, either from himself or any other Person, being thereof convicted by the Oath of one Witness, or on his own Confession, before the Governor or Deputy, shall be by him committed to the County-House of Correction, there to remain till discharged by due Course of Law.

Manner of admitting into the County-House of Correction.   XXVI. That when any Person shall be brought to the County-House of Correction, by a Mittimus to the said House, he shall be immediately confined within the Fasting-room, there to remain with no other Maintenance than Bread and Water during the Space of Twenty-four Hours; after which he shall be put to hard Labour with the other Prisoners, unless he shall give any Marks, by his Words or Behaviour, of any outrageous Degree of Reprobacy; in which case the Keeper of the said County-House of Correction shall inform the Governor or his Deputy thereof, who shall convene the Party before him, and may at his Discretion remand the said Person to the aforesaid Fasting-room, or may confine him alone in a Cell, to be supported with Bread and Water only, till such Time as he shall behave in a more orderly Manner; or, in default thereof, till the next Sessions. And all Persons committed to the County-House of Correction, shall there remain and be put to hard Labour till they be discharged at the Sessions, in such Manner as in this Act is directed, unless in Cases where a shorter Confinement is appointed by the Act itself.

Rules and Orders of the House.   XXVII. That the Bell of the County-house shall be rung every Morning at four throughout the Year, and Prayers shall begin in the Chapel precisely at five; at the Conclusion of which, on every *Wednesday* and *Friday*, some short Lecture, or Exhortation of Morality shall be read to the People; and if any Person, unless on Account of Sickness, or for some other reasonable Cause to be allowed by the Governor or his Deputy, shall be absent, he shall be guilty of a Misdemeanor, to be punished as hereafter. Hour of Prayer.

XXVIII. That the Hours of Work in the County-House of Correction shall be every Day from six in the Morning to seven in the Evening, allowing half an Hour for Breakfast, and an Hour for Dinner; and in the County-house the said Hours of Work shall be daily from six in the Morning till nine, from ten to one, and from two till six in the Evening, except on *Thursdays*, when two Hours in the Afternoon are to be otherwise employed, as hereafter is appointed, such Holy-days likewise excepted, as hereafter are mentioned; that Prayers shall again be read in the Chapel every Evening at seven. of Work.

XXIX. That the Bell of the County-house shall be rung every Evening at nine, that all Fires and Lights shall be then put out, except in the Infirmary and in the Apartments of the Officers; that all the Gates and Doors of both Houses, except as aforesaid, shall then be shut and fastened, the Keys delivered to the Governor or Deputy, and the Watch shall be set. —of Rest.

XXX. That the Keepers or Under Keepers of both Houses, shall by Turns constantly attend and supervise the Labourers, and shall take an Account of any Neglect of Work, or other Misbehaviour; the Keepers of the County-house shall likewise take Account of any extraordinary Diligence in any of the said Labourers, and shall faithfully report the same twice in every Week, to the Governor or his Deputy, at their Court, which is hereafter appointed to be holden, and that one of the Labourers of the best Morals and Demeanor, shall in every Room be appointed to supervise the Conduct of the other Labourers, and to report the same.

XXXI. That as often as may be, the Labourers in the County-house shall be permitted to refresh themselves in the inclosed Ground, contiguous to the said House, in the Presence of two at least of the Keepers and Under Keepers, particularly on *Sundays* and on every *Thursday* in the Year, when two Hours Labour in the Afternoon shall be remitted for that Purpose; the same Liberty shall be granted to any one or more of the Prisoners in the House of Correction, provided that the Surgeon or Apothecary shall certify to the Governor or his deputy, that such Refreshment is necessary for the Health of the said Prisoners, who shall on all such Occasions be sufficiently guarded, and none of the Labourers to be present at the same Time, provided that *Christmas*-day, and the three subsequent Days, *Twelfth*-day, *Ash-wednesday*, *Good Friday*, *Monday* in *Easter* Week, *Monday* in *Whitsun* Week, *Michaelmas*-day, *Gunpowder Treason*-day,[2] and his *Majesty's* Birth-day, —of Recreation.

---

[2] Anniversary commemorating the exposure of the plot to blow up the Houses of Parliament, 5 Nov. 1605.

shall be Holydays in the County-house, and the Labourers may recreate themselves on those Days; which shall likewise be Days of Rest in the County-House of Correction.

Order for the Sick.

XXXII. That no Person shall be removed from either of the said Houses, to the Infirmary, unless by an Order signed by the Governor or his Deputy, to be obtained by the Certificate of the Surgeon or Apothecary, that such Person is in a sick and languishing Condition; and that Notice of such Removal, shall be immediately given to the Receiver and Store-keeper, who shall minute the Day of such Removal, as they shall likewise the Recovery or Death of the Party, (of which they shall also have Notice) in the same Page where the Person's Name shall have afore been entered.

—and dead.

XXXIII. And as often as any of the Labourers or Prisoners, in either of the said Houses shall happen to die, the Governor shall take Order for the Burial in the cheapest Manner consistent with Decency, in the Burying-ground belonging to the said House; unless any of the Relations of the Deceased shall be desirous of removing the Body to be buried elsewhere at their own Expence:—After which an Account shall be taken of any Cloaths, Money, or other things, of which the Deceased shall die possessed, as well as an Account taken of what was due from the Receiver to him, or from him to the Receiver; and if on the Balance any thing shall appear to have been due to the Deceased, such Balance, together with his Cloaths, &c. shall carefully and faithfully be delivered to his lawful Representative: All which shall be entered in the Book of the Receiver and Store-keeper, in the same Page where the said Party's Name was above ordered to be entered.

Advancement to the Labourers in the County-house.

XXXIV. That as often as any Person shall be committed or admitted to the County-house, the Receiver shall immediately advance to him or her, if desired, the Sum of two Shillings, and so weekly the same Sum, until the first Sale of the Manufacture wrought by such Person; after which it shall not be lawful for the said Receiver to make any farther Advancement, without a special Order from the Governor or Deputy, specifying the Sum to be advanced, opposite to which shall be entered the Letter O; and such Order shall likewise be filed, as a Voucher for that Purpose. All these Advancements to be afterwards deducted by the Receiver, after the Rate of Fourpence in the Shilling, out of the Monies due to the said labourer from the Sale of his Manufacture, till the whole shall be repaid.

—To the Prisoners in the County-House of Correction.

XXXV. That to all Persons committed to the County-House of Correction, at their Commitment thither, shall be advanced by the said Receiver the Sum of one Shilling, and so weekly the said Sum during their Continuance there.

Deductions from the Labourers.

XXXVI. That from all those who are committed to the County-house, the Sum of Twopence in every Shilling shall be deducted out of the nett

Profits arising from their Labour; but from those who voluntarily come thither, no more than one Penny in every Shilling.

XXXVII. That immediately after every Sale the Receiver shall make up the Accounts thereof with the Governor or Deputy, which Accounts shall be examined with and checqued by those kept by the Store-keeper; after which the Receiver shall presently distribute to the several Labourers in the County-house, all such Sums as shall by him be received for their several Manufactures, having first made such Deductions as are herein before appointed; all which Deductions shall be forthwith paid into the Hands of the Treasurer of the said House. *Accounts to be kept.*

XXXVIII. That the Receiver and Store-keeper shall keep an exact Account of all Implements, Materials, &c. from Time to Time brought to the said House, of those which are delivered to the Labourers, and those which remain in the Hands of the said Store-keeper. The same exact Account to be likewise kept of all the Manufactures which shall be wrought in the said House, and by whom; with the prices for which the said Manufactures were sold, the Monies paid to the Labourers, and the Deductions: All which shall be entered in two Books by the Receiver and Store-keeper, allowing a separate Page to every Man.

XXXIX. That all such Accounts shall be examined by the Governor, and shall be afterwards laid before every Quarter-Sessions; at which Time the Receiver and Store-keeper shall swear to the Truth thereof: To which said Sessions the Treasurer shall likewise transmit an Account of the Monies then in his Hands, and if there shall at any Time appear to be less than the Sum of one Thousand Pounds remaining with the Treasurer, the Deficiency shall be made up by a County-rate, together with so much more as by the best Computation shall be thought necessary for mean Expenditures, so that there may still remain the said Sum of one Thousand Pounds Capital Stock in the Hands of the said Treasurer, at the ensuing Quarter-Sessions: And if any considerable Excess of the said Capital Stock, over and above what shall be necessary for paying the Salaries of the Officers, and other Expences concerning the said Houses, shall be in the Treasurer's Hands, such Redundancy shall then be applied in aid of the parochial Rates, in the several Parishes of the said County. *Governor to inspect Accounts, and Sessions.* *How Deficiencies made up.* *How Redundancies employed.*

XL. That for the better Instruction of the Labourers in the Manufactures and Mysteries now exercised in this Kingdom, as well as for the Introduction of foreign Manufactures and Mysteries into the said Kingdom, it shall be lawful for the Governor to expend annually, during the first three Years, the Sum of   and every subsequent Year annually the Sum of for the Pay and Encouragement of Persons to teach our own and foreign Manufactures to the said Labourers. All such Disbursements to be entered *Teachers of Manufacture to be hired.*

in a Book to be kept for that Purpose, attested by the Party receiving the same, and by the Governor and one Deputy at least, as well as by the Receiver; and such Book to be constantly inspected and examined into by the Justices as they shall think fit.

Labourers may be let out to Service.

XLI. Upon Application made by any Nobleman, Gentleman, Merchant, Tradesman, Farmer, or substantial Housholder, dwelling within the County of *Middlesex*, or within twenty Miles of the said County-house, to the Governor or Deputy, signifying that such Nobleman, &c. is desirous to take into his Service any Labourer or Labourers then confined in the said County-house, it shall be lawful for the Governor or Deputy, and he is hereby required to deliver over the said Labourer or Labourers to such Person so applying, and to deliver to each of the said Labourers a Certificate, in the Words following,

County-house *Middlesex*,
    A. B. is delivered to *C. D.* as his servant, to serve him until
and then to return to the said House. Dated the 5th of *August*, 1753.

                    E. F. Deputy-Governor.

Provided nevertheless, that where such Servant shall be hired for a Year certain, the Clause relating to his Return shall be omitted; and when any Labourer shall be so hired as aforesaid for any less Time than one Year, the Person so hiring such Labourer shall deposit in the Hands of the Receiver of the said House one Half of the Labourer's Wages for the Time he shall be so hired: And if he shall be hired for any longer Time than two Months, then one Month's Wages to be deposited; which Money so deposited shall be paid by the Receiver to every such Labourer immediately upon his Return to the said House, deducting one Penny in every Shilling. And if such Labourer shall depart, or be lawfully discharged from his said Service, before the Wages so deposited shall become due, the Receiver shall return the whole to the Person depositing the same, deducting only as above; but if the said Labourer shall abide with his said Master during the limited Time, and shall not return within two Days after the Expiration thereof, (Sickness, or other lawful Impediment excepted) then shall the Money deposited be forfeited to the Use of the said House; of all which Retainers, Deposits, Repayments, and Forfeitures, a double Entry shall be made by the Receiver and Store-keeper.

And if any Person so hiring any Labourer as aforesaid, shall discharge the same before the Expiration of the Term for which he was so hired, he shall forfeit the whole Money deposited by him as above; which Money shall be paid to such Labourer, at his Return to the said House.

Provided that it shall be lawful on reasonable Cause shewn to the Satisfaction of any one Justice of the Peace, either by the Master or

Labourer, for such Justice to discharge such Labourer, and to send him back to the County-house, or order him to the County-House of Correction, at his Pleasure; and if such Labourer shall have been hired into any foreign County, the Justice of such County may, if he pleases, commit him to the House of Correction there: Provided likewise, that if such Labourer shall by Sickness or any Accident be rendered incapable of working; it shall be lawful for his Master, at his Expence, to return him to the County-house, to be provided for in the Infirmary of the said House; in which Case, the Money deposited shall be paid to him to whom it shall appear to be due.

And if any Labourer so hired as aforesaid for less Time than one Year, shall not, at the End of his Term, return to the said House; or if any Labourer whatsoever, so being hired, shall run away or depart from his Master's Service before the Expiration of his Term, unless for some Default in his Master or Mistress or shall assault his Master or Mistress, or shall refuse to work at the Command of his said Master, or his Agent, or be guilty of any Misdemeanor in his said Service, it shall be lawful for any Justice of the Peace, if such Masters shall reside in the County of *Middlesex*, to commit the said Labourer to the County-House of Correction, there to be first severely whipt, and to remain to hard Labour till the next Sessions, when he may be farther dealt with by the Justices at their Discretion: Or if the said Master shall reside in any other County, then to be sent by a Justice of that County to the House of Correction there, to be severely whipt, and to remain for any Time not exceeding three, nor less than one Calendar Month. Provided that no Person who comes voluntarily to the said House shall be forced into such Service contrary to his own Consent and Option.

XLII. That if any Persons, to the Number of three or more, shall conspire together to break the said County-house, or County-House of Correction, and shall have provided themselves with any Kind of Arms or Weapons for that Purpose, and shall all or any of them do any Act whatsoever in pursuance of such Conspiracy, and with a manifest Design of executing the same, in consequence of which Act any Officer belonging to either of the said Houses shall be killed, maimed, or wounded, this shall be Felony without Clergy[3] in all the Conspirators.

Crimes cognizable before the higher Courts of Justice.

1. Conspiracies to break the Prison.

2. To beat, wound, &c. the Officers.

XLIII. That if any Persons, to the Number of three or more, whereof all or any Part shall be confined within either of the said Houses, shall maliciously beat and bruise, or wound any Officer belonging to either of those Houses, in such manner that the Surgeon or Apothecary appointed to

---

[3] By the 16th century, benefit of clergy (originally a privilege of clerics to be tried by ecclesiastical rather than by civil authorities) effectually had become in common law a means whereby first offenders could escape capital punishment for many offences. In the 16th, 17th, and 18th centuries, statute after statute removed benefit of clergy from specified offences so as to ensure, as Fielding wants to do here, the death penalty.

attend the said Houses shall on Oath declare, that the Life or Limb of such Officer was brought into Danger thereby, such Persons being lawfully convicted of such Offence, shall suffer Death as Felons without Clergy.

3. Assaults on the Governor, &c.

XLIV. That every Person confined within either of the aforesaid Houses, who shall assault the Governor, Deputy Governor, or Chaplains, tho' not then in the Execution of their Office; or who shall assault, beat, and bruise, or wound any of the Officers belonging to either House, any wise, on account of, or in the Execution of their several Offices; or who shall actually break either of the said Houses, and escape therefrom; being lawfully convicted of any of the said Offences shall be transported for fourteen Years.

4. Conveying Arms, &c. into the Houses.

XLV. That all Persons who shall convey any Fire-arms, or any mischievous Weapon or Tool, to any of the Labourers or Prisoners within either of the said Houses, without the Privity of the Governor or Deputy Governor, shall be guilty of Felony; and being lawfully convicted thereof, shall be transported for seven Years.

5. Refusal to work.

XLVI. That all Persons committed to the County-House of Correction, who shall absolutely refuse or neglect to labour, after a Fortnight's Confinement in the said House; and having during that Time received the Discipline of the same, being lawfully convicted of such absolute Refusal or Neglect, before Justices of Oyer and Terminer, or Goal-delivery,[4] shall be transported for   Years; provided that it may be lawful for any Officer of the Army to receive the Body of such Offender, and to convey him to serve his Majesty in any of his Forces in the *East* or *West Indies*.

6. Frauds in the Officers.

XLVII. That any Receiver, Storekeeper, Clerk, or other Person, who shall knowingly, and with a fraudulent Design make any false Entry in any of the Books by this Act ordered to be kept, and in which Entries are here ordered to be made, such Offender being lawfully convicted thereof, shall be deemed guilty of Felony, and transported for seven Years.

Accused Persons to be committed to the County Goal.

XLVIII. That all Persons lawfully accused, by the Oath of one credible Witness, of any of the aforesaid Crimes before the Governor or his Deputy, shall by him be committed to the County Goal, there to remain till discharged by due Course of Law. In the same Manner shall be committed all Persons accused of Felony in either of the said Houses, or of giving any Maim, dangerous Wound, Bruise, or Hurt, to any Person within the said Houses.

Lesser Crimes.
1. Introducing spirituous Liquors into the Houses.

XLIX. That if any of the Officers, or any Person having Liberty to sell their Wares within the said Houses, shall sell or give to any of the Labourers in either of the said Houses, any Quantity, how small soever, of spirituous Liquors, without the Order or Direction of the Surgeon or Apothecary, such

---

[4] See *Charge*, p. 6.

Persons being lawfully convicted thereof before the Justices at their Sessions, shall be deemed guilty of a Misdemeanor, punishable by the Justices with Fine and Imprisonment: And all such Persons being so convicted, shall be incapable of bearing any Office, or selling any of their Wares within either of the said Houses for the future: And all those who shall be charged on Oath before the Governor with the said Crime, shall be bound with sufficient Sureties to appear and answer the same at the next Sessions.

L. That all Persons wilfully and maliciously destroying, spoiling, or injuring any of the Furniture belonging to either of the said Houses, or any of the Implements, Tools, Materials, Manufacture, or Stock being therein, shall, when lawfully convicted thereof before the Justices at their Sessions, be deemed guilty of an infamous Crime, and may, besides Fine and Imprisonment, receive any corporal Punishment, not extending to Life or Limb, at the Discretion of the said Justices. *2. Destroying Work, &c.*

LI. That every Person escaping from the County-House of Correction, shall, on his being apprehended, be brought before the Governor or Deputy, and being thereof convicted before him, shall be by him recommitted to the said House; there to be severely whipt, and then confined during the Space of ten Days in one of the Cells belonging to the said House, and to have only Bread and Water for his Support: After which he shall remain in the House of Correction subject to the Rules of the House as before, with this likewise, that he shall on no Account be liable to be discharged from the same until the next Sessions which shall be held after the Expiration of six Calendar Months. *3. Escape from the County-House of Correction.*

LII. That every Person escaping from the County-house shall be committed to the County-House of Correction, and shall be whipt at his Entrance into the same. *—From the County-house.*

LIII. That twice in every Week, that is to say, on every Monday and every Thursday in the Forenoon, the Governor or his Deputy shall hold a Court within the said County-house; in which the said Governor or his Deputy shall have Power to hear and determine any of the following Offences. *Jurisdiction of the Governor.*

1. Quarrels amongst the Labourers, where no Maim, Wound, violent Bruise, or other dangerous Hurt is given or done; but where the Injury consists in some slight Blow or Kick, or of contumelious and provoking Language. *Petty Offences.*

2. Profane Swearing or Cursing, or other profane Discourse, and all Kind of Indecency in Word or Act.

3. Drunkenness.

4. Absence from Chapel without Cause, or irreverent Behaviour there.

5. Absence from Work, Idleness at it, or negligently spoiling the same.

6. Obstinate Disobedience to any of the Rules of the House.

All which are hereby declared to be Offences against the true Intent and Meaning of this Act, and to be punishable by the said Governor or Deputy, by Rebuke, small Fine, or Confinement for any short Time, not exceeding three Days; allowing only such Sustenance as shall be thought proper for the first Offence; for a second Offence the Confinement may be enlarged to a Week; and for a third, the Offender may be committed to the House of Correction, there to remain till the next Sessions, or for any less Time; and may likewise be ordered to be whipt. And in case of a third Offence committed by any of the Prisoners in the House of Correction, the Governor or Deputy may, besides the Punishment of Whipping, confine such Person in one of the Cells, there to remain till the next Sessions; or if such Offence be an absolute Refusal or Neglect of Work, may commit him to the County Goal, there to remain till he be discharged by due Course of Law: Provided that the second and third Offence above mentioned is here intended to be an Offence of the same Kind with the first. All Convictions to be on the View of the Governor or Deputy, Confession of the Party, or on the Oath of one credible Witness.

Of what the Governor, &c. to enquire.

2dly, The Governor or Deputy shall at such his Court enquire of all Persons who have behaved themselves so as to merit Reward; and shall minute their Names in a Book to be kept for that Purpose, which shall be produced to the Justices at the next Sessions.

3dly, They shall enquire of the Conduct of all the Officers under them, and if they find any of them deficient in their Duty, or guilty of any Cruelty, Corruption, or other atrocious Fault, such Officer shall be suspended from his Office till the next Sessions, when the same shall be presented before the Justices.

4thly, They shall enquire of all Offences within this Act, and of all other Offences of which the Persons lawfully accused are to be committed to the County Goal; and such as are so accused they shall commit thither.

5thly, They shall from Time to Time enquire into the Prices of Provisions brought into the said House, and regulate the same, subject to the Supervisal of the Sessions. And if any Exactions shall have been made on the Labourers or Prisoners, or any unwholesome Provisions introduced into the said Houses, or other Default be in the Victuallers, they shall report the same to the Sessions.

Jurisdiction of the Sessions.

LIV. That on one of the Days on every Sessions to be holden at *Hicks's-Hall*,[5] the said Sessions shall be adjourned to the County-house, there to be holden within five Days next after such Adjournment; at which Sessions at the County-house the Justices shall have Power to enquire,

[5] General sessions for the county of Middlesex were mainly held at Hicks's Hall, St John Street, Clerkenwell. See *Charge*, p. 12, n. 2.

1st, Of all Neglects, Corruptions, or other Misdemeanours, in any of the Officers of the said Houses, and to punish the same, (unless in the Governor or Deputies, or Chaplains of the said House,) by Reproof, Fine, or Dismission, as they shall think meet; and if by Dismission, then to place some other fit Person in the Room of the Officers so dismissed.

2dly, They shall enquire into the general Conduct of the said House, and if they shall find any Default in the Governor, Deputy Governors, or Chaplains of the same, they shall report such Default before their Brethren at the next ensuing Sessions at *Hicks's-Hall*, where the Governor, *&c.* shall have Notice to appear, and make his Defence; and if such Default shall seem to the Majority of the Justices of the said Sessions to be well proved, and to be of such a Nature as to merit any severe Censure, they may, if they please, report the same to the Lord High Chancellor of *Great Britain*, who shall have full Cognizance of the Matter, and may remove the Governor, *&c.* from his Office, or fine him at his Pleasure.

3dly, The Justices shall enquire of the Prices of Provisions, *&c.* which shall be brought into the said Houses, and shall regulate the same at their Discretion, altering, if they see fit, the Orders taken by the Governor herein; and may hear the Report of the Governor touching any Default in the Victuallers, and may punish the same by Fine or by turning out such Victualler at their Pleasure.

4thly, They shall enquire of the Behaviour of all Persons confined within the House of Correction, and such as they shall find, by the Report of the Keeper on his Oath, or by other Evidence, to have behaved themselves orderly, and to have applied closely to their Labour, the Justices may enlarge from that Confinement, and commit them to the County-house, to be there kept till the ensuing Sessions; and such as they shall find to have behaved in a less orderly Manner, or to be lazy or negligent in their Work, they may order to remain till the next Sessions in the House of Correction, where they then are; but such as they shall find to be utterly reprobate and ungovernable, and to refuse all Kinds of Labour, the Justices are hereby required to commit to the County Goal, there to remain till discharged by due Course of Law.

5thly, The Justices shall likewise enquire by the Recommendation of the Governor, Deputy Governor, or Rector, or by the Oath of other Evidence, of the Behaviour of the several Labourers then confined within the County-house; and such as shall appear to have behaved themselves decently and orderly, and to have been diligent in their Work, the Justices may, at the Desire of the Party, enlarge from their Confinement: provided, that such Party shall make out to their Satisfaction, that there is any reasonable Cause to hope or expect that such Labourer will be able to maintain himself in an honest Manner at his own Home; in which Case the Justices shall give the

Party a Pass, to enable him to travel thither without Molestation: Provided that no Person shall be discharged from the County-house while he shall remain indebted to the Receiver of the said House.

And such Persons as shall have behaved themselves in a less becoming Manner, or who shall have been idle and negligent in their Work, or who shall not be able to make it appear to the Satisfaction of the Justices, that they would be capable of procuring an honest Livelihood at their own Homes, or shall remain indebted to the said Receiver, the said Justices shall order to continue in the said County-house till the next Sessions. And if it shall appear to the said Justices, by any of the means aforesaid that any of the said Persons have behaved themselves in a notorious and outrageous Manner, or have totally neglected or refused to work, then it shall be lawful for the said Justices to commit such Persons to the County-House of Correction, there to remain till the next Sessions, with hard Labour, and with other such Correction and Punishment as they shall think proper.

6thly, The Justices shall inspect all the Accounts relating to the said House, and shall have Power to examine on Oath the Treasurer, Receiver, Store-keeper, with their several Clerks, or any other Person touching the same; and if the said Accounts shall appear to them to be fair and just, they shall then sign the same: Which Accounts having been first examined and signed by the Governor or Deputy, and so passed and counter-signed by the said Justices, shall be good and effectual to all Manner of Purposes: But if there shall appear to the Justices upon their said Examination to have been any gross Mistakes, or any Kind of false Entry, Fraud, or Collusion, shall appear upon the Face of the said Accounts, the said Justices may, if they please, examine into and finally determine the same; as likewise may suspend or dismiss any Officer who shall to them appear to have been guilty of any such false Entry, Fraud, or Collusion; or may, if they shall see more convenient, adjourn over the further Hearing and Determination of the same to the next Sessions: To which they may bind over all Parties, and in the mean Time may, if they shall think fit, suspend the suspected Person from the Exercise of his Office, and may appoint another to officiate in his Room.

Lastly, They shall have Power to enquire into the Behaviour of any of the Labourers, who shall have so behaved themselves as to merit Rewards, and may proceed to order them severally such Reward as to them shall seem proper: All which shall be publickly paid to the said Labourers in open Court by the Governor, who shall draw on the Treasurer for the same; such Reward to be paid in the Presence of all who are to receive any Punishment at that Time.

Governor, &c. to inspect Punishments.   LV. Whereas the Punishment of Whipping is inflicted in some Cases in this Law, which Whipping is always intended to be severe and exemplary, the Governor, or his Deputy, is always to be present at the inflicting the same.

LVI. That the Governor, Deputy Governors, Chaplains, Treasurer, Receiver, Keeper of the House of Correction, and all other the Officers and Ministers attending the same, shall be chose at the Sessions at *Hicks's-Hall*, by the Majority of the Justices there present, by Ballot; and before any of the said Justices shall be admitted to ballot he shall take the following Oath:

> You do swear that you will give your Suffrage in the Ballot now to be made, impartially, not out of Favour or Affection, nor on account of any Promise made by you or to you, nor by the Force of any Recommendation whatsoever; but as you are persuaded to the best of your Knowledge or Belief, that the Person for whom you shall give your Suffrage is better qualified than any other of his Competitors (*if there be any, otherwise say only is qualified*) for the Discharge of the Trust for which he now appears a Candidate. So help you God.

In like Manner shall all Vacancies be supplied from Time to Time.

LVII. That all Fines and Forfeitures to be imposed or to accrue by Virtue of this Act, not otherwise disposed of, shall be paid to the Treasurer of the County-house, and be applied to the Use of the said House.

LVIII. The Governor may make By-laws with the Consent of the Justices, the same to be approved by the Lord Chancellor.

LIX . Persons tried, *&c.* shall plead this Act, *&c.*

ARGUMENTS

IN

Explanation and Support

OF THE

Foregoing PROPOSALS.

Paragraph I, &c. to XIV. *The Appointment of a County-house and County-House of Correction, with the Regulation thereof.*

PAR. I. *In* Middlesex, &c.] It is proposed to make the Trial first in the County of *Middlesex*, as I am best acquainted with the State of the Poor in that County, and as the well regulating them there is of the greatest Moment to the Public; but if the Plan should be approved by Experience, it will be very easy to extend it over the Kingdom.

Ibid. In some convenient Place.] This should be at some little Distance from *London*; nor will it be difficult among the many Wastes which lie within a few Miles, to fix on some convenient Place for the Purpose. I do not know myself any so proper as a Common near *Acton-Wells*, the Purchase of which, tho' of three Hundred Acres Extent, would be very reasonable; it being at present allotted to the Use of the Poor of *Fulham*, who derive very little Benefit from it.[6] I may add, that this is a very healthy Spot, and most commodiously situated; being at no great Distance from any Part of *Middlesex*, and not five Miles from *Hyde Park* Corner.

II. *The County-house to be large enough*, &c.] As whatever is perfectly new is apt to affect us with Surprize, and as this Surprize is increased and attended with Doubt and Incredulity in proportion to the Greatness of the Object, I am well aware of the Impression with which the Largeness of this Building will strike many Minds: The Idea of a Body of Men united under one Government in a large City, must have been amazing when it was first propounded to Men who lived a wandering Life, scattered in single

---

[6] Thomas Wilford (see General Introduction, p. lxxxviii) came to London from the Fulham Workhouse. Fielding's workhouse would not have been far from his retreat near Ealing or from Richardson's country house in Fulham.

Families, or collected in very small Numbers together; tho' indeed our Astonishment is not quite so excuseable, as we see not only the possibility of such Union, but the Advantages arising from it.

In the present Case, however, I think to make it appear from Reason, Authority, and Experience, that to answer the Ends proposed, *to make the Poor useful Members of the Society*, we must bring them as much as possible together; at least so as to collect the Poor of a single County.

First, It is a great Work, and requires many great Qualifications in the Person who is principally to direct it: Such Men are not to be found in every Parish in a County; nor if they were found, could they be induced to employ their Time this Way by any Reward which the Parish could bestow on them: For not much less Time and Trouble will be requisite to the directing and supervising a small Body of Men, than a Body twenty Times as large, when once this is brought into Regularity and Order. The same Abilities and the same Trouble which can well order and govern a small State, will suffice for the Government of a large Kingdom. To manage the Poor so as to produce the Ends proposed in this undertaking, is a Task to which very few are equal; and those who are equal to it will scarce undertake it, unless they are well paid for their Pains.

2dly, The Expence and Difficulty of carrying this Purpose into Execution will always increase in proportion to the Smallness of the Body of People by whose Hands it is to be executed. And this is the Reason why Work-houses (more properly called Idle-houses) have by Experience been found to produce no better Effect:[7] For if the Masters of these Houses had a real Disposition to set the Poor to work, and if they had all adequate Capacities for that Purpose, they would by no Means be able to effect it. One or two or three Manufactures will not suffice to employ the various Talents, Skill, and Strength of a small Body of Men, especially when this Body is eternally changing. Many Inconveniences will necessarily attend such Houses: The Manufacturer will sometimes stand still for Want of Work; and at others, the Materials will be spoiled for Want of Hands; whereas in such a Number of Persons as are here proposed to be collected together, some will be found capable of every Manufacture, and of every Branch of it; and as from a Certainty of finding such Hands, all Kind of Materials and all Kind of Tools will be provided, both the Mischiefs above complained of will of course be avoided. I have here supposed the Existence of Parish Work-houses at least, (whereas in Reality there are but few of these where any Number of Poor are lodged, and much fewer where they are in any Manner employed) for as to those Parishes where the Poor are left at large, it is utterly impossible that they should be made in any Degree useful, or indeed any other than a heavy

---

[7] See General Introduction, p. lxxiii and n. 2.

Burthen on their Neighbours; some of whom, (by the Way) are often little richer than themselves. In a large Body alone the Materials can be sufficiently supplied, the Hands properly adapted, new Manufactures taught, and the Work well disposed of to the Emolument of the Public, and the proper Encouragement of the Labourer.

3dly, As the Industrious cannot so well be employed, so neither can the Lazy be so efficaciously compelled to work in Parish Work-houses; the Care of which must be intrusted to Persons of mean Consideration, where there can be no proper Authority to inflict Punishment, nor any adequate Force to execute it on those who are most reprobate and desperate.

4thly, The Poor cannot be so well nor so cheaply provided for in many Bodies, as they may be when collected into one.

5thly, They will not be so commodiously confined. In small and crowded Work-houses, where there are no Courts nor Outlets to admit the Air, the Poor are often so distempered, that their Keepers are obliged by common Humanity to let them frequently out; in which Case, the certain and immediate Use which these Wretches make of their Liberty, is to increase the Number of Beggars.

6thly, The Proposal for Amendment of their Morals, by instilling into them Notions of Religion or Morality, (a Matter as it appears to me of the highest Consequence) is only consistent with the Scheme of bringing them together; to which Scheme indeed all the Rules and Orders of this Plan are directed, and with which alone they will, on Examination, be found compatible. Every Thing, therefore, which I shall say on the present Occasion, may be applied as an additional Reason on this Head.

And in this Case, Authority will be found to be on the same Side with Reason. My Lord Chief Justice *Hale*, perceiving that the Poor of a single Parish could not be well provided for by themselves, advises a Coalition of several Parishes for this Purpose. This was clearly seeing the defect in the Statute of *Elizabeth*, tho' it was not carrying the Remedy far enough.[8]

The Author of an Essay on the Bills of Mortality (said to be the famous Sir *William Petyt*, under the borrowed Name of *Graunt*) having discoursed on the Evil of Beggars, of *reforming their Morals, curing their Impotencies, and teaching them to work according to the Condition and Capacity of every Individual*,[9]

[8] *A Discourse Touching Provision for the Poor* (London, 1683), p. 25. Hale proposed 'That the Justices of the Peace at the Quarter Sessions do set out and distribute the Parishes in their several Counties into several Divisions, in each of which there may be a Work-House for the common use of the respective Divisions, wherein they are respectively placed, *viz*. one, two, three, four, five or six Parishes to a Work-House, according to the greatness or smallness, and accommodation of the several Parishes.'

[9] John Graunt (1620–74), *Natural and Political Observations on the Bills of Mortality* (London, 1662), reprinted in *A Collection of the Yearly Bills of Mortality from 1657 to 1758 Inclusive* (London, 1759), ch. III, p. 11. Fielding paraphrases Graunt, who in fact argues against state employment of beggars because that would deprive the industrious poor of work. *Observations* is in Baker, no. 543. William

concludes in these Words, "But I say none of these can be effected without bringing them together; or if it could be effected at all, neither so well nor so cheaply*."[1]

The great Sir *Josiah Child* (for great in his Province he certainly was) proposes, "that the Cities of *London* and *Westminster*, Borough of *Southwark*, and all other Places within the usual Lines of Communication described in the weekly Bills of Mortality, may, by Act of Parliament, be associated into one Province, or Line of Communication for the Relief of the Poor."[2]

He proceeds, among other Powers to be given to his Corporation, "that they, and such as they shall authorise, may have Power to purchase Lands, erect and endow Work-houses, Hospitals, and Houses of Correction," &c.[3]

Here is almost as populous, if not as large a District, as the County of *Middlesex* itself. It is true, he doth not expresly mention the bringing these Work-houses, Hospitals, and Houses of Correction together into one Place; but this will appear, I think, to have been his Intention, or he would not have concluded in the following Manner:

"If it be here objected to the whole Purpose of this Treatise, that this Work may as well be done in distinct Parishes, if all Parishes were obliged to build Work-houses, and employ their Poor therein, as *Dorchester* and some others have done with good Success:

"I answer, that such Attempts have been made in many Places, to my Knowledge, with very good Intents and strenuous Endeavours; but all that ever I heard of proved vain and ineffectual, except that single Instance of the Town of *Dorchester*, which yet signifies nothing to the Kingdom in general; nor does the Town of *Dorchester* entertain any but their own Poor only, and whip away all others: Whereas that which I design, is to propose such a Foundation as shall be large, wise, honest, and rich enough to maintain and employ all Poor that come within the Pale of their Communication, without enquiring where they were born," &c.[4]

---

* *Graunt* on Bills of Mortality, Chap. 3.   † *Child* on Trade, &c. Chap. 3.

Petty (see below, p. 262, n. 8) was thought by many to have written *Observations*, but authorship is uncertain (see Geoffrey Keynes, *A Bibliography of Sir William Petty . . . and of Observations on the Bills of Mortality by John Graunt* [Oxford, 1971]). William Petyt (1641?–1707) wrote *The Antient Right of the Commons of England Asserted* (1680). Fielding has been confused by the similarity of names. He repeats this error below, p. 263–4.

[1] This sentence is not in *Observations*.

[2] *A Discourse about Trade* (London, 1690), pp. 65–6 (Baker, no. 27). Sir Josiah Child (1630–99), whom Fielding calls a 'truly wise and great Man' (*Enquiry*, p. 115–6), was a large stockholder in the East India Company and one of the wealthiest merchants of his time. William Letwin in *Sir Josiah Child: Merchant Economist* (Cambridge, Mass., 1959) denies theoretical importance to Child's economic thought but notes that he was the 'most widely read of seventeenth-century English economic writers' (p. 26). See also Letwin's chapter on Child in *The Origins of Scientific Economics: English Economic Thought 1660–1776* (London, 1963), pp. 3–47.

[3] Child, *Discourse*, p. 67.

[4] Ibid., pp. 77–8. After 'vain and ineffectual', Fielding omits '*as I fear will that of Clerkenwell*'.

These are great Authorities, and will, I doubt not, much more than counterbalance any Opinions which can be produced on the other Side, if indeed there are any such.

Lastly, Experience, the Instructor of those who can learn of no other Master, might, of itself alone, convince us of the Truth for which I am contending. I will not here repeat what I have said in the Introduction, relating to the wretched State of the Poor under the present Establishment; all which may be urged as an Argument on this Head, since it will, I think, appear, that the scattered State in which the Poor were left by the Statute of *Elizabeth*, is the principal Reason why this Law hath produced no better Effect. It is true indeed, the Management of the Poor was by that Statute intrusted to very improper Hands; but this will not universally account for the Evil, since many worthy and good Men have, in divers Places, taken upon themselves the Charge of the Poor, and have employed much Time and Trouble therein to very little or no Purpose. The true Reason therefore that the Poor have not yet been well provided for, and well employed is, that they have not yet been drawn together. Of this Opinion were the great Writers whom I have cited, and both Reason and Experience may convince us, that the Matter can be accomplished no other Way.

But perhaps an Objection may suggest itself of the contrary Kind, and to which it may at first Sight appear more difficult to give an Answer. It will perhaps be said, that I have computed the Poor at too small a Number, and have not proposed a Method of providing for one half of them. Indeed if we are to estimate the Poor by the Overseer's Books in the several Parishes as they now stand, and add to these the Inhabitants of *Bridewell*, with all those who ought to be Inhabitants of that Place, I readily grant I have not provided for Half, nor perhaps for half a Quarter of the Poor of this County. But the Objector will be pleased to observe, that a great Number of the latter Part do not properly belong to this County; but are Vagabonds from all Parts of the Kingdom: Witness the great Expence to which this County is put, by passing one in a Hundred perhaps back to their own Homes.[5] Some of these are at present drawn hither from those Counties where their Labour is often wanted, by the great Encouragement which this Town affords to Beggars and Thieves. Others come up with honester Views at first, in which being commonly disappointed, they betake themselves to the same Means of procuring the Bread of Idleness: but when instead of such alluring Prospects, a Work-house or a *Bridewell* shall present itself to their Eyes, this Swarm, it may easily be supposed, will soon cease, and the two Houses will be little filled with such Vagabonds. And as to the proper Poor of the

---

[5] Beggars and vagabonds could be sent or 'passed' back to the parish where they had a legal settlement (see *Enquiry*, p. 139). Fielding's 'one in a Hundred' calls attention to the ease with which country poor migrated to the slums of Westminster and the out parishes of London.

County, when we deduct the Aged, the Infant, and the accidentally Impotent, who are not the Objects of my Plan, the Building proposed will perhaps be found capable of receiving the rest. But let us allow the Objection its full Force, and what doth it assert? Why, that there are more able Poor in the County of *Middlesex*, who are at present idle, tho' capable of being employed, than I have provided an Accommodation for. The Result of this would certainly be, that the means of Accommodation should be enlarged; and this I apprehend, if it should appear to be necessary, may very easily be effected.

III. *Men and Women to be kept separate.*] The Utility of this Provision needs no Comment: Our present Houses of Correction, for Want of this Regulation, are Places of the most infamous and profligate Debauchery.

IV. *&c.* to the IXth inclusive.] These are only loose Sketches of what it may perhaps be unnecessary to insert in the Bill, and which may be left to the Discretion of those to whom the Legislature shall think proper to intrust the Care of the Building. The Nomination of the Commissioners I likewise submit to the Legislature.

XI. *A Sum to be raised.*] I have not ventured to particularize any Sum; but it must undoubtedly be a large one. And yet large as it will be, when we consider the great Utility proposed, of effectually providing for the Poor, and of relieving the Public from Beggars and Thieves, it must appear moderate, or even trifling.

But farther: It is not only the Redress of an Evil, by the relieving the Poor from their Misery, and the Public from the Poor, which is the Object of this Plan; much of positive Good is designed by it to the Society. If 6000 Hands which now sit idle can be employed, the Advantages resulting hence to the Public need not be explained to any who have the least Notion of Trade, or of the Benefits arising from it.

An excellent Writer on our Constitution observes, that *of the three main Supports of the Riches of a People, two of them consist in improving their natural Commodities, and in setting the Poor to work**. The former indeed is only the Consequence of the latter; nay, as he himself says, *The Improvement of the natural Commodity can never enrich the Kingdom so long as many Mouths are fed upon the main Stock, and waste the same in Idleness and Prodigality.*[6]

---

* *Bacon's* Disc. on Law and Government, Part II. p. 39.

[6] Nathaniel Bacon (1593–1660), *The Continuation of an Historicall Discourse on the Government of England* (London, 1651), ch. VII, 'Concerning Trade', pp. 66–7 (Fielding owned a 1739 edition, Baker, no. 277). According to Christopher Hill, the puritan Bacon's *Historicall Discourse* was 'the most ambitious work produced during the Interregnum on the historical theory of the constitution' ('The Norman Yoke', in *Puritanism and Revolution* [1958; New York, 1964], p. 72). Fielding also cites Bacon in the *Enquiry*, p. 132.

The great Mr. *Law*, in his little Treatise called Money and Trade considered, explains this more fully. His Words are these, "An Addition to the Money adds to the Value of the Country. So long as Money gives Interest, it is employed; and Money employed brings Profit, tho' the Employer loses. If 50 Men are set to work to whom 25 *s.* is paid *per* Day, and the Improvement made by their Labour is only equal to, or worth 15 *s*, yet by so much the Value of the Country is increased; but as it is reasonable to suppose their Labour equal to 40 *s.* so much is added to the Value of the Country, of which the Employer gains 15 *s.* 15 may be supposed equal to the Consumption of the Labourers, who before lived on Charity, and 10 *s.* remains to them over their Consumption†."[7]

Nor will it bear, I think, any rational Doubt, whether Employments may be found for this, or indeed a much larger Number of Hands. Sir *William Petyt*, in that excellent Work called his Political Arithmetic, affirms, and proves too, that there were in his Days spare Hands among the King's Subjects to earn two Millions more than was actually earned.[8] He farther affirms, that there was two Millions Worth of Work to be done, which the King's Subjects did neglect to do*; for without this latter could be proved, the former, as he himself admits, would serve to little Consequence.[9]

Now the Number of Hands here to be provided for, may surely be computed at a very low Rate (for so I would make the Computation) to do, one with another, Work to the Value of 10 *l. per Annum*, this will amount to 60000 *l.* the Advantage of which to the Public will be readily acknowledged. Here then the Evil of the Poor will not only be removed, but it will be converted into a very great Emolument.

But there is yet another Light in which this Sum may perhaps appear more palatable; and that is, by comparing it with the Sum now paid to the Poor-Rate, which in this County of *Middlesex*

---

† Money and Trade considered, p. 22.
* Polit. Arithmetic, Chap. VIII.

[7] John Law (1671–1729), *Money and Trade Consider'd* (1705; London, 1729), pp. 11–12 (this work is not listed in Baker). Law, a Scotsman, established the first French bank (1716) and was appointed controller-general of French finances in 1720. After the failure of his 'Mississippi Scheme', he fled France and died in poverty.
[8] Sir William Petty (1623–87), *Political Arithmetick* (London, 1691), p. 107: '. . . there are spare Hands among the Kings Subjects to earn two Millions more than they do'. (Fielding owned this edition; Baker, no. 546.) Petty's *Economic Writings* have been edited by Charles Henry Hull, 2 vols. (Cambridge, 1899). A friend of Hobbes and one of the founders of the Royal Society, Petty 'wrote with equal facility of trade, coinage, population, mathematics, medicine, music, shipbuilding, the art of dyeing, clothmaking, and much else' (James Sutherland, *English Literature of the Late Seventeenth Century* [Oxford, 1969], p. 372).
[9] *Political Arithmetick*, p. 108: 'Now if there were spare Hands to Superlucrate Millions of Millions, they signify nothing unless there were employment for them; and may as well follow their Pleasures, and Speculations as Labour to no purpose; therefore the more material Point is, to prove that there is two Millions worth of Work to be done, which at present the Kings Subjects do neglect.'

amounts annually to upwards of 70,000 *l.*[1] as I am informed: Of which five Parts in six are, I believe, applied to the Use of those poor who are the Objects of the Law proposed in this Plan.

They are the able Poor, either such as cannot procure Work, or such as will not do it, who are the great Burthens of the Society. Of those who are absolutely impotent, the Number is truly inconsiderable. Sir *William Petyt*, whom I shall beg Leave to cite once more, in his Political Anatomy of *Ireland*[†], computes, that there is in Nature but one in 500 at most who is blind, lame, or under any incurable Impotence, as old Age, *&c.* To every Individual of these he allows 6 *l. per Annum*; which, he says, would maintain them without Scandal.[2] A very large Allowance, when we consider the Place of which he speaks, and the Time in which he wrote. A less Sum would, I believe, answer the Purpose among us.

According to this Computation, if the People in *Middlesex* amount to 1,200,000, the impotent Poor will be 2400: the Expence of maintaining which Number will be 13,600 *l.*[3] The above excellent Author estimates the Children under seven Years of Age at the Rate of one Fourth of the People:[4] These then, according to my Estimate in *Middlesex*, will be 300,000. Of these, I presume, not above one in 150 will be a Burthen on the Public.[5] This Number then will be 3000; for whom 3 *l.* each, one with another, will be sufficient; and which will make the Sum of 9000 *l.* The whole Expence therefore of the impotent Poor in *Middlesex* will be 22,600 *l.* about the fourth Part of what it now is. And if the Number of Hospitals, Infirmaries, and various donative Charities within this County of *Middlesex*, do not reduce this Sum, so as to bring the whole Expence to one Sixth Part of what it now is, I am greatly deceived, or those must be grosly misapplied.[6]

I have endeavoured in a former Essay[*] to shew, that such Objects as these, so cheaply to be provided for, might with great Safety be left to voluntary Contributions: Nor shall I add anything more to the Arguments I have there used, especially as this Part of our Poor have since fallen under the

---

[†] Polit. Anat. of *Ireland*, p. 11.
[*] Enquiry into the Causes of the Increase of Robberies, &c. [p. 109].

---

[1] Accurate information does not exist, but the Webbs cite contemporary figures that indicate the poor-rate for the nation at mid-century was nearly £700,000 and that one tenth of this sum was levied in the metropolitan London area (Sidney and Beatrice Webb, *English Local Government*, vii. [London, 1926], 153). For other estimates see *Enquiry*, p. 99, n. 1.
[2] Sir William Petty, *The Political Anatomy of Ireland* (London, 1691), p. 10 (Fielding owned a 1719 edn.; Baker, no. 355): 'There is in Nature but one in 500 at most who are Blind, Lame, and under incurable Impotence; so as not above 2000 in Ireland, whom 1200£ would maintain without Scandal.'
[3] The figure should be £14,400.
[4] *Political Anatomy of Ireland*, p. 11.
[5] Another error. If Fielding had estimated 'one in 100' instead of 'one in 150', his figure of 3,000 would work.
[6] See *Enquiry*, p. 99 and n. 3.

Consideration of two very honourable and learned Persons, for whom I have a very high Respect and Esteem.[7]

If either of these Bills, with that proposed in this Plan, should pass into a Law, the Poor-Rate would then entirely cease of course; and the Statute of *Elizabeth*, with all Laws for providing for the Poor as to this County, might be utterly repealed. The same indeed would be the Case, if the impotent Poor were trusted to voluntary Contributions, as they possibly might, tho' with less Advantage to the Public, especially as to the Education of the Infants, which is a valuable Part in the Schemes of those honourable Persons.

I conclude this Head therefore with asserting, (for so I surely may) that whoever considers my Plan only in this last Respect, and compares the Expence proposed in it with that which is at present annually incurred, must view the Sum of 100,000 *l*. (beyond which the whole Expence of building, furnishing, and providing all Kind of Implements, will not rise) as a trifling Sum well laid out in a cheap and valuable Purchase. Private Interest, from this Respect alone, will to every wise Man recommend a Scheme, by which he may propose to be so great a Gainer, to his fullest Consideration; and this Motive, in proportion as he is a good Man, will be greatly enhanced by those Arguments which relate to the Public. There are none so stupid as not to prefer the Payment of 20 *l*. once, to the yearly Payment of that Sum; and few so entirely void of all public Spirit, as to be totally indifferent whether that Money which is levied on them be applied to the Good of the Community, or squandered away, as it now is, to no Manner of Purpose.

If there be any Enemies therefore to my Plan, they must be such only as doubt its Efficacy. To these I answer, that absolute Certainty with regard to a future Event, is not in the Nature of Human Affairs: but let them examine the Plan with Fairness, Impartiality, and Candour; let them well and duly weigh every Part of it, and I am greatly deceived if the Result will not be a strong Opinion of the Probability of its Success; tho' indeed a very small Degree of this Probability would in our present Situation be almost a sufficient Encouragement to the Undertaking.

[7] Sir Richard Lloyd (?1696–1761) and Wills Hill (1718–93), Earl of Hillsborough, later Baron Harwich. Lloyd was a government supporter, sitting for Maldon, and a member of the Committee of 1751. In 1752 he had introduced a bill 'for the better Maintenance and Employment of Poor Children' which advocated a workhouse for their care and education and which was to be financed by a lottery. He became solicitor-general in 1754 and baron of the Exchequer in 1759. He was one of the king's counsel in the libel trial that was part of the aftermath of the Westminster election of 1749.

Hillsborough, at first an opposition Whig and adherent to Dodington, was a government supporter by 1749 sitting for Warwick. His bill for 'the Maintenance and Employment of all sorts of Poor, as well the Aged as Children; Lame, Blind, Ideots, Sick . . .' would have established a hospital-workhouse in each county in England (see the *London Magazine*, xxi. [Apr. 1752] 153–4). Cross incorrectly identified Lord Hardwicke as the sponsor of this bill. Hillsborough was to enjoy many high posts under George III, including secretary of state for the southern department.

According to Thomas Alcock, who dates his pamphlet 10 Feb. 1753, 'The passing either of those Bills into a Law indeed was purposely suspended . . . that during the Recess of Parliament the Matter might be more thoroughly canvassed and considered'. Neither bill became law.

I have hitherto supposed, that this Sum was to be immediately raised among the present Inhabitants of *Middlesex*, by an additional Poor-Rate; But this is not necessary; for as the Benefit of this Plan is to extend to Posterity, it is equitable that they should contribute towards the Expence. If the Money therefore was granted by a Vote of Credit, at Three and an Half *per Cent.* and only a twentieth or thirtieth Part of the Principal paid off yearly with the Interest, the annual Charge on the County would be so small, that it would scarce be felt; nay, perhaps, if this was done by way of Lottery, it might be so contrived, as to reduce the whole Expence to little or nothing.[8]

XII. *The Appointment of Officers.*] Any Alteration may be made with regard to these, if it shall appear proper. The Number, I think, which I have here mentioned will not be found extravagant, any more than the Salaries allotted to each, when we consider the Trust which they are severally to undertake.

XIII. *The Powers of the Governor.*] Perhaps some further Powers may be found necessary; as to *that of holding a Market*, &c. such open Sale of the Commodities will give great Encouragement to the Labourers, and may be moreover one Means of preventing Frauds, which, in all public Institutions, can never be too well-guarded against, too often, or too strictly enquired into, or too severely punished.

Par. XIII. *&c.* to XXIII. *Who to be sent or admitted in the County-house*, &c. *with the Manner of sending them.*

XVI. *Persons accused of Petit-Larceny to be committed to the said Houses*, &c.] By the common Law Petit-Larceny is Felony, and it is not within the Power of the Magistrate to compound the Offence, tho' it be ever so trifling, or the Party should appear to be in the highest Degree an Object of Mercy.[9] The Prisoner is therefore to be committed to Goal, where he must often lie in *Middlesex* many Weeks, in other Counties many Months before he is brought to his Trial.[1] During this Time, his Morals, however bad, are farther corrupted; his Necessities, however pressing before, are increased; his Family, if he hath any, made more wretched; and the Means of providing for himself and them rendered more difficult, if not impossible, for the future,

---

[8] If Fielding's suggestion of a lottery seems inconsistent with his criticisms of the abuses of that institution (see for example *The Lottery* [1732]), it was not impractical. According to Lecky, Westminster Bridge 'was built chiefly from the produce of lotteries' and 'in 1753 lotteries were established to purchase the Sloane collections and the Harleian manuscripts, which were combined with the Cottonian collection and deposited in Montague House under the name of the British Museum' (*History of England*, i. 566).

[9] Larceny may be *simple* ('plain theft') or *compound* (accompanied by 'atrocious circumstances'), the punishments for the latter being much more severe. Petit larceny, whatever the circumstances, was classified as simple larceny (Blackstone, *Comm.* iv. 229 ff.).

[1] Awaiting one of the twice-yearly visitations (after Hilary and Trinity terms) of the assize judges with their commissions of oyer and terminer and general gaol delivery. On the Northern Circuit judges went once a year, and it was possible for a prisoner to wait eleven months for his trial.

by the total Loss of his Character. If he be acquitted on his Trial, as he often is by the Mercy of the Jury, against clear and positive Evidence, he is again turned loose among the Community with all the Disadvantages I have mentioned above; to which, if he be convicted and whipt, I may add the Circumstance of Infamy, the Marks of which he will be sure to carry on his Forehead,[2] tho' the Hangman very seldom, I believe, leaves any on his Back. What must be the Situation of this Wretch I need not mention; such in Truth it is, that his second Theft is in reality less criminal than the first. This was perhaps Choice; but that will be Necessity. A late Act of Parliament hath indeed put it in the Power of the Court to transport these Pilferers;[3] but this, tho' probably it may be real Mercy, hath such an Appearance of extreme Severity, that few Judges are willing to inflict such a Punishment on such an Offence.[4] But if it should be the Interest of a Wretch in these Circumstances, to be banished from a Country where he must steal or starve, it is scarce the Interest of the Public to lose every Year a great Number of such able Hands. By the means I have proposed, it seems to me, that the Offender will receive a Punishment proportionable to his Offence; he and his Family may be preserved from utter Ruin, and an able Member, instead of being entirely lost to the Public, will be rendered more useful to it than he was before. ·

XVII. *That it shall be lawful to seize all suspicious Persons*, &c.] I have observed in another Place*, that tho' we have had several Laws against Vagrants, by which many Misdemeanours have been called and constituted Acts of Vagrancy; yet Vagrancy itself, or wandering about from Place to Place, is not of itself alone punishable. This is an egregious Defect in this Part of our Constitution, and hath been one great Cause of the Increase of Beggars and Thieves. To prevent the wandering of the Poor was the great Purpose, as I have shewn, of the Laws of *Alfred*. It was this which gave that Strength and Energy to those Insitutions, which have been praised by so many Pens, both of Lawyers and Historians. Hence it was, that Travellers, as we are told, might pass through the whole Kingdom with Safety; nay, that Bracelets of Gold might be hung up in the public Roads, and found at a

---

* Essay on Robberies [p. 142].

[2] The 'Marks' must be metaphorical. Burning 'the most visible part of the left cheek, nearest to the nose' as a punishment for *grand* larceny was ended in 1706.

[3] 4 Geo. I, c. 11; 6 Geo. I, c. 23; and 16 Geo. II, c. 15 are all directed to transportation of petty offenders.

[4] John H. Langbein observes that 'juries fairly frequently [downvalued] from grand to petty larceny in order to turn transportation into whipping, especially when the goods were of relatively small amount or when the accused was a married woman or a family man' ('Shaping the Eighteenth-Century Criminal Trial: 'A View from the Ryder Sources', *University of Chicago Law Review*, 50 [1983], 54). The fear of transportation is illustated by Moll Flanders's Lancashire husband who, offered the possibility of transportation, tells Moll 'that he thought the passage into another state much more tolerable at the gallows'.

distant Time by the Owner in the Place where they were left.[5] Upon these Principles I have formed this Clause, and without it I will venture to say, no Laws whatever for the Suppression of Thieves and Beggars will be found effectual.

I should scarce apprehend, tho' I am told I may, that some Persons should represent the Restraint here laid on the lower People as derogatory from their Liberty.[6] Such Notions are indeed of the enthusiastical Kind, and are inconsistent with all Order and all Government. They are the natural Parents of that Licentiousness which it is one main Intent of this whole Plan to cure; which is necessarily productive of most of the Evils of which the Public complains; of that Licentiousness, in a Word, which among the many Mischiefs introduced by it into every Society where it prevails, is sure at last to end in the Destruction of Liberty itself.[7]

As the Clause now stands, I have drawn it with much Caution, and have qualified it with such Restrictions, that I own I cannot see any Inconvenience which can possibly attend it; if any such should appear, it may be qualified yet farther. But if we must on no Account deprive even the lowest People of the Liberty of doing what they will, and going where they will, of Wandring and Drunkenness, why should we deny them that Liberty which is but the Consequence of this; I mean that of begging and stealing, of robbing or cutting Throats at their good Pleasure: For if these be Evils, they cannot be effectually abolished but by some such Law as this; a Law which hath not only the Sanction of such an Authority as *Alfred*, but of an Act of Parliament in the Reign of Queen *Elizabeth*.[8]

XVIII. *The Poor to travel with a Pass.*] This Method of permitting the Poor to go abroad to work, &c. under a Pass, is taken from an Act of Parliament of *Elizabeth*.[9] I have through this Plan proposed short Precedents of Orders, &c. a Method which it would be well if the Legislature would pursue in all Acts relating to the Office of a Justice of Peace.

XX. *Poor to be passed to the County-house.*] Tho' every Commitment by the Magistrate may carry with it some Notion of Delinquency, yet I would not have the County-house supposed to be a Place of Infamy, or a Confinement there to be so much intended for Punishment as Preservation. It is true indeed, that I have, to avoid Confusion, left it in the Breast of the Magistrate to which House he will commit; but surely he will never extend this discretionary Power so far, as to send Persons to the County-house who are

---

[5] For Fielding's celebration of Alfred's England see General Introduction, pp. lxiv ff.

[6] Perhaps an allusion to 'Ben Sedgly's' *Observations on Mr. Fielding's Enquiry* (see General Introduction, pp. lxvii ff.).

[7] Cf. Fielding's discussion of liberty in the *Enquiry*, p. 73.

[8] 39 Eliz., c. 4.

[9] 5 Eliz., c. 4. sect. 10.

convicted of any higher Crimes than barely Wandering and Idleness; which are not infamous in themselves, and therefore should not, nay, cannot be rendered so by any Punishment. The County-house is indeed a Place contrived for the Promotion of Industry only, and is therefore a proper Asylum for the Industrious of their own Accord to fly to for Protection.

XXIII. to XLIII. inclusive. *The Method of receiving the Poor, putting them to Work, and ordering them in these Houses.*

XXIII. *Double Entry to be made.*] Through this whole Plan I have endeavoured as much as possible to guard against Fraud, to which human Nature, without proper Checks, is but too liable.

XXIV. *None to depart,* &c.] As it would be hard absolutely to confine Volunteers like Prisoners, so on the other Hand it would be altogether inconvenient to give such Persons full Right of rambling where they please. This might fill the Highways with Thieves and Beggars, and one great Evil which the Plan intends to abolish, might be increased by it.

XXV. *A Badge to be worn.*] As Persons sent hither by the Justices, must be supposed guilty of some Crime (Idleness at least) it may be proper to distinguish them from those Labourers who are entirely guiltless. And this Distinction is moreover necessary to inform the Officers, whom they are to let out at their Pleasure.[1]

XXVI. *Prisoners to be confined on Bread and Water during twenty-four Hours.*] Scarce any Person will be committed hither who would not by the Law as it now stands have been committed to *Bridewell*, where the Allowance is no more than a Penny Loaf a Day, with Water. To be confined therefore with such Sustenance for twenty-four Hours, cannot be well thought a severe Punishment. The particular Reason why I have inserted it here, is, that the Party, before he be let loose among the other Prisoners, should be perfectly cool; which is seldom the Case when profligate Persons are brought before the Justice, and by him committed to the House of Correction. And if at the Expiration of that Term, the Prisoner should still retain any Signs of outrageous Reprobacy, it will be much more proper to confine him by himself, than to suffer him to reinfect those who may possibly have made some Advancement in their Cure: And indeed there can be no more effectual Means of bringing most abandoned Profligates to Reason and Order, than those of Solitude and Fasting; which latter especially is often as

[1] Badging, common at least since Tudor times, was fiercely resented by the poor (see Marshall, *The English Poor in the Eighteenth Century*, pp. 102 ff.). Swift thought it an effective way for a parish to identify its own beggars (*Works*, ed. Davis, ix. 207). Gibbon observed that the Romans once thought to distinguish their slaves by a 'peculiar habit' but 'it was justly apprehended that there might be some danger in acquainting them with their own numbers' (*Decline and Fall*, ed. William Smith [New York, n.d.], i. 266 [ch. ii]).

useful to a Diseased Mind, as to a distempered Body: To say Truth, this is a very wholesome Punishment, and is not liable to those ill Consequences which are produced by Punishments attended with Shame:[2] For by once inflicting Shame on a Criminal, we for ever remove that Fear of it, which is one very strong Preservative against doing Evil. Indeed, however this may have been admitted into the Punishments of all Countries, it appears to me to contain in it no less Absurdity, than that of taking away from the Party all Sense of Honour, in order to make him a good Man.

XXVII. *Prayers every Morning*, &c.] Nothing can I think appear more strange, than the Policy of appointing a Chaplain to *Newgate* and none to *Bridewell*. On a religious Account it is surely very fit to have a proper Person for preparing Men for Death; but in a political View it must seem most extremely absurd to provide for the Regulation of those Morals in which the Society are no longer concerned, and entirely to neglect the Correction and Amendment of Persons who are shortly to be let loose again among the Public, and who are even confined for the Purpose of Correction. The Correction of the Body only was doubtless not the whole End of the Institution of such Houses; and yet it must be allowed a great Defect in that Institution, to leave the Correction of the Mind to the same Hands. In real Truth, Religion is alone capable of effectually executing this Work. This *Solomon* asserted long ago, and the excellent Archbishop *Tillotson*, in a Sermon on his Words,[3] which *Solomon* might have himself preached, hath very nobly expatiated on the Subject.

"Religion (says he) hath a good Influence on the People, to make them obedient to Government, and peaceable towards one another. To make them obedient to Government, and conformable to Laws, and not only for Wrath and out of Fear of the Magistrate's Power, which is but a weak and loose Principle of Obedience, and will cease whenever Men can rebel with Safety, and to Advantage; but out of Conscience, which is a firm, and constant, and lasting Principle, and will hold a Man fast when all other Obligations will break. He that hath entertained the true Principles of Christianity, is not to be tempted from his Obedience and Subjection by any worldly Considerations; because he believes, that who ever resisteth Authority, resisteth the Ordinance of God, and that they who resist shall receive to themselves Damnation.

"Religion tends to make Men peaceable one towards another, for it

---

[2] Allworthy refuses to gratify the 'good-natured Disposition of the Mob' by sending Jenny Jones to the bridewell where she would have been 'sacrificed to Ruin and Infamy by a shameful Correction' (I. ix. 59). The infliction of shame as a punishment is apparently the equivalent of capital punishment for the gypsies in *Tom Jones* (XII. xii. 669).

[3] The text for Tillotson's sermon is, 'Righteousness exalteth a nation, but sin is the reproach of any people' (Proverbs 14: 34).

endeavours to plant all those Qualities and Dispositions in Men which tend to Peace and Unity, and to fill Men with a Spirit of universal Love and good Will. It endeavours likewise to secure every Man's Interest, by commanding the Observation of that great Rule of Equity, whatsoever ye would that Men should do unto you, do ye even so to them, by injoining that Truth and Fidelity be inviolably observed in all our Words, Promises and Contracts; and in order hereunto, it requires the Extirpation of all those Passions and Vices which render Men unsociable and troublesome to one another; as Pride, Covetousness and Injustice, Hatred and Revenge and Cruelty; and those likewise which are not so commonly reputed Vices, as Self-Conceit and Peremtoriness in a Man's own Opinions and all Peevishness and Incompliance in Things lawful and indifferent.

"And that these are the proper Effects of true Piety, the Doctrine of our Saviour and his Apostles every where teaches us. Now if this be the Design of Religion to bring us to this Temper, thus to heal the Natures of Men and to sweeten their Spirits, to correct their Passions, and to mortify all those Lusts which are the Causes of Enmity and Division, then it is evident, that in its own Nature it tends to the Peace and Happiness of human Society. And that if Men would live as Religion requires they should do, the World would be a quiet Habitation, a most lovely and desireable Place in Comparison of what it now is; and indeed the true Reason why the Societies of Men are so full of Tumult and Disorder, so troublesome and tempestuous, is because there is so little of true Religion among Men; so that were it not, for some small Remainders of Piety and Virtue which are yet left scattered among Mankind, human Society would in a short Space disband and run into Confusion, the Earth would grow wild and become a great Forest, and Mankind would become Beasts of Prey one towards another, &c."[4]

So far this great Preacher, the Truth of whose Doctrine I might confirm by Quotations from almost every good Writer, who hath treated of the Rules and Laws of Society, as well as by the Example of all those Legislators by whom the several Societies, which have ever been extant in the World, were first instituted; and therefore as the learned *Diodorus* long since observed, all great Lawgivers, among whom he includes *Moses*, derived their Commissions from Heaven, and mixt religious Rites with civil Institutions, well knowing how necessary the former were to strengthen and give a proper Sanction to the latter.[5] Nay the very Deist and Atheist himself, if such a Monster there

[4] Tillotson, 'Sermon III, The Advantages of Religion to Societies', *Works*, 3rd edn. (London, 1701), p. 46. John Tillotson (1630–94), Archbishop of Canterbury, was one of Fielding's favorite divines (see *Tom Jones*, III. ix. 145 and n.).

[5] Diodorus Siculus, *History*, i. 94. Diodorus mentions several lawgivers who ascribed the laws to the gods, observing 'among the Jewes Moyses referred his laws to the god who is invoked as Iao. They all did this either because they believed that a conception which would help humanity was marvellous and wholly divine, or because they held that the common crowd would be more likely to obey the laws

be, must acknowledge the Truth of this Doctrine, since those who will not allow Religion to be a divine, must at least confess that it is a political Institution, and designed by the Magistrate for the Purpose of guarding his Authority, and of reducing the People to Obedience; "therefore, (says the learn'd Archbishop) Magistrates have always thought themselves concerned to cherish Religion, and to maintain in the Minds of Men the Belief of a God in another life; nay that common Suggestion of atheistical persons, that Religion was at first a politic Devise, and is still kept up in the World as a state Engine to awe Men into Obedience, is a clear Acknowledgment of the Usefulness of it to the Ends of Government, &c."[6]

Indeed if this solemn Truth wanted any further Proof, it might be easy to make a Melancholy Experiment of it on the present Occasion; since whoever should attempt, without the Assistance of what I here contend for, to preserve any Order or Decency among such a Body of People as is proposed to assemble together; would, I am convinced, find himself very egregiously, and perhaps very unfortunately Mistaken: If indeed such a Body of Men could be kept together at all, and refrained from the most violent and inordinate Outrages, this could be only effected by a strong and constant military Force; in short by the same Degree of Coercion, as would restrain the Fury of wild Beasts, which are possibly as easy to be governed as wild Men.

That Religion is a very cold and unavailing Motive to Action in the World, is, I am afraid, neither easy to be denied, or difficult to account for. Some there are who are too wise, (I mean in their own Opinions) to believe any of the Truths of it; many more are too far immers'd in the Pursuits of Business or Pleasure, and many, almost all indeed who are the Objects of this Plan very seldom or never hear the Word Religion mentioned; but Heaven and Hell when well-rung in the Ears of those who have not yet learn't that there are no such Places, and who will give some Attention to what they hear, are by no Means Words of little or no Signification. Hope and Fear, two very strong and active Passions,[7] will hardly find a fuller or more adequate Object to amuse and employ them; this more especially in a Place where there will be so little of Temptation, to rouse or to gratify the evil Inclinations of human Nature; where Men will find so few of Those good things, of this World, for which the other is every Day bartered; and where they will have no Encouragement, from the Example of their Betters, to make so prudent an Exchange. In such a Place, and among such a People, Religion will, I am

if their gaze were directed towards the majesty and power of those to whom their laws were ascribed' (Loeb).

[6] Tillotson, Sermon III, p. 47.

[7] Cf. *Amelia*, III. v. 313, where Doctor Harrison demonstrates the truth of Christianity on the basis of its appeal to our strongest passions, hope and fear. Fielding employs the 'active' passion of fear in *Examples of Providence*.

satisfied, have a very strong Influence in correcting the Morals of Men; and I am no less persuaded, that it is Religion alone which can effectually accomplish so great and so desireable a Work.

XXVIII. XIX. Need no Explanation, but may be altered as the Legislature pleases.

XXX. *The Keepers, &c. to report the evil or good Behaviour of the Labourers.*] Tho' it be the Duty of every Man to obey the Laws of his Country, and no Man is entitled to any Reward for the Performance of his Duty; and therefore Legislators are not to be accused of Severity in annexing Punishment to the Breach of their Laws, while they have assigned no Reward to the obedient: However, I am inclined to think they have not omitted the latter so much from this Perswasion, as from foreseeing the great Difficulties in which it would have involved them: for tho' it be impossible in large and extended Societies, to preserve a general Course as well of rewarding as punishing, yet the wisest Governments have endeavoured as far as in them lies, to avail themselves of the Force of Allurement, as well as of Terror. Hence, that Indulgence in all Nations to the Wealth and Luxury of their great Men, which *Gallus Assinius* in *Tacitus* calls *Delinimenta Curarum & Periculorum*.[8] Hence all those Titles and Honours, with which Politicians have baited for the Ambition of Mankind; and hence, when the public Stock could afford no more of real Value, those gewgaw trifling Distinctions, which, in spite of all the Ridicule of the Witty and Scorn of the wise, the greedy Appetite of Vanity will be always ready to swallow.

In large Societies, however, all these can reach but a little Way, and can be shared by very few. Of great Armies, scarce the hundredth Part can partake of any Reward for the most notable Exploits, and most complete Victories. The rest must content themselves with the Consciousness of having done their Duty, and of having escaped that Punishment to which Cowardice would have subjected them, and of which they fail not of seeing sufficient Examples.

I much question whether the outrageous Indecency of the lowest Part of Mankind among us, can be derived from a truer Cause than this. As they have no Hopes of Reward, be they as good as they will, why should we wonder that they are as bad as they can be, when they have no Fear of incurring Punishment? And very bad indeed they may often be, without any such Danger. For their Idleness at least this will very sufficiently account. From this there is neither Hope of public Reward to allure, nor Fear of public Punishment to deter; What Wonder then, if those who are inclined to Idleness, should indulge their Inclination, and betake themselves to begging,

---

[8] Tacitus, *Annals*, ii. 33: 'relaxations [compensating for] . . . responsibilities and . . . dangers' (Loeb). *delenimentis* in the received text.

a better Trade perhaps than any to which Industry can tempt them to turn their Hands.

Now, in the Society here proposed, there will be no less Opportunity of rewarding Industry, than of punishing Idleness;[9] nor need these Rewards be very expensive to the public Chest, since they will be so extremely honourable to those who receive them. By a very moderate and judicious Distribution of such Rewards for Industry, and a very gentle Infliction of Punishment for Idleness, I make no Doubt but that in the County-house the former might be rendered as honourable, and the latter as infamous as any Virtue and Vice have ever been held in any Nation upon Earth.

XXXI. The Utility, and, I think, Necessity of this Paragraph may be suffered to speak for itself, and so shall the two next.

XXXIV. *Money to be advanced*, &c.] As many of the Persons to be committed hither, or who may voluntarily come hither, will possibly be Pennyless, some Advancement to them will be necessary for their Support. The *Quantum* is submitted to the Legislature, as well as the Method which I have proposed for the Repayment.

XXXV. *Prisoners to be allowed one Shilling weekly.*] This is somewhat less than 2d *per Diem*; which is much larger than the present Bridewell Allowance;[1] but as the Intent is, that they shall be really kept to hard Labour, it will be necessary to support them somewhat better, than when they were suffered to remain in Idleness.

XXXVI. *Deductions to be made*, &c.] As the Society have a Right to the Labour of Delinquents, by Way of Punishment, allowing them only a necessary Support; and as they here exercise this Right in the Case of those who are committed to the House of Correction; so the Defalcation from Persons committed to the County-house, will, I believe appear very reasonable; as these are in some Degree Offenders, and the Objects at least of some small Punishment. As to the Deduction of one Penny from the Volunteers, it should be considered as a reasonable Price for Lodging, Fire, Candles, *&c.* which are here provided for them.

XXXVII. *The Receiver to make up his Accounts after every Sale.*] I have endeavoured to shut out Fraud as much as possible through this whole Plan, if any stronger Bars can be added, I hope they will.

XXXVIII. *An Account to be kept in separate Pages.*] In order to have these

---

[9] Among the 'peculiar' laws and customs of Lilliput that Gulliver was tempted to say something in justification of was the practice of rewarding good behavior as well as punishing ill. 'And these people thought it a prodigious defect of policy among us, when I told them that our laws were enforced only by penalties without any mention of reward' (i. vi.).

[1] 'No more than a Penny Loaf a Day, with Water' (see above, p. 268).

Accounts well and often inspected, they must be rendered easy. The Method I have chalked out, was the best I could invent for this Purpose; but perhaps a much better may be found by some who are more versed in these Matters.

XXXIX. The several branches of this Paragraph need no Comment.

XL. *The Labourers to be instructed in all kinds of Manufactures.*] Upon the right Management of the Power given in this Paragraph, depends in a great Measure the Utility of the whole Plan: and the Improvement of those Advantages which I propose from bringing the Poor together. It is this principally which will require great Capacity in the Governor; and that he should be always a Man of much Knowledge and Experience. Which Qualifications if he should possess, and will do his Duty, in applying them, I doubt not but most of the advantageous Manufactures of Europe, may be by these Means introduced into the Nation.

XLII to XLVI *inclusive. Crimes with their Punishment.*

XLIII. XLIV. As the Crimes mentioned in these two Paragraphs must be guarded against with the utmost Precaution, the Punishment of them cannot possibly be less than that *Ultimum Supplicium*,[2] which is here allotted to them. This, I think, no Man can have any Doubt of, who considers the Numbers and Nature of the People here to be assembled. The same Consideration will remove all Appearance of Severity from the Punishments inflicted in the 38*th* and 39*th* Paragraphs.

XLVI. The Persons who are here to be transported, seem of all others the most proper Objects of that Punishment. This, however, some of them may possibly avoid by the Alternative proposed, which is perhaps the only Method of converting a Fellow to some Use, who would be otherwise good for nothing. It is to be hoped that the military Gentlemen will, on this Occasion, depart a little from their usual Nicety, with Regard to the Morals of their Recruits;[3] since a Man may have great military Qualifications, and may yet be very properly turned out of a civil Society.

XLIX. This is taken from the last Gin Act, with little Variation, and is of the utmost Consequence to all the Purposes of this Plan.[4]

L. LI. LII. Are submitted, without any Comment.

---

[2] Caesar, *Civil Wars*, i. 84: *ad ultimum supplicium*: 'to the extreme of punishment', that is, capital punishment.

[3] Fielding's irony here is underlined when one remembers the scene in *Tom Jones* where Tom is recruited with a 'tippler' (VII. xi).

[4] 24 Geo. II, c. 40 (1751). Sections XIII, XIV, and XV deal specifically with the sale of spirituous liquors in prisons, houses of correction, and workhouses.

LIII. *Judicial Power of the Governor,* &c.]

LIII. Nothing conduces more to the good Order of any Society, than the moderate Punishment of small Offences; this is properly called Correction, since by it the Manners of the Party are often corrected, and he is prevented from the Commission of greater Crimes. Such Punishments should be always attended with Reproof, and an Endeavour to persuade the Offender that he is corrected only for his own Good. It must be remembered however, that they are the better, and milder Dispositions which are to be much amended in this Way; and therefore Shame should, as little as possible, be mixed with such Correction. The Articles here subjected to the Governor's Jurisdiction, are for the most part Peccadillos, and therefore he can scarce be too mild or moderate in his Correction for the first Offence, especially if attended with Contrition. Indeed his Power of punishing here is but small, and savours more of a Master than a Magistrate. On a second Offence he may be a little more severe, and it may commonly be proper to go to the Extent of his Power. But a third Offence of the same kind, and within the Time limited, argues an incorrigible Temper, and savours of the Spirit of Resistance to Government: Here he punishes as a Magistrate, and the Punishment is of the exemplary Kind, tending rather to raise Terror in others, than to work the Reformation of the Party himself.[5]

Among other Powers, the Governor hath that of regulating the Price of Provisions. The Method of supplying the Labourers with these is a problematical Question, and it may admit of much Debate, whether it would be better to provide for them, or to suffer them to provide for themselves? In behalf of the former Method it may be urged, that many Persons joining together in a Mess, may be provided for at a much cheaper Rate than the same Number separately.

2. That possibly they may not of themselves chuse to join; and it may therefore be proper to compel them by a coercive Power.

3. That if they should for the most part agree to mess together, the Savings on that Account should be preserved to the Use of the House.

4. That some of them, when they are Masters of their own Money, will chuse to stint themselves of Food, in order to be more plentifully supplied with Drink; which, besides causing Disorders, will tend to weaken their Bodies, to incapacitate them for Labour, and render them sickly, *&c.*

On the other Side it may be answered, 1. That allowing the Expediency of their messing together, it can hardly be supposed but that in such a Body sufficient Numbers will always be found for that Purpose.

2. That when this is voluntary, it will be much more eligible than when it is by Coercion, which, where the Spirits of Men are so fired with Freedom

---

[5] Cf. *Enquiry,* above, p. 166.

as in this Nation, is never submitted to in small and unaccustomed Matters, without Uneasiness and Heart-burning.

3. That by the Power of constantly regulating the Prices of Provisions, condescending to particularize every minute Article, there will be little Difference between employing Servants or employing Sutlers, in the manner as is here appointed; and the latter will be attended with much the less Confusion.

4. That the Liberty of providing for themselves, at their own Discretion, and of laying out their own Money, is but a reasonable Liberty; and the Refusal of it savours too much of the Treatment of Children: Nor is it without some Tincture of Injustice, for those who eat less will by such means be obliged to pay equally with those who eat more.

5. That as to the Restraint from laying out too much of their Money in Drink, this Restraint seems needless, while they receive the Allowance of the House; and when by their own Industry they become possessed of Money, it will be altogether as ineffectual: Besides, proper Care is taken on this Head, by absolutely prohibiting the Introduction of spirituous Liquors, and by punishing any Kind of Drunkenness.

Upon the Whole, the Method here proposed seems to me the better; but perhaps it will be most proper to leave this Matter open to the Discretion of the Governor and Sessions, who may act therein as they shall find most convenient.

LIV. *The Jurisdiction of the Session.*]

I submit this whole Paragraph, with any Alterations in it which may be thought proper, without a Comment: Nor doth the Residue of the Plan seem to want any Explanation.

Thus have I laid my Plan before the Public, with all that I have to say in its Support or Recommendation. They will, as they please, receive it in the Whole, or in Part; will alter, amend, or entirely reject it, at their Discretion. Whatever shall be the Fate of my Labour, it will not find me quite unprepared: and though my Plan should be treated by some as an impossible, by others as an absurd or ridiculous Scheme, it will neither spoil my Stomach, nor break my Rest. I do not affect an absolute or Stoical Indifference on this Occasion; I mean no more than to be as little solicitous as it is possible about Events, whatever Trouble I have taken in using the Means; a Temper of Mind for which I am not a little obliged to my great Master's Advice,

> *Quem sors dierum cunque dabit, lucre*
> *Appone.*[6]

---

[6] Horace, *Songs*, I. ix. 14–15: 'set down as gain each day that fortune grants' (Loeb).

And again,

Grata superveniet quæ non sperabitur hora.[7]

The forming which into a general Precept, and then reducing that Precept into a Habit, hath cost me more Pains than I have employed in composing the foregoing Pages; nor is the former Labour thrown away, whatever may become of the latter.

Besides the fair Opponents mentioned in the Introduction, and those whom the Imperfections of my Plan may raise, I am to apprehend, I am well convinced, many who will be interested in the Opposition. Some are Enemies to all Schemes whatever, and some to all Schemes but their own; others there are, who find an Advantage in the present wretched State of the Poor, and in the numerous Laws concerning them. Lastly, I sometimes flatter myself, that I have some few Enemies; Men who do me the Honour of thinking better either of my Parts, or of my Fortune, than I do myself; and who consequently hate me from the only Motive which can prompt a Man to hate those who have done him no Injury: These will, I presume, not only deny all Merit to the Execution of my Design, but to the Design itself; and will discover, that instead of intending a Provision for the Poor, I have been carving out one for myself, and have very cunningly projected to build myself a fine House at the Expence of the Public. This would be to act in direct Opposition to the Advice of my above Master; it would be indeed

Struere domos immemor sepulchri.[8]

Those who do not know me, may believe this; but those who do, will hardly be so deceived by that Chearfulness which was always natural to me; and which, I thank God, my Conscience doth not reprove me for, to imagine that I am not sensible of my declining Constitution. In real Truth, if my Plan be embraced, I shall be very easily recompenced for my Trouble, without any Concern in the Execution. Ambition or Avarice can no longer raise a Hope, or dictate any Scheme to me, who have no farther Design than to pass my short Remainder of life in some Degree of Ease, and barely to preserve my Family from being the objects of any such Laws as I have here proposed.

Note. There are several little Mistakes in the foregoing Proposals, such as *his* or *her* for *their*, and *vice versa*: which escaped Correction in the Hurry in which this Pamphlet was printed:[9] they will, it is hoped, be

---

[7] Horace, *Epistles*, I. iv. 14: 'Welcome will come to you another hour unhoped for' (Loeb).

[8] Horace, *Songs*, II. xviii. 18–19 (. . . *sepulcri / Immemor struis domos*): to 'build Houses of five hundred by a hundred Feet, forgetting that of six by two', according to Fielding's playful translation in *Tom Jones* (II. vii. 109).

[9] See General Introduction, p. lxxvi.

excused in a rough Sketch, where the Author intends only to convey his Meaning, to be amended and improved, and not to form the regular Draught of a Law.

F I N I S.

BOOKS printed for A. MILLAR, *and written by* HENRY FIELDING, *Esq.*

1. MIscellanies in Profe and Verfe, 3 Vol. Octavo, Price 15s.

2. The Hiftory of the Adventures of Jofeph Andrews and his Friend Mr. Abraham Adams, 2 Vol. Price 6s.

3. The Hiftory of Tom Jones, a Foundling, 4 Vol. Price 12s.

4. Amelia, 4 Vol. Price 12s.

5. An Enquiry into the Caufes of the late Increafe of Robbers, &c. Price 3s. bound, or 2s. 6d. fewed.

6. The true State of the Cafe of Bofavern Penlez, who fuffered on Account of a Riot in the Strand, in July 1749. Price 1s.

7. A Charge addreffed to the Grand Jury at the Seffions of the Peace held for the City and Liberty of Weftminfter, the 29th of June, 1749. Pr. 1s.

8. Examples of the Interpofition of Providence in the Detection and Punifhment of Murder, containing above thirty Cafes, in which this dreadful Crime has been brought to Light, in the moft extraordinary and miraculous manner. Price 1s.

The following by his Sifter.

1. The Adventures of David Simple. 2 Vol. Price 6s.

2. Familiar Letters between the principal Characters in David Simple, and fome others. 2 Vol. being the 3d and 4th of David Simple, Pr. 6s.

3. The Adventures of David Simple, Volume the laft, wherein his Hiftory is concluded. Price 3s.

4. The Governefs, or little Female Academy; calculated for the Entertainment and Inftruction of young Ladies in their Education. Pr. 2s. 6d.

The fame Book on a fmaller Letter. Pr. 1s. 6d.

7. Advertisement appearing at the end of the *Proposal*, 1753

A

CLEAR STATE

OF THE

CASE

OF

ELIZABETH CANNING,

Who hath fworn that fhe was robbed and almoft ftarved
to Death by a Gang of Gipfies and other Villains in
January laft, for which one MARY SQUIRES now
lies under Sentence of Death.

---

*Quæ, quia funt admirabilia, contraque Opinionem
omnium ; tentare volui poffentne proferri in Lucem, &
ita dici ut probarentur.*

CICERO. Parad.

By HENRY FIELDING, Efq;

LONDON:
Printed for A. MILLAR in the *Strand.*
M.DCC.LIII.

(Price One Shilling.)

A

CLEAR STATE

OF THE

CASE

OF

ELIZABETH CANNING,

Who hath fworn that fhe was robbed and almoft ftarved
to Death by a Gang of Gipfies and other Villains in
January laft, for which one MARY SQUIRES now
lies under Sentence of Death.

---

*Quæ, quia funt admirabilia, contraque Opinionem
omnium ; tentare volui poffentne proferri in Lucem, &
ita dici ut probarentur.*

CICERO. Parad.

By HENRY FIELDING, Efq;

THE SECOND EDITION.

LONDON:

Printed for A. MILLAR in the *Strand.*
M.DCC.LIII.

(Price One Shilling.)

THE
CASE

OF

ELIZABETH CANNING, &c.

There is nothing more admirable, nor indeed more amable, in the Law of *England*, than the extreme Tenderness with which it proceeds against Persons accused of capital Crimes.[1] In this respect it justly claims a Preference to the Institutions of all other Countries; in some of which a Criminal is hurried to Execution, with rather less Ceremony than is required, by our law, to carry him to Prison; in many, the Tryals (if they may be called such) have little of Form, and are so extremely precipitate, that the unhappy Wretch hath no Time to make his Defence, but is often condemned without well knowing his Accuser, and sometimes without well understanding his Accusation. In this happy Kingdom, on the contrary, so tender is the Law of the Life of a Subject, so cautious of unjustly or erroneously condemning him, that according to its own Maxim, *De Morte Hominis, nulla est Cunctatio longa,*[2] it proceeds by slow and regular Gradations, and requires so many antecedent Ceremonies to the ultimate Discussion[3] of a Court of Justice, that so far from being in Danger of a Condemnation without a fair and open Tryal, every Man must be tried more than once before he can receive a capital Sentence: By the Law of *England*, no Man can be apprehended for Felony, without a strong and just Suspicion of his Guilt;[4] nor can he be committed to Prison, without a Charge on Oath

---

Title-page] 'State': 'Statement'. Often so used in a legal context.

Title-page] Cicero, *Paradox Stoicorum*, 4: 'These doctrines are surprising, and they run counter to universal opinion . . . so I wanted to try whether it is possible for them to be brought out into the light [of common daily life (*id est in forum*)] and expounded in a form to win acceptance' (Loeb). Cicero refers to the 'doctrines styled *paradoxa* by the Stoics'.

[1] Cf. Fielding's praise of English legal institutions in the *Charge*, p. 3 ff.; and p. 11, n. 6. A good brief account of criminal courts and procedures is J. H. Baker's 'Criminal Courts and Procedure at Common Law, 1550–1800', in *Crime and England, 1550–1800*, ed. J. S. Cockburn (Princeton, NJ, 1977), pp. 1–48. For a much fuller account of actual trial practices and procedures, see two articles by John H. Langbein, both in the *University of Chicago Law Review*: 'The Criminal Trial before the Lawyers', 45 (1976), 263–316; and 'Shaping the Eighteenth-Century Criminal Trial: A View from the Ryder Sources', 50 (1983), 1–136.

[2] Concerning the death of a man no delay is long.' The maxim appears in Coke, *I Inst.* fo. 134 b.

[3] 'Trial'.

[4] In undertaking the *Treatise on the Office of Constable* (see *Enquiry*, p. 145, n. 3), Fielding set out to describe one part of the very complicated laws governing arrest.

before a lawful Magistrate.[5] This Charge must be again proved on Oath, to the Satisfaction of a large Number (Twelve at least) of the better Sort of his Countrymen;[6] (except in the Case of an Appeal of Felony, which is now obsolete, and where the Proceedings are still more ceremonial and tedious;)[7] before the Accused can be required to answer to it, or be put on his Defence;[8] and after all these Preparatives, the Truth of this Charge is to be tried in an open Court of Justice, before one at least and often many Judges,[9] by twelve indifferent[1] and unexceptionable Men: I may truly say unexceptionable, since it is in the Prisoner's Power to except against twenty-four without showing any Cause,[2] and as many more as he can show a reasonable Cause of Exception against.[3] These, after a patient Hearing of the Witnesses against him, and after attending to his Defence (in the making which, the Law prescribes that every Indulgence shall be shewn him, and that even his Judge shall be his Council and assist him)[4] must all concur in declaring on

---

[5] A justice of the peace was 'to take the examinations of felons (without oath,) and the informations of accusers or witness (upon oath,)' (Hale, ii. 52).

[6] Before a case went to the petty jury, a majority of twelve or more grand jurors (usually twenty-three were empanelled), all substantial freeholders, must find the bill 'true', i.e., determine that the crown had a case that should go forward. See Fielding's *Charge*, especially, p. 4 and n. 6; and pp. xxiv–xxv.

[7] An *Appeal* was a prosecution of a heinous crime (larceny, arson, rape, or murder) at the suit of the subject (the appellant) instead of the usual prosecution by way of indictment in the name of the crown. The ancient origin of this process is suggested by the appellee's right to demand trial by battle (an appeal was last claimed in 1818, and the appellee did in fact throw down his glove in court and demand trial by battle). Blackstone remarked that prosecution by an appeal was still in force but 'very little in use' (*Comm.* iv. 312).

[8] 'Defence, in its true legal sense, signifies not a justification, protection, or guard, which is now its popular signification; but merely an *opposing* or *denial* (from the French verb *defender*) of the truth or validity of the complaint. It is . . . a general assertion that the plaintiff hath no ground of action, which assertion is afterwards extended and maintained in his plea' (Blackstone, *Comm.* iii. 296–7).

[9] The number of judges before whom a criminal case could be tried ranged from a single King's Bench judge sitting at the Middlesex Sessions or at the Old Bailey to the legal splendor of an assize bench composed of the two commissioned assize judges joined by all of the principal justices of the peace of the county. Elizabeth Canning was tried before five common-law judges, the recorder of London, the lord mayor, and ten aldermen.

[1] 'Impartial'.

[2] In a felony trial, the accused had only twenty peremptory challenges (Hale, ii. 269; Hawkins, ii. 414; Blackstone, *Comm.* iv. 354).

[3] That is, there was no limit to the number of challenges for cause.

[4] Though one on trial for a misdemeanor was allowed counsel, one on trial for a felony was allowed counsel only when a point of law was debated (Hawkins, ii. 400), a circumstance Blackstone considered 'not all of a piece with the rest of the humane treatment of prisoners by the English Law'. (*Comm.* ii. 355). The judges' obligation to see that trial proceedings were properly legal palliated the felon's disadvantage, and, moreover, by the 18th century they commonly allowed counsel to advise on matters of fact as well as on matters of law.

But Partridge's comment in *Tom Jones* on a trial conducted by Sir Francis Page ('the Hanging judge') should be recalled: 'It is indeed charming Sport to hear Trials upon Life and Death. One Thing I own I thought a little hard, that the Prisoner's Counsel was not suffered to speak for him, though he desired only to be heard one very short Word; but my Lord would not hearken to him, though he suffered a Counsellor to talk against him for above half an Hour. I thought it hard, I own, that there should be so many of them; my Lord and the Court, and the Jury, and the Counsellors, and the Witnesses all upon one poor Man, and he too in Chains' (VIII. xi. 459–60).

their Oaths, that he is guilty of the Crime alledged against him; or he is to be discharged, and can never more be called in Question for the same Offence, save only in the Case of Murder.[5]

It seems, I think, that the Wit of Man could invent no stronger Bulwark against all Injustice, and false Accusation, than this Institution, under which not only Innocence, may rejoice in its own Security, but even Guilt can scarce be so immodest as to require a fairer Chance of escaping the Punishment it deserves.

And yet, if after all this Precaution it should manifestly appear, that a Person hath been unjustly condemned, either by bringing to Light some latent Circumstance, or by discovering that the Witnesses against him are certainly perjured, or by any other Means of displaying the Party's Innocence, the Gates of Mercy are still left open, and upon a proper and decent Application, either to the Judge before whom the Tryal was had, or to the privy Council, the condemned Person will be sure of obtaining a Pardon, of preserving his Life, and of regaining both his Liberty and Reputation.[6]

To make therefore such an Application on the Behalf of injured Innocence, is not only laudable in every Man, but it is a Duty, the Neglect of which he can by no Means answer to his own Conscience; but this, as I have said, is to be done in a proper and decent Manner, by a private Application to those with whom the Law hath lodged a Power of correcting its Errors, and remitting its Severity; whereas to resort immediately to the Public by inflammatory Libels against the Justice of the Nation, to establish a kind of a Court of Appeal from this Justice in the Bookseller's Shop, to re-examine in News Papers and Pamphlets the merits of Causes which, after a fair and legal Tryal, have already received the solemn Determination of a Court of Judicature, to arraign the Conduct of Magistrates, of Juries, and even Judges, and this even with the most profligate Indecency, are the Effects of a Licentiousness to which no Government, jealous of its own Honour, or indeed provident of its own Safety, will ever indulge or submit to.[7]

---

[5] One found innocent on an indictment for murder could still be tried on an appeal of murder.

[6] The possibility of appeal to a higher court for reversal of judgment did not exist in the 18th century. A judgment could be set aside on a writ of error or by Parliament, or, the action Fielding has in mind here, the felon could be pardoned. Usually an appeal for the king's pardon, which had to be sealed with the Great Seal, was directed to one of the secretaries of state or to the Privy Council. A pardon rendered a felon 'a new Man, and gives him a new Capacity and Credit' (Hawkins, ii. 395).

[7] Fielding's strictures here probably recall the furor surrounding the case of Bosavern Penlez as well as anticipate the impending commentary on Canning, Wells, and Squires. The grounds of his anticipation lay in rumors (accurate) of Sir Crisp Gascoyne's dissatisfaction with the conviction of Squires and in John Hill's 'Inspector' columns in the *London Daily Advertiser* (see General Introduction, pp. cii–ciii).

He may also have had in mind the publicity preceding the trial of Mary Blandy a year earlier (Feb. 1752). One of the judges at this trial acknowledged in court that the activities of the press had been 'improper' and 'scandalous', and Blandy's counsel referred to 'unjustifiable and illegal methods . . . used to prejudice the world against Miss Blandy' (*State Trials*, xviii. 1167–8 and 1170). In the

Sensible as I am of this, I should by no means become an Aggressor of this Kind; but surely when such Methods have been used to mislead the Public, and to censure the Justice of the Nation in its Sagacity at least, and grossly to misrepresent their Proceedings, it can require little Apology to make use of the same Means to refute so iniquitous an Attempt. However unlawful a Weapon may be in the Hands of an Assailant, it becomes strictly justifiable in those of the Defendant: And as the Judges will certainly excuse an Undertaking in Defence of themselves, so may I expect that the Public, (that Part of it, I mean, whose Esteem alone I have ever coveted or desired) should shew some Favour to a Design which hath in View not a bare Satisfaction of their Curiosity only, but to prevent them from forming a very rash, and, possibly, a very unjust Judgment. Lastly, there is something within myself which rouses me to the Protection of injured Innocence, and which prompts me with the Hopes of an Applause much more valuable than that of the whole World.

Without this last Motive, indeed, it may be imagined I should scarce have taken up my Pen in the defence of a poor little Girl whom the many have already condemned. I well know the extreme Difficulty which will always be found in obtaining a Reversal of such a Judgment. Men who have applauded themselves, and have been applauded by others, for their great Penetration and Discernment, will struggle very hard before they will give up their Title to such Commendation. Though they, perhaps, heard the Cause at first with the Impartiality of upright Judges, when they have once given their Opinion, they are too apt to become warm Advocates, and even interested Parties in Defence of that Opinion.[8] Deplorable, indeed, and desperate is the Case of a poor Wretch against whom such a Sentence is past! No Writ of Error lies against this Sentence, but before that tremendous Court of the Public where it was first pronounced, and no Court whatever is, for the Reasons already assigned, so tenacious of the Judgments which it hath once given.

In Defiance, nevertheless, of this Difficulty, I am determined to proceed to disclose, as far as I am able, the true State of an Affair which, however inconsiderable the Parties may be in their Station of Life, (though injured Innocence will never appear an inconsiderable Object to a good Mind) is now become a Matter of real Concern and great Importance to the Public; against whom a most horrible Imposture, supported by the most impudent as well as impious Perjury is dressed up, either on the one Side or on the other: To discover most manifestly on which Side it lies seems to be within the

---

'*Proceedings at the Court of* Censorial Enquiry' (*CGJ*, i. 204–5), Fielding sternly rebuked pretrial judgment of Blandy. See *Examples of Providence*, p. 214.

[8] The first of several allusions to Sir Crisp Gascoyne, lord mayor of London 1752–3, who was largely responsible for the pardon of Squires and the subsequent trial of Canning (see General Introduction, p. cii ff.).

Power of the Government, and it is highly incumbent on them to exert themselves on this Occasion, in order that by the most exemplary Punishment they may deter Men from that dreadful Crime of Perjury, which in this Case either threatens to make the Sword of Justice a Terror to the Innocent, or to take off all its Edge from the Guilty; which of these it is likeliest to do in the present Instance, I will endeavour to assist the Reader, at least, in forming a probable Conjecture.

Elizabeth Canning, a young Girl of eighteen Years of Age, who lived at *Aldermanbury* Postern,[9] in the City of *London*, declares, That on *Monday* the 1st of *January* last she went to see her Uncle and Aunt, who are People of a very good Character, and who live at *Saltpetre Bank* near *Rosemary-lane*; that having continued with them till towards nine in the Evening, her Uncle and Aunt, it being late, walked a great Part of the Way home with her; that soon after she parted with them, and came opposite to *Bethlehem-gate* in *Moorfields*, she was seized by two Men who, after robbing her of half a Guinea in Gold, and three Shillings in Silver, of her Hat, Gown, and Apron, violently dragged her into a Gravel-walk that leads down to the Gate of *Bethlehem* Hospital, about the Middle of which one of the Men, after threatening to do for her, gave her a violent Blow with his Fist on the right Temple, that threw her into a Fit, and intirely deprived her of her Senses. These Fits she says she hath been accustomed to; that they were first occasioned by the Fall of a Cieling on her Head; that they are apt to return upon her whenever she is frightened, and that they sometimes continue for six or seven Hours; that when she came to herself she perceived that two Men were hurrying her along in a large Road-way, and that in a little time after she was recovered, she was able to walk alone; however, they still continued to pull and drag her along; that she was so intimidated by their Usage that she durst not call out, nor even speak to them; that in about half an Hour after the Recovery of her Senses they carried her into an House where she saw in the Kitchen an old Gipsy Woman and two young Women; that the old Gipsy Woman took hold of her by the Hand, and promised *to give her fine Cloaths if she would go their Way*, which Expression she understanding to mean the becoming a Prostitute, she utterly refused to comply with; upon which the old Gipsy Woman took a Knife out of a Drawer and cut the Stays off this *Elizabeth Canning*, and took them away from her, at which time one of the Men likewise took off her Cap, and then both the men went away; that soon after they were gone, and about an Hour after she had been in the House the old Gipsy Woman forced her up an old Pair of Stairs, and pushed her into a Back-room like a Hay-loft, without any Furniture

---

[9] The places mentioned in this paragraph are clearly represented in the map reproduced between pp. 8 and 9 of de la Torre's *Elizabeth is Missing*. Aldermanbury Postern was about a half mile from the Guildhall. Salt-Petre Bank is now Dock Street.

whatsoever in the same, and there locked her up, threatening that if she made the least Noise or Disturbance, the old Gipsy Woman would come up and cut her Throat, and then fastened the Door on the Outside and went away. She says, that when it was Day-light, upon her looking round to see in what dismal Place she was confined, she discovered a large black Jug, with the Neck much broken, filled with Water, and several Pieces of Bread, amounting to about the Quantity of a Quartern Loaf scattered on the Floor, where was likewise a small Parcel of Hay. In this Room she says she continued from that time till about half an Hour after four of the Clock in the Afternoon of *Monday* the 29th Day of the same Month of *January*, being in all twenty-seven Days and upwards, without any other Sustenance than the aforesaid Bread and Water, except one small Minced-pye which she had in her Pocket which she was carrying home as a Present to her little Brother. She likewise says, that she had some Part of this Provision remaining on the *Friday* before she made her Escape, which she did by breaking out at a Window of the Room or Loft in which she was confined, and whence having escaped, she got back to her Friends in *London* in about six Hours, in a most weak and miserable Condition, being almost starved to Death, and without ever once stopping at any House or Place by the Way. She likewise says, that during her whole Confinement no Person ever came near her to ask her any Question whatever, nor did she see any belonging to the House more than once, when one of the Women peeped through a Hole in the Door, and that she herself was afraid to call or speak to any one. All this she hath solemnly sworn before a Magistrate and in a Court of Justice.[1]

Such is the Narrative of *Elizabeth Canning*, and a very extraordinary Narrative it is, consisting of many strange Particulars, resembling rather a wild Dream than a real Fact.[2] *First*, It doth not well appear with what Motive these Men carried this poor Girl such a Length of Way, or indeed that they had any Motive at all for so doing. *Secondly*, that they should be able to do it is not very easy to believe; I do not mean that it is not within the Strength of two Men to carry a little Girl (for so she is) ten Miles, but that they could do this without being met, opposed, or examined, by any Persons in the much frequented Roads near this Town, is extreamly strange and surprising. *Thirdly*, the Gipsy Woman doth not seem to have had any sufficient Motive to her Proceedings. If her Design was to make a Prostitute or a Gipsy, or

---

[1] Elizabeth first (31 Jan. 1753) swore to her story before Thomas Chitty, an alderman of the city of London, who issued a warrant for the arrest of 'Mother Wells' (the warrant is printed in *State Trials*, xix. 376; Chitty's 'minutes' of her statement appear on pp. 374–5); the 'Court of Justice' of course was at the trial of Squires and Wells.

[2] In what follows, Fielding clearly is responding to already commonplace objections to Elizabeth Canning's story. *Select Trials* (ii. 266–8) lists nine reasons for the dissatisfaction of the attorney and solicitor-general and 'other Gentlemen' with Canning's story. Fielding's seven objections are among them.

both, of this poor Girl, she would, in all Probability, have applied to her during her Confinement, to try what Effect that Confinement had produced. If her Design was Murder, she had many easier and better Ways than by starving, or if she had chosen this Method of destroying the Girl, it seems impossible to account for the conveying to her that Bread and Water, which could serve for no other Purpose but to lengthen out the Misery of a Wretch against whom the Gipsy Woman had, as appears, no Foundation whatever of Anger or Revenge, and might have increased the Danger of discovering the whole Villainy. *Fourthly*, That *Elizabeth Canning* herself should have survived this Usage, and all the Terrors it must have occasioned, and should have been kept alive with no other Sustenance than she declares she had, are Facts very astonishing and almost incredible. *Fifthly*, That she should so well have husbanded her small Pittance as to retain some of it till within two Days of her Escape, is another very surprising Circumstance. *Sixthly*, that she should undergo all this Hardship and Fasting without attempting sooner to make her Escape, or without perceiving the Possibility of making it in the Manner in which she at last says she did effect it, seems to be no less shocking to Reason and common Sense. *Lastly*, that at the Time when she dates this Escape, she should have Strength sufficient left, not only to break her Prison in the Manner she declares, but to walk eleven or twelve Miles to her own Home, is another Fact which may very well stagger our Belief, and is a proper Close to this strange, unaccountable, and scarce credible Story.

Thus have I set the several Particulars of this Narrative in as strong a Light against the Relater, and in one as disadvantageous to the Credibility of her Relation, as I think they can fairly be placed. Certain it is, that the Facts seem at first to amount to the very highest Degree of Improbability, but I think that they do not amount to an Impossibility; for as to those Objections which arise from the Want of a sufficient Motive in the Transactors of this cruel Scene, no great Stress I think can be laid on these. I might ask what possible Motive could induce two Ruffians, who were executed last Winter for Murder, after they had robbed a poor Wretch who made no Resistance, to return and batter his Skull with their Clubs, till they fractured it in almost twenty different Places.[3] How many Cruelties indeed do we daily hear of, to which it seems not easy to assign any other Motive than Barbarity itself? In serious and sorrowful Truth, doth not History as well as our own Experience afford us too great Reason to suspect, that there is in some Minds a Sensation directly opposite to that of Benevolence, and which delights and

---

[3] Fielding alludes to Randolph Branch and William Dessent who were tried for murder in Sept. 1752 and executed shortly after their trial. After knocking their victim helpless to the ground they continued to beat him on the head. The surgeon's account of the injuries suggests an extraordinarily barbarous and wanton assault. See *Select Trials*, ii. 207 ff.

feeds itself with Acts of Cruelty and Inhumanity?[4] And if such a Passion can be allowed any Existence, where can we imagine it more likely to exist than among such People as these?

Besides, though to a humane and truly sensible Mind such Actions appear to want an adequate Motive, yet to Wretches very little removed, either in their Sensations or Understandings, from wild Beasts, here may possibly appear a very sufficient Motive to all that they did; such might be a Desire of increasing the Train of Gipsies or of Whores in the Family of Mother *Wells*. One of these appears to have been the Design of the Gipsy Woman from the Declaration of *Elizabeth Canning*, who, if she had said Nothing more improbable, would certainly have been intitled to our Belief in this, though this Design seems afterwards not to have been pursued. In short, she might very possibly have left the Alternative with some Indifference to the Girl's own Option; if she was starved out of her Virtue, the Family might easily apprehend she would give them Notice; if out of her Life, it would be then Time enough to convey her dead Body to some Ditch or Dunghill, where when it was found it would tell no Tales: Possibly, however, the Indifference of the Gipsy Woman was not so absolute, but that she might prefer the Girl's *going her Way*, and this will account for her conveying to her that Bread and Water, which might give the poor Girl a longer Time to deliberate, and consequently the Love of Life might have a better Chance to prevail over the love of Virtue.

So much for the first and third Objection arising from the Want of Motive, from which, as I have observed above, no very powerful Arguments can be drawn in the Case of such Wretches: As to the second Objection, though I mentioned it as I would omit none, the Reader, I presume, will lay so little Weight upon it, that it would be wasting Time to give it much Answer. In Reality, the Darkness of the Night at that Season of the Year, and when it was within two Days of the New Moon, with the Indifference of most People to what doth not concern themselves, and the Terror with which all honest Persons pass by Night through the Roads near this Town, will very sufficiently account for the Want of all Interruption to these Men in their Conveyance of the poor Girl.[5]

With regard to the fourth Objection, How she could survive this Usage, &c? I leave the Degree of Probability to be ascertained by the Physicians:[6]

---

[4] Cf. *Tom Jones*, VI. i. 270: '. . . there is in some (I believe in many) human Breasts, a kind and benevolent Disposition, which is gratified by contributing to the Happiness of others.'

[5] At Canning's trial a turnpike keeper testified that he had seen Canning and her abductors the night of 1 Jan. 1753. When asked why he had not assisted her, he replied, 'There were two men with her, and we are fearful in our business; except they ask us any questions, we never meddle with such; and I was then alone' (*State Trials*, xix. 525).

[6] Shortly after Fielding wrote, two physicians published accounts of their examination of Canning: James Solas Dodd, *A Physical Account of the Case of Elizabeth Canning* (London, 1753); and Daniel Cox,

Possible, I think it is, and I contend for no more. I shall only observe here, that she barely did survive it, and that she, who left her Mother in a plump Condition, returned so like a Spectre, that her Mother fainted away when she saw her; her Limbs were all emaciated, and the Colour of her Skin turned black, so as to resemble a State of Mortification; her Recovery from which State since, is a Proof of that firm and sound Constitution, which supported her, if she says true, under all her Misery.

As to the fifth Objection, she answers, That the cruel Usage she had met with, and the Condition she saw herself in, so affected both her Mind and Body, that she eat scarce any Thing during the first Days of her Confinement, and afterwards had so little Appetite, that she could scarce swallow the hard Morsels which were allotted her.

The sixth Objection hath, in my Opinion, so little in it, that had I not heard it insisted on by others, I should not myself have advanced it; common Experience every Day teacheth us, that we endure many Inconveniencies of Life, while we overlook those Ways of extricating ourselves, which, when they are discovered, appear to have been, from the first, extremely easy and obvious. The Inference which may be drawn from this Observation, a moderate Degree of Candor will oblige us to extend very far in the Case of a poor simple Child, under all the Circumstances of Weakness of Body, and Depression and Confusion of Spirits, till Despair, which is a Quality that is ever increasing as its Object increases, grew to the highest Pitch, and forced her to an attempt, which she had not before had the Courage to undertake.

As to her accomplishing this, and being able to escape to her Friends, the Probability of this likewise I leave to the Discussion of Physicians: Possible it surely is, and I question very much, whether the Degree of Despair, which I have just mentioned, will not even make it probable; since this is known to add no less Strength to the Body than it doth to the Mind, a Truth which every Man almost may confirm by many Instances.

But if, notwithstanding all I have here said, the Narrative should still appear ever so improbable, it may yet become a proper Object of our Belief, from the Weight of the Evidence, for there is a Degree of Evidence, by which every Fact that is not impossible to have happened at all, or to have happened in the Manner in which it is related, may be supported and ought to be believed: In all Cases, indeed, the Weight of Evidence ought to be strictly conformable to the Weight of Improbability; and when it is so, the wiser a Man is the sooner and easier he will believe. To say Truth, to judge well of this Conformity is what we truly call Sagacity, and requires the

An *Appeal to the Public, in behalf of Elizabeth Canning* (London, 1753). Dodd argued, partly on the evidence of recorded cases of near starvation, that Canning's story was medically possible. Cox reported that she had never borne a child and that there was no sign of venereal disease. At Canning's trial Dr Eaton, who had cared for her on her return home, testified that her physical condition was consistent with her story (*State Trials*, xix. 522–4).

greatest Strength and Force of Understanding. He, who gives a hasty Belief to what is strange and improbable, is guilty of Rashness; but he is much more absurd, who declares that he will believe no such Fact on any Evidence whatever. The World are too much inclined to think, that the Credulous is the only Fool; whereas, in Truth, there is *another Fool*[7] of a quite opposite Character, who is much more difficult to deal with, less liable to the Dominion of Reason, and possessed of a Frailty more prejudicial to himself and often more detrimental to Mankind in general.

To apply this Reasoning to the present Case, as we have, it is hoped, with great Fairness and Impartiality, stated all the Improbabilities which compose this Girl's Narrative, we will now consider the Evidence that supports them. And when we have done this, it will possibly appear, that the credulous Person is he who believes that *Elizabeth Canning* is a Liar.

First then, there is one Part of this Story, which is incontestably true, as it is a Matter of public Notoriety, and known by almost every Inhabitant in the Parish where her mother dwells. That is, that the Girl, after the Absence of a Month, returned on the 29th of *January*, in the dreadful Condition above-described. This being an established Fact, a very fair Presumption follows, that she was confined some-where, and by some Person; that this Confinement was of equal Duration with her Absence; that she was almost starved to Death; that she was confined in a Place, whence it was difficult to make her Escape; that, however, this Escape was possible; and that, at length, she actually made it: All these are Circumstances, which arise from the Nature of the Fact itself. They are what *Tully* calls *Evidentia Rei*,[8] and are stronger than the positive Testimony of any Witnesses; they do, indeed, carry Conviction with them to every Man, who hath Capacity enough to draw a Conclusion from the most self-evident Premises.

These Facts being established, I shall oppose Improbability to Improbability, and first I begin by asking, Why did this Girl conceal the Person who thus cruelly used her? It could not be a Lover; for among all the Cruelties, by which Men have become infamous in their Commerce with Women, none of this Kind, can, I believe be produced. What Reason, therefore, can be assigned for this great Degree of more than Christian Forgiveness of such barbarous Usage, is to me, I own, a Secret; such Forgiveness, therefore, is, at least, as great a Degree of Improbability as any which can be found, or which can be feigned in her Narrative.

Again, What Motive can be invented for her laying this heavy Charge on those who are innocent? That Street-robbers and Gipsies, who have scarce even the Appearance of Humanity, should be guilty of wanton Cruelty without a Motive, hath greatly staggered the World, and many have denied

[7] Glancing at an old antagonist, the writer of 'The Fool' (see *Bosavern Penlez*, p. 34, n.).

[8] Cicero, *Academica*, II. vi. 18: *evidentium rerum*: 'the evidence of things'.

the Probability of such a Fact: Will they then imagine, that this Girl hath committed a more deliberate, and, therefore, a more atrocious Crime, by endeavouring to take away the Lives of an old Woman, her Son, and another Man, as well as to ruin another Woman, without any Motive whatever? Will they believe this of a young Girl, hardly 18 Years old, who hath the unanimous Testimony of all who ever knew her from her Infancy, to support the Character of a virtuous, modest, sober, well-disposed Girl; and this Character most inforced by those who know her best, and particularly by those with whom she hath lived in Service.[9]

As to any Motive of getting Money by such an Attempt, nothing can be more groundless and evidently false than the Suggestion; the Subscription which was proposed and publicly advertised, was thought of long after the Girl's Return to her mother, upon which Return she immediately told the Story in the Presence of Numbers of People, with all the Circumstances with which she hath since, without any Variation, related it. The real Truth is, that this Subscription was set on foot by several well-disposed Neighbours and very substantial Tradesmen, in order to bring a Set of horrid Villains to Justice, which then appeared (as it hath since proved) to be a Matter which would be attended with considerable Expence,[1] nor was any Reward to the Girl then thought of; the first Proposer of which Reward was a Noble and Generous Lord, who was present at the last Examination of this Matter in *Bow-street*:[2] So that this Charge of the Gipsy Woman, and the rest, if a false one, was absolutely without any Motive at all. A second Improbability which rises as much higher than that to which it is opposed, as the Crime would be higher, since it would be more deliberate, in the Girl, and as her Character is better than that of Street-robbers and Gipsies.

Again, as the Girl can scarce be supposed wicked enough, so I am far from supposing her witty enough to invent such a Story;[3] a Story full of Variety of

---

[9] There was abundant testimony at her trial to Canning's good character, including that of her employers, John Wintlebury, respectable alehouse keeper; and Edward Lyon, carpenter to the Goldsmith's Company.

[1] *The Case of Elizabeth Canning*, a broadside, was published and circulated early in Feb. 1753, to encourage contributions to prosecute a 'nest of villains'. It is reprinted in [Allan Ramsay], 'A Letter to the Right Honourable the Earl of ——— Concerning the Affair of Elizabeth Canning' (London, 1753), pp. 24–7. Ramsay's pamphlet is reprinted in his *The Investigator*, London, 1762.

[2] The 'Noble and Generous Lord' is probably Montfort (see below, p. 306 n. 2), and the 'last Examination' 14 Feb. (below, p. 304). Some time after 14 Feb., however, Fielding met with a 'gentleman' with Canning present to consider how money collected for her should be used (below, p. 306).

There were apparently numerous instances of casual donations to Canning. The 'Historical Chronicle, March 1753' of *GM*, for instance, states that 'Elizabeth Canning was sent for [on 2 Mar. 1753] to Whites' chocolate house, and had upwards of 30£ collected for her there.' De la Torre estimates that nearly £300 was collected for Canning. At her trial, the prosecution suggested that 'golden hopes' led her to stick to her improbable story (*State Trials*, xix. 299).

[3] Hill ridiculed Fielding's suggestion that the invention of such a story as Canning's required wit, characterizing it as 'absurd, incredible, and most ridiculous': 'A Piece of contradictory Incidents, and

strange Incidents, and worthy the invention of some Writer of Romances, in many of which we find such kind of strange Improbabilities that are the Productions of a fertile, though commonly a distempered, Brain;[4] whereas this Girl is a Child in Years, and yet more so in Understanding, with all the evident Marks of Simplicity that I ever discovered in a human Countenance; and this I think may be admitted to be a third Improbability.

A *Fourth* seems to me to arise from the Manner in which this poor simple Girl hath supported this Story; which, as it requires the highest Degree of Wickedness of Heart, and some tolerable Goodness of Head to have invented, so doth it require no small Degree of Assurance to support, and that in large Assemblies of Persons of a much higher Degree than she had ever before appeared in the presence of: Before Noblemen, and Magistrates, and Judges, Persons who must have inspired a Girl of this kind with the highest Awe. Before all these she went through her Evidence without Hesitation, Confusion, Trembling, Change of Countenance, or other apparent Emotion. As such a Behaviour could proceed only from the highest Impudence, or most perfect Innocence, so it seemed clearly to arise from the latter, as it was accompanied with such a Shew of Decency, Modesty, and Simplicity, that if these were all affected, which those who disbelieve her must suppose, it must have required not only the highest Art, but the longest Practice and Habit to bring it to such a Degree of Perfection.

A *Fifth* Improbability is, that this Girl should fix on a Place so far from home, and where it doth not appear she had ever been before. Had she gone to this Place of her own Accord, or been carried thither by any other than the Person she accused, surely Mother *Wells* would have told this, as it must have acquitted her of the Fact laid to her Charge, and would indeed have destroyed the whole Character of *Elizabeth Canning*, and of Consequence have put an End to the Prosecution; but Mother *Wells*, on the contrary, denied absolutely that *Elizabeth Canning* had ever been in her House, or that she had ever seen her Face before she came there with the Peace Officers.

In this Point, *viz.* That *Elizabeth Canning* was not acquainted with Mother *Wells*, or her House, nor ever there, in any other Manner than as she herself hath informed us, her Evidence stands confirmed by the best and strongest Testimony imaginable, and that is by the Declaration of the Defendant *Wells* herself. It is true indeed, that as to her being confined there, *Wells* utterly denies it, but she as positively affirms, that this *Elizabeth Canning* was never there at any other Time, nor in any other Manner. From this Point then so established, will result an utter Impossibility; for unless this poor Girl had

---

most improbable Events, a waking Dream, the Reverie of an Idiot: A Relation that could not be allowed a Face of Likelihood; and that would have taken no hold on any, but as it pleaded to their Compassion' (*The Story of Elizabeth Canning Considered*, pp. 16–17).

[4] For similar comment on 'romances' see *Tom Jones*, IV. i and IX. i; and *Joseph Andrews*, III. i.

been well acquainted with the House, the Hayloft, the Pitcher, &c. how was it possible that she should describe them all so very exactly as she did, at her Return to her Mother's, in the Presence of such Numbers of People?[5] Nay, she described, likewise, the Prospect that appeared from the Hayloft, with such Exactness as required a long Time to furnish her with the Particulars of. I know but two Ways of her being enabled to give this Description; either she must have been there herself, or must have had her Information from some other. As to the former *Wells* herself denies it; and as to the latter, I leave to the Conjecture of my ingenious Reader, whether it was Mother *Wells* herself, the Gipsy Woman, *Virtue Hall*, or who else that instructed *Elizabeth Canning* in all these Particulars.

In the mean time, I shall beg leave to conclude, either that we must account for the Girl's Knowledge one of the Ways which I have mentioned; or, *Secondly*, we must believe an Impossibility; or, *Thirdly*, we must swallow the Truth of this Relation, though it be as hard a Morsel as any which the poor Girl fed on during her whole Confinement.

And now I come to a Piece of Evidence which hath been the principal Foundation of that Credit which I have given to this extraordinary Story. It appeared to me at first to be convincing and unsurmountable, in the same Light it appeared to a Gentleman whose Understanding and Sagacity are of the very first Rate, and who is one of the best Lawyers of his Time;[6] he owned that this Evidence seemed to him to be unanswerable, so I acknowledge it yet seems to me, and till it shall receive an Answer, I must continue to believe the Fact which rests upon it.

In order to lay this Evidence before the Reader in a fair and just Light, it will be necessary to give a brief Relation of the Order of Proceeding in this Case, down to the Time when *Virtue Hall* appeared first before me.

Upon the Return of *Elizabeth Canning* to her Mother's House in the Manner above set forth, and upon the Account which she gave of her unprecedented Sufferings, the visible Marks of which then appeared on her Body, all her Neighbours began to fire with Resentment against the several Actors concerned in so cruel a Scene; and presently some of the most substantial of these Neighbours proposed to raise a Contribution amongst themselves, in order, if possible, to bring the Villains who had injured this poor Girl to exemplary Justice: As soon therefore as she was able to bear the Journey they put her into a Chaise,[7] and, taking with them proper Peace

---

[5] There was abundant testimony at her trial to show that her initial description of Wells's house and the room in which she was supposedly imprisoned was vague and/or inaccurate. Her later testimony before Chitty, Tyshemaker, and Fielding, and at the trial of Squires and Wells was inconsistent (see *State Trials, passim*). These inconsistencies need not have been apparent to Fielding writing in mid-March.

[6] Unidentified. Perhaps Fielding's cousin, Henry Gould, whom Canning at one point petitioned to be her counsel (Jones, p. 230 n.).

[7] 1 Feb. 1753.

Officers, conveyed the Girl along the *Hertford* Road,[8] to see if she was able to trace out the House where she had been confined: for she at that Time knew not the Name of the Place, nor could she sufficiently describe the Situation of *Wells's* House, though she had before so exactly described the Inside of it. Possibly indeed she might never have been able to have discovered the House at all, had it not been for a very extraordinary Incident, and this was, that through the Chinks or Crevices of the Boards of the Hayloft she saw, at a Distance the *Hertford* Stage Coach pass by, the Driver of which she knew, though he past not near enough for her to call to him with any Hopes of Success, and by this extraordinary Circumstance she came to know that the House stood on the *Hertford* Road.

When they arrived at this House[9] the poor Girl was taken out of the Chaise, and placed on a Table in the Kitchen, where all the Family passed in Review before her; she then fixed on the Gipsy Woman, whom she had very particularly described before, and who is, perhaps, the most remarkable Person in the whole World;[1] she charged likewise *Virtue Hall*, whose Countenance likewise is very easy to be remembered by those who have once seen her.

The whole Family, however, though no more were positively charged by *Elizabeth Canning*, being put all into a Cart were conducted before Mr. *Tyshemaker*, who is a Justice of the Peace for the County of *Middlesex*, who having first examined *Elizabeth Canning* alone, but without taking from her any Information in Writing, did afterwards examine all the Parties, and in the End committed the Gipsy Woman and *Wells*, the former for taking away the Stays from *Elizabeth Canning*, and the latter for keeping a disorderly House.[2]

And here the Reader will be pleased to observe these Facts:

First, That *Elizabeth Canning* did not make any Information in Writing before this Justice.

Secondly, That the History of the Fact[3] that she related to the Justice was not in the Presence of *Virtue Hall*.

Thirdly, That *Elizabeth Canning*, so cautious is she in taking her Oath, declared, That she could not swear to the Gipsy's Son, as the Men's Hats were flapped over their Faces in the House, and as when she was first assaulted it was so very dark she could not distinguish their Countenances,

---

[8] Now roughly the A10/A1010 that runs north from the city of London past Edmonton, Enfield Wash, and Hertford to Cambridge.

[9] Wells's house was still standing in 1874, on the right-hand side 'a little beyond the tenth milestone on the Hertford road' (John Paget, 'Elizabeth Canning', *Paradoxes and Puzzles* [London, 1874], p. 322).

[1] That Elizabeth had failed to specify before Alderman Chitty the striking physical features of her supposed attacker was one of the telling points against her at her trial.

[2] Merry Tyshmaker (who regularly appears as 'Tashmaker' in *State Trials*), owner of Ford's Grove in Edmonton, committed Squires to New Prison in Clerkenwell and Wells to the adjoining bridewell.

[3] 'Crime' (*OED*); cf. 'after the fact'.

nor did she charge *Wells* with any Crime at all, except that which resulted from the Tenor of her whole Evidence of keeping a disorderly House.

Lastly, That *Virtue Hall* did, at that Time, absolutely deny, that she knew any Thing of the Matter, and declared, that *Elizabeth Canning* had never been in *Wells's* House, to her Knowledge, till that Day, nor had she ever seen her Face before; the Consequence of which Declaration was, that the Gipsy's Son, whom this *Virtue Hall* hath since accused of the Robbery, was discharged by Mr. *Tyshemaker.*

Elizabeth Canning, with her Friends, now returned home to her Mother's House, where she continued to languish in a very deplorable Condition; and now Mr. *Salt*,[4] the Attorney who hath been employed in this Cause, advised the Parties to apply to Council, and upon this Occasion, as he hath done upon many others, he fixed upon me as the Council to be advised with.

Accordingly, upon the 6*th* of *February*,[5] as I was sitting in my Room, Counsellor *Maden*[6] being then with me, my Clerk[7] delivered me a Case, which was thus, as I remember, indorsed at the Top, *The Case of* Elizabeth Canning *for Mr.* Fielding's *Opinion*, and at the Bottom, *Salt*, Solr. Upon the Receipt of this Case, with my Fee, I bid my Clerk give my Service to Mr. *Salt* and tell him, that I would take the Case with me into the Country,[8] whither I intended to go the next Day, and desired he would call for it on the *Friday* Morning afterwards; after which, without looking into it, I delivered it to my Wife,[9] who was then drinking Tea with us, and who laid it by.

---

[4] Not further identified. He disappeared quickly from the case and by 13 Mar. another lawyer, John Miles, was active on Elizabeth's behalf. Perhaps Virtue Hall's confession of perjury had made Salt nervous.

[5] A Tuesday.

[6] Martin Madan (1726–90) was called to the bar in 1748 and led a life of fashionable dissipation until converted to Methodism in 1750. The 'lawyer turned divine' attracted considerable attention in 1750 when he preached his first sermon. 'Counsellor' was an ironic title commemorating his legal past. In 1784 he published *Thoughts on Executive Justice, with respect to our Criminal Laws* in which he argued for a more rigorous application of even the harshest laws. He recommends Fielding's *Enquiry* to 'every order of magistrates within the kingdom' (2nd edn., p. 83), approves of his sentiments on the frequency and effects of pardons (pp. 127–9), and commends his establishment of 'a public office, open at all times for the examination and commitment of offenders' (pp. 131–2). Madan's views were called cruel and unmerciful in a charge delivered to the grand jury for the county of Surrey by Sir Richard Perryn (see Appendix to *Executive Justice*, 2nd edn., London, 1785).

[7] Joshua Brogden had been Sir Thomas de Veil's clerk and apparently he was with Fielding from his first tenure in office, for he witnessed Fielding's assignment of copyright in *Tom Jones* to Millar on 25 Mar. 1749. Fielding unsuccessfully asked for a magistrate's commission for Brogden in July 1749 (Cross, ii. 243–4). Brogden assisted with the reporting of criminal cases in the *Covent-Garden Journal* and, according to Cross (ii. 371), he and William Young were part of the 'permanent editorial staff' of the paper. Fielding alludes to Brogden in *Voyage to Lisbon* (Introduction, p. 34 and n.), complimenting his industry and character.

[8] Probably Fordhook farm at Ealing, then a village, now a western stop on the Central and District Underground lines. Fielding had purchased this house in the summer of 1752 as a country retreat (Cross, ii. 289–90) and it was from Fordhook that he began his journey to Lisbon (*Voyage to Lisbon*, p. 43).

[9] Fielding's second wife, Mary Daniel.

The Reader will pardon my being so particular in these Circumstances, as they seem, however trifling they may be in themselves, to shew the true Nature of this whole Transaction, which hath been so basely misrepresented, and as they will all be attested by a Gentleman of Fashion, and of as much Honor as any in the Nation.[1] My Clerk presently returned up Stairs, and brought Mr. *Salt* with him, who, when he came into the Room, told me, that he believed the Question would be of very little Difficulty, and begged me earnestly to read it over then, and give him my Opinion, as it was a Matter of some Haste, being of a criminal Nature, and he feared the Parties would make their Escape. Upon this, I desired him to sit down, and when the Tea was ended, I ordered my Wife to fetch me back the Case, which I then read over, and found it to contain a very full and clear State of the whole Affair relating to the Usage of this Girl, with a *Quere* what Methods might be proper to take to bring the Offenders to Justice; which *Quere* I answered in the best Manner I was able. Mr. *Salt* then desired, that *Elizabeth Canning* might swear to her Information before me, and added, that it was the very particular Desire of several Gentlemen of that End of the Town, that *Virtue Hall* might be examined by me relating to her Knowledge of this Affair.

This Business I at first declined, partly, as it was a Transaction which had happened at a distant Part of the County, as it had been examined already by a Gentleman, with whom I have the Pleasure of some Acquaintance, and of whose Worth and Integrity I have, with all, I believe, who know him, a very high Opinion;[2] but principally, indeed, for that I had been almost fatigued to Death, with several tedious Examinations at that Time, and had intended to refresh myself with a Day or two's Interval in the Country, where I had not been, unless on a *Sunday*, for a long Time.

I yielded, however, at last, to the Importunities of Mr. *Salt*; and my only Motives for so doing were, besides those Importunities, some Curiosity, occasioned by the extraordinary Nature of the Case, and a great Compassion for the dreadful Condition of the Girl, as it was represented to me by Mr. *Salt*.

The next Day, *Elizabeth Canning* was brought in a Chair to my House, and being lead up Stairs between two,[3] the following Information, which I had never before seen, was read over to her, when she swore to the Truth and set her Mark to it.

---

[1] Madan's gentlemanly credentials were excellent. His father was an MP and supporter of the Prince of Wales; an aunt married the master of the robes and keeper of the privy purse to George II; his mother was niece to Lord Chancellor Cowper (Sedgwick, ii. 239).

[2] Probably Merry Tyshmaker (see above, p. 296, n.).

[3] John Wintlebury (see above, p. 293, n. 9) and Robert Scarrat, hartshorn rasper and neighbor of Canning, who may have suggested the name of 'mother Wells' to Canning (see General Introduction, p. xcvii).

Middlesex.] *The* INFORMATION[4] *of* Elizabeth Canning *of* Aldermanbury
Postern, London, *Spinster, taken upon Oath, this* 7th *Day of*
February, *in the Year of our Lord* 1753, *before* Henry Fielding, *Esq,*
one of his Majesty's Justices of the Peace for the County of Middlesex.

This Informant, upon her Oath, saith, That on *Monday*, the First Day of
January last past, she, this Informant, went to see her Uncle and Aunt, who
live at *Saltpetre Bank*, near *Rosemary-lane*, in the County of *Middlesex*, and
continued with them until the Evening; and saith, That upon her Return
home, about Half an Hour after Nine, being opposite *Bethlehem-gate* in
Moorfields, she, this Informant, was seized by two Men (whose Names are
unknown to her, this Informant) who both had brown Bob-wigs[5] on, and
drab-coloured Great-coats; one of whom held her, this Informant, whilst the
other, feloniously and violently, took from her one Shaving Hat,[6] one Stuff
Gown,[7] and one Linen Apron, which she had on; and also, Half a Guinea in
Gold, and Three Shillings in Silver; and then he that held her threatened to
do for this Informant. And this Informant saith, That, immediately after,
they, the same two Men, violently took hold of her, and dragged her up into
the Gravel-walk that leads down to the said Gate, and about the Middle
thereof, he, the said Man, that first held her, gave her, with his Fist, a very
violent blow upon the right Temple, which threw her into a Fit, and deprived
her of her Senses, (which Fits, she, this Informant, saith she is accustomed
and subject to, upon being frighted, and that they often continue for six or
seven Hours.) And this Informant saith, That when she came to herself, she
perceived that she was carrying along by the same two Men, in a large Road-
way: And saith, That in a little Time after, she was so recovered she was able
to walk alone; however they continued to pull her along, which still so
intimidated and frightened her, that she durst not call out for Assistance, or
speak to them. And this Informant saith, That in about half an Hour after
she had so recovered herself, they, the said two Men, carried her, this
Informant, into a House (which, as she, this Informant, heard from some of
them, was about Four o' Clock in the Morning, and which House, as she,
this Informant, hath since heard and believes, is situate at *Enfield-wash* in the
County of *Middlesex*, and is reputed to be a very bad and disorderly Bawdy-
house, and occupied by one —— *Wells*, Widow) and there this Informant
saw, in the Kitchen, an old Gipsy Woman, and two young Women, whose
Names were unknown to this Informant; but the Name of one of them, this

---

[4] Canning's information before Fielding was introduced at her trial as evidence of her perjury. It
was proved by Joshua Brogden (*State Trials*, xix. 428–30).

[5] A wig with the bottom locks turned up into 'bobs' or short curls (*OED*).

[6] '? A hat made of shavings' (*OED*). Described as a 'chip hat' at her trial: a hat made of thin strips of
wood.

[7] A gown made or lined with wool' (*OED*).

Informant hath since heard, and believes is *Virtue Hall*, and saith, That the said old Gipsy Woman took hold of this Informant's Hand, and promised to give her fine Cloaths if she would go their Way; (meaning, as this Informant understood, to become a Prostitute) which this Informant refusing to do, she, the said old Gipsy Woman took a Knife out of a Drawer, and cut the Lace of the Stays of her, this Informant, and took the said Stays away from her; and one of the said Men took off her Cap, and then the said two Men went away with it, and she, this Informant, hath never since seen any of her Things. And this Informant saith, That soon after they were gone, (which she, this Informant, believes was about Five in the Morning) she, the said old Gipsy Woman, forced her, this Informant, up an old Pair of Stairs, and pushed her into a back Room like a Hay-loft, without any Furniture whatsoever in the same, and there locked her, this Informant, up, threatening her, this Informant, that if she made the least Noise or Disturbance, she, the said old Gipsy Woman, would cut her Throat, and then she went away. And this Informant saith, That when it grew light, upon her looking round to see in what a dismal Place she was, she, this Informant, discovered a large black Jug with the Neck much broken, wherein was some Water; and upon the Floor, several Pieces of Bread, near in Quantity to a quartern Loaf, and a small Parcel of Hay: And saith, That she continued in this Room, or Place, from the said *Tuesday* Morning, the second Day of *January*, until about Half-an-Hour after Four of the Clock in the Afternoon of *Monday* the twenty-ninth Day of the same Month of *January*, without having, or receiving, any other Sustenance, or Provision, than the said Bread and Water (except a small Minced-pye, which she, this Informant, had in her Pocket) or any Thing to lie on, other than the said Hay; and without any Person, or Persons, coming to her, altho' she often heard the Name of Mrs. and Mother *Wells* called upon, whom she understood was the Mistress of the House. And this Informant saith, That on *Friday*, the twenty-sixth Day of *January* last past, she, this Informant, had consumed all the aforesaid Bread and Water,[8] and continued without having any Thing to eat, or drink, until the *Monday* following, when she, this Informant, being almost famished with Hunger, and starved with Cold, and almost naked during the whole Time of her Confinement, about Half-an-hour after Four in the Afternoon of the said twenty-ninth Day of *January*, broke out at a Window of the said Room, or Place, and got to her Friends in *London*, about a Quarter after Ten the same Night, in a most weak, miserable Condition, being very near starved to Death. And this Informant saith, That she ever since hath been; and now is, in a very weak and declining State and Condition of Health, and altho' all possible Care and Assistance is given to her, yet whatever small Nutriment

---

[8] Canning was to say later that she drank the last of the water just before her escape, a discrepancy the crown emphasized at her trial.

she, this Informant, is able to take, the same receives no Passage through her, but what is forced by the Apothecary's Assistance and Medicines,

The Mark of

E C

Sworn before me,   *Elizabeth Canning.*[9]
this 7th of Feb.
1753.
H. FIELDING.

Upon this Information, I issued a Warrant against all who should be found resident in the House of the said *Wells*, as idle and disorderly Persons, and Persons of evil Fame, that they might appear before me, give Security for their good Behaviour; upon which Warrant, *Virtue Hall* and one *Judith Natus* were seized and brought before me, both being found at Mother *Wells's*: They were in my House above an Hour or more before I was at Leisure to see them, during which Time, and before I had ever seen *Virtue Hall*, I was informed, that she would confess the whole Matter. When she came before me, she appeared in Tears, and seemed all over in a trembling Condition; upon which I endeavoured to soothe and comfort her: The Words I first spoke to her, as well as I can remember, were these, Child, you need not be under this Fear and Apprehension; if you will tell us the whole Truth of this Affair, I give you my Word and Honour, as far as it is in my Power, to protect you; you shall come to no Manner of Harm. She answered, that she would tell the whole Truth, but desired to have some Time given her to recover from her Fright; upon this, I ordered a Chair to be brought her, and desired her to sit down, and then after some Minutes began to examine her; which I continued doing, in the softest Language and kindest Manner I was able, for a considerable Time, till she had been guilty of so many Prevarications and Contradictions, that I told her I would examine her no longer, but would commit her to Prison, and leave her to stand or fall by the Evidence against her, and at the same Time advised Mr. *Salt* to prosecute her as a Felon,[1]

---

[9] The prosecution showed at her trial that Canning was able to sign her name. The implication was that setting only her mark to her information before Fielding was intended to enforce her appearance of simplicity: 'Who would have thought, upon reading the pamphlet, which that good magistrate was pleased to oblige the world with, containing the information at large, with such ingenious remarks upon her stupidity;—who would have dreamt, that this "child in years, more so in understanding," was able to write a fair, legible hand?' (*State Trials*, xix. 631).

[1] On 8 Mar. two days after she had recanted her testimony taken before Fielding, Hall was again examined by Gascoyne before aldermen, 'people of fashion', and Canning. When asked why she had forsworn herself, she replied, ' "when she was at mr. *Fielding's* she at first spoke the truth, but that she was told that *that* was not the truth, and was *terrified and threatened to be sent to* Newgate *and prosecuted as a* felon, *unless she would speak the truth*" ' (Gascoyne, *An Address to the Liverymen of the City of London* [London, 1754], p. 11). Gascoyne disapproved of Fielding's method of interrogation and in a note quotes Fielding's own description of the interview and also a notice from the *Publick Advertiser* for

together with the Gipsy Woman; upon this, she begged I would hear her once more, and said that she would tell the whole Truth, and accounted for her Unwillingness to do it, from the Fears of the Gipsy Woman and *Wells.* I then asked her a few Questions, which she answered with more Appearance of Truth than she had done before; after which, I recommended to Mr. *Salt,* to go with her and take her Information in Writing; and at her parting from me, I bid her be a good Girl, and be sure to say neither more nor less than the whole Truth. During this whole Time, there were no less than ten or a dozen Persons of Credit present, who will, I suppose, testify the Truth of this whole Transaction as it is here related.[2] *Virtue Hall* then went from me, and returned in about two Hours, when the following Information, which was, as she said, taken from her Mouth, was read over to her and signed with her mark.

> The INFORMATION *of* Virtue Hall *late of the Parish of* Enfield *in the County of* Middlesex, *Spinster, taken upon Oath this* 13*th Day of* February 1753, *before me* Henry Fielding, *Esq; one of his Majesty's Justices of the Peace for the County of* Middlesex.

This Informant upon her Oath saith, That on *Tuesday* the second Day of *January* last past, about Four of the Clock in the Morning, a young Woman, whose Name this Informant hath since heard is *Elizabeth Canning*, was brought (without any Gown, Hat, or Apron on) to the House of one *Susannah Wells* of *Enfield-Wash* in the County aforesaid, Widow, by two Men, the Name of one of whom is *John Squires*,[3] the reputed Son of one *Mary Squires*, an old Gipsy Woman, who then, and some little time before, had lodged at the House of the said *Susannah Wells*, but the Name of the other of the said two Men this Informant knows not, she this Informant never having seen him before or since to the best of her Knowledge. And this Informant saith, That when she the said *Elizabeth Canning* was brought into the Kitchen of the said *Wells's* House, there were present the said *Mary Squires*, *John Squires*, the Man unknown, *Katharine Squires*, the reputed Daughter of the said *Mary Squires*, and this informant; and this Informant does not recollect that any one else was in the said Kitchen at that time: And saith, That immediately upon her the said *Elizabeth Canning's* being brought in, the said *John Squires* said, here Mother take this Girl, or used Words to that Effect; and she the said *Mary Squires* asked him where they had brought

---

Saturday, 10 Feb. 1753: 'this girl was brought before Mr. *Fielding* on *Thursday* evening, and was under examination from *six* till *twelve* at night; when, after *many hard struggles*, and *stout denials* of the *truth*, she *at length*, confessed the whole; *by which means* it is not doubted but that all the actors of that cruel scene will be brought to the fate they deserve' (loc. cit.).

[2] Including some of Fielding's Bow-Street Runners. According to de la Torre, the men present were later maliciously referred to as 'thief-takers' and 'Newgate solicitors' (*Elizabeth is Missing*, p. 73).

[3] A mistake for George Squires.

her from? and *John* said from *Moorfields*, and told his said Mother that they had taken her Gown, Apron, Hat, and half a Guinea from her, to the best of this Informant's Recollection and Belief: Whereupon she the said *Mary Squires* took hold of the said *Elizabeth Canning's* Hand, and asked her if she would go their Way, or Words to that Effect; and upon the said *Elizabeth Canning's* answering no, she the said *Mary Squires* took a Knife out of the Drawer of the Dresser in the Kitchen, and therewith cut the Lace of the said *Elizabeth Canning's* Stays, and took the said Stays away from her, and hung them on the Back of a Chair, and the said Man unknown took the Cap off the said *Elizabeth Canning's* Head, and then he, with the said *John Squires*, went out of Doors with it. And this Informant saith, That quickly after they were gone she the said *Mary Squires* pushed the said *Elizabeth Canning* along the Kitchen, towards and up a Pair of Stairs leading into a large Back-room like a Loft, called the Workshop, where there was some Hay; and whilst she the said *Mary Squires* was so pushing her the said *Elizabeth Canning* towards the Stairs, she the said *Susannah Wells* came into the Kitchen, and asked the said *Mary Squires* what she was going to push the Girl up Stairs for, or Words to that Effect, and to the best of this Informant's Recollection and Belief the said *Mary Squires* answered, What is that to you, you have no Business with it? whereupon the said *Susannah Wells* directly went out of the Kitchen into an opposite Room called the Parlour, from whence she came, as this Informant believes. And this Informant saith, That the said *Mary Squires* forced the said *Elizabeth Canning* up Stairs into the said Workshop, and buttoned the Door at the Bottom of the Stairs in the Kitchen upon her, and confined her there. And this Informant saith, That about two Hours after a Quantity of Water in an old broken mouthed large black Jug was carried up the said Stairs, and put down upon the Floor of the said Workshop at the Top of the Stairs, to the best of this Informant's Recollection and Belief. And this Informant saith, That soon after the said *Elizabeth Canning* was so put into the said Workshop, and the said *Susannah Wells* was returned into the Parlour, the said *John Squires* returned again into the Kitchen, and took the Stays from off the Chair and went away with the same, and in about an Hour's time returned and went into the Parlour with the said *Susannah Wells*. He the said *John Squires* came again into the Kitchen, and then this Informant went into the Parlour to the said *Susannah Wells*, and the said *Susannah Wells* there said to this Informant *Virtue*, the Gipsy Man (meaning the said *John Squires*) has been telling me that his Mother had cut the Girl's (meaning the said *Elizabeth Canning's*) Stays off her Back, and that he has got them; and further said, I desire you will not make a Clack of it, for fear it should be blown, or used Words to that or the like Effect. And this Informant saith, That from the Time of the said *Elizabeth Canning's* being so confined in the Morning of the said second Day of *January* in manner as aforesaid, she the said *Elizabeth Canning* was not missed or discovered to have escaped out of the said Workshop untill *Wednesday* the 31st Day of the same Month of *January*, as she this Informant verily believes; for that to the best of this Informant's Recollection and Belief, she was the Person that first missed the said *Elizabeth Canning* thereout. And this Informant saith, That the said *Susannah Wells* harboured and continued the said *Mary Squires* in her aforesaid House from the Time of the said *Mary Squires's* robbing the said *Elizabeth Canning* of her Stays untill *Thursday* the first Day of *February* last past, when the said *Susannah Wells, Sarah* her Daughter, *Mary Squires, John Squires*, his two Sisters *Katharine* and *Mary Squires, Fortune Natus*, and *Sarah* his Wife,[4] and this Informant, were apprehended on account thereof, and carried before Justice *Tyshemaker*. And this Informant saith, That *Fortune Natus* and *Sarah* his Wife, to the best of this Informant's Recollection and Belief, have lodged in the House of the said *Susannah Wells* about eleven Weeks next before *Monday* the fifth Day of *February* Instant, and layed on a Bed of Hay spread in the Kitchen at Night, which was in the Day-time pushed up in a Corner thereof, and continued lying there, when at home, untill *Thursday* the said first Day of *February* when before the said Mr. *Tyshemaker*, all except the said *Susannah Wells* and *Mary Squires* were discharged, and then that Evening the said *Fortune Natus* and *Sarah* his Wife laid up in the said Workshop where the said *Elizabeth Canning* had been confined, so that, as this Informant understood, it might be pretended that they had lain in the said Workshop for all the Time they had lodged in the said *Susannah Wells's* House. And saith, That on the Day on which it was discovered that the said *Elizabeth Canning* had made her Escape out of the said Workshop, by breaking down some Boards slightly affixed across the Window-place, the said *Sarah*, Daughter of the said *Susannah Wells*, nailed up the said Window-place again with Boards, so that the said Window-place might not appear to have been broke open. And lastly, this Informant saith, That she, this Informant, hath lived with the said *Susannah Wells* about a Quarter of a Year last past, and well knows that the said *Susannah Wells*, during that time, hath kept a very notorious ill governed and disorderly House, and has had the Character of doing so for many Years past; and that the said *Susannah Wells* well knew and was privy to the Confinement of the said *Elizabeth Canning*.

Sworn before me,	*her*
this 14th February	*Virtue + Hall.*
1753.[5]	*Mark.*
H. FIELDING.	

[4] A mistake for Judith.

[5] Although it is 7 Feb. in the chronology of Fielding's narrative here, he prints the statement that Virtue Hall swore to before 'several Noble Lords' on 14 Feb. (see below, p. 306), a discrepancy which

The Reader will be pleased to consider the Nature of this Information truly taken in the Manner above set down, to compare it with the Evidence given by this *Virtue Hall* at her Tryal, and lastly, to compare it with the Evidence of *Elizabeth Canning*, and then I am much mistaken if he condemns either the Judge or Jury.

After I had finished the Examination of *Virtue Hall*, one *Judith Natus*, the Wife of *Fortune Natus*, whom I apprehend to belong to the Gipsies,[6] and who was found in the House with *Virtue Hall*, being examined upon her Oath before me, declared, That she and her Husband lay in the same Room where *Elizabeth Canning* pretended to have been confined during the whole Time of her pretended Confinement, and declared, That she had never seen nor heard of any such Person as *Elizabeth Canning* in *Wells's* House. Upon this *Virtue Hall*, of her own Accord, affirmed, as she doth in her Information in Writing, these two Persons were introduced into that Room, to lie there, by Mother *Wells*, to give a Colour to the Defence which *Wells* was to make, and which these People, in the Presence of *Virtue Hall*, had agreed to swear to.

Upon this some Persons, who were present, were desirous that this *Judith Natus* should be committed for Perjury, but I told them that such a Proceeding would be contrary to Law, for that I might as well commit *Virtue Hall* upon the Evidence of *Judith Natus*. However, as I confess I myself thought her guilty of Perjury, I gave her some little Caution, and told her that she ought to be very sure of the Truth of what she said, if she intended to give that Evidence at the *Old Bailey*, and then discharged her.

The next Day[7] *Virtue Hall* came again before me, but nothing material passed, nor was she three Minutes in my Presence. I then ordered Detainers[8] for Felony against the Gipsy Woman and *Wells* to be sent to the Prisons where they then lay upon the Commitments of Mr. *Tyshemaker*, and thus ended all the Trouble which I thought it was necessary for me to give myself in this Affair; for as to the Gipsy Woman or *Wells*, those who understand the Law well know I had no Business with them.[9]

confused some pamphleteers and which led others to suspect Fielding had tampered with the evidence. The date at the head of Hall's information (13 Feb.) and its unnatural language indicate that it was one prepared beforehand, presumably by Salt.

[6] Fortune Natus was, according to his own description, 'a poor labouring man' employed at Waltham Cross (*State Trials*, xix. 400). Neither he nor his wife was associated with the gypsies. His character, however, was not good. When asked if Fortune Natus would lie when nothing was to be gained by it, one of his neighbors replied, 'I think he would, he hates truth' (*State Trials*, xix. 589). Judith Natus was characterized as a 'drunken beast' (loc. cit.).

[7] 8 Feb.

[8] A writ detaining one already held for prosecution. Squires and Wells were being held for prosecution on Canning's information taken before Tyshemaker. Virtue Hall's information taken before Fielding constituted additional ground for prosecution.

[9] The processes of arrest and imprisonment having already been executed, the presentment of the bill to a grand jury would duly follow without further action on Fielding's part.

Some Days afterwards, however, upon my Return to Town, my Clerk informed me, that several Noble Lords had sent to my House in my Absence, desiring to be present at the Examination of the Gipsy Woman. Of this I informed Mr. *Salt*, and desired him to bring *Elizabeth Canning* and *Virtue Hall*, in order to swear their several Informations again in the Presence of the Gipsy Woman and *Wells*, and appointed him a Day[1] for so doing, of which I sent an Advice to the noble Lords.

One of these, namely Lord *Montfort*,[2] together with several Gentlemen of Fashion, came at the appointed Time. They were in my Room before the Prisoners or Witnesses were brought up. The Informations were read to the two Prisoners; after which I asked the Prisoners a very few Questions, and in what Manner I behaved to them let all who were present testify; I can truly say, that my memory doth not charge me with having ever insulted the lowest Wretch that hath been brought before me.

The Prisoners and Witnesses left the Room while all the Company remained in it; and from that Time to this Day I never saw the Face of *Virtue Hall*, unless once when she came before me with *Canning*, to see a Man who was taken on Suspicion of the Robbery,[3] and when I scarce spoke to her; nor should I have seen *Elizabeth Canning* more, had not I received a Message from some Gentlemen desiring my Advice how to dispose of some Money which they had collected, to the Use of *Elizabeth Canning*, in the best Manner for her Advantage; upon which Occasion I ordered her to be sent for, to meet one of the Gentlemen at my House:[4] And had I not likewise been informed since the Tryal, that a great Number of Affidavits, proving that the Gipsy Woman was at *Abbotsbury*[5] in *Dorsetshire*, at the very Time when *Elizabeth Canning* had sworn that she was robbed by her at *Enfield-washe*, were arrived at my Lord Mayor's Office.[6] Upon this I sent for her

---

[1]   14 Feb. It is this second recording of Hall's 'Information' that Fielding quotes above (p. 302 ff.). The reason for printing the information of 14 Feb. rather than that of 7 Feb. is given in *A Refutation of Sir Crisp Gascoyne's Address . . . By A Clear State of the Case of Elizabeth Canning, In A Narrative of Facts* [London, 1754]: 'Hall was afterwards brought before Mr. Fielding, and confronted with Wells and Squires and Canning, in the presence of several persons of distinction, and still confirmed the account she had given with great calmness and consistency; and signed and swore a second information, in which she related many particulars, that in the hurry of the first, which was drawn at twelve o'clock at night, were omitted' (p. 10).

[2]   Henry Bromley (1705–55), MP for Cambridgeshire 1727–41, lord lieutenant of Cambridgeshire 1730–42, created Baron Montfort 1741. He managed Cambridgeshire elections for Walpole and was a 'useful speaker for the Court'. Bromley was a notable gambler, 'the sharpest genius of his time', but his suicide 1 Jan. 1755 was apparently the result of extraordinary debts and 'an estate out of repair and in a very ruinous condition' (Sedgwick, i. 492–3). Fielding praises him in passing in 'Of Good Nature' (*Miscellanies* [1743], p. 35).

[3]   Virtue Hall was being maintained in the Westminster Gatehouse prison by friends of Canning to identify George Squires, should he be apprehended.

[4]   See above, p. 293, n. 2.

[5]   On the Dorsetshire coast half-way between Weymouth and Lyme Regis.

[6]   Sir Crisp Gascoyne began collecting affidavits supporting Squires's story shortly after the trial (Squires and Wells were convicted 21 Feb. 1753; sentenced 26 Feb.). On 6 Mar. Virtue Hall recanted

once more; and endeavoured by all Means in my Power to sift the Truth out of her, and to bring her to a Confession if she was guilty; but she persisted in the Truth of the Evidence that she had given, and with such an Appearance of Innocence, as persuaded all present of the Justice of her Cause.[7]

Thus have I very minutely recited the whole Concern which I had in this Affair, unless that after I had discharged my whole Duty as a Justice of the Peace, Mr. *Salt* came again to consult with me concerning the Crime of which *Wells* was accused, and the Manner of prosecuting her, upon a Point of Law, which is by no means a very easy one, namely that of Accessaries after the Fact in Felony, upon which I gave him my Opinion.[8]

And now having run through the Process of the Affair as far as to the Tryal, which is already in Print,[9] I come to lay before the Reader that Point of Evidence on which, as I have said, so great a Stress ought to be laid, a Point on which indeed any Cause whatever might be safely rested: This is the Agreement, in so many particular Circumstances between the Evidence of *Elizabeth Canning* and *Virtue Hall*. That *Virtue Hall* had never seen nor heard the Evidence of *Elizabeth Canning* at the Time when she made her own Information, is· a Fact; nay, had she even heard the other repeat it once over before a Justice of Peace, that she should be able, at a Distance of Time, to retain every particular Circumstance so exactly as to make it tally in the Manner her Information doth with that of *Elizabeth Canning*, is a Supposition in the highest Degree absurd, and those who can believe it can believe that which is more incredible than anything in the Narrative of *Elizabeth Canning*.

The only Way therefore to account for this is, by supposing that the two Girls laid this Story together. To the Probability and indeed Possibility of this Supposition, I object,

First, That from the whole Circumstances of this Case it appears

---

her testimony supporting Canning. Two Abbotsbury witnesses appeared before Gascoyne 13 Mar., and he issued a warrant for Canning's arrest on a charge of perjury the same day. By 10 Apr. he had collected abundant evidence supporting Squires's alibi, which he presented to the king. Squires was granted a six-week respite on that date. See General Introduction, p. cii ff.

[7] Supporters of Canning cite this last interview with Fielding as evidence of the truth of her story: 'With this view [to detect her in a falsehood] Mr. Fielding examined her several hours, in the presence of many persons, after Hall had made her recantation; endeavouring by turns to sooth and terrify her, and using every art which he had acquired by an universal acquaintance with mankind, and many years experience as a magistrate' (*A Refutation of Sir Crisp Gascoyne's Address*, p. 3).

[8] The indictment of Susannah Wells charges that she 'did then and there feloniously receive, harbour, comfort, conceal, and maintain, against his majesty's peace, and against the form of the statute' the felon Mary Squires (*State Trials*, xix. 262).

[9] Criminal trials were regularly and swiftly published under the title *The Proceedings on the King's Commissions of the Peace, Oyer & Terminer, & Gaol Delivery* . . . (better known as the *Old Bailey Sessions Papers*), a series which also contains the 'dying speeches' of malefactors. The articles by John H. Langbein (cited above, p. 283, n. 1) are partly based on his study of the *Old Bailey Sessions Papers* and provide an excellent account of them. See especially 'The Criminal Trial before the Lawyers', pp. 267–72; and 'Shaping the Eighteenth-century Criminal Trial', pp. 3 ff.

manifestly that they had never seen the Face of each other (unless *Canning* be believed as to the Time when she was brought into *Wells's*) before the Persons came to apprehend her, nay *Wells* herself declared before me, that *Canning* had never been in her House, and the other scarce ever out of it during the whole Month in Question.

Secondly, If we could suppose they had met together so as to form this Story, the Behaviour of *Virtue Hall* before Mr. *Tyshemaker* would intirely destroy any such Supposition, for there this *Virtue Hall* was so far from being in the same Story with *Elizabeth Canning*, that she there affirmed she knew nothing of the Matter, and she had then no Reason to apprehend any farther Examination; nor is it possible to conceive that these two Girls should afterwards enter into any such Agreement. From the Day of the Examination before Mr. *Tyshemaker*, till *Virtue Hall* came before me, the two Girls never saw the Face of each other, the one remained sick at her Mother's in Town, the other continued at *Wells's* House at *Enfield*, in Company with those who yet persist in their Friendship to *Wells* and the Gipsy. In reality, I never yet heard a Fact better established in a Court of Justice than this, that *Elizabeth Canning* and *Virtue Hall* did not lay this Story together, nay even she herself doth not, as I have heard, since her Apostacy,[1] pretend to say any such thing, but imputes her Evidence to her being threatened and bullied into it, which to my own Knowledge, and that of many others, is a most impudent Falsehood; and, secondly, ascribes her agreeing with *Elizabeth Canning* to having heard her deliver her Evidence, which, besides being impossible, can be proved to be another notorious Falsehood, by a great Number of Witnesses of indisputable Credit.

So that I think I am here intitled to the following syllogistical Conclusion.

Whenever two Witnesses declare a Fact, and agree in all the Circumstances of it, either the Fact is true or they have previously concerted the Evidence between themselves:

But in this Case it is impossible that these Girls should have so previously concerted the Evidence:

And therefore the Fact is true.[2]

---

[1] See above, p. 301, n. 1.

[2] The point that Fielding stresses is surprisingly weak. Hill was quick to point out Salt's opportunity to shape Hall's confession and sneered at Fielding's logic: 'Now, Syllogist where is your Argument! Can two Persons who swear the same thing agree in all particulars, and yet that thing be false? Yes certainly, if one has heard the other's Story. As certainly if the same Hand drew up both the Informations, and both that swear are perjured. This is the true state of the Question: You beg too much, as you have put it' (*The Story of Elizabeth Canning Considered*, p. 37).

At Canning's trial Edward Willes (son of Chief Justice Sir John Willes), counsel for the crown, took note of the argument 'That Canning and Virtue Hall were never together before Virtue Hall's examination, and yet they agree in almost every circumstance of the story, and therefore Canning's

The Reader will be pleased to observe, That I do not here lay any Weight on the Evidence of *Virtue Hall*, as far as her own Credit is necessary to support that Evidence, for in Truth she deserves no Credit at all;[3] the Weight which I here lay on her Evidence is so far only as it is supported by that Evidence of Fact which alone is always safely to be depended upon as it is alone incapable of a Lye.

And here, though I might very well rest the Merits of the whole Cause on this single Point, yet I cannot conclude the Case of this poor Girl without one Observation, which hath, I own, surprized me, and will, I doubt not, surprize the Reader. It is this, Why did not the Gipsy Woman and *Wells* produce the Evidence of *Fortune Natus* and his Wife in their Defence at their Tryal, since that Evidence, as they well knew, was so very strong in their Behalf, that had the Jury believed it, they must have been acquitted? For my own Part, I can give but one Answer to this, and that is too obvious to need to be here mentioned.[4]

Nor will I quit this Case, without observing the pretty Incident of the minced Pye;[5] which, as it possibly saved this poor Girl's Life, so doth the Intention of carrying it home to her little Brother serve very highly to represent the Goodness, as well as Childishness and Simplicity of her Character; a Character so strongly imprinted in her Countenance, and attested by all her Neighbours.

Upon the whole, this Case, whether it be considered in a private or in a public Light, deserves to be scrutinised to the Bottom; and that can be only done by the Government's authorising some very capable and very indifferent Persons,[6] to examine into it, and particularly into the *alibi* Defence of *Mary Squires* the Gipsy Woman. On the one Side here is the Life of a Subject at Stake, who, if her Defence is true, is innocent; and a young

evidence must be true'. He went on to observe that 'it is very remarkable, that Virtue Hall's confession was not taken at first (for what reason I know not) *viva voce* before Justice Fielding. She was thrust out of the room to retire with her solicitor, who was also Canning's solicitor: her information was reduced into writing, and was two hours in preparing. After this, what mighty wonder is there, that when she came into the justice's presence again, she should repeat her lesson without the least hesitation?' (*State Trials*, xix. 317.)

[3] Though in law Virtue Hall might still be technically an admissible witness, the prosecution at Canning's trial wanted nothing to do with her. It was the defence, curiously, which called for her appearance, presumably because her testimony might further confuse matters (see *State Trials*, xix. 449 ff.).

[4] At Canning's trial, both Fortune and Judith Natus testified that they had been subpoenaed to appear at the trial of Squires and Wells but a court officer and the mob had kept them from entering the court room.

[5] Because a younger brother had 'huffed' her, Elizabeth had withheld his Christmas penny. On the day of her disappearance she had relented and purchased a penny mince pie for him.

[6] Perhaps Fielding glances at Sir Crisp Gascoyne, whose activity on behalf of Squires seemed to the supporters of Canning unnaturally zealous. When the grand jury indicted Canning for perjury, her lawyers concealed her until Gascoyne's mayoralty expired lest he again sit on the bench. At the trial of the three Abbotsbury witnesses in Sept. 1753 (see Introduction, p. cx), Gascoyne was careful to quit the chair and retire out of court.

Girl, guilty of the blackest, most premeditated, and most audacious Perjury, levelled against the Lives of several innocent Persons. On the other Side, if the Evidence of *Elizabeth Canning* is true, and Perjury should, nevertheless, prevail against her, an innocent young Creature, who hath suffered the most cruel and unheard-of Injuries, is in Danger of being rewarded for them by Ruin and Infamy; and what must extremely aggravate her Case, and will distinguish her Misery from that of all other Wretches upon Earth, is, that she will owe all this Ruin and Infamy to this strange Circumstance, that her Sufferings have been beyond what human Nature is supposed capable of bearing; whilst Robbery, Cruelty, and the most impudent of all Perjuries, will escape with Impunity and Triumph; and, therefore, will so escape, because the Barbarity of the guilty Parties hath risen to a Pitch of wanton and untempted Inhumanity, beyond all Possibility of Belief.

As to my own Conduct in this Affair, which I have deduced with the most minute Exactness, I know it to be highly justifiable before God and before Man. I frankly own, I thought it intitled me to the very Reverse of Censure. The Truth is, the same Motive prevailed with me then, which principally urged me to take up my Pen at this Time, a Desire to protect Innocence and to detect Guilt; and the Delight in so doing was the only Reward I ever expected, so help me God; and I have the Satisfaction to be assured, that those who know me best will most believe me.

In solemn Truth, the only Error I can ever be possibly charged with in this Case is an Error in Sagacity. If *Elizabeth Canning* be guilty of a false Accusation, I own she hath been capable of imposing on me; but I have the Comfort to think the same Imposition hath passed not only on two Juries, but likewise on one of the best Judges that ever sate on the Bench of Justice, and on two other very able Judges who were present at the Tryal.[7]

I do not, for my own Part, pretend to Infallibility, though I can at the same time with Truth declare, that I have never spared any Pains in endeavouring to detect Falsehood and Perjury, and have had some very notable Success that Way.

In this Case, however, one of the most simple Girls I ever saw, if she be a wicked one, hath been too hard for me; supposing her to be such she hath indeed most grossly deceived me, for I remain still in the same Error: And I appeal, in the most solemn Manner, to the Almighty for the Truth of what I now assert. I am at this very Time, on this 15th Day of *March* 1753, as firmly persuaded as I am of any Fact in this World, the Truth of which depends solely on the Evidence of others, that *Mary Squires* the Gipsy Woman, IS

---

[7] Three justices presided at the trial of Squires and Wells: Martin Wright (1691–1767), judge of the King's Bench (1740–55); Nathaniel Gundry (1701?–54), MP for Dorsetshire (1741–50) and judge of the Common Pleas (1750–4); and Sir Richard Adams (1710–73), baron of the Court of Exchequer (1753–73). 'One of the best Judges' must be Martin Wright, the most senior of the three, a neighbor when Fielding lived in Boswell Court, and a subscriber to the *Miscellanies* (Cross, ii. 11).

GUILTY of the Robbery and Cruelty of which she stands convicted; that the *alibi* Defence is not only a false one, but a Falsehood very easy to be practised on all Occasions, where there are Gangs of People, as Gipsies, *&c.* that very foul and unjustifiable Practices have been used in this whole Affair since the Tryal; and that *Elizabeth Canning* is a poor, honest, innocent, simple Girl, and the most unhappy and most injured of all human Beings.

It is this Persuasion alone, I repeat it again, which occasioned me to give the Public this Trouble; for as to myself, I am, in my own Opinion, as little concerned in the Event of this whole Matter as any other Man whatever.

Whatever Warmth I have at last contracted in this Matter, I have contracted from those who have been much warmer on the other Side; nor can any such Magistrate blame me,[8] since we must, I am persuaded, act from the same Motive of doing Justice to injured Innocence. This is surely the Duty of every Man, and a very indispensible Duty it is, if we believe one of the best of Writers. *Qui non defendit, nec obsistit, si potest, injuriæ, tam erit in vitio quam si parentes, aut amicos, aut patriam deserat.*[9] These are *Tully's* Words, and they are in the most especial Manner applicable to every Magistrate.

To the Merit of having discharged this Duty, my Lord Mayor as well as myself have a just Title at all Events. And for my own Part, as I do not expect to gain, so neither do I fear to lose any other Honour on the final Issue of this Affair: For surely the Cause is of such a Nature that a Man must be intolerably vain who is ashamed of being mistaken on either Side. To be placed above the Reach of Deceit is to be placed above the Rank of a human being; sure I am that I make no Pretension to be of that Rank; indeed I have been often deceived in my Opinion of Men, and have served and recommended to others those Persons whom I have afterwards discovered to be totally worthless. I shall, in short, be very well contented with the Character which *Cicero* gives of *Epicurus. Quis illum neget & bonum virum & comem & humanum fuisse!*[1] And whoever will allow me this, which I must own I think I deserve, shall have my Leave to add, *tamen, si hæc vera sunt non satis acutus fuit.*[2]

In solemn Truth, so little desirous am I to be found in the right, that I shall not be in the least displeased to find myself mistaken. This indeed I ought, as a good Man, to wish may be the Case; since that this Country should have produced one great Monster of Iniquity, is a Reflection much less shocking than to consider the Nation to be arrived at such an alarming

---

[8] Again glancing at Gascoyne.

[9] Cicero, *De officiis*, I. vii. 'He who does not prevent or oppose wrong, if he can, [is] just as guilty of wrong as if he deserted his parents or his friends or his country' (Loeb).

[1] Cicero, *De Finibus*, II. xxv. 'Who . . . denies that Epicurus was a good man, and a kind and humane man?' (Loeb.)

[2] Ibid. 'But if what I say is true . . . he was not a very acute thinker' (Loeb.)

State of Profligacy, and our Laws and Government to lie in so languishing a Condition that a Gang of Wretches like these should dare to form such an impudent Attempt to elude public Justice, nay rather to overbear it by the Force of associated Perjury in the Face of the whole World; and that this audacious Attempt should have had, at least, a very high Probability of succeeding.

This is the Light in which I see this Case at present. I conclude, therefore, with hoping that the Government will authorise some proper Persons to examine to the very Bottom, a Matter in which the Honour of our national Justice is so deeply concerned.

POSTSCRIPT.

In the extreme Hurry in which the foregoing Case was drawn up, I forgot to observe one strange Circumstance which will attend the Case of *Elizabeth Canning*, if it should be admitted to be a Forgery; this is, that she should charge the Gipsy Woman when she must have known that Woman could prove an *Alibi*, and not *Susannah Wells*, who could have had no such Proof. This will be very strong if applied to the Evidence of *Canning*, but much stronger when applied to the Evidence of *Virtue Hall*, who lived in the House the whole Time.

This appears to be very simple Conduct; and, as such, indeed, is consistent enough with her Character. So is not the artful Manner in which the Charge was brought out; first *Canning* accused the Gipsy Woman, and went no farther, then *Hall* brought the rest upon the Stage, all in such Regularity, and with such Appearance of Truth that no *Newgate* Sollicitor ever ranged his Evidence in better Order. But, perhaps, I might have spared my Reader these Observations, as I can now inform him that I have this very Afternoon (*Sunday* the 18th instant) read over a great Number of Affidavits corroborating the whole Evidence of *Canning*, and contradicting the *Alibi* Defence of the Gipsy Woman.[3] I shall only add, that these Affidavits are by unquestionable Witnesses, and sworn before three worthy Justices of the County of *Middlesex*, who live in the Neighbourhood of *Enfield-Washe*.

FINIS.

[3] John Miles, who replaced Salt as Canning's solicitor, conveyed over twenty witnesses from the neighborhood of Enfield Wash on 15 and 16 Mar. 1753 to view Squires in Newgate (de la Torre, *Elizabeth is Missing*, pp. 116–22). Testimony at Canning's trial makes it clear that some of these witnesses were among those who contradicted Squires's alibi. Miles had placed advertisements for witnesses, such as the following, in the newspapers: 'Whereas there are various scandalous and malicious Falshoods raised and reported of *Elizabeth Canning* by several Persons, particularly by Mr. *Hill* and his *Associates* . . . thereby imposing on the Publick, and to the great Injury of *Canning*; I do hereby take upon me to declare, that several Persons . . . are daily informing me of . . . Circumstances [which prove] her Innocence . . . And as it [is] apprehended there are Numbers of other Persons that have not yet been heard of by *Canning*, or her Friends, who know of Matters material and relative to her Case, the Favour will be greatly acknowledged, if *such Persons* will give *Information* thereof to John Myles, Attorney, in Birchin-Lane' ('*Canning's' Magazine*, p. 82).

APPENDIXES

In Appendix V, Bibliographical Descriptions, the different states or impressions of *Bosavern Penlez, Examples of Providence,* and *Elizabeth Canning* have been distinguished by the symbols *, †, or ‡ to avoid the implication of chronological sequence that numbers or letters would give.

The copy text for each pamphlet in this edition is the one listed first in 'copies collated' (Appendix V).

W stands for the present Wesleyan edition.

APPENDIX I

List of Substantive Emendations

CHARGE

29. 3 is] W; if

BOSAVERN PENLEZ

56. 1 the] W; *om.* 1–2

ENQUIRY

67. 12 above] 2; have above 1
72. 2 this] 2; yet this 1
72. 16 it] 2; its 1
76. 26 is] 2; are 1
78. 6 Proportion] 2; probable Proportion 1
80. 4 called] 2; really called 1
81. 23 natural] 2; certain natural 1
94. (note) 158] W (from *errata*); 174 1; 58 2.
96. 17 to] 2; *om.* 1
124. (note) of the] 2; the of 1
126. 10 still] 2; perhaps still 1
131. 10–12 *Arabia*. For . . . discovered] 2 (*from errata*); *Arabia. om.* 1
131. 14–15 Evil, namely . . . Poor, and] W (*from errata*); Evil, namely, . . . Poor, and 2; Evil, *om.* and 1

135. (note) Tourn] W (*from errata*; Town 1–2
164. (note) *om.*] W; † Disc. l. 3. c. 3. 1; *om.* 2
165. 4 *Machiavel* **] W; ~ ₌ 1–2
165. (*note*) ** *Disc. l. 3. c. 3*] W; *om.* 1–2
173. 19 in the Thirty-fourth of] 2; in *om.* 1
173. 26 (¶) N.B. Books containing a full Account of the Office, are now to be had at it.] 2; *om.* 1

PROPOSAL

230. (note) Members] W; Member
263. (note) Causes] W; Cause

ELIZABETH CANNING

285. 28 Judges] 2; of Judges
286. 5 Means] 2; Ends
287. 29 an] 2; a

APPENDIX II

List of Accidentals Emendations

CHARGE

8. 11 *Institute*] W; Institute
8. 14 Act (says Lord COKE)] W; Act, says Lord COKE,
13. 29 *Book of Assises*] W; Book of Assises
17. 7 *Pleas of the Crown*] W; Pleas of the Crown
20. 5–6 last-] W; ~ ∧
22. 6 Kind] W; kind
22. 11 thirty-] W; thirthy-
25. 20 This∧] W; ~,
27. 25 *Politics*] W; Politics

BOSAVERN PENLEZ

35. 5 Falsehood] W; Falshood 1–2
37. 3 War∧] W; ~, 1–2
37. 10 here (says Lord *Coke*)] W; here, says Lord *Coke*, 1–2
37. 11 this (says he)] W; this, says he, 1–2
37. (note) *Hawk.*] W; Hawk. 1–2
37. 20 *Bailey*] W; *Baily* 1–2
38. 4 Lord∧ Chief∧] W; ~-∧-~- 1–2
38. 5 *Reports*] W; Reports 1–2
38. (note) *Hale's*] W; Hale's 1–2
39. 12–13 Case (says Lord *Coke*)] W; Case, says Lord *Coke*, 1–2
39. (note) *And*] W; And 1–2
39. (note) *Poph.*] W; Poph. 1–2
40. 13 ∧This is ...] *no paragraph* 2; "This is ...]
40. (note) *And*] W; And 1–2
40. (note) *Hale's*] W; Hale's 1–2
42. 32 Twelve] W; twelve 1–2
43. 10 Chapel] W; Chap-|pel 1–2
43. 17 Let] W; Lett 1–2
*47. 14 That] 2; that
*47. 18 there∧] 2; ~,
49. 24 Fire] W; fire 1–2 (*see also* 51. 34, 51. 35)

50. 23 Welch] W; Welsh 1–2
52. 17 Three] W; three 1–2
52. 20 Twelve] W; twelve 1–2
55. 15 *street*] W; *Street* 1–2
56. 14 *wit*,] 1 (*cw*); ~; 1 (*text*)
58. 14 undoubtedly] W; undoubtledly 1–2
60. (note) *Bailey*] W; *Baily* 1–2

ENQUIRY

66. 8 Body,] 2; ~;
66. 17 Historians∧] 2; ~,
67. 13 before mentioned] 2; beforementioned
67. 15 Soul (says *Simmias* in *Plato*)] W; Soul,' says *Simmias* in Plato, 1–2
68. 19 men (says Lord *Coke*)] W; men,' says Lord Coke, 1–2
76. 30 Cheating] 2; cheating
76. 31 Thieving] 2; thieving
76. 31 Robbing] 2; robbing
80. 8 Divine] 2; divine
80. 10 *Feast of the unleavened Bread*] 2; *no ital.*
80. 10 *Feast of the Weeks*] 2; *no ital.*
80. 11 the *Feast of the Tabernacles*] W; *the ... Tabernacles* 2; *no ital.* 1
80. 11 is] 2; it
80. 24 Entertainment] 2; En-|tainment
80. 25 *Romans*,] 2; ~∧
81. 17 Remission (says he)] W; Remission, says he, 1–2
81. (note) *Saturnalia*] 2; *Saturnal.*
84. 27 Lewdness] W; Leudness 1–2
86. 6 Ale-houses] W; Alehouses 1–2
87. 30. to] 2; ro
97. 21 Laws] 2; laws
102. 15 Indeed (says he)] W; Indeed, says he, 1–2
103. 12 Emolument;] 2; ~.

103. 16 which (says he)] W; which, says he, 1–2

104. 15 objected (says he)] W; objected, says he, 1–2

105. 32 entered] 2; entred

106. 25 it,] W; ∼ₐ 1; ∼; 2

113. 26 Daysₐ] W; Days ‡ 1–2

113. 28 void. ‡] W; ∼ₐ 1–2

115. 6 illegalₐ] 2; ∼,

116. 6 Here (says he)] W; Here, says he, 1–2

121. 28 *Bridewell*] W; Bridewell 1–2

124. 20–1 Provision (says Lord *Hale*)] W; Provision, says Lord Hale, 1–2

126. 2 Pawnbrokers] 2; Pawn-brokers

134. 8 established (says *Rapin*)] W; established,' says *Rapin*, 1–2

134. 13–14 Peace (says Lord *Coke*)] W; Peace,' says Lord *Coke*, 1–2

138. 13 Increase] 2; Encrease

141. 37 Ale-houses] W; Alehouses 1–2

142. 8 4.] 2; ∼,

143. 4 Ale-houses] W; Alehouses 1–2

146. 5 That] 2; that

146. 11 Intent (says the Statute)] W; Intent, says the Statute, 1–2

146. 21 or,] 2; ∼ₐ

146. 21 Necessity,] 2; ∼ₐ

147. 13 Attempt] 2; attempt

148. 14 Robberies] 2; Robberys

153. 25 Forₐ] 2; ∼,

153. 25 who,] W; ∼ₐ 1–2

158. 15 is (says he)] W; is,' says he, 1–2

165. 8 Severity (says *Machiavel*)] W; Severity, says *Machiavel*, 1–2

166. 1 raising] 2; rasing

168. 16 Latter] W; latter 1–2

170. 25 believe,] 2; ∼;

170. 30 Divines;] 2; ∼,

171. 1 Death (says the same Author)] W; Death, says the same Author, 1–2

171. 16 *Bailey*] W; *Baily* 1–2 (see also 171. 25)

EXAMPLES OF PROVIDENCE

177. 15 distinguished] W; dstinguished

181. 27–8 Herod (says Eusebius)] W; Herod,' says Eusebius,

182. 13 Christians] W; christians

183. 17 *Plutarch's*] W; Plutarch's

183. 17 *Solin.*] W; Solin.

192. 24 lived] W; ived

192. 26 poison] W; oison

194. 6 so] W; so so

194. 38 killed] W; kiled

198. 5 Christinetta] W; Christenitta

199. 11 Masserina] W; Nasserina

199. 36 Albemare] W; Albemane

200. 9 Albemare] W; Albemane

204. 14 stolen] W; stoln

205. 2 dunghill] W; dung-hill

211. 7 servants] W; servant's

PROPOSAL

220. 4 Chapel] W; Chaple

220. 20 Chaplains] W; Chaplaims

225. 20 consider (says he)] W; consider,' says he,

227. 10 Part (says he)] W; Part, says he,

**237. 11 County-House] W; ∼ₐ∼ (*see also* 237. (*margin*); 237. (*margin*); 238. 7, 238. (*margin*); 240. 4, 240. 12; 246. (*margin*), 246. 36; 249. 18; 249. 27; 250. 16)

237. (*margin*) Suttling-houses] W; ∼ₐ∼

241. 11–12 Peaceₐ Officer] W; ∼-∼

**241. 16 County-house] W; County-House (*see also* 241. 23, 253. 26)

241. 18 at] W; at at

**243. 9 County-House] W; County-house (*see also* 243. 17; 243. 39; 244. 21, 244. 23, 244 (*margin*); 244. 29, 244. 35; 245. 6; 246. 3; 249. 2; 256. 6)

246. 9 minute] W; mintue

246. 11 Person's] W; Persons

249. 16 Misdemeanor] W; Misdemeaonr

250. 13–14 Deputyₐ Governor] W; ∼-∼ (*see also* 253. 7, 253. 35, 255. 3)

**251. (*margin*) County-house] W; Countyₐ House (*see also* 273. 8, 273. 27)

251. 40 irreverent] W; irreverend

252. 11 Whipping] W; whipping
252. 25 atrocious] W; attrocious
252. (*margin*) Jurisdiction] W; Jurisdic|ion
253. 34 5thly] W; 4thly
254. 11 outrageous] W; outragious
254. 16 6thly] W; 5thly
254. 29 Hearing] W; hearing
260. 24 Overseer's] W; Overseers
269. 5 *Indeed,*] W; ~‸
269. 9 XXVII] W; XXVIII
269. 24 Religion (says he)] W; Religion,'
   says he,
269. 27 Magistrate's] W; Magistrates
270.9 Hatred] W; hatred
270. 29 Writer] W; Wriger
270. 36 Atheist] W; Athest
271. 7 Suggestion] W; sugjestion
271. 18 inordinate] W; inordinat
271. 23 afraid,] W; ~‸
271. 25 Pursuits] W; Persuits
275. 11 Peccadillos] W; Peccadillo's
276. 1 submitted] W; submited

ELIZABETH CANNING

283. 9 Execution] 2; execution
286. 2 Kind] 2; kind

286. 9 desired‸] 2; ~,
286. 30 nevertheless] 2; neverthertheless
286. 31 State] 2; state
286. 33 Mind‸] W; ~, 1–2
288. 35 Gipsy] 2; Gipsey (*see also* 299. 35)
290. 8 Gipsies] 2; Gypsys
290. 28 Answer] 2; answer
292. 35 Improbability] W; Imbrobability 1–2
293. 16 well-disposed] W; ~‸~ 1–2
293. 26 Street-robbers] W; Street-Robbers 1–2
297. 3 *Virtue*] W; *Vertue* 1–2 (*see also* 297. 7, 298. 17, 300. 1, 301. 12, 301. 15, 302. 10)
*297. 7 Gipsy's] 2; Gipsey's
298. 2 trifling] W; triffling 1–2
298. 28 importunities] W; Importuities 1–2
299. 7 *Saltpetre‸ Bank*] W; ~-~ 1–2
299. 7 *Rosemary-lane*] W; *Rosemary-Lane* 1–2
300. 23 twenty-ninth] W; twenty-ninty 1–2
301. 9 all‸] W; ~, 1–2
302. 19 Four] W; four 1–2

* This change was made in standing type.
** The copy-text initially maintains with considerable consistency an orthographic distinction between the two parts of Fielding's workhouse, the 'County-house' (for minor offenders) and the 'County-House' of Correction (for the 'unruly' poor). The emendations necessary to maintain this useful and apparently intentional distinction have been made in the Wesleyan text.

APPENDIX III

Word-Division

1. *End-of-the-Line Hyphenation in the Wesleyan Edition*

[Note. No hyphenation of a possible compound at the end of a line in the Wesleyan edition is present in the copy-text except for the following readings, which are hyphenated within the line in copy-text. Hyphenated compounds in which both elements are capitalized are excluded.]

CHARGE
23. 17 Well-being

BOSAVERN PENLEZ
40. 25 Dove-house
41. 13 Conduit-heads
41. 17 Dove-houses
55. 1 Watch-house
58. 31 Gaming-houses

ENQUIRY
89. 5 Twenty-four
136. 6 Sun-setting
156. 11 ill-judging
156. 25 good-natured

EXAMPLES OF PROVIDENCE
183. 6 with-held
210. 29 ill-founded

PROPOSAL
237. 17 Store-rooms
239. 31 Store-keeper's
246. 14 Burying-ground
253. 36 County-house

ELIZABETH CANNING
292. 17 above-described
299. 24 Road-way
299. 33 Bawdy-house
306. 26 *Enfield-washe*

2. *End-of-the-Line Hyphenation in the Copy-Text*

[Note. The following compounds, or possible compounds, are hyphenated at the end of the line in the copy-text. The form in which they have been given in the Wesleyan edition, as listed below, represents the usual practice of the copy-text in so far as it may be ascertained from other appearances.]

CHARGE
13. 15 wherever
19. 12 Forefathers
28. 18 Right-hand

BOSAVERN PENLEZ
41. 18 Fish-pond
48. 3 Watch-house
49. 4 Night-Prison
50. 23 *High-Constable*
55. 7 *White-friars*

55. 15 *Carey-street*
55. 22 Watch-house

ENQUIRY
94. 20 Twelve-month
99. 11 Alms-houses
101. 9 Grandfather
103. 24 Workhouse
105. 17 Churchwardens
127. 28 out-lawed
131. 29 Burghholder

141. 4 Handicraft
141. 27 Patent-Gatherers
143. 27 *Shoreditch*
153. 17, 153. 22 Thief-catcher
154. 13 Thief-catchers

EXAMPLES OF PROVIDENCE

180. 30 abovementioned
187. 23 Gravesend
189. 2 macebearer
192. 9 ill-placed
202. 7 maid-servant
205. 3 cow-house
205. 22 Lutterworth
211. 7 snow-balls
212. 21 self-defence
214. 28 bare-fac'd

PROPOSAL

237. 7 County-house (*see also* 242. 27;

244. *margin*; 244. 39; 245. 14; 246.
  26; 252. 38; 268. 3)
241. 3 Victualling-house
241. 18 Headboroughs
242. 10 Churchwarden
243. 39 County-House (*see also* 246. 3)
244. 25 Fasting-room
247. 11 Store-keeper
247. 23 County-rate
254. 2 counter-signed
260. 24 Overseers
260. 37 Work-house
271. 5 Archbishop

ELIZABETH CANNING

287. 11. *Rosemary-*
287. 15 *Moorfields*
303. 13 Back-room

3. *Special Cases*

[NOTE. The following compounds or possible compounds are hypenated at the end of the line both in copy-text and in the Wesleyan edition.]

CHARGE

13. 20 last- |mentioned (i.e. last-mentioned)
24. 7 over- |sanctified (i.e. over-sanctified)

BOSAVERN PENLEZ

37. 22 Bawdy- |houses (i.e. Bawdy-houses)

EXAMPLES OF PROVIDENCE

204. 7 Queen- |hithe (i.e. Queen-hithe)

PROPOSAL

245. 8 County- |house (i.e. County-house)

APPENDIX IV

Historical Collation

BOSAVERN PENLEZ

35. 23 Pulton] Poulton 2
38. 24 Examples] Example 2
41. 6 ure] use 2
47. 14 That] that 1
47. 18 there] ~, 1
48. 1 In- | formant] In- | fomant *, †;
    In-| ofomant ‡

ENQUIRY

70. 17 the] that 2
77. 18 aim] am 2
80. 4 it] if 2
82. 4 tells] tell 2
84. 10 repaird] repaid 2
87. 11 for] of 2
93. 7 Temptations] Temptations 2
94. (note) 158] 174 1; 58 2

96. 3 forfeiting] om. 2
100. 40 Goal] gaol 2
111. 12 43] 43d 2
111. 19 2.] 2d 2
114. 34 Deduction] Deductions 2
115. 3 4.] om. 2
131. 29 Tithingman] Tithingham 2
135. 9 velut] velat 2
136. 30 County] Country 2
138. 18 1.] 1st 2
138. (note) 5 Eliz.] om. Eliz. 2
139. 19 last] om. 2
143. 10 Giles's] Giles 2
162. 26 to] om. 2

ELIZABETH CANNING

295. 25 In] It 2 (cw)
297.7 Gipsy's] Gipsey's 1

APPENDIX V

Bibliographical Descriptions

CHARGE

Title-page: A facsimile of the title-page is found on page [1].

Collation: 8⁰: A1 [=I2] B–H I² (–I2); $2 signed; 30 leaves, pp. [2] [7] 8–64

Press Figures: (sig.-page-fig.) B-13-2, C-16-2, D-28-3, E-36-3, F-43-1, G-51-1, H-61-4

Contents: A1: title; A1ᵛ: vote of the Sessions; B1: HT '[Woodcut, 3cm. × 8.1cm] | A | CHARGE | Delivered to the | GRAND JURY, &c.' and text (init.⁶) headed '*Gentlemen of the Grand Jury*,' ending on I1ᵛ with '*FINIS.*'.

Notes: (1) Copies collated: British Library (T. 1858), Bodley (g. Pamph. 1172 [12]), William Andrews Clark Library (*PR3454 C41), Huntington Library (123367), Lilly Library, Indiana University (spec./JN 787/.F4).

(2) Both the quarto and octavo printings of Murphy's 1762 edition of Fielding's *Works* include the *Charge*. Only minor variations exist between these two printings. Both omit the 'Vote of the Sessions' and integrate Fielding's marginal notes into the body of his text. The text in both formats has been collated with the 1749 *Charge* but has been found to be an unauthoritative reprint, and its variants have not been recorded for this edition.

BOSAVERN PENLEZ

(1) THE FIRST EDITION

Title-Page: A facsimile of the title-page is found on page [31].

Collation: 8⁰: A1 [=H4] B–G⁴ H⁴ (–H4); $2 (–E2) signed; 28 leaves, pp. [2] 1–54 (1–8, 25–32, 41–52 within [ ]; 9–24, 33–40, 53–4 within ( )).

Press Figures: (sig.-page-fig.): B-2-4, C-16-1, D-22-3, E-32-4, F-39-2, G-44-1

Contents: A1: title (verso blank); B1: HT '[head-piece] | A | TRUE STATE | OF THE | CASE | OF | *BOSAVERN PENLEZ*.' and text (cap.³) ending on H3ᵛ with '*FINIS.*'

Note: (1) Copies collated: British Library (1417. f. 14. and 518 g. 28), University Library, Cambridge (z. 23. 56⁴), William Andrews Clark Library (*PR3454/T81), Huntington Library (123354), Lilly Library, Indiana University (spec./DA503/.F43).

(2) THE SECOND EDITION

State *

As in the First Edition except: E2 signed; *Press figures*: B-8-4, D-22-3, E-30-3, G-44-1, H-52-2; *Pagination*: 1–8, 15–40, 53–4 within ( ); 9–14, 41–52 within [ ]; HT: different head-piece.

Note: (1) Copy collated: Bodley (g. p. 1919 [14]).

State †

As in state * except: added press fig.: F-39-3

Note: (1) Copy collated: Huntington Library (123353).

State ‡

As in state † except: last line of text on H3 moved to first line of text on H3ᵛ.

Note: (1) Copy collated: Newberry Library (Case/E5/.P378).

For the second edition

Note: signatures B1–4ᵛ (1–8), C3 (13), C4 (15), C4ᵛ (16), E1ᵛ (26), E4 (31) were reset; the rest was printed from standing type.

ENQUIRY

(1) THE FIRST EDITION

Title-Page: A facsimile of the title-page is found on page [61].

Collation: 8⁰: A–I⁸; $4 (−I3) signed; 72 leaves, pp. [i–iii] iv–xv [xvi], [1] 2–127 [128].

Press Figures: (sig.-page-fig.): A-xi-3, A-xii-4, B-2-4, B-13-2, C-26-3, D-47-3, E-50-3, E-61-4, F-68-2, F-79-4, G-93-2, G-94-3, H-108-3, H-111-4, I-123-1, I-128-4

Contents: A1: title (verso blank); A2: dedication: 'TO THE | RIGHT HONOURABLE | Philip Lord Hardwick, | Lord High Chancellor of *Great Britain*.' and text (cap.⁴) headed 'MY LORD,' ending A2ᵛ signed 'HENRY FIELDING.'; A3: preface '[double rule] | THE PREFACE.' ending A8 (verso blank); B1: HT '[double rule] | AN | ENQUIRY | INTO THE | CAUSES of the late Increase of | ROBBERS, &c. | [rule]' and text (cap.⁴) headed 'INTRODUCTION.' ending on I8 with '*FINIS*.' and seven line errata; I8ᵛ: 'TO THE PUBLIC'.

Notes: (1) Copies collated: British Library (T. 1858 [2]), Newberry Library (Case/4A/872), University Library, Cambridge (Yorke. d. 639¹), Bodley Law Library (L Crim./500/F459), William Andrews Clark Library (*PR3454/E51), Huntington Library (106882), Lilly Library, Indiana University (PR3454/.E5).

(2) Both the quarto and octavo printings of Murphy's 1762 edition of Fielding's *Works* include the *Enquiry*. Only minor variations exist between the two printings. Both appear to follow the *Enquiry* first edition, though a few corrections from the second edition are accepted (or made independently), and the changes indicated by the first edition errata list are incorporated. Collation of both Murphy texts shows them to be unauthoritative reprints and their variants have not been recorded for this edition.

(2) THE SECOND EDITION

Title-page: A facsimile of the title-page is found on page [62].

Collation: 12⁰: A¹² b⁴ B–I¹² K⁶; $6 (−A1, A2, A5, D4, D6; + K3) signed; 118 leaves, pp. [i–x] xi–xxxii, [1] 2–199 [200] 201–3 [204]

Press Figures: (sig.-page-fig.): A-xiii-2, A-xv-3, B-13-2, C-40-2, C-46-3, D-64-3, E-94-1, F-118-2, F-120-3, G-130-3, G-132-2, H-166-2, H-168-3, I-178-2, I-180-3.

Contents: A1: HT 'AN | ENQUIRY | INTO THE | CAUSES of the late Increase | of ROBBERS, &c. | WITH SOME | PROPOSALS for Remedying | this Growing Evil. | [Price 3*s.* bound, and 2*s.* 6*d.* sew'd.]' (verso blank); A2: title (verso blank); A3: dedication '[double rule] | TO THE | RIGHT HONOURABLE | PHILIP LORD HARDWICK, | Lord High Chancellor of *Great Britain*.' and text (cap.³) headed 'MY LORD,' ending on A5 signed 'Henry Fielding.' (verso blank); A6: preface '[double rule] | THE | PREFACE.' and text (cap.⁴) ending on b4ᵛ; B1: HT '[head-piece] | AN | ENQUIRY | INTO THE | CAUSES of the late Increase | of ROBBERS, &c. | [rule]' and text (cap.⁴) headed 'INTRODUCTION.' ending on K4 with '*FINIS*.' (verso blank); K5: '[head-piece] | TO the PUBLIC.' and text (cap.²) ending on K6 with orn. (verso blank).

Note: (1) Copies collated: British Library (291 d 41), University Library, Cambridge (Acton. d. 25. 482), Newberry Library (Case/I/2045/.29). Lilly Library, Indiana University (PR3454/.E5/1751).

EXAMPLES OF PROVIDENCE

State *

Title-page: A facsimilie of the title-page is found on page [175].

Collation: 12⁰: π1 [=I6] A² B–H⁶ I⁶ (−I6); $3 signed; 50 leaves, pp. [2] i–iii [iv], [1] 2–94

Press Figures: (sig.-page-fig.) B-2-3, C-23-1, D-30-1, E-43-2, F-56-4, G-67-1, H-84-4, I-88-3

Contents: π1: title (verso blank); A1: dedication '[double rule] | TO THE | Right Rev. Father in God, | ISAAC | Lord Bishop of | WORCESTER.' and text (cap.²) headed 'My Lord,' ending A2 signed 'HENRY FIELDING.' (verso blank); B1: HT '[head-piece] | EXAMPLES | OF THE | Interposition of Providence in | the Detection and Punishment | of Murder.' and text (orn. cap.⁶) ending on I5ᵛ with *'FINIS.'*.

Note: (1) Copies collated: British Library (19347), Bodley (55. c. 154), Huntington Library (123332), Lilly Library, Indiana University (PR3454/ E.96).

State †

As in state * except: press figures: (sig.–page-fig.) B-2-4, C-23-2, E-43-2, F-56-4, G-67-2, H-84-3.

Note: (1) Copies collated: University Library, Cambridge (7100 e. 193), William Andrews Clark Library (*PR3454 E91).

PROPOSAL

Title-page: A facsimile of the title-page is found on page [219].

Collation: 8⁰: (folded plate) A² B–F⁸ G⁶; $4 (−G4) signed; 48 leaves, pp. [i– iii] iv, [1] 2–13 [14–17] 18–56 [57] 58–91 [92]

Press Figures: (sig.-page-fig.): A-ii-7, B-2-1, C-29-3, D-43-3, E-52-3, E-62-4, F-77-1, F-78-7, G-86-1

Contents: folded plate: architect's plan for workhouse signed 'Tho.ˢ Gibson Arch.ᵗ J. Mynde Sculp.'; A1: title; A1ᵛ: 'EXPLANATION of the PLAN.' A2: dedication '[double rule] | TO THE RIGHT HONOURABLE | HENRY PELHAM, | Chancellor of his Majesty's Exchequer.' and text (cap.²) headed 'Sir,' ending on A2ᵛ and signed 'Jan. 19 1753. Henry Fielding.'; B1: HT '[double rule] | A | PROPOSAL | For making an effectual Pro- | vision for the POOR, &c. | [rule]' and text (cap.³) headed 'INTRODUCTION.' ending on B7 (verso blank); B8: section title 'PROPOSALS | For Erecting | A County Work-house &c.' (verso blank); C1: section '[double rule] | PROPOSALS | For Erecting | A County Work-house, &c.' and text ending E4ᵛ; E5: section heading '[double rule] | ARGUMENTS | In | Explanation and Support | Of The | Foregoing Proposals. | [rule]' and text ending on G6 with 'FINIS.' (verso: advertisement).

Note: (1) Copies collated: British Library (CT 102), University Library, Cambridge (7200 d. 11.), Bodley (G. Pamph. 1174. [12]), Newberry Library (Case/I/3045/.279), Huntington Library (123349), William Andrews Clark

Library (*PR3454 P91), Lilly Library, Indiana University (HV6665/G7F4).

ELIZABETH CANNING

(1) THE FIRST EDITION

Title-page: A facsimile of the title-page is found on page [281].

Collation: 8⁰: *A*1 [=I4] B–H⁴ I⁴ (−I4); $2 signed; 32 leaves, pp. [2] 1–62

Press Figures: (sig.-page-fig.) B-7-1, D-24-1, E-28-3, G-47-2

Contents: A1: title (verso blank); B1: HT '[two double rules] | THE | CASE | OF | *ELIZABETH CANNING*, &c.' and text (cap.³) ending on I3ᵛ with '*FINIS.*'.

Note: (1) Copies collated: British Library (1415. e. 15), University Library, Cambridge (H h.h. 355⁴; Yorke. c. 227⁴), and Lilly Library, Indiana University (HV6248/.C2F4).

(2) THE SECOND EDITION

State *

Title-page: A facsimile of the title-page is found on page [282].

Collation: 8⁰: *A*1 [=I4] B–H⁴ I⁴ (−I4); $2 signed; 32 leaves, pp. [2] 1–62

Press Figure: (sig.-page-fig.) G-47-2

Contents: A1: title (verso blank); B1: HT '[two double rules] | THE | CASE | OF | *ELIZABETH CANNING*, &c.' and text (cap.³) ending on I3ᵛ with '*FINIS.*'.

Note: (1) copies collated: Bodley (24728e. 64 [10]), Newberry Library (ES. c1662). British Library (6496 aa 8) mispaginates: 1–58 60 59 61–2.

State †

As in state * except: added press figure E-28-3.

Note: (1) Copy collated: Huntington Library (E–PV/352830–41).

Note: For the Second Edition, signatures B–C⁴ (1–16) were reset. On the title-page (A1) a rule and 'THE SECOND EDITION' were inserted below Fielding's name in an otherwise reprinted sheet. The rest was printed from standing type.

INDEX OF NAMES, PLACES AND TOPICS

IN INTRODUCTIONS, TEXT, AND NOTES

(Coverage of topics and statutes is selective. Fielding's own notes are designated by an asterisk in front of the number.)